GOVERNMENT AND REVOLUTION
IN VIETNAM

The Royal Institute of International Affairs is an unofficial body which promotes the scientific study of international questions and does not express opinions of its own. The opinions expressed in this publication are the responsibility of the author.

The Institute gratefully acknowledges the comments and suggestions of the following who read the manuscript on behalf of the Research Committee: Dr Coral Bell and Professor Hugh Tinker.

GOVERNMENT
AND REVOLUTION
IN VIETNAM

DENNIS J. DUNCANSON

Issued under the auspices of the
Royal Institute of International Affairs

1968

OXFORD UNIVERSITY PRESS

NEW YORK AND LONDON

Second printing, 1968

© Royal Institute of International Affairs 1968
Library of Congress Catalogue Card Number 68-19954
Printed in the United States of America

Anonymous eleventh-century commentary on the defeat of an army from China (*Kham-dinh Viet-su*, 1960, p.101).

O'er hills and streams of southern clime
  A southern monarch reigns;
    His sov'reign state

On bamboo slips engraved by Time
  The Writ of Heav'n ordains.
    Dare you, 'gainst Fate,

Thrust in, his turbulence to quell?
Beware!—for *you* will sound the knell.

CONTENTS

ABBREVIATIONS

AFP:	Agence France Presse.
AID:	Agency for International Development.
Ann. stat.:	*Annuaire statistique du Viet-Nam.*
Ann. stat. Indochine:	*Annuaire statistique de l'Indochine.*
Ann. Statist. B.:	USOM, *Annual Statistical Bulletin.*
AP:	Associated Press.
BAVH:	*Bulletin des Amis du Vieux Hué.*
BEFEO:	*Bulletin de l'École Française d'Extrême Orient.*
BSEI:	*Bulletin de la Société des Études Indochinoises.*
CIA:	Central Intelligence Agency.
CIDG:	Civilian Independent Defense Groups.
CIP:	Commercial Import Program.
Cmnd. 9239:	*Further Documents relating to the discussion of Indo-China at the Geneva Conference . . .1954.*
Cmnd 2834:	*Documents relating to British Involvement in the Indo-China Conflict, 1945–65.*
Cochinchine française:	Cochinchina, Comité Agricole et Industriel, *La Cochinchine française en 1878.*
Contribution:	Indochina, *Contribution à l'histoire des mouvements politiques de l'Indochine française* (1934).
DRV:	Democratic Republic of Vietnam.
FULRO:	Front Unifié pour la Lutte de la Race Opprimée.
ICC:	International Control Commission (International Commission for Supervision and Control in Vietnam).
ICP:	Indochina Communist Party.
JEO:	*Journal d'Extrême Orient.*
JMBRAS:	*Journal of the Malayan Branch of the Royal Asiatic Society.*
JP:	Justice of the Peace.
KMT:	Kuomintang.
MAAG:	Military Assistance Advisory Group.
MACV:	Military Assistance Command, Vietnam.
MSUG:	Michigan State University Group.
NCNA:	New China News Agency.
NFLSV:	National Front for the Liberation of South Vietnam.
NYHT:	*New York Herald Tribune.*

NYT:	*New York Times.*
PMS:	Pays Montagnards du Sud.
PRP:	People's Revolutionary Party.
Thirty Years:	DRV, *Thirty Years of Struggle of the Party* (1960).
RIJE:	*Revue Indochinoise Juridique et Économique.*
RVN:	Republic of Vietnam.
SDN:	*Saigon Daily News.*
SEPES:	Service des Études Politiques, Économiques et Sociales.
SP:	*Saigon Post.*
TVN:	*Times of Vietnam* (Saigon).
USIS:	US Information Service.
USOM:	US Operations Mission.
VC:	Vietcong.
VNA:	Vietnam News Agency (Hanoi).
VNP:	Vietnam-Presse (Saigon).
VNQDD:	Viet Nam Quoc Dan Dang.
VWP:	Vietnamese Workers' Party.

PREFACE

PERSONAL observation and experience have contributed the major part to the construction of this book; but, on such a subject, the reader has good cause to be cautious of unsupported personal testimony. Wherever I could, therefore, I have sought out confirmation from other observers already in print. The text of the book has been written as impersonally as possible, but I should like to express my gratitude to those I have quoted, to others from whose ideas, not committed to print, my own have benefited, and to the many who have helped me in one way or another to turn it all into a book.

In the first place I mention my wife, who from the beginning encouraged this unsubventioned undertaking and in practical ways helped it forward. I am grateful to Chatham House editors and readers for suggestions how to improve form or content, all of which have been valued and heeded—even the ones I have not felt able to incorporate. Next come the staffs of libraries: Chatham House again (including the Press Archives), the Royal Asiatic Society, the Royal Anthropological Institute, the School of Oriental and African Studies, the Buddhist Society, the British Museum Reading Room (all in London), and, most particularly and generously, the Société des Études Indochinoises down the road from my office in Saigon.

It is to friends and colleagues in Vietnam that my deepest debt of gratitude is owed. First the handful of my fellow countrymen formerly in Malaya, headed by Sir Robert Thompson, the threads of whose collective thinking I have worked without attribution into the wider fabric of the book. Then there are my numerous Australian and American collaborators, civil and military. I would pay special tribute to Public Administration Advisor Gustav C. Hertz—kidnapped and agonizingly held hostage under repeated threat of death, out of retaliatory spite against the proper course of justice. I have to thank Vietnamese leaders and officials, in uniform or out, who during five years aired their problems with me. Here also one name stands out—that of the protagonist in the tragedy, President Diem. As many of his compatriots might admit today if in the East one dared to speak one's mind about fallen politicians, he was the embodiment of his country's soul, for good no less than for bad; the reader may judge from the acknowledgements I have recorded in the footnotes the value to me of his notorious monologues lasting four, five, or six hours.

It would give me the greatest satisfaction to thank by name the members of the Vietnamese civil service to whom I owe so much information, some of it volunteered explicitly for incorporation in my text. But, whether they are still at home or now in exile, my tributes might one day serve them ill, and so I must be content to express generally my appreciation of their friendship and my admiration for the stoicism with which I have watched them face public anxieties, personal sorrows and physical hardships. It is to the *Cong Vu*—the public services—as a body that I would dedicate this book if the gesture did not seem, in present circumstances, an impertinent sentimentality.

London, August 1967   D. J. D.

EDITORIAL NOTES

Place names

Over the centuries there have been many changes in the names not only for Vietnam as a country but also for its constituent parts and for its towns and villages. For the sake of simplicity, one name has been used for each throughout this book, and Vietnamese readers are asked to pardon any disregard of their susceptibilities on this account or any anachronisms that result. Their indulgence is called for especially on account of the use of the names for the regions: current Vietnamese use of *North*, *Centre*, and *South*—there are in use no fewer than four different ways of conveying even that simple notion—is particularly confusing for foreigners at a time when the country is partitioned between North and South in another sense; *Tonkin*, *Annam*, and *Cochinchina* have been used consistently even though they are foreign, in default of native names of equal precision. *Tourane* has been used through most of the book because, in the historical period, it is not always certain whether references are to the modern site of Danang or to Hoi An (Faifo) near-by; in the last chapter, Danang—which incidentally is not of Vietnamese derivation either—has been employed because of its present currency in the US.

Personal names

Vietnamese personal names are not all formed on the same pattern, and native practice as to employment of capital letters for the second, third or (if any) fourth component, and of hyphens between them, varies. In this book it has seemed desirable to fix on a single standard, more particularly because of the need to distinguish Vietnamese names from Chinese ones. Although the most widespread usage in Vietnam is *Ngo-dinh-Diem*, the less common pattern *Ngo Dinh Diem* is adopted here instead because it is more familiar to Western readers and because it avoids any violation of grammar or logic entailed by extending the commoner pattern to names composed on a different basis. The reader will be able to recognize Chinese names by their hyphen (*Chiang Kai-shek*).

Vietnamese printing

Although the Vietnamese language is nowadays written for all purposes in its romanized alphabet, that entails the addition of a great wealth of diacritical marks to the type. Unfortunately, problems of printing rule out the presentation of names and phrases in their proper form, even though the omissions make both correct pronunciation and comprehension almost impossible. The reader is therefore asked to bear in mind that many of the apparent homonyms would be clearly distinguished if the words bore their full indications of vowel value—there are three each for *a* and *o*, two each for *e* and *u*—and of the six different tones. The consonant *d* has two values, and readers may wish to know that in the name *Ngo Dinh Diem* only the first one is a true *d*; the second one is pronounced either *z* (Annam and Tonkin) or *y* (Cochinchina). Given the difficulty of printing, a full note on Vietnamese pronunciation has seemed pointless, but it may perhaps be mentioned that, whereas *kh* and *ph* are nowadays pronounced respectively as in English *khanate* and *philosophy*, *th* represents *t* followed by *h* as in Chinese *t'*.

Calligraphy

The poem on the flyleaf is not reproduced in explicitly Vietnamese calligraphy, for the reason that no samples of antique Vietnamese calligraphy are extant. It is, however, in a style fashionable in China at the time when the poem is supposed to have been written.

Glossary

For the interest of readers familiar with Chinese but not with Vietnamese, a list of romanized equivalents of key Sino-Vietnamese words and phrases will be found on pp. 417–19.

References and supplementary notes

Letters of the alphabet in the text refer to footnotes, figures to the Supplementary Notes on pp. 381–416.

In order to avoid long footnotes, references to sources are restricted to the name of the author, or in some cases to a short title (see Abbreviations, pp. ix and x). The date of publication is given at the first reference only unless it is included to distinguish different works by the same author. The system used for official publications is to give the name of the country as author (but not the issuing department) and a brief title. Full references to all works cited are given in the Bibliography.

GOVERNMENT AND REVOLUTION
IN VIETNAM

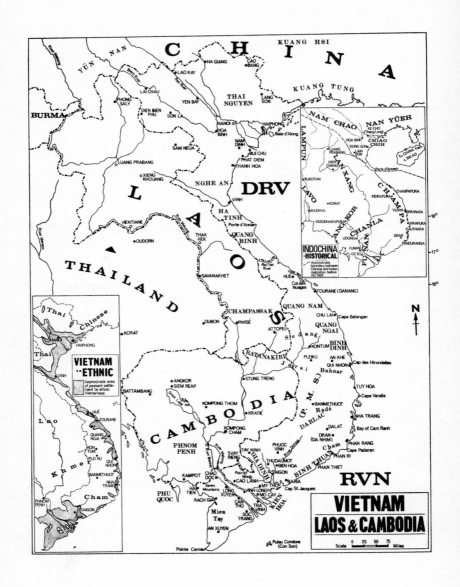

1

VIETNAM AS A WORLD
PROBLEM

I. INTERNATIONAL ANXIETIES AND STRATEGIC INTERESTS

FEW internal conflicts in modern times have received as much publicity and been as little understood as the fighting in Vietnam; few have aroused so much humanitarian sentiment abroad and so little at home; few have been the object of so much solicitude in the diplomatic world, and of foreign intervention on such a massive scale, with so little apparent effect on the course of events. In fact, under all three heads, Vietnam is probably unique. Sooner or later the conflict must come to an end, for all conflicts do; and yet it can be demonstrated with almost mathematical certainty that no viable settlement is possible. So baffling is the Vietnamese enigma that public opinion in many countries is tempted to fall back on proposals to leave the Vietnamese to come to terms among themselves. The admonition on the fly-leaf of this book, ancient and proud, seems to be addressed to friend as well as foe. Yet, at the stage now reached, non-intervention is itself a form of intervention—the withholding of support as positive a pressure as increasing it: in the Vietnamese conflict there is no longer a neutral position.

Military casualties

There can be no question that the cost of the conflict in human suffering, as in the dissipation of material resources, has been very great. The full extent of the casualties cannot be ascertained because so many of those who have been hurt have belonged to categories it was nobody's business to concern himself with; there are no coroners in Vietnam. During that phase of the conflict we know as the Indochina War, the forces under French command lost almost 95,000 men killed out of a total casualty figure variously estimated between 175,000[a] and a quarter of a million.[b] As much for motives of secrecy and fear of adverse publicity as because of the informality and the unaccountability that generally characterize the manage-

[a] Fall (1961), p. 313.　　[b] Le-thanh-Khoi (1955), p. 483.

ment of their affairs, the Communist authorities in Vietnam have published no information about their losses. But it is obvious that in the engagements in which they pitched 'human waves' against artillery, tanks, or machine guns the slaughter must have been terrible; at the single battle of Dien Bien Phu their adversaries estimated their dead to have been 20,000.[a] In the conflict since independence battle casualties have been bigger still. A Vietnamese Government estimate in the middle of 1962 put the figure for all casualties on both sides since 1 January 1957 at almost the million mark.[b] The single year 1964 saw 28,000 killed in action,[c] the twelve months 1 June 1965–31 May 1966 some 32,000;[d] the Communist dead for the calendar year 1966 were of the order of 50,000—nearly 1,000 a week.[e] There is no precision about these figures, and they are not complete; but it seems certain that not fewer than a quarter of a million combatants lost their lives during the Indochina War, between 1946 and 1954, and more like half a million since. The total population of Vietnam is about 30 millions. For the Vietnamese soldier or guerrilla who survives it unscathed, every battle, win or lose, is a prelude to the next. Where neither victory nor defeat can bring decision, fighting becomes an end in itself and the 'score' of kills the barometer of achievement on both sides; the Vietcong actually set themselves targets—20,000 Americans alone to be killed during 1966.[f]

Civilian casualties

But it is not only combatants who are killed. Civilian casualties have never been recorded by any authority in Vietnam; there is reason to believe they may have equalled, or even exceeded, the battle casualties.[g] There are the victims of systematic murder or acts of terrorism (derailed trains, mined motor-buses, mortared villages, hand grenades in markets and cinemas); there are those who have been caught in the cross-fire of ambush or pitched battle; and there are the unknown numbers killed or maimed in air raids on sup-

---

[a] Navarre (1956), p. 228.   [b] AFP, Saigon, 30 Aug. 1962.
[c] Vietnam-Presse, Saigon, 5 Jan. 1965.
[d] The sum of figures issued weekly by the US Command.
[e] US military spokesman in Saigon at the end of the year.
[f] Text of speech by the late Gen. Nguyen Chi Thanh, Commander-in-Chief, at HQ Congress 'somewhere in South Vietnam' in Mar. 1966, captured by US army ten months later (USIS communiqué, Saigon, 30 Mar. 1967, p. 3). In fact 5,008 Americans were killed during 1966 (*The Times*, 26 May 1967).
[g] The opinion, for instance, of the US General in charge of medical aid to Vietnam (press conference quoted in AP file, Washington, 6 Jan. 1966).

posedly hostile villages in South Vietnam since 1961 or (probably the smaller number) in the bombing of military targets in North Vietnam since 1965. Not all have lost their lives at the hands of the Vietcong or the South Vietnamese Government or US forces; at least some have been victims of the Sects, of bandits, or of political or private feuds arising out of the main conflict or sheltering behind the anonymity it confers on evildoers. We can only guess the total. Yet hospital statistics tell us something. During 1965 the provincial hospital at Can Tho in Cochinchina performed 8,783 surgical operations of various kinds; 7,202 were for the repair of wounds.[a] That figure does not include people who either died or recovered without surgical intervention—presumably not less than an equal number. There were at least ten other provincial hospitals just as busy at the time, so that one might expect civilian casualties that year to have exceeded 100,000.[b] And for the peasant it is as for the fighting man: a ravaged crop, a burnt-down house and dispersed or slaughtered livestock must be made good, like his torn flesh, by his own efforts, until the war comes his way a second time, or a third or a fourth.

Cost of the war

The cost of the conflict in public treasure has been hardly less alarming. The burden on France was 53 milliard francs in the first full year of fighting, 1947; by 1952 that figure had multiplied more than ten times and accounted for a third of the national budget.[c] At the end, the Indochina War had cost France 2,385 milliards[d] and the United States over $1,500 million;[e] what it had cost the two Vietnamese Governments is not calculable, but in the zones controlled by the Communists every public resource had been thrown into the war effort to the total sacrifice of public well-being. For the period since 1954 it is difficult to separate defence from economic expenditure in either the national budget of the Republic of Vietnam or the contribution in the form of loans, grants or direct expenditure borne by the US. However, for the former it has been estimated that by 1964 the war was already consuming a quarter of the gross national product of South Vietnam;[f] US appropriations for

[a] Figures obtained privately; the RVN Government does not generally publish this kind of information.
[b] The official estimate for 1966, admitted to be conservative, was 48,000; it was based on a one-day count in sixty hospitals (*The Times*, 28 Dec. 1966).
[c] Despuech (1953), p. 31.   [d] Le-thanh-Khoi.   [e] Lancaster (1961), p. 417.
[f] USOM, *US Assistance Program* (1965), p. 7.

Vietnam have risen from under $400 million in 1958–9[a] to $20,000 million in 1966–7[b]—virtually the whole of the increase being in response to the gathering momentum of Communist hostilities. Once again, what the conflict has cost the Democratic Republic of Vietnam cannot be ascertained, but the destruction of communications and the expenditure on armaments for use in the South as well as at home in the North, whatever proportion may be covered out of Russian and Chinese contributions,[c] cannot but be a severe strain on a country with such meagre industrial capacity.

Danger for world peace

To the anxiety of world opinion over this mounting waste and human suffering is added anxiety over the threat to peace between Communist and non-Communist powers which steadily intensifying hostilities are felt to entail. It is this second anxiety perhaps more than humanitarian concern for the Vietnamese themselves that explains the unceasing appeals of national and of world leaders since 1964 to the heads of the combatant governments to agree to a ceasefire as the prelude to negotiation of a lasting peace; for these appeals date, not from when the fighting first became acute, but from when the US began to take a direct hand in it, first with her punitive retaliations from sea and air against North Vietnamese installations, and second with her commitment of land forces to the defence of South Vietnamese territory. The direct engagement of a great power on one side could lead to a balancing engagement on the other.

Strategic factors

That none of the combatants is willing to heed these appeals unilaterally, and the DRV not even bilaterally, is a measure of the value they set on the strategic factors involved in their struggle. The inference is that both sides regard these as equally important and take the same view of what consequences would follow from a decision either way. The view which the South Vietnamese Government takes of its interests is well known; its existence as an independent state was sanctioned by the Geneva Agreements of 1954, and no arrangement short of the total withdrawal of forces of all kinds under the formal command of, or voluntarily obedient to, the North Vietnamese Government will safeguard its continued existence. The North Vietnamese point of view is that the separate exis-

[a] Assuming military equipment supplied was not in excess of $200 m.
[b] *The Times*, 29 Nov. 1966.   [c] See note 98.

tence of South Vietnam was a temporary measure, due to end in 1956; that it is itself the sole legitimate successor both to the realms of the Nguyen emperors and to the suzerainty and the sovereignty exercised by France over the three regions of Vietnam; that it has every right to engage in hostilities aimed at unification under its own authority; and that the US, in rallying to the support of secessionary South Vietnam, is an aggressor with no rights in the matter and with whom therefore there is nothing to negotiate.

Falling dominoes

The strategic interest in Vietnam of which the US sees herself as the champion on behalf of the Western, and indeed the whole non-Communist, world—the Dullesian 'global conflict'—is twofold. The first aspect is that the countries of southeast Asia might be successively toppled by Communist penetration, like 'falling dominoes' in the metaphor of ex-President Eisenhower. The reality of the peril can be deduced from the very arguments of the DRV: both France and the Nguyen emperors before her had claims to suzerainty over the other peoples of French Indochina, the Laotians and the Cambodians, and the North Vietnamese Communists have in the past claimed a parallel paramountcy over the Communist movements of those countries.[a] The army of the DRV invaded Laos at the end of 1952, and the revolutionary movement of the Pathet Lao is an offshoot of the resulting Vietnamese military occupation of the Sam Neua province of Laos; the Pathet Lao has continued to be supplied and in part manned from Hanoi, and its periods of activity are relatable to calls for reinforcements along the 'Ho Chi Minh trail' for Communist forces operating in South Vietnam. Unification of Vietnam under DRV leadership must therefore be expected to presage a revival of Vietnamese irredentism in regard to the rest of the former Indochina Union and be interpreted in the rest of southeast Asia as a definitive shift in the balance of power in favour of the Communist nations. Prince Norodom Sihanouk showed that this opinion is shared inside Indochina when he wrote to the *New York Times* in May 1965: 'After the disappearance of the USA from our region and the victory of the Communist camp, I myself and the People's Socialist Community that I have created would inevitably disappear from the scene.'[b]

[a] The point is discussed on p. 170 below; see also DRV broadcast on 13 Apr. 1953 (quoted Central Office of Information fact sheet on Laos, R.5489, London, 1963).
[b] *NYT*, 4 June 1965.

World revolution

The other aspect of the strategic interest which has involved the US so deeply in Vietnam is the danger that underdeveloped countries farther afield than southeast Asia would view Communist success in the same light. The technique of revolutionary warfare, starting as it does with the harnessing to an external political cause of organized crime in countries lacking police forces adequate to detect and check its progress, is an insidious means of aggression presenting few if any targets for conventional political or military measures of defence. It is not hysterical alarm that has given the US Government such a keen flair for incipient revolutionary wars in Africa or Latin America: the Chinese Defence Minister, Marshal Lin Piao, in his much-publicized article in 1965, spoke of revolutionary warfare in future as a method for 'using the underdeveloped countries to encircle the developed, as once we used the country to encircle the towns.'[a] The Minister of Defence of North Vietnam, General Vo Nguyen Giap, was affirming at the same time that 'South Vietnam is the vanguard fighter of the national liberation movement in the present era . . . and the failure of the special war unleashed by the US imperialists in South Vietnam would mean that this war can be defeated anywhere in the world.'[b] American determination to 'contain' these ambitions is no mere issue of chauvinistic prestige. Both sides agree how much is at stake.

Strategic interests of the Communists

Less obvious, but not much less certainly supported by historical precedent, are the strategic interests in Vietnam of the Communist powers ranged behind the DRV and keeping her afloat logistically. Fear in the West of a victory in Vietnam for revolutionary warfare finds its counterpart in China, and to a large extent in the Soviet Union as well, in a converse fear of the consequences of a defeat: those who claim to be repositories of absolute truth cannot compromise without loss of command over their own people, not to speak of their influence with the intended 'domino' peoples. To this has to be added the fanaticism of the North Vietnamese leaders who have come so far along the path of violence and are unlikely to be turned back by revulsion against bloodshed from the attainment of their goal, in a land where life is cheap. But the crucial factor for the Communists—at least the Chinese—is again geography, and es-

[a] NCNA (Peking), English broadcast, 2 Sept. 1965.
[b] Vo-nguyen-Giap (1965), pp. 69–70.

pecially the protection of China's own southern flank from penetration, if not by military forces, then still by ideas and perhaps foreign agents. China has suffered invasion through Tonkin in all these ways in the past and well within living memory; as the Soviet Union has demonstrated in Europe, a Communist state cannot feel safe if its frontiers march with hostile, or even with neutral, regimes —security depends on a cordon of satellites.

Consequently, the urgency of achieving a settlement of the conflict in Vietnam is offset by the irreconcilability of the interests that have to be satisfied. Perhaps that is no novel predicament for diplomatists committed to peacemaking and engaged in peacekeeping. Unfortunately, in the case of Vietnam the problem is rendered all the more intractable by being, to a large extent, the result of a previous attempt to make and keep the peace, the reasons for whose failure would have to be avoided somehow if another attempt were made.

2. FAILURE OF PEACEKEEPING IN THE PAST

The model for peace efforts in Vietnam is the Geneva formula which brought the Indochina War to an end in 1954. The main features of that formula were a cease-fire between the Communists and French-commanded forces, a regrouping of these on either side of a ten-mile-wide demilitarized zone along the 17th parallel of latitude (which divided the country almost into equal halves at its narrowest point), the provision of facilities for civilians also to follow the armed forces of their choice, and the setting up of an International Commission for Supervision and Control (ICC) to see fair play. Subsidiary clauses tried to secure the basis for a more lasting political settlement according to which, among other details, free elections would be held simultaneously in North and South within two years under international supervision.[a] Generally speaking, the main features of this agreement were carried out,[b] and to that extent it was a success; but the very fact that hostilities broke out again is evidence of the failure of its political provisions. Few people expected otherwise at the time it was drawn up: in the West it was fully expected that, whatever the majority will expressed in a free election might turn out to be, the Communist Party of Vietnam (or of Indochina) would not willingly relinquish the dominion over the

[a] The text of the 1954 Geneva Agreements is contained in Cmd. 9239.
[b] *4th Interim Report* (1955).

North for which it had secured international recognition at Geneva nor rest content until, by foul means if not by fair, it had gained dominion over the South as well. Every public pronouncement by DRV leaders since that time confirms that they would not themselves have acquiesced in the agreement if they had not fully expected that by its means they could complete their assumption of power throughout the country without further armed struggle. Thus, whereas for everybody else the Geneva armistice was a deal to establish peace through territorial concessions, for the DRV it was a formula to gain territory through the concession of peace to an enemy who acknowledged defeat: in different minds the means and the ends were interchanged.

Limitations of the Agreement

The principal architect of the agreement was the British Foreign Secretary, Mr Anthony Eden, now Lord Avon; he has recognized more than once that the flaws in the agreement were apparent to him at the time; but it was the best that could be negotiated at that moment in history.[a] The story of the diplomacy and the military events that led up to the agreement is a complicated one and will be summarized in a later chapter. The essential points to be dealt with here are of two kinds: the inherent (however unavoidable) weaknesses of the agreement itself, and—even more significant—the elements in the situation in Vietnam which it did not, and perhaps at the time could not, take account of. At the head of the first category must be put doubt who the parties to the agreement really were. The Geneva Conference was held under the joint chairmanship of the Foreign Ministers of Britain and Russia; the delegations attending represented France, the US, the People's Republic of China, the DRV, and each of the Associated States of Indochina (Viet-Nam, Cambodia, and Laos). The territory pretended to by the DRV and the State of Viet-Nam was, of course, one and the same. The various delegations had assembled, except for the last three, primarily to discuss conditions for the reunification of Korea (over which they arrived at no conclusion), the problem of French Indochina being an afterthought.[b] The signatories to the armistice were delegates of the Generals in command of the combat forces—of the forces of the DRV on one side of all three agreements (there were separate ceasefires in Vietnam, Cambodia, and Laos) and of the forces of France on the other side of the Vietnam and Laos agreements, of the Khmer

[a] e.g. Eden (1964).   [b] Berlin agreement of 18 Feb. 1954 in Cmnd 2834, p. 65.

National Army on that of the Cambodian one. The US and the State of Viet-Nam were not in control of combat forces and consequently could not in logic have been parties to the cease-fire. Nobody signed the Final Declaration relating to a permanent political settlement, and both South Vietnam and the US recorded caveats, the former against partition, the latter against unification as an imposed sequel to elections. In little over eighteen months France had ceased to have any responsibilities within Vietnam, and with her one party to the agreement simply disappeared. It is on the agreement that the US and the successive Governments of South Vietnam have, despite their original dissociation from it and the caveat of the South Vietnamese against partition, based their insistence on the sovereign independence of the South and on the obligation of the North, as the sole surviving signatory to the armistice, to respect it. The North on its side insists on its right to unification and, since the elimination of the other signatory to whom the duty of fulfilment should have fallen, on its right to use force as the only means to bring unification about[a]—if not by direct invasion, at least in support of an insurrection in the South dedicated to that aim.

The ICC

Similar confusion has arisen over the ICC. Composed of delegations from Poland, Canada, and India under the chairmanship of the last, the Commission was invested only with the right to station observer teams at ports and frontier posts and a few other points in the two halves of the country; it disposed of no executive arm and depended for the discharge even of its limited functions on the goodwill of the two Vietnamese Governments. Once the Geneva Conference had dispersed, there was no body the Commission was responsible to or whose support it could invoke; the custom developed of submitting periodical reports to the Foreign Ministers of Britain and Russia as ex-co-chairmen, but this had no basis in the agreements, nor had the recipients any sanction they could apply even if they were at one over the course that should be followed. As an apparatus for giving effect to the cease-fire, the ICC was reasonably successful because the various armed forces were themselves willing co-operators; but when it came to permanent peacekeeping, the Commission was impotent as an arbiter between the conflicting in-

[a] At the conclusion of the Geneva Conference, the representative of South Vietnam engaged his Government, in spite of its caveat, not to disturb the arrangements in the agreement by resort to force; so did the representative of the US. The representative of North Vietnam evaded the question (Cmnd 9239, pp. 6–7).

terpretations of the Final Declaration and could only deplore the prevarications it detected. Even detection of prevarications was made difficult by the tendency of the Polish Delegation to take the part of the North or of the Canadian, in compensation, to take the part of the South; this has led on several occasions to majority and minority reports, with the Indian Chairman leaning now towards one, now towards the other—as often, one may suspect, out of diplomatic considerations as out of objective ones. On such questions as whether subversion by criminal methods constituted a resumption of hostilities or whether preventive detention of professional agitators amounted to reprisals against former participants in the Indochina War, the Commission arrived, when these issues were crucial to preparations for the second Communist uprising (from 1956 to 1959), at no agreed doctrine; even if it had, it could have taken no action. In its role as observer, the Commission was also at a disadvantage by comparison with more conventional peace-keeping forces; it soon found it was not the military contingent placed between separately identifiable armies which the demarcation line was intended to make it, but a political observer inside an unfamiliar society in a state of revolutionary turmoil. It would have taken more than a few lessons in the Vietnamese language (which hardly any of them took anyway) to equip the officers of the ICC even to investigate thoroughly the complaints that the two Vietnamese Governments plied them with—usually with the most partisan disregard for objectivity—before attempting to be watchdogs of fair play on their own initiative in the villages of either North or South. There was some substance, to quote one practical illustration, in the reproach of the South Vietnamese Government that the teams were not qualified to say whether persons they saw leaving Qui Nhon for Tonkin under DRV control in 1955, at the same time as the regrouping of fighting forces, were embarking voluntarily or were victims of coercion.[a]

In fact the Geneva Agreements and the Control Commission they created were a fruit of the Cold War at the stage it had reached in 1954. In one important respect this was an advantage: without the general desire to relax tension that found expression at the Berlin Conference in February 1954, the Geneva Conference would probably not have been convened, whilst since then Communist China has shown herself progressively less willing to co-operate in international negotiations of a political kind with non-Communist

[a] RVN, *Violations* (1959), p. 80.

countries. On the other hand, the Cold War context out of which the Geneva Conference arose focused attention on the international aspect of the Vietnamese conflict to the exclusion of issues originating from the country's domestic situation; in reality many other internal stresses have been involved with the Cold War to thwart the purpose of the peacemakers at Geneva.

3. CIVIL STRIFE AND THE COLD WAR

There has been no lack in the West of appreciation that domestic issues were involved. The duration of the fighting, and at times its intensity, have been interpreted as signs that those engaged, far from being pawns in an international power struggle, must have been fired by deeply-felt emotions of their own.[a] In the US it was early decided that the growth of Communist strength in Indochina must be due to the force of anti-colonial feeling there; all territories under the yoke of colonialism shared the same bitter resentment, felt by Americans themselves in the eighteenth century; but in Indochina the colonial power was France, and she was believed in America to have been specially selfish and incompetent as an administering power. Not a few French voices made themselves heard in confirmation of the rightness of this American deduction, and the progressive slackening of French political and administrative control in response to the growth of insurgent strength implied some degree of official endorsement of it in Paris. Throughout the first Indochina War—fought mainly in North Vietnam—insurgent propaganda insisted on the priority of nationalism among its aims and of patriotic fervour as the sole motivation of its manpower; according as they did with Western expectations, these claims sounded perfectly plausible; they were, moreover, strongly supported by anti-Communist intellectuals in Vietnam who had worked at first with the Communists, later deserted them, and thereafter felt the need for a personal justification.

The 'Resistance'

This near-unanimity of interpretation has not been preserved during the second outbreak of fighting, which took place this time in South Vietnam; but still the opinion has generally persisted that an idealism in which Marxism had little or no part to play must be

---

[a] These paragraphs are deliberately not documented in the manner followed in the rest of the book because it is not desired to take issue directly with other writers.

postulated to account for the success of the insurrection in commanding such widespread popular support and such willingness among the guerrillas to go on getting hurt. The ingredients of the idealism could not be quite the same as formerly, because colonialism had now disappeared; nor was the issue of reunification a very credible cause for which men would risk being killed; but the reputation which Ngo Dinh Diem, first Prime Minister and later President of the new Republic of Vietnam (that is, the South), quickly acquired for high-handed administration suggested the possibility of a new motive for rebellion, namely the intolerability of his tyrannical rule. The explanation was strongly urged by writers of French nationality. Its main points gained widespread currency in American circles, including eventually the entourage of President Kennedy. The insurgents, both before and after they began to call themselves the National Front for the Liberation of South Vietnam (NFLSV), also adopted this slogan, adding to it, however, that they were at the same time 'resisting'—the word retained the aura of its world war connotation—an American conspiracy to re-establish a colonial regime in South Vietnam. Americans, who had always gone more than halfway to trust the sincerity of Vietnamese insurgents, even while being shot at by them, could not in logic subscribe to this last explanation, since they knew the falseness of the fact alleged. In its place, therefore, American official opinion has tended to draw a distinction between the rank and file of the insurgents in the South, who might be fighting bravely because they believed these things in error, and the leaders who, deliberately misleading them, could henceforward be branded outright Communists dedicated to the international interests in play in the Cold War. For the second time, it seemed, a general grievance (the tyranny of Ngo Dinh Diem, not colonial ambitions on the part of the US) had taken hold of the Vietnamese people and provided a national power base for Communist intrigue.

Idealism in warfare

If one accepted any of these explanations at its face value, there would be little more to find out about the nature of the conflict in Vietnam and no more to say in this book. It is difficult, however, not to feel certain reservations about them, if only because they cannot all be true so long as there are inconsistencies between them and all rest equally on deduction from Western historical experience. Is it really necessary to postulate an idealistic cause, and enthusiasm for it, as the motivation of the insurgents' rank and file? This is not to say no such cause exists, but only to question whether its existence has to be assumed *a priori*. The fighting in Vietnam that it is sought to explain, even when by way of guerrilla warfare, has been of a kind calling for regular supplies and a good deal of discipline; it is a commonplace that embodied troops fight better if they 'know what they are fighting for', but it is the experience of most soldiers that they have fought their battles day by day primarily because they were 'in it' and that, the longer time goes on, the less often causes are remembered and the more strongly unit morale and thoughts of victory or defeat for their own sake come into play. Nearly all the fighting men in Vietnam, on both sides, have been conscripts, if only to the degree that volunteers have been retained in their respective forces indefinitely whatever their own original idea—a circumstance that goes far, incidentally, to account for absences without leave (rarely amounting in reality to 'defections') on both sides; among the bravest soldiers of all in Indochina were the French Foreign Legion. So it may be that the initial postulate is not well founded.

Objections

On further reflection, positive objections to these idealistic explanations suggest themselves, on both general and specific grounds. In the first place, whatever we may personally believe about the motivation of leaders and of soldiers in the great wars of Europe in the past, one would look far in East Asia before one found a war that had not been a pretty crude power struggle; it is customary to explain the internal wars of China by the wickedness of the courts of successively decadent dynasties, yet those who have overthrown them have without exception been barefaced brigands.[a] It may be that the advent of Communism to the Asian scene has raised warfare to a nobler level, but that it should have done so cannot be taken for granted without evidence. In the second place, the argument cuts both ways, and if we are going to count the Vietnamese who have stood ready to sacrifice life or limb in the fighting, we find the insurgents in a minority— in a minority not better than one to four; so that, at best, the ideal, whatever it is, is one which a minority are trying to impose

[a] The Elizabethan rhyme —'Treason doth never prosper: what's the reason?
For if it prosper, none dare call it treason'—
has an even older Chinese equivalent: 'Who loses is a brigand, who pulls it off a prince' (*Pai-chê wei k'ou, ch'êng-chê wei wang*).

on the majority, fired likewise (*a priori*) by an ideal of their own.

Persuasion or coercion?

Indeed, their minority standing is perhaps the strongest objection against looking for an idealistic motivation for the insurgents, since we cannot ignore the means of persuasion available to them and actually used by them. In the 1930s the Communists and other revolutionary movements in Vietnam published newspapers, through which it was possible for them to convert people to their way of thinking—although that is still not to say they did so in fact; from the 1940s onwards presses and newsprint have not been available, either to the insurgents in the North before 1954 or to those in the South after 1954, and at best they have possessed means to produce leaflets by cyclostyle; there were virtually no wireless receivers in the Vietnamese countryside until about 1960. Persuasion could therefore only be by word of mouth, and who is to know just what was said? This particular activity is invariably called in the books of the insurgents '*armed* propaganda'—in those of Truong Chinh and Vo Nguyen Giap the word 'propaganda' hardly occurs on its own; but if propaganda is armed, its cogency is more likely to repose in the weapon than in the argument. This would not be consistent with the image of a movement motivated by spontaneous enthusiasm. Indeed, if terror was employed at all it must surely undermine that image; and not only has it been employed at every stage in the conflict, but the fact is publicized and boasted of, as if to do so advanced the movement in some way—as obviously it would if the driving force were intimidation, not argument. The object of 'armed propaganda' in 1945, we are told, was 'suppression of puppet officials and traitors';[a] what quality of investigation and of judgement preceded these 'liquidations?'—and is the fair presumption that they were prompted by ideals of impartial justice or that they were acts of terror to make the watchers fearful for themselves? In the most recent period we may be helped to identify the positive side of the Liberation Front by the exultation with which its clandestine transmitter recounted the mortaring of Saigon central market late in 1966 (in which eight people died and forty-two were maimed) as a 'resounding exploit' showing the insurgents' 'perfect creative spirit'.[b] The kindest interpretation of such boasts would be that they are Freudian betrayals of subconscious thought—less kind that they are meant to bully and frighten their listeners.

Front and Party

No less baffling than the question of rank-and-file motivation has been that, at least since 1960, of the weight to be ascribed to the Communist element in the NFLSV. The publicity of that body tells us that it is truly a front, in which the Communist element, represented by the People's Revolutionary Party, is large but not dominant; that the Front is entirely independent of the Government of North Vietnam, for all the 'fraternal solidarity' vouchsafed it from that quarter; that it arose from non-Communist initiatives to overthrow the Diem tyranny and free the country from foreign domination (by the US); and that its objectives, Diem having been overthrown by other hands, are to free South Vietnam from those who have succeeded him (no less objectionable as puppets), to set up a 'liberal regime' with a neutral foreign policy, to evict US forces, to transfer ownership of big estates to the 'tillers', and to enable the people of the South to 'progress towards reunification with the North'.[a] Again, French writers tend to confirm the independence of the Front from the Government of the North and, originally, of Communist influence—to the point of telling us that the insurgent bands sprang up in South Vietnam from 1959 onwards by a sort of spontaneous generation, driven to it in self-defence against an oppressive Government; that the Communists founded the People's Revolutionary Party (*Dang Nhan Dan Cach Mang*) to take over leadership of these bands almost reluctantly; and that the Government of Ho Chi Minh had to be shamed into giving them moral and other support. Here also certain reservations suggest themselves.

Propaganda and fact

It is curious—however possible—for a Communist government to have to be shamed into supporting a movement beyond its borders dedicated to turning over to it territory it had all along claimed was its by right. But it is, more than that, quite impossible that half a dozen insurrections should begin simultaneously in a small area independently of one another and without preparation or organization: it takes a guiding hand even to arrange a riot in a crowded township. If the 'Marxist-Leninists' (as they call themselves), in founding the People's Revolutionary Party, had to be

[a] Originally six points (e.g. Gettleman, 1966, pp. 265–8), the same matter was later rearranged as ten (*Daily Worker*, 26 June 1965); the points not mentioned here advocated social services, equality of sexes and races, freedom of press and religion, a national army, etc. etc.—all of which could be claimed by their adversaries to exist already.

pushed forward from a state of modest retirement to take on the leadership of a guerrilla Front they had had no part in setting in motion, the question demands an answer what they had been doing since the days when they were the 'majority party' in the Vietminh; if they had been letting the grass grow under their feet, they were poor Marxist-Leninists. Nor is the publication of slogans and manifestoes by Front or Party in itself evidence of much weight: a Communist writer in China has pointed out that slogans adopted by rebels in Chinese history had habitually been hypocritical excuses for rebellion;[a] when Professor Lucien Pye interrogated sixty surrendered Communist insurgents in Malaya he found that only seven of them had supposed the movement's slogans were to be taken at their face value—and they had been subjected to ridicule by their comrades for their ingenuousness.[b] Doubt is similarly cast over the sincerity of the Front's slogans: what popular appeal is to be expected from a published programme demanding social services that exist already but whose shortcomings are visibly due to the armed insurrection whose object purports to be to create them? The apparent illogicality of this position is cleared up if we consider the slogan on land reform: we know about it because we read the *Daily Worker*, but if instead we had obtained our information about the Front's land policy from simultaneous broadcasts by Liberation Radio, we would have learnt something rather different, namely that by October 1965 3 million South Vietnamese peasants living in the 'liberated areas', and already owners of the land they tilled, 'had been grouped into mutual-aid teams, the first step towards collectivization'.[c] Evidently the Front has two voices, one advocating land *to* the tillers and the other land *from* the tillers, and its published statements cannot be taken on their own as evidence of fact.

Two voices

At least in this particular example, the difference between the Front's two voices lies in the audience addressed: to the Western world the Front, and the armed insurrection it leads, seeks sympathy by appearing as a respectable form of civil strife, manned by the enthusiastic masses smarting under their grievances and wanting only what is best for their nation; but before the Communist world the Front emphasizes its Marxist-Leninist orthodoxy and reassures its friends that its struggle is fully in line with their common

[a] Sun Tso-min, quoted by Harrison (1965, p. 100).   [b] Pye (1956), pp. 225–6.
[c] Rebroadcast by Radio Hanoi, 30 Mar. 1966.

Cold War interests. As General Vo Nguyen Giap explains the Front's position to his Communist audience, if the Front in the South has truck with the middle classes and the bourgeoisie and espouses the slogan of 'neutrality', that is only out of expediency, to make use of 'the nationalism of the largest majority of the people' against the US notwithstanding their 'class' objections to the movement's real Marxist aims; the achievement of the latter will be helped, not hindered, by this supping with the Devil, a necessary preliminary to uniting the South with the Communist North and aligning it with the Communist bloc—'Vietnam has ever been one and indivisible'.[a]

4. GOVERNMENT AND REVOLUTION

The unsatisfactoriness of the current explanations of the conflict in Vietnam show the need to probe deeper beneath the surface in search of the perplexing unseen factors which have frustrated peacekeeping by the ICC and have resulted in horrifying loss of life, stultifying Vietnam's development as an independent country and disappointing the hopes at Geneva in 1954 that the country would cease to be a threat to international peace.

Scope of this study

The study of which the following chapters are the fruit began nearly a year before the NFLSV announced its foundation at the end of 1961; it has been made almost wholly in Vietnam. From the chronological point of view, the greater part of it was made backwards, starting from the present situation and working towards its causes; but the events described in Chapters 6 and 7 were lived through as they happened. The conclusions reached have determined the arrangement of the material; since the study is an inquiry into causes, influences, and motives rather than a chronicle of events —many of the more spectacular of which, judged from the international point of view, have been peculiarly irrelevant to the course of Vietnam's domestic drama (that 'Writ of Heaven')—, the arrangement is partly chronological and partly topical. In order to bring out as many as possible of the factors that have contributed to the country's predicament today, none has been explored in full detail; the biggest economies of treatment have been made at the expense of the diplomatic and military aspects of the conflict be-

---

[a] Vo-nguyen-Giap (1965), p. 50.

cause these, being conditioned largely by forces external to Vietnam, are the ones best covered in an already copious literature. (It is regrettable that none of this literature comes from the pens of Vietnamese, save for about four Communist leaders[a]—another unexpected fact whose explanation is sought hereafter.) As the inquiry is directed to discovering the internal factors at work, fuller treatment is given to topics the author has been able to see at close range or even from the inside.[b]

The argument

The argument is that the NFLSV, like the Vietminh before it, is none other than the old ICP, and that that Party, far from having been founded spontaneously by local men converted to Marxism through intellectual curiosity and conviction, was from the outset a subversive movement introduced into Vietnam by the Communist International out of considerations that held no interest for, and were marked at the time by little interest in, the Vietnamese people; that the Party's success was owed to the accident of the Second World War, not to its own popularity; and that this foreign-orientated movement adapted itself only gradually, albeit skilfully in the end, to the social structure of the country and to the traditional patterns of behaviour of Vietnamese peasant life. In order to understand peasant behaviour, a look must be taken at the historical and geographical factors that have shaped it. The influence of China has been immense—greater than the influence of India on the neighbouring lands of Indochina—but it has not all been connected with the fine art and noble thought for which China stood, until the other day, in the eyes of the West. China has bequeathed to Vietnam her own perennial conflict, at the level of the village commune, between the stabilizing forces of central government and the disruptive elements of revolution. The extraordinary shape of the national territory as finally settled by the ethnic Vietnamese (1,500 miles long, but in places barely two miles wide, with the two main concentrations of population more than 1,000 miles apart) has further weakened central government and national cohesion, leading to repeated partitions at points between the 16th and the 18th paral-

---

[a] Caution is called for in accepting even these as works of personal authorship: all share a common style, issue under a single imprint and could be the work of ghost writers in the propaganda factory. We shall see later that 'Ho Chi Minh' may not originally have been a single person (note 55).

[b] For a different reason, no attempt has been made to record developments in North Vietnam since 1956; information is hard to come by (see however the treatise of Le Chau, 1966), and the internal conflict there is at an end for the foreseeable future.

lels for nearly half a millennium; the present division is, by historical criteria, normal not exceptional.

Rulers and allies

In fact, to Vietnam's turmoil today, when viewed from the inside, the issue of peace or war is incidental to the millenary conflict within the village commune between government and revolution. French colonial rule—the hackneyed judgements about whose worth do not help towards an accurate understanding of the country's problems—affected Vietnamese life profoundly but did not, in the end, solve this ancient problem. When one looks at the facts more closely, Ngo Dinh Diem (who is the central figure in this book) is seen to have erred, not by imposing too much government on his people, but too little. Moreover, like generations of Vietnamese rulers before him, he was deeply xenophobic, to the point of supposing foreign powers wanted only to annex his land, until, just as typically of his predecessors at the head of the state, it suited him to call on foreign aid himself from an ally he thought he could use more than it used him. Ho Chi Minh, in the same tradition, was pursuing a similar policy at the same time; both of them mistrusted France at the delicate moment of colonial emancipation lest, if the other should call on her as well (as unabrogated, if disregarded, protocol agreements with her required), it would be the other she would intrigue with and favour more; so in her place each chose the friend with most to give, and the link between their civil strife and the Cold War became indissoluble. But the Cold War was not the essence of the matter, and, if historical precedent is anything to go by, it is probable that, even if there had been no Communist factor, independence would have been followed just the same by regional partition and by attempts of each half to get the better of the other through manipulation of ethnic minorities and religious or other factions with real, imaginary or trumped-up grievances against the authority on the spot.

Revolutionary warfare

The method by which the Communist movement, started so long ago for Russian reasons of state, did adapt itself successfully to the Vietnamese ecology, after several failures, was learnt in the Chinese school of revolutionary warfare. Whilst too much significance ought not perhaps to be attached to the writings of Mao Tsê-tung—or even to those of his Vietnamese disciples, Truong Chinh and Vo

Nguyen Giap—, for they contain large doses of propaganda and of explanation *post factum*, there is in all these works an underlying line of thought that is significant: it can be appropriately labelled 'Tagorism'. Rabindranath Tagore seems to have been the writer who first comforted Chinese intellectuals forty years ago for their country's inadequacy to stand up to foreign armies equipped from Western technology with the idea that, in the long run, the laws of history will ensure the triumph of the moral values and the spiritual civilization of the East against the ruthless materialism of an over-mechanized West.[a] This idea, though rejected by Chinese thinkers of other persuasions,[b] has sustained both Chinese and Vietnamese Communists, for all their wish to be materialists, through dire tribulation, and the spectacular Communist victory over France has lingered in Vietnamese memories as evidence of its correctness in spite of subsequent experiences to the contrary. In 1954 the leaders of the DRV might conceivably have set about triumphing over the separate regime in the South by making the North more attractive to the masses in economic terms; paradoxically—for Tagore's intentions were pacifist—the Tagorist depreciation of technology strengthened their preference for guerrilla warfare as the way to make the most effective use of an abundant but unskilled manpower. We shall see how occasions for the practical application of Tagorism to guerrilla fighting have arisen under the heads both of morale and of logistics. From this point of view, guerrillas must not seek material rewards for successful endeavour on behalf of the revolution because the movement will never have the resources from which to bestow them; instead, they must in the first place get their guns for themselves through ruthless application of the spiritual qualities of guile, stealth, and daring, in order to prove they are worthy of their meagre share of the sustenance extorted from the masses and, later, of the strictly rationed armaments and supplies sent in through laborious channels by fraternal People's Democracies far away. Their pride must be in the impalpable rewards that accrue from their leaders' wits and their own toil to the cause of the *Party*—which is going to win anyway because it forces upon them these virtues of austerity and self-effacement—, and they must show contempt for the regular soldiers opposing them, who are rendered soft and craven-hearted, as well as slow-footed, by the superior weapons and outsize impedimenta that have been slung about their slender shoulders by their rich wellwishers. If the guer-

---

[a] Wright (1959), p. 119.   [b] e.g. Hu Shih (1934), iii. 3.

rillas can snatch from their opponents even a fifth of their equipment, the forces are henceforward evenly matched.

American intervention

The reasons why America's unprecedentedly altruistic help—there should be no mistake about its motives—failed to make her ally in the South viable stem from inability to sever at an early stage the symbiotic relationship between government and revolutionary forces, and likewise from misunderstanding of the persuasiveness of the Tagorist outlook. In the life of the Vietnamese peasant there are no free choices: he has no practical prospect of determining his own destiny, and if now and again he does choose not to comply with the wishes of the power he estimates will prove the stronger in the end, it is out of fear of some more immediate intimidation. The pillars of support America fashioned for Ngo Dinh Diem rested on the contrary assumption that the peasant could exercise a free choice and that his support could be won by appeal to ideology and material comforts. In order that the effect of financial aid and of a powerful army (the two principal pillars of aid) should be greater than just their sum, they were closely tied together; it will be argued in this book that it was that bond which destroyed the leader it was meant to uphold. The chain of events that actually brought about Ngo Dinh Diem's destruction owed less to his 'tyranny' or his religious prejudice than the outside world was led to believe; the decisive factor was more prosaic—his ignorance how to administer the ordinary machinery of government over which he presided and which a more statesmanlike leader might have so disposed as to prevent revolutionary activity from reviving in his territory at all, formidable though the Marxist-Leninist leadership and methods had always been. Executive presidents need to know their business better than do kings and titular presidents whose ministers can share constitutionally their heavy responsibility. The US tried to redeem the calamitous consequences of Diem's downfall—calamitous from the Cold War point of view—by multiplying many times its financial and military efforts without changing their direction or upsetting the symbiotic balance. Those efforts aggravated the economic disintegration of urban life and held out new opportunities for factional disputes, but they did little to solve the fundamental problem facing the country—the protection of the individual villager from the intimidation, immediate or in prospect, of revolutionaries brought up on that first principle of Marxism-

Leninism, 'Every Communist must grasp the truth that political power grows out of the barrel of a gun.'[a]

Envoi

The story of the stages by which Vietnam has declined into her present condition makes no more cheerful reading than does the description of the condition itself. It is hardly surprising to find that it has been brought about otherwise than by display of heroism and exercise of wisdom. The faults of the Vietnamese people and their leaders, the exposure of which through the presence in their homeland of so many foreigners has put them out of countenance, may be judged not different in kind or degree from shortcomings detectable in a number of other newly independent countries; but the Vietnamese face perils those other countries do not face, and it is that circumstance which makes their sins and mistakes a serious matter. If for this reason few palms fall to be awarded in the following pages, it is not the chronicler who should be blamed.

[a] Mao Tsê-tung (1965), ii. 224.

2

THE HERITAGE FROM CHINA

IF there is one proposition that unites all Vietnamese, whatever else divides them, it is the negative one that their country is not to be regarded on any account as a dependency of China; they may disagree about what Vietnam is or ought to be, but all are at one that what it is not is that. And yet China has been a factor in every period of Vietnam's history and overshadows her national life today the same as ever. She overshadows Vietnam geographically, demographically, linguistically, culturally, politically. Other influences may intrude for a while, but China is present always. There is no aspect of the domestic life of the Vietnamese people that has not been touched by influences from China. In whatever external problem Vietnam becomes involved, the parties will invariably have an eye to China in its solution, even when China herself evinces no concern. Whilst generalizations about China are frequently invalid for Vietnam, China is nevertheless a constant point of reference in talking about Vietnam.

Geographical links

Considering the geographical ties between the two countries first of all, there is, besides their common frontier, a striking resemblance between the serpentine coastline of Vietnam and that of China: as one Western writer has put it, Vietnam is 'the lesser Dragon'.[a] Historically, the origins of political development are traceable in both countries to the settlement of alluvial river valleys and estuaries and to a 'social contract' catering primarily for the regulation of irrigation. Even more significantly, the history of Vietnam has been shaped, among other influences, by the same tendency as the history of China for population to drift southwards: the Chinese did not settle their southernmost coastal regions until the eleventh century, nor the Vietnamese theirs until the eighteenth. More than that, there may have been some connexion between the parallel migratory movements, the Vietnamese people having originated,

[a] Buttinger (1958).

like many other southeast Asian peoples, in what is today Chinese territory. In both cases the absorption of more southerly peoples has left its mark on the inhabitants of the southern provinces alike in physical characteristics and in a tendency to seek political autonomy from the traditional centres of civilization and of authority in the north. Southward migration remains even today a feature of Vietnamese demography with its bearing on the Communist struggle. The North enjoys a prestige of intellect and leadership— the French sited both the capital and the university of Indochina at Hanoi—which overawes the far South and makes the people there sensitive and suspicious lest the North should try to 'colonize' them. The prestige of Peking and of northern speech among the Chinese is a close parallel, but, in the case of Vietnam, Hanoi and Tonkin owe their prestige to their closeness to China as the fountainhead of Vietnamese culture, in addition to being the cradle of the nation.

Chinese sovereignty

Only in the most modern period of Vietnamese history has China ceased to be the suzerain at least of the northern half of the country, if not of the people themselves, wherever they thrust southwards to settle—only, in fact, since the treaty of Tientsin in 1885, by which France forced China to cede the protectorate over Tonkin. For 900 years before that the Vietnamese sovereigns ('emperors' in their own parlance, 'princes' in that of the Chinese) had held their throne by virtue of the seal issued by the Sons of Heaven and at regular intervals acknowledged their subordination by payment of tribute. Although a tribute mission sent to Peking in 1877 proved to be the last, the notion of the relationship of under-king to suzerain (*la tutrice morale*, as one French scholar describes it),[a] derived ultimately from the remote example of relations between the Chinese princelings and the Chou Emperors before even the time of Confucius, persisted at the Vietnamese court, with a sentiment akin to pride, in defiance of the French point of view, right on until the Throne of Heaven itself went under in the Chinese revolution of 1911. Beyond the ceremonial of this suzerainty, China has at many periods played a significant part in Vietnamese political life more or less indirectly. Vietnamese kings deposed by their rebellious subjects would appeal to the Son of Heaven for help in regaining their throne, and responses to such appeals have been the commonest

[a] Gaultier (1933), p. 18.

motive for invasion by Chinese armies. On the other hand, Vietnamese rebels who had been unsuccessful would also seek sanctuary in China. This latter custom, from the 1880s onwards, has put Vietnam in touch with the intellectual movements of modern China and with their important political undertones. It was not until after the First World War that France displaced China as the main source of ideas about government, either political or administrative; until that time, Western writers (not excluding French ones) were commonly read by the Vietnamese intelligentsia in Chinese translation rather than in French. The flow of ideas out of China has played an important part in the development of Vietnamese Communism.

Chinese immigration

Vietnamese émigrés have, however, been numerically the smaller element in the migration between the two countries, and immigration to Vietnam from China has been a steadier and more prolonged movement. The hilly borderlands of Tonkin have been a sanctuary for Chinese brigands since time immemorial, and these have often intervened at moments of crisis in Vietnamese history, from the thirteenth century to the twentieth; similarly, the towns were a haven for political refugees from China and an exile for transported criminals. Chinese travellers were recording journeys to more southerly and westerly parts of Indochina as far back as the third century, and the middle stretches of the coast of Annam have attracted merchants (or pirates—they were often indistinguishable) at least since the sixteenth century. During the seventeenth century there were Chinese physicians on the staff of the royal court at Hanoi,[a] and refugees from the Manchu invasion of China did much of the pioneering work in Cochinchina by means of which sovereignty over the Mekong Delta passed, bit by bit, from Cambodia to Annam between 1650 and 1750. These latter refugees, originating in a particular region of China, have left their mark on the folk culture of southern Vietnamese society: to their influence can be attributed, in part at least, the prevalence of clandestine organizations among the rural population which has so favoured the growth of the Communist movement. Chinese migration attained its greatest momentum after the advent of colonial rule; all over southeast Asia, European political control not only provided many more opportunities for commerce but also created both new demands for

[a] Marini (1663), p. 148.

labour and the shipping and financial facilities, through indenture, by which Chinese peasants uprooted in the aftermath of the Taiping Revolt of the 1850s and 1860s in their own country could take advantage of them. At the present day it is estimated that about a million 'overseas Chinese' live in Vietnam and have Vietnamese citizenship—a smaller proportion of the total population than in some neighbouring countries, but a no less self-conscious and self-perpetuating community, racially distinct. They do not labour much on estates, as they do in Malaysia and Indonesia, but play an important part in banking and moneylending, the wholesale marketing of rice, the retailing of non-perishable goods, and in foreign trade; one or two Chinese peasant groups in the Mien Tay, notably near Rach Gia, are reckoned by their Khmer and Vietnamese neighbours to be the oldest inhabitants of the locality.[1]

Invasions of China

It would be wrong, however, to think of China's attitude towards Vietnam as entirely passive. In the modern period at any rate, China has had cause to be apprehensive, not at the risk of invasion by the Vietnamese themselves, but lest Vietnamese territory be used by third parties to penetrate her own. Japanese merchants, excluded from direct trade with China in the sixteenth century, established entrepots at 'Ke Cho' (Hanoi) and at Tourane. The occupation of Cochinchina by the French had, as one of its original motives, the erroneous belief that the River Mekong would prove to be a navigable route into western China by which the limitations placed on European shipping up the Yangtze could be circumvented and the heart of the country be reached for purposes of trade in defiance of the policy of the Chinese Government of the day. When it was discovered that the Mekong was navigable only up to a point still far removed from the nearest Chinese territory, French mercantile interest switched to the Red River; it was only after exploration had confirmed that this route, on the contrary, would give access to Yunnan that the French declared their protectorate over Tonkin as superseding China's. During the Second World War, after the fall of France, Japan was able to use Vietnamese territory for the extrication of troops beleaguered in China and threatened later to fight her way back in by the same route. Today, it is obvious that a united Vietnam in alliance with the West at a time when the West is hostile to China—even if the hostility is caused by China's aggressiveness—would bring with it the threat of twentieth-century style penetration. This is the source of China's active interest in Vietnam at the present time.

China's frontiers

In one way or another, therefore, the Chinese presence is an enduring feature of Vietnamese national life, not substantially more preponderant for one generation than for another—always maintaining itself but never taking over completely. The fact is that China is only in the modern period becoming a defined area of territory, with permanent and certain edges beyond which lie quite distinct states and cultures. Traditionally China was a cultural core, radiating its influence wider and wider over the centuries as it reached out from the Yellow River Basin, so that at a given moment of history it would only be in degree that the Chineseness of the speech and the customs of Kuangtung, for instance, would differentiate them from those of Hainan or Tonkin—the latter always betraying some measure of assimilation, the former never totally sinicized. To land in Vietnam today from the West is to feel that one has arrived in the Chinese world; but to arrive instead from the East is to be aware of having already left China behind. However deeply one gets to know country and people in the course of time, this baffling impression always persists—that two viewpoints are valid on the Chineseness of Vietnam, depending upon which way the observer happens to be facing at the time.

2. VIETNAMESE BEGINNINGS

The ultimate home of the Vietnamese is to be sought in China, but in the southwestern regions of that country and at a time before there were Chinese inhabitants in them; the emergence of a self-conscious ethnic unit identifiable as Vietnamese is most probably a result of the expansion of the Chinese southwards during the last half-millennium BC. These earliest origins are shrouded in doubt, and recourse to a good deal of conjecture is needed if the scattered pieces of evidence are to be reduced to a system. Speaking archaeologically, the whole Indochina peninsula had attained a certain cultural unity by the time metals came into use; this cultural area, which reached as far as Indonesia in the south and into what is now southern China in the north, is known after a type-site, Dong Son, situated on the borders of Annam and Tonkin. By this criterion, the land of the Vietnamese would not differ from the rest of Indochina but would be distinct from most of China. By about the fourth century BC the Chinese were in touch with a principality in Tonkin which they called Chiao Chih, and this is claimed by the modern Vietnamese, very plausibly, as a native kingdom of their own. They have legends to carry the national history back much farther, especially to a state called Van Lang and a line of monarchs called Hung Vuong or 'Hero-Princes', followed by a dynasty called Hong Bang (meaning 'vast and overflowing') that lasted 2,500 years; but these legends are so coloured by details taken from Chinese mythology as to obscure rather than illuminate the facts of Vietnamese origins.

The name Viet

The same can be said for the very name *Viet*. We know it from Chinese books even earlier than the fourth century BC, when it was written, more or less arbitrarily, by borrowing either of two ideograms which appear always to have been pronounced the same way (modern Chinese *yüeh*) although they had unconnected meanings. The name was applied to peoples the Chinese regarded as alien to themselves anywhere down the seaboard from the Shantung peninsula to the Gulf of Tonkin, so vaguely that in the time of Confucius reference was frequently made to the 'Hundred (that is, numerous) Viets'.[a] One might infer that *Viet* stood for the native name of a widely spread people, all of whose descendants have since been absorbed by the Chinese save those of Tonkin.[b] An alternative hypothesis would be that a single people is indeed involved, but that they are spoken of at different points on the coast at different periods because they were gradually migrating southwards all the time, perhaps under Chinese pressure; thus one French scholar identifies the early Vietnamese with the Hoklo of Swatow and Hong Kong.[c] But no evidence is put forward in support of this, and there is no trace in the Vietnamese language of the survival of any original native form for *Viet*. The truth is almost certainly that it is the name itself that has migrated; ethnic names have a curious way of doing that (*Indian, Ethiopian, Dutch*), and the Chinese have always displayed a somewhat contemptuous imprecision, if not ignorance, about foreign peoples—all the more so when these called themselves by names which the Chinese, hampered by a restricted phonology, could not pronounce. Many Chinese authors contented themselves with referring to barbarians vaguely by the quarter of the

[a] T'ao Wei-ying (1959), p. 27.   [b] Aurousseau (1924), p. 23.
[c] Madrolle (1937), p. 329.

compass in which their homes were supposed to lie, and in fact *Viet* was at times interchangeable with *Yi* denoting simply 'barbarians to the East'.[a] The addition of the word *nam* meaning 'south' would be explained by the need to distinguish Tonkin from the provinces farther up the coast, also included in the general designation *Yüeh*. The fact that the Vietnamese adopted this Chinese political term for themselves instead of using an indigenous ethnic name is attributable to their heterogeneous make-up, upon which a political unity was finally imposed under some sort of Chinese influence and under a Chinese label, rather than by internal forces.

Thai peoples

The most plausible of the available explanations of Vietnamese origins, and the one most generally accepted nowadays, is that we have here a mixture of the common Indochina stock with an overlay of Thai, or else of a tribal people connected with the Thais. The Thais are believed to be related ultimately to the Chinese but to have separated from them a long time ago and to have been gradually pushed out by them from the southwestern provinces of modern China; an early offshoot would have migrated to the southeastern provinces of modern China to constitute the Chuang people of Kuanghsi province, as well as the aristocratic element in the formation of the first Vietnamese state of Chiao Chih. If this was so in fact, Vietnam conforms closely to the general ethnic composition of the Indochina peninsula: a basic population of proto-Indonesian stock, speaking some kind of Malay language or of Mon–Khmer, constantly retreating before the southward pressure down the Salween, Menam, Mekong, and Red River valleys of successive waves of Thais (known by many other names—Tho, Lao, Shan, Siam) who have either driven them out of the irrigated valleys into the less hospitable hill country or have set up states in which the natives are incorporated but subject to social disadvantages. Ethnic distinctions have subsequently been obliterated by the common adoption, on the one hand of the cultural heritage of India, on the other of that of China. Since these latter influences have not penetrated the hill country at all, the more apparent division of peoples in the area today is less one of biological descent than of culture between civilized, literate plainsmen cultivating 'wet'-paddy *sawahs* and more backward, unlettered hill tribes practising slash-and-burn cultivation of 'dry' paddy.[2]

[a] T'ao Wei-ying, p. 28.

Indian civilization

Although it was the introduction of a Hinduized culture which made possible the organization of big states in the plains of Indochina, there was no political domination from India, which lay such a long way away by sea. In this India's influence was on a different footing from China's. How it penetrated the region is still not very clear, but most scholars discount suggestions that it could have resulted from actual migration from India on any considerable scale without leaving clear evidence of the fact; a simpler explanation is that it was a by-product of trade, the date at which it appears to have begun—the first century AD—corresponding closely to the discovery of the monsoons and the known opening of extensive navigation across the Indian Ocean by vessels of Middle Eastern, Indian, and Chinese construction; Western artifacts of Roman date, and Roman coins, have been unearthed in the Mekong Delta.[a] The Indonesian archipelago was affected as much as the mainland of southeast Asia, but the effects made themselves felt only gradually on continent and islands alike; it may be significant that, in addition to their common underlying wet-paddy agriculture, all the Hinduized states, continental and insular, were from the beginning seafaring and able to maintain contact with India over long periods by themselves, whether or not Indian travellers continued to show interest in southeast Asia. What we know of the earlier stages of the process of indianization comes not from native sources, for writing was one of the elements in the new culture to be copied more slowly, but from the records of visitors from China; in later centuries also, when these states were eventually compiling their own chronicles, there are many gaps in their history which can be filled only from Chinese sources, none from Indian ones.[b]

Funan and Chanla

Three states arose under Indian influence on territory destined later to belong to Vietnam; one of them, Chanla, is known only from Chinese records until the moment when, in the seventh century, it conquered the second of them (but the first in point of age), Funan. The third is Champa, called by the Chinese *Linyi*. None of these states can have been truly a nation-state, for the area over which they wielded authority at any given time was scattered and uncertain and rarely homogeneous even linguistically. Funan was

[a] Malleret (1951), pp. 86–87.
[b] With the exception of Burma (Saletore, 1960, *passim*).

the most important as well as the earliest. Largely Malay by race, with colonies of its own merchants as far away as the Malay peninsula and the Menam valley in modern Thailand, it had its capital on the present Vietnamese-Cambodian frontier beside the River Bassac, whence in those days access to the open sea through broader, unsilted channels was doubtless easier than it would be today. The territory of Funan included southern Cambodia and all of southern Vietnam as far up the coast as Cape Varella. Chanla lay to the north of Funan, inland up the Mekong valley, and was inhabited by Khmer-speakers, doubtless akin to the modern Bahnar and Sedang tribes of the Annamite Chain but more strongly influenced by Indian civilization. Their conquest of Funan gave the latter its definitively Khmer character, and it was at this time that the name 'Kambuja' was adopted, also from India;[a] from the revitalized empire, now centred on Yasodharapura, there developed by the eighth century the kingdom of Angkor, destined to dominate the region for 700 years, until overthrown by the Thais of Siam. The descendants of the Chanla are still an important element in the population of Cochinchina, and the limestone outcrops of the capital region of Funan which they overran, known now as the Seven Mountains, have been a significant sanctuary and recruiting-ground for insurgents allied to the Communists.[3]

Champa

The third of the Hinduized kingdoms on what today is Vietnamese soil, Champa, stretched along the coast from north of Nha Trang to the Col des Nuages at the sixteenth parallel; calling itself by the borrowed Buddhist name Amaravati,[b] it had its spiritual centre at an inland place in Quang Nam province nowadays called My Son, but in those days Indrapura; the king's residence was Champapura, modern Dong Duong. Champa was Malay by stock and language, and apparently more aggressive than its neighbours, dispatching war fleets in course of time up the China coast, down to Sumatra and the great Malay kingdom of Srivijaya, and through the Mekong waterways to the Great Lake and the city of Angkor. Like its neighbours, it adopted Indian religion at court, with changing fashions of devotion to Buddha (down to the eighth century),[c] Shiva, Vishnu, and the phallic cult of the Linga a constant subordinate element. Yet the architecture of the surviving ruins of

---

[a] Hall (1964), p. 90.   [b] Champa as well is an Indian place name, in West Bengal.
[c] Parmentier (1906), p. 5.

places of worship, though usually Indian in decoration, exhibits notable non-Indian elements: the Hindu veneer of the state worship was perhaps not deepseated and began only at a later date to affect the lives of common people. The indigenous folklore of animism and propitiations by means of magic still today constitutes a common heritage of the unlettered peasantry throughout Indochina. Moreover, although far-away India might be the source of such political notions as those early kingdoms knew, it was to China that the Indochinese kings sent their periodical tribute and from China that they sought the recognition on which their local prestige rested to some extent; it was with China that part at least of their trade was conducted, more persistently than with India, and the presence of Chinese resident communities is attested all through the Middle Ages.[4]

Chinese conquest

The political interest of China in southeast Asia began as one of the manifestations of the expansion achieved under the exuberance of the Han dynasty, which, as has often been pointed out before, was fully equal, as a centre of civilization culturally, militarily, and politically, to its contemporary in the West, the Roman Empire. The relations between the Han empire and the less advanced peoples along its borders were similar to those of Rome in that they were marked by a gradual radiation of cultural, commercial, and political influence through the unconscious agency of political fugitives, adventurers, and settlers, as well as of traders, leading by stages to assimilation and eventually absorption. Conscious Han interest in Tonkin begins with the establishment in the third century BC of suzerainty over Chiao Chih; already modelling themselves in some respects on Chinese manners,[a] it would be natural for the princelings of the area to come to terms with the, at that time, novel phenomenon of a united Chinese monarchy. But when the Great Emperor annexed the region of Canton to China permanently, he extended his realm also to Tonkin, at that period scarcely distinguishable racially or culturally from its northeastern neighbour; for the previous hundred years or so, the two had together made up a single, partially-sinicized but politically-independent, state called by the Chinese *Nan Yüeh* (*Nam Viet*). This happened as early as 111 BC, and the territory thus brought under some sort of

---

[a] The *Shih Chi* (the earliest of China's dynastic histories) mentions a prince from the region who was brought up at the Han court (Li Chêng-fu, 1945, p. 23).

Chinese rule extended to isolated settlements on the coast as far down into Annam as the pass known as Porte d'Annam at the eighteenth parallel. During the next 150 years, Chinese political control remained for the most part indirect, it is generally believed, with a native feudal aristocracy in control, itself much influenced by Chinese ways, with the mass of the populace still living a 'Dongsonian' existence in all essentials. But a revolt of uncertain proportions against Chinese authority in the year AD 40, led according to tradition by two sisters of the surname Trung, marked the absorption of Tonkin for the next 900 years administratively into the Chinese state. There was, however, one interruption, in the sixth century; during the chaos that prevailed in southern China under the Liang dynasty, a Tonkinese principality appeared calling itself quaintly 'Eternal Spring' (*Van Xuan*). But the founder, Ly Bon, was of Chinese extraction, and his collaborators were largely refugees from China,[a] so that the authenticity of this insurrection as a Vietnamese one is perhaps in doubt. After reconquest by the Sui dynasty, Chinese rule continued uninterrupted until the end of T'ang.

Sinicization

The formative effects of this experience on the Vietnamese as a nation were destined to manifest themselves only at a future date when other factors arose to set them on the march. But it is most probably to these centuries, not earlier, that the fusion of the Tonkinese into one people speaking one language, with its profound Chinese flavour, belongs; it was then that they learned a system of government whose principal function was to regulate drainage and irrigation, and it was then that the Tonkinese became so completely imbued with the Confucian social and political philosophy which has persisted down to the present day alongside the primitive beliefs, as well as certain of the religious practices of Buddhism, which they share with their Indianized neighbours. It was during the ninth and tenth centuries that the new factors arose in Indochina from which Vietnam drew her separate national identity.

3. ACQUISITION OF THE NATIONAL TERRITORY

There were three factors at work to change the face of Indochina from about AD 800 onwards. The first and perhaps most important

[a] Durand (1954), pp. 439–40.

is the least precisely known about: it was a great increase in population, affecting the Hinduized Khmers and Chams and the Vietnamese no doubt in equal manner. In the region as a whole, there was abundant untilled land to be brought under cultivation, but the transfer of population from one place to another to take advantage of it led to centuries of warfare. The second factor came as an aggravation of the first: it was the arrival of fresh Thai immigrants —themselves doubtless impelled by overcrowding under conditions of inefficient agriculture in their upland homes—in many small and disunited groups, to swell the pressure in the valleys and plains between the Annamite Chain and the frontiers of modern Burma. The Vietnamese were descended in part from an earlier wave of Thais, and by the eighth century Tonkin was under pressure from a second wave, which had formed a principality calling itself Nam Chao and having its centre in Yunnan. In 862–3 this pressure culminated in the sacking of Hanoi, inadequately defended by the Chinese,[a] and gave the Tonkinese another reason for turning their eyes southwards. A third wave brought the ancestors of the Siamese down the Menam, those of the Lao down the Mekong. That infiltration was for the most part a slow process, and in the western parts of Indochina it was not until the thirteenth century that total numbers had grown enough for Thai states to be constituted and to challenge the authority of the indigenous kingdoms. The third of the three new factors was the collapse of the T'ang dynasty (of which the overrunning of Hanoi by Nam Chao was a small but locally-significant symptom), and the temporary disintegration of the Chinese empire which followed; China never again quite enjoyed her former pre-eminence in the East as a political force, even under the Manchus, although her cultural pre-eminence has remained to this day unimpaired.

Champa against Angkor

For 500 years, from 900 to 1400, Indochina was dominated by Angkor and Champa. Vietnam was destined to swallow up successively all the territory of the latter and most of the territory of the former, although French intervention eventually restored national identity to the Khmers in their heartland round the Great Lake. But it is unlikely that the astonishing expansion of Vietnam towards the south (the *Nam Tien*, as it was called) in the 500 years from 1400 to 1900 could have begun unless Champa had been weakened first

[a] Li Chêng-fu, p. 105.

in its wars with Angkor, and Angkor in its with Champa and with the encroaching Thais. The detail of the recurrent outbreaks by which this historical process was carried on has only an indirect bearing on the development of Vietnam; yet for much of the period the growing power of Vietnam as a potential ally from time to time was a factor in them, as perhaps was the ultimate referee, China. Angkor reached its zenith in the twelfth century, when its man-power was divided between the conduct of its military campaigns, the maintenance of the vast irrigation system comprising the heart of the capital region, and the building in stone (whereas the Chinese and Vietnamese built only with timber) of the huge monuments, among the canals and reservoirs, of Suryavarman II (Angkor Wat) and Jayavarman VII (Angkor Thom)—Indian in name and con-cept, native in design, and incongruously primitive in architectural execution. In the same period, Champa endowed what is modern Annam, if not with irrigation works, still with monuments of similar inspiration, though less ambitious construction—the towers, in brick, called *kalans* which occur beside many of the estuaries of Southern Annam, in the hills of Darlac and all round Indrapura, referred to before.[5]

Vietnam against Champa

The Chams had made raids into the northernmost part of Annam as early as the fifth century. The effect of the collapse of the T'ang dynasty was to remove the Pax Sinica from the region, both by de-priving the Vietnamese of its protection and by relaxing restraints on migration of their excess population in the opposite direction. The seesaw struggle for possession of modern Quang Binh and Thua Thien, stretching southwards from the Porte d'Annam at the 18th parallel to the Col des Nuages almost at the 16th, was not finally resolved in favour of the Vietnamese until about 1330, and even then, between Vietnamese raids as far as Qui Nhon, the Chams were able several times to sack Hanoi, the last occasion being as late as 1390. The decisive factor in the transfer of this territory was very probably colonization by Vietnamese peasants. The Chams were a typical Malay folk, more interested in the sea than in the land; in this they differed notably from the Vietnamese peasants, who cared much less for the sea and continued to penetrate Cham territory, and to cultivate it, independently of the military or political ar-rangements made by their princes. There was thus an insidious sapping of the Cham position at home going on all through the period of the great exploits against Angkor, from about 1150 to 1350.[6]

Champa subdued

Once the Vietnamese had secured a permanent foothold south of the Col des Nuages, by overrunning Indrapura and Champapura, all was quickly over. The Cham princes made concessions to and alliances with the Vietnamese court, but the advance of Vietnamese settlement in the coastal lands, which was both more intensive and more efficient than that of the natives, inevitably tended to undermine the authority of the Brahminized Cham court among its easy-going subjects. The process by which the Vietnamese gained possession of the Cham lands (unofficial encroachment, followed by formal cession, followed by the implanting of colonies of soldiers, banished rebels or merely landless peasants, whose grandchildren started the whole process over again) has set on the national character a pattern of colonization still followed today; it also left its mark on the close configuration of village settlement in Annam, which contrasts in its emphasis on the requirements of defence against surprise attack with the more open and scattered pattern that was to prevail eventually in Cochinchina, which for the most part lacked an indigenous population.

Fate of the Chams

After a short halt in their expansion when they were themselves reconquered by the Chinese, the Vietnamese finally evicted the Chams from Vijaya (Binh Dinh) in 1471, massacring those who could not get away[a] and confining those who did to the lands south of Cape Varella. The Vietnamese continued to recognize the hereditary status of Cham princes at Nha Trang and Phan Rang until nearly 1800, and an embassy from Champa received official Chinese recognition at Nanking as late as 1543.[b] In 1833–4 the surviving Chams were concentrated, under the supervision of Vietnamese villagers, in the arid area between Phan Rang and Phan Thiet, but most then emigrated en masse over the mountains to live among the Khmers on the middle or lower Mekong, or else assimilated themselves in small groups to the near-by hill tribes. Although about two-thirds of the groups who stayed in Annam retain traces of the

[a] Chesneaux (1956, p. 40) says 40,000 Chams were put to death; G. Maspéro (1928, p. 237) puts it at 60,000.

[b] Le-thanh-Khoi, p. 265; the *Wan-li hui-tien* still claimed in 1587 that Champa was sending tribute every three years (Fairbank & Têng, 1960, p. 123).

Hindu practices of long ago (the Cham Harat), the remainder have all become Muslims (the Cham Bani),[a] presumably by the same process that won their cousins in Malaya and Indonesia: reaction to the ostentation of the court religion, contrasting with the hardships that followed from the collapse of the central authority, would enhance the attractions of a simpler egalitarian faith. Although the Chams have gradually become identified in Cambodia with later Malay settlers from Kelantan, the memory of Champa's one-time glory is still cherished by those who have stayed in Vietnam; not only is much of the ancient regalia of their princes treasured by custodians recognized by the authorities near Phan Ri on the coast and at Dran in the mountains,[b] but when the Radé hill tribe, related racially to the Chams and no doubt recalling a 300-year integration with Champa long ago,[c] rebelled against the independent Vietnamese Government in 1959 and again in 1964–5, one of their demands was for the revival of Champa as an autonomous state. They have left their mark on the Vietnamese nation by adding to the general racial mixture, and also on the language, especially of the South, and not least, it is said, on Vietnamese music.

Decline of Angkor

The elimination of Champa brought the Vietnamese into direct contact, and conflict, with the Khmers. Already in the heyday of Angkor, Suryavarman II had in the 1120s invaded Annam from the Mekong and briefly held a wedge of the coastline of the Gulf of Tonkin between Vietnam and Champa. The decline of Angkor under the onslaught of the Chams and the Siamese Thais, as well probably as from the internal strains connected with the spread of quietist Theravada Buddhism among the common people, resulted in a drift of Khmer population southwards in the direction of the Mekong Delta which the Vietnamese were approaching simultaneously down the coast. The capture of Angkor by the Siamese Thais in 1431 made the Khmer kings retreat to the neighbourhood of Phnom Penh; but it also marked a general break-up of the Khmer state and the independence of rival petty princes—much as in the last days of Champa—who became an easy prey for Siamese and Vietnamese intrigue right down until the advent of French control over the area.

[a] Lafont (1964), pp. 157–8.   [b] Nghiem Tham (1960), p. 150.
[c] From about 1150 to 1450 (Bourotte, 1955, p. 19).

Vietnamese annexation of Cochinchina

Like the Chams earlier on, the Khmers were spread thinly over their part of the coastal plain, and their total population in the still forested Mekong Delta around 1700 was estimated in the official Vietnamese gazetteer of the region, the *Gia Dinh Dong Chi*, at below 40,000 families.[a] There were already Japanese, European, and other foreign settlements in the neighbourhood of Bien Hoa and Gia Dinh, and to them was added a Chinese colony at Cho Lon (the 'Great Market') about 1670.[b] In fact, Vietnamese penetration of Cochinchina was greatly helped by Chinese merchants and money-lenders, who settled before them and laid the foundations of a re-lationship that has persisted as a feature of Cochinchinese society down to the present day; the Chinese no doubt found the Viet-namese pioneers a more industrious people to finance than the native Khmers. The first Vietnamese claim to suzerainty over any of the Khmer lands dates from 1658;[c] in 1698 the Vietnamese ob-tained the formal cession of Bien Hoa and Saigon from the Khmer prince of Cap St Jacques, while ten years later they extended nominal protection to a Chinese settlement at Ha Tien, on the Gulf of Siam, which the Khmer princes at Phnom Penh had proved un-able to protect from the exactions of the Siamese. Further Vietna-mese demands on Phnom Penh in 1755 led to the cession of the country between Saigon and the Bassac. Altogether, the effective occupation of the vast alluvial plain between Saigon and Ha Tien took the Vietnamese another 150 years; extensive areas of it, es-pecially the Transbassac (Mien Tay) from modern Can Tho down to Pointe Camau, were only settled by the Vietnamese after the establishment of French colonial rule. Although about half a mil-lion Khmers remain today in the Mekong Delta, keeping their language and culture, many others have accepted assimilation to the Vietnamese way of life, with a consequent hybridization of the latter that is discernible in physical features, especially deeper skin pigment.

Limits of Vietnamese expansion

The present frontiers of Vietnam are not, however, the limit of historical Vietnamese expansion. As early as the fifteenth century, after the decline of Nam Chao had left their Thai neighbours in the hills of Tonkin less able to defend themselves, the Vietnamese pene-trated to the plateau areas of Sam Neua and Phong Saly in modern

[a] Aubaret (1863), p. 6.   [b] Boudet (1942), pp. 115–32.   [c] Hall, p. 399.

Laos and thence established their 'protection' over the Lao peoples of Vientiane—an historical precedent for the occupation of those same provinces by the Vietminh in 1952 and the launching from them of the Pathet Lao, who also constitute a threat to Vientiane at the present day. Similarly in the south, the opportunity of a suitable base in the Mekong Delta, combined with apprehension at the continued expansion of the Siamese Thais into Khmer territory, led the Vietnamese to advance in the 1830s to a point west of Phnom Penh, as well as up the Mekong behind the Annamite Chain, and to partition Cambodia for a while with Bangkok. On the other hand, within their frontiers the Vietnamese have never settled, and rarely administered, the mountain areas covering the greater part of the territory that is today recognized internationally as being their country: these and the residual lands of the Chams, separated from Cochinchina by a further inhospitable belt of low jungle country offering few possibilities for wet-paddy agriculture, have stretched internal lines of communication beyond the acceptable limit for national unity; from the fall of Vijaya until the present day, there have only been about three decades when the whole Vietnamese territory was under a single government.

4. CHINESE SUZERAINTY AND OFFICIAL CULTURE

The emancipation of the first Vietnamese state from Chinese rule in the tenth century is usually explained in modern histories as a nationalist uprising against an early type of colonial rule; but a closer look at the events attending the collapse of the T'ang dynasty does not bear out this explanation, nor is it compatible with the subsequent course of Sino-Vietnamese relations. It was the Thais of Nam Chao who evicted the Chinese from effective control of Tonkin in 863, not any popular uprising of the Vietnamese, and the fall of Canton in 878 or 879 to the rebel Huang Ch'ao which broke the links and brought Chinese officials (a particular target for plunder and murder by the rebels) in headlong flight to Tonkin—together, incidentally, with hundreds of Arab and other 'Western' merchants.[a] The Chinese 'Governor' whom the first Vietnamese leader, Ngo Quyen, displaced in 939—from which date the independence of the Dai Viet state is usually reckoned—was, though nominally a representative of the so-called Southern Han dynasty, no less a local warlord than Ngo Quyen himself. Vietnam became independent

[a] Levy (1955), pp. 28 & 110–13.

because China, in a state of anarchy, abandoned it. Only in 960, the year in which the Sung dynasty re-established law and order in China, over an area much smaller than had been ruled by the T'ang, was a true government of their own set up by the Vietnamese.[7]

Later Chinese invasions

The first phase of Vietnamese national history coincides with the Sung dynasty in China. The Sung recognized the first Vietnamese king, Dinh Bo Lanh (his given name seems to have meant 'Securer of the Mountain Ranges'), as a vassal ruler over 'Dai Co Viet'. When his family was turned out by the Le a few years later, the Sung Government tried to intervene, but their troops were defeated—the occasion which prompted the verse on the flyleaf of this book. There followed a period of 200 years during which successive Vietnamese usurpers turned out the ruling families recognized by the Chinese court, a progressively feebler China championed the legitimate side unsuccessfully, and finally the usurpers in their turn secured Chinese recognition. This cycle was repeated four times before the vigorous Tran family, often regarded itself as being of Chinese descent, put down a rebellion on behalf of the ruling Ly and then, in 1225, seized power on its own account.[a] They carried Vietnam a stage farther along the road of organization as a separate country. Previous 'dynasties', as we have seen, had battled victoriously against both Champa and Angkor; it now fell to the Tran dynasty to hold the Mongols at bay for thirty years. One tribe of the latter had subdued northern China in the twelfth century—an event which had encouraged Angkor to attempt the subjugation of both Champa and Dai Viet—, and the horsemen of Genghis Khan appeared in Tonkin for the first time in 1257, twenty years before they captured Hangchow and set up the Yüan dynasty in China. Indochina was saved by its climate from the ravages wrought by the Mongols in temperate latitudes, from eastern Europe to Korea. Although their expeditions by land and sea to conquer all the countries whose names the Chinese were able to give them, from northern Burma in an arc down to Java, were on the whole victorious—the Tran were driven out of Hanoi twice, on the second occasion by an army forcing its way overland to conquer Champa—their objectives scarcely went beyond glory and plunder. Eventually the treachery of the Chinese mariners on whom the Mongol fleets in southeast Asia de-

[a] Tran-trong-Kim (1964), p. 115.

pended, and the depredations of dysentery among their ill-acclimatized armies, spent the momentum of Kublai Khan once and for all. The last Mongol force invaded Tonkin by sea in 1287, got trapped in the inland waterways, and was slaughtered by the guerrillas of the redoubtable national hero of the North Vietnamese, Marshal Tran Hung Dao.[8] Thereafter, the Mongol dynasty in China took little interest in Indochina.

The Ming Conquest

The Tran eventually fell victims themselves to a family of usurpers from among their own warlords, the Ho, and the old pattern of reactions ensued. By now the Mongol yoke had been thrown off in China by the native dynasty of Ming, to whom the Tran were sending triennial tribute missions.[a] The great Yung Lo Emperor once more championed Tran legitimacy, sending an army to occupy Tonkin. But this time Chinese intervention took the form of a permanent reoccupation. While reviling the Mongols for their 'militarism' towards Indochina, the Emperor was ambitious to 'restore the arts of civilization, fallen so low from the standards of former times' in Vietnam, and even to 'dominate by his virtue' all of southeast Asia.[b] Hanoi was reduced to its ancient status under a Chinese Governor, Li Pin; Vietnamese mandarins who had been associated with the Ho against the Tran were replaced by Chinese officials, but those who were loyal to the Tran seem to have been left in office, sometimes with Chinese 'advisers' (*t'ung chih*) to watch over them.[c] But the new officials displayed a zeal and a highhandedness in the furtherance of administrative reform that went down ill with native ruling interests.[d] However, even this might have been accepted by most of the people but for the fiscal levies that were demanded to pay for it. The Chinese made their presence felt in the countryside only indirectly, and lawlessness became general. Out of the anarchy a new Vietnamese leader arose, Le Loi, to proclaim himself 'Prince of Pacification' (*Binh Dinh Vuong*); in the space of five or six years, from a base in the Lam Son hills in northernmost Annam, he worked up a guerrilla force which split up and, in 1427, surrounded the Chinese garrison, although allowing the defeated remnant to take flight back to Kuanghsi. Next year he held a public ceremony at which he proclaimed himself successor to the Tran and invited the

---

[a] Fairbank & Têng, p. 123. Regular three-yearly embassies seem to have begun in 1127 (Li Chêng-fu, p. 124).
[b] *Ming Shih* 321 (quoted in Li Chêng-fu, pp. 138–9).   [c] Ibid. p. 148.
[d] Ibid. p. 141.

people to take part in an elaborate oathswearing of national loyalty.[a9]

The Le and the chuas

It was the momentum of this renewed national effort that carried the Vietnamese on into the Thai country on one hand and the last strongholds of Champa on the other. Le Loi personally was soon overthrown in his turn, but the dynasty he founded was eventually recognized by the Ming in 1462[b] and remained the titular ruler of the Vietnamese until 1788. Many upheavals broke the peace in the meantime. It was exactly 100 years until, in 1527, another usurper appeared, Mac Dang Dung. For a century and a half the Mac maintained their hold over much of Tonkin, and it is interesting to note that the Le made use of the Lao provinces as a base in the early days of the struggle, while the Mac received support from Chinese bandits in the borderlands, making their last stand at Cao Bang, a traditional frontier stronghold for outlaws. The Le owed their survival to a family of majordomos, the Trinh, who, taking the title of *chua* (overlord), set up a kind of shogunate in Tonkin and put an end to Mac independence in 1677. But the consolidation of Trinh authority in Tonkin was achieved at the cost of losing Annam, where their cousins, the Nguyen, set up a rival regime of *chuas*—but not a rival throne[10]—at Hué. Thus Vietnam had absorbed Champa only to split again near the old dividing line. At first the Trinh were content to leave the Nguyen alone, in exchange for tribute and a supply of rice for always overpopulated Tonkin, already unable to produce enough for its needs.[c] But both sides were able to mobilize huge armies,[d] and fighting broke out between them in 1627; it lasted until 1673, when they made peace on the basis of the *status quo*, freeing their resources to cope with other internal stresses and, in the case of the Nguyen, to resolve these by pursuit of their drive into the lands of the Khmers. The Nguyen built a wall from the sea to the foothills across the coastal plain near Dong Hoi, a little north of the 17th parallel, which was respected by the Trinh for the next 100 years, before fighting broke out on a larger scale between the rival factions once more. As an old Sino-Vietnamese saying summed up the policy followed by the Nguyen, '*Hoa bac, tien nam*'—'When at peace with the North, push on in the South'.

a *Ming Shih* 154 (ibid. p. 153).   b Ibid. p. 159.
c Borri (1631), p. 83.
d The Nguyen 80,000 (ibid.), the Trinh 120,000 (Rhodes, 1651, p. 27).

Chinese suzerainty

It is not easy to argue from the succession of dynastic changes any very certain theory of Chinese suzerainty over Vietnam. The Dragon Throne was a kind of Papacy, both in its own sight and in that of its clients. Its moral prestige, if not its political power, was strong enough for the Hindu states of Indochina and Indonesia to seek its recognition in support of their new dynasties and kings. The collapse of dynasties in China invariably heralded trouble between neighbours in Indochina, while a return to strong government in one restored the balance of power in the other, through channels of influence it is no longer easy to discern. In the case of Vietnam, the relationship was more intimate; originating in the conquests of Han times, Chinese suzerainty, right down to the nineteenth century, was asserted in regard to Vietnamese territory rather than the Vietnamese people and thus was quite definite in Tonkin (which alone had formed part of the *ling t'u* or 'contiguous land' of the Han and the T'ang), much less certain in Annam, and never asserted at all in regard to Cochinchina. Yet the evidence is against the modern Vietnamese complaint that China would at all times have liked to swallow up Tonkin and was only prevented by the patriotic ardour and the valour of the people. Without exception, Chinese interventions after Vietnam became independent had as their object the restoration of Vietnamese princes deposed by their subjects, and the issue of legitimacy can be traced as a Chinese concern right through to the modern period. Even the action of the Yung Lo Emperor in 1407 was clearly intended to take a disorderly vassal in hand, when its ruler appealed for help, and to put it firmly in order once for all.

China and Vietnamese society

It is to the Yung Lo episode, for all its short duration, that many of the Chinese features in the structure of the Vietnamese state can be put down. Not a great deal remained from the earlier period of Chinese domination, except the dykes and canals, and even those had had to be rebuilt under the Tran. Although the administration of the T'ang empire had been more complex than any known in the world before, Chiao Chih had been only a distant province and had had only a provincial government; it had, moreover, covered a very small area—possibly 80 miles by 120. There was a gap of a whole generation between the last T'ang governor and the first Vietnamese. Chiao Chih had always been an alien, and therefore a backward, province with no written language of its own and possessing a class literate in Chinese whose numbers were exiguous by comparison with China's own educated class. Vietnamese society had adopted a Confucian aspect, especially no doubt in so far as Confucianism was the codification of a traditional ethical system common to the ancestors of both Chinese and Vietnamese: the family, comprising past and future generations equally with the present one, constituted the only recognized unit of society and, rooted in its land, provided a model of behaviour for the state, which was itself thought of as an extended family. The following of Chinese official ritual at family and agricultural shrines involved the knowledge of only a limited Chinese vocabulary of symbols and emblems, but the shortage of men learned enough to keep records must have placed severe limitations on administrative practice. It is significant that the considerable literature of China on topics of government produced under the T'ang, and even more, after the invention of printing, in Sung times, awoke hardly an echo among the Vietnamese.[a]

China and Vietnamese government

The Tran had introduced a system of education after the Chinese pattern to produce administrators, all the same, as well as recruitment by public examination;[b] now the Le dynasty took the process of modelling the Vietnamese state after China a step or two further. They adopted for themselves the style 'Son of Heaven' as well as 'Emperor' and manned their court with officials having specific administrative and ritual functions; below these they installed territorial 'mandarins' to administer provinces, districts, and villages as well; but these last, the *xa quan* (village mandarins), who had been employed earlier for a few decades by the Tran, gave way to local-born *xa truong* (village leaders) recognized after the sixteenth century as the sole authority within the commune.[c] The Le sovereigns kept up the system of land tenure, registration, taxation, and liability for military and labour service introduced during the Yung-Lo occupation. Besides specific enactments from time to time, a new general code of laws provided norms for family life and inheritance, as well as a wide range of penal sanctions; it was largely modelled on

[a] For the brief literary flowering of the Hong Duc period (1470–97), however, see p. 69 below.

[b] Texier (1962), p. 8. There is of course no way of knowing whether such measures were really carried into effect or remained mere statements of intention; the private literature by which these things are known about in China does not exist for Vietnam.

[c] Phan-huy-Chu (1821/1957), p. 98.

the T'ang Code[a]—perhaps because the latter was the last Chinese legislation felt to be properly applicable in Vietnam, despite its supersession in China several times over. The use of paper money came in.[b] Yet notwithstanding these measures, Vietnam at this time continued to fall far short of the sophistication of China in both government and cultural achievement. In the first place, the Le court lost its momentum and its energy rather as did the Ming court itself, and from similar causes, namely irresponsible pleasure-seeking and the corruption of eunuchs in positions of command, content to pay lip-service to institutions, rituals, and codes of law with a Chinese cachet, but not much concerned for their practical application. In the second place, the frontier life of fighting the Chams and Khmers and of pioneering new lands rapidly carried a big segment of the Vietnamese people away in space as well as time from the influence of Ming China and beyond the reach of the Tonkinese administration the latter had inaugurated. And, finally, other cultural influences, though largely of Chinese origin too, were at work below the surface to prevent the development, still less the maintenance, of a unitary state in Vietnam after the Chinese pattern.

5. CHINESE RELIGION AND UNOFFICIAL CULTURE

The Chinese have long drawn a distinction between their official culture and their unofficial culture. The distinction is a far-reaching one: in literature it is something like the Western contrast in taste and style between classicism and romanticism, although it is to be noted that in China all poetry is regarded as classic whereas we would consider it romantic; in ceremonial the royal, the agricultural, and the family observances associated with Confucianism count as official, orthodox, dignified, and the way of life of the gentleman, the scholar, and the mandarin; whereas both magic and religion, even when practised quite openly by the monarch, as well as all art or philosophy inspired by non-Chinese ideas, such as Buddhism, are reckoned unofficial, heterodox, private, popular, and undignified. In the West we are familiar with the restraint and refinement of Chinese painting, calligraphy, and ceramics inspired by the philosophy of the Middle Way; but in China itself there exists side by side with all that an intimate, gaudy world of baroque decoration and grotesque mythology frequented by the common

[a] Deloustal (1908–23); Vu-van-Mau (1956).
[b] It may, however, have been the currency of China (Li Chêng-fu, p. 177).

people, which the foreigner may only become aware of at a theatrical performance, or if he peers closely at the roof-ridge of a Buddhist or Taoist temple. In the social history of China the first of these two complexes of ideas and concepts is associated with government, the second with revolution: bandits, swashbucklers (often horrifyingly cruel), refugees from natural calamities, the pilgrims who fetched the *Three Baskets* of Buddhist classics from Bengal, fortune-tellers and priests—all these move together in an ill-assorted outworld, portrayed on the Chinese (or identical Vietnamese) stage and in such novels as those known in English as *The Three Kingdoms*, *Monkey*, or *All Men are Brothers*—an unsociety that periodically in history breaks into the introvert and ethnocentric society of Confucianism to chastise with the wrath of Heaven the dishonest or the inefficient in high places; royalty has never been revered in China for its blue blood.[11] The Vietnamese people have inherited from China on the whole rather more under the unofficial head than under the official, and their nationhood has been moulded as much by Chinese traditions of rebellion as by the traditions of social harmony and unity of the ideal Confucian state.

Vietnamese religion

One of the consequences in both China and Vietnam of the disestablishment of religion to the point of classifying it with the forces of disorder rather than with those of order, as in the West, is that religions rarely command the undivided faith of their devotees: 'Worship wherever there is a god' (*Thieng dau, tho day*), runs a popular Vietnamese saying. The struggle of Christianity to consolidate the faith of its converts by fostering the autarky of self-contained *chrétientés* has been a source of friction in Vietnamese society on and off since the seventeenth century; a small number of such communities (*xu khuon*) already existed in Tonkin in obedience to the Buddhist rule, but apart from them Buddhism, though having a somewhat tenuous history in Vietnam 1,000 years longer than that of Christianity, has never achieved domination of the people's minds and provides only one among several sources of their beliefs and of their religious practices. Underlying Buddhism throughout Indochina is a mass of animistic belief, found in its more primitive forms among the hill tribes, but also expressing itself in daily taboos and propitiations among the more advanced plainsmen; there lurks a spirit in every tree and rock and water-course, ready to pounce if unpropitiated and to thwart any human endeavour. One sometimes does not have to look far below the surface to detect animism operating as a guide to personal conduct among the modern Chinese either, often in the guise of Taoism. Similarly widespread in Vietnam, if less so in other parts of Indochina, is the practice of shamanism or fortune-telling and healing through the consultation of spirit mediums in trance. It is not possible here to conjecture how far belief in animism and the practice of shamanism are indigenous to Vietnam or introduced from China;[a] their importance in the present context is that they combined with Buddhism to produce a store of symbolism, ritual, and ideology out of which new religions and quasi-political movements have been liable to grow all through Vietnamese history.

Buddhism

Knowledge of intellectual Buddhism reached Tonkin in early times both through China and through the Indianized states, for Chiao Chih is mentioned as a stop after Funan on the journey made by holy men passing between China and India during the third and fourth centuries.[b] From both directions the early Vietnamese learnt about the 'Greater Vehicle' or Mahayana branch and its classics in medieval Sanskrit. Its interest in the souls of the dead fitted well the ancestor worship prevalent all over the Far East, but it addressed itself to the upper classes and had little impact on the common people of Indochina; at Angkor particularly it became confused with the Hindu worship of Shiva as identified with the person of the reigning monarch. This *devaraja*, or god-king cult, though like the phallic cult that went with it repugnant to the ideas of China, where Confucianism, with its practical view of politics, inimical to mysticism, was too well entrenched, nevertheless did spread from Angkor to Vietnam, and Emperor Ly Cao Tong (1175–1210) ordered that he was to be looked upon as identical with Buddha, doubtless in imitation of his contemporary at Angkor, Jayavarman VII.[c] The other great branch of Buddhism, the *Hinayana* or 'Lesser Vehicle', commonly referred to by the name of its only surviving subdivision, the *Theravada* or 'Ancient Doctrine', with its classics in Pali, arose in Ceylon and spread to Indochina through Burma; encouraging simplicity and poverty, it seems to have become the

[a] Shamanism had been practised in China at least from the time of the Mongol conquest; it enjoyed a fresh vogue after the Manchu conquest (e.g. Hummel, 1943, p. 891).
[b] *T'ai-p'ing yü lan*, quoted in Li Chêng-fu, p. 84.
[c] Tran-van-Giap (1943), p. 258. A Chinese precedent during the sixth century is, however, mentioned by Wright (p. 61).

popular faith at Angkor while the court was still Mahayanist,[a] but in the end displaced it and today is the established religion of Cambodia, Thailand, and Laos. The Vietnamese who eventually colonized Cochinchina did so at a time when Mahayana Buddhism was all but eclipsed in Tonkin[b] and before it had made any headway in Annam, whither the first educated Buddhist missionaries only arrived from China after the Catholics from France, about 1700.[c] Until the 1930s such Buddhism as was to be found among the South Vietnamese had been learnt from Theravada bonzes among the Khmer population; these have had a substantial part to play in the political movements of the region during the last fifty years.

The bonzes

The key to understanding religion in Vietnam is not the doctrine of Buddhism at all, whether Mahayana or Theravada, but the personal figure of the *sai* or rustic bonze. If this is not so true of neighbouring countries where Buddhism has long been institutionalized as well as established by the state, it is none the less true of China. The bonze's self-appointed function is to minister to the spiritual or superstitious needs of the peasantry; whether in doing so he invokes the lore of Taoism or the philosophy of Buddhism depends upon his own whim. He tells fortunes, makes up and sells talismans called *fu*, advises in which direction to site houses, and intones incantations at funerals; he may be a recluse on a hilltop or he may manage a pagoda in a busy city street; he may take any name suggestive of holiness, learning, wisdom, or occult powers that he thinks fit; the fact is that no hierarchy and no authority exists to control him. When bonzes group together under a leader, they may form a community for purposes of meditation and ascetic living, and then they will constitute a sect (a *mon* or 'doorway') with a rule and with the discipline of a *sangha* or 'community', with its generations of *thichs* (*shakyas*) in the best traditions of Buddhist monasticism. But as Vietnam expanded southwards, the pioneers, who would rarely be able to read or write, were, like the mandarins in relation to Confucianism, carried farther and farther from the sources of intellectual Buddhism in China and from the sophistication and respect-

---

[a] Coedès (1948), p. 364; cf. also the spread of Islam among the Chams during the same period (p. 37 above).
[b] Buddhism was proscribed in Tonkin in the 1660s, at the same time as Catholicism (Coulet, 1930, p. 93); similar proscriptions were being issued in contemporary China, where likewise popular Buddhism was already in decline.
[c] Cadière (1958), i. 3.

ability of the three or four historically-famous sects of Tonkin. Traditionally, relationships among the adherents of any Vietnamese sect, religious or secular, are democratic, growing from the ground up, not by proselytizing from a higher centre, and the individual members will often join and depart again with scant formality: ordination rarely consists of any rite more solemn than submission to the tonsure and donning of the robe.

Secret societies

The influence of the bonze, thus undisciplined, in a credulous and superstitious agricultural society, dispersed far from the centres of authority, has been the bane of every regime in Vietnamese history. Secret societies founded for banditry or piracy have been one of the most persistent features of the Chinese social scene, dominating the seafaring vocation, for instance, with their 'justice', right down to modern times.[a] Always making show of loftier purposes, and trying to sublimate their bullying practices into heroics, the promoters have centred themselves from time immemorial in Chinese history on temples, pretending to relive the feats of legends like *The Three Kingdoms*; one such society, several hundred years old, was the Elder Brother Society (*Ko Lao Hui*), with which in modern times Chairman Mao Tsê-tung was once connected.[b] We find the same custom in the hill regions of Tonkin: there is a logical affinity perhaps between the practice of magic, with a view to getting round the laws of nature, and association in secret societies, with a view to getting round the laws of the king.[c] The bonze, in satisfying the popular demand for fortune-telling and for talismans,[d] is able in any case to influence his clients to join or support the bandits, threatening real or supernatural sanctions for those who hold back, and acting as go-between, informant, and courier for the gang. Not infrequently, successful bands are able to espouse a political cause their peasant supporters never dreamt of when they first listened to the bonze, and swiftly an exalted mob is giving itself over to looting, and from looting gets committed to a full-scale rebellion. Chinese rulers have been trying to protect their state from the political consequences of organized superstition at least since the fifth century,[e] and Vietnamese history also has been much affected by recurrent

[a] Favre (1933), pp. 178–82.   [b] p. 147 below.
[c] Observation of Prof. Coulet (1926, p. 26).
[d] A study of the indispensability of the *fu* in the social life of the Overseas Chinese peasant at the present day has been made by Park (1963, pp. 207–8).
[e] According to the *Wei Shu*, quoted in De Groot (1903), p. 29.

upheavals starting in the same way; such were the antecedents of the Ly 'dynasty' in the eleventh century,[a] and Le Loi, when he was driving the Chinese out of Tonkin in 1427, drew support in his early days from the bonzes who considered themselves to be persecuted under their shortlived subjection to anti-Buddhist rule by the Ming authorities—anti-Buddhist in policy notwithstanding the Ming founder's own origin as a Buddhist bonze when he first raised *his* standard of revolt against the Mongols.

The Triad Society

It is not merely the social structure and the ideas conducive to the formation of secret societies which Vietnam has inherited from China, but in one important instance the society itself: that is the notorious, Mafia-like Triad Society.[12] The society appeared in the Fukien province of southeast China after the Ming dynasty was overwhelmed by the Manchus in the 1640s. Fukien had become Chinese only under the T'ang dynasty, and both the people and their dialect, to this day, have remained imperfectly assimilated to China. Foochow, the capital, became a great centre for the practice of the Confucian arts; but the countryside has nurtured many rebellions, down to Mao Tsê-tung's 'soviets' in the 1930s, and Amoy, the other big port in the same province, has been a nursery for all manner of religious sects, especially the cult of the 'Pure Land' afterlife, of Kuan Yin (the 'Goddess of Mercy' in European popularizations) and half-secret vegetarian associations for women in general and for spirit mediums in particular. Many Chinese peasants displaced from other provinces by poverty—the *liu min* or *yu min*, 'vagrant folk'—have in the past halted a while at Amoy on their way to settle abroad and have found in joining these cults and societies comfort, security, and the hope of ultimate return home, if not in life then in a funeral jar in the care of their association or *hui*. The last stand of the Ming dynasty was in Fukien, and the Triad Society arose among its supporters at the moment of defeat, vowed to its restoration by oaths and symbols picked up among the local bonzes. Destined to spawn innumerable subsocieties in the countries to which its members emigrated, till from Formosa down to Java it was impossible for a Chinese to do any sort of business without its 'protection', the Triad also acted as the vehicle for exporting to Vietnam a whole new wave of popular Chinese cult elements.[b]

[a] Coulet (1930), p. 27.

[b] Some part in this emigration was also taken by more learned Buddhists (a very small number) who contributed to a revival in education (Gaspardone, 1940).

Large numbers of these emigrants took to piracy for a living, and one group, under the notorious 'Koxinga' who preyed on the Dutch merchants, conquered Formosa and brought it for the first time under a Chinese rule of sorts.

The Minh Huong

Within a generation or so of the Manchu conquest of China—by about 1675—the Fukinese were arriving in Annam, where they formed a community at Faifo near modern Tourane; they lived by a combination of trade and piracy (ennobled by the ostensible political motive of harrying the Manchus) that had already characterized this coast in Cham times, and they intermarried with the Vietnamese, forming a self-contained community known as *Minh Huong* or Ming Settlement.[a] It was these groups which provided most of the manpower for the new Chinese colonies in Cochinchina mentioned previously as paying the way for Vietnamese pioneering. What is recorded of the leader of the Ha Tien settlement, Mo Chiu (Mac Cuu), himself actually a Cantonese, makes him sound like a Triad Society *kapitan China* typical of the organization of Chinese emigrants to Indonesia, Malaya, and other countries of southeast Asia. He obtained a concession over the small tin mines of the neighbourhood, managed gambling dens, became a middleman in much of the country trade with Siam, and was a law unto himself in all the affairs of his followers to such an extent that it was not until the death of his son, who succeeded to his position of power, that, in 1780, the last of the Nguyen overlords, the future Emperor Gia Long, was able to incorporate Ha Tien, but now much decayed, in his personal domains.[b] The influence of the Triad Society lived on after the disappearance of the *kapitan China* who had introduced it and has been one of the factors shaping the underworld of Cochinchina in the twentieth century.

The Tay Son

The Triad Society played a small part in the greatest and bloodiest of all Vietnamese rebellions, that of the so-called Tay Son at the end of the eighteenth century, which was the only one until the Communist uprising of 1945 to engulf the whole country within its final frontiers. The Tay Son were three brothers of the surname Ho

[a] This is a Chinese pun and more commonly written to mean 'Perfume arising from Ming'.
[b] Boudet, *passim*.

(Nhac, Hue, and Lu) who lived at Binh Khe in the foothills of the Annamite Chain thirty miles west of Qui Nhon, whence no doubt their style meaning 'Western Hills'.[a] They were the fourth generation of a family transported by force from northern Annam for being troublemakers there too. Their father had once been a Catholic, and Ho Hue, it was said, a bonze.[b] The revolt began in 1771, directed against the Nguyen overlords, whose place the brothers aspired to take. The legitimacy of the authority of the *chuas*, both Nguyen and Trinh, was challengeable on the grounds that it derived from the arbitrary captivity of the Le Emperors; during the thirty years of civil war which followed, the Nguyen were known as the Dong Son or 'Eastern Hills'[c] which can be taken perhaps as a sign that the struggle was viewed even by those taking part as of a purely factional nature, between rival usurpers, and not over any matter of right or principle.

The three brothers began by changing their surname to Nguyen as more prestigious, and then, leaning characteristically at first on bonzes, both nominally Buddhist ones and nominally Taoist ones,[d] the movement tried to be all things to all men and to set up a 'Pure Land' or 'Kingdom of Heaven' on earth. Offering land reform to the Vietnamese peasants, restoration of their former dignities to the Cham princes, and various advantages according to their tastes to the hill peoples, the Tay Son gained the population of Saigon by authorizing the massacre of Chinese immigrants and the looting of their property[e] at the same time as they were making a deal with the Triad Society bravo, Ts'ai Ch'ien, for joint pirate raids up the China coast as a source of foreign money with which to buy arms abroad.[f] The object of the rebellion was the carving out of an empire at a moment, after forty years of minor disturbances, when government in Vietnam was even weaker than usual. When one of the supercargoes of the East India Company was sent from Calcutta in 1778 to find out what was going on in Annam, Nguyen Nhac received him at Binh Khe and told him he was out to make himself master of the whole country, and of Cambodia too; all he could usefully ask from the Company was recognition and shipping.[g] Not

---

[a] During the presidency of Ngo Dinh Diem, an elaborate monument to the Tay Son was erected at Binh Khe, now a stronghold against revolutionaries.
[b] Louvet (1885), p. 387.   [c] Schreiner (1901), p. 148.
[d] Chesneaux, p. 60.   [e] Purcell (1965), p. 184.
[f] *Shêng Wu Chi*, quoted by Devéria (1880, p. 48) and by Fang Chao-ying in Hummel (p. 447); Le-thanh-Khoi, p. 312.
[g] Lamb (1961), p. 43.

Nhac, but Hue, very nearly brought it off. The Tay Son rebellion has a modern ring about it and has been elevated in Communist propaganda to the dignity of precursor of the Vietminh, much as the Chinese Communists claim spiritual descent from the Taiping Rebellion of the 1850s—in which also, incidentally, the Triad Society took a hand and a 'Kingdom of Heaven' was declared, but an Evangelical, not a Buddhist, one.

Nguyen Hue

The wars by which the Tay Son brothers did bring about the downfall first of the Nguyen and next of the Trinh, only to be vanquished in the end by a revival of the fortunes of the scion of the Nguyen, Phuc Anh, were not guerrilla wars, like so many Vietnamese struggles before and since, but wars of big formations and long sieges of strongholds like Qui Nhon and Hué; elephants were used on both sides. How the French came to be involved, and the British nearly, belongs to the next chapter. More interesting than the details of the fighting is their outcome. At first the three brothers were content to divide their conquests between them, along lines not far from the three regional divisions of Vietnam today; but gradually they fell out, and Nguyen Hue, the youngest, proved the strongest and became master in turn of both Annam and Tonkin. He never ruled Cochinchina because Nguyen Anh had by that time reconquered it from Nhac. The Trinh surrendered Hanoi to Nguyen Hue in 1787, and the next year he declared himself Emperor of a new dynasty with the reign-title Quang Trung. China, still under the aged Manchu Emperor Ch'ien Lung, reacted in customary fashion by sending an army of 10,000 to Tonkin to restore, not the Trinh, but the legitimate Le sovereign. Hanoi fell to this Chinese army in 1788, but, by a characteristic stratagem which earned him renown as a national hero, Nguyen Hue infiltrated his own men into the capital on Chinese New Year's Eve (*Tet*) 1789 and set upon and routed General Sun Shih-i and his men next morning while they were still sleeping off their carousal. Ch'ien Lung accepted this situation with habitual grace, and after an exchange of prisoners issued the customary seal—since 1660 always bearing the emblem of a camel[a]—in recognition of the titles that Quang Trung had assumed. The latter is credited with some ideas for reform—notably repudiation of the Confucian ceremonial at court and use of vernacular Vietnamese in official documents—but did

[a] Devéria, p. 9.

not live to carry them out.[13] His son reigned after him but was finally defeated by Nguyen Anh, by now the Emperor Gia Long, in June 1802. The official culture of China had weathered its most serious storm ever in Vietnam and was to emerge strengthened by this vindication.

6. STATE AND NATION UNDER THE NGUYEN DYNASTY

The historic role of Gia Long (1802–20) was to consolidate the Vietnam created by the forces and influences, and the weaknesses, described in the previous pages; the task his descendants set for themselves right down to Bao Dai, who brought the monarchy to an end in 1945, was to preserve what Gia Long had consolidated. Conservatism was the keynote of Nguyen policy from start to finish. Buddhism was already at a low ebb when Gia Long mounted the throne, and identification with Confucianism and the official culture of China became the policy of his state; not only were Chinese ways copied more closely than ever before, but the suzerainty of China was sedulously upheld by the court—to a degree that has cost the dynasty the esteem of modern generations—in the face of the European encroachment both countries had to face during the course of the nineteenth century.[14] But it was a decadent China the Nguyens were turning to, and one whose own standards of government, under alien rulers, were year by year proving less able to withstand the pressures of the West and the internal disorders that coincided with them. For sixty years the first four Nguyen Emperors followed a model in, and both sought and received the political support of, an overlord already vowed to self-destruction. More than any previous Vietnamese dynasty, the Nguyen followed the fateful cycle of the dynasties of China: an energetic founder, one or two competent successors, and then a long decline through several generations of quickly-debauched heirs brought up in a self-indulgent court dominated by concubines and eunuchs, each of whom represented a factional interest and swayed public policy in directions that served it. Only the French conquest saved the Nguyen from the extremes of degradation attained by the Manchus.

Gia Long's realm

Gia Long began by disposing of the Tay Son in a manner calculated to deter imitation of them: the bones of Quang Trung were exhumed and dishonoured in a specially disgusting fashion in the presence of his captive son, and the latter was thereupon made to suffer the fate of St Hippolytus, except that Gia Long employed elephants instead of horses, perhaps to make death slower.[a] Even so, his position was not secure: in separatist Tonkin he was widely regarded as a usurper who ought not to have repudiated the Le—an objection the Emperor met, in time-honoured manner, by bestowing favours on those who voiced it.[b] Next he took certain symbolic steps to affirm the unity of the realm: during the previous centuries of expansion and division there had been no need for a single name, but now he combined *Viet Thuong* with *Annam* to make *Vietnam*;[15] he established the capital once and for all at Hué, its mid-point, where he built a 'Great Within' or Forbidden City more or less on the lines (but only a fraction of the scale) of the Manchu palace at Peking; he built an Altar of Heaven (the *Nam Giao* or 'Southern Suburb'), at which annually to purify himself in the sight of Heaven, as prescribed in the Confucian canon of China, and secure a good harvest for his people—a custom kept up, latterly at three-year intervals, until 1943; and he adopted for himself a reign-title commemorative of his reconquest of the country from south to north, for *Gia* was taken from Gia Dinh (Saigon), whilst *Long* was taken from Thang Long (one of the Vietnamese, as distinct from the Chinese, names for Hanoi). In so doing he incidentally paid the compliment of imitation to his suzerain, the successor of Ch'ien Lung, who had adopted a reign-title beginning with the same Chinese character— 'Chia Ch'ing'. The remnants of both Le and Trinh were fugitives in China, where they took service with the Manchus;[c] recognition in the same quarter of his own legitimacy in their stead was important for Gia Long, not only in committing China not to intervene again in Tonkin, but still more in the eyes of his own subjects. Chia Ch'ing confirmed by proclamation in 1803 both the change of name of the country and Gia Long's own title as Ruler (Prince) of Vietnam.[d] However, as had happened in the case of Quang Trung,[e] the document evidently was drawn up merely by the Governor of Kuanghsi[f] and conveyed by hand of a district judge, while Gia Long had by contrast to journey himself to Hanoi to receive it with exaggerated pomp.[g] Once back in Hué, however,

[a] Lemonnier de la Bissachère (1812), ii. 193.   [b] Gaultier (1933), pp. 171-2.
[c] Fang Chao-ying, in Hummel, p. 681.   [d] Ch.-B. Maybon (1919), p. 377.
[e] Devéria, p. 37.   [f] Fang Chao-ying, in Hummel, p. 684.
[g] Gaultier (1935), pp. 26 & 31.

Gia Long was Emperor again, and in his turn received tribute from Laos and invested a Khmer prince as ruler of Cambodia.[a] These symbolic acts served as a reminder of the enduring vassalage of Indochina, and at the same time as an assertion that Vietnam had now taken on the position within Indochina once enjoyed by Angkor.

Administrative structure

Gia Long's domestic policy, and that of his successors, was likewise centred on China. Nothing remained of the Le court, and the Tay Son had scarcely been administrators; but a few of the never-numerous mandarins of the old regime were still in office, and on this nucleus the Emperor based a central Government consisting of an Executive Council and six ministries resembling those of the Manchus. A territorial administration (the *Ngoai nhiem*) of provincial and district mandarins (a corps of about 150 only), bearing current Chinese titles, represented the court outside the capital. Staff were recruited by public examination in Chinese in subjects of classical Confucian learning. The need for a proper civil service was greater now than when the Tran and Le had proclaimed similar rules: the country had grown in extent, and so had its requirements for an administrative framework. The system remained in effect until 1918. In China the ideals of the civil service and the principle of free competition to join it, however much they were abused in practice, had blossomed into an institution that was not only effective functionally but served as a force binding distant provinces and different social classes into a self-conscious nation-state possessing a characteristic civilization. Gia Long's desire to revive this Chinese institution was a laudable one, therefore, especially at a time when no other model for government lay to hand; that the attempt did not meet with success was due as much to the lack of supporting social infrastructure and to the difficulties of using Chinese as the language of education and administration as it was to the later Nguyen emperors' personal failings and inability to see policies through to the end. With the official use of Chinese went the bodily re-enactment of the Manchu Legal Code in 1815, as an act of sovereignty by a new dynasty; it showed even less regard for native custom or the applicability to Vietnam of certain of the provisions than did the laws of the Le borrowed from the T'ang Code. Laws drawn up in Chinese had in any case only a limited prospect of being

[a] Ch.-B. Maybon (1919), pp. 381 & 385.

understood even by the literate few, who knew them from manuscript copies open to error; consequently the praiseworthy intention of restoring order to the affairs of the nation by laying down
norms applicable to all classes and all areas became self-defeating
and only confirmed the remoteness and irrelevance of Hué in matters of local concern.

Village government

The effect of the reforms of Gia Long and his successor, Minh
Mang (1820–41), was to emphasize the symbolic unity of a national
state but to do little to secure it by practical means. Great stress was
laid on the need for the Emperor to approve, by the issue of certificates of appointment analogous to the one he received himself from
the Son of Heaven, the tutelary spirit (usually a dead leader or benefactor of the locality) to be worshipped in each village, in accordance with Confucian custom, as a way of confirming village harmony and obtaining prosperous harvests. But when the vermilion
signature and seal had been appended, it was as if the Emperor had
thereby discharged his responsibility for good government in that
particular village once and for all: he could fall back on the com-
fortably ancient Confucian maxim, 'Like the boiling of a small fish,
the government of a large state should not be overdone.' By the end
of the Le dynasty the development of self-government in the *xa*,
noted earlier as a departure from Chinese precedent,[a] had gone so
far that the commune was the only legal entity with which the
Government had dealings. It had become so much more important
than the family that even penal responsibility was deemed to be collective; whereas great attention was paid in China to inquests into
crimes of violence in order to establish identity and the extent of
personal culpability,[b] in Vietnam the discovery of a corpse on the
village's land (which included not just the houses but also fields and
forest up to the territory of the next commune) could lead to the up-
rooting of the village and banishment of its members[c] or to the levy-
ing of such a crushing collective fine that the villagers chose to
abandon hearth and home of their own accord and flee elsewhere,
far from the reach of the authorities.[d] So too with taxation: the
central Government assessed its requirements for revenue (which in
earlier times had been derived from rent on the personal domains

[a] p. 44 above. For the limitations on self-government in Chinese village administration,
see Ch'ü T'ung-tsu (1962), p. 4.
[b] Ibid. p. 119; Van der Sprenkel (1962), pp. 71–73 & 140–1.
[c] Nguyen-huu-Khang (1946), p. 145.   [d] Lemonnier, i. 286.

of the sovereign tilled as common land by the villagers)[a] and for *corvée* (*cong dich*), and these were apportioned downwards through the hierarchy of regions, provinces, and districts. Since the 1660s, though possibly not earlier,[b] the district mandarins assessed the total share to be met by the commune, and it was left to the notables (*huong dich*) to apportion its incidence on households, themselves remaining exempt.[c] Demands for *corvée* and for the provision of local materials for road-making or for building garrison posts—both heavy during Gia Long's reign—fell on rich and poor in equal measure.[d]

Arbitrary administration

Under such a regime, custom inevitably became the rule rather than law, and what was important was the customary view of who had the right to bully whom. The luckless individual was at the mercy of cliques, and even if a complaint did reach the mandarin, he had no means and little incentive to put it right, save in response to some greater pressure. Even in China, the mandarin might be made by his superiors to answer for the disturbance of social harmony within his jurisdiction which the very occurrence of a dispute revealed;[e] as a result, accommodations based on compromise between pressures, masquerading as equity, often took the place of true judgements. All the same, in its home country the system of government did not always work unfairly; there was more direct assessment of taxes by the mandarins in China, a more certain law of land tenure and a stronger sense of duty and honesty in the administration, notwithstanding all the recorded lapses. In Vietnam the tradition was not native, and in no dynasty had the Vietnamese kings quite matched up to the role of Son of Heaven upon which everything in China rested.[f] The apparatus of the Confucian state was alien—remote in space, superfluous in purpose, and more often than not in conflict with the commune's interests or those of its leaders. Whereas in China a vigorously self-conscious official culture, and the monarchy and mandarinate which gave it institutionalized form, were native to the people it governed, for the Vietnamese the culture was not their own and the institutions of mandarinate and monarchy, ever aware that they were acting a part, had never, in 900 years, quite outgrown the feeling of being

[a] Ibid. p. 297.   [b] Khang, p. 42.   [c] Lemonnier, p. 298.
[d] Ibid. p. 299.   [e] Escarra (1936), p. 70.
[f] A Vietnamese endorsement of this opinion is contained in Vu-quoc-Thong (1952), p. 34.

understudies for the real actors who had temporarily left the political stage during the anarchy of the T'ang–Sung interregnum. Whereas, therefore, China was decidedly centripetal, Vietnam, amid the hazards and uncertainties of a perpetual frontier existence the length of her narrow waist and in the pioneering plains of the Donnai and the Mekong, was no less decidedly centrifugal, her people insecure and devious. With no authority available to settle what was equitable between them, families and individuals—particularly the *dan lau*[a] or 'unsettled' farmers who were at the mercy of the *dan bo* or 'registered' stakeholders for their livelihood—would gang together for mutual protection under the leadership of occult sect or secret society. Large numbers of people in the South lived in what amounted to extraterritorial communities under the sway of such organizations more or less all the time, their common interest further cemented by superstitious bonds. Under dynamic leaders they became revolutionary movements which there existed no police force to detect; the provincial mandarins had an interest in concealing information that anything was amiss within their jurisdiction, and the first the central Government would learn of impending disorder would be if and when the malcontents took up arms and challenged a garrison somewhere.

The Army

In these conditions, the army took on an importance rather greater than in China. At his accession, Gia Long is said to have had a force of 140,000 men, and also a fleet of 100 ships with supporting armament.[b] Garrisons were quartered in citadels built on the plan of the 'star forts' of Vauban, and the Emperor's whole force had benefited from the training and equipment he had obtained from foreign (mainly but not exclusively French) sources; superficially at least, it had been modernized far in advance of the Chinese forces of the day, even if its operations were still subject to the interference of military astrologers.[c] After the throne, the army rather than the mandarinate was the principal institution of the state—a detail which has continued down to the present to distinguish Vietnamese from Chinese attitudes. The army kept up its strength by conscription, the notables in each village being required to find 1 infantryman (a *linh*) for every 3 (in Annam), 5 (Cochinchina) or 7

[a] The Vietnamese form of Chinese *liu min* (p. 50 above).
[b] Lemonnier, ii. 310–11.
[c] Schreiner, iii. 115–17, and Giran (1912), p. 210 n. 2.

(Tonkin) 'registered' inhabitants.[a] Although the practice was expressly forbidden,[b] those who were chosen by the notables tended to be the 'unsettled' and landless, but upon demobilization soldiers were encouraged, as in earlier generations, to found fresh *don dien* (agricultural colonies), especially in the South; these were supposed to constitute pockets of loyalty in otherwise unreliable regions. How far loyalty really was secured by this device must, however, remain an open question, for desertion even from the colours was notoriously widespread,[c] and rebels seemed to flourish in the vicinity of the *don dien* just the same.

Nguyen economics

The economic condition of the Nguyen empire was, if anything, more stagnant than that of China. Whereas in China commerce had come to be regarded as an alternative, both profitable and respectable, to investment in land, Vietnamese in all walks of life continued long into the twentieth century to put their surplus into rentable land alone. Manufactures received no investment, and even handicrafts were further discouraged because the court requisitioned all outstanding talents that came to notice for the embellishment of the capital.[d] By the middle of the century, if not earlier, food had become an item of maritime trade in the Far East, but the Vietnamese Emperors, endeavouring to monopolize overseas commerce for government-freighted shipping,[e] stifled any gain that might have accrued to the rich delta areas of Vietnam on this account by placing a ban on the export of rice.[f] It is likely that this ban originated in observance of the ancient precept of Confucian economics (going back to the era of Mencius, about 300 BC, if not earlier), the so-called 'ever-even granary', whereby grain surpluses in good years should be bought up by the Government when prices were low and sold again to equalize the market in bad years when prices were high. Tonkin especially had mineral resources, but the product was exported unchecked, the Emperors being satisfied with the arbitrary royalty paid them once and for all by Chinese concessionnaires;[g] tin had not featured as a commodity in the days when Mencius laid down the laws of Chinese political economy for all time, and so there was no inherited precept for administering its extraction. Individual Vietnamese who began to travel to Europe about 1850 and

---

[a] Pasquier (1929), p. 127.   [b] Ibid. p. 128.   [c] Luro (1876), p. 117.
[d] G. Maspéro (1929–30), i. 201.   [e] Tarling (1966), pp. 29 ff.
[f] Schreiner, ii. 284.   [g] Gaultier (1935), p. 266.

came home with more enlightened ideas were quickly silenced.[a]

Minh Mang

Gia Long's system of government kept the peace more or less for the remainder of his lifetime, but it was not adequate to subdue for good the endemic forces of disorder, and rebels showed their hand again as soon as he and his prestige had passed away. Minh Mang was his designated heir but, in spite of his reign-title (which meant 'Clear right to the Succession'), offered in his person a ready pretext to rebels in that he was the child of a concubine. His ambition was to extend the empire of his father throughout Indochina to lands where there was as yet no effective Vietnamese settlement, but while his armies were pushing to the Mekong on a broad front reaching from central Laos down to Phnom Penh, Tonkin was invaded in his rear by a new bandit army, to be known in southwest China for the next fifty years as the Black Flags and at first incorporating in its ranks old supporters of both the Le and the Tay Son. The bandits intimidated some areas of Tonkin with a combination of secret-society and guerrilla activities, whilst in others a Vietnamese Robin Hood called Nguyen Hanh led a band of peasant bravoes on looting raids which distracted the attention of the garrison forces. Nevertheless, after a bad start when he wasted his resources in futile 'sweeps' behind invisible marauders of the night, the Imperial commander, Truong Van Minh, did succeed in capturing Nguyen Hanh, having him dismembered, and restoring order in the Red River Delta.[b]

Cochinchinese separatism

But it was in Cochinchina that the most serious threat to the Nguyen state arose. This was the product of all the weaknesses in the regime we have described, and, in addition, of the growth of regional rivalry—a tendency in which the foreign Catholic missions became caught up. Although Gia Long had tried to improve communications along the great length of the realm by building a 'Mandarin Route' out of Hué north and south to Hanoi and Saigon, like the four great routes radiating from Peking, it proved of limited usefulness. Whereas the postal service of China was a charge on the central exchequer,[c] both the maintenance of its Vietnamese equivalent and the manning of the relays were by *corvées* levied on the vil-

[a] Buttinger, p. 282.   [b] Gaultier (1935), pp. 189–205.
[c] Fairbank & Têng, p. 9 n. 19.

lages along the way and liable consequently, over such an enormous length, to be both neglected and resented at the same time. The administration of Tonkin and of Cochinchina was entrusted to *Tong Doc* (regional viceroys) with unspecified powers, and this on the other hand tended to make for autonomy in practice, to a much greater degree than in China, where the title came from but the authority of the throne was held in greater awe. Gia Long, though never converted to Christianity, had tolerated foreign missions out of gratitude for Catholic help against the Tay Son; but when he died the missions backed Minh Mang's rival for the throne as a promising subject for conversion.[16] Awareness that the Church entertained this preference no doubt combined in Minh Mang's mind with apprehension that in any case Catholicism was, even more than Buddhism, a threat to the fabric of Confucian society—a fear shared by the Emperors of China throughout the nineteenth century. The new Emperor therefore, from 1825 onwards, forbade preaching and banished certain individual missionaries. The Catholics were shielded by the *Tong Doc* of Cochinchina, Marshal Le Van Duyet who, as one of Gia Long's generals, had worked closely with the French and, like his late sovereign, was also moved by loyalty towards them.

Le Huu Khoi's revolt

So long as Duyet lived Minh Mang's decrees remained a dead letter in Cochinchina—as for other reasons they largely did in Tonkin as well[a]—but there was no revolt. After his death, however, his adopted son,[b] Le Huu Khoi, felt no such scruple: himself a Tonkinese and former Black Flag with the remnants of the Tay Son whom Duyet had won over, Khoi made a bid for regional independence on his own account. To the grievances of the *dan lau* against the *dan bo* which were common to much of Vietnam there was added in Cochinchina the servitude of the local *ta dien* or tenant farmers on the estates of absentee Annamite landlords;[c] the latter would take an excessive share of the crop, returning part of it as a loan at exorbitant interest near sowing-time and thus binding the *ta dien* to them by a never-extinguished debt. It was this system of agricultural credit that the Minh Huong had financed in order to support the pioneering of the region a hundred or more years before. Offering once more all things to all men, like his Tay Son masters, Le Huu

a Taboulet (1955–6), i. 326.   b Duyet was a eunuch.
c Gaultier (1935), p. 112.

Khoi had most of the mandarins of the region suddenly murdered and declared himself 'Supreme Pacifier of the South'. Khoi's revolt was supported with supplies of arms by the Siamese, who hoped to divert Minh Mang's forces from Laos. It lasted from 1833 to 1835. But in the end the rebels made the mistake of shutting themselves up in the citadel of Saigon, counting on supplies by water from a countryside hostile enough to the royal authority but over which Khoi had not properly consolidated his control before taking up arms; much of the population was Khmer, took fright on the approach of the Annamite army and fled to Cambodia, never to return.[a] The Imperial army under Truong Minh Giang ultimately wore down the isolated rebels and massacred 500 survivors. Khoi was already dead, but the French missionary who had comforted him and ministered to the Catholic nucleus among the rebels, Père Marchand, was seized and executed at Hué by the agony of 'slicing', as prescribed for traitors in Chinese law.

Corruption

Thanks to its army, the Nguyen dynasty had preserved its position in both North and South. But so far it had achieved little to establish a firm nation-state: the causes of disruption and disorder still remained, and the apparatus of the Confucian state, in its attenuated Vietnamese guise and with its backward-looking quest for remedies, only aggravated them. Conspicuous among these was a particularly rapacious degree of corruption among narrowly self-seeking officials which often rendered totally ineffectual any form of government expenditure. In order to rebuild Tonkin in some measure after the ravages of Nguyen Hanh and his bands, Minh Mang dispatched relief supplies for the villages that had suffered most; not a string of cash or a sack of rice ever got through the greedy hands of the intermediate authorities. No more surprising was the royal reaction to news of this frustration: three of the many mandarins implicated were singled out and, with excessive severity, put to death without semblance of a trial, while the remainder went unpunished —and the intended beneficiaries of the public assistance uncompensated.[b]

Decline of the Nguyen

Although the third and fourth Emperors, Thieu Tri (1841–7) and Tu Duc (1847–83), survived further revolts, especially in Ton-

---

[a] Bourotte, p. 40.   [b] Gaultier (1935), p. 204.

kin, the dynasty would surely have gone under before long—like, in the end, the Manchus in China—if France had not stepped in during the later of these two reigns and saved the Nguyen (incidentally, not deliberately) from the consequences of mounting internal strains, which her own external pressure had, for fifty years, been making so much worse. At the same time it was only in the negative object of resistance to French invasion that national unity of a kind was shown by the Vietnamese in the Nguyen period; the extent even of that expression of national consciousness is often exaggerated.

7. THE VIETNAMESE LANGUAGE

Among the historical forces that have shaped the modern state and nation of Vietnam are to be reckoned the influences that have formed the language, and in this too China has played a predominant part. Possession of a common language, whether exclusively or not, is usually regarded as one of the more obvious marks of nationhood. The capacity for internal cohesion of a nation-state is often measured by the volume and qualities of its literature. In the case of Vietnam, the form of the language is a mirror reflecting closely the extent, the intimacy, and the subtlety of the links that bind Vietnam to China over a wide cultural field.

Language families

The mixture of races in Indochina has given rise to a similarly confused distribution of languages—so much so that speakers of all the big language families of southeast Asia (Burmo-Tibetan, Mon-Khmer, Malay, Thai, and Chinese itself) are to be found in every one of the modern countries into which Indochina is divided politically. Inevitably, the dialects spoken today have influenced one another extensively by adoption of common vocabularies for cultural elements they share, above all in the spheres of magic and of religion. All the languages of the region, with the partial exception of the Malay group, are monosyllabic and most are tonal, though not the Mon–Khmer and Malay groups, which, in Vietnam, account between them for Cham and all the hill dialects of Annam. The hill dialects of Tonkin are almost universally Thai. So probably is Vietnamese, at bottom, despite the smallness of the Thai element in its vocabulary and its much more extensive use of Chinese words. Every word contained in the vocabulary of Chinese can be used in

Vietnamese, whose strictly native vocabulary, even when the few words taken from Cham and Khmer are counted in as native, makes up only a third or so of that whole.[17] Chinese words make up what might be called the learned vocabulary, non-Chinese the popular vocabulary; thus two words for the same idea often exist side by side, although quite a few of those in the popular vocabulary are no more than deformations of the same Chinese roots as occur in the learned vocabulary, representing in some cases perhaps an earlier stratum of influence. The criteria by which French linguists have classed Vietnamese with Thai[a] are, firstly, the tone system of the older non-Chinese elements, and, secondly, the rather characteristic word order, which places the attribute after the substantive—a characteristic shared by other southeast Asian languages, not only Thai —and consequently is the opposite of that found in Chinese. Phrases composed of all-Chinese elements get incorporated into Vietnamese sentences, sometimes in their original Chinese order, sometimes in the Thai order;[b] as word order is the basis of grammatical relationships in monosyllabic languages, this hesitation presents great problems for modern educationists developing a system of education in which Vietnamese is used up to the highest levels in preference to Chinese or French.

Systems of writing

Writing reached Indochina as part of the general cultural influence from India on the one hand and from China on the other. For a long time the only modes of writing practised in the area were the derivatives of Sanskrit or else Chinese. It is an indication of the general level of civilization reached by the native peoples that not until the twelfth century or later did any need arise to write about anything but the abstractions of religion or government for which those classical languages provided all the ideas. But by 1150 adaptations of the classical script to write the Indochinese vernaculars became general: Khmer, Cham, various branches of Thai, and Vietnamese all began to develop their own writing systems about the same time. In the case of each of the Indianized languages, a new script was evolved from the phonetic writing of Sanskrit, developing a distinct form for each language; but a phonetic writing for Viet-

[a] For instance H. Maspéro (in G. Maspéro, 1929–30, p. 75). The general opinion is challenged, however, by Goloubew (1937), and Haudricourt (1954), who both favour a Mon–Khmer origin.
[b] The difference is analogous to that between English (which is like Chinese in this respect) and French (which is like Vietnamese).

namese had to await the first contacts with Europeans. Until then Chinese ideograms continued to be used for learned words, of Chinese origin, while new ideograms were made up for popular words, of non-Chinese derivation; this was done by putting two Chinese ideograms together—one to suggest the order of ideas and the other the pronunciation as indicated by some already-existing and well-known Chinese ideogram. Occasionally a non-Chinese word would be read to a Chinese character, as is common in Japanese, faced with the same basic problem. Since the great majority of Chinese characters are already composed on this radical-cum-phonetic principle, as it is called, the resulting *chu nom* (southern script)[a] of Vietnamese, as distinguished from the *chu nho* (Confucian script) of pure Chinese, made up of two such composite characters, looked very complicated indeed. The system became even more cumbersome in practice because no definite usage prevailed as between possible options; its inadequacy was certainly one of the factors accounting for the comparative poverty of Vietnamese literature before the modern period. No Vietnamese author ever compiled a dictionary of the *chu nom* that might have established a standard, and very few writers in this idiom were prepared to adopt the forms worked out by their predecessors and build further developments of the national language upon them. The chaotic state of the written language had serious disadvantages for the mass production of books, for though it would matter less so long as printing was done by carved wood blocks in which the whole page had to be incised specially anyway, lack of standardization precluded the use of movable types and so of modern presses; at the beginning of the nineteenth century it appears there was only one printing press in the realm, at Hanoi—with a project for one at Hué—and that only official publications had yet been printed in Vietnam, works of literature by private authors circulating down to that time solely in manuscript.[b]

Romanization

The necessity of accommodating the characters to movable types favoured the eventual adoption of the romanized system of writing, known as *quoc ngu* or 'national (that is, non-Chinese) speech'. Originally romanization was an invention of the Jesuits early in the seventeenth century; they found that, as with Chinese, they needed

---

[a] The word *nom* is of uncertain etymology, but there are analogies for equating it with *nam*, 'south'.

[b] Lemonnier, ii. 127–8.

a system for their private use by which to recall the pronunciation of the ideograms. The great French missionary of their Order, Alexandre de Rhodes, realized the scope of romanization in catechizing peasant converts: it bestowed an effective degree of literacy more quickly than the traditional way of writing, and furthermore a literacy that did not extend beyond the tracts and prayer-books composed in it; it made the compilation or translation of these very much easier for the missioners. The system of Rhodes has, since his day, undergone some small modifications to accommodate changes in pronunciation, but in all essentials—including a remarkably precise indication of the tones—it is the system which, between about 1880 and 1920, finally superseded the ideograms throughout Vietnam except for use on monuments and good-luck charms and for a few religious purposes.

Modern Vietnamese

The adoption of the romanized script to write modern Vietnamese followed pressure from the French administration, but it has furthered the interests of a national education.[18] On the other hand, it has not put an end to the traditional dependence of Vietnamese for new words on Chinese coinage: the links remain as strong as in the days of the characters. The explanation lies in the problem of modernization common to all the languages within the cultural orbit of China: the choice for these languages lies between bodily incorporating foreign words in speech and text, where they will be hard to pronounce and frequently misunderstood, and trying to absorb them by translation as living elements of the language.[19] Japanese, Korean, and Vietnamese have all chosen the latter course. The remarkable intellectual achievement of translating Western concepts in philosophy, politics, and science into an entirely unrelated vocabulary is the work of writers in China and Japan, but Korea and Vietnam have shared in the general enrichment of the common stock. In the case of Chinese, language reform has extended to grammar as well, and the decades from 1860 to 1930 saw the progressive substitution, for the laconic obscurities of the classical style, comprehensible only to a small educated class, of a grammar closer to the spoken language and comprehensible to all classes. For Vietnamese the corresponding reform has involved, first, romanization, and secondly, not so much a change of grammatical style, for which there were not the same grounds, as a change of taste in vocabulary: too much use of Chinese words where non-Chinese ones were available came to be regarded as pedantic, like preferences for Latin roots to Anglo-Saxon in English. On the other hand, the strict monosyllabism of the Vietnamese has, if anything, reaffirmed the necessity of taking the vocabulary for modern concepts from Chinese—in some cases that meant ultimately from Japanese—since European words could not be digested and few alternatives were available within the native stock of Vietnamese itself. By and large, therefore, Chinese influence has regained on balance almost as much as it has lost through romanization in the Vietnamese language reform. The Vietnamese form even of French names passes through the Chinese crucible first, and we read *Ba-li* for Paris, as being the Vietnamese pronunciation of the ideograms used in Chinese, despite the fact that the Chinese themselves say '*Pa-li*' and Vietnamese actually possesses both *pa* and *ri* in its phonology; in this instance it would have no difficulty in reproducing the French pronunciation exactly, yet it prefers a Chinese garb.

Vietnamese names

The Vietnamese language therefore has a definite identity and is no mere dialect of Chinese, as the originally distinct vernaculars, for example, of Fukien and Hainan have become; and yet it is almost wholly dependent on Chinese for its semantic development and all but impervious to what we think of as international words coined in the West.[20] The same is true of Vietnamese proper names. In Chinese there are few names that are not meaningful words, and in Vietnamese, except for nicknames, it is unusual for any but Chinese words to serve as names. The general Chinese trisyllabic pattern of a surname followed by two given names—or alternatively a double surname followed by one given name—prevails in Vietnamese, but with some important differences. Whereas Chinese recognizes about 4,000 family names, of which 400 or more are in common use, Vietnamese uses only about 100, of which barely a score are common, and a good third of the population share the single surname *Nguyen* (Chinese *Yüan*).[21] Middle names are similarly chosen from a severely limited range. The choice of third name is theoretically unlimited, and, as in Chinese, there is no absolute distinction between names suitable for men and those suitable for women. But the most un-Chinese characteristic of Vietnamese personal names is the employment of the third name when addressing a person shortly. This feature is found in other southeast Asian languages, in which people are known by their given name rather than by a family name or a patronym. It is as if their surnames did not belong to the Vietnamese quite so intimately as to the Chinese, perhaps because they were acquired in the first instance, not through physical descent, but through the relationship of local clients to Chinese landowning families.

Vietnamese literature

The peculiarities of the language have handicapped the development of an original Vietnamese literature. In the remoter historical periods the educated élite of the official class presumably did a certain amount of reading of Chinese books in the Confucian library, if only to sit for their examinations whenever those were in force, while the Chinese versions of the Buddhist *sutras* were available for proselytizing the common people as soon as printing began in China in the tenth century; but we have no texts to show that these literatures were contributed to by the Vietnamese themselves. According to the historian Le Quy Don who, writing in the 1740s, is our main source of information, Vietnamese historical compositions were commissioned by the Ly and Tran in the thirteenth century; they included both annals and topical treatises on government modelled on the *t'ung tien* and *hui yao* that were being compiled or republished at that time in Sung China.[a] But these works, which Le Quy Don believed might have numbered as many as 100 (a doubtful claim), were never printed, and the manuscripts were lost when the Chams destroyed Hanoi in 1371. At the time of the conquest of Champa in its turn 100 years later, the Le Emperor Thanh Ton considered his Hong Duc reign period an auspicious one for reconstituting the national heritage, in emulation of Yung Lo a generation earlier in China. Some texts were reconstituted from extant fragments,[b] and the contemporary dynasty's own laws and regulations codified.[c] But this output also remained unprinted, and Le Quy Don complained that students who might have made their own copies wasted their time copying instead the commentaries of crammers because they were interested only in passing examinations.[d] He wrote his own national history on the Sung plan, but again we cannot be sure how far its present incomplete condition is due to himself or to the carelessness of later generations; similar uncertainty surrounds the work of Phan Huy Chu in the reign of Minh Mang.[e] Such authors were solitary figures in their times.

[a] Trans. in Tran-van-Giap (1937), p. 45. [b] Ibid. p. 42. [c] *Hong Duc* (1959).
[d] Tran-van-Giap, p. 43. [e] Phan-huy-Chu.

Unofficial literature

A popular Vietnamese literature, written mostly in verse and in the *chu nom* rather than Chinese, began also in the Hong Duc period, attaining its peak at the end of the eighteenth century. It was then that the poet Nguyen Du composed the principal national classic *Kim Van Kieu*, a long and melancholy epic of Buddhist renunciation, of great pathos and subtlety of expression, but with an episodic plot set in China and frankly taken from Chinese sources. The nineteenth century saw the continuation of this *nom* literature, but little change of fashion, until translation from Western books, together with the introduction of romanization, began to break the confining bonds of Chinese scholasticism and to stimulate a wider intellectual freedom. Even so, the modern output has been meagre in quantity for the size and sophistication of the population.

Intellectual traditions

The accidents of Vietnamese history can thus be seen to have deprived the country of a vigorous intellectual tradition with a national focus. The civilization of China, rich in ideas and modes of expression under both its official and its unofficial facets, has always been available to the Vietnamese, but they have not participated in its further development, in the way the Japanese did. Enjoying few periods of stability and prosperity, isolated and at the same time disturbed internally by the Nam Tien, and scattered over a wide territory, the Vietnamese developed no centres of learning (or indeed of commerce) within their own frontiers. It seems probable, from what evidence there is, that the literate classes were always fewer proportionately than in China; since the adoption of romanization, the proportion able to read the characters has dwindled still further, and yet without that knowledge the associations of ideas behind the words used for things of the mind can, in a monosyllabic language with hundreds, even thousands, of homonyms, only be grasped imperfectly. Contributory causes there may also be, but it is to the characteristics of the Vietnamese language that we must look first to explain why it should only be in the framework of Chinese thought (of Liang Ch'i-ch'ao, Ch'ên Tu-hsiu, Hu Shih), and inside China, that the initiative of a modern Vietnamese thinker like Pham Quynh could arise;[a] his contribution, though ex-

---

[a] p. 123 below. The list of Chinese names might include the shortlived vogue for Bertrand Russell, promoted in China by Liang Ch'i-cha'o, but there is no evidence that Pham Quynh met him during his celebrated visit in 1921.

pressed in Vietnamese, had no following. Whatever else may divide the Sects and parties of the present day, it is hardly ideas—and it is not ideas because their leaders do not write. Even the Communist literature of North Vietnam is of negligible proportions, and it is not ideas that distinguish them either from their fellow countrymen. In both North and South there are many signs that French still dominates the conceptual framework in educated peoples' minds. Ngo Dinh Diem and Ngo Dinh Nhu seemed to be aware of this problem and to have hoped to see a nationally-centred intellectual tradition begin to flower; but neither of them was the man to plant the seed.

3

THE LEGACY OF FRANCE

I. FRENCH CIVILIZATION AND FRENCH CATHOLICISM

THE establishment of the French colony and protectorate over Vietnamese territory, between 1862 and 1885, brought about no abrupt transition from Chinese influence to French; not only did Chinese influence continue all through the colonial period in various ways, but French influence had already been at work for more than two centuries earlier than that—in fact, since long before the consolidation of the modern Vietnamese state in its full Chinese garb, reaching to its final frontiers. France even contributed in some measure to that consolidation; the new factor of her political domination brought about a change in the relative intensities of French and Chinese influences in political and cultural aspects of the national life, but hardly a change of kind. There are, moreover, some striking parallels between the cultural influence France has exerted on the Vietnamese people and the influence exerted by China. Chinese thought and French thought both lean, especially in their treatment of social and political questions, towards scholasticism rather than empiricism. Speculation on these matters, whether it is in the Cartesian tradition or the Neo-Confucian, argues from *a priori* principle in preference to observation and experience. There may be many exceptions to this generalization discoverable in the intellectual heritage of either country, yet the common effect of both upon the mind of Vietnam has been to discourage a practical approach to the responsibilities, and the art, of government. Bureaucratic conservatism amounting to pedantry among administrators goes with personal detachment from the social problems of their environment among lawyers, doctors, and teachers as a characteristic of Vietnam in her post-colonial independence. A feature common to the legacy of France and to the heritage from China, the scholastic outlook, of which these failings are the expression, has played its part in weakening national solidarity in the face of Communist anarchy. The patriarchy of Ngo Dinh Diem was a synthesis of French and Chinese influences in the sphere of moral philosophy rather than a practical machine for governing the country.

Church and State

The coming of French influence to Vietnam was the fruit of a French national purpose, her *mission civilisatrice*. At the heart of that purpose lay Catholicism—specifically French Catholicism. The Church has long been disestablished in France, and at times anti-clericalism has coloured state policy; but such periods have constituted no exception to the general truth that, for 350 years, Catholicism has remained constantly at the centre of the *présence française* overseas—a focus and a justification for the *geste française*. Conversely, already in the earliest years, when the missionaries were the only representatives of France in Vietnam, the purpose of procuring conversions was coloured by the wish to see them associated with French values in other fields than that of religious faith. Although both the Spaniards and the Portuguese had somewhat similar hopes when they secured from Rome an explicitly national—or at least royal—patronage over the missions and hierarchies of certain areas of the globe newly explored (indeed, French intrusion was offensive to the Portuguese *Padroado no Oriente*),[a] their clergy remained subject to the discipline of Orders with an international organization and an international field of recruitment. This was not so in the case of the French missions, whose secular foundation facilitated a more single-minded loyalty to the interests of the sovereign who licensed them, Louis XIV and his successors, royal or republican.

The Jesuits

Portuguese and Spanish missionaries, as well as soldier-adventurers, visited parts of Indochina from time to time in the sixteenth century, but the first organized missionary activity in Vietnam was that of the Jesuits. In 1615 the Superior of Macau chose the neighbourhood of Tourane, in Annam, as a suitable alternative pastoral field to Japan, which had been closed to Catholics the previous year.[b] The attraction of Tourane was that, among the foreigners living there, were to be found a number of Japanese engaged in the trade with China, and through them Japanese-speaking European priests could hope to gain access to the native people.[22] Another mission was opened in the territory of the Trinh, in Tonkin, in 1626. It was in the ranks of the Jesuits that the first Frenchman came on the

---

[a] The principal field of rivalry was China, but even in Vietnam missioners under the patronage of France and of Portugal behaved towards each other with ungodly malice, as if their nations were at war (e.g. Navarrete, 1962, pp. 371–2).
[b] Marucci (1651), p. 94.

scene, Alexandre de Rhodes, developer of the romanized script.[a]
In part because of his representation of the damage suffered by the
propagation of the Faith from the rivalry of the Orders, in part for
reasons connected with the struggle between Jesuits and Jansenists
at the French court, the Société des Missions Étrangères was
founded by royal charter in 1659, to be free of the Orders and of the
struggles for ecclesiastical jurisdiction which dogged the Spanish
Church in the Philippines; the new missionaries were to be the servants of the French Crown as much as of the Holy See.

Louis XIV

Support of the French Fathers by Louis XIV over the remaining
decades of the seventeenth century fitted in closely with that monarch's policy of building a network of links with oriental countries—
links in which the interests of commerce were subordinated, in a
manner unusual in the age of mercantilism, to the purpose of establishing the prestige of France as a centre in the West of cultural
achievement that Eastern potentates would deem it useful to have
relations with, in competition with the centres of civilization in
India and China. The intrigues by which Louis's agents tried to
thwart the oriental trading ventures of the Protestant Dutch, and
to a lesser extent of the English, involved ramifications reaching
from Turkey through Egypt, Ethiopia, Persia, India, and Siam as
far as Tonkin. It was in Siam that the French Fathers made their
first base for action in Vietnam, and their seminary for training
native clergy remained there for a hundred years. Two bishops were
put in charge at first, one of them nominally to look after Tonkin
and the other Annam, because of the state of war already known to
exist between the Trinh and the Nguyen overlords. They did not
long retain the monopoly of the royal favour at home, however, for
Louis was obliged to heal his quarrel with the Jesuits and to transfer
to them the realization of his political aims in Siam. In the end, the
French Fathers kept the cure of Annam, and incidentally of Cochinchina not yet Vietnamese, while the Jesuits were temporarily reassigned Tonkin.

Success of the Missions

The Catholic mission to Vietnam, arising from the accident of
exclusion from Japan, was destined to meet with the most immedi-

[a] Strictly speaking, being born at Avignon, he was a temporal subject of the Pope, not
of the King of France.

ate, far-reaching and enduring success of any mission on the continent of Asia. In contrast to the rebuffs encountered in the neighbouring Theravada countries and the indifference of China, conversions in Vietnam were made in hundreds at a time, until by 1650, before the French entered the field, there were 200,000 in Tonkin alone and ten years later nearly twice as many.[a] These claims are not to be disbelieved, and when we find the numbers had dwindled in the latter half of the eighteenth century, only to burst forth a second time in the big self-contained communities of the nineteenth, we may be sure that the early Fathers had somehow touched a motor nerve of Vietnamese society, charged with its own internal variations of dynamism.

Healing and conversions

In the first place, as was their practice in other Asian countries, the Jesuits tried to make converts among the mandarins and at the two courts; they converted some royal personages and secured early toleration for their activities by their ability to predict eclipses, as they did in China.[b] The success of the two missions' appeal among the common people was due in large part, as the Jesuits observed, to the circumstances of a poor, rustic society in which monogamy was the rule and many young people, especially women, were accustomed to the idea of celibacy and chastity—the themes about which, after theology, the Fathers had most to say.[c] But they seem to have owed a great deal more to the attraction from the start of hundreds of bonzes, about whose place in society they could not be expected to have any prior knowledge. In the seventeenth century, whatever differences of theology separated them, Europeans and Vietnamese were at one in supposing illness to be due to possession by evil spirits; a system of religious practices able to demonstrate its potency in restoring health, without demanding money, was sure to win the hearts of simple peasants. Borri described vividly how 'devils', to be seen walking through the streets, were kept at bay by sight of the Agnus wax and were unable to touch any person protected by it—unable to get nearer than the front door of anybody who, in addition, had been baptized.[d] In some cases, children were offered for

---

[a] Rhodes, p. 318; Marini, p. 263.   [b] Borri, pp. 174–5.
[c] Marucci, p. 93; the observation is repeated many times by all the Fathers. The *Tam Phu* ('Three Realms') sect for unmarried women has been the leading spirit-medium cult in Tonkin for several hundred years; adepts would be susceptible to the idea of personal dedication to the B.V.M.
[d] Borri, pp. 209–12.

baptism by the Church as a prophylactic for their parents' state of health rather than their own.[a] Although the Fathers came to be regarded later on as rivals by the spirit mediums of Tonkin,[b] other bonzes whose principal activity was as healers flocked to the mission houses to apply for baptism themselves and, one may surmise, for access to holy water, much in use in their own exorcisms.[c] Many of them were chosen to become catechists, distributing holy water for carrying about the person in a little bottle, as a *bua* or amulet, or else giving it to sick people to drink or sprinkle over themselves; the effect was so convincing that one enterprising catechist, we are told by one of the Fathers, found a veterinary application for it and cured a number of sick elephants in the military stables at Hanoi.[d] It was presumably such helpers who persuaded the Jesuits to adopt the Buddhist and Taoist word for reverence (*duc*) when speaking of Catholic luminaries, to call holy water *nuoc phep*,[e] and to use *phep* on its own—a word with superstitious undertones—to translate 'sacrament', thereby unwittingly confirming, one might expect, the misapprehension Rhodes complained had been prevalent that Christianity was a new system of magic.[f] Ex-bonzes made the most constant proselytes,[g] yet it may be wondered how canonical, in the circumstances described by the Fathers, would be the doctrine they imparted. It was fervently believed by the Jesuits none the less that their catechists had been invested by Providence with power to work miracles, restoring sight to the blind and even raising the dead.[h]

The Church and the authorities

Before setting out as catechists to conquer new flocks of souls for the Church, the bonzes often were able to muster for baptism the whole of their previous sect or clientele, running to hundreds at a time.[i] The Faith also spread rapidly through family loyalties,[j] and on one occasion the missioners acted on the invitation of a wealthy landowner to attend to the peasants of his village, whose imminent death from some epidemic would have left him with no agricultural labour.[k] The authorities became alarmed: to the Nguyen and the

---

[a] Fr. Courtalin, in Taboulet, i. 46.   [b] Marini, p. 149.   [c] Giran, p. 285.
[d] Marini, p. 266.
[e] The modern Catholic usage is *nuoc thanh*, more literally 'holy water'; for their own water, bonzes seem to use *nuoc thai* (cleansing water), but it is quite possible that *nuoc phep* was already in use before the missionaries entered the country.
[f] Rhodes, in Taboulet, i. 11.   [g] Rhodes, p. 165.   [h] Ibid. p. 268.
[i] Borri, pp. 190–6.   [j] Marini, p. 369.   [k] Rhodes, p. 185.

Trinh, what the Catholics were bringing about appeared less a mass conversion than a mass subversion; the missionaries' incautious association with the bonzes would be enough to put the *chuas* on their guard that here was another revolutionary sect in the making. Suspicion over the popular foundations the Catholic movement was gaining was reinforced by the unconcealed abhorrence of the priests for various forms of courtly self-indulgence, by the ban they put on the practice of usury among the faithful at a time when this was already the basis of the country's agricultural economy, and by the intolerance shown by the French Fathers (though not by the Jesuits), at least from the date of a synod held at Tourane in 1672, over continued performance of the simple daily rites before the family altar prescribed by Confucianism in honour of the ancestors.[23] The new faith inevitably made converts among the soldiers fighting in the war between the rival *chuas*, which broke out in 1627, and when these met on the battlefield they forbore to kill each other.[a] All such factors added up to a threat to the fabric of Vietnamese society, as well as to the prerogatives of the ruling powers. Moreover, toleration of missionaries at both Hanoi and Hué was bound up closely, as in other parts of Asia at the time, with the earliest of all questions of technological aid: the willingness or ability of missionaries to procure arms for the rulers. Writing of the years before 1622, Borri attributes the success of the Nguyen overlords in resisting the superior manpower of the Trinh to their possession of 100 or more pieces of artillery bought or salvaged from European ships and to the outstanding skill of their gunners, which he rates above that of their European counterparts.[b24] Rhodes was banished in turn from Annam and Tonkin, and on the latter occasion it was because Portuguese transports had failed to arrive on time with cannon promised from Macau[c]—a misfortune that befell the mission more than once.[d]

Banishment and persecution

Banishment of missionaries led on to persecution of converts, and although much could be done to alleviate the severity of official measures through judicious placing of gratifications,[e] the general effect was to drive Christianity underground. An anonymous priest of the French mission described the life of his colleagues about 1675, going from village to village barefoot by day, attending to the

[a] Marini, p. 308.   [b] Borri, p. 81.   [c] Rhodes, p. 211.
[d] Nguyen-huu-Trong (1959), p. 83.   [e] Mgr Pallu, in Taboulet, i. 29.

spiritual needs and devotions of the faithful at night, to have Mass finished by dawn and be away before the authorities (presumably the *xa truong*) awoke to what was going on.[a] French priests continued to land in the country, only to be turned out again, and the Trinh martyred a few of the more persistent ones. The numbers of Vietnamese remaining true to the Faith declined under pressure, but revived many times; the last general persecution took place in 1750 in Annam,[b] but in 1759 there were still 120,000 Catholics in Tonkin.[c] That Catholicism survived so well was due in the main to the French society's foresight—doubtless connected with its early Jansenism—in ordaining a native clergy from the beginning;[25] the first two Vietnamese priests (elderly catechists of the Jesuits and therefore perhaps ex-bonzes) took Orders in Siam in 1668.[d] While the French priests stayed in the background, the native parishes took root as a permanent feature of the sectarian, factional society of Vietnam; but French Catholicism had got itself linked with the heterodox, barbarian forces of revolution, unlike that of the Jesuits in China, who had deliberately associated themselves with the official culture of the Confucian Government and, contrary to their expectations, came to grief as a result.

The Bishop of Adran

The revival of Catholic fortunes after the persecutions came at the end of the eighteenth century under the leadership of Mgr Pigneau de Behaine, titular Bishop of Adran, and was bound up closely with the internal politics of the country. The French Fathers by this time enjoyed a clear field throughout Vietnam: the Jesuits had been expelled from Tonkin once and for all in 1750 (and suppressed as an Order at home in 1773), whilst the Khmer population of Cochinchina, as obdurate in the face of Christianity as all Theravada Buddhists then and since, were rapidly being surrounded or displaced by the immigrant settlers from Annam, who were more amenable to conversion. Pigneau's chance came with the Tay Son rebellion. When Nguyen Anh was driven in 1777 down to the Gulf of Siam, he applied in vain to the Chinese at Ha Tien for support,[e] but the Bishop was able to offer him the shelter of the way-stations along the French Fathers' own 'Alexandre de Rhodes trail' leading back to their base in Siam. Pigneau proposed a French military alliance to the *chua*, by which, in exchange for small territorial con-

---

[a] Quoted ibid. p. 43.   [b] Ibid. p. 99.   [c] Mgr Néez, quoted ibid. p. 104.
[d] Trong, p. 197.   [e] p. 51 above.

cessions for purposes of trade on Pulau Condore and at Tourane, royalist France would dispatch ships, men, and arms to help Nguyen Anh recover his lost territory. This scheme was in the tradition of Louis XIV.[26] The young *chua* was ready to agree, but the French Revolution frustrated the plan.[a] The Bishop also ran into opposition from the Commander-in-Chief at Pondicherry. Undaunted, however, and prompted perhaps by knowledge of the success unofficial aid and volunteers from France had recently had in the early stages of the American War of Independence, he set about raising a privately-financed expedition, paid for by French commercial interests in India and manned by officers attracted away from the colours by adventure or mercenary inducement.[27] This first Western military mission to Vietnam, commanded by a Catholic bishop, constituted a highly romantic episode in the historical relations between the two countries and, incidentally, set the seal on the identification of Catholicism in Vietnam with the French nation. By the time Pigneau returned from his odyssey to get help, the *chua* had rallied most of Cochinchina back to loyalty to himself without outside assistance. His French advisers now set about helping him consolidate his hold over the food supplies and the manpower of this area, based on a citadel they built him at Saigon, and from it to reconquer first Annam—where Qui Nhon (the stronghold of the Chams) had to be taken twice before there was a breakthrough to Hué—and, after ten more years of patient campaigning, Hanoi and Tonkin. Pigneau de Behaine died too soon to witness the final victory and the elevation of his protégé to the Imperial throne, with sway over a reunited and enlarged Vietnam.

Achievement of Behaine

It is easier to describe than to weigh the achievement of the bishop and his Frenchmen. They were not numerous—100 perhaps, at most—and few even of those stayed in the country more than two or three years;[b] but they brought modern ideas to the Vietnamese army in organization, in weaponry, in shipbuilding, and above all in the strategy associated with the name of Vauban, the engineer in Louis XIV's army who developed the star-shaped *place-forte* as the pivot of frontier defence. This concept of conventional warfare was adapted by Colonel Olivier du Puymanel to the problems of

---

[a] Amongst other difficulties resulting from that event was the suppression of the Société des Missions Étrangères in 1791, which threw Pigneau onto his own resources. The Society was revived temporarily in 1805–9, permanently from 1815.
[b] Taboulet, i. 240–2.

internal defence faced by Nguyen Anh. None of Puymanel's citadels has survived—the biggest was the one at Saigon demolished
after Le Huu Khoi's revolt in the 1830s—but the remains of half a
dozen others, copied from them after 1804, can still be visited in
parts of Annam. The palace Gia Long built at Hué at the beginning
of his reign owes rather more in its zigzagged external wall and its
gateways to the Vauban tradition than to the Forbidden City at
Peking whose purpose it was meant to imitate. The intervention of
the French Catholics, though small, evoked the gratitude of the new
Emperor, and he rewarded his advisers, if they stayed on in the country, with mandarinal office at court (Vannier, Chaigneau). But in
the end the cost of dependence upon foreign aid had to be paid in the
customary currency of diminished prestige in the eyes of his subjects.

Chrétientés

Pigneau de Behaine's breadth of mind and qualities of leadership
died with him; within two or three decades of Catholicism's temporary attainment of recognition we have glimpses again of a fur-
tive mission back nearly to the point where the Bishop had come on
the scene. There was no more mass proselytizing, as in the seventeenth century, and no more misplaced trust in bonzes, but instead
previously-converted agents were sent quietly into villages where
advance intelligence indicated the community as a whole was dis-
contented and might be won; if things went well, a catechist would
follow, then a native priest, and finally the French Father himself
would arrive to bestow the blessing of parish status on the new *ho
duong* or *chrétienté*.[a] Henceforward, the compact, as far as possible
self-sufficient, parish became the unit of Catholicism in Vietnam,
and its evolution was undoubtedly one of the successful consequences of the secular character of the French mission. Like the
similar, though less numerous, communities of Buddhists, the *xu
khuon* (on which it may in part have been modelled), the *chrétienté*
offered the converts mutual support against bullies, extortionate
moneylenders, and the bailiffs of absentee landlords, in a land
where the Government could not yet be counted on to keep order
or to uphold law, and it afforded that organization for mutual defence against both brigandage and abuse of authority which other
Vietnamese, especially in Cochinchina, sought in occult sects or the
Chinese in their secret societies. Inevitably, to the Government,
Catholicism began once more to take on the appearance of an *im-*

[a] Gaultier (1935), pp. 84–87.

perium in imperio, and episodes such as the insurrection of Le Huu Khoi, during which the priests again showed lack of caution, led to renewed banishments and persecutions—those in turn to methods of conversion by stealth hardly distinguishable, however laudable their purpose, from further subversion, until the Faith was stamped out by the harshest repression.

French intervention

But as the nineteenth century advanced, it was no less inevitable that the Western power with patronage over the persecuted missioners, at that time undergoing a strong Catholic revival at home under the rule of Napoleon III, should step in to set the wrongs to right. Pleas from the French Fathers multiplied for a quarter of a century after Minh Mang's general edict for the suppression of Catholicism in 1833 and, when successive envoys dispatched to Hué to negotiate a revocation of the edict failed even to obtain a hearing from Thieu Tri or Tu Duc—and after Tourane had been bombarded in turn by French (1844) and American (1847) men-of-war[a]—Napoleon III sanctioned, in 1858, a unilateral seizure of Vietnamese territory as a pledge for a return to Gia Long's policy of toleration. As if to justify the French Emperor's decision after it was taken, but actually before it could be carried into effect, the Vietnamese Emperor committed his greatest folly: all told, nine French Fathers and five Spanish Dominicans had already been put to death since 1833, in addition to thousands of native converts, and now Tu Duc ordered (or at least connived at) the execution of the Apostolic Vicar of Tonkin, Mgr Diaz, who happened to be Spanish, just at the moment when France and Spain had fleets in the Far East, along with Britain, poised for an attack on China. Modelling his own intransigence on that of Peking, Tu Duc invited the same reaction as Peking. However, in her reaction to Vietnam France's original purpose of championing the persecuted Catholics by now had other facets as well, reflecting the coincidence of interest between the Church in Vietnam and the colonial ambitions of the Second Empire.

2. THE CONSOLIDATION OF FRENCH POWER

The aims of colonial powers, during the hundred years modern colonialism lasted, evolved only stage by stage. France was no ex-

[a] Hall, p. 610; Tarling, p. 31.

ception, and in 1858 Napoleon III's intentions were still far from being more than a limited annexation of Vietnamese territory. Rivalry with Britain, chiefly as a question of prestige, was also a strong incentive behind French policy towards Vietnam, even if Britain was herself unaware of any grounds for competition with France and was now, for the moment, an ally and close associate in the Far East. Both the rivalry and the collaboration arose at this date over China.

France and the 'open door'

For seventy years the Western powers, led by Britain and latterly including America in second place, had been demanding that China should grant them freedom to trade, freedom to proselytize, and the right to maintain diplomatic missions at Peking which could treat with the Chinese Government, over these freedoms and other questions, on a basis of sovereign equality. The story of the China Wars, the second of which was fought between 1858 and 1860, is well known. In the case of Britain the prior objective was trade, and the missions an afterthought, putting to spiritual advantage the channels of penetration—principally the new Treaty Ports —opened in the interests of the merchants. For France, for a number of economic and historical reasons, the balance went the other way,[a] and it was the desire to secure toleration of Catholic missions for the future, as well as amends for the judicial murder of French priests in the interior of China in the recent past—for the Vietnamese Emperor had only been acting in accordance with Chinese precedent—that furnished the motive for her joint naval action with Britain. Another related difference between British and French aims may be noted, both at this time and at most others: whereas Britain (and America) sought the 'open door', by which all foreign nations should enjoy freedom to trade, preach, and maintain diplomatic missions, France constantly sought exclusive rights and privileges. The French annexation of Indochina is, similarly, interpretable as a gesture of separateness from the other powers—though hardly of independence, since a moment was chosen when both British and Spanish support was on hand—and, specifically, as a means to more successful competition with Britain in the future. This point is stressed because, in so acting, France was once again carrying on a long-standing policy of exclusiveness and one she has

---

[a] Brunschwig (1960, p. 15) quotes a Chinese official source of about 1850 as evidence that the difference between the two 'aggressors' was appreciated there.

adhered to ever since, both in the protectionist measures that marked her administration of Indochina and in the direction her contribution to its ultimate settlement took when colonial regimes were being liquidated. The demand made upon Tu Duc was the opposite of the 'open-door' policy: it was the exclusive right to preach for French Catholic missions.

France and Britain

Franco-British rivalry did, however, also arise over Vietnam more directly. All through the eighteenth century the struggle had been waged between the two powers for supremacy in India, and the final discomfiture of France induced in her a hankering after territorial compensations that would restore her political, if not commercial, status; the idea that Indochina could satisfy this debt, as it were, which the world vaguely owed her, is expressed many times by French writers both before and after 1858—the year which, significantly for this French attitude, saw the consolidation of an 'Indian empire' by Britain and the assumption of direct administration over it by the Crown as a consequence of the Sepoy Mutiny. Britain's penetration of Burma after 1850, and the greater headway made by her prestige than France's in the 'protection' of an aggressive Siam, was another inducement to seek a counterweight in the area. Finally, there was the perennial question of a trading station on the Vietnamese coast. Although in 1748 there had been a French proposal for plantations to grow sugar or silk-worm mulberry,[a] there was little trade to be expected in Vietnamese products; but both French and British travellers had repeatedly pointed to the possibility of using a factory on the Bay of Tourane, or on one of the islands, as an entrepot to which Chinese junks could be attracted— as they had been in earlier centuries—and the vexations visited on foreign merchants at Canton circumvented.[28] A second demand made to Tu Duc by the French Admiral, Rigault de Genouilly, in 1858, was therefore for the cession of a site at Tourane.

Pressure on Tu Duc

The Admiral's third demand was the one for admission of a French consul to reside at Hué. There had been a French consul at Hué previously in the person of Jean-Baptiste Chaigneau, one of Behaine's men and concurrently a mandarin at the court; the termination of his consular functions by Minh Mang had rankled with

[a] Ch.-B. Maybon (1910), p. 60.

France for a long time. But this demand, like the other two, was resisted by Tu Duc, who was guided in part by what was going on simultaneously in China; the Admiral likewise took his cue from the same direction, where the allies had just occupied Canton in order to exert pressure on Peking, and himself seized Saigon in order to exert pressure on Hué. Unsuccessful in his immediate objective, however, Rigault was then called away to rejoin the equally unsuccessful allies in their attack on North China. It was two years before the French ships came back again and, seizing Saigon a second time, went on to occupy three provinces to the east and west of it. Tu Duc was now weaker: he had done nothing to improve the defences of Saigon or of Tourane, where a landing was made at the same time; China, his suzerain, had had to give way to Britain and France on the same three issues; a new French Admiral, Charner, was able to cut off the flow of rice by junk from Cochinchina to Annam and Tonkin, both already deficit regions by this period; and, to crown all, another revolt had broken out in various parts of Tonkin, led by one Ta Van Phung, who claimed to be descended from the Le, and certainly was a Catholic, with substantial support from the *chrétientés* still suffering from the effects of persecution. In June 1862 the Emperor gave way on all points, ceding half of Cochinchina to France and undertaking (like China) to pay an indemnity, of which most went to Spain. He sent his most outstanding mandarin, Phan Thanh Gian, on a goodwill mission to Paris (the first Vietnamese diplomatic mission abroad) to stay a chain of events whose course could already be foretold from the experience of the 'unequal treaties' in China; Phan Thanh Gian returned empty-handed and was appointed Governor of what remained of Cochinchina. The mandarins in the French-occupied provinces did little to keep out the guerrilla bands that now constantly attacked the French forces from Phan Thanh Gian's provinces, and in June 1867 the whole region was taken over and brought under a direct French administration.

French annexations

This tale of progressive involvement by energetic and often ambitious local commanders, with uncertain authority from home, has been characteristic of much of the colonial expansion of other European countries as well as France, including Britain. Cambodia became a French Protectorate in 1863, without the prior consent of Paris, and the consummation of France's hold over Vietnam resulted, in 1874, from the activities of a French gun-runner who tried to force his cargo up the Red River, occupied at this time by the Black Flags called in by the Annamite court,[a] on the sole authority of the Chinese Governor of Yunnan and without reference to Hué. It is true that the French authorities in Saigon were inclined to be ashamed of this last incident and disowned the capture by French filibusters of the citadel of Hanoi in which it ended; but that did not deter them from settling the matter finally by forcing upon Tu Duc another treaty ('of peace and alliance') whose terms confirmed their occupation of Cochinchina by transferring full sovereignty from Vietnam to France and, at the same time, gave them a protectorate over both Tonkin and Annam guaranteeing, among other things, internal security. The meaning of this last provision was that the *chrétientés* had been implicated, of their own accord or by their parish priests, in both the rebellion of Ta Van Phung and the recent *coup de main* at Hanoi and thereby invited a renewal of reprisals against Catholics generally by the court if they were not shielded by France. As was to be expected, China protested against the new treaty, which ignored her suzerainty over Tonkin and Annam. The position of Cochinchina—never subject to Chinese administration, not yet fully integrated into Vietnam and inhabited by a numerous minority of Khmers—was of much less concern to the Manchus. Only in 1885 was France able, after blockading Formosa and putting down the last big rising of the Black Flags, now reinforced by remnants of the Taipings from central China and armed and led at Tu Duc's invitation from across the frontier, to browbeat China into the formal renunciation of her rights, and obligations, in these territories.

Laos and Siam

The enlargement of French ambitions during these twenty-five years was due in no small degree to the activities of the other powers in the Far East and to the continuing desire to match or forestall British expansion, actual or supposedly intended. French designs upon Vietnam broadened into designs upon Indochina as a whole —an area whose western limits were not fixed by any obvious geographical or historical criterion. Under the Third Republic, humiliated at the hands of Prussia in 1870 and led by Napoleon III's ferocious antagonist Prime Minister Jules Ferry, it was no longer a question of France's protecting persecuted missions, but of straight

[a] Morse (1913–19), ii. 349.

imperialism to refurbish her tarnished glory.[a] For ten years, from 1884 to 1893, under the leadership of Auguste Pavie, a series of actions was undertaken to intimidate Siam into renouncing her own expansionist policy towards the territory of Laos lying on the east bank of the Mekong.[29] In so doing, France claimed to be acting as protector of the Emperor of Vietnam and therefore invested with his rights of suzerainty over Laos—in curious inconsistency with the repudiation, on that same Emperor's behalf, of his centuries-old obligation of tribute to China.

Colonial policy

The consolidation of France's hold over Indochina was contemporary with the consolidation of her possessions in Africa, and the government she introduced, as well as the social and economic measures it carried out, were determined more and more, as time went on, by standardized policies worked out to suit French interests in all the colonies and protectorates as a whole. The process of standardization began in 1870, when the largely indirect rule of the Ministry of Marine came to an end and Indochinese affairs were entrusted to a civilian governor, Le Myre de Vilers, under the Ministry of Colonies, with explicit instructions to promote *assimilation*.[b] By this was meant the raising, or the modernizing, of the standards of native life to a level which would permit the territories' absorption sooner or later into the French Republic and the adoption of the people, individually, as fully-fledged citizens of Catholic, egalitarian, France.[c] This was the policy eventually carried out by the United States in the greater number of her overseas possessions. But whereas such a policy was workable in regard to the small creole communities of the French island empire—the American empire also was an island one—, it had little hope of success when applied to large continental possessions, especially if these were also the home of advanced indigenous civilizations. Moreover, the ambitious transformation of Vietnamese life and society that the policy implied would have required public expenditure far in excess of the resources of local taxation in an age when massive investment by metropolitan governments for such philanthropic purposes, with no direct return, became acceptable to public opinion at home only after the opportunity for it had passed.[d] Consequently, in the early

---

[a] Brunschwig, p. 177.   [b] Le Myre de Vilers (1908), p. 1.
[c] Betts (1961), p. 26.
[d] Criticism voiced earlier by Sarraut (1931, p. 215), later by Mus (1952).

1900s, the doctrine of *assimilation* gave way in French official thinking to that of *association*.[a] The revised policy envisaged a partnership between races and between their institutions which should be of equal benefit to both parties, but in which the colonial power would be the ruler more or less in perpetuity and the subject people could aspire to self-determination only by identifying themselves individually with the French way of life—which of course meant *assimilation* again. The benefits to be shared would no longer be confined to knowledge of Christianity, but would extend to all the worldly advantages to be derived from an enlightened legal and judicial system and from modern agriculture, mineral and plantation exploitations, from commerce and perhaps industry. This joint venture, guided and developed by the genius of France, was to be a high moral enterprise which it was unthinkable the subject peoples should wish ever to dissolve—provided, the authors of the policy freely recognized, France remained true to her values. But in a society and economy dedicated to free enterprise, the new doctrine implied, more than partnership between races, a partnership between French administrators on one hand, more or less imbued with those values, and French *colons*, capitalists, and adventurers on the other with minds only for the more immediate gains of a narrower enterprise, not for the higher enterprise at all. Conflict between these latter partners was to dog the French administration of Vietnam till its end in 1954. French politicians never ceased to look over their shoulders with a combination of envy and disgust at the slow preparation of British India for independence through self-government.[b]

3. FRENCH COLONIAL RULE: THE MACHINERY OF GOVERNMENT

The policy of *association* was supposed to be guiding the French administration of Indochina from 1907 until the suspension of direct French rule by the Japanese in March 1945. Throughout the period, the powers of the Governor-General were available, and were repeatedly exercised, to overrule the nominal autonomy of the component territories, not only on matters of policy but even in dealing with individual cases. In no part of the French colonial empire were the two parties to the *association* on an equal, or even a de-

[a] Harmand (1910), p. 159.
[b] The last French High Commissioner condemned Britain's pursuit of this policy as 'selfish'—that is, selfish in relation to other European colonial powers (Ély, 1964, p. 323).

fined, footing; in Indochina, although native sovereignties continued to be recognized in certain formalities, in practice they were considered to be overridden by the authority—the actual sovereignty, in the opinion of some jurists[a]—of the French state.

Status of territories

The territories which made up the *Union Indochinoise* were Cochinchina, Annam, Tonkin, Cambodia, and Laos. Annam and Tonkin were protectorates reigned over, if not ruled, by the Emperor of Vietnam, whom however the French were careful to refer to only by the more limited title of Emperor of *Annam*, while he himself still considered himself Emperor of *Dainam*.[b] Cambodia also was a protectorate, with one member of the royal family recognized as king where formerly brothers and cousins had ruled their principalities independently of each other. The frontiers of Annam with Tonkin, Cambodia, and Cochinchina were adjusted several times, by unilateral French decision.[30] Laos was also a protectorate, but it lacked any clear internal constitution: separate princes continued under the French to reign at Paksé and Vientiane and a king at Luang Prabang; there was scarcely any native administration, the public services being furnished by French administrators. Only in 1946 did Laos gain a definite identity when France recognized the King of Luang Prabang as monarch over all the provinces and paramount over the other princes. Although Annam and Tonkin remained under native sovereignty, the two ports of Tourane and Haiphong, and also the city of Hanoi, were early made the objects of 'concessions' to France, on the pattern of European concessions in China, and later ceded as *concessions en toute propriété* (whatever that meant) in 1888 by the Emperor Dong Khanh. Thus, all the protectorates of Indochina were nominally under native princes. The French Government, undoubtedly with its eye on British 'paramountcy' in India, read into the overriding authority which it derived from the treaties these princes had signed, and which, by unilateral decision, it vested in the Governor-General of the Union in 1887, the right also to make and unmake kings as might suit itself, as if they were petty African chiefs. In none of the royal houses concerned were rules of succession very definite, and all of them were accustomed to intrigue and interference by neighbouring powers. But the French behaved in their dealings with them in such a way as to emphasize the princes' dependent status. Successors to

[a] Tran-chanh-Thanh (1943), p. 451.   [b] See note 15.

the throne at Phnom Penh not merely required to secure French recognition but were designated and actually crowned by the republican Governor-General as if he were a Pope.[31] At Hué, France interpreted the rights of protection ceded to her by China under the 1885 treaty as entitling her, not only to approve the succession of a new king upon the death of the old, as the sovereign of China had done before her, but to remove kings in mid-reign, appoint successors at will, and then remove them in their turn if they threatened to give trouble. At the higher of the echelons of government, therefore, the policy of *association* operated to reduce to insignificance the key symbol of the subordinate partner's identity.

Indirect rule in Annam

The internal administration of Cambodia and Laos is not of concern here. In all three regions of Vietnam the French found it more practical to preserve a number of features of indirect rule, even in Cochinchina, which they regarded as an area suitable for indirect rule in most respects. The administration was most indirect in Annam; here the Emperor retained intact his ministries and territorial authorities, all staffed by mandarins as in pre-French times. A French *Résident-Supérieur* resided at the court (latterly at Dalat); the functions of this official were political rather than administrative and were centred as much on preventing the Emperors from asserting too much independence of France as on making sure they governed wisely. Eventually, in 1925, the *Résident-Supérieur* was actually installed as chairman of the Annamite Council of Ministers and, in 1930, the process was taken so far that he became, in addition, president of the Council of the Royal Family.[32] In the provinces of Annam there were also *Résidents*, who however concerned themselves mainly with French interests in the area and with the prevention or suppression of uprisings. But this regime was installed only in the lowlands of Annam, while the highlands, inhabited by the vestiges of Champa and other hill tribes, were administered directly by French officials as a unit called the *Pays Montagnards du Sud* (PMS). This region was not effectively administered before 1920 and even then was treated at once as an ethnological reserve and as a reserve for exploitation by European concessionnaires; the Vietnamese had always disliked the highlands as much as the hill tribes disliked the plains, and, by common consent (what was known as the *politique de race*),[a] few persons of Vietna-

[a] Bourotte, p. 80.

mese race went to reside there save as migrant labourers, as government clerks, or as employees of the Catholic missions. The latter meanwhile conducted an intensive and successful penetration of the pagan villages.

Tonkin and Cochinchina

The French regime in Tonkin was more direct than that in Annam. Here too the mandarinate remained and was responsible, for a decade or so after the protectorate was set up, to a representative of the Emperor residing in Hanoi; but then the office was abolished, and the mandarin in charge of each province came directly under the *Résident-Supérieur* of Tonkin, who henceforward governed the Protectorate in the name of the Emperor, but without consulting him.[a] The mandarins of Tonkin were required constantly to seek, and always to follow, the advice of their French *Résident*, and it was to him that their reports were addressed 'under flying seal' to their Vietnamese superior; in Annam, on the other hand, the *Résident* was specifically precluded from taking any active hand in public business, although he was allowed to report and comment to the *Résident-Supérieur*.[b] In the days before village notables became elective, it was the mandarin who appointed or confirmed them in Annam, but the *Résident* in Tonkin.[c] During long periods the same French officer acted as *Résident-Supérieur* of Annam and Tonkin simultaneously. In Cochinchina, during the 1860s and 1870s, the French likewise had attempted to run the provinces indirectly through any Vietnamese mandarin they could induce to collaborate, like a territory occupied temporarily by a military force; but the intrigues and non-cooperation of the latter had made the system unworkable, so that, with the advent of civil government and a more definite colonial policy, French *Chefs de Province* were substituted. In both the protectorates and the colony alike, the provinces gradually came to be divided into districts over which a Vietnamese district chief had charge, but without powers of his own and as little more than a sub-agent of the French provincial authority. Throughout Vietnam the municipalities were entirely under French authority and management.

[a] Gen. Catroux served as a young man in the Indochina administration shortly after this arrangement was made; when he became Governor-General himself he condemned it as an unworthy trick to deprive the Emperor of part of his domains (Catroux 1959, p. 33).

[b] These details were laid down in the Conventions, e.g. one of 6 June 1884, quoted in Jean (1944, p. 451).

[c] Blet (1950), p. 228.

Territorial administration

This territorial framework of administration no doubt owed something to the Napoleonic system in France itself, under which local autonomy was balanced by the *Préfet*, who represented the central Government in each *département* and was charged especially with preventing political upheavals. It did not differ in its essentials either from the structure adopted in other colonies generally, whether French or not, or from the Chinese system which had been found in operation in the country: a common paternalism inspired colonialism and Confucianism alike. Whether direct or indirect rule resulted from these arrangements would depend on the powers that were exercised respectively by the French and the Vietnamese authorities, and on the ways in which they were exercised. The feature that gave the French system most positively the character of indirect rule was the preservation of the village autonomy of the commune or *xa*. Although there were some details (such as land registration) over which practice differed between colony and protectorates, the main features of traditional government by notables and of internal allocation of liability for property tax, of liability for *corvée* and for military service continued much as before.[33] Also retained from precolonial days were the extraterritorialities: the Chinese were left to manage their affairs through five *bangs* (translated into French as *congrégations*, the term formerly used in France for Jewish communities), differentiated by the Chinese dialect of their members, as was the practice in all colonial territories of southeast Asia; French administrators in Cochinchina appear actually to have been less concerned on the whole than their Dutch or British counterparts with the persistence of secret societies which that particular extraterritoriality tended everywhere to give rise to.[34] French nationals as well enjoyed another kind of extraterritoriality in that they were subject to special legal and judicial provisions and were not subject to Vietnamese jurisdiction in any respect, even whilst in Annam. Thirdly, the *chrétientés* were encouraged in the autarky desired by their priests, and in practice—though not in law—were often administered in questions affecting land, in the provision of health and education services, as well as over the payment of taxes and performance of obligatory services, through their parish priest, with whom alone the authorities—very often, that is, the French authorities over the head of the Vietnamese—would deal as they would with the notables of a *xa* or with the headman of a *bang*. In two areas of Tonkin that were solidly

Catholic, the dioceses of Phat Diem and Bui Chu, the bishops were *de facto* temporal administrators. Finally, natives of one territory in Indochina were subject to special restrictions and special jurisdictions whenever they moved to another territory, even as between the three regions of Vietnam.

Legislation

The allocation of powers to legislate in French Indochina, and the laws themselves, were clouded by uncertainty all through the colonial period, and the writings of French jurists on the subject frequently contain frank condemnations of official neglect to clarify the position. An enactment of Napoleon III in 1854 was interpreted, despite its repeal by the Third Republic in 1870, as reserving the right to legislate for all dependent territories of France, as an act of sovereignty, in the hands of the Head of State of the metropolitan power—a parallel to Order-in-Council procedure for British dependencies. In regard to Indochina, this formula was used for the enactment of fundamental laws, though not consistently; in addition, many metropolitan statutes were extended to the Union by fiat of the Governor-General, if no local legislation covered the subject, or else were taken account of in the courts on an equity basis. Until after 1945 legislation was mostly enacted by the Governor-General, subject to disallowance by the Minister of the Colonies, although the constitutional validity of this procedure was in some doubt.[a] The sovereigns within their Protectorates had the theoretical power to object, and in some cases (for example, the Labour Code)[b] to express their assent, but they could not initiate legislation, save on the proposal of the *Résident-Supérieur*. In any case, the powers of the sovereign in Tonkin had already been absorbed by the *Résident-Supérieur*, and the latter was subordinate to the Governor-General. Regulations applicable only to the Protectorate of Annam continued to be enacted by the Emperor in the form of edicts—*du*, as distinct from basic laws, *luat*, adopted formerly from China and now from France. Minor regulatory powers were held by municipalities and by province authorities.

Advisory councils

At each of these political and administrative levels consultative councils were set up, but their function never developed beyond the advisory stage, and legislation did not require their endorsement.

[a] Jean, p. 79.   [b] Indochina, *Réglementation du travail* (1937).

At the lowest level, the elective principle was introduced for village councils from 1921 onwards, and from 1927 in Cochinchina (1941 in Tonkin, 1942 in Annam) statutes were given them in the hope of bringing some order to the chaos of communal administration; the main effect of this measure was to invest a limited number of notables in each *xa* with responsibility for actual performance, in substitution for the informal gatherings of the past in which all the notables had had a voice but no responsibility. The councils collected the direct taxes on behalf of the central Government in all three regions, deriving their own revenue to meet local expenditure from the tithe they were allowed to demand over and above the figure named in the tax-roll—an arrangement unsatisfactory because it smacked of tax-farming, to which it did in fact owe its origin hundreds of years before. The experiment in other ways also appears to have been a failure, for it increased rather than diminished the bickering, corruption, and local factionalism that were traditional to Vietnamese village life.[a] Provincial councils had come earlier (Cochinchina 1882, Tonkin 1886, Annam 1913) and underwent many changes of statute in an effort to give them a useful role in government; but although they enjoyed some reality of power in that they levied rates and taxes in townships, they suffered from the same fundamental weakness as village councils. At the central Government level, Cochinchina had a *Conseil Colonial* from as early as 1880, composed half of Frenchmen and half of Vietnamese, with the latter elected on a limited suffrage. Native councils existed also in Annam and Tonkin, but in none of the three regions were any effective powers conceded to them, and, furthermore, all discussion of a political nature was excluded, as was attendance by the press and the public. Finally, from 1928 onwards, right at the top of the pyramid there existed a *Grand Conseil des Intérêts Économiques et Financiers de l'Indochine*, composed of 28 French members and 23 native (usually 17 or 18 of them Vietnamese, the remainder Cambodian or Lao), as a referee on applications for public-utility concessions and on the all-Indochina budget; but in its discussions on the latter, the effective fiscal authority of this Council was curtailed by a rule that all proposals to reduce taxation or increase expenditure must be accompanied by compensating proposals to make good the deficit under another head on the same side of the account: the Council had no power to increase expenditure and then raise more revenue to pay for it, or alternatively to cut out some un-

[a] The opinion of both Pinto (1946, pp. 38–42) and Mus (1952, pp. 24–26).

wanted item of expenditure and reduce taxes accordingly. Consultation of the wishes of her Indochinese subjects from village up to federal level was thus never developed by France into a methodically-phased plan for the gradual devolution of power; such a policy would have been inconsistent with the aims of either *assimilation* or *association*, and even in the last days of French rule, consultation was never allowed to grow into control, and legislation continued to be by decree of the executive.

State of the laws

Under French rule, the state of the laws in Vietnam as a whole was in many particulars confusing, and procedure before the courts, criminal as well as civil, tended to be complicated and dilatory. During the first decade and a half in Cochinchina, passed nominally under military administration, the mandarins were left to apply the customs and the laws of Hué as far as they knew them in the absence of printed texts; even French administrators, though permitted to apply French law if they thought it more equitable, tried to apply the Nguyen Code as made available to them in translation by their enterprising colleague Aubaret;[a] when this was not clear, they might refer to the antecedent Hong Duc Code of the Le, giving, from case to case, conflicting judgments on such fundamental questions as whether a married woman could dispose of property independently of her husband.[b] The more gruesome forms of punishment prescribed in the Nguyen Code were soon modified, but not under the Admirals.[c] The advent of civil government led to other reforms: French administrators were substituted for the mandarins, and the humaner Penal Code of France became the basis of criminal law, until a version modified to suit local conditions was brought out in 1912. Many statutes enacted in France were interpreted as applying automatically to Cochinchina, as to other full colonies. The Civil Code of France was followed by the French courts from the same period onwards, although local modifications were published as early as 1883, but of doubtful applicability to natives. The uncertainties characteristic of the laws of Cochinchina persisted much longer in the Protectorates of Tonkin and Annam: the *jus receptum* from former times remained in an undefined state of coexistence with the laws of France until a Code of Criminal Procedure was

---

[a] Aubaret (1865).
[b] Judge Le Tai Trien in a public lecture at Saigon on 25 Aug. 1965.
[c] Decree of 24 Mar. 1877.

brought out in Tonkin in 1917, a Penal Code in 1921, and a Civil Code in 1931 (all by authority of the Governor-General of Indochina) and a Penal Code in Annam, with a Procedure Code, in 1933 and a Civil Code in three parts between 1936 and 1939 (all by authority of the Emperor).[a] The applicability of these codes was not by territorial jurisdiction, however, but *ratione personae*; that is to say, each individual carried his own law with him, and the regional codes applied only to natives of the region, while strangers (for instance an Annamite student at Hanoi University) were subject to their own law in civil disputes, to French law—as were French citizens and other foreigners—if charged with a criminal offence. To a limited degree, this form of extraterritoriality was a matter of personal choice, in that French law was always available to any who sought its protection—by right in Cochinchina and Tonkin, by custom in Annam, where the Emperor's constitutional prerogative of legislating for his own subjects was protected by treaty.[b] On commercial questions, as in many other spheres of modern life, native law was of course silent, whilst, as time went on, metropolitan French law also proved inadequate for local conditions; both single statutes and general codes applicable to all Indochina came to be enacted in substitution for it. Thus, the consolidated Land Code of 1925 and the Labour Code of 1936—the former generally applicable to French and Vietnamese alike, the latter in certain particulars only.[35]

Application of the law

The language of the statutes was French; but whereas the Nguyen Code had been drawn up in Chinese, the modern *du* which began to be promulgated in the name of the Vietnamese Emperor after the turn of the century, and especially the new codes for Annam, had French and Vietnamese versions together—the latter printed in *quoc ngu* instead of the ideograms. This represented a gain for the emancipation of Vietnamese government from the traditional Chinese incubus, and also for the Western view of the law itself as published for the knowledge of all it applied to, against the obscurantist attitude of the mandarins, who had kept their texts as secretly as a quack doctor his recipes.[c] An attempt was made in 1921 to resolve many of the uncertainties in the laws, but at the cost of

[a] The French drafting officers went to great lengths to ascertain conscientiously what Tonkinese and Annamite customs really were and to exclude inconsistent provisions carried over into the Nguyen Code slavishly from Chinese texts (Judge Trien, loc. cit.).
[b] Camerlynck (1937), esp. p. 114.   [c] Aubaret (1865), p. ii.

increasing the complexities.[a] The *corpus juris* was indexed in 1916, but the edition was small and soon went out of date; the laws themselves were never collected or edited in the light of amendments. It is small wonder that this state of affairs encouraged the growth of a class of lawyers, some French some Vietnamese, who showed more interest in promoting litigation than in securing justice, or that French administrators, having already a certain national attachment to social and economic freedom amounting to *laisser-faire*,[36] but rarely any specific powers or duties written into the statutes, tried to limit abuse by administrative action in preference to enforcement of the law, whose applicability was so open to embarrassing challenge by advocates. The effect, and the effectiveness, of the laws was in any case tied up with the structure of the judicial system and with the question of citizenship.

The courts

The dualism of the legal system was matched by dualism in the judicial system. There were French courts and Vietnamese courts, but the former enjoyed an overriding jurisdiction in accordance with the overriding sovereignty of the French state; and yet the origin of the protectorate system in the extraterritoriality of China was echoed in the designation of French courts as *tribunaux consulaires*. The native courts comprised only the courts of the provincial administrators sitting as magistrates or judges, as they had sat under the Chinese system of the Nguyens; and in Cochinchina, as well as the three 'concessions' of Tourane, Hanoi, and Haiphong, these administrators were Frenchmen. However, although the mandarins had disappeared from the judicial scene in Cochinchina in 1879, new Vietnamese magistrates were appointed from 1921 onwards to hear cases according to French penal law but in the vernacular language of the accused.[b] The only courts of higher or appellate status had to be French since the only procedure for appeals under the traditional system was by petition to the throne. Especially after 1928, when the Judiciary was brought into line throughout the French empire,[c] the courts of the *justice française* were much as in France itself. There was one high court at Hanoi for the northern half of Indochina, which included Laos, Tonkin, and Annam down to the Col des Nuages, and a second at Saigon for

---

[a] Decree of 16 Feb. 1921.   [b] Decree of 15 Feb. 1921.
[c] *Décret du Conseil d'État* of 22 July 1928 cited in Indochina, *Organisation judiciaire* (1938–9).

the southern half, including the rest of Annam as well as Cochin-china and Cambodia. The appeal court for all Indochina sat, not at Hanoi, but at Saigon. There were latterly administrative courts as well, and the *Conseil d'État* of the French state exercised ultimate re-view of the rights of individuals infringed by the Government. The supreme judicial appeal was to the *Cour de Cassation* in Paris. Save in Annam, where the exclusive right of the sovereign to dispense jus-tice between his Annamite subjects (though not between his Anna-mite and Tonkinese subjects) was regularly upheld by the French courts,[a] litigants had a choice of civil jurisdictions between French and Vietnamese judges, even when the law they sought to be governed by was customary law in preference to the statutes of the colonial regime; however, if one party was not Vietnamese, juris-diction fell obligatorily to the French court. Also, in penal matters, the jurisdiction of Vietnamese magistrates was restricted to accused persons native to the region: a charge against a Tonkinese on a visit to Vinh, for instance, could be brought only before a French magis-trate (just as it could only be brought under French law), even though a Vietnamese magistrate invested with equal powers might be sitting in the next room. In practice, therefore, French domina-tion of the Judiciary made few concessions to native participation or to the avowed policy of *association*: the involved jurisdictions and procedures to which its progressive standardization gave rise from 1880 onwards were an inducement to bypass the rules and, in times of emergency when serious disorder threatened, to set up special courts in the Protectorates to try persons charged with offences against the interests of France.[37] To treat common crimes com-mitted by malcontents as political misdemeanours in this way tend-ed at the same time to make martyrs of the culprits[b] and to under-line the divergence of interest between the protecting and the native authorities to which the two parts of the Judiciary were separately answerable.

Personal status

One might have expected that the detachment of Cochinchina from the realms of the Emperor of Annam and its incorporation into the territory of France—so intimately that, like other juridical colonies, it elected a member to the *Chambre des Députés*—would have conferred French citizenship on the natives; but it did not, and

[a] Tran-chanh-Thanh, pp. 483–7; for cases, Camerlynck, p. 110 n. 2.
[b] For instance, in Annam in 1932—see below p. 130.

the Cochinchinese gained no advantage from their colonial status not available equally to Indochinese from the Protectorates. Thus, every Vietnamese was born a *sujet* in Cochinchina (or *sujet protégé* in the Protectorates)—subject, that is, to the *régime de l'indigénat*: liable in the countryside for what remained of the *corvée*, allowed to travel any distance only upon production of identity papers issuable by the village authority (ostensibly to certify that he was not a tax-debtor, but often in practice arbitrarily or corruptly) and subject to the indignity of imprisonment up to five days for causing displeasure (undefined) to any personage invested with magisterial powers—a rather petty procedure reckoned to be administrative, not judicial, and consequently not subject to revision or appeal[a]— and liable to detention indefinitely and to confiscation of all property by order of the Governor-General though with the partial safeguard of review by the Minister of the Colonies.[b] The status of *citoyen* could be acquired, even by those born on French soil, only by an act of naturalization; and the qualification for that was the degree of *assimilation* reached by the applicant. The usual roads to *assimilation* were adoption into a French family, marriage to a French national, possession of a French secondary-school certificate, or service in the French army.[c] Birth in a *chrétienté* or conversion to Catholicism made the path to assimilation easier but did not, of course, figure among the regulations. Senior positions in the government service of Cochinchina and of the federal departments of Indochina, as well as membership of representative councils, were open only to *citoyens*, but as late as 1938 there were still only 2,600 *naturalisés* in all Vietnam, three-fifths of them in Cochinchina.[d]

Police

The criminal courts of Indochina were supported by a police organization that was narrowly functional, with different bodies of police entrusted with different duties to all intents and purposes in isolation from one another. Framing charges in connexion with even quite minor criminal proceedings before the justices was the responsibility of officials of the court, not of the police. The keeping of order in the bigger towns—traffic control, control of vice, superintendence of markets and so on—was taken care of by urban police under the local *préfet*. The *Gendarmerie* operated in Indochina, with

---

[a] Jean, p. 106.   [b] Decree of 11 Oct. 1904, in Pinto, p. 74.
[c] Decrees of 25 May 1881, 26 May 1913, and 4 Sept. 1919.
[d] Devillers (1952), p. 33 n. 5.

the quasi-military discipline and with certain guard and escort duties similar to those it had in France; it was in fact incorporated into the *Gendarmerie* of France but had a number of native auxiliaries.[a] The key body to which police functions were entrusted, however, was the *Sûreté*. Like the *Gendarmerie*, the *Sûreté* was a pan-Indochina service, owing loyalty solely to the state interests of France, not of the native sovereigns, of whose territories it had nevertheless a free run. The *Sûreté* was primarily a detective body. In the French system, the initiative in criminal investigation falls to the magistrate himself, employing bailiffs to make overt inquiries about simple matters in dispute; but more subtle inquiries, calling for a measure of professional sophistication, were carried out by the *Sûreté*. In practice the bulk of the work done by the *Sûreté* was not criminal investigation at all but political control—its full title was *Direction des Affaires Politiques de la Sûreté Générale*—, and its agents, not trained as professional detectives with clearly-prescribed answerability before a judicial authority, generally stood in low public esteem; they were never concerned with safeguarding the personal safety and private property of Vietnamese villagers and seem to have considered themselves primarily as a network of agents to watch over the interests of the French state. The scope for graft latent in many Asian societies was aggravated in Indochina by the dependence of French police officers, in their almost universal ignorance of the native languages, upon the inquiries and operations of a class of Indian, Chinese, Eurasian, and other non-native informers whose venality became a byword. Worst of all, the *Sûreté* was not averse to operating for 'reasons of state' beyond the terms of the law itself and tended to bring the legal and judicial system of the French administration into disrepute as hardly preferable to the arbitrary Chinese system it had supplanted. The system proved little suited to dealing with subversion through intimidation. Down in the village, the traditional organization was intact, and the *xa* continued to be responsible for its own internal law and order, as in the days of the Nguyen (except for the limitation of collective penal responsibility in Annam to cases of riot[b] and its dropping altogether from the laws of Tonkin and Cochinchina), with no impartial representative of the central Government to whom the aggrieved or intimidated could turn for protection: the village constable was simply one of the local notables, and he had no certain police powers, nor the wherewithal to exercise any. This neglect of the

[a] Galembert (1931), p. 340.　　　[b] Penal Code of Annam, art. 95.

interests of the individual native, posing as self-determination for the village commune, was regarded as an aspect of indirect rule implicit in the policy of *association*, at the other end of the political scale from the retention of the titular sovereignty of the Emperor at Hué. It was also a factor in the continued flourishing of occult sects and secret societies offering the protection which ought to have been available from the police and the legal system.

Paramilitary forces

Like the Nguyen before them, the French reckoned to forestall uprisings in Indochina at the instigation of sects and political movements by the establishment of garrisons at strategic points. The garrisons were made up part of army, part of paramilitary forces. The army comprised both wholly French units at various times and, all the time, units whose ranks were Vietnamese (never, apparently, Lao or Cambodian) but whose officers, from sergeant upwards, were French (or at least *citoyens*). There appear to have been Vietnamese volunteers in the native battalions, but the bulk of the strength was maintained by the traditional form of conscription, now called *l'appel*: quotas were set for each village and filled, in Annam and Tonkin, through designation by the notables, in Cochinchina by drawing lots; any deserters (who were as numerous after the French conquest as they had been before)[a] were replaceable by the same village. Soldiers received their pay and, in addition, regular privileges like exemption from taxes (at village, not state, expense), as well as occasional ones like the granting of honorific titles in the Protectorates or, in Cochinchina, favoured consideration for sinecure employment after demobilization.[b] None of these arrangements were innovations of the French colonial regime; they too could be made out to perpetuate native tradition in conformity with the indirect rule implicit in *association*. Nor did the imperial army of the Nguyen disappear altogether from the Protectorates: it survived in attenuated state in both Tonkin and Annam, but with duties that were purely ceremonial; theoretically it came under Vietnamese command alone, but in practice even this concession was too risky for French mistrust, and French officers supervised the units closely.[c]

There were several paramilitary forces, all independent of one another and ostensibly concerned with internal security, but without legally-prescribed powers or duties. Described generally as

---

[a] p. 60 above.   [b] Based on Galembert, pp. 350–5.
[c] Galembert, p. 868.

milices and commanded by the territorial administration in normal times—by the French *Résident*, that is, in both Tonkin and Annam, not by the Vietnamese mandarin[a]—they were subject to military command during a declared emergency. Apart from a *Garde Urbaine*, the two most important paramilitary bodies were the *Garde Indigène de l'Indochine* and the *Garde Civile de Cochinchine*—the former stationed in the Protectorates and the latter in the Colony. The *Garde Indochinoise* was a French-officered corps, but with natives in all ranks up to regimental sergeant-major; its establishment was quite small— 5,300 for Tonkin and 3,100 for Annam. The men were mostly volunteers, but their numbers too had sometimes to be made up by *appel*; besides their pay (met from the Protectorate budget), they were also in receipt of privileges such as tax exemption at the expense of their fellow villagers. The *Garde Civile* was an all-Vietnamese corps, but, except for training and administration, had— perhaps for that very reason—no Colony-wide command; individual units came under the French *Chefs de Province* and were paid three-fifths from his budget, two-fifths from the budget of the village where the political situation was sufficiently unreliable for a platoon to be posted to it—an arrangement which unhappily gave a punitive tone to relations with the villagers. Both *Gardes* were regulated by a decree of the French President. which specified their duties as being police ones but conferred no actual powers on them.[b] Their training seems to have been confined to drill and combat and to have paid no attention to legal refinements; all the same, the civil authorities retained command over them very jealously, in spite of military pretensions to command them which were quashed by an injunction of the *Conseil d'État* in Paris in 1886.[c]

Technical departments

The technical services made a more impressive showing than the security services in the French apparatus of government in Indochina; technical efficiency was essential in the public sector if the chosen economic policy was to be carried through. From 1887 onwards the Post Office, Public Works and Communications (including the railway and the telegraphs) were centralized as all-Indochina departments, as was the collection of Customs duties and of a few other forms of indirect taxation designated to pay for these major enterprises and for the administrative expenditure of the

[a] Jean, p. 211.   [b] Decree of 20 June 1915, amended 21 May 1931, esp. art. 4.
[c] Daufès (1933-4), i. p. xi.

Gouvernement-Général. French education, which included all forms of post-primary schooling, was similarly centralized, together with control of mining, forestry, and other natural resources. Public Health, vernacular education, the land administration, agriculture and engineering works in connexion with land development fell to each *Gouvernement* separately—except that their work was subject to inspection by officers of the *Gouvernement-Général*[a]—and were paid for out of direct taxes, of which by far the most productive was land revenue, with poll taxes next and income and business taxes assessed *pro rata* only as a much later feature of French administration.

Public services

Both technical and administrative services were staffed by a hierarchy of French and Indochinese *cadres* whose structure varied from one decade to the next as the policies of different Governor-Generals changed. The changes reflected swings of a pendulum between what were considered to be the interests of efficiency (of benefit to French and natives jointly) and the ideal of associating educated natives—principally Vietnamese even when the public services of Laos and Cambodia were in question—with the administration of their own country; they were not connected with the progressive devolution of office to native personnel. Common to all the arrangements, in fact, was the principle that natives could not aspire to higher posts, whatever their technical qualifications; despite the more liberal efforts of such Governor-Generals as Vannier, Pasquier, and Robin—and even Admiral Decoux during the Second World War—there was a tendency, as public services expanded and reached new fields of public life, for Frenchmen to be recruited to provide them and incidentally to take over ever more of the humbler positions, to such an extent that their numbers doubled during the seven years 1919–25.[b] This process was the reverse of the tendency in other colonial territories, including some of those under French rule. Generally speaking, what in British usage would be called the administrative grades of all the technical services were filled by members of the empire-wide French Colonial Service; this applied to the executive grades as well of certain departments such as the Treasury, Customs, Public Works, and the *Sûreté*. Local *cadres* provided men for middle and lower ranks of other services. The French Colonial Service was a unified body, so that, in accordance with the policy of ultimate *assimilation*, the members of the French

[a] Jean, pp. 135–41.   [b] Chesneaux, p. 198.

cadres, unlike their British counterparts, were employees of the metropolitan Government and owed their loyalty to it, not to the people they were administering. This orientation was even more marked among the very select top men sent to Indochina to fill politically sensitive posts for a while who were members of the *Grands Corps de l'État*—that is to say, home civil servants with a specific mission to pull Indochinese affairs back into a course suiting metropolitan interests.[38] According to Pinto,[a] no Vietnamese, however fully assimilated and technically qualified—and the qualifications for entry to the mandarinate in Tonkin and Annam were very high—could, even though a *citoyen*, occupy any position reserved to members of the empire-wide *Services Généraux*, and cases were quoted of Indochinese with top marks from the Grandes Écoles in France returning home to serve under Frenchmen with much lower qualifications, or none at all, and on a salary approximately a fifth of what would be paid to a European doing the same work.[39] Harmand, writing in 1910, characterized as folly a decision of British policy in India, taken as far back as the 1820s, that public office must be open to European and Asiatic on an equal footing;[b] three times as many Frenchmen were employed in 1937 to run Indochina, with a population of 30 millions, as Britons to run India, which had more than ten times the population,[c] so that France's policy came to look as if it had been dictated as much by a desire to find employment for the sons of her own middle classes as by any political wisdom in furtherance of the joint interest of colony and metropolis.[d]

4. FRENCH COLONIAL RULE: SOCIAL AND ECONOMIC DEVELOPMENTS

The transformation wrought in the way of life of the Vietnamese people by this machinery of government during the eighty years it lasted was remarkable in certain directions. One of these was the spread of Catholicism. Although the Christian faith never displaced Confucianism as the orthodox ideology of Vietnam, it was adopted eventually by not fewer than a tenth of the population: in certain provinces the proportion rose to between twenty and fifty.[40] The sectors in which the missionaries were most successful were the coastal provinces of Tonkin, the non-Vietnamese highlands, and

[a] p. 27. [b] Harmand, p. 229.
[c] About 1,400 in India, 4,654 in Indochina (*Ann. stat. Indochine, 1938,* p. 240).
[d] The Chesneaux's charge (p. 158). Minister of Colonies Albert Sarraut went even further: 'Au début . . . l'on n'y exilait que les déchets métropolitains' (1931, p. 209).

the upper classes in the big towns. In many hamlets the entire community belonged to the Church, and the parish priest became not only a spokesman in dealing with the authorities, but the real decision-maker in aspects of social and economic activity in which the authorities had no part, so that persistent dissenters tended to drift away from the village.

Population

A second direction in which Vietnamese life was transformed was the absolute growth of the population. This more than doubled between 1870 and 1950, although the figures cannot be given with confidence because no proper census was ever taken.[41] In 1870 the population of Cochinchina was well under 2 million,[a] that of Annam under 4, that of Tonkin (not yet French) under 5, but by 1943 —the last year the French authorities were in sufficient control to make a count—these three estimates had risen respectively to $5\frac{1}{2}$, 7, and 10 million.[b] The disproportionate increase for Cochinchina reflects internal migration; the historical *nam tien* was further stimulated by economic development, and at times organized under French auspices, at a rate up to 25,000 a year,[c] in spite of unsatisfactory working conditions that led many to go back to Tonkin at the first opportunity.[d] In addition to internal migration, there was an important movement into and out of Vietnam. In the outward movement it was once again the Tonkinese who furnished the bulk of the manpower. Indentured labour was exported, under arrangements similar to those for British Indians labouring in Ceylon or Malaya, to work on French estates, particularly in New Caledonia. Tonkinese labourers were also taken to France by the thousand between 1914 and 1917—more or less under constraint—to help make good the loss of labourers to the French army. But neither of these forms of emigration was permanent, for the majority of labourers came home sooner or later. Immigration into Vietnam brought French settlers (they numbered about 30,000 in 1937,[e] but barely 8,000 again by 1963)[f] and also both Indians and Chinese. The Indians were never numerous but came as cloth merchants and moneylenders (*chettyars*) through the French settlements on the Indian mainland; few penetrated farther afield than Cochinchina, whither individual Indians also were posted in the French Colonial

[a] *Cochinchine française* (p. 101) gives it as barely 1,500,000.
[b] *Ann. stat. 1949–50*, p. 23.   [c] ILO, *Problèmes du travail* (1937), p. 47.
[d] A. Maybon (1931), pp. 126–8; also Mus (1952), pp. 106–7.
[e] Robequain (1944), pp. 21–23.   [f] *Ann. stat. 1963*, p. 28.

Service. The rise and fall of Chinese immigration belong more to the history of the Overseas Chinese generally than to that specially of Vietnam; the total number rose from an estimated 36,000 in Cochinchina at the beginning of the colonial period (presumably not counting the *Minh Huong*)[a] to over 400,000 on the eve of the depression of 1931, declined again when large numbers were back to China,[b] and then rose again from 1936 onwards to 466,000 in 1943.[c] Like the Indians, the Chinese have stayed predominantly in Cochinchina, where under French rule they further strengthened their position in the financial life and the overseas trade of the country; even the small groups of Chinese retailers who did settle in Annam and Tonkin during the colonial period were, apart from the port of Haiphong, to be found mostly in out-of-the-way markets, often in the hill country.

Schools

The French record in providing social services for the expanding population of Indochina was, for the period, a very good one. By 1938, despite chronic shortage of trained teachers,[d] over 750,000 children were receiving elementary education free, in government schools in the three regions, without counting private and missionary schools or the traditional schools in villages;[e] and even if we do not accept at its face value the official claim that this meant that 75 per cent of all children of elementary-school age were at school,[f] it is possible that that proportion did receive some schooling, if only for a year or two. The educational principle common to France's dependencies—to France itself—was followed: 'Instruire la masse et dégager l'élite.'[g] Vietnamese was the medium of instruction in elementary schools, with French as a subject and, down to about 1900, Chinese as well. Secondary education developed more slowly and, despite experiments with Vietnamese, usually with French as the medium, for the reason that it was a responsibility of the Union Government and designed primarily for *citoyens*, actual or in the

[a] *Cochinchine française.*   [b] Robequain, pp. 34–43.
[c] *Ann. stat. 1949–50*, p. 23. The figure for 1966 is unofficially estimated at over a million.
[d] Cultru (1910), p. 399 (writing about the 1880s) compared with A. Maybon (1931), p. 151 (writing about the 1920s).
[e] According to Virginia Thompson's informants (1937, p. 301), there were in 1931 village schools in all but 115 out of the 1,419 *xa* in Cochinchina, even if quality was, according to Prof. Coulet who was in charge, very low (Coulet, 1930, p. 199).
[f] France, *Premier rapport* (1948), p. 10.
[g] Statement attributed to Governor-General Carde of French West Africa by Hailey (1945, p. 1263).

making.[42] After the closure of classical Confucian schools in 1919, there was, until well on into the 1930s, no secondary education in Annam, but the native authorities there paid for promising children to be sent to schools in Tonkin.[a] In the country as a whole, however, over 3,000 Vietnamese children were attending *lycées* by 1938, and in that year about 200 received the *baccalauréat* (450 in 1944).[b] Nearly as many children again were at the same time attending so-called technical schools,[c] but the latter were merely trade schools for mechanics, fitters, and carpenters.

Higher education

The élite were at least as well looked after as the masses. In the 1930s 100 or more Vietnamese were sent annually to universities in France, or else to the Grandes Écoles, at government expense, and an even bigger number went on their own. The French-speaking University of Hanoi began in 1902 with a Faculty of Medicine, to which in 1907 was added a Faculty of Law—a broader field of study in French usage than in English or American, including economics and public administration. The University soon had to be closed again because of subversive agitation among the students, but from 1917 onwards it functioned fully, taking in Arts and Science as well. The standard aimed at was the equivalent of a European university, with no concession to any popular desire for easy degrees, and, perhaps because of that, the number of graduates remained a low proportion of the number of students for some years; by 1930 there were still not 300 fully-trained doctors.[d] By 1939, however, the figure had risen to 580.[e] The conservation of the ruins of Angkor and the sixty-odd volumes of the *Bulletin* of the École Française d'Extrême Orient, founded at Hanoi in 1899, are two impressive monuments to French concern for the preservation of the elements of Indochinese civilization. Opportunities for a modern education open to Vietnamese youth under French tutelage were thus anything but illiberal; what sometimes was lacking was the willingness, or the incentive, to profit by them in a spirit of public service. Too many of those who gained higher diplomas preferred to stay in, or go to, metropolitan France to practise their profession, or else not to practise it at all but to regard it as an attainment of worth purely for prestige—as a qualification for naturalization as *citoyens*, perhaps— while they continued to live by their private means.

[a] Indochina, *Annam scolaire* (1931), p. 92.   [b] France, *Premier rapport*, p. 57.
[c] Ibid.   [d] Indochina, *Indochine scolaire* (1931), p. 25.   [e] Isoart (1961), p. 253.

Medical services

This attitude to medical training tended to keep the health and medical services understaffed in relation to the material facilities available through French planning. The first government hospital, the Cho Quan at Saigon, had been opened as early as 1864,[a] but it was another fifty years before enough doctors were available to set up a regular medical and health service (in 1914).[b] In 1938 there were over 25 general and 7 specialist hospitals in the country,[c] besides many hundreds of dispensaries, lying-in wards, orphanages,[43] and homes for the aged. There were only 250 Vietnamese doctors, and 150 French, to run these establishments[d] (although there were several hundred other doctors in wholly private practice) and 1,300 nurses,[e] but in that one year they cared for 365,000 in-patients, dealt with 13 million out-patients and gave inoculations against smallpox or cholera to well over half the population.[f] As with education, the medical and health services were free and represented a standard of welfare not surpassed for the time anywhere in southeast Asia.

The economy

The social services were the fruit of an economy which, in spite of booms and slumps, was sustained well by its agricultural foundation through most of the period, until the world crisis in 1931. Several studies of the French Indochina economy are available, and it is only possible here to mention certain features of it. The division of function between the various sources of finance were similar to those of other colonies: major hydraulic works, communications (an ever-present concern, in the special geography of Vietnam), and social services were provided from public funds, while all forms of production were left strictly to private enterprise, albeit a private enterprise encouraged by a larger measure of protectionism on national lines than was the policy, for instance, in British, American, or Dutch dependencies. Capital works fell mainly within the competence of the all-Indochina budget, as did the technical departments to carry them out, and powers to raise loans on the Paris market were vested in the Governor-General alone: regional governments and municipalities were dependent for loan capital upon subsidies from the federal exchequer—a restriction no doubt im-

[a] Vial (1874), i. 336.   [b] Isoart, p. 253.
[c] France, *Premier rapport*, p. 58; number of beds not stated.   [d] Ibid.
[e] Isoart. His claim that there were 15,000 hospital beds in Vietnam in 1939 must contain a misunderstanding of the official figures.
[f] *Premier rapport*, p. 58.

posed from the best of motives but one which failed to accustom Indochinese leaders, or the educated public, to the exercise of responsibility in the context of modern state finance. Consistently with this approach in the public sector, banking was developed in the private sector always with guarantees of solvency the first, and almost sole, consideration in the issue of licences. Thus, although the British Far Eastern banks (the Chartered, the Mercantile, and the Hongkong & Shanghai Banking Corporation) had from the beginning financed Cochinchinese trade with other southeast Asian ports,[44] Paris banks were encouraged to form a consortium, the Banque de l'Indochine (1875).[a] The latter was granted a monopoly of the note-issue when in 1878 the piastre replaced the franc as the currency of Indochina,[45] and thanks to it the authorities secured more easily than through freely-competing banks the type of finance that suited their development policy with minimum risk of bank failures, of which the Far East has experienced so many. A consequence of this policy quite acceptable to the French was that no native banks were ever founded—unfortunately banking was a Chinese art the Vietnamese had failed to pick up for themselves—and, right down to the moment of independence, no banking facilities at all were available in the provinces, either to receive deposits or to make advances.

Overseas trade

Early French hopes of obtaining a bigger share of trade with the interior of China by way of the Red River met with scarcely greater success than the hopes they had placed earlier in the Mekong, and Indochina never competed with Singapore and Hong Kong as a Far Eastern entrepot. Instead, the pattern of trade was always determined by the export of Indochinese products and the importation of consumer commodities, vehicles, appliances and, latterly, oil fuel. In the earliest days of Cochinchina, the principal trading partners were China and Hong Kong, but increasingly metropolitan France took the lead on both sides of the account, until by 1950 she was buying 45 per cent of Vietnamese exports and supplying almost 80 per cent of Vietnamese imports.[b] Sooner or later, imperial preference became the doctrine of all colonial powers; in the case of France a more active form of protectionism had been enshrined in the doctrine of Colbert, as far back as Louis XIV, that colonies should be incorporated directly into the economy of the

[a] *Cochinchine française*, p. 301.   [b] *Ann. stat. 1949–50*, pp. 242–3.

metropolis, supplying the latter with raw materials and buying its manufactures. The same idea had been formulated by Jules Ferry in the 1880s when he told the French parliament that 'la politique coloniale est fille de la politique industrielle'.[a] Yet it was only after 1928 that full protection was made a reality and in 1930 that the piastre was transferred from the silver standard (which had linked it, together with other currencies of the area, to China and involved it in the silver crisis of the 1920s) to a gold standard and hencefor-ward quoted in terms of the franc.[b] Many forces were no doubt in play at that time, including metropolitan manufacturers,[c] but dominant among them was pressure from settler interests in Indo-china itself.[d] The significance of this pressure is that it reflected a shift of weight in French investment, without any absolute reduc-tion in the interest in commerce, towards ownership of agricultural estates, rubber plantations, and other exploitations of the land. Not only China, but the other countries of the Far East and southeast Asia as well, tended to be replaced as customers for Indochinese ex-ports by France and French dependencies; although Japan always bought the bulk of Tonkinese coal (not an important item in the Vietnamese economy anyway), nearly all the rubber produced and close on half the rice stayed within the French empire.[e]

Land policy

The strength of the *colons* as a body claiming its rights from the French administration, but less conscious of its duties towards the people of Indochina,[f] grew directly from the land policy pursued in furtherance of the objectives of *assimilation* and of *association*; to the same cause is attributable in large measure the agrarian crisis of 1931, which provided the seed-bed for the rise of the Communist movement. Although a certain amount was done to facilitate native agriculture, especially in Tonkin and Cochinchina, the problems of land use and tenure were never tackled in a resolute manner. The central concept behind the policy pursued was *mise-en-valeur*. This meant, in effect, three things: making the maximum possible area of land available, making the maximum use of it, and putting an exchange value into land hitherto looked upon by its native owners only in terms of the crop raised on it. The principal measure in furtherance of the first aim was the execution and maintenance of

[a] Ferry (1890), p. 38.   [b] A. Maybon, p. 109.   [c] Bernard (1934), p. 39.
[d] Robequain, pp. 132–3.   [e] *Ann. stat. 1950–1*, pp. 234–47.
[f] The complaint of both Harmand (p. 159) and Sarraut (1931, p. 209).

extensive hydraulic works in the river deltas and estuaries; the other two aims were sought through the combination of concessionary grants of state land and the facilitation of mortgages on private land—a combination it was hoped would tend to bring arable land, through operation of the economic forces of free enterprise, under the most modern and expert management, to the mutual advantage of French and Indochinese partners in the *association*.

Land improvement

Great engineering effort was expended on land improvement. Beginning as early as the Admirals' administration of Cochinchina, untilled tracts of the alluvial plain of the Mekong, especially the Transbassac, were crisscrossed with new canals. The principal function of these was to make possible rapid transit of the swamps by security forces, but drainage of the flood plains and transport of goods later assumed the major importance. In Cochinchina close on a million cubic metres of earth were being excavated by manual labour annually by 1897 and were adding 30,000 hectares a year to the area of arable land through resultant drainage.[a] The process continued throughout the colonial period, though with manual labour increasingly supplemented by machinery, so that the total area of land under paddy alone rose from half a million hectares in 1880 to $2\frac{1}{4}$ million in 1937,[b] while the total length of navigable canals exceeding 25 feet in bottom width eventually reached some 1,200 miles.[c] Two features unfortunately marred these monumental works: the first was that the labour was commandeered, was often unpaid and ill fed and frequently fell victim to epidemics;[46] the other was that plans were not always prepared methodically, and often the drainage of new land proved detrimental to the old.[d] In Annam works of this kind were less spectacular, and in the whole French period less than 100,000 hectares were reclaimed.[e] In Tonkin the figure was smaller still—50,000–60,000;[f] but there the great effort was put into dyking the courses of the rivers, some of which flood in spring, some in autumn, and a third group in both. Until the 1920s further improvements of the traditional earthworks had been meagre, for there were already 2,400 kilometres of dykes

[a] France, *Premier rapport*, pp. 20–21.
[b] Robequain, p. 220; a higher figure still is given by Bernard (1937, p. 29).
[c] UN & others (1959), p. 206; most of these in fact had bottom widths between 50 and 200 ft, while the mileage of channels dug merely for drainage, and regularly spaced across the Delta, ran to several thousand.
[d] Peautonnier (1946), pt. 2.   [e] Masson (1950), p. 104.   [f] Ibid.

before the French annexed Tonkin (representing a displacement, it was calculated, of 156 million cubic metres of earth);[a] thus the whole region was already regulated. However, the alignment of dykes had been governed by considerations of geomancy (*phong thuy*) as much as by observation and experience, and, as in China where these ideas originated, the notables had not been above suborning the geomancers for private advantage.[b] In 1926 an unprecedented flood carried all away, and the reconstruction offered an opportunity to improve the system; the dykes were thickened and heightened severalfold[c]—this time by requisitioned, but properly-paid, labour. Agriculture in Vietnam generally also benefited from agronomical experiments—for example, by the specialization of 'floating' rice, whose stalk grows as fast as the flood rises; but it never extended to badly-needed soil and fertilizer studies[d]—in parts of Cochinchina there are chronic problems of alkalinity, largely tidal—with the result that rice yields in Indochina as a whole remained about the lowest in southeast Asia.[47] Even so, total production of rice rose enormously during the colonial period; although satisfactory comparative figures are lacking for Tonkin and Annam, the increase in Cochinchina was fivefold, from about 600,000 tons in the 1870s to over 3 million in 1930.[e] As populations rose, Cochinchina was thus able to supply the ever bigger deficiency in Annam and Tonkin, which paid for it by services, in addition to providing, along with Cambodia, the bulk of Indochinese rice exports overseas.

Alienation of state land

This much of the land and agricultural policy was, therefore, a success in that the total quantity of food available more than outstripped the growth of population and afforded a valuable export as well. But the concession-and-mortgage side of the policy was not such a success. Since there was at no time any prospect that Indochina could become a *colonie de peuplement*—that is to say, one in which French nationals would settle permanently—settlement land was never set aside for purposes of colonization; any arable land was regarded as alienable so long as it had no native claimant. The annexation of Cochinchina and the conquest of Tonkin both occurred during periods of social turmoil, which the advent of French troops, as was to be expected, at first aggravated. Thou-

---

[a] Pasquier, p. 299.   [b] Chesneaux, p. 72.   [c] Gourou (1940), p. 221.
[d] Peautonnier, pt. 4.   [e] Henry (1932), i. 333; *Cochinchine française*, p. 263.

sands of peasants in both regions abandoned their cultivations, and in many villages tax and land registers, traditionally the first casualties in civil disturbances, were destroyed. The view was then taken that abandoned land, as soon as the tax was no longer being paid, was forfeited to the state under Chinese law, applicable to Vietnam in this convenient context if in no other. In reality this was a principle neither in Chinese law[a]—whose supposed applicability in this isolated circumstance was special pleading—nor in Vietnamese law. But on the basis of this misunderstanding of the rights of the state, title was freely given by the French authorities in the early days of the annexation to Europeans who were little better than squatters. In Cochinchina, where squatting on new land was easy, little irreparable harm was done if a native owner reappeared; but in Tonkin, where land was scarce, the population was for long terrorized by both Black Flags and armed French *colons* who, in 1888, secured the enactment of regulations sanctioning concessions on the supposed domain-by-escheat and thereby legalized their squatters' 'rights'. These regulations must have been drawn up without consultation of the Annamite authorities, but, although they were subsequently called in question as *ultra vires*, French courts were upholding French concessions against Tonkinese proprietors as late as 1908.[b]

Mortgage and foreclosure

At the same time as these virtual expropriations in favour of settlers were taking place, other native riceland was changing hands by mortgage, although under this head Indian and Chinese moneylenders were as often beneficiaries as French settlers.[48] By the middle of the nineteenth century dependence, especially of new cultivators in Cochinchina, on the never-extinguished debts of agricultural credit had brought large areas under various kinds of traditional mortgage as a less onerous source of finance than loans at extortionate rates of interest then prevailing; however, under this customary law foreclosures or other irreversible transfers of ownership were rare.[c] So long as peasant borrowers continued to obtain credit from Vietnamese lenders, the advent of French administration and law would make little difference to the situation; but French or Indian mortgagees automatically, Chinese optionally,

[a] The law and practice of China at this period are described by H. Maspéro (1950, pp. 190–1).

[b] Boudillon (1915), pp. 178–82.   [c] Luro, pp. 238–9.

brought the transaction within the scope of the Civil Code of France, and, as we have seen, it became policy to put a money value into the native's land by facilitating mortgages. Interest rates on mortgages were, on the face of it, more reasonable than on loans, the procedure (by notarial deed) was simple, and the temptation of easy money for social display, gambling—or of course to meet the contingencies of a poor crop—could prove irresistible to a peasant who did not realize that the mitigations of customary tenure would no longer be accessible to him. No statistics are available to show the extent of foreclosures, but, with the scales unavoidably loaded against the impoverished native in the face of an unassailable right before a foreign judge, they were common enough in both Cochin-china and Tonkin to cause concern in Paris and to result in the in-quiry into land tenure conducted by M. Boudillon, just quoted.

Land registration and concessions

Up to that time the only forms of land registration had been the *dia bo* or village registers—subject to every conceivable error and fraud—and the French *Conservation des Hypothèques*; no general land survey had been attempted. It was now proposed (in 1925, that is, after obstruction to the Boudillon proposals had been overcome) to begin a cadastral survey, which would register land by lot instead of by person, and would make possible the issue of unchallengeable titles; at the same time, whilst making permanent alienations of newly drained and irrigated ricelands in Cochinchina, concessions were to be available for rubber, tea, or coffee planting in the thinly-populated eastern parts of Cochinchina, the PMS, and a few hilly areas in Tonkin. The cadastral survey in the event occupied itself only with the determination of the extent of the state domain; it did little to solve any of the mortgage or other problems of land tenure in long-settled areas. In the coastal plains of Annam, up to 1940, it had still hardly taken in more than the townships; in Tonkin and the PMS it was content to ascertain that there were no encum-brances on lands applied for in concession. Only under the direct colonial regime of Cochinchina did the cadastral survey set out to cover all land irrespective of status, and even there the overriding concern with encouragement of concessions, for both rice and rub-ber, meant that not much above a third of the arable area was regis-tered by lot when French control came to an end. Effort was con-centrated on big estates, and these associated the land registry with the interests of Europeans and the small minority of Vietnamese *assimilés* because, in fulfilment of the policy of getting land into the hands of cultivators likely to manage it the most efficiently, concessions could only be granted to *citoyens*;[a] the peasant proprietor and the tenant, captive to outmoded forms of tenure, were left to fend for themselves. Production benefited in certain directions; though relatively a late starter in Indochina, rubber eventually reached 70,000 tons a year[b]—enough to supply all the needs of France and leave some for export elsewhere; but tea and coffee were not such a success, and the granting of concessions to grow them in the PMS, together with the importation of landless Vietnamese plainsmen to do the work, if only seasonally, laid the foundations for long-standing resentment among the hill tribes.

Tenure in Tonkin and Annam

The problem of land tenure in Annam and Tonkin arose from overcrowding, for growth of population outstripped the benefits from hydraulic works. When Yves Henry, the Inspector-General of Colonial Agriculture, conducted his inquiry in 1931, he found the Tonkinese were having to feed themselves, on average, from the product of just over a third of an acre of paddy land a head, and in some localities on that of barely a fifth; Annam was marginally better off.[c] Pressure of population had resulted in such fragmentation of holdings that the biggest to be found in Tonkin was not much over three acres in extent, while two-thirds of all holdings were three-quarters of an acre or less.[d] Although foreclosures and forced sales did bring extensive acreages into the hands of single creditors,[e] there was no economic gain of the sort French policy-makers had expected because the new proprietors were financiers, not better-skilled and equipped agriculturalists, and the scattered plots unworkable as an entity. In Annam urban creditors disposed of less liquid cash, and the lot of the peasant was a little less onerous as a result. In both regions some relief was available through common land (*cong dien*), which added on average a fifth to the arable of a village in Tonkin, a quarter in Annam. Yet here too abuse was rife, for the notables who annually allocated the common land habitually kept back the best for themselves;[f] whilst in some areas groups like the Catholics would be favoured, in others they would be discriminated against. In Annam at least, whatever was left went, not

---

[a] Long-standing practice was given legislative force by Governor-General's *arrêté* dated 4 Nov. 1928.
[b] Note 83.   [c] Henry, i. 8 & 23.   [d] Ibid. pp. 108–10.   [e] Gourou, p. 230.
[f] Henry, i. 44.

to the most needy or to all by rotation, but to the highest bidder in an auction held to benefit the village budget and to reduce the taxes falling on the better-off.[a] The only remedy available to French Protectorate officials moved by social conscience, but lacking administrative powers in such matters, was to facilitate migration of surplus labour to the mines, the new plantations, Cochinchina, or overseas.

Tenure in Cochinchina

In Cochinchina the problems were different: here land was still abundant, but, far from nearly every peasant owning his minute and barely-economic share of it, ownership was concentrated in fewer hands, while the majority of peasants were *phan canh* (share-croppers) or *ta dien* (tenants).[b] Over the decades, indebtedness had continued to concentrate ownership of the older lands, whilst the Government denied grants on the new land created by drainage to all who lacked capital with which to manage it efficiently;[c] schemes for the employment of surplus labour were left to private enterprise and the traditional formulae of *phan canh*, *ta dien*, or daily hire. Although the Indian chetty is less bitterly complained of at this period, little else had changed, and his place had been taken, as in Tonkin, by the capitalistically-minded native landowner. The purpose of the concession policy might well be to encourage more scientific cultivation through bigger units of tillage, but in practice concession-naires, whether French or Vietnamese *citoyens*,[49] worked the big estates on the new lands of the Transbassac simply by farming them out in one-family plots resembling, in their neatly-quadrated strips, Roman *latifundia*; with the colonial administration thinly spread, the landowners ran their estates on a system amounting to extra-territoriality.[d] Even in the older provinces of the Mekong proper, merchants, officials, and other town-dwellers without alternative investment for their savings—there were no industrial stocks to invest in—had begun to buy up agricultural land, whose management they were content to leave to bailiffs with all the vices of middle-men, and to be rid of any personal responsibility for crop or tenant, so long as the latter's indebtedness could be counted on for a steady cash income.[e] In many cases Henry found that a *ta dien* tilling

---

[a] This detail does not seem to be recorded by contemporary French writers, but it was a long-standing custom and is followed still.

[b] According to Le-Thanh-Khoi (p. 423), 57 per cent of the agricultural population cultivated on *ta dien* terms.

[c] Peautonnier, pt. 1.   [d] Henry, i. 57.   [e] Ibid. p. 102 and ii. 310.

a 5-hectare *rizière* retained for himself as little as a twentieth of the crop he raised and therefore could not subsist save by setting himself and his family to off-season employment elsewhere. For ten or twenty years the Colony Government had tried to reduce indebtedness by opening various funds for agricultural credit in place of the money-lender; but these made loans only against security, and the real debtor had none to give. The money tended to stick with the landowners, who were not above passing it on to their clients at the usual exorbitant interest.[a50]

The depression

The world economic crisis of 1930–1 hit southeast Asia hard, and the slump in world markets for every one of Indochina's products brought a severe deficiency in public revenue. Rice moved in sympathy with rubber: from over 13 piastres a quintal at Saigon in April 1930 it drifted steadily downwards to barely 3 piastres in November 1933.[b] Social repercussions could not fail to be far-reaching. Nearly 36 million piastres were reckoned to be owed in cash loans on 427,000 hectares of land; ruin faced individuals at all levels of the social scale. French companies operating rice and rubber concessions lost all their capital and were taken over by new financial interests from home, to the tune of several thousand million francs, but fortunately a moratorium on debts secured by land reduced the extent of the foreclosure to which smallholdings were exposed,[c] while the imposition of a drastic limitation on interest rates to some extent safeguarded the habitual debtor's future, in law if not always in practice. For thousands of tenant farmers, however, the choice lay between resigned acceptance of further prolongation of their debt bondage and either absconding or making common cause with the bandits, secret societies, and political movements for whom the crisis was a godsend. Indochina did recover from the depression, and by 1937 financial stability had returned; but this outcome was due for the most part to world recovery, not to the tackling of social problems in the Vietnamese countryside, where the lot of the peasant farmer, at best minutely less oppressed than his neighbour in the Philippines,[d] was relieved by no new hope, but was on the contrary on the point of being exploited in the most brutal yet of a long series of insurrections against the colonial power

a Speech by Gov.-Gen. Pasquier in the *Grand Conseil des Intérêts Économiques et Financiers* on 25 Nov. 1931, quoted by Chesneaux (p. 208).
b Isoart, p. 280.   c Robequain, p. 175.
d The opinion of Prof. Hall (p. 728).

in which the peasant had been, and would continue to be, the chief sufferer.

5. VIETNAMESE REACTIONS TO FRENCH COLONIAL RULE

Seen in retrospect from the vantage point of today's interests and attitudes, the Vietnamese reaction to colonialism is usually portrayed as one of unmitigated hostility. Yet, by and large, French rule was, at worst, acquiesced in and, at best, enjoyed the co-operation of the Vietnamese upper and middle classes in its efforts to preserve law and order in the face of unceasing banditry in the countryside, just as in the days before French rule, and continual revolutionary movements nourished by banditry; social reformers like Sarraut and Varenne were genuinely admired by Vietnamese intellectuals, who desired nothing more than to share French standards and the French way of life; the French authorities could not have carried on without the support of native uniformed and civil services. Three elements are traceable in the revolutionary movements: nationalism, brigandage, and influences from outside Vietnam—both foreign political ideas and deliberate foreign intrigue on the part of China, Japan, and Russia. Although today all the upheavals against the French are ascribed to nationalism on its own, those who were entrusted with putting down outbreaks of rapine and slaughter can perhaps be pardoned for viewing them primarily as crimes against the victims and for awarding more significance in their own minds to the foreign encouragement that was often behind them than to social conditions under their own jurisdiction which provided the occasion and the excuse.

Resistance to annexation

The French annexation of Cochinchina had to face two apparently independent insurrections, and in doing so received little or no co-operation from the Vietnamese mandarinate through which the military authorities had hoped to govern. The *Tong Doc*, Phan Thanh Gian, had owed his appointment two years earlier to the fact that his native province of Vinh Long, where he now had his residence, was threatened by irredentist claims by displaced Khmers[a] and, at the same time, by an outbreak of brigandage among some of the Vietnamese; at Hué he was thought to be the right man to deal with both problems.[b] At the approach of Admiral

[a] Le-thanh-Tuong (1938), p. 51.   [b] Ibid. p. 95.

Lagrandière to Vinh Long in 1867, he committed suicide, to the chagrin of the French,[a] while his subordinates threw in their lot with the brigands, who set up a base in the Plain of Reeds and harried French garrisons between Saigon and My Tho for a while. But the ordinary people seem to have taken little part—on the contrary, some had been only too ready to enlist for service with the French colours in the attack on Tourane,[b] as, ten years later, the Tonkinese also joined up[c]—and the remnants of this revolt were absorbed by the contemporary insurrection led by one Pu Kombo, a Khmer bonze, which drew its strength primarily from Cambodia. The resistance which the establishment of the Protectorate met in Tonkin twenty years later was both harder to deal with and compounded of a tangle of forces harder to unravel. Tu Duc had little popular support outside Hanoi, partly because the Nguyen were still unforgiven for their usurpation of the throne and for the transfer of the capital to Hué, in part because of dishonesty among the mandarins from Annam.[d] It was to China therefore that Tu Duc turned for reinforcement against France; but this was forthcoming in the first place through the indirect agency, easier to disown, of the Black Flags, now swollen by recruits from the defeated Taipings (whom China was happy to see out of mischief at home) and commanded by a skilled frontier partisan, Liu Yung-fu, whose sobriquet 'Liu Yi' suggests he may have been a Triad man.[e] The prowess and the renown of Liu were due to his tactics and to the organization of his guerrillas with supplies obtained by terrorizing the Tonkinese villages and using them as hideouts from which to lure French columns away from their strong-points, ambush them and seize their weapons. Units of the Chinese regular army also occupied northern Tonkin in conjunction with the Black Flags during the later period of open hostilities in 1883 to 1885. Although the withdrawal from this position which France forced on Peking in 1885 included the Black Flags, who were there by agreement between Peking and Hué,[f] the irregulars none the less hung on for several more years. They did so until the French army learnt to

---

[a] Vial describes the French doctors' efforts to save his life (1874, ii. 144–51).
[b] *Cochinchine française*, p. 221.   [c] Dutreb (1924), p. 92.
[d] Roberts (1929), p. 441.
[e] Huang Hai-an (1955), p. 169. Liu Yi's followers were 'unemployed and vagabonds' from Kuanghsi bound together by an oath of secrecy and loyalty sworn over a potion of cockerel's blood mixed with wine (ibid. p. 251). According to Pouvourville (1905, p. 55), elements of both Triad (Taoist) and White Lotus (Buddhist) secret societies were mixed up in the Black Flags.
[f] Morse, ii. 345–9.

abandon its flag-showing and punitive 'sweeps', punctuated by in-discriminate 'executions' of suspects,[a] in favour of the 'oil-spot pacification' adapted from Equatorial Africa by Colonel Galliéni and the future Maréchal Lyautey of Moroccan fame. The plan was for a systematically-expanding security framework of villages find-ing their own militia, but armed and trained by the Government; the latter showed itself concerned to facilitate the revival of agri-culture and local trade and to afford police protection against ban-ditry and terrorism.[b] The parallels with Vietminh and Vietcong campaigns revealed by French officers' memoirs of the time are illuminating, and one can only regret that the undoubted humani-tarianism of the French military should have been marred during the following decade, as was noted earlier, by the civil authorities' shortsighted land policy.

Revolt of the Mandarins

Meanwhile, Tu Duc had died in 1883, bequeathing a struggle for power in the pavilions of the Great Within which resolved itself into pro and anti-French factions. One after another infant princes were butchered,[c] until a war party, gathering round the adolescent Ham Nghi, fled with him from Hué and took to the hills, at the height of the Black Flag confusion, proclaiming him legitimate successor to the throne. Almost the entire mandarinate and 'scholar' class de-clared its adherence to this 'War of the Civil Officers' (Giac Van Than),[d] and the senior man on the establishment, Phan Dinh Phung, took command. The direst vengeance was wrought by the 'scholars' on the chrétientés for their abetting of French aggression: the lowest of the estimates for the slaughter the mandarins licensed at this time is 20,000.[e] But no popular bases had been organized capable of surviving after the withdrawal of Chinese forces; Ham Nghi was betrayed to the French by one of the hill tribes, and the revolt, dependent on proceeds from the liquidation of the royal treasure[f]—for the exhausted villages opted for French pacification —came to an end when the leading commander, Cao Thang, was defeated in battle and killed by a contingent of Vietnamese soldiers loyal to the French;[g] Phan Dinh Phung himself, now 74, succumbed

[a] Lyautey (1921); Chesneaux, p. 140.   [b] Galliéni, quoted in Lyautey, p. 639.
[c] Lancaster, p. 48.
[d] Sometimes referred to in Vietnamese as the 'Royalist Movement' (Phong-trao Can Vuong).
[e] That of Blet (p. 216).   [f] Chesneaux, p. 138.
[g] Nguyen-phut-Tan (1964), p. 266.

to the rigours of living rough. The new court of Emperor Thanh Thai took the bloodiest of reprisals against those who gave themselves up.[a] However, just as the mandarins had taken advantage of the Black Flag troubles, so now another moss-trooper arose in turn in the lee of them. He was known as 'De Tham'[b] and set up his headquarters in the hills of Thai Nguyen, astride the eastern trade route from Hanoi into China. The interest of his insurrection, which also had claims to nationalist inspiration, is that the French authorities were unable to make their 'oil-spot' of pacification reach as far as De Tham's domain, and so they gave him an unofficial concession over it, with the implied condition that he would abstain from raids on the Delta. The reign of this Vietnamese warlord lasted thirty years, interspersed with periodical break-outs,[c] whose true purpose most probably was to chastise defaulters among subscribers (including French concessionnaires)[d] to his system of 'protection' for the frontier traffic; in the latter it may be guessed opium was a valuable item. Just thirty more years were to elapse before the Vietminh reoccupied De Tham's retreat.

Pu Kombo

Underground movements in Cochinchina during the early phase of French rule followed a course independent of Hué and Hanoi; beyond the factor of distance, organized superstition, strong throughout Vietnam, was at its strongest in the far south. At the moment of the French disembarkation in Cochinchina, a new cult was being spread by Pu Kombo, already mentioned. He was a native of the Bassat region of the Transbassac, the Seven Mountains, which had been the heart of the Khmer kingdom of Funan; in the reign of Minh Mang, Bassat became the haunt of a 'Bonze from the Western Regions' called Nguyen Van Quyen, famous for the practice of Chinese acupuncture as well as various black arts.[e] Quyen is credited with prophesying the overthrow of Minh Mang by Europeans and their displacement in turn by a reincarnation of a favourite wraith of romance and secret-society lore, Minh Vuong—none other than the T'ang dynasty Emperor Ming Huang, legendary lover of Yang Kuei-fei and patron of the Sino-Vietnamese theatre. Pu Kombo claimed both descent from the ancient Khmer kings and mastery of these black arts and gained a reputation for selling

[a] Gosselin (1904), p. 314.
[b] Truong Van Tham, alias Hoang Hoa Tham (Nguyen-phut-Tan, p. 281).
[c] Coulet (1926), p. 14.   [d] Blet, p. 218.   [e] Savani (1953), p. 98.

charms (*bua*) at Chau Doc on the Bassac.[a] Resistance to the French stirred up by the mandarins created a demand in the Plain of Reeds for *bua gong*—the charms made by Cambodians (there is a national monopoly of the magic) which render the wearer invulnerable even against bullets. From *bua gong* Pu Kombo graduated to arms smuggling,[b] and soon he was at the head of a new 'inner (that is, secret) sect' (*dao noi*), to which he gave the name Dao Lanh, 'The Way of the Meek', and whose adherents were being taught to handle firearms by Tagal (Philippine) deserters from the Spanish fleet that had joined the French from Manila.[c] Caught up with the Vietnamese followers of the mandarins in revolt, Pu Kombo came to grief in the end with them; he was captured on another mystical limestone mountain of the Khmers, the Nui Ba Den at Tay Ninh, after a final fruitless bid to capture Phnom Penh and enthrone himself as King of Cambodia.[d]

From Dao Lanh to Hoa Hao

But the Dao Lanh lived on after the death of Pu Kombo, in competition with other sects like itself,[e] thriving on a combination of superstition with intimidation and 'protection' of all within its chosen area. It was anti-French because it was anti-authority, and the colonial Government declared it illegal in 1873.[f] Thereupon it changed its name to Dao Phat Duong, or the 'Way of Buddhism in the Home'.[g] Various branches of this association renewed themselves over the next sixty years by the same processes and continued to offer to any political agitators who won over the leading bonze of the moment inviolable repositories for arms in its holy places and a reservoir of manpower, held together by local and family ties as well as by a mixture of physical and of superstitious fear; if fighting was called for, religious exaltation and faith in the personal safety conferred by the *bua gong* that were invariably handed out would take the place of reasoned appreciation of the agitators' political aims, which were not necessarily made known at all.[h] In 1915, when there was a wave of anti-French agitation in Cochinchina, one of the prime movers was Phan Xich Long; besides learning how to make explosives while on a visit to Siam,[i] he too had received in-

---

[a] Vial, ii. 15.   [b] Thomazi (1934), p. 90.   [c] Vial, ii. 63.   [d] Bourotte, p. 69.
[e] Chesneaux, p. 118. Prof. Coulet (1926, pp. 25–48) mentions some connected with Dao Lanh, others independent of it; one, around 1910–15, called itself *Nghia Hoa Duong*, the 'Boxers', but probably had no more connexion with its namesake in China than the borrowing of a name in the news.
[f] Coulet (1928), p. 9.   [g] Coulet (1926), p. 122.   [h] Ibid.   [i] Ibid. p. 39.

itiation into the practice of magic from a son of Phan Thanh Gian at the Pagoda of the Western Regions on the rocky hill overlooking Chau Doc.[a] At the same time a bonze calling himself Thay Phung appeared at the head of the Dao Lanh at the village of Hoa Hao, between the Mekong and the Bassac; it was from this village a generation later that the ultimate blossoming of Dao Lanh arose, under the inspiration of Huynh Phu So of that village. Like Pu Kombo and Thay Phung, So underwent at the Pagoda of the Burning Hillside (Tra Son) in the Seven Mountains a novitiate in the acupuncture and black arts of the Bonze of the Western Regions, and then reappeared at Hoa Hao in 1939, exalted and transfigured, to go into trances, utter prophecies, work miraculous cures, and issue a fresh call for 'Buddhism in the home'.[51] The speed with which the Hoa Hao sect spread along the two rivers of the Delta from the Cambodian frontier to Can Tho, there to stop abruptly, as it has for twenty years, leaves little doubt that it is a revival of the long-established *dao noi* Dao Lanh. The role the Hoa Hao has played in Cochinchinese politics will be told in subsequent chapters.

Chinese Reform Movement

A more intellectual strand of reaction to French colonial rule arose from the Reform Movement in China. The principal circumstances, and the reactions to them, which marked this intellectual movement in China were reproduced in Vietnam. The crucial question was whether Confucian society and institutions of government could rise to the challenge of Western intellectual and technological competition with equal moral and spiritual forces of Eastern inspiration and so halt the humiliations inflicted by Western aggression. By 1890 the challenge patently was not being met. Did the remedy lie in reform or in total revolution—in the addition of the knowledge of science and the processes of technology to Confucian ethics and institutions, or in the total overthrow of the Manchu dynasty (or the Nguyen) and the substitution of a republic modelled on European ideas but not under European domination? Japan was an example for the revolutionaries, but the intellectual material which was used in their debates came from Europe, much of it from France; the Encyclopaedists of the eighteenth century were translated into Chinese and, in that language, read in Vietnam as well as China. The Reform Movement had its short-lived triumph in China during the 'Hundred Days' of 1898; it failed because it tried

[a] Coulet (1926), p. 39; also Nguyen-van-Tam (1949), p. 59.

to appeal, in the European manner, through its ideas and programmes alone; having no disciplined popular organization at its
command, it had no power base and was easily thrust aside again
by the Manchu Empress Dowager. However, this point of view retained its following in Vietnam. Its chief proponents there were first
Phan Chau Trinh and later Pham Quynh—the latter being the
leading literary figure of modern Vietnam; the big editions Pham
Quynh's books ran to leave little doubt that he had a wide if im-
passive audience. But his Constitutional Party had no popular
organization either, and although the Emperor Khai Dinh, over
whom he exerted a considerable influence, went to Paris in 1922 to
ask for more Vietnamese participation in political affairs through
native institutions modernized under French auspices, and through
universal education in French, the *colons* saw to it that this inoffen-
sive approach was rebuffed—as was another by Bui Quang Chieu
four years later—and the movement lost its momentum.[a]

Phan Boi Chau

As in China, so in Vietnam, the tide was with the revolutionaries,
not the reformers—with the conspirators, not the constitutionalists;
the Chinese fashion for cutting off pigtails in defiance of the Manchus was copied in Vietnam by the cutting of *chignons* as an un-
spoken sign of being *avant-garde*.[b] Apart from the obvious necessity
of organizing without the knowledge of the authorities the revolution was supposed to overthrow, the new middle class had no contact with the peasants and turned more naturally to a political
movement organized as a secret society, terrorizing individuals into
support of a small élite held together by interests other than abstract
political ideas.[c] In his preparations for the Chinese revolution in
1911, Sun Yat-sen leant heavily on the Triad Society's ability to
raise funds by coercion among the Chinese communities abroad,
and at the same time upon the masonry of 'pan-Asian' interests in
Japan.[d] Vietnamese students also went in increasing numbers to
Tokyo,[e] as well as Canton, and there came under the spell of Sun's
intellectual and less violent contemporary, Liang Ch'i-ch'ao; they

[a] Devillers (1952), pp. 40–41. [b] Daufès, p. 148.
[c] The character of the support behind these political movements is surveyed in Chesneaux (pp. 186–9).
[d] Jansen (1954), p. 59; their organization was the Social Democratic Party.
[e] Organized in Hanoi by the Dong-kinh Free Academy; wool was pulled over the
authorities' eyes by the equivocation that *dong-kinh* meant both Tonkin and Tokyo
(Nguyen-phut-Tan, p. 313).

returned for the most part to Saigon, where also the Triad was at the peak of its influence over the Chinese and where numerous purely Vietnamese associations of the same kind were available to draw the essentials of money and a ready-made clientele from the countryside, itself in need periodically of a safety valve.[a] The symbolic leader of the students in Tokyo was a descendant of Gia Long, Prince Cuong De,[b] and the effective leader Phan Boi Chau, a native of Vinh, the traditional home of Vietnamese revolutions in northern Annam. The controller of the Triad in Cochinchina at this time was a government employee called Gilbert Chieu, Chinese by race but French by naturalization. These three combined to start the Reform Association (*Duy Tan Hoi*), financed by a business house[c] under cover of whose name they collected funds, circulated inflammatory leaflets, and plotted the spectacular, if futile, gesture of trying to poison the French garrison of Hanoi,[d] at the same time implicating so many students at the newly-opened University that the French authorities closed it again.

The Quang Phuc Hoi

After 1911 the Triad lost its *raison d'être* and the Reform Association was reorganized (at Canton) into the Vietnam Restoration Association (*Viet Nam Quang Phuc Hoi*). It attained its apogee during the First World War. Drawing into its ranks the young Emperor, who had taken the appropriate reign title Duy Tan, and with the help of German subventions, it is said,[e] Phan Boi Chau brought together the resources of more than one secret society in Cochinchina;[f] his emissary with the young Emperor was another practitioner of magic and *phong-thuy* geomancy called Tran Cao Van, recently released from detention on Pulau Condore for complicity with Gilbert Chieu.[g] Whether or not there was in truth widespread resentment over the recruitment of young men for military service behind the lines in France (100,000 were taken), the local French forces were depleted and the recruits waiting to embark were good material for subversion. Early in 1916 twin attacks were launched on the garrisons at Hué and Saigon, and in the latter a secret society mob, brought in from the countryside and fortified with *bua gong*, captured an armoury and released the convicts from the Chi Hoa prison.[h] But there was no plan for further action, order was quickly

[a] Coulet (1926), p. 24.   [b] See note 16.   [c] Nguyen-phut-Tan, p. 313.
[d] Coulet (1926), p. 11.   [e] Nguyen-phut-Tan, p. 320.   [f] Coulet (1926), p. 33.
[g] Ibid. p. 21.
[h] Ibid. p. 34; the mob were devotees of Phan Xich Long (p. 121 above).

restored, and the ringleaders were detained on Pulau Condore, except for Chau himself who was arrested in Canton.[52] The historical importance of Phan Boi Chau and the *Quang Phuc Hoi* is to be seen less in what they achieved directly, however, than in the help they afforded unconsciously to even more extremist groups, notably the Communists. They established a sort of 'underground railroad' by which Vietnamese students (most were from better-off homes, few from the villages) could get secretly to China for further (particularly political) studies and, from about 1920, receive military training at the Whampoa Military Academy outside Canton or, further afield, go to Tokyo, Paris or Moscow, the organization also produced a steady flow of political tracts for circulation at home, and it was undoubtedly from this source that many of Vietnam's future revolutionaries gained their first ideas of politics.[a]

Cao Dai

It was out of these movements in which the leaders were intellectuals, and after the disappointments of the constitutional movement, that another *dao noi* emerged in Cochinchina in 1926, the Cao Dai.[b] Although subsequent events have led Cao Dai along similar paths to Hoa Hao—even into some competition for territory—they contrasted sharply in their origins. Cao Dai began about 1920 with the district administrator of Phu Quoc Island, one Ngo Van Chieu. His heart's desire was a transfer to Saigon, but routine applications were all rejected. He had read books about Taoist mediumship and also about the type of European spiritualism associated with Colonel Olcott and the Theosophists.[c] From these two sources he concocted his own occult procedures, which duly secured him his transfer.[d] Arrived in Saigon, Chieu demonstrated his methods to a widening circle of colleagues in need, like himself, of resolution of the cultural contrast between French education and their Chinese traditions—of reconciliation perhaps of their loyalty to alien chiefs with all the social pressures surrounding their daily lives. They began to contact spirits from both the West and the East of the Other World.[e] About 1925 two other officials joined the group and perceived the scope for developing and propagating such ideas; they

[a] Nguyen-phut-Tan, p. 321.
[b] The official name of the Sect is *Dai-dao Tam-ky Pho-do* (Faith in the Third Salvation) and the official Cao Dai translation 'Third Amnesty of God in the Orient' (Tran-quang-Vinh, 1953).
[c] Gobron (1948), pp. 14–18.   [d] Nguyen-van-Tam, p. 44.
[e] *Histoire sommaire* (1956), p. 8.

were Le Van Trung and Pham Cong Tac. A whole new syncretic religion was built up and gathered dogmas as it gathered adherents. The speed and sophistication with which this was done was owed, here too, to secret-society affiliation: Tac already controlled a blood-brotherhood several thousand strong—of which presumably he was the founder since they were called *Pham Mon*[a]—while Trung was a labour contractor who, it is claimed, was able to muster 50,000 'followers' for the inauguration at Tay Ninh in 1928;[b] one of the early names they used was *Thien Dia Hoi* (Heaven and Earth Society), and it is therefore likely that they took over some part of the Vietnamese Triad, whose headquarters was at that time at Thu Dau Mot,[c] not far from Tay Ninh. Trung and Tac also attracted, among other French people, a well-to-do widow called Mme Monnier, who bought them at Tay Ninh (already a centre for pilgrimages, resort of spirit mediums, and home of a succession of occult organizations since Pu Kombo's day) a site for a 'Vatican'. Trung became the first 'Pope' (*Giao Tong*), whilst Tac assumed the Vietnamese title *Ho Phap*, which means either 'Defender of the Faith' or 'spirit medium' as one wishes; 100-odd 'bishoprics' and 'archbishoprics' were handed out to selected adherents, presumably according to the size of the following they could collect to make up a 'diocese'.

The object of worship was Cao Dai, 'High Altar', a sort of French-Revolutionary *Être Suprême*, represented in architecture and on the priests' 'canonicals' by Victor Hugo's Eye of Conscience[d] enclosed in a triangle symbolic of the three faiths of China (Confucianism, Taoism, and Buddhism), while their principal intercessionary spirit was, incongruously, again Minh Vuong, patron of the theatre. The founders of all other religions the Cao Daists know about are 'saints' for them, and a thousand fragments of folklore of local and foreign origin have been stuck on to the phantasmagoric plaster-work of the *Den Thanh* or 'Basilica' at Tay Ninh. Robes of priests and initiates are reminiscent, save for the Eye, of those of the Triad. Wherever it had a community, the Sect took over or founded friendly societies and welfare schemes in the aftermath of the economic depression of 1931; these included a land-settlement scheme with Government approval at Tay Ninh itself. Among the social needs that Cao Dai met was evidently one to unify the secret socie-

---

[a] Savani, p. 88.   [b] Nguyen-van-Tam, p. 47.   [c] Coulet (1926), p. 272.
[d] From the poem *Cain*; other explanations also are given sometimes, e.g. *Histoire sommaire*, p. 12.

ties spawning to both east and west of Saigon, no doubt in difficulties over meeting the demands of their members in the crisis; many agricultural debts will have been 'voluntarily' extinguished as soon as the debtor had this novel and forbidding eye of conscience on his side. The welfare schemes were linked together by the transmission of 'divine' messages, which in later years began to convey political innuendoes and admonitions to the faithful.[a] By 1938 the faithful numbered 300,000, and this astonishing offspring of the *politique d'association* might have become an even graver threat to public order than eventually it did, in spite of its respect early on for authority, had Trung not had to be unfrocked for blatantly squandering the endowments, while other schisms—some personal, others probably along old secret-society boundaries[b]—put a brake on its leaders' ambitions. Like Hoa Hao, Cao Dai attained its ultimate strength by favour of Japan during the Second World War.

VNQDD origins

Contemporary with Cao Dai in Cochinchina, and to some extent fulfilling a similar psychological need, there arose in Tonkin the *Viet Nam Quoc Dan Dang* (VNQDD) or 'Nationalist Party of Vietnam'. Although the knowledge of Chinese became rarer in Vietnamese intellectual circles after the First World War as romanized Vietnamese took hold and education in French became the rule, the flow of ideas, and modern vocabulary, from China was little reduced.[53] As with the reform-versus-revolution debate in China twenty years before, it was now the turn of the inner struggles of the Kuomintang (KMT), the Nationalist Party of China, to reproduce themselves south of the common frontier. The Government, and party, of Sun Yat-sen, having failed to obtain financial support for its efforts to subdue the warlords in North China, had acceded to overtures from Soviet Russia. A Bolshevik mission to the provisional capital at Canton, under Michael Borodin, had reorganized the party on Leninist lines and as, primarily, a youth movement; but, within a year of Sun Yat-sen's death in 1925, a right wing under Chiang Kai-shek had broken with Borodin and expelled the Communist wing of the party; within two more years the warlords had been subdued and China reunited. KMT prestige stood high in Tonkin and Hué at the moment when Vietnamese demands for con-

---

[a] Savani, p. 90.

[b] This was certainly the case as between the sub-sects at Mo Cay and Ba Tri in Kien Hoa province, which originated as secret societies founded about 1915 by Le Van Khanh (Coulet, 1926, p. 33).

stitutional advance had been brusquely turned down in Paris; the
KMT, moreover, has always been a zealous heir to Manchu China's
resentment and contempt towards France. The foundation at
Hanoi in 1927 of a party bearing the same name, likewise primarily
as an instrument for activating youth, and with a programme to
embarrass and undermine French rule, but in opposition to the
various Communist groups beginning to appear at the same time,
could only be welcomed at Nanking, whither the Nationalist capital had been moved. For the next twenty years branches of the
KMT in the provinces bordering on Tonkin, in an arc from Canton
to Kunming, were at the disposal of young Vietnamese brethren of
the same persuasion as a refuge and base for their clandestine
operations.

Revolt of the VNQDD

The first home of the VNQDD in Vietnam was a publishing
house ostensibly producing popular literature,[a] but it would be a
mistake to imagine that divulgation of the printed word was intended to be the road to independence: the business was merely a
cover for the activities of the founder, Nguyen Thai Hon,[b] and
when it was closed by the Sûreté the underground core of the organization remained intact. Neither in Tonkin at this period, nor in
Annam, where also the VNQDD was active, was it a question of
taking over existing secret societies, but the party was basically a
secret society itself. The KMT in China consisted of a Leninist drill-
book of techniques for 'masses activation' in association with a
Triad-type blood brotherhood held together by family, school
class, and similar ties and with a loyalty oath the sanction for whose
forswearing was assassination. So it was with the VNQDD.[c] The
party obtained money by the usual method of extortion from the
well-to-do and manpower by lending these funds to peasants who
then owed it a moral debt of obedience in lieu of interest. The
VNQDD was not a popular movement that members joined by
application; like other secret societies, and like Communist parties,
its members joined by invitation, issued because they could perform
some service the movement had a use for. The leaders were convinced that France could be evicted from Vietnam at a favourable
moment by a single-blow revolution, as were the Communists at

[a] The Nam-dong Thu Xa; see note 53.
[b] Devillers (1952), p. 56. Thai-hon, it may be noted, means exactly the same thing as
Gandhi's epithet Mahatma.
[c] Nguyen-phut-Tan, p. 361.

this time, and no doubt believed, like the Communists, that capitalism and imperialism were about to crumble from within because of the world economic crisis; there was discontent enough, and to spare, at this time among university graduates without jobs, a small but growing industrial proletariat as yet unprotected by legislation or trade unionism and the deepening hardships of the agrarian crisis. In the event, the VNQDD leaders, who hoped for outside aid from KMT China,[a] misjudged badly. Ever more frequent acts of anonymous terrorism, culminating in an attempt on the life of the Governor-General while he was on a visit to Canton,[b] had in 1930 put the *Sûreté* on to the network of cells when a French labour contractor, in deep water over the recruitment of indentured labour for rubber estates in Cochinchina, was murdered. Some of these cells had subverted units of the *Garde Indochinoise*, and, to protect their identity, the VNQDD called for a general mutiny. In fact it was complete only at Yen Bay, where all the French officers were murdered. The Government reacted swiftly, and the VNQDD leaders fled into China; most of them remained there until the height of the Second World War, and some received commissions in the Nationalist army.[c] It is clear from what happened when they came back, however, that the groundwork they had so energetically laid in the space of only three years survived any efforts made by the *Sûreté* to eradicate it.

The Communist rebellion

The flight of the VNQDD leaders soon turned out to be only the beginning of the episode. The Communists, who also had come on the scene in 1927, had been working on parallel lines to subvert students, mineworkers, and rubber-estate labour, as well as peasants. They too entertained high hopes from the economic crisis and set about exploiting the commotion within the French administration over Yen Bay. Rural misery in northern Annam, after a succession of bad harvests, seemed to offer the best tinder for the 'agitprop' spark. Strikes and bomb outrages in the towns were synchronized with hunger marches by distressed peasants in the countryside, often at pistol-point[d] and to the accompaniment of several hundred murders (some of them sickeningly gruesome);[e] the movement reached its peak in a 'declaration of soviets' (somewhat in-

[a] Devillers (1953), p. 56.   [b] Dang-chan-Lieu (1947), p. 63.
[c] For example, 'Gen.' Nguyen Hoa Hiep, Minister of the Interior at Saigon, Feb.–June 1965.
[d] Viollis (1949), p. 90.   [e] *Contribution*, v. 31.

substantial)[a] and an attempt to take the town of Vinh by storm.[b] In several places, including Vinh, the French authorities panicked; villages were bombed,[c] and in the general atmosphere of excitability French soldiers, including drunken and rowdy elements of the Foreign Legion,[d] took it upon themselves to conduct private punitive expeditions of their own.[e] Under the threat of famine, the French *Résidents* had to find food for as many as 80,000 victims at one time,[f] and even then the Communists continued to have stocks destroyed;[g] a French government doctor estimated later that 10,000 died of starvation, while 60,000 more required treatment for oedema.[h] Three thousand criminal charges were made by the *Sûreté*; 100 murder trials ended under the guillotine; 10,000 suspects were detained without trial for lack of willing witnesses.[i] For the moment, the Communist organization was disrupted,[j] but the principal cost fell upon the peasants, and they were expendable; on the credit side for the revolutionaries—although they were still far from appreciating its psychological value[k]—was the acceptance, in France and other countries, that what had just taken place was a nationalist uprising and that its suppression was an act of colonial tyranny. The outcry in France was joined by the Right as well as the Left, and within a few months all persons detained without trial were released—the ringleaders to fight many another day.

6. THE VIETNAMESE NATION AT THE OUTBREAK
OF THE SECOND WORLD WAR

French rule in Indochina has been the object of more published criticism than the colonial record of any power in any other single country. It is to the credit of the French people that nine-tenths of this criticism has issued from the pens of French writers—and not simply of doctrinaire anti-colonialists or of politicians with an axe to grind, but often of professional men whose opinions command a hearing; in a number of works drawn on in this book the critics were the officials responsible for administration—even makers of policy

---

[a] *Thirty Years*, p. 31.   [b] Roussel (1947), p. 50.   [c] Blet, p. 231.
[d] Dorsenne (1932), p. 54.   [e] Viollis, pp. 149–52.   [f] Ibid. p. 90.
[g] *Contribution*, v. 33.   [h] Viollis, p. 91.   [i] *Contribution*, iv. 40.
[j] Lancaster, p. 83.
[k] The Party was still narrowly preoccupied with the doctrine of class struggle at this period (*Thirty Years*, p. 26), scorning as impossible the independence demanded by the nationalist groups.

themselves. It is to the political controversies of the 1880s inside France that the world owes the coining of *colonialisme* as a pejorative term. On the other hand, from outside France the Vietnamese people have been helped to see themselves as the victims consistently of misrule and exploitation at the hands of France. The late Mr Bernard Fall documented the effect which uninformed and generalized condemnation of France had on the mind of President Roosevelt at decisive moments in the war;[a] unfortunately the condemnation, the generalization, and the ignorance have persisted into the period of America's own tutelage over the destiny of Vietnam. It is not proposed here to hazard a complete judgement of France's achievement in Vietnam, but only to point to the consequences of her action in the light of the challenges which the Vietnamese nation has had to face since the withdrawal of France. The balance is struck in the year 1939 for two reasons: the first is that after the outbreak of the Second World War France never again had a free hand in Indochina—indeed almost the whole of what she had built there, materially and morally, had been shattered by August 1945—so that her policies after that date became a response to external events in which others made the running; and the second reason is that by 1939 all the eventual actors in Vietnam's inner drama of today—the parties, Sects, and group interests— were already on the stage and identifiable.

Exploitation by France

Two questions should be disposed of first: did France exploit for selfish gain her dependencies in Indochina, and was she more unenlightened than other colonial powers in not preparing the Indochinese peoples for independence? A recent writer on colonial history in general has pointed out how modest was the return to French investors in the colonial territories as a whole when compared with interest and dividend rates available at home or from foreign investment.[b] No doubt individual Frenchmen in the public services or in commerce found a livelihood in Indochina on a higher standard than they might have expected at home, and in numbers far exceeding, for instance, their British or American counterparts; but this hardly amounted to selfish exploitation. The moneylenders

---

[a] Fall (1963), pp. 51–54. The President is defended, on the other hand, by Mr Schlesinger (1967, p. 11).
[b] Fieldhouse (1966), p. 388.

and financiers behind the exploitation of basic farming in Cochin-china were French nationals but not usually Frenchmen, and the companies owning concessions lost much or most of their invest-ment in the crash of 1931—and a second time in the compulsory acquisitions of 1955. On the other hand, it was psychologically bad policy to permit and even foster European involvement in estab-lished native agriculture at all—just as, conversely, it was bad policy to exclude the Vietnamese, especially smallholders, from sharing in the profits to be made from rubber. In the public sector, contribu-tions for defence were levied by the Paris Government on the Indo-china budget (12 per cent in 1931, down to 5 by 1938);[a] but the sums were a mere token of what was being spent, and the source from which they were drawn was indirect taxation, mostly from customs duties on commodities consumed by Europeans and better-off Indochinese. Like most overseas dependencies of colonial powers, Indochina was in the main a charge on the metropolitan exchequer, not the other way round, and it has been shown that be-tween 1907 and 1929, for example, France recouped in trading profits a bare 18 per cent of her outlay, private investment taken with public expenditure:[b] the interest of France in her colonies was, as we have seen, not financial but political. In answer to our second question, it is certain that by 1939 France had done nothing to pre-pare Indochina for independence, or even what was then called 'home rule'. The policy of *association* envisaged no terminal date, for the reasons we have given, and the only road to emancipation open to individual natives was *assimilation*—a road leading to settlement in France which an unknown, but large, number did take (headed by Emperors Duy Tan and, much later, Bao Dai) and a much larger number would have liked to take if they, or their parents, could have afforded the preliminaries. Events have proved France to have been wrong. Were those countries, such as Britain and America, who now turn out to have been right, really so much more farseeing in 1939? At the time, it was not always the British policy which commended itself to native opinion in her colonies: the colonial administration in Nigeria was criticized for not opening up to Africans the opportunities for *assimilation* open to their neigh-bours under the French flag.[c]

[a] Robequain, p. 150.
[b] Southworth (1931), pp. 124 & 131; much of the expenditure on civil projects was not reported to Parliament and is therefore not even included in this heavily adverse balance (ibid. p. 42).
[c] Prof. L. P. Mair (1936), quoted by Crowder (1964, p. 204).

Aims and achievements

What perhaps tells most against the French achievement in Indochina is its failure to reach the objectives it set itself. Of these the dominating ideas were the unity of Indochina, the 'modernization' of the economy, and the substitution of law for the arbitrary exercise of power by the authorities of an Asian state, theoretically tempered by humane considerations but in practice checked only by the balance of vested interests. Such aims were, perhaps, over-ambitious in any circumstances: no other colonial power ever ventured to take on a people of Chinese culture, except as immigrant minorities. Yet more might have been done, and to the advantage of the different races of Indochina, if there had not been failures in French performance: there was unhappily a gap between intention and fulfilment.[a] Even in the economic sphere, where a neutral ground of common interests might have been prepared against social and political prejudice, neither unity nor modernization appears to have guided policy in practice. The adoption of a policy of imperial protection after 1928 was allowed to stand in the way of development of local industry, for which Tonkin was a promising location; such development might have contributed much to making the *Union Indochinoise* a reality on the economic plane. The activities of French enterprise in Vietnam, it has been pointed out,[b] were carried on without regard to development of the Vietnamese economy: products needed for the latter were exported to France, while imports bought in exchange barely percolated down to the Vietnamese middle classes, leaving the life of the mass of the people unbenefited. The land policy pursued consistently, whatever claims to be reforming it were made from time to time, far from ensuring the transfer of Vietnam's arable to the most efficient hands, led to no improvement in farming methods whatever, so that an official report could say, at the end of the period, that the average income of a native farmer was insufficient even to feed him, let alone allow him a decent standard of living.[c] The great works of drainage and irrigation were all public works, not benefits that can be put down to private investment or improved farming, and even there the criticism can be advanced that the scientific bunding of the Tonkinese Delta was delayed until the disaster of 1926; it ought to have been undertaken long before. The slow development of the railway from Hanoi to Saigon (completed in 1936) proved, in disturbed times at

[a] Mus (1949), p. 267.   [b] France, *Premier rapport*, p. 67.
[c] Devillers (1952), pp. 48–49.

home as much as in time of war, a fragile substitute for a modern coastwise shipping line.

Constitutional backwardness

The indictment by France's critics takes clearer shape when we turn to the constitutional plane. The separation of Cochinchina and Tonkin from Annam had, 100 years ago, more justification than patriotic Vietnamese can be expected to admit at the present day: Cochinchina was mostly uninhabited, and it is debatable whether the Vietnamese, lawless and unsettled, made up even half of what population it did have; as for Tonkin, the Nguyen were recognized as sovereign there by both France and China, but by no means so certainly by the Tonkinese. However, once the decision had been made to dismember Vietnam, no steps were taken either to strengthen the prestige of the Nguyen in their native region of Annam or to develop the *Union Indochinoise* as a wider horizon for common loyalty and co-operation. Instead, the undoubted shortcomings of the princelings available from the *Que That* (the 'Gynaeceum' at Hué) was used as an excuse for continual kingmaking, while the federal Government operated, on the one hand as the administrator of common 'modern' services managed solely by Frenchmen, and on the other as a super-sovereign identified with the interests of metropolitan France and liable to intervene unpredictably in any public matter—to intervene predictably in questions of public order. Official French publications about Annam constantly refer to the Royal and the Union administrations as if there were two Governments in the region, whilst, on occasions like the VNQDD and Communist disturbances in 1930–1, special French courts were set up over the heads of the native judges, even if a few Vietnamese magistrates did also take part in the inquiries. There was omission here to associate the Vietnamese officials, still less the public, with the preservation of law and order, with either union or modernization, and it is hardly surprising if the Vietnamese consequently saw in the *Union Indochinoise* only an instrument of metropolitan dominion and attributed to their partners in the *association* a determination to keep them divided the more easily to dominate them; at least they were provided with an easy excuse for shirking responsibility towards their own people (or for giving in to intimidation) over the maintenance of law and order.[a] Thus a worth-while ideal was left unrealized.

---

[a] As complained by the *Sûreté*, for instance, in *Contribution*, iv. 34.

Reform and modernization

No colonial power can claim to have pursued always consistent policies; it was to be expected in Indochina that the aim of administrative modernization would sometimes be in conflict with the French attitude of *laisser-faire* in regard to social questions even at home and, still more, with the particular aim of preserving indirect rule. Under the influence of the Reform Movement in China, resentment against the incompetence and dishonesty of the mandarinate in Tonkin became acute in the 1900s: an outdated Annamite despotism, due for reform, must not be preserved through the protection of France, wrote the *Résident-Supérieur* to his French subordinates in 1913,[a] and even in the modern period we find a Vietnamese civil servant admitting in retrospect that it was the French element in the administration which tended to contribute the necessary dynamism.[b] Yet the remedy was not sought in the gradual turning of the mandarinate into a modern civil service, but in setting up provincial councils instead, with power to criticize but no answerability (unless to an electoral college of untutored village notables), which added to the complexities of administration but led to no improvement; in fact, in this choice of remedy is to be seen evasion on the part of the French administrators of the difficulties of modernizing the mandarinate. Similarly they shrugged their shoulders and allowed the notorious corruption prevalent among Vietnamese officials all over Cochinchina (French sovereign territory) to go uncorrected to the end.[c] Introduction of an *État Civil* to register births and deaths and maintain a census of sorts enabled tax-rolls to be rationalized and a fuller contribution to be levied to pay for the public services of a modern state; but the dishonesty with which the notables administered it was exploited by agitators to procure false identity papers,[d] and the system, in reducing the notables' opportunities to make a percentage on the collection of taxes, antagonized them, diverted their avarice to other channels— though France cannot be blamed for a Vietnamese vice—and effected no general amelioration of the ill.[e]

Confusion and neglect in the law, explained earlier in this chapter, militated against respect for it, whilst the entrusting of large areas of Tonkin to military governors for almost the whole duration of the Protectorate, like resort to special tribunals and extra-legal procedures, undermined in practice the principles of government im-

[a] Vu-quoc-Thong, p. 78. [b] Nghiem Dang (1966), p. 128. [c] Pinto, p. 34.
[d] Vanlande (1930), p. 41. [e] Mus (1952), pp. 24–25.

plicit in *modernisation* and the *mission civilisatrice*. In the mechanics of administration, the idea of keeping honest records and exercising controls was certainly introduced; but procedures did not long remain up to date, and the accountancy regulations, for example, were not modernized further after 1912. Poor judgement, added to administrative bungling, sometimes frustrated progressive or humanitarian measures, and in 1930–1 opened unexpected doors to Communist opportunism: Province Chiefs and *Résidents* were authorized to remit agricultural and poll taxes those years at discretion; in the Mien Tay of Cochinchina the administrators had no efficient means of notifying the peasants quickly, and Communist agitators who had wind of the decision organized marches to some of the towns to demand, and get credit for, what they knew had already been granted;[a] next season the Communists planned similar marches and demands in the Ha Tinh and Nghe An provinces of Annam, but the *Résidents*, not wanting to be made fools of like their colleagues in Cochinchina by appearing to heed Communist agitation, decided to refuse the remission of tax; hardship then went unrelieved, and the Communists were given an even more powerful pretext.[b] Finally, the indifferent ethical and intellectual standards of a large proportion of French officials (often patently at the beck and call of irascible *colons*) complained of by many French authors,[c] combined with the exclusion of Vietnamese officials from the making of decisions and the exercise of responsibility because efficiency was believed to call for a Western touch not even the *assimilé* possessed, tended to perpetuate the cynical opinion often encountered in the Chinese world that all government, even when not alien, is simply a machine for exploitation—'usurious and prebendal', as Chesneaux summed it up.[d]

Nationalism and criminality

It is primarily that traditional attitude which explains the many insurrections that took place against French rule; the alien quality of French rule could be pointed to as a justification for rebellion, but it was not so certainly its actual cause. The mandarins of the *Giac Van Than* were unquestionably resisting the establishment of French rule, and even if we suspect that preservation of their own position weighed with them as heavily as preservation of Vietnamese national freedom, obviously that particular revolt would

---

[a] Ibid. pp. 140–2.   [b] Dorsenne (1932), p. 49.   [c] Harmand, p. 182.
[d] p. 158.

not have occurred without the French annexation. On the other hand, the resistance in Tonkin was directed not only against France but equally against the Nguyen dynasty and the Annamite mandarinate whose authority France was endeavouring to buttress, even if that served also as a façade for her own dominion.[54] Every subsequent revolt was the work of organizations brought and held together by criminal methods, often with shocking brutality, always with callous cynicism. Secret societies were the foundation of their strength without any exceptions, and at the very least private gain, if not some more criminal motive, was associated with their criminal methods: the bonze, the magician, the 'protector', the pirate, and the political agitator belonged historically in Vietnam to the same vocation. The victims of their terror were other Vietnamese, not Frenchmen. Blame is not due to France for her repression of movements thus inspired and led when they took up arms; at worst she failed to educate them out of Vietnamese society.

Nationalism and factionalism

By their chosen designations the more recent of these movements appear to foreigners—at least, their 'fronts' do—as political parties or religious sects; yet there have been extremely few individual Vietnamese, if any, who have belonged to both such a party and such a sect. The reason is that all were mutually-competing factions, patriotic no doubt if the issue came up, but primarily seeking power and influence by force, whether their names were political or religious, the established Government native or alien; and force included supernatural sanctions (blood covenants and oaths of secrecy sworn at an altar) whether the names were religious or political. For the leaders of such organisms, constitutional paths to political influence were simply not a congenial route, even if any had been open to them; if the French, on their side, had been less obstinate than they were, there existed among these bodies none that could have been trusted to collaborate honestly in any democratization of government, still less devolution of executive authority. If there was misery in the countryside, it was turned to advantage, but of proposals for relieving it the agitators gave no hint; no movement produced any programme for the exercise of power if once it had it, until the Communists issued a manifesto in 1929 which proclaimed land reform, labour reform, and nationalization of banks and rubber estates; but even that document went no further than the list of slogans, proffering neither detail nor argument, and seems to have been meant to be read in France, while in Vietnam separate *Struggle Programmes* said nothing about reform but demanded abolition of taxation, of the monarchy and of all forms of regulation[a] while proclaiming 'support for the Soviet Union'.[b]

Nationalism and French education

If there was a lack of public debate over public issues, the banning of political discussion from representative councils does not explain the near silence over social and economic problems. It was not censorship that stifled the press: the authorities in Annam and Tonkin may have been hypersensitive to what constituted sedition, but this explanation could not be pleaded in Cochinchina, which both stood in greatest need and enjoyed the freedoms of French sovereign territory. A highly intelligent and educated professional class was established by 1939 in all corners of Vietnam, enjoying the friendship and sympathy of their European colleagues; these men had the capacity and the means to ventilate the practical griefs of their nation, but did not. The content of French education, emphasizing the intellectual and scientific aspects of French culture above the didactic, coupled with the financial rewards of assimilation, drew the young professionals towards metropolitan France rather than towards the service, and betterment, of their native society; at home remuneration was unacceptably discriminatory. French training, if not education, did not produce Vietnamese experienced in industrial and financial management; universal exclusion of local men from management deprived the nation, in a sphere analogous to government and linked with it, of a reservoir of manpower experienced in the shouldering of public responsibility.

Neglect of village government

In the country, at the other end of the social scale, the weaknesses of government which characterized the Vietnamese state under Gia Long and Minh Mang persisted under French rule. At its conclusion the autonomous commune, answerable for its own internal order, was still the unique institution, if anything further enfeebled by opportunities to split and break away that arose from French agricultural enterprise and from expansion of the *chrétientés*, as well as by the activities of sects and secret societies.[c] French failure to

---

[a] *Contribution*, iv. 55–57.   [b] *Thirty Years*, p. 27.
[c] Other causes as well for this phenomenon are suggested in Indochina, *Annam scolaire*, p. 56.

strengthen village government in such a way as to provide intimidated individuals with an authority to turn to for protection—the basic duty of government as much in the political philosophy of France as in that of the Confucian state—preserved untouched the traditional grazing grounds for the forces of revolution and anarchy.

4

THE ANARCHY OF
HO CHI MINH

1. ORIGINS OF THE VIETMINH

In the beginning, the Communist movement in Vietnam differed from other political movements in an important respect: it was a subversive movement launched from outside Vietnam by the Soviet Government as an instrument for embarrassing France. Other political movements arose from initiatives inside the country; even the VNQDD, whose appearance coincided with Chiang Kai-shek's break with the Communists in China and which in its first twenty years of life leaned heavily on support from China, was founded at Hanoi by Tonkinese, apparently of their own accord. The ICP was founded on the initiative of the Communist International—a fact we know from its official history.[a] Furthermore, in its earlier stages its aim was not the national emancipation of Vietnam from French rule—that aim did not emerge until the defeat of France by Germany in 1940—but the building-up of a 'bolshevized' Marxist-Leninist party on the class-struggle pattern of the Russian party.[b] As the Party grew, it drew considerable—as we shall see, essential—political support from China, not from the Chinese Communists, with whom communications were physically difficult, but by subterfuge from the Chinese Nationalists. Moral support, on the other hand, was forthcoming at crucial moments from the Communist Party of France; the latter did not espouse colonial emancipation as good in itself but expected that colonies would become Communist in course of time through revolution in the metropolis, with which they would keep the same kind of relationship after the revolution as before.[c] Indeed, the ICP not only was not a Vietnamese nationalist party but was almost anti-anti-colonial: Mao Tsê-tung as well was on record at this time as declaring revolutionary warfare in a

---

[a] *Thirty Years*, p. 25.   [b] Ibid. pp. 18 & 28.
[c] Resolution at the 7th Congress of the French Communist Party in 1930, quoted in Walter (1948), p. 377.

colonial territory to be 'a phenomenon that cannot occur',[a] and, in the belief that 'Indochina is a colony whose economy is dependent on the imperialists and could not develop independently',[b] the Party did its best to 'become divorced from "nationalist" influence.'[c] The VNQDD and other nationalists have long made political capital to the Vietnamese Communists' disadvantage out of these facts and out of the Communists' readiness from time to time to compromise temporarily with left-wing Governments in Paris while consolidating their organization and building their strength; to this day anti-Communist propaganda in Vietnam has been able with some point to bracket 'Communists and Colonialists' as an unholy alliance thwarting the plans of 'true patriots' both on the international stage and in the internal struggle for independence. The one connecting link running through the whole history of the Vietnamese Communist movement has been the personal struggle for power of Ho Chi Minh; the achievement of his lifelong career as a revolutionary has been to canalize alternately French and Chinese support so as to transfer the movement's centre of gravity from its original foreign bases to the heart of the Vietnamese countryside where it now lies and to transform himself from the obscure international agent of a foreign state into the national leader of his own. He has adapted Communist method to the social scene of Vietnam and thereby harnessed local resources of many kinds to his struggle for power; he has exploited, with rarely-failing skill, the traditional weakness of government and the traditional strength of forces of anarchy and revolution.

The Comintern

'Ho Chi Minh was the first Vietnamese Communist.'[d] A native of Nghe An province, of which Vinh is the chief town, he hailed from a locality close to the homes of Le Loi and of the Tay Son brothers. The other way round from the latter, he bore the surname *Nguyen* at birth and later changed it to *Ho*; he has employed half a dozen different given names and pseudonyms; between 1920 and 1943 he was best known as Nguyen Ai Quoc, *ai-quoc* meaning patriotic in Sino-Vietnamese.[55] Born in 1890, he went to sea as a ship's steward and was in Europe by about 1910; he seems not to have revisited his

[a] In 1928 (Mao Tsê-tung, 1963, p. 11); Mao's later editors give the credit for Ho Chi Minh's achievement of this 'impossible' objective in 1945, correctly, to the unintended help he received from Japanese intervention (ibid. p. 17).
[b] *Thirty Years*, p. 26.   [c] Ibid. and again on p. 28.   [d] Ibid. i. 18.

native country again until 1944. By the end of the First World War he had joined the French Socialist Party in Paris and was one of the members at the Tours Conference in 1920 making up the Communist wing which voted to transfer the party's affiliation from the Second to the Third International.[a] It is clear he was by now a seasoned recruit, for he was sent on a tour round France to harangue the camps of Vietnamese soldiers waiting to go home after their war service. He was also supplied with funds to run an anti-colonial periodical called *Le Paria*, and as colonial expert of the new French Communist Party he took part in the inauguration of Krestintern, the 'Peasant International', at Moscow in 1923; he attended the *agitprop* school there calling itself the University for the Toilers of the East, where he no doubt trained as a trainer for his next employment on behalf of the Comintern.[b] Outwardly he was an employee of Borodin's mission to the KMT Government at Canton,[c] but his real function was to foster a Communist movement, subject to Comintern discipline, among the southeast Asian émigrés of various nationalities collected there. It was Russian policy in the 1920s, especially Stalin's, to subvert the overseas dependencies of the nations of western Europe as a means of weakening the home countries, whose wealth was derived—or so Lenin had taught—from exploitation of their 'surplus value'. It was from the 'Southeast Asia Sub-bureau of the Comintern', with Ho Chi Minh in charge, that the multi-racial Nanyang Communist Party was started in Singapore to cause labour trouble in both Malaya and the Dutch Indies, in the belief that the economies of the metropolitan countries could be affected sufficiently to cause unemployment and discontent there in turn.

Brotherhood of Revolutionary Youth

Since his rise to power, Ho Chi Minh has told us that, although it was patriotism that first led him to Lenin and the Third International, once caught up in the 'struggle' he became a thoroughgoing Marxist-Leninist vowed to 'emancipating workers and downtrodden people all over the world'.[d] Not surprisingly, however, his biggest success in spreading Communist influence in this period lay not in his activities among Asians of other nationalities so much as

[a] *Thirty Years*, i. 18.
[b] These early details are common ground between Communist and non-Communist writers; see in particular Fall (1960), pp. 20 ff.
[c] p. 127 above.   [d] Ho-chi-Minh (1960).

in the subversion of young Vietnamese being sent to Canton by such clandestine bodies as that of his fellow townsman, Phan Boi Chau, for training at the Whampoa Military Academy. By the time of Chiang Kai-shek's break with the Communists, Ho Chi Minh had subverted some 200 *can bo* (cadres) and either sent them to Moscow with the Chinese Communist contingent for further training, alongside Vietnamese arriving via Paris,[a] or straight back to Vietnam, as members of the 'Brotherhood of Revolutionary Youth' (*Cach Menh Thanh Nien Dong-chi Hoi*). These were the first Communists working in Vietnam to establish, by a process they called 'bead-stringing',[b] a conspiratorial 'people's network' (*luoi nhan dan*) to be used, at a suitable moment, for 'masses activation'.[c] Individuals who changed their minds, especially any induced to favour the KMT–VNQDD line in the recent ideological schism inside China, were given away to the *Sûreté*;[d] this was a trick to which the professional deficiencies of that body noted before continued to lay it open for many years to come. It was already plain at this stage that the purpose the Communists had in mind was to lay the foundations of an organ for seizing power, rather than to advance any definite ideology.

Indochina Communist Party

Ho Chi Minh's enforced return to Moscow when Borodin was asked to leave Canton severed his links with Tonkin and with his 'revolutionary brethren'. He soon returned to the East, however, with a more peripatetic way of life than before now that he was a marked man in the eyes of both Chiang Kai-shek's Government and the colonial powers in control at the same time of the territories of southeast Asia and of the foreign concessions in China. His new position seems to have been as an assistant within the Far East Bureau of the Comintern—located at Shanghai and operating behind the cover of the Pan-Pacific Trade Union Secretariat, but managed through the French, not the Chinese, Communist Party; he was entrusted with links to the underground movements in Vietnam and, more important, among the Overseas Chinese communities in Malaya and Indonesia, whose language the French agents presumably did not know.[e] When Ho Chi Minh required a sanctuary from time to time he found it among the small Tonkinese communities established for several generations on the west bank of the

[a] Dorsenne (1932), p. 536.   [b] Hoang-yan-Chi (1964), p. 48.
[c] *Dan-trung van-dong/RDM*, or *dan-van* for short.
[d] Fall (1962), p. 93.   [e] Roussel, p. 50; McLane (1966), pp. 135–6.

middle and upper Mekong, on Siamese territory.[a] During the 1920s knowledge of Marxian political economy spread among the young intelligentsia of Vietnam through French and Chinese publications, while independent 'associations', often very small, began to urge Communist economics and an interest in the 'Soviet experiment'; they did not have a definite revolutionary purpose, and the majority were Trotskyist and a divisive influence on the work promoted by the Comintern.[56] The cadres trained at Moscow or Whampoa were subject to dissensions of their own anyway, like all Vietnamese movements.[b] The result was that, on the eve of the world economic crisis, several mutually antagonistic 'Communist Parties' were in competition inside Vietnam. Apparently at the behest of Ho Chi Minh's Comintern employers, representatives of these groups met him in Hong Kong on 6 January 1930. They agreed to amalgamate into a single 'Vietnam Communist Party'; but Moscow objected to the nationalist flavour of this title and, among other instructions, told them to rename themselves 'Indochina Communist Party' because 'the Vietnamese, Cambodian and Laotian proletariat have politically and economically to be closely related in spite of their difference in language, customs, and race.'[c] The new Party was inaugurated with international proletarian pretensions as an 'autonomous branch of the Communist International';[d] but none of the other races of the region were actually represented, and total Vietnamese membership came only to 211, of whom 54 were not in the country.[e]

The 1931 Putsch

The violent disturbances centred on Vinh in 1931 were the work of this organization and belong to the general *putsch* in the Far East by which Stalin evidently hoped to undermine Britain, France, and Holland, in fulfilment of Lenin's expectations, now that all the southeast Asian colonies were in the grip of the great depression. To Communists all over the world, as a matter of fact, this was an apocalyptic moment. Lenin was in error, but that did not stop colonial Governments from reacting with unusual vigour and even rarer cooperation over their common interest. Besides smaller fry, two key

---

a Roussel.
b A fault complained of repeatedly within the Comintern (McLane, pp. 149–53).
c *Thirty Years*, pp. 25 & 27.
d A Party programme printed in Vietnamese at Berlin in 1932 refers to it by this title (*Dang Cong San Dong Duong—chi bo doc lap quoc te Cong San*); see also Fischer (1956), p. 179.
e *Thirty Years*, p. 24.

French officials in the Comintern fell foul of the police in Singapore and Hong Kong, and Ho Chi Minh was caught and sent to prison for two years in the latter place.[a] The Comintern network and a good deal of the workings of the front organizations within the colonial territories was laid bare—so much so that the *Sûreté* in Vietnam was able to round up virtually the entire framework of cadres. The Comintern links, thus exposed, could not be revived, and Ho Chi Minh disappeared for the next few years after his release from Hong Kong, sitting out the period of the Popular Front in France until better, more disturbed, times should inevitably dawn again and capitalism fall victim to its own 'internal contradictions' in the context, unpredictable as yet, of Japanese aggression and colonial emancipation.

The Popular Front

The Communists convicted by the French courts for capital offences had, unlike the partisans of the VNQDD, mostly been non-members of the Party, while the leaders, at worst, not being implicated in the criminal acts they had incited, got away with preventive detention and were given their liberty again under the 1933 amnesty. The setback of 1932 dictated withdrawal from policies of extremism and reversion to the 'doctrine of temporary alliances' with 'bourgeois' bodies of opinion[b] wherever common ground could be found to exploit; doctrinally the policy was justified by expectation of a 'bourgeois democratic revolution' in France like that of Kerensky in Russia. The Communist-supported *Front Populaire* elected in France in 1936 confirmed this tendency, for it coincided with small French concessions to the demand for higher positions in the public services than before for Vietnamese nationals, and that in turn took the wind out of the sails of those government employees who had surreptitiously given money to the Communist Parties, or to the VNQDD, out of conviction, or from a wish to insure with both sides, rather than from the more prevalent traditional motive of fear of the sinister hand of clandestine 'protectors'. In Cochinchina two Communists actually campaigned openly for, and won, Vietnamese seats on the Municipal Council, one as a Stalinist, the other as a Trotskyite, and the two factions jointly ran a French-language newspaper in the atmosphere of sweet reasonableness now prevailing; but the policy of the paper, *La Lutte*,[c] was strictly Marx-

[a] Dorsenne (1932), pp. 75–76.
[b] Propounded by Lenin in 1920 (McLane, p. 14).   [c] Hammer (1954), p. 89.

ist, the ideological class struggle, eschewing political revolution and only loosely connected with the subversive activities of the Party continuing underground at the same time.[a] The policy of apparent legality was maintained until the Nazi-Soviet Pact of 1939.

Vietnamese Leninism

During these six or seven years, however, the real leaders of the Party—dedicated to the vocation of the revolutionary and resisting the comforts of legality (except for a small nucleus living in Macau)[b] and the blandishments of the rest of the left wing to collaborate against the new enemy, Fascism—were digesting the lessons of 1930–2 and adapting their Leninist methodology to the social setting of Vietnam. The major lesson was that the French regime could not be unseated by civil disobedience and rioting alone: some other hand or circumstance had to do the hatchet work for them, as the Great War had done it for Lenin; the VNQDD's puny effort had been an infantile first step towards a Communist take-over. A second lesson was that, in order to be prepared when the lucky moment of destiny should come, they must have sources for essential supplies, and a network of communications, already organized: manpower, food, weapons, intelligence, and, above all, money. The important thing was not the social class of the people they would be counting on for these supplies—for instance, whether they were peasants or proletarians—nor their ideological convictions, but the organization for its own sake and the methods by which an armed revolutionary machine could be rooted reliably in the local economy.

Preliminaries for revolution

The steps by which these preparations were actually made thirty years ago have, in the main, to be inferred from the situation in later years; however, the outline of subversive activity is admitted in the Party history. It seems there was still no attempt at subversion in every part of the country, but only at selected points—whether by design or because trustworthy cadres were few. The major effort went, not into propaganda as one might expect, but into finance; existing trade unions were penetrated and new ones sponsored among the small industrial and estate population ('taxing' wage

[a] At a meeting on 29–30 Mar. 1938, the secret Central Committee of the Party called the legal organs to order as properly subordinate, at all Party levels, to their underground counterparts (*Thirty Years*, p. 58).
[b] Ibid. p. 46. They published a periodical significantly called *Bolshevik*.

increases obtained through strikes), while, in other localities, mutual-aid associations were started in the rural areas, especially of the overcrowded Annamite provinces of Nghe An, Tinh Ha, and Quang Ngai.[a] In Tonkin cadres were planted along the two main trade and infiltration routes from Hanoi into China through Cao Bang and Lao Cay and reoccupied the guerrilla base formerly used by De Tham in Thai Nguyen. The future General Vo Nguyen Giap, with future Prime Minister Pham Van Dong, supported this activity with a legal front association they called the 'Indochina Democratic Front'.[b] In distant Cochinchina the Communist leadership, represented by a necessarily autonomous director, Tran Van Giau, in 'temporary alliance' with the leading Trotskyite, Ta Thu Thau, seem to have kept away from established secret societies, neither infiltrating them nor quarrelling with them—a course which accorded with the policy of the Chinese Communists in southeast Asia and distinguished them from the KMT[c]—and established their three-cadre cells at points where there would be no competition. In spite of the contemporary growth of the Cao Dai and the Hoa Hao, corners could be found close to Saigon where a mutual-aid association or youth organization could be introduced, or, farther off in the Plain of Reeds, in the estuaries and in the Camau peninsula, in places where villages of recent settlement were still unadministered by the colonial Government and could be brought under the influence of a persuasive cadre back from Whampoa, much as they might have come under the influence of bonze or fortune-teller. Students were ideal contacts with isolated district officers, who themselves were first-class sources of information. Intimidation was not much used at this period (except for discipline within the Party), probably out of fear of discovery, and although some well-to-do supporters of French rule considered it wise to subscribe and keep in with them,[d] the Communists generally contented themselves in this period with the recruits they could get by their helpfulness—in suitable cases by appeal to a sense of adventure in young people with more education and ambition than prospects— but without appealing for support in furtherance of a revolution.

[a] Burial, dining, and football clubs also were exploited as a 'tactic to recreate the Party's primary organizations', and money was raised from 1938 onwards in the name of helping China against Japan (*Thirty Years*, pp. 44 & 58).

[b] Devillers (1952), p. 70.

[c] In China itself, on the other hand, Mao Tsê-tung at one time had close relations with the great rival of the KMT-supporting Triad Society, namely the *Ko Lao Hui* or Elder-Brother Society (Schram 1966, quoting from Mao's own writings).

[d] Or so it was at the beginning of the period (Dorsenne, *RDM*, 1932, p. 543).

They had no single message; they were all things to all men—
neither nationalism nor land reform were urged at this time[a]—and
asked only for solidarity and reasonable contributions in return for
whatever service they performed.

The Communist network

Thus, by the outbreak of the Second World War, the Party had,
besides its legal and overt organization (which the French Government declared illegal after the Nazi-Soviet Pact and the outbreak of
war in Europe), a tenuous and scattered, but connected, network
of cells with radiating spheres of information and influence in villages, schools, unions, government departments, paramilitary
forces, and associations of various kinds in many, though not yet all,
parts of the country. The Party kept its publicity abreast of the times
by continually changing the names of the 'fronts' it worked behind;
in November 1939 it made the biggest change of all in connexion
with an 'Indochinese Anti-Imperialist National United Front'; the
Bolshevik past was finally repudiated by suppression of the old
slogan 'Found Soviet power by the workers, peasants and soldiers'
and substitution of 'Found the Democratic Republic of Indochina'
(not yet quite of Vietnam).[b] The organization was still a long way
from being able to undertake an insurrection, but it had two important assets: first, it had largely purged itself of idealistic and self-
deceptive notions that power would fall into its hands at one drama-
tic moment by mere operation of Marxian historical laws—patience
discipline, austerity, and ruthlessness were the indispensable price
of power; second, it had at its command, besides considerable sums
of money and (in the South) a few firearms, a potential intelligence
network without precedent or equal in Vietnam. It was the entry of
Japan into the war that gave this second asset its rentability and did
the hatchet work Ho Chi Minh had been waiting for.

2. THE INTERVENTION OF JAPAN

Japan had ancient connexions with Vietnam: one of the mandarins from China who governed Chiao Chih in the eighth century was
Japanese by race;[c] excluded from direct trade with China in later
centuries, Japanese merchants had used Vietnamese ports as places
at which to meet Chinese merchants and get round the ban.[d] In the

---

[a] This omission is noted as being an 'incorrect line' in *Thirty Years* (p. 61).
[b] Ibid. p. 65.   [c] Daudin (1965).   [d] p. 73 above.

modern period, however, apart from the regular purchase of the bulk of the coal produced by the mines of Tonkin, Japanese interest in Vietnam has been political. The asylum found in Japan by Prince Cuong De and those around him was sought by the émigrés themselves, as it was in the case of the Chinese intellectual refugees, rather than offered spontaneously by their hosts. But that did not prevent Japanese financial groups with ambitions for the expansion of their country's political influence from putting the émigrés in Japan's debt, and the ground had been prepared for many years before 1941.[a] The outbreak of the Second World War found Japan with two objects in Indochina. Firstly, there was the immediate purpose, arising from her attempt to conquer China, of putting a stop, once she had sealed off Canton and other ports in South China from the interior, to the use of the Tonkin railway from Haiphong to Kunming to convey supplies from the outside world to the Chinese armies—if possible of obtaining the use of the railway herself as an additional invasion route. Secondly, there was the long-range purpose of evicting the Western powers from their southeast Asian colonies and substituting her own or puppet administrations—the policy of the 'Co-Prosperity Sphere' of 'Greater East Asia'. The Franco-German armistice in June 1940 placed Indochina at Japan's mercy, for it brought to an end all possibility of military reinforcement and supply from Europe and, at the same time, brought the colonial administration under a Ministry at Paris that was more or less acquiescent towards Axis behests. The moment of France's defeat was chosen to serve the Governor-General, at that time General Catroux, with an ultimatum to stop supplies to China and to accept a Japanese Control Commission on French soil to supervise shipping. Catroux gave way,[57] and was replaced a few days later by Admiral Decoux, who, faced with further Japanese demands, had ultimately to accept a *de facto* Japanese military occupation; French sovereignty was recognized and the existing government machinery allowed to function normally, but Japan stationed in Tonkin and Annam a military force numbering 25,000 troops, together with naval and air force units and certain propaganda and administrative services which included the notorious *Kempeitai* or 'Military Police'. Further concessions giving them access to the colonial territory of Cochinchina were signed by Vichy in July 1941.[b]

[a] Nguyen-phut-Tan, p. 453.   [b] Mordant (1950), p. 12.

Admiral Decoux's administration

Japanese intervention had taken place in pursuit of the more immediate of her two aims, but it contributed enormously to the second aim by bringing home to the Vietnamese urban population, including the public services, the extent of France's humiliation and her weakness. When Siam made attacks on Laos and Cambodia in November 1940, which the French forces were insufficient to repel, some of the Communist outposts read the signs to mean their moment of destiny had arrived, and those in the Plain of Reeds made simultaneous attacks on the *Gendarmerie* garrisons at My Tho and Cao Lanh.[a] They were unsuccessful because their rising was not coordinated with moves in other parts of the country, and they lost many prisoners, sent to Pulau Condore; but the incident is of interest because the Communists made use for the first time of the flag later adopted by the Democratic Republic of Vietnam,[b] whose propagandists sometimes date the outbreak of the Indochina War from that isolated episode.[c] Admiral Decoux reacted with punitive air raids on villages[d] but took the warning to heart and made a renewed effort to attach the Vietnamese civil service to his regime. Between 1940 and 1944 he voted funds for 4,800 new schools, extended the use of *quoc ngu* in public business, provided many new facilities for sports, and doubled the Vietnamese entry to the higher ranks of the civil service.[e] At the same time, he embarked on a unified Penal Code for all Vietnam and drew up a scheme for absolute parity of emoluments and other terms of service between Vietnamese and expatriate staff, although none of these measures went into effect before the end of Decoux's regime.[58] Beneath a surface of comparative calm all through these years, however, and while the war was raging all round Indochina, many separate interests were engaged in subverting townsfolk or peasants.

Japanese subversion

From the moment of Pearl Harbour, if not earlier, the biggest effort to undermine French authority was directed by the Japanese, relying largely on the psychological impact of their naval and military victories. Prince Cuong De was taken out of moth-balls as a focus for Asian patriotism, and at the same time the Buddhists of Cambodia and of Tonkin were invited to join in a xenophobic re-

---

[a] Decoux (1949), p. 240.   [b] Chesneaux, p. 225.
[c] Though not the official Party history, which is reluctant to yield honours to Cochinchina (*Thirty Years*, p. 69).
[d] Devillers (1952), p. 80.   [e] Ibid. p. 85.

ligious movement affiliated to the Buddhists of Japan.[a] These two tendencies ran together at many points, and most notably through the Cochinchinese Sects. Pham Cong Tac had secured a special statute in 1939 recognizing Cao Dai as an incorporated religion but had subsequently taken to prophesying in his 'divine messages' the return of Cuong De;[b] he was probably already in somebody's pay, and as soon as the *Kempeitai* was established overtly in Cochinchina he made things so difficult for the French authorities that it could be said that autonomous districts were taking shape under his control.[c] Decoux declared the Sect illegal and had Tac deported to the Comoro Islands. Some time later the *Kempeitai* brought the head of a rival offshoot of Cao Dai, Tran Quang Vinh, from his 'temple' at Phnom Penh to start training an irregular, explicitly anti-French, militia for the Sect—a development which seems to have gone undetected at the time.[d] Huynh Phu So was no less alert than others to read the signs of the times, and the Hoa Hao took on such a violently anti-French colour, and, like Cao Dai, seemed so certain to carve itself out a fief of control and exploitation, that Decoux ordered the seizure of the 'Mad Bonze' as well; this time, however, the *Kempeitai* intercepted the French police and gave So their protection, as well as practical help, such as supplies of quinine, with which to carry on his faith-healing miracles and his crusade.[e] Many ephemeral patriotic associations, vaguely presided over by Cuong De from Tokyo, were set up with Japanese funds in different parts of the country, although they probably lost their attraction whenever the money ran out; two of them nevertheless were destined to become permanent, the *Dai Viet Quoc Dan Hoi* (Greater Vietnam Republic Association) and the *Dai Viet Cach Menh Dang* (Greater Vietnam Revolutionary Party), later fused with it.[f] Various political leaders were given *Kempeitai* protection against possible arrest by the French; Ngo Dinh Diem was of their number.[g] The *Kempeitai* paid, and protected with its 'military' identity cards, every kind of rogue on the streets of Saigon as an agent of one sort or other; the young thugs were dubbed 'local Japanese'. Even Communist cadres, it would seem, were not above distributing patriotic propaganda against the Axis Powers with one hand[h]—more accurately, against the Anti-Comintern Pact—while accepting the Mikado's yen with the other.[i]

[a] Decoux, p. 236.   [b] Ibid, p. 235.   [c] Savani, p. 90.   [d] Ibid. p. 91.
[e] Nguyen-van-Tam, p. 61.   [f] Devillers (1952), p. 93.   [g] Ibid.
[h] Devillers, p. 96.   [i] Masson, p. 115.

French prestige in decline

Years later, as he wrote his apologia in prison, expiating his collaboration with the Japanese and his mistaken recognition of Marshal Pétain as temporary repository of the glory, honour, and destiny of France, the Admiral was to pride himself on having watched the tricolour flutter over the palaces in Hanoi and Saigon sunset after sunset almost till the end of the war; he would assuredly not have had that soldier's satisfaction if, in 1940, he had given the young French officers on the half-dozen ships in his flotilla in the Saigon River their head to strike the tricolour, raise the white ensign, and sail to chance their luck with the Royal Navy at Singapore.[a] Yet it was in those years, and under his Fascist administration,[59] during which so many concessions were made to Vietnamese aspirations to take part in their own government—although 'control, command, and security were held tightly in French hands'[b]—that respect for French authority in Indochina, and for authority as such, was gradually eaten away underneath. For the time being, the corruption, the double dealing, the deepening economic crisis of wartime isolation, the consequent black marketeering, the breakdown of internal transport and communications under the effects of American bombing,[c] and the paralysis of established order in many rural areas, all created an atmosphere indirectly helpful to the Allies in the war at sea against Japan by multiplying the opportunities for espionage.

Rival intelligence networks

The principal consumer of military intelligence about Japanese movements was the US fleet, but it had to depend for collection of intelligence on agents inside the country. These were controlled, necessarily, by French networks or by Chinese ones. Many Frenchmen caught in Indochina sympathized with General de Gaulle, and after the liberation of Paris in 1944 their numbers grew fast. A network for gathering intelligence was easily organized among them, and this was in touch by wireless both with the Free French Command at Calcutta and with a smaller French unit attached to Allied Headquarters for the China theatre at Kunming. Allied aircraft parachuted French liaison officers into Tonkin and Cochinchina,

---

[a] That is what he boasts he prevented from happening (Decoux, p. 39).
[b] Ibid. p. 390.
[c] It is interesting that the targets of American bombing in 1965 were often identical with those of 1945.

and a full-scale 'resistance' movement was organized (on paper), through which, at the end, even Admiral Decoux double-insured with the US. This emotional rather than practical French underground deliberately and ill-advisedly stayed aloof from the Vietnamese.[60] There were two main Vietnamese groups: the VNQDD and the Communists. The former had a few cells only in Tonkin, and their leaders had been fugitives in China almost continuously since 1931, gradually falling out of touch with home; but on the other hand they were politically reliable from the point of view of the Chinese High Command. The Communists had, as we have seen, a a far wider, and always widening, network several thousand strong, but were distrusted by Chiang Kai-shek.

The first guerrillas

Ho Chi Minh had returned to southwest China by mid-1941, evidently with a clear eye for the opportunities to make another bid for power if Japan unseated the Decoux regime.[61] This was the period of superficial united front against Japan between KMT and Chinese Communists, and, once again, Ho Chi Minh took his cue from the situation in China and called on various other émigrés to join in a *Viet Nam Doc-lap Dong-minh Hoi* (Brotherhood for an Independent Vietnam), or *Viet Minh* for short. For some reason, possibly carried over from his work with Borodin, he was put in prison in August 1942. A year later, however, after he had been marched in chains ceaselessly from town to town,[a] the ineptitude and spitefulness among themselves of the Vietnamese nationalists led the warlord who had been thus tormenting him, Chang Fa-k'uei, to give him his freedom again as the price of making Communist intelligence from Indochina available to the American mission in China. It was at this moment that Ho Chi Minh first adopted that name.[b] He accepted the funds proffered, and also the opportunities first to revive his alliance with the other émigrés by changing the full title of the Vietminh slightly,[c] and second to set up a small guerrilla base on Tonkinese soil near to Cao Bang and the possibility of quick retreat back into China. We have already seen the Cochinchinese Communists armed and organized militarily at My Tho and Cao Lanh; on the frontiers of Tonkin the ease with which American

[a] According to his *Prison Diary* (Ho-chi-Minh, 1966). He none the less found time to compose this remarkable record of his experience in a 100 short poems in Chinese; one suspects retouching at a later date in emulation of Mao Tsê-tung's fame at versification.
[b] *Thirty Years*, pp. 17 & 74.
[c] *Doc-lap* (Independent) became *Cach-menh* (Revolutionary).

arms and training were available through the unintegrated command of the KMT[a] had been put to use for two or three years to form a guerrilla nucleus, ostensibly to fight the Japanese again,[b] out of Vietnamese soldiers who had already deserted once from French command, overawed by the reputation of the Japanese. Vo Nguyen Giap (future commander at the battle of Dien Bien Phu) was at the head of this band, which he expanded by bringing in some of the Tho tribesmen of Tonkin,[c] until by the beginning of 1945 he disposed of a force of several thousands.[d]

Conflicting war aims

For the American Command there was a single objective, the defeat of Japan, which would be the end of the affair; but for the Chinese and the Vietnamese the defeat of Japan would be incidental and little more than the beginning of a further struggle between KMT and Communists inside China and to the ousting of France from Indochina. It was hoped that America would finish Japan off somewhere far away—which is what happened in the sequel—and meanwhile they were all prepared to gather and transmit to the Americans intelligence useful to that end, and to help extricate American pilots beginning to be shot down by the Japanese over Vietnamese territory, in exchange for money and arms, ostensibly also for the same purpose, but in the hope they could be laid by. For their part, Americans in China regarded the aspiration for ultimate emancipation spoken of by the Vietminh as an additional recommendation that their motives were righteous ones and the Vietnamese more rewarding collaborators than the prickly French, who had less to offer and made difficulties about even that.[e] The Vietminh's studious avoidance of engagement with Japanese forces could, unlike similar KMT avoidance, be put down to unpreparedness to take on a professional army—an unpreparedness it was in American interests to help the Vietminh overcome by reinforcing their first bases in Tonkin.

Internment of the French

It was at this stage in the unfolding of Vietminh fortunes that the Japanese decided to destroy French authority in Indochina altogether. By the beginning of 1945 it was plain that victory would go

---

[a] A well-documented account of the disorganization of Chiang Kai-shek's army and its operations during the war is given by Ch'ên (1965, pp. 241–3).
[b] Devillers (1952), p. 104.   [c] Hammer, p. 97.
[d] Vo-nguyen-Giap (1961), p. 51.   [e] Lancaster, p. 122.

to the Allies. The Free French organization was now receiving important airdrops of weapons and approaching the moment of expanding its intelligence operations into a *coup de force* to annihilate the Japanese garrison, with or without a concerted American landing from the by now reoccupied Philippines. The economy of the country was fast breaking down under the combined effect of Japan's own pressures, of American sinking of sea transports, and of American bombing of internal communications: with shipments of rice from Cochinchina almost at a standstill, northern Annam and Tonkin faced famine. But the decisive consideration for the Japanese was the desire, even if they could not hold on to Indochina themselves, to deprive the colonial power of it, as was their policy in Indonesia and Burma. Consequently, on 9 March 1945, while the Free French were still screwing up their courage to strike, the Japanese Ambassador informed Admiral Decoux that he was taking over the Government; simultaneously Japanese units moved into all government offices and garrison camps. The entire French community was disarmed and interned, except for one French column already in the jungle which fought its way out to Yunnan. The psychological effect of this action was exactly as intended: the peoples of Indochina who witnessed the disarming of French soldiers concluded that French rule was at an end for all time, and with it the whole system of government and apparatus of law and order for which France had stood.

Japanese occupation

Having locked up the French officials, the Japanese inaugurated a quasi-military administration of their own.[62] At Hué they confirmed the Emperor Bao Dai in his sovereign rights over Annam and Tonkin and supported his proclamation two days later of the end of the French Protectorate. A Prime Minister and Cabinet were hastily installed, and to them the Japanese allowed a free hand so long as military interests were not infringed: there was already popular clamour for the appointment of Ngo Dinh Diem in Hué, some believe, but he prudently declined, and a lawyer, Dr Tran Trong Kim, took over with the support of the Dai Viet Party and other pro-Japanese groups. Dr Kim's was, however, purely a shadow administration: at the end its sole achievement proved to have been adoption of the flag and national anthem which are still those of the Republic of Vietnam; its writ never ran beyond the towns;[a] in the

[a] Devillers (1952), pp. 126–8.

country administrative inertia sustained the mandarinate and the *Garde Indochinoise* despite the removal of their French chiefs, and the Japanese did not interfere so long as the war levy ('rice for the bowls of Greater East Asia') came in on time. Japan did not include Cochinchina in the territory recognized to be under Bao Dai's sovereignty, and in this, whatever her motives, she was adhering to the usages of war: sovereignty in Annam and Tonkin had always vested in the emperor, but Cochinchina was French soil which could not be disposed of by an occupying power. Instead, the military filled with their own officials the few posts they regarded as vital and promoted junior Vietnamese in others, while areas of no military value and little economic value were left to themselves and to the mercies—or the mercilessness—of the Sects. Over the next few months, as the imminence of defeat loomed larger, all sense of responsibility for keeping order among the population faded from Japanese thinking and they became more and more detached from what was going on, much as in their other occupied territories— Philippines, Malaya, Dutch Indies.

Administrative breakdown

On all sides, the end first of French rule in Vietnam, and now of Japanese, signalled the end of regulation and restraint of any kind; there was an administrative void[a] which 'the flexible tactics of the Indochina Communist Party' aggravated and turned to advantage in order to 'sow confusion in the enemy ranks'.[b] The courts and police ceased to function, and criminals, as well as political agitators, found their way out of confinement[c] to seek out and avenge themselves on law-abiding villagers ('traitors') whose evidence they knew or merely suspected had caused their imprisonment. Disorder and unofficial measures for self-protection stimulated one another. Cao Dai and Hoa Hao—both of them dedicated to not taking life—expanded their armed bands under their two leaders' new and belligerent lieutenants, Tran Quang Vinh and Tran Van Soai; Vinh's operations were, on the whole, defensive, but Soai's were aimed fanatically at commanding the obedience of village authorities—the only ones left in the countryside—over as wide an area and as swiftly as he could.[d] Firearms were short, but the Japanese had supplied a number to Huynh Phu So, and both Sects extorted

[a] Devillers (1952), pp. 126–8.   [b] Truong Chinh (1962), p. 27.
[c] Lancaster, p. 138. For the Communist role in this, Truong Chinh (1961), p. 16.
[d] Vinh was Assistant Curator in the Museum at Phnom Penh (Savani, p. 91) and Soai a taxi-driver (Nguyen-van-Tam, p. 63).

money from villagers with which to buy more from Japanese soldiers. Into the turmoil of Saigon there stepped a new factor for lawlessness—a body calling itself 'Binh Xuyen Bandits'.[a] These were hooligans from the riverside swamps led by an unregenerate gangster, Le Van Vien, who dispensed with any mumbo-jumbo and made it his job to protect, and tax, Chinese enterprises in Cholon. The Communists in Cochinchina used these months to consolidate their youth movement, which took over much of the strength of Admiral Decoux's youth organization, left in the air by the internment of its promoters.[b] In Annam Communist cadres conducted a campaign of threats to hang as 'collaborators' all officials who did not act on their instructions.[c] In Tonkin, now in the grip of famine, the Vietminh leadership, supported logistically by the Americans and the French through China as well as by the Chinese,[63] and employing 'propaganda by armed units and suppression of puppet officials, paved the way for the setting up of revolutionary power' and declaration of a 'liberated zone' on 4 June 1945;[d] besides Thai Nguyen, the 'zone' reached in a horseshoe through the hills surrounding the Delta. The Delta in turn was saturated with Communist cadres, who, in the name of 'People's Salvation Committees', organized the looting and selective distribution of what supplies there were,[e] sweeping aside as 'Fascists' all who stood in their way, to the slogan '*Doc-lap!*' (Independence!).[f] With both French and Japanese authority destroyed by the beginning of August, outside Hanoi, Haiphong, Nam Dinh, and the two Catholic dioceses, the Vietminh was the nearest thing there was to a public administration, and a Red Army under Vo Nguyen Giap had taken shape on this foundation; on all hands the mandarinate and the militia were disarmed, and village elders deferred to the ICP's cadres as the new fountainhead of authority.[g]

3. FRENCH REVENDICATIONS

The suddenness of the Japanese surrender found the Allies—to whom as victors responsibility for re-establishing order fell—politically, militarily, and logistically unprepared all over southeast Asia; the forces of disorder, on the other hand, required no previous

[a] Lancaster, p. 127.   [b] Fall (1962), p. 48.
[c] Devillers (1952), p. 135; admitted also in *Thirty Years*, i. 88.   [d] *Thirty Years*, i. 88.
[e] The foundation for all the other activities according to Truong Chinh (1962), p. 28.
[f] Truong Chinh (1961), pp. 11–15.   [g] Vo-nguyen-Giap (1966), p. 74.

planning for their work of destruction and set to with a will, each to grab what pledges for the future he could. Ho Chi Minh and his comrades immediately moved down from their caves to Hanoi to occupy the power vacuum and, declaring themselves to be a National Liberation Committee, set in train a series of rapid moves purporting to establish an independent Government. On 25 August they persuaded the Emperor Bao Dai at Hué to denounce the treaties with France and then to abdicate.[a] Tran Trong Kim and his pro-Japanese colleagues had faded away already, and Bao Dai, henceforward plain Prince Vinh Thuy, returned to Hanoi with the Communist emissary, Tran Huy Lieu, to join in the proclamation of the Democratic Republic of Vietnam by Ho Chi Minh on 2 September. The Communists' procurement of the Emperor's abdication was most probably prompted less by foresight than by the doctrinaire example of the Russian Revolution; yet it proved a masterstroke, for it gave the long-planned insurrection instant and unlooked for constitutional legitimacy: in Annam and Tonkin at least, the Communists were from now on the sovereign Government, by right of a sovereign act of the previous monarch. Politically, however, their boldness had little foundation; it rested in part on the prestige they drew from exaggerated claims to the support of the Allies[b]—for recognition by foreign powers was as vital to acceptance of an independent Government inside Vietnam at this stage of history as it has been in the 1950s and 1960s[c]—and in part from the 'armed propaganda' of its People's Committees all over the country to keep the initiative in informing the population of the course of national events in its own terms and to stifle any initiatives on the part of the local authorities. To allay suspicions of its true intent, the Vietminh (by now ostensibly a united front of Communist and non-Communist émigrés) put out on 11 November 'the Party's declaration of its dissolution (in reality the Party went underground)'[d] and invited into the new Cabinet a minority of other interests, including the Catholics.[64]

Chaos in Cochinchina

As at other moments in this story, conditions were different in the

[a] Devillers (1952), p. 139.
[b] Some American officers of the Office of Strategic Services, predecessor of the CIA, were present at the proclamation of the DRV, whose preamble borrowed extensively from the Declaration of Independence.
[c] There is a Vietnamese proverb which says 'No influence penetrates deeper than a foreign influence' (*Phong trao o ngoai vao*).
[d] The words of the Party's Secretary, Truong Chinh (1963), p. 23.

South. Despite a last-minute reversal by the Japanese of their earlier opinion over the question of sovereignty,[a] Bao Dai had no following and no standing in Cochinchina. The Communists as well were in a weaker position than in the North; there had been no opportunity to consolidate their scattered nuclei in the countryside, cut off more and more by the rapid growth of Cao Dai and Hoa Hao, both of which now declared their own autonomous areas. The Communists had no disciplined organization either, and the Trotskyite minority of Ta Thu Thau was still active; affiliation to the Vietminh was uncertain, as was the constitutional claim of the Hanoi 'Government' to rule Cochinchina. Even in Saigon the Communists' reservoir of strength was the mobs who came on to the streets to celebrate, with looting and violence, the end of the Japanese (and French) occupation. Tran Van Giau, who represented the Vietminh and the Indochina Communist Party, tried with limited success to discipline these mobs through the cadres of what survived of the youth movement.[b] The Japanese, still answerable internationally under the usages of war even though defeated, tried to turn over authority to a United National Front of politicians of all colours, including the Sects; but nobody was listened to or had any machinery for keeping order. All through September the turmoil continued, with well-to-do Vietnamese as well as French people (now back in their homes) the victims; Giau endeavoured in his public statements to limit the personal violence against Europeans,[c] but in secret he invited the Binh Xuyen (unsuccessfully) to liquidate a list of *viet gian* (traitors to Vietnam).[d] The tale of looting, of robbery with murder or other violence, and of political assassination, which could be paralleled from other Japanese-occupied territories at the time, spread rapidly to the whole of the Vietnamese lowlands; among its victims at Hué, whence all government had withdrawn with Bao Dai, were the elderly constitutionalist Pham Quynh and Ngo Dinh Khoi, elder brother of Diem, who himself narrowly escaped.

The British occupation

In handing over authority to local *ad hoc* bodies, however, the Japanese had not surrendered; this they could do only to the Allied Commanders-in-Chief, who were Lord Mountbatten for southeast Asia and General Chiang Kai-shek for the China theatre. The Pots-

[a] Hammer, p. 52.   [b] Ibid. p. 107.   [c] Ibid. p. 106.
[d] Lancaster, p. 137.

dam Conference fixed the boundary between the two commands at the sixteenth parallel; nobody had any foreknowledge of conditions inside the country, and the line was arbitrary. A token British force numbering 750 men landed at Saigon to take the Japanese surrender there and ensure the safety of Allied personnel, while Chinese troops entered Tonkin for the same purpose. French troops might have been assigned the British task had there been any available from home—those in internment being tainted with collaboration—but not the Chinese task: the distaste of America, dominant ally in the China theatre, for the return of colonial regimes was notorious, while China demanded that territory wrested from her under the 'unequal treaties' and recently delivered, without a blow struck, to her invaders, must fall to her in the general triumph. On arrival, the British contingent found Vietnamese public opinion ranged against the rioters and the Vietminh behind them,[a] but the Commander-in-Chief was loath to sanction the extension of the contingent's mission to that of keeping order in Saigon; he was overridden from London, however, and the local British Commander proclaimed his assumption of responsibility for order as far north as the sixteenth parallel, issuing arms to the freed French forces to help him. Calm gradually returned to the towns, but there was no British military administration, and it was the French who took charge of government buildings.[b]

The Chinese occupation

The Chinese occupation of the North was reminiscent of the days of the Black Flags. The operation was entrusted to General Lu Han, who, like his 180,000 troops,[c] shared that indeterminate status in the army and command of China that had always characterized the forces of warlords: they were in alliance with the KMT rather than subordinate to the orders of the Nationalist Government. Like the British, the Chinese too avoided a military administration involving them in direct responsibility for government, but (contrary to the laws and usages of war) brought in their train the VNQDD and other émigrés, whom they helped to supplant with their own followers the Vietminh's People's Salvation Committees in the 'liberated zones' and helped to take office in the ostensibly United Front Government of the DRV. General Lu Han took the view of

[a] Donnison (1956), p. 409.   [b] Cmnd 2834, pp. 7–8 & 47–49.
[c] Sainteny (1954), p. 119.

Indochina which the Russians were at that moment taking of Manchuria: that it was enemy territory and that all industrial equipment, as well as private property found in Japanese hands, was legitimate booty. French nationals were soon drawing their piastres out of their bank accounts to buy back from the Chinese military their possessions looted by the Japanese while they were interned; the Chinese then exported the piastres to the money markets of Macau and Hong Kong. By the same token, this huge army claimed rations on an inflated scale off the land, despite famine conditions aggravated by collapse of the untended dykes—followed by drought—so that the surplus could be sold on the black market. Subventions were demanded from the Bank of Indochina, eventually totalling 400 million piastres, on account of 'costs of occupation'.[a] The proceeds of the operations were distributed among the Chinese troops.[b] Nor were those the only sources of gold for this Fafner ensconced in the Governor-General's palace: Ho Chi Minh had to maintain his precarious occupation of public buildings in Hanoi in the teeth of demands by the VNQDD for fulfilment of Vietminh promises to make room for them in the United Front Government;[c] the VNQDD addressed themselves to Lu Han as occupying power and as their KMT protector, and he in turn prodded Ho Chi Minh who, it has been alleged, bought him off with offerings of gold which (their life's savings) the cadres browbeat the masses into voluntarily surrendering.[d]

The French reoccupation

French wisdom in fighting back at this stage has been questioned, in France as much as in America. Yet apart from considerations of loss of prestige and of property, no colonial power could willingly have surrendered its responsibility for the destinies of Vietnam, and of Indochina, to such anarchy as we have just described. Ho Chi Minh has admitted since that his followers at this time still only numbered 5,000;[e] whatever 'popular support' they commanded was commanded visibly at gun point. Consequently, Commissioners charged with safeguarding French public responsibilities and private interests as best they could were sent out by air to Saigon and, a little later, to Hanoi. During October they were fol-

[a] Ibid. pp. 143 ff.   [b] Lancaster, p. 126.   [c] Célerier (1950), pp. 40–50.
[d] Lancaster, p. 126.
[e] Speech at 3rd Party Congress, reported by NCNA, 10 Sept. 1960.

lowed by General Leclerc and a force of French infantry, who disembarked in contingents at Saigon, reoccupied the provincial capitals of Cochinchina, and landed civilian officials at Nha Trang and at Tourane to take possession of Hué. A period of simultaneous negotiations then began in Hanoi and Chungking during which Leclerc at Hanoi and the French Ambassador at Chungking secured (in exchange for free port rights at Haiphong for China and other adjustments to Franco-Chinese relations)[a] Chiang Kai-shek's agreement to end the military occupation. At the same time Ho Chi Minh agreed to the temporary return of a French garrison to Tonkin in place of the Chinese, in exchange for French recognition of the DRV and its nucleus of an army as a 'Free State within the Federation of Indochina and the French Union'; this meant continuation of the political *status quo*—the DRV would administer the North, the French the South, with no line fixed between them.[b] Early in March 1946 French troops landed at Haiphong—though not without exchanges of fire with both Chinese and Vietminh soldiers—, and the Chinese withdrew with the last of their 35,000 Japanese prisoners. From their own point of view, the French were giving effect to the declaration of General de Gaulle in March 1945 that, after the war, Indochina should have her own armed forces (always a vital issue with the Vietnamese) and a new political statute within the French Union.[c] But although the provisional accommodation at Hanoi sounded like concession of the major step towards colonial emancipation, it did not in fact create a Vietnamese national state. France was still thinking in terms of a 'nation' embracing all of Indochina, and substantive negotiations would be needed before the permanent constitutional future could be worked out to cover, above all, the difficult question of Cochinchina. It was not predictable when that might be possible on the French side: though aligned on the winning side in the war, the French had been defeated and now plunged in Indochina into witchhunts among themselves between *collaborateurs* and *résistants*, between *colons* and recruits from home,[d] while Paris was too much absorbed by its own scandals and purges to face up to the problems resulting in Vietnam from the breakdown of government, let alone a longer future. The provisional accommodation consequently reflected no firm policy on the part of France, but only a need to temporize on the part of Leclerc.

[a] Cole (1956), pp. 7–9.   [b] Sainteny, p. 177.   [c] Hammer, pp. 111–12.
[d] Sabattier (1952), pp. 332–4.

The Party on the tightrope

Although he is often said to have come in for bitter criticism from his own extremists for agreeing to reoccupation of Tonkin by French troops, Ho Chi Minh had as compelling reasons as Leclerc for temporizing on his side. The Communist Party was a minute body of men and had to build up a measure of disciplined military strength before it could act independently of the alliances represented by its various fronts; that meant playing off Japanese, Chinese, and French against each other—there was still hope of a Communist Government in postwar Paris—while retaining American sympathy for Vietminh slogans of independence, democracy, and fulfilment of the recent Atlantic Charter. On the domestic stage, the war had left Marxism no longer a fashionable ideology, and the class struggle afforded too narrow a base for consolidation of the Party's power: the latter had to 'change its watchwords, forms of propaganda, organization and struggle'.[a] On doctrinaire grounds, power could not be expected without struggle, and struggle would call for a Red Army capable of taking on the French army; the needs of this necessarily 'self-reliant' guerrilla force would have to be supplied locally, and that meant a shift of its centre of gravity from its émigré origins, first to selected guerrilla bases,[b] later to the heart of every Vietnamese *xa*. Intellectuals with technical skills and capacity for leadership must be attracted to the cause; that meant obliterating the Comintern and Bolshevik traces: the Comintern itself had been wound up in Moscow, and the two Bolsheviks who had kept the Red Flag flying in Cochinchina through the years of waiting, Ta Thu Thau the Trotskyite and Tran Van Giau the Stalinist, were (the former literally, the latter figuratively) buried. The financial resources of landowners would have to be tapped, and 'with a view to winning a number of landlords over to the anti-imperialist cause, the watchword Agrarian Revolution was omitted' from Vietminh pronouncements;[c] obviously it was more convenient to tax a few landlords than to distribute their land and then have to collect the money from hundreds of former tenants. This new policy of 'flexible tactics' embraced the staging in January 1946 of a 'nation-wide' election for a National Assembly; the communications and administrative resources necessary before such an election could really be held did not exist in fact, but it is reported to have been conducted 'with enthusiasm' at least at certain places in

[a] Truong Chinh (1962), p. 25.   [b] Vo-nguyen-Giap (1961), pp. 101–3.
[c] Truong Chinh, p. 26.

Tonkin.[a] Two-thirds of the seats in the Assembly were allocated—evidently in advance of whatever balloting actually took place—to parties other than the Communists;[b] the Party's control was assured, however, by delegation of the Assembly's authority at the only meeting it held to a Cabinet in which the Party held the vital portfolios.[c]

Franco-Vietminh negotiations

These internal manœuvres put the Vietminh in a stronger position, during the course of 1946, to embark on several conferences with the French Government over a more permanent settlement; whether Ho Chi Minh and his Party colleagues expected to gain more than recognition of their status as a provisional government, and a breathing space while they armed, is not clear. The first conference took place at the hill station of Dalat in Annam. It was presided over by the new French High Commissioner, Admiral Thierry d'Argenlieu,[65] whilst the DRV was represented, not by a Communist, but by the leader of the VNQDD, Nguyen Tuong Tam. No agreement was reached on any matter in dispute. A second conference was held at Fontainebleau, and this time the DRV rearranged its leadership in Hanoi under yet another 'transitory organization' called the Lien Viet or 'Vietnamese Alliance', to include selected Buddhists, Catholics, and others as a front for the Party element;[d] the DRV leader at Fontainebleau was the present Prime Minister, Pham Van Dong, but Ho Chi Minh was invited to Paris at the same time without taking part directly. At both conferences, apart from relatively minor issues like nationalization of the Tonkinese coal mines, the insuperable obstacles were French efforts to keep Cochinchina out of an independent Vietnam and insistence on the continued overriding authority of the all-Indochina administration, both of which were seen by the Vietminh as measures to deny full sovereignty to a Vietnamese national state and, no less, the right to establish a Communist regime in it. To make agreement more difficult, Admiral d'Argenlieu chose that moment to give way to the *colons* (and to Catholic and other southern autonomists) by proclaiming, entirely on his own authority—the extent of

[a] Le-thanh-Khoi, p. 467.   [b] Fall (1960), p. 47.
[c] Ibid. p. 49. Official accounts of the period compiled in later years to establish that the Party has never really deviated for a moment from the path of Marxism-Leninism, in spite of its decision to go underground, do not mention the National Assembly but only, vaguely, 'occasions for the people to realize universal suffrage' (Truong Chinh, p. 29).
[d] Devillers (1952), p. 272; Hammer, p. 199.

his powers as High Commissioner had never been laid down, it would appear[a]—a Provisional Republic of Cochinchina, with all essential powers reserved to himself. One of the demands of the Vietminh delegation at Fontainebleau was that a referendum should be held in Cochinchina on unification; the French refusal had been soundly argued—that prevailing terrorism precluded free choice until order was restored[b]—but the monk-Admiral's action suggested more sinister motives, to which he invited further attention when, immediately afterwards, he declared another 'autonomous republic' of the hill tribes of the PMS.

Preparations for war

Although the Fontainebleau Conference broke down, like its predecessor, because both sides believed they had time and superior reserve force on their own side, after it was over Ho Chi Minh of his own accord signed a *modus vivendi* with M. Georges Bidault—there had been another change of French Prime Ministers in the course of the Conference—which, besides prolonging the *status quo* on military and political questions, would permit resumption of French commercial enterprise in the North and, most important, collection by France of the customs duties which were the biggest item in the all-Indochina budget.[c] These were paid largely by French citizens, and the Vietminh had counted on collecting them to make good the revenue lost when local taxes, paid by the peasants, were giddily abolished some months earlier.[d] Ho Chi Minh's statesmanship was ill received in Tonkin, and the VNQDD, with the Japanese-sponsored Dai Viet, in league with gangs of bandits, tried to 'liberate' their own base areas along the Chinese frontier.[e] Vo Nguyen Giap's elimination of these pockets during the summer of 1946 was a rehearsal for the bigger tussle with the French army. This broke out finally in December. Repeated disputes over collection of customs, as well as French efforts to control the export of currency redeemable in francs by Chinese speculators[f] and of illicitly-mined coal[g]—both of which were sources of foreign exchange for the Vietminh—led to reinforcement of both sides' garrisons at Haiphong, until the French rashly bombarded the encroaching Vietminh positions on 23 November, wantonly killing as many as

---

[a] Originally a personal nominee of Gen. de Gaulle, he was in the peculiar position of not being answerable to the Minister of Colonies (Hammer, p. 189).
[b] Ibid. p. 199.   [c] Lancaster, p. 162.   [d] Fall (1963), p. 139.
[e] Devillers, pp. 275 & 311.   [f] Sainteny, p. 314.   [g] Célerier, p. 148.

6,000 people.[a] Tension rapidly rose amid skirmishing in many parts of the country as both sides prepared their positions for an inevitable general appeal to arms. The French, who had thus far refrained from reoccupying Annam with their military forces, landed troops at Tourane and Nha Trang. Bao Dai fled to Hong Kong, and after dark on 19 December 1946 the Vietminh attacked the French garrison at Hanoi, wounding the French Commissioner, Sainteny; in Annam they tried to lay waste the path in front of the contingents advancing from Tourane and Nha Trang (the 'scorched earth policy' of the Chinese Communists still believed in in those days) by setting fire to and gutting the main pavilions of the Dai Noi at Hué and completely destroying the township of Qui Nhon.[b]

'General uprising'

The Vietminh's decision to take to the hills and launch the open hostilities for which strenuous but not yet complete preparations had been in train was probably influenced by the failure of the Communist Party in France to obtain the majority hoped for at the first elections under the constitution for the Fourth Republic in November. This defeat put an end to expectations that the DRV would succeed to the control of Vietnam through constitutional recognition by a Communist Ministry in Paris; there was no longer any answer to the Leninist firebrands who insisted that there must be a 'general uprising'—that revolution must be violent or it would not be revolution.[c66] Further delay in the face of hardening intransigence on the part of France would have belied the claim to be moved by nationalist aims alone: Ho Chi Minh was already criticized for wanting power for its own sake,[d] even at the price of protracted subservience to France. There was, finally, the practical consideration that the later stages of the build-up of strength would be hampered by the continuing need for secrecy, but facilitated by a declaration of war and the justification which war brought with it for exacting maximum sacrifices from the masses.

---

[a] Sainteny, p. 216.

[b] Intent on wooing the Catholic hierarchy, the Communists spared the Cathedral and other ecclesiastical property at Qui Nhon.

[c] It may be debated whether the Chinese revolution entailed at any moment a 'general uprising' as envisaged by Lenin, but the Vietnamese Communists borrowed a Chinese phrase for it (*khoi nghia*) used historically in China for successful revolts that had brought to an end the anarchy of one dynasty in decline and themselves founded the next.

[d] Sainteny, p. 208; Célerier (p. 137) on the other hand inclined to the opinion that the publicized criticisms were part of an elaborate bluff.

4. THE DEMOCRATIC REPUBLIC OF VIETNAM

From now on, the Vietminh was both a Government and a revolutionary movement at the same time; it tried to be a kind of Government-in-exile in its own 'liberated zones', and a revolution in what came to be called the 'free zones' still under French control. Yet the agencies through which it worked, and their methods, were the same ones for the discharge of both these conflicting functions, and the DRV was ruled for eight or more years by machinery designed primarily for the disruption of government. This contradiction was made to work, at the cost of the ordinary duties of a government, by concentrating on mobilization of the masses and of every public and private resource, with no possibility of dissent, for prosecution of the war.[a] The reproach of the Trotskyites in 1932 that under these same leaders 'terrorist activity had taken precedence over proletarian organization, brigandage over the economic struggle of the workers'[b] became even truer now than when it was made.

Extent of the DRV

In the exercise of its powers as a Government, the DRV did not proclaim territories over which it had the right to rule, for in its own eyes it was rightful ruler of all Vietnam, even if it had no seat of government. Nevertheless, informal boundaries did establish themselves early between 'free' and 'liberated' zones for such purposes as the circulation of currency. The DRV, somewhat ill-advisedly, issued their own currency, on the example of the distinct currency zones of divided Germany and as a symbol of their status as a Government. After the Chinese Communists appeared on the frontier at the beginning of 1950, the garrison towns on the Tonkinese side were lost to France, as was the 'autonomous republic' of the Thai hill tribes; the latter had been set up hastily in 1948 in the same way as the 'autonomous republic' farther south, in the PMS, had been in 1946 in accordance with the French policy of weakening the Vietnamese by splitting off the strategically-placed hill tribes.[c] But apart from these particular transfers of territory, the zones remained stable right through the Indochina War.[67] The stability was, however, more apparent than real and was to be explained by the guerrilla nature of the fighting: the French military were able

[a] Truong Chinh (1966), pp. 139–45; Vo-nguyen-Giap (1961), p. 98.
[b] Sacks, in Trager (1960), p. 129.
[c] The move was also tied up with promotion of autonomous warlords and with the traffic in opium (see note 77).

to penetrate the Communist zones from time to time with their heavily armoured columns, while the Vietminh cadres and guerrillas had the run of the free zones, at least at night, to tax the peasantry and the middle classes—as they had done for so many years—, to subvert supposedly loyal officials, and to sabotage essential installations under the borrowed cachet of respectability that these things amounted to a continuation of wartime *résistance*.[a] In Annam the French held a 'free' zone between the 17th parallel and the 16th; the Vietminh to the south of it, though militarily unshakable, were beyond the reach of administrative control from Ho Chi Minh's limestone caves in Tonkin, and beyond Cape Varella again the Communists had no foothold at all. The Vietminh of Cochinchina, though subject to orders from the North in a general way, made little pretence of representing the DRV as a Government.

Central government

Within this disjointed area authority was nominally divided between two agencies. The officers of the mandarinate who had not been murdered in 1945 were all turned out of office and in the majority of cases escaped sooner or later to the 'free' zone. Their place was taken by Administrative Committees (*Uy Ban Hanh Chanh*), changed later to Resistance Committees (*Uy Ban Khang Chien*), answerable in theory to the political machinery of a ministerial executive and an elected legislature that were supposed to have taken the place of the Protectorate Governments and the all-Indochina departments of the prewar French administration. The hierarchy and the jurisdictions of these committees coincided with those of the territorial administration they replaced, but the old channels of communication had disappeared. The DRV legislature (the National Assembly supposed to have been elected in January 1946) met only twice during 1946, voted a parliamentary constitution (in which, however, all powers were vested in a Standing Committee, as in other Communist countries), and was thereafter defunct.[b 68] The Cabinet also existed primarily in order to convey the image of a Government recognizable as such abroad, and secondarily to provide the appearance of a political coalition for national unity; it had no administrative duties, and the members disposed of no ministerial machinery. The second agency sharing the DRV's

[a] Agent cells worked in the native forces under French command; on the surface they were exemplary soldiers (Lacheroy, 1957, p. 37).

[b] It is supposed to have met the next time in 1953 (Chesneaux, p. 301); but in fact no secretariat had existed in the meantime to keep touch with members.

authority was, of course, the Party, represented in the country as a whole by its cadres; these were distinguished from the personnel of the Committees (whom they nominated for formal election by the inhabitants)[a] by being outsiders to the region, whereas the members of the Committees were local people.

Local government

On the surface village government, always democratic in a sense, might seem to have been little affected by the revolution; down to about 1951 the village assembly was in many, though not all, localities still elected as under the French. But titles were made to conform to Communist patterns ('People's Assemblies'), the revolutionary upheaval had eliminated all traditional village elders (many of whom very properly had helped the French authorities identify their persecutors in the disturbances of 1930–2[b] and were therefore classed as 'traitors' in the 'Red Terror' of 1945) in favour of Vietminh nominees,[c] and management of village affairs had to be delegated to the Administrative (or Resistance) Committee at the basic echelon. The cadres had no formal authority even under the hastily-drafted 'Constitution' of 1945, but they were nevertheless the real Government. They mobilized all the inhabitants of town or village into vocational, age-grade, or similar associations; the associations purported to be voluntary and to promote spontaneous initiatives, but in practice the cadres assigned to them such tasks in support of the war effort as might be indicated by the higher echelons. Appropriate resolutions were then endorsed by acclamation at mass meetings 'under Party leadership'—the whole procedure making up the political principle known as 'democratic centralism'.[69] The combined body of these associations or 'masses organizations' constituted the Lien Viet, like the Corporate State of Fascist theory. The cadres had a monopoly of communications, and the Administrative Committees could act only under their direction and in conformity—and here the point was laid down by law[d]—with instructions received from the higher echelons.[70] Even technical subjects such as the administration of education were entrusted to them in the interests of the revolution, which meant the war effort. As time went on, the growing demands of the latter led to re-

[a] Ginsburgs (1962), p. 190. Elections for administrative office differed from those for the legislature by not being by universal suffrage but by electoral college, members of the lower Committees making up the college to elect the next higher Committee.
[b] Mus (1949), p. 265.   [c] Devillers (1952), p. 183.
[d] Decrees of 1948 and 1949 quoted by Fall (1960, p. 80).

placement even of bodies charged under the 1945 Constitution with judicial and regulatory functions by 'temporary organs' of a distinctly military colour.[a] When laws were said to have been passed— the constitutional legislature having been dispersed—such as the Civil Code of 1950, they appear to have been intended primarily as a more intimidating authority with which to override obstinate traditional resistance to the process of democratic centralism or to the Party's administrative policies.

The Party

That such resistance was a serious matter for the Government of the DRV is shown by the embarrassment expressed by the leadership over the standing of the cadres upon whom the whole apparatus depended. The cadres owed their position and authority to supposed membership of the ICP, but that, officially, had been dissolved.[b] As with the identity of President Ho Chi Minh, so with the identity of the Party: cadres had been instructed to let its continued existence be taken for granted behind the façade of the Lien Viet, but not to talk about it. Presumably, for practical purposes, the situation did not differ much from that prevailing under the 1938 Directive, when overt Communist activities were admitted to have been controlled by the secret wing of the Party.[c] The erasing of the name of the ICP had been necessitated by the switch from Marxism to nationalism as the Party's ideology; with this change went the emancipation—in theory, that is, for in practice there was little to emancipate—of the Cambodian and Laotian divisions of the Party as the nationalist Khmer Issarak and Lao Issara respectively.[71] But by 1951 the lack of an explicitly Party chain of command was sharply felt in the DRV—possibly, although this is not said expressly in the Directive, to balance the growing military predominance—whereas there was no longer cause to be quite so circumspect about Communist control. The Party decided 'to reappear officially' as the Vietnamese Workers' Party (VWP—Dang Lao Dong Viet Nam); it was explained that the name was a compromise to

[a] Ginsburgs, p. 195, quoting a Russian authority.
[b] The details in this paragraph are taken, where not otherwise stated, from a Party Directive issued in Mar. 1951. Understandably, the Party has never published it, although its central message has been admitted many times in later Communist books (e.g. Vo Nguyen Giap 1961, p. 35). Its existence is well known in South Vietnam and is mentioned in Fall (1956, p. 40), Brimmell (1959, p. 180), and Honey (1963, p. 22). Quotations here are from a translation made by the French authorities in Nov. 1951.
[c] p. 146 above.

satisfy convinced Marxists on one hand without, on the other, offering property owners who had been subscribing to the Vietminh as a
patriotic duty the excuse to break away that the name 'Communist
Party' would have given them. This possibility must have been quite
a real danger at the time, for cadres were authorized to admit, only
where it was 'safe' to do so, that the VWP was still the old ICP, that
it even retained right of supervision over the Issarak and the Issara,
and that when conditions were ripe it would change its name back
to Communist Party, true to its undeviating Marxist-Leninist 'line'.
It is probable that the convinced Marxists demanding satisfaction
on this last point were Chinese rather than Vietnamese: the Peoples'
Republic in China was two years old now, and, as the Vietnamese
conflict became polarized by the Cold War, Chinese logistical support was becoming a factor in it that could be neither refused nor
dispensed with; Chinese support entailed a less equivocal posture
over Marxism-Leninism than heretofore.

Law and terror

   The official reappearance of the Party in fact foreshadowed a
hardening of its line towards the masses all round. Although democratic centralism gave the appearance of voluntary conformity and
co-operation on the part of the people, the situation from now on
demanded obedience of the most rigid kind: acute shortages of food
had to be made good; a growing and unproductive military machine had to be equipped and maintained for an indefinite period;
and the proximity of the 'free' zones placed the 'liberated' zones
under the constant twin threats of penetration by French agents
and of escape by badly-needed workers, both of which dogged the
DRV down to 1954. However strongly developed the popular
nationalistic fervour enlisted in support of the DRV might have
been, it would at all times have been folly to rely on that alone, for
opinions could differ over the best course of action in pursuit of the
nationalist aim. Since the Marxist-Leninist line was for the DRV
leaders not just a method but an end in itself, fear was the soundest
of the possible bases for the security of the regime. As in Communist
China, whose experiences were quite explicitly studied and re-
enacted by the DRV after 1950, fear of the regime was kept up in
part by permanent security agencies, in part by periodical campaigns of terror. Long accustomed to being preyed on by secret
societies and bandits, and with the example of Communist ruthlessness during 1945 fresh in their minds, the Tonkinese might have

been expected to acquiesce totally in the demands of the cadres; yet the DRV maintained a fully-staffed *Cong An* or *Sûreté*, as well as a military body of Chinese inspiration, the *Trinh Sat* (literally 'reconnaissance'), which from time to time brought persons accused of so-called 'common-law' offences—for the most part hoarding, evading *corvée* or military service or forms of disobedience classifiable as sabotage—before either the military or the local civil courts. Both types of court were set up *ad hoc* and normally had three judges on the bench, of whom one would be a professional (that is to say, a cadre with some formal instruction in law but not necessarily very much) and two would be laymen—soldiers in the one case, simple villagers in the other.[a] If the laws were often in doubt in French times, such courts as these could not be expected to have more than the haziest grasp of them, whilst the means of carrying out the punishments laid down in the laws, such as imprisonment, were simply not available. The function of the courts was in any case not so much to apply the laws as to render harmless the 'enemies of the people'[b] and deter other potential 'dissidents'.[c]

The Land reform

The periodical campaigns of systematic terror, to ensure obedience and loyalty, followed the succession of ideas put into practice in China. As early as 1946 the Party itself is said to have practised 'struggle' in private, and after about 1950 'self-criticism' (*kiem thao*) was extended to the masses organizations to bring about 'thought reform'—that is to say, indoctrination to the point where the subject responds to circumstances as he knows the Party wishes without needing to be ordered.[d] In 1945 village murders of alleged traitors had been perpetrated out of hand as acts of vengeance; from 1951 onwards the purpose of terror became indoctrination in this sense, and victims were picked out by denunciation, more or less at random, according to their social standing, to be made examples of at people's trials.[e] (Actual misdemeanours continued to fall within the jurisdiction of regular courts.) But the greatest of the terror campaigns in the DRV did not begin until 1953—not, that is, until the decisive phase of the fighting against France, after the advent of Chinese advisers in large numbers and after the effects of similar campaigns in China (the Five Antis, the Three Antis, the Land Re-

[a] Fall (1960), p. 97.   [b] Circular instruction quoted by Fall (1960, p. 98).
[c] Educated Vietnamese on both sides continued to classify one another in the wartime French categories of *résistants* and *dissidents*.
[d] Hoang-van-Chi, p. 118.   [e] Ibid. p. 101.

form, the Thought Reform) had taught their sinister lessons. The tale of these campaigns in China has been told often; they were aimed at purging from all ranks of society individuals whose livelihood might give rise to some interest that was in conflict with the regime and the Party line, and they taught the rest of the populace to make sure they too never 'deviated'. In the DRV the intention seems to have been less the elimination of any particular class of people than eradication from everybody's mind, without distinction of class, of any desire to own private property or to pursue any private purpose. On the face of it, the campaign was a land reform. The need for this had been urged so often in Communist propaganda in China that many well-disposed foreigners had been misled into interpreting it as the chief or sole purpose of the Vietminh uprising; in reality, land reform had not been a slogan of either ICP or Vietminh—a fact Truong Chinh condemned as an error.[a] Land reform was one of the subjects invested with the legislative sanction of various empowering decrees from 1949 onwards whose effect would be to reduce rents, cancel indebtedness, and redistribute large estates; landlords subscribing to the Vietminh were not affected at first.[b] As was to be expected from the severe penury of administrative resources, added to the systematic destruction of records of land tenure during the previous decade, these decrees remained virtually a dead letter;[c] moreover, big holdings, which they were designed to split up, were extremely rare in Tonkin anyway.

Early in 1953, land reform was transferred to the extra-legal scope of a 'struggle' campaign of great violence. Cadres—many of them soldiers out of uniform[d]—were sent to classify the population district by district, ostensibly into social categories, but actually according to their possessions; information was obtained by exploiting petty jealousies and other 'internal contradictions' within the village and quickly developed, like the Five Antis, into a persecution of alleged tax-evaders. Thence to denunciations of landowners was an easy step in villages where almost everybody owned a small plot and one could buy his safety by denouncing another. People's courts, set up by the visiting teams of cadres and conducted with similar cowardly hysteria to those of China, demanded quotas of denunciations by the villagers and ordered on-the-spot destruction of property and 'execution' of the owners by various unjudicial

---

[a] Truong Chinh (1962) (written originally in 1946), p. 23.
[b] Quotation in Fall (1960), p. 266.
[c] Vo-nhan-Tri (1960), p. 358.   [d] Fall (1966), p. 97.

barbarities: besides tens of thousands who lost their lives,[a] many more were made outcasts from their village communities. Although, after the end of the period covered by this chapter, the DRV had, as a direct consequence, to put down an insurrection against itself in Northern Annam in 1956, while many others of the victims have individually become its implacable enemies in South Vietnam, these drawbacks were a small price to pay for the psychological achievements of the campaign. The Government, not officially answerable for Party cadres or the 'spontaneous struggle' of the indoctrinated masses, was able to switch the terror off suddenly[72] and instantly earn the gratitude of all who felt they were up to then still in jeopardy. Taking its line from the 'destalinization' in Russia which followed the Polish and Hungarian uprisings, and also from the 'Rectification' in China, the DRV Government 'freely confessed' the gravity of the 'mistakes' made;[b] but the issue remained a Party one, and no judicial action was taken, or restitution made; reprisals taken by a few undaunted spirits among the victims similarly went unpunished.[c] The psychological shock to the community was effective for more than a decade, and obedience to the Party became established in far corners of the country where previously no *chi-bo* cells had yet taken root.[d] In China, on the other hand, the taps of 'struggle' have had to be turned on again several times during the same period of time.

Masses mobilization

This manipulation of fear as a disincentive to ownership of property or to the pursuit of individual inclinations is the key to the 'masses mobilization' by which the Vietminh transferred its centre of gravity from outside the country into the village communities and made sure of a system of logistical support for its guerrilla warfare that would be immune to French interception; those who were mobilized were told the services they provided were an extension of wartime 'resistance'. Service with the regular fighting forces was, paradoxically, not the most important; although compulsory military service was written into the 1946 constitution of the DRV,[e] mobilization was a revolutionary activity of the cadres, not a docu-

---

[a] Hoang-van-Chi (p. 166) gives the figure as 100,000; in the total absence of public records from the DRV (Le Chau, p. 150), guesses by eyewitnesses who later escaped from the DRV are the only source of information.

[b] *Nhan Dan* (31 Aug. 1957) admitted that 30 per cent of persons liquidated as landowners did not own any land.

[c] Le Chau, pp. 141–150.   [d] Ibid. p. 137.   [e] Fall (1960), p. 52.

mented administrative procedure. Moreover, a substantial proportion of the 300,000 strength eventually attained[a] was recruited from the 'free' zone. The most important support services required for the fighting were food production—to offset French control of nearly all the cultivated plains—and manual labour for transport in the absence of motor vehicles. Men engaged on these tasks, which could be made to sound like traditional *corvée*, were at the same time given military training for local guerrilla operations; in the later stages, losses among the regular forces were made good largely by promotion from this militia (the *Tu Ve*)[b]—often, perhaps a welcome release from drudgery. It was essential that all of what Marx would have called the population's surplus value should be available for the revolutionary war effort; the assessments of what that surplus amounted to were, once more, not an administrative function but one for the cadres playing one peasant off to inform on, or accuse, his neighbours.[c]

Tactics and morale

The rank and file of the Liberation Army were recruited in the main by conscription, therefore, if only through the informal procedures of masses mobilization and 'volunteering' after indoctrination in a body.[d] In a country where traditionally no disgrace attached to desertion, the maintenance of loyalty might have proved very difficult. One reason why it did not was the problem that faced any deserter of finding sanctuary; the French military authorities had no adequate organization for psychological warfare or reception of surrendered personnel, whereas the long arm of the Party reached into every corner of the country and would not hesitate to take reprisals against the families of 'traitors'. But the principal binding force within all the Vietminh's fighting units was the high morale generated by actual guerrilla tactics: strict observance of the military doctrine of never engaging the enemy save with the advantages of surprise, speed, and immediately-overwhelming strength was a tremendous source of confidence among the men and of trust in their commanders. It was an easy doctrine for an Asian peasant army, with neither defence commitments nor complicated logistical requirements, to apply against an enemy weighed down with both. Former officers of the Liberation Army who have since

[a] Tanham (1962), p. 56.   [b] Truong Chinh (1966), p. 41.
[c] Hoang-van-Chi, p. 77.
[d] Informal, for example, in such respects as that the recruit did not undergo any preliminary medical examination.

broken with the Communists still speak with pride of the 'Tagorism' (though not by that name) and 'self-reliance' which, taught by the Vietminh leadership, was such a large ingredient in their patriotic opposition to the *Corps Expéditionnaire*; their tales of guerrilla exploits echo the accounts of Captain Gosselin, of Le Loi, and of the *Romance of the Three Kingdoms*.[a] It is significant that the one period when the Vietminh had to contend with numerous defections was the aftermath of a nearly disastrous attempt by Vo Nguyen Giap, in the first half of 1951, to cut the corners, in mistaken imitation of Mao Tsê-tung finishing off the armies of Chiang Kai-shek. Other psychological influences were in play at the time, but the dominant consideration for the defectors was certainly a decline in their faith that (in Truong Chinh's words) the 'Resistance would win'.

Arms and supplies

The Vietminh had obtained its first weapons and equipment from the KMT army in China, from the other Allies, and—by far the biggest quantity—from the Japanese. As the war spread and intensified, the DRV had to count on three sources: local improvisation, capture or theft from their adversaries, and purchase abroad.[b] Since the DRV still keeps its oldest secrets and its transactions went unrecorded, it is never likely to be possible to speak of these sources except in general terms. Purchase abroad depended on supplies of cash, and although at the beginning gun-running from Siam, where there was a big and previously penetrated Vietnamese community, was fairly dependable, this source dried up after the overthrow of the Pridi Phanomyong Government, tolerant of Communist activity, in 1948.[c] Capture on the battlefield seems to have yielded fewer weapons to the Vietminh than it did later to the Vietcong, but the French command was unable to stop entirely the drain from their armouries organized by the cadres active behind their lines. Improvisation, helped by a number of escaped Japanese prisoners of war[d] (like Pu Kombo's Tagals) and of French Foreign Legion deserters,[e] was probably the main source of small-arms ammuni-

[a] pp. 119, 41 & 49 above. Le Loi was compulsory reading for Vietminh officers, according to Truong Chinh (1966, p. 128).

[b] Tanham (1962), p. 67.

[c] Brimmell, p. 242. It was doubtless this setback that prompted Gen. Giap's complaint that 'importation was impossible, the neighbouring countries being hostile to the DRV' (Vo-nguyen-Giap, 1961, p. 52); taken literally, this sentence is undoubtedly a prevarication. Pridi Phanomyong later went to live in Communist China.

[d] Tanham, p. 69.

[e] Several of them, possibly Communists infiltrated deliberately from Europe, subsequently published memoirs of their experiences.

tion, medical supplies, and the one indispensable item of technical equipment, radio sets. However, the gradual mechanization and improved fire power of the French forces from 1951 onwards (the first year of American aid), whilst increasing the scope for Vietminh parasitism, would probably have tipped the scales against the Communist forces if the Central People's Government had not come to the rescue. Something like 40,000 DRV soldiers received training in China,[a] while instructors and technicians were sent both to base areas and to accompany regular units of the Vietminh forces in the field.[73] Chinese artillerymen took part in the final battle of Dien Bien Phu in 1954 as combatants.[b] The quantity of supplies received from China rose from under 20 tons a month in 1951 to 4,000 by the end of the war.[c] It was in the road building and porterage for these supplies, which meant supporting each Vietminh division of 10,000 combatants with an army of 40,000 coolies,[d] that the real achievement of the DRV regime in the way of masses mobilization stood revealed.

Popular support

It is not easy to judge whether the Communists may have had some justification for claiming to the outside world that the vastly laborious effort they demanded of the Tonkinese masses during the Indochina War was undertaken all the same by willing hands. The inner core of cadres, who explicitly thought of themselves as Communists and members of the Party, were the students and trade unionists recruited in the 1930s. 'Bead-stringing' made easy progress in the confusion of the last phases of the war, when the Party was alone in having a programme and its 'armed propagandists' the ruthlessness to put it into effect; no authority was left to protect anybody inclined to argue. Small numbers of volunteers continued to join the Vietminh from Annam and Cochinchina after 1945, out of enthusiasm, adventure, or unemployment; but once a semblance of order had returned to the towns, the University of Hanoi had reopened (in 1947), and recruitment to the public services had resumed, the flow of volunteers dried up, and those already in, like the civil servants of the Tonkin mandarinate, fled to the free zone when opportunities arose. Comintern doctrine had in any case long been 'against creating a single national revolutionary party based

[a] Tanham, p. 63. The officer-training 'academy' in China was nominally under a Vietnamese General, but the instructors were Chinese (Nguyen-phut-Tan, p. 590.)
[b] O'Ballance (1964), p. 218 (and other writers).   [c] Ibid. p. 69.
[d] Tanham (1962), p. 71.

upon individual adherents', and the Party preferred 'co-operation' with pre-existing organizations it could lean upon and guide.[a] Although in 1945 the Party declared uncompromising war on the Dai Viet and decimated its clandestine affiliates in the villages, it did by contrast, through the Vietminh alliance, win groups of VNQDD cadres and retain them down to the end of the fighting—a few for good—even though the original alliance had ended upon the outbreak of hostilities. The Catholics, who as a body also supported the Vietminh from August 1945, were slower than the VNQDD to break with it, and when Bao Dai fled to Hong Kong his place as so-called Supreme Counsellor to the DRV was taken by the senior bishop.[b] Catholics remembered past persecutions for collaboration with France, and alien rule, whether it offended their patriotism or was a matter of indifference to them, must some day come to an end; the Church broke with the DRV when the conflict began to take on its Cold War aspect and, because Bao Dai had come back, an alternative native regime was available as a focus of loyalty, buttressed during 1951 by the short-lived military successes of General de Lattre de Tassigny. But for the peasant masses in the villages, who were hardly less vulnerable in the 'free' than in the 'liberated' zone, it was not even a question of weighing up which side was going to win in the end: the People's Army could not afford to leave its essential supplies, its intelligence, or its security to personal choice. All possibility of dissent or half-heartedness was therefore ruled out in the 'liberated' zone by the administrative machinery described in the previous paragraph and in the 'free' zone by the *dich van* and their 'armed propaganda'.

5. THE STRUGGLE IN THE SOUTH

Despite the constant insistence of the DRV leadership at the Conferences at Dalat and Fontainebleau that Cochinchina must be incorporated into an independent Vietnam under their control, its isolation from the main territory imposed limitations on Vietminh operations there. Not only was it beyond the reach of supplies from China, but although the leaders possessed an excellent radio network,[c] the conduct of the fighting could not be directed from what in reality was an ever-shifting hide-out in the north of Tonkin, even if this did give itself out to be the capital of the DRV. Whereas the

---

[a] *Pravda*, 17 Oct. 1928, quoted in Fall (1956), p. 40.   [b] Hammer, p. 276.
[c] Devillers (1953), p. 206.

Communists were strongest near to China, the French were stronger near the port of Saigon; politically also the status of Cochinchina as French sovereign territory still counted for something among local educated Vietnamese, reinforcing regional sentiment—or at least regional apathy towards the fate and aspirations of Tonkin. The task assigned to the Communist organization in the South was therefore unspectacularly to second the main effort to 'liberate' Tonkin; this was to be done both negatively, by causing diversionary mischief for the French in the political, economic, and military, spheres, and positively, by milking the human and material resources of the richer South to contribute secretly to the sustenance of the North—taxing the 'white' areas to pay for administration of the 'red'.[a] In the end it was the circumstances and course of events in the South that led to the refinement of the techniques of revolutionary warfare from the principles of Leninism, through the intermediate stage elaborated by Mao Tsê-tung, which Truong Chinh the theoretician and Vo Nguyen Giap the commander put into practice in Tonkin, into the characteristically Vietnamese form described later in this book that they have taken on since 1960.

Nguyen Binh

After removing the prewar Stalinist leader Tran Van Giau, Ho Chi Minh appointed in his place a China-trained Tonkinese called Nguyen Binh[b]—a seaman recruited first by the VNQDD and later 'turned' by the Communists while in prison for his part in the Yen Bay uprising.[c] A nucleus of cadres forming the inner core of the organization were Tonkinese like himself, drawn from the rubber estates, and round them had been gathered other bands of tappers when the detention of estate managers by the Japanese in March 1945 threw them out of work. Some of these groups procured firearms from the surrendering Japanese a few months later.[d] Nguyen Binh inherited the uneasy alliance with the Cao Dai, Hoa Hao, and Binh Xuyen which had resulted from the so-called United National Front; all through 1946 he kept up relations with them. Simultaneously he was building up the previous base in the swamps of the Plain of Reeds, northwest of Saigon, and extending also the areas in

---

[a] What in China, before the Long March, Chiang Kai-shek's blockade had prevented Mao Tse-tung from bringing off (Ch'ên 1965, p. 179).

[b] Like 'Truong Chinh', this is a nickname (*Nguyen* is in a different tone from the similar family name); it means 'The Plains' and may perhaps be the name of the man's birthplace. Giau had been known in the Party as 'Ha Nam' (Chinese *Ho Nan*).

[c] Lancaster, p. 139; Chesneaux, p. 252.   [d] Gourou (1947), p. 26.

which the 'armed propaganda' and 'phantom attacks' (the phrases are General Giap's) of his cadres made conditions in the villages so frightening for the militia garrisons that they withdrew to the towns, closely followed as a rule by the village notables. The place of the withdrawing authorities was then taken by new village committees, under the control of Communist cells, whose duties were not the continuation of village administration but the prevention of the re-establishment of Government authority and the extension of Communist domination to neighbouring villages. Already at this early date, it is said, the followers of Nguyen Binh were borrowing the metaphor of Maréchal Lyautey about 'the oil-spot pattern of pacification'. The process was slow and held out little promise of a consolidated zone of the sort that had been consolidated in Tonkin; it was still thought in Communist circles, on the example of the Yenan Border Region in China, that such a base was necessary before terms could be dictated to the French. Although Communist domination of the Plain of Reeds and of the Camau peninsula was fairly complete, there was little prospect of linking these across the territory of the Hoa Hao, while other promising areas, like Kien Hoa, in the mouths of the Delta, were disputed with the Cao Dai.

The Sects

The two Sects, though less certain than the Communists about their ultimate aims, had been working along similar lines to take advantage of the period of confusion, and a mob of Hoa Hao, several thousand strong, fortified with *bua gong* and out for trouble, had once come to blows with armed bands of the Vietminh at Can Tho and lost several hundred dead or wounded.[a] But by the time the fighting broke out in Tonkin in December 1946, the Hoa Hao disposed of a standing armed militia of about 1,000[b] among a following (some voluntary, many coerced) of several hundred thousand; it was in a position to 'protect' and tax the big riceland concessions in the Mien Tay, as well as the entire marketing of the paddy as it passed along the waterways or crossed the ferries leading to Saigon. The fact that the trade was in the hands of a small number of Chinese merchants made the extortion of dues all the easier. The Cao Dai militia was more numerous than the Hoa Hao, and its total following well over the million mark;[c] but the domain it controlled was situated in the 'old' provinces of Cochinchina, less susceptible to direct financial exploitation. The two Sects concluded a sort of

a Savani 1953, p. 103.   b Nguyen-van-Tam, p. 64.   c Ibid. p. 57.

non-aggression and non-encroachment pact in January 1947;[a] the Hoa Hao, feeling the need to count at least some intellectuals among its leaders, took up with a group of Saigon professional men calling themselves the Social Democratic Party (*Dan Chu Xa Hoi Dang*),[b] and who were in search of manpower to draw on—a situation reminiscent of the insurrection in 1916. Within Saigon itself, the Binh Xuyen, hankering after plunder rather than power, had battened on the Chinese community and the profits from the wholesale trade it controlled, which promised profits from postwar reconstruction. The Vietminh's allies were therefore becoming rivals: if they continued to wax at the same rate, they would threaten the pre-eminence of the DRV; on the other hand if they could be captured, they might add decisively to the political power and the financial resources of the Vietminh. Nguyen Binh laid a series of traps to get the Sect leaders into his power and impose on them individually terms for stricter collaboration in the future.[c] Huynh Phu So of Hoa Hao was the first to be enticed into the Plain of Reeds, but somehow he was done to death, although his body was never recovered.[d] Le Van Vien was next to receive an invitation as head of the Binh Xuyen, but he was on his guard and retired for the moment to his own fastnesses.[74] The Cao Dai Pope could not be got at because he was still interned in the Comoro Islands, but his museum-director deputy, Tran Quang Vinh, was ambushed by the Communists; what his fate might have been is not known, for he escaped again, but he and his followers believed Nguyen Binh's true intention was to kill him too.[e]

Anarchy of the Sects

Treachery and butchery, unaccompanied by supporting measures or further plans, were in the tradition of Yen Bay and, by hardening opposition to the Vietminh, proved as complete a fiasco. Ho Chi Minh eventually dismissed Nguyen Binh in his turn, and he died in 1951 in an ambush set by the French security forces, many have suspected, on information laid by emissaries from Party headquarters. Huynh Phu So became an object of deeper veneration in

---

[a] Ibid. p. 58.

[b] A name that may possibly contain a hint of Japanese associations.

[c] The Communist plot was an echo of the capture of Chiang Kai-shek at Sian in 1936 by which Mao Tsê-tung had, through an intermediary warlord, procured the suspension of KMT hostilities against the Chinese Communists.

[d] Leroy (1955), p. 127; it could be So's own followers who concealed the corpse, in order to foster the Barbarossa-like legend current ever since.

[e] Savani, p. 91.

death than in life, and his surviving lieutenants made common cause
immediately (in May 1947) with the French authorities against the
Vietminh, to be followed by the Binh Xuyen and the Cao Dai. Of
the three, however, only the Binh Xuyen remained united, helped
no doubt by the fact that it never tried to enlarge its domain. Both
Hoa Hao and Cao Dai split into rival factions—in the case of the
Cao Dai, if not so certainly in that of the Hoa Hao, along the lines of
its constituent secret societies. A dozen 'dissident' sub-sects emerged
and although they were ready to co-operate in this or that political
or military enterprise over the next few years, they did not accept
a central discipline any more, and each continued to consolidate its
following in its own area, until the movement reached a stable
membership of a million and a half.[a] The Hoa Hao split into three;
little secret is any longer made that their schism was not doctrinal
but over division of the spoils. Tran Van Soai's personality—ably
supported by his fearsome wife who acted as treasurer and commanded an armed women's contingent[b]—kept him in the forefront,
but unity of action only returned to the Sect after independence,
when the scope for racketeering narrowed again. Although the
Vietminh attempts to capture the Sects intact had failed, they continued their efforts in two other directions: subversion of subordinate leaders and penetration of the areas controlled by leaders who
refused to co-operate. The first policy earned them the adherence
of one each of the dissident sub-sects of the Cao Dai[c] and the Hoa
Hao (the former drawing support from the rubber estates, the latter
based on Thot Not in the Mien Tay and the French-managed agricultural concessions of that locality), and this solidarity is the more
remarkable for its having lasted down to the present day. The extent
of the Communists' success in secretly milking the dominions of the
Sects is no longer ascertainable, but it certainly increased as the
fighting in the North developed in their favour. The very existence
of the Sects, and the *de facto* autonomy of their 'administrations',
helped the Vietminh cause by undermining respect for government,
perpetuating the wartime confusion of authority, and creating
fresh opportunities in the general anarchy for corruption, 'protection', and smuggling.

[a] Savani, p. 97.
[b] Lancaster, p. 183. This lady's reputation for unfeminine ferocity was not unique;
Vietnamese women generally have had a bigger hand in their country's violent history
than have Chinese women.
[c] The Communist Cao Dai called themselves the 'Eleven Unified Sects', but that was a
hope rather than a fact.

Vietminh exploitation

From 1947 until the Geneva Agreement, the main effort of the
Vietminh in the South was directed to the maintenance of this state
of anarchy and to its exploitation for supplies of arms, food, and
above all piastres to send to the DRV. The ingenuity and the integration which were displayed in the course of their operations were
astonishing. In the earlier years, action tended to be straightforward: to obtain arms, garrison posts of the security forces were
stormed head-on by 'human waves', after little tactical preparation
and with horrible consequences for the assault party. To obtain
foreign exchange, peasants were rounded up, according to one
authority,[a] and transplanted to an agricultural settlement on the
sparsely-populated fringes of the Camau swamps; the rice surplus
they harvested was shipped to Bangkok and traded by Vietnamese
merchants there, until the traffic was stopped after 1948,[b] for arms
to be sent direct to Tonkin through Laos.[c] But soon the direction of
Vietminh military activity became subtler and shifted towards
sabotage and harassment of French forces in such a way as to encourage reinforcement and new schemes of pacification; small-
scale ambushes designed to capture rifles became common, while
public-works contractors, estate managers, transport companies,
and all who had to operate in isolated places were invited, and even
helped, to carry on in exchange for a percentage of their resources in
kind or money, for which regular receipts were issued.[d] Anybody so
foolhardy as to refuse what amounted in most cases to a modest demand, unlikely in itself to make much difference, was certain to be
knifed sooner or later by the cadres of the *ban dac-cong*—the 'Special
Service Teams'. 'Bonds' bearing a portrait of Ho Chi Minh were
sold by the cadres like lottery tickets and bought by people who
could afford them as a kind of insurance policy. Direct theft offered
its contribution, as did blackmail of officials and merchants corrupted by the scope for bribery and profiteering beginning to be
opened up by the slackness within government departments. The
rubber boom which followed from the Korean War, and was
handled in Malaya as a weapon against the Communist insurgents
there, turned in Cochinchina to their advantage as offering a much
higher yield from 'taxes' on labour, supplies and contracts.[e] The
proceeds of these transactions were negotiated through Chinese
finance houses in Saigon (under pressure to double-insure against

[a] Bodard (1963), p. 158.   [b] p. 176 above.   [c] Despuech (1953), p. 132.
[d] Bodard, p. 184.   [e] Despuech, p. 135.

Cold War contingencies) for credits in Paris, Hong Kong, or elsewhere on behalf of nominees of the DRV, who used them for arms
smuggling or to back their otherwise worthless internal currency.[a]
The remittances were made possible by French toleration of the
abuse of exchange dealings, almost uncontrolled, as an incentive
for their own forces to volunteer for service in Indochina, and
for the wealthy Cochinchinese to support the war effort on their
side.[75]

6. FRENCH STRATEGY AGAINST THE GUERRILLAS

In the Indochina War the strategy was mainly on one side and the
tactics mainly on the other. The initiative in taking up arms lay
with the Vietminh, and yet they never acquired, and never expected
to acquire, the military means to crush their enemy: they counted
on so exploiting his resources and his weaknesses (especially political
ones) that he would lose heart and give up—if not his soldiers, then
his public at home. 'Time', says Truong Chinh, 'is our best strategist.'[b] The arts of the guerrilla are practised locally, immediately,
and swiftly; they are essentially tactical. By contrast, in combating
the Vietminh, as had become notorious, the heavily-equipped
French forces had in their drill-book too little tactical lore and were
worsted over and over on that account. But the French Generals
had clearer military objectives than their critics have given them
credit for, and a strategy for attaining them—one that remained
essentially unchanged all through the war. This was to bring the
main forces of Vo Nguyen Giap (his *chu luc*) to battle in circumstances that would expose them to the superior weaponry of the
French army, and thereby destroy their military potential. This
would oblige the DRV to seek negotiations for a political settlement
of the future of Vietnam in which France would retain, for the sake
of her prestige, some part of her former standing. Since General
Giap's main forces were concentrated in Tonkin, the principal
battlegrounds must be sought there and the Vietminh prevented
from spreading west into Laos or south into highland Annam. At
the same time the Tonkinese Delta was to be protected against
sneak attacks in the hope that life would return to normal after the
famine and violence of the end of the Second World War and bring
a state of 'pacification' in its wake. The strategy for Annam amounted to no more than holding on to Hué, Tourane, and also the high-

[a] Despuech, pp. 131 & 139.   [b] Truong Chinh, p. 112.

lands and coast south of Cape Varella. In Cochinchina there was no major military threat, and no operations by big formations were called for; but pacification involved the preservation of law and order by whatever forces could be spared from the North.

French deployment

The seven years of fighting witnessed half a dozen changes in the French Commander-in-Chief and a considerable expansion, and turnover, of the *Corps Expéditionnaire*; its ultimate strength was about 190,000.[a] The development of the bulk of this force in Tonkin was in two parts: the smaller was used, according to the intended strategy, to man a ring of forts and seal off the periphery of the Delta, which coincided with the informal frontier between DRV and 'free' administrations. The Vietminh would be cut off, by what came in the end to be known as the 'De Lattre Line',[b] from their sources of supply in the Delta villages, would have to fight for their food, and so would present a target for the main French force, held in readiness to strike as soon as the Vietminh appeared in concentration. Down to 1950, before the Chinese Communists reached the Tonkinese frontier, the intended strike forces (the *groupes mobiles*) were fully occupied in convoying supplies through the 'liberated' zone to the fortress towns on the border—often sustaining considerable losses in men and weapons on the way. By the time this drain was stemmed by withdrawal from the fortresses, however, the terrorist domination by the Vietminh of the Delta redoubt had gone so far that they were able to extort all the supplies they could use. Their guerrillas, far from being brought to battle, were able to sabotage communications and installations on such a scale that almost the entire French strike force was put on the defensive.[c] During the years 1950 to 1952, influenced by the outbreak of the Korean War, both sides in turn attempted to take a more conventional offensive, but each time to the advantage in the end of their adversaries. By 1953 it was estimated that there were 35,000 Vietminh guerrillas permanently within the Delta perimeter, tying down 100,000 of the defence forces[d]—and the best trained of the defence forces at that, because unskilled men could not handle the sophisticated equipment given them in order that they should lack no ad-

[a] Navarre, p. 46 n. 3.
[b] After the most celebrated of the French Generals in Indochina, and the most successful, Jean de Lattre de Tassigny; he died prematurely of an incurable illness, never to be replaced adequately.
[c] Navarre, p. 22.　　[d] Tanham (1962), p. 102.

vantage.[a] Yet no pitched battles took place, and the equilibrium might have been prolonged indefinitely.

Pacification in Tonkin

Superficially, this equilibrium gave the impression that normal conditions had returned to the Delta in fulfilment of French hopes; it was 'pacification' that was slow to follow. Repairs to irrigation works, normalization of inland trade, speeding of deliveries of rice and other commodities from the South, and restoring the technical services of government were all pushed ahead by the French administration. Everything was done that could be to make life more attractive in the 'free' zone than in the 'liberated' zone and thereby to dissuade peasants and townfolk from working for the Vietminh. After some time special villages, picturesquely called *agrovilles*, were built on the perimeter and equipped with quasi-urban amenities calculated to attract peasants away from the hardships and fear prevailing in the 'free' zone. This policy was called 'pacification by prosperity' and owed much to Galliéni and Lyautey; the financing of it was also one of the earliest objects of American aid to France after the outbreak of the Korean War.[b] It met with some success in attracting peasant settlers, thanks mainly to the scope for smuggling and spying it afforded between the two zones, but it could never be decisive because the settlers continued to feel insecure—a feeling which the numerous French guard posts along the perimeter could do little to dispel so long as the 'Special Service Teams' operated at night, anonymously, and held all village authorities in the same state of dread as ever.

Garrisoning Cochinchina

In Cochinchina there was no definite perimeter and no 'free' zone beyond, so that all military activity there was directed towards 'pacification'. No engagements of more than company strength on the Vietminh side were fought in the South. Here the concept of the perimeter line was given a second dimension to form a whole grid of garrison posts, varying in strength from battalions in big towns down to one-man watchtowers to fill in the gaps between platoons, placed within visual and hailing distance of one another.[c] Readers of Mr Graham Greene will know what befell the luckless

[a] Navarre, p. 146.
[b] About US $200,000 appear to have been spent on the 'show' *agroville* at Dong Quan (private Vietnamese source).
[c] The author of this plan was called appropriately Gen. de Latour.

wardens of those outposts; the smaller ones, far from helping re-store law and order, could maintain their daunting vigil only by negotiating their own particular *modus vivendi* with those whose comings and goings they were there to intercept. Bigger posts fared better but, usually commanded by French senior n.c.o.s with no local background and manned by Vietnamese gendarmes or militia, they were exposed to every kind of treachery.[a] They too endured in vain the terrors of surprise attack, besides the unending barrage of taunting propaganda, for, on balance, their presence con-tributed more to the logistical supplies of the Vietminh than to the restoration of law and order: they had neither legal powers nor pro-cedure to rely on, and when the villagers did put them on the trail of some alleged miscreant, the chances were that the Communists were themselves authors of the information, and the victim—of whom the post commander had no means of disposing unless by having him shot out of hand—an enemy of theirs. Needless to say, the presence of the grid offered little hindrance to the tax-gathering which was the principal aim of the Vietminh. This strategy, as one French military writer has put it, failed to focus the defence on the proper target, the guerrilla himself, but instead focused it on the guerrilla's targets, namely the defence's own strongpoints.[b] He might have added that the defensive posture reflected the dilemma of all armies charged with the restoration of order on their own and not in support of a civilian authority with reliable local intelligence at its disposal; it has proved one of the enduring features of the Vietnamese conflict.

Sects as warlords

However, the difficulty which impressed itself most on General Latour's mind was that he had not enough forces to man his grid. The quarrel between Nguyen Binh and the Binh Xuyen and the Sects offered the General a chance to swing to the side of the authori-ties a large area for whose pacification he was responsible, to-gether with not negligible armed manpower, if ill-trained and un-disciplined. The incongruity of the ruffians who had enlisted in these bands being employed as agents of the law paled before the promise of their loyalty born of supposed hatred of the common foe.[76] The Cao Dai were the first to 'rally to the national cause', by a pact con-

[a] The life of the wretched n.c.o.s has been eloquently chronicled by Bodard (1963, *passim*).
[b] Trinquier (1964), p. 55.

cluded in January 1947. Their loyalty was cemented by the grant of
political office when the 'Pope', newly brought back from his wartime internment, was able to nominate his 'political adviser', Dr
Le Van Hoach, to become 'Chief Minister' in Saigon,[a] and Latour
underwrote in cash the support costs of 1,500 Cao Dai fighting
men;[b] the Sect was tacitly granted a monopoly of all administrative offices within its territorial domain. The Hoa Hao were netted
within a fortnight of the assassination of the Mad Bonze; their rewards for loyalty included a completely free hand to levy transit
dues on canals and roads, the payment and re-equipping by the
French military authorities of 2,000 men, and the recognition of
their administrative machinery in parts of the Mien Tay as the
Government authority there.[c] The rewards thus seen to crown
loyalty so promptly brought one of the dissident branches of the
Hoa Hao into the fold in 1948, but some of *its* component leaders
insisted on making their own deals direct with the French; one of
them, celebrated some years later under the nickname 'Ba Cut', re-
asserted his loyalty (against payment on the nail) on five occasions,
defecting again each time in between.[d] The opportunity to manifest
their loyalty to the best advantage of all was reserved ultimately for
the Binh Xuyen, but for the moment they declared against the
Vietminh in exchange for recognition by the authorities of their
illegal bodyguards and armed bands and for a free hand to organize
gambling and vice in the capital, catering especially for the French
troops.

Other private armies

In order to complete the process of what has with justification
been called feudalization in the countryside of Cochinchina,
potential *condottieri* were encouraged (with unaccountable public
funds) to create private armies *ad hoc*. The best known among these
swashbucklers was a Eurasian, 'Colonel' Jean Leroy, who was given
arms and a free hand by the French High Command (in the conviction that its authority prevailed by both right and reason over
that of the Vietnamese civil administration now in charge of Saigon,
which disapproved of Leroy), to organize a Catholic militia in the
Kien Hoa province on the basis of self-accounting collections of
revenue and administrative disbursements. So successful were the
'Colonel's' shoot-at-sight procedures in reducing Vietminh inci-

---

[a] Lancaster, p. 182.   [b] Savani, p. 92.   [c] Ibid. p. 105.
[d] Bodard (1963), p. 150.

dents that he was soon allotted the adjacent provinces to pacify, but there he ultimately fell from grace.[77] The fashion for private armies was allowed to spread, until every Province Chief was running his own militia from a vast, unaudited 'goat-bag', and the protection of rubber estates and agricultural concessions was entrusted to anybody prepared to provide suitable 'arrangements', with few questions asked.

Private armies in Tonkin

In Tonkin as well warlordism was given official recognition in the Thai highlands on the far side of the territory of the DRV;[78] the Dai Viet Party was allowed a free hand in almost any locality of which it could gain control,[a] on condition there were no Vietminh incidents in it. The two Catholic dioceses, Phat Diem and Bui Chu, once they had broken with the DRV, were provided with a Vietnamese garrison under French command, but were granted complete administrative autonomy and were helped to form their own militia.[b] Each of these private armies, in Tonkin and in Cochinchina, was held together by its own internal discipline and fought for its own reasons, in the traditions of Ta Van Phung or De Tham or Pu Kombo, under its own private standard—the Tonkinese Catholic militia under the flag of the Vatican. Such forces could not be allotted a role in an overall defence plan: they were not subject to the High Command and so could not be drawn on to fight outside their own territory, while regular troops venturing into their domain to reinforce them would have been taking a grave operational risk. The system only gave the impression of working, therefore, because the Vietminh chose not to attack in strength, but accepted that these areas were for the time being a no man's land; this strategy made no contribution to pacification and the restoration of law and order. In fact each group's defence of its own satrapy, measured by non-occurrence of incidents, was won at a cost to the general defence, for few cared what happened to their neighbour or would risk their own skins to stop supplies flowing to Communist units operating on the neighbour's ground. The unhappy reality was that French impotence was legalizing an anarchy perfectly adapted for exploitation by a subversive movement, and that the flourishing of the latter was all the more truly a symbiosis because the Sects, the warlords, and certain Province Chiefs themselves flourished only so long as the conflict lasted. France was trapped.

[a] Hammer, p. 273.   [b] Ibid. p. 276.

7. DEVOLUTION OF POWER AND TRANSFER OF OFFICE

The French Generals, politicians, and administrators were fully alive to the limitations of a purely military defence against the Vietminh, whatever strategy or tactics might have been devised to carry it through. They were no less alive to the factors making some measure of devolution of power imperative and urgent: the anti-colonial temper of world opinion, justified by the example of British India, could not be disregarded—still less anti-colonial feeling in America as the moment loomed up, in the course of 1949, when it was going to be necessary to ask for American aid in order to carry on the war. On the domestic front the French Government appreciated the necessity to find a native authority to set against the DRV and provide a nationalist focus for native forces under direct command or under that of the Sects and factions. The Government's hesitations to act on these promptings are generally (and, on the whole, correctly) attributed to reluctance to relinquish political and financial control. Yet there was the administrative factor to consider, and this confronted the ministers in Paris with a very real dilemma: it was the general breakdown of government that had enabled the Vietminh to plant their roots in the villages—behind the defence perimeter in Tonkin as much as in the 'old' provinces of Cochinchina—and no army, however numerous and massively equipped, would be able by itself to afford protection to individual victims of intimidation or, in part because of that, reverse the notorious balance of intelligence which gave every advantage to the aggressor. The security intelligence that only a civilian administration could provide was a prerequisite even for strictly military operations. Thus proposals for devolution of power, inspired mainly by considerations external to Vietnam, were largely irrelevant to the root cause of the internal trouble, except that, if they were followed by a further weakening of the administration, they could make the trouble worse instead of better.

Republic of Cochinchina

Negotiations with Ho Chi Minh in 1946 had never advanced beyond irreducible disagreements over broad political principle, but when the DRV began open hostilities the French Government were left with nobody to talk to even about that. The behaviour of the Emperor—first abdication, then flight—left them with no constitutional basis for a future settlement, and indeed with no stand-

ing, save in Cochinchina, for such limited government action as
they were able to carry on. Political endeavour after 1946 consequently had two aims: on one hand to enlist Cochinchinese support
for the 'Provisional Republic' hastily set up by Admiral d'Argenlieu, and on the other to find a formula by which Indochina—retaining if possible its federal structure—could be given a substantial
measure of self-government but yet not leave the French Union
altogether. The arguments advanced in the various negotiations
have been fully recorded elsewhere; they are not repeated here because they proved to be of no lasting consequence. Much the same
can be said about the personalities who took part in them, mostly
for short periods, as members of the Cabinets of the Cochinchinese
Republic. The first Chief Minister, Dr Nguyen Van Thinh, committed suicide from the chagrin of realizing his powerlessness between Vietnamese pressure groups and French administrators still
holding the purse-strings.[a] Some of those who succeeded him still
have places on the political stage of Saigon today, but hardly by virtue of noteworthy services at that time. The Republic consisted of a
nominated *Conseil de Cochinchine*, without specific constitutional
powers, and of ministerial heads of departments with little or no
practical control over the French civil servants, whose numbers
were increasing much faster than those of the Vietnamese and who
still took their instructions from the Commissioner and Commis-
sioner-General of France. The latters' powers were in effect unabated from the days when they had been called Governor and
Governor-General. The Vietnamese ministers' control outside
Saigon, such as it was, worked through political channels of their
own, not through administrative ones, for these remained an exclusive French preserve.

The State of Viet-Nam

The question of Indochinese common interests was never settled
under French auspices, but once France had given way on the two
issues of unification for the three regions of Vietnam and of complete
self-determination,[b] it proved possible—after a year of negotiations
during which the French side was universally thought to be drag-
ging its feet—to persuade Bao Dai to return from his voluntary exile
and preside over a *Quoc Gia Viet Nam* (State of Viet-Nam). Though

[a] Lancaster, p. 164.
[b] By act of the French parliament of 21 May 1949. The Communist deputies voted
against and, by implication, favoured perpetuating the colonial status of Cochinchina
(Célerier, pp. 252–3).

retaining the style 'His Majesty',[a] he was no longer Emperor—he had after all renounced the throne—but simply Head of State (*Quoc Truong*). An outwardly self-governing Vietnam came into existence on 1 January 1950 and received recognition from France, Great Britain, and the United States, followed by the Vatican and one or two other Western countries. The Soviet Union and China (where the People's Government was barely three months old) reacted by recognizing the DRV, although it was destitute of a state mechanism. By reason of these contrasting acts of foreign recognition the Vietnamese conflict was subtly 'escalated' from a colonial dispute, the internal affair of France, into an aspect of the Cold War. The relations of the new state to the French Union still fell some way short of independence: not only were defence and external relations reserved to France's control, but so too were responsibility for internal security, until 'pacification' should be complete, while an attenuated protectorate was to be exercised by France over the hill tribes of all three regions (including the 'autonomous' PMS) until the Head of State should enact an agreed statute for their administration and the safeguarding of the tribesmen's rights under majority rule.[b][79] Given the unpreparedness for self-government of the Vietnamese nation as a whole, the arrangements could not well have been otherwise if the existing anarchy in the country was not to deteriorate into chaos; unfortunately political parties in Paris, no doubt connected with financial interests in Vietnam, were said to be taking advantage of the situation for undercover manipulation of the Vietnamese personalities about to inherit political responsibility.[c] Further negotiations took place during 1950 (the Pau Conference) to settle financial and economic questions between French interests and the three 'Associated States of Indochina'— for Laos and Cambodia were henceforward self-governing as well as Vietnam—but the arrangements were marked by pettifogging bickering over sovereignty[d] and did not survive the final French withdrawal in 1954–5.

Transfer of power

The significant details of the Élysée Agreement setting up the State of Viet-Nam were its subsidiary conventions relating to defence and public administration. Vietnamese of all political colours had been united in regarding possession of a national army as the

---

[a] *Duc* (see p. 72 above).   [b] France, *Accords Franco-Vietnamiens*, 1949.
[c] Devillers & Lacouture (1960), p. 22.   [d] Lancaster, p. 212.

most precious of all marks of independent sovereignty and were no doubt predisposed to this point of view by the military traditions of their past. For their part, the French were divided on the benefits to be expected in the struggle against the Vietminh: some Generals showed more hesitation about entrusting the French interest in the fighting to an unseasoned national army than they had about en-trusting it to private armies, but De Lattre de Tassigny, and the politicians with answerability for finance, attached more weight to the prospect of relieving the metropolitan taxpayer of some of the burden. Under the Convention on defence, Vietnamese national forces were to be formed (air as well as land), paid, and equipped from the Vietnamese budget—but trained and commanded by French officers, save where Vietnamese officers already serving in the French forces could be seconded for the purpose, in particular to serve on a Joint General Staff; the Vietnamese forces were to be responsible primarily for internal security, the *Corps Expéditionnaire* taking their place in this role until training should be further ad-vanced.[a] Military establishments were to be transferred to Viet-namese ownership as soon as they were taken over by Vietnamese forces, but were to be paid for. Thus on the military front there were few immediate signs of any change of control. The conventions on the different aspects of public administration unfortunately gave a similar impression of being more concerned with the protection of French interests than with the viability and independence of the Vietnamese state; astonishingly, they were silent on constitutional questions, for instance, and made no provision for the legislative process. The duality of the judicial system was retained, except that the French courts were to give way gradually to mixed courts as Vietnamese magistrates and prosecutors became available.[b] The police and the *Sûreté* were to pass under Vietnamese command im-mediately, except for residual duties vested temporarily in certain agencies under the French High Commissioner (as the Commis-sioner-General now became).[c] The departments of government were to be transferred to Vietnamese ministries in their entirety as these became ready to take them over; French personnel were to be allowed to retire, compensation for loss of career being payable (on a not very generous scale) by the Vietnamese exchequer to any who could not be absorbed by the home civil service—this option being open also to Vietnamese personnel.[d]

[a] France, *Convention inter-États, 1949.* pp. 13–24.   [b] Ibid. pp. 79 ff.
[c] Ibid. pp. 111–15.   [d] Ibid. pp. 47–65.

Central government

More important than the letter of these conventions was the manner of their execution and the reaction to them of Vietnamese leaders and people. The tone was set by the Head of State: no drama or excitement over this historic moment for which, the world had been led to believe, the Vietnamese people had waited eighty years. Instead, His Majesty retired to his establishment in the mists and pinewoods of Dalat to hunt, to meditate, and to hold court in the most paltry of senses—not to reign over, still less inspire, progressive government or to grapple with the appalling crisis of the civil war, but to bestow remunerative office, much as his forefathers had been content to issue patents for tutelary spirits. Under him, and answerable only to him in the absence of either legislature or political parties, came the Prime Minister[a] and a Cabinet of other Ministers who, working without any clear principle of responsibility, nevertheless represented the extension to Annam and Tonkin of the writ of the former Cochinchinese Provisional Government rather than the setting up of an administration with a nation-wide horizon.[80] The lack of a national budget, and consequent uncertainty about the destination of French subsidies, led in 1952 to a scandal in the French parliament,[b] but also to the adoption of proper estimates for the next year; in presenting these to the Head of State, the Vietnamese Prime Minister said they should be seen as an indication of the country's qualification for nationhood and of her gratitude to other countries now giving her aid.[c] Regional accounts, though published, revealed such random anomalies as half a million piastres spent on personal emoluments in Annam for the upkeep of royal tombs in 1950, beside only 12,000 for Prisons Staff but almost 6 millions for equipment and supplies for the prisons.[d] If procedures for the keeping of public accounts were disregarded, procedures for the conduct of other public business simply did not exist, and, in the face of persistent reluctance of Vietnamese officials to accept the responsibility along with the emoluments and prestige of office, attempts by their French advisers to keep the machine on the rails were inevitably decried as reluctance to hand over.

[a] Nguyen Van Tam.   [b] Lancaster, p. 349.   [c] *Budget de l'année 1953*, p. 6.
[d] *Ann. stat. 1949–50*, p. 220. The royal tombs were not mentioned in later years, but in 1952 Prisons in Annam show 6,000 piastres for staff, 3 m. for *matériel* (*Ann. Stat. 1951–2*, p. 189)—the same disproportion, although both figures had been halved.

Territorial administration

Provincial government fared no better. Tonkin had had no central administration for several years (only a French-manned *Comité de Gestion Administrative* with a Vietnamese figurehead whose title, *Tong Tran*, was an old-fashioned word for 'Area Commander'). It was too far away to be governed effectively under present circumstances—the railway was interrupted, shipping was erratic, and air travel still expensive—as an integral part of the new Saigon-based state; but the head of the Dai Viet, Nguyen Huu Tri, declared his support for Bao Dai and in return was appointed Governor[a]—by accession, as it were, rather than appointment. He presided, however, only over the municipalities and his own party machine, for there was not in reality any administration in the countryside, even inside the security perimeter. The Catholic dioceses also declared their allegiance to Bao Dai, whilst retaining practical autonomy, as we saw earlier in the military connexion. In Cochinchina the support of the Sects had been one of Bao Dai's prior conditions for resuming the throne at all (if that was what he had done—it was not altogether clear). Their forces were attracting so many of the unemployed and the refugees at a loose end because of Vietminh terror in their home villages that, by 1952, their strength had risen to 35,000.[b] The advent of self-government did not transfer the subvention of the private armies from the French to the national exchequer, however, and the Sects, as they played off their various friends against each other, gave least of all the groups practical signs of pride in the establishment of a national Government exercising no command or other control over them. The Binh Xuyen went from strength to strength, and in 1953 they were given the task of keeping 'open' the main road from Saigon to the sea. Le Van Vien attained his final apotheosis as a Vietnamese Vautrin the following spring, when Nguyen Van Tam, who was personally opposed to the French policy of feudalization, was replaced as Prime Minister by one of Bao Dai's uncles, Prince Buu Loc, and a nominee of the Binh Xuyen, Lai Huu Sang, was appointed Director of the Saigon Police. Mai Huu Xuan, the incumbent, took away with him into the national army several hundred of his subordinates, leaving their offices in a clean sweep to members of the Binh Xuyen.[c]

[a] Hammer, p. 284. His Vietnamese title was *Thu Hien* (Chief Magistrate), which emphasized the provisional character of the new arrangements no less than of the old.
[b] Savani, p. 83.   [c] Lancaster, p. 307.

The National Army

The least unsatisfactory of the Élysée Conventions in its effects was the one concerning the national army. There was no absolute shortage of manpower, and by the early summer of 1953 the target of 150,000 trained men under arms had been reached.[a] Conscription, introduced to speed up recruitment, had, however, the opposite effect, frustrated to some extent by the Sects[b] and the Province Chiefs, who offered a quieter life if not better pay.[c] By the spring of 1954, and with the Geneva Conference in prospect, the call-up netted only one in ten of those liable for service.[d] A more serious difficulty was to find officers; although a small number of Vietnamese had reached field rank in the French forces and others could be drafted from the paramilitary forces (the *Garde Indochinoise/Cochinchinoise*, now called the *Bao An*) or from among the police officers of Mai Huu Xuan, these were insufficient for the imposing conventional army most Vietnamese politicians pictured themselves reviewing on parade. Promotion of other ranks to commissions was (and still is) socially abhorrent to the Vietnamese middle classes, who were not above procuring deferment of their sons' military service in the ranks so that they could attend military academies in France and qualify for higher rank in the army on their return without having to earn it by service.[e] Fortunately, the French view that the Vietnamese army should concern itself with pacification, leaving the *Corps Expéditionnaire* to tackle the main forces of the Vietminh in Tonkin,[f] prevailed with Prime Minister Tam, and so the new battalions, trained for more limited engagements, were officered satisfactorily for immediate requirements.[g]

Vietnamese attitude to office

In spite of this relative success, however, the phased transfer of responsibility for the provinces in all the regions from French to Vietnamese hands which ought to have been speeded up by it—a process involving both provincial administration and police and garrison duties—ran into fresh difficulties. The programme was based on the supposition that, as time went on, the countryside would gradually be pacified—administration would be restored and, with it, stability and confidence. In the event, the opposite

---

[a] Navarre, p. 46.   [b] Lancaster, p. 233.
[c] The French authorities controlled rates of pay to prevent crimping.
[d] Navarre, p. 140.   [e] Ély, p. 268.   [f] Bodard (1963), p. 171.
[g] Navarre, p. 142.

tendency became apparent. Vietnamese *doc phu* (district officers) had been promoted to Province Chiefs since 1948, but their position was a very difficult one: before they had a chance to establish themselves in the public eye as the equals of the colonial authority they had superseded, they became the butt of Vietminh vilification and intimidation. Many of them kept going by reaching a discreet *modus vivendi* of their own with the local Sect or the Vietminh bravo —and also, it is alleged,[a] with the comfort of personal subsidies that were intended to compensate them for the risk of assassination but, presumably, were likewise liable to be mulcted. The imminence of the call to accept responsibility alone for security, with the help of a small private army—to shoulder personally in the area of their jurisdiction, as it really meant, the whole burden of national independence—before their provinces had been pacified under French auspices, led to procrastinations[b] and even one or two premature retirements from the civil service. With few exceptions, from His Majesty down to the sergeants and clerks, to the shopkeepers and the bonzes, national independence was understood in terms of personal interests in influence, power and money, whilst France's new-found haste to grant it was interpreted as an undignified flight from colonial responsibility on her part, and that in turn further undermined public confidence.

8. THE FRENCH LOSS OF NERVE

Vietnamese criticism of France on this last score was well founded. French domestic resources were feeling the strain, and one at least of the Communist objectives was within sight: France was having to withdraw reserves from the Cold War front in Europe and deny them to her administrations in North Africa, also confronted by 'national-liberation movements'. France's first priority was to hold the already permeated perimeter in Tonkin. The struggle in Indochina had become a permanent feature of the life of the Fourth Republic, whose procession of ephemeral policies had still produced neither a defence plan nor practical proposals for the future of the region, in or out of the French Union. In June 1953 M. Joseph Laniel took office and, judging public opinion to be ripe, gave the signal, in a parliamentary statement on 3 July, for disengagement. Arguing from an enumeration of political, administrative, and military progress achieved in Indochina, whose falseness laid bare

[a] Bodard (1963), p. 171.   [b] Navarre, p. 142.

to Vietnamese observers the collapse of French resolve it was meant to cover up, he announced a series of conferences whose agreements would 'complete (*parfaire*) the independence and sovereignty of the three states'.[a] The outgoing Cabinet had very recently appointed General Navarre as Commander-in-Chief in succession to General Salan,[81] and he had been commissioned to draw up a defence plan which would hold the line while an 'honourable way out' was evolved on the international political plane.[b] M. Laniel confirmed these instructions but added a new emphasis on building up the Vietnamese army as the price of American political support and financial aid.[c] The 'Plan Navarre' which emerged therefore envisaged a year of holding, to be followed by an offensive against the elusive Vietminh (subject to their being located, of course) to put the French Union in a position to negotiate from strength,[d] the whole to be conceived so as to secure further increases in American aid.

Military deadlock

Not many alternatives were open to the General. The balance of military strength was against the Vietminh, but only just: 400,000 of them to half a million of the defence forces. But whereas the Vietminh were all wholly mobile, if only on foot, the bulk of the defence was still rooted to the protection of its grid of blockhouses. Whilst therefore the Communists had the run of the 'free' zone, at night if not in the daytime, and the defence was powerless to prevent them —although it could and did impede them—, they had little prospect of becoming strong enough to evict the *Corps Expéditionnaire* from the country. But General Navarre could not expect reinforcements on a worth-while scale: France, beset more and more by trouble in North Africa, had already given all she could, and the frame of mind within Vietnam was not such as to incur the sacrifices which might have broken the military deadlock. The Communist colour of the Vietminh was by now undeniable; as the miseries of land reform began to make themselves felt, the flow of families escaping from DRV rule increased steeply and filled the mass of the people in the 'free' zone with foreboding lest Communist dominion should creep nearer; but there was nothing to be done privately about that in the absence of resolute government leadership, French or Vietnamese, and the best thing was to make what hay could be made while the sun still shone.

[a] Laniel (1957), pp. 11–12.   [b] Catroux, p. 124.   [c] Laniel, pp. 16–18.
[d] Navarre, p. 82.

The financial drain

The war had saddled Indochina with a prodigious adverse balance of payments, whose exact amount was unknown,[a] and with a financial spiral from which the French authorities could find no way out. Having all along pursued a policy of tolerating profiteering and other abuses in order to retain the support of both French and Vietnamese vested interests, from the banks to the Sects, the Paris Government had finally devalued the piastre shortly before General Navarre took command. In 1945 the piastre had been revalued at 17 francs, but on the open market it had been worth around 10; in the following years French servicemen had been the chief—and intended—beneficiaries, for the possibility of reconverting their pay into francs with a gain of 70 per cent made postings to Indochina worth the hardship at a time when all were volunteers. But the exchange control was in French banking (not official) hands, and maintenance of franc-piastre convertibility was part of the Élysée Conventions; these two circumstances precluded regulation of the traffic by law, although efforts were made from time to time to hinder it by creating arbitrary obstacles.[b] Vietnamese interests (headed, it is alleged, by His Majesty)[c] and big French companies had also taken advantage of the favourable rate in order to transfer (and augment) their war-damage compensation, the profits of the rubber boom, and proceeds from the liquidation of capital assets in anticipation of a French defeat, or at least withdrawal.[d] Coupled with extensive smuggling of US dollars—a practice rife at the time all over the Far East—, the traffic in piastres offered perfect cover for the illicit transactions of the Vietminh, which gained the same 70 per cent augmentation of the initial holding in piastres as everyone else.[e] The traffic also transferred to the French exchequer most of the Indochina deficit and led to a drain on France's dollar holdings; it was largely the restoration of the latter that M. Laniel sought through increased American financial aid for the war, especially when it was found that the devaluation of the piastre to 10 francs merely antagonized the Vietnamese Government, who had not been consulted, while the traffic went on just the same on the basis of a black-market rate of 6 francs.

[a] Estimated at 140,000 m. francs by the end of 1951 (Despuech, p. 49).
[b] Ibid. pp. 51–54.   [c] Ibid. p. 64.
[d] Including, we are told on good authority (e.g. Lancaster, pp. 413–14), the Bank of Indochina's estates in Cochinchina built up through foreclosures after the collapse of credit in the 1930 crisis.
[e] Despuech, p. 132.

The Geneva Conference

The outcome of the 'Plan Navarre' was the opposite of its intention: negotiations for a political settlement of the conflict began on the international stage long before any military advantage could have been looked for, and the military advantage, when it did take shape, went entirely to the enemy. During the course of the unsuccessful Berlin Conference on Germany and European defence early in 1954, the Russian Government proposed a five-power conference on Korea and Indochina, whose chief interest to the Communist world was a diplomatic one—the inclusion of China in the discussions and the recognition of her Government that participation would imply. The US Government of the day, though apprehensive about coming to terms with Communist China and her satellite before the expected military advantage had become a certainty, acquiesced: France seized the chance to disengage. The Conference was arranged to take place at Geneva in April 1954. Despite assurances not to commit the future of the Associated States unilaterally, the French Government had still been haggling over terms for granting the final stages of sovereignty.[a] On the eve of the international conference it tried to rush through two treaties by which France would acknowledge Vietnam's independence and Vietnam would simultaneously adhere to the French Union. But, as the only way to stop fighting and extricate the *Corps Expéditionnaire*, there was already talk that France intended to support the partition of Vietnam, although this would deprive the new state of self-determination at the very moment of independence. The US made no secret of her willingness to underwrite a continuation of the struggle by direct aid to Vietnam, and Bao Dai, who flew to Paris to strengthen his delegation's hand as soon as French haste for an armistice looked like degenerating into panic at the prospect of a military disaster in Tonkin,[b] refused to sign the French drafts already initialed by his negotiators.[c] That is how it came about that the Geneva Conference, whose original purpose had been simply to bring hostilities to an end, became the arbiter *de facto* of the terms of Vietnamese independence.

Battle of Dien Bien Phu

The military disaster duly befell, at the battle of Dien Bien Phu. This 'bitter fruit of an error of strategy on the part of General

---

[a] Devillers & Lacouture, p. 106.   [b] Lancaster, p. 306.
[c] Drafts were initialed in Paris on 4 June 1954 but never ratified.

Navarre', as the official investigator judged it,[a] was the culmination of the military doctrine of Vauban and the *place-forte* at grips with an enemy whose tactics eluded the comprehension of the conventional strategist of those days. Navarre, fresh from occupied Germany and the traditional concepts of Franco-German defence, had no previous knowledge of the Indochina War and, dominated by anxiety not to 'lose' ground, rose to the bait of rushing his mobile forces, as part of his holding action, to any corner of northern Indochina where his jack-in-the-box enemy momentarily bobbed up. The most serious of these threats at the end of 1953, he judged, was in Laos; the best strategy for meeting it was to build an entrenched camp at Dien Bien Phu, on the Tonkinese side of the border and 'commanding' the valleys down to Luang Prabang and the upper Mekong, but accessible only by air across nearly 200 miles of uncontrolled country. If the enemy could be drawn into a pitched battle here at last, in sparsely populated terrain, the weight of superior French weaponry would crush his main forces, deprive him of further fighting strength, and oblige him to negotiate. Navarre committed to the Dien Bien Phu camp, whose drill-book ingenuity 'evoked the enthusiasm' of the senior American liaison officer, General O'Daniel,[b] 16,000 men. Giap and his Communist Chinese advisers saw in this step an opportunity to trap the *Corps Expéditionnaire*, in a manner foreshadowed in *their* drill-book, and score a victory of little strategic value perhaps, but of great demoralizing effect in France. They themselves committed to the siege three and a half divisions and over 70,000 Vietnamese coolies,[c] at least 20,000 Chinese army personnel[d] and a wealth of war material, some of which was reputed to have been captured from American forces in Korea. Giap timed the battle for April to coincide with the Geneva Conference, and on 8 May the gallant defenders were finally overrun by a combination of artillery and of ruthlessly-sacrificed human waves. The DRV lost some 20,000 men, half of them killed, and France all her 16,000, of whom 1,500 were killed[e] and the survivors doomed to the deliberate torment of Japanese-style death marches and concentration camps.[f] To the strategy of the war, the battle was almost irrelevant; to the French public, for whom, as we have seen repeatedly, Indochina had always been a symbol of national prestige, the defeat was charged with

[a] Catroux, p. 120.   [b] Navarre, p. 196.   [c] Ibid. p. 213.
[d] Chinese sources quoted by O'Ballance, p. 225.   [e] Navarre, pp. 228–9.
[f] Fall (1961), pp. 264 ff.

emotions far deeper than the loss of a financial investment made out by their detractors to have been their sole interest. The Laniel Government was dismissed and General Navarre relieved of his command. Fortunately, the Vietminh were exhausted by their superhuman—or rather, multi-human—effort and were left no less eager than France for a respite.

The Geneva Agreements

Against this background, the five Great Powers worked out their compromise at Geneva, with delegations from the DRV and each of the Associated States, under the joint chairmanship of Mr Molotov and Mr Eden. The representatives of the DRV and of Bao Dai both claimed to speak for the whole Vietnamese nation. Bao Dai's representatives asked for a single state under the monarchy, elections under United Nations supervision as soon as the Security Council determined that 'conditions of freedom were fulfilled', and incorporation of the Vietminh forces into those of Bao Dai.[a] What was actually negotiated, on 21 July, fell far short of these hopes. An Agreement on the Cessation of Hostilities was signed by representatives of the French and of the Vietminh Commanders-in-Chief.[b] It provided for regrouping of the two armies on either side of the 17th parallel, with a demilitarized zone in between; evacuation of military units each from the territory of the other as so demarcated; liberation and repatriation of prisoners of war and civilian internees; transfer of members of the population not wishing to live under one regime to the territory of the other; eventual unification of the country through general elections; a ban on reprisals or discriminations; a ban on introduction of fresh troops or arms or new military bases; a ban on military alliances with outside Powers; and the setting up of an International Commission for Supervision and Control in Viet-Nam, composed of India, Poland, and Canada with the Indian presiding, to report to the British and Russian Co-Chairmen of the Conference, now terminated, on the execution of the agreement.[c] There was then a Final Declaration, which nobody signed and from which the representatives of the US and of the State of Viet-Nam expressly dissociated themselves, calling for the elections mentioned in the agreement to take place under the supervision of the ICC within two years (i.e. by 1956), after discussion be-

[a] Cmnd 2834, pp. 72–73.
[b] A similar agreement was signed in respect of Laos and one between the same Vietminh General and a General of the Khmer National Army for Cambodia.
[c] Cmd. 9239, pp. 27–40.

tween the two parties over arrangements beginning one year earlier
(July 1955).[a]

No formal treaties ended French rule in Vietnam, therefore—
only these cease-fire agreements, signed on the French side by a
Brigadier, while the State of Viet-Nam was not even a party to
them. The ignominy and multiple humiliations attending France's
final laying down of her colonial charge, after she had identified her
national pride so intimately with it, tended to confirm Vietnamese
scepticism about the political institutions and principles of government cherished in the West—a scepticism that has marked the conduct of public affairs ever since Geneva, in the South almost as much
as in the North.

[a] Ibid. pp. 9–11.

5

THE PATRIARCHY OF
NGO DINH DIEM

I. ON THE THRESHOLD OF INDEPENDENCE

VIETNAMESE independence is usually dated from the Geneva
Agreements, but really this is arbitrary. For the DRV it may be
justified to the extent that, before that date, in spite of the high-
sounding titles assumed by Communist leaders since 1945 and of
recognition by the Communist powers since 1950, there had existed
neither a seat of government nor any real state apparatus; both of
those the DRV now acquired. But the agreements in themselves
conferred on Bao Dai's State of Viet-Nam no constitutional advance: they settled issues between France and the DRV, but not between France and the South.[82] More subtly, the agreements
brought a tacit end to Bao Dai's undertaking in 1949 only to look
beyond France for aid on occasions when France was unable to give
it;[a] July 1954 saw the balance of tutelage tilt from the side of France
to the side of the US. American aid and protection had been growing steadily in significance since 1950, and those of France had
several more years to run; July 1954 transferred the weight from one
foot to the other, but there was no constitutional event to justify seeing in this a revolutionary change from 'colonialism' to 'independence', and much of what might have been the magic of an otherwise historic moment was lost. It is of course true of the DRV as well
that its leaders' assumption of responsibilities for government and
for management of the economy of partly-industrialized Tonkin did
not diminish but increased their dependence on foreign advice; they
had to seek technical assistance from eastern Europe in place of the
cruder kinds of aid—weapons and unskilled labour in furtherance
of the 'liberation' war—which hitherto had been the monopoly of
Chinese tutelage.

Effects of the war

Many of the problems that had faced the Bao Dai Government

a Lancaster, p. 188.

before July 1954 continued to face it after that date, or else were exchanged for just as perplexing new ones. It is impossible to arrive at an accurate statistical assessment of the condition of the country at the moment of the cease-fire. For a decade the cracked apparatus of government had been papered over at many points by the recording of statistics that were not necessarily measured on the ground, especially when they were linked to budgetary credits; other records relating to 1954 or earlier years have in many cases been destroyed since 1954, and it is therefore necessary to be content with generalizations.[a] The physical scars of war were not conspicuous: the principal fighting had been in the North, and material damage waiting to be made good in the South consisted primarily of the railway (interrupted in the Vietminh areas though not much sabotaged elsewhere), roads and road bridges in districts under the control of the Vietminh and of the Sects, and public buildings in the villages— that is to say, schools and *dinh* (temple-offices) burnt down as acts of terror. There had, of course, been little regular maintenance. More serious was the financial aftermath of the war: the new state had started its life in 1950 with no loan charges on its budget, but also with negligible cash reserves with the banks. The collection of direct taxes had become so erratic—as much on the excuse of insecurity as because of the reality of it[b]—that even the Municipality of Saigon had to be subsidized by the central Government to the extent of 25 per cent of its expenditure in 1954,[c] while the profits tax in Cochinchina actually brought to account (not necessarily the amount collected, still less that which was due) fell, inversely to the soaring of profits, from 160 million piastres in 1952 to only 6 million in 1953.[d] Tax delinquency was thus added to the all-devouring costs of defence to remove financial independence beyond the realms even of dream.

State of the economy

Superficially, the national economy was sound. Rubber had become the principal export thanks to the boom caused by the Korean War, production being little affected by the activities of the Vietminh—in fact it was 'protected' by both Cao Dai and Binh Xuyen by arrangement with the managements—, and the estates, although

[a] By the end of 1964 there were no staff records available to the Director-General of the Civil Service earlier than 1956.
[b] This is the hint of Prime Minister Nguyen Van Tam in Viet-Nam, *Budget de l'année 1953*, p. 4.
[c] *Ann. stat. 1952–3*, p. 195.   [d] Ibid. p. 187.

entirely under French management, made up a national asset in first-class condition and adequately financed.[83] Rice, considered as a staple subsistence foodstuff, had been little affected by the war; even where a crop was lost in some locality, the consequences did not last beyond that year.[a] Although exports of rice had dwindled to 100,000 tons in 1953,[b] it could be expected that they would recover at least to the 1951 figure of 275,000 tons[c] even without action by the Government, especially if the previous annual shipment of 100,000 tons to Tonkin could be diverted to the export market in future as well. On the whole, loss of Tonkin was an economic advantage to the South in the short run because the cost of rehabilitating it would have exceeded the immediate value of its assets; but in the long run it meant loss of the proceeds from the export of minerals (among which coal for Japan had come to represent the third most valuable export from Vietnam)[d] and, more serious, loss of the industrial production of Tonkin, the chief item of which was textiles. This industry had been expanded in the course of the Indochina War to produce cheaper commodities as a contribution to 'pacification by prosperity'. Here was another factor adding to the new state's dependence on foreign resources, to make good immediately the shortage of manufactures and, in the future, the industries themselves. Along with the country's industrial endowment, the State of Viet-Nam was cut off by partition from the University of Indochina and other leading schools and technical colleges, most of which were located at Hanoi.

Refugees from the North

But it was the human problem which commanded most attention in the latter half of 1954. First, there were the peasants who had fled from their villages at different times—often more than once— to get away from aerial or artillery bombardment, from terrorist outrages or from intimidation at the hands of the Vietminh or of the Sects. In central Annam were to be found large camps of prisoners held by the Vietminh as unreliable, and now with bitter scores to pay off. In the far south of Cochinchina there were captive communities, transported there by the Vietminh in the prevailing anarchy to grow food for them, in the manner of the Dao Lanh and

[a] The *Ann. stat.* gives figures for production year by year, but these could only be guesswork and were sometimes contradictory.
[b] *Ann. stat. 1952–3*, p. 224.   [c] Ibid. *1950–1*, p. 234.
[d] In 1953 248,000 tons out of 306,000 were exported; all exports taken together, Japan took the lead as Vietnam's best customer (ibid. *1952–3*, pp. 207, 222, & 235).

other movements before them. But the biggest groups of displaced persons were those now wanting to exercise their right under the Geneva Agreement to be 'regrouped' with the rival armies from South to North or from North to South. About 30,000 people presented themselves at the reception centres in the South for transfer to the North;[a] but those fleeing imminent absorption into the DRV overtopped the million mark[b][84] and included not a few who had already taken refuge in the 'free' zone from the 'liberated' zone at various stages of the war and dared not face the reprisals of a second liberation. Some thousands of the refugees were professionals or skilled workers, but most were peasants who knew no other labour than that of the paddy field. The transport and reception of these unfortunates was paid for by France and the US; but their permanent settlement in the South—partaking to some extent of a temporary resumption of the *nam tien* before the gates shut indefinitely—combined with the problem of the local fugitives to open up the whole question of land tenure and the need for changes of custom, if not of law, which had defeated—or been neglected by—the French administrators for so many decades, but for which both Vietminh and, in Cochinchina, the Sects had been finding their own interested solutions for nine years.

Government staff

Although the Geneva Agreement set no time limit to the process in so many words, the transfer of office and of the technical services from French to Vietnamese personnel had now to be speeded up if it was to be completed in time for unification in 1956; it had also to be arranged so as to take back control of areas which the French had not reoccupied since the events of March 1945. The task of planning these operations presented forbidding difficulties, for the fate of many of the staff, and the intentions of others, remained unknown until they actually reported for duty; it was only possible to compile the files in 1955 by taking a census of the staff found at their desks.[c] It then became evident that a few public servants in Tonkin had stayed behind; any who were still with the DRV in 1954 had had little chance of getting away at the last moment, but no senior staff, and few juniors, chose to go North if already in the South. The

[a] Mr Fall believed (1966, p. 76) the correct figure to be 80,000.
[b] Including 120,000 members of the national army and ancillary units—Bui Van Luong (Commissioner for Refugees), in Lindholm (1959), p. 60.
[c] RVN, *Ann. Report 1958*, p. 8; even so, only a round figure of 82,000 employees of all grades was arrived at. Three years later this number had risen to 140,000 (ibid. p. 18).

manning of health and education services in the towns was not too difficult because both had always been staffed predominantly by Vietnamese,[a] and the call for personnel for the reoccupied provinces of Annam was more than met from staff inherited from the all-Indochina services, now dissolved, or from those of Tonkin; but the shortage of trained staff to man junior grades, in the service of provinces or villages, was acute, mainly because of the opportunities for more remunerative work offered by the wartime boom. On the other hand some senior personnel, whose numbers have not been revealed, had been exercising their option as naturalized *assimilés* to retire to France on the attainment of independence and could no longer be counted on; they were mostly from the legal and judicial services but also included other professions. The number of qualified graduates who returned to Saigon in response to appeals to discharge their patriotic duty was stated much later to have been 361;[b] the number who refused to heed these appeals, or instead responded to those of the DRV, cannot have been fewer than twice that figure.[c]

Reactions to independence

Thus an apparatus of government was to hand, but it was disorganized, unevenly spread, and still in process of adapting its regulations and procedures to control from Saigon instead of Paris or Hanoi. It remained to be seen whether its personnel yet possessed the experience and the esprit de corps to shoulder the moral burden of either the immediate or the long-term problems of full self-government. There was no general rejoicing[d] and no spirit of national renewal noticeably sweeping the country; no young intellectuals were rushing into print with programmes and policies to meet the challenges of the moment or of the future; the political parties, so called, issued no manifestoes and made no secret of their faith in factional intrigue as the best-mapped road to power. There were grounds for apprehension lest public officials, who had felt themselves excused from conscientious discharge of public duties and honest handling of public money so long as political direction

---

[a] Out of 426 doctors registered on 31 Dec. 1952, 61 were French and 9 Chinese, the rest Vietnamese (*Ann. stat. 1951–2*, p. 42).

[b] VNP, 1 June 1961.

[c] There are commonly reputed to be at the present time about 350 Vietnamese doctors in practice in various parts of France and hundreds more in other professions; but the majority are Tonkinese by birth.

[d] There was evidently none in Hanoi either (Lancaster, p. 362).

remained 'colonialist', would continue in their bad habits on the grounds that these were not so unpatriotic if foreign aid was on tap to substitute for revenue not brought to account. And the tap of foreign aid was kept open by the risks of further war latent in the peace contrived at Geneva. Its terms had been drawn up with the peace terms of Korea in mind, and the 17th parallel evoked the same fears and also the same hopes as had been evoked by the 38th parallel. The danger that General Giap might, after a respite, strike south again with his People's Army was estimated as serious enough to make quite certain that the taps of foreign aid would be left on for some time yet. This danger also turned attention to the armed forces; the uncomfortable facts in that quarter were that the army was still technically under the command of the French High Commissioner, General Ély, and that, although its units had fought quite as gallantly as their French comrades at Dien Bien Phu, battalions fighting under their own senior officers at the same time in central Annam had proved 'timorous',[a] not out of disloyalty so much as low unit morale and poor discipline. The desertion rate of the new Vietnamese army, albeit homewards rather than towards the enemy's lines,[b] was as high as it had been under Gia Long.

French and American attitudes

The situation was precarious, and the world at large, though imperfectly informed about its details, showed little faith that the State of Viet-Nam was going to survive. In French eyes, the best hope lay in preserving as much as possible of the French connexion—in education, in the civil service, in the armed forces, and even in modelling political life on that of the Fourth Republic—although France could not offer to foot the bill. Only Frenchmen, however, discerned in this opinion any element of altruism; to Vietnamese and Americans it appeared that France had had her chance—that her rule was dead but claiming the right not to have to lie down. Asking nothing better than to have to foot the bills, American public opinion considered France had failed to defend the interests of the free world and that it behoved her to stand decorously aside—the more so since, in Asian eyes, she had already lost the Mandate of Heaven by 1945 and had disregarded the signs of history at her own peril. In American eyes, the 1950 devolution of administrative authority, even though reinforced by the traditional sanction of Bao Dai's

[a] O'Ballance, pp. 208–9.
[b] Vietminh efforts to subvert the army were a failure, in Gen. Ély's opinion (p. 195).

monarchy, had already proved itself inadequate to fire national enthusiasm; what was required from now on to pull South Vietnam together was a leader with an ideology, to set against Ho Chi Minh and Communism—to be, if not a second Chiang Kai-shek, another Syngman Rhee—one whom the United States could support financially and help to establish himself among his own people as the focus of loyalty for politicians and soldiers. It was with these two classes of Vietnamese that the future of their ally as a sheet-anchor in southeast Asia of resistance to Communist aggression would more assuredly lie than with the civil servants, who stood, most Americans considered, for little more than the frailties of an outdated colonialist bureaucracy. The leader who now came forward to fit this specification was Ngo Dinh Diem. His private ideology was Catholicism; the ideology his regime was going to purvey would be called, in English, Personalism.

2. THE IDEOLOGICAL BASES OF THE PATRIARCHY

The dictatorship of Ngo Dinh Diem grew out of the constitutional vacuum in which the Geneva Agreement left the State of Viet-Nam. As the Geneva Conference approached its climax, during June 1954, and the *Corps Expéditionnaire* drew in its defensive perimeter round a tighter nucleus of the Red River Delta, the lack of public confidence in Prince Buu Loc as upholder of the country's interests, in harness with a France whose resolve was so obviously faltering, led Bao Dai, by now in Paris himself, to offer the premiership instead to Ngo Dinh Diem. Diem accepted it on 19 June, the day Laniel gave way to Mendès France, and was thus already head of the Government when the agreements were concluded. There was no other procedure whereby a Prime Minister and Cabinet could come to office at that time. Accounts of what prompted Bao Dai to make his choice vary, for neither he nor any other Vietnamese has recorded his version of these events. The most plausible explanation is perhaps that Bao Dai, sensing the imminent shift of his country's destinies from French to American tutelage, acted spontaneously, to appoint a man he knew would enjoy American confidence even at the cost of French.[a]

Diem's earlier career

Ngo Dinh Diem was a likeable man, perpetually good humoured;

[a] Lancaster, pp. 327–8.

although his policies have been so universally condemned, it was rare to hear anyone speak ill of him personally. In this he contrasted with his brother Nhu, of whose policies more approved than would admit today, although he was disliked on all hands. At this time Diem was 53 and unmarried.[a] The family originated, like Ho Chi Minh's, from the 'cradle of revolt', the Nghe An province of Annam of which Vinh is the chief city.[b] They had been Catholic for more than two centuries, and the father, Ngo Dinh Kha,[c] was first principal under the French Protectorate of the school for training the sons of mandarins to succeed their fathers, the *Quoc Hoc*; it was a secondary school, with no intellectual pretensions and not in any way comparable to the University of Hanoi, although it harboured similar anti-French feeling.[d] Diem was educated there himself and was taught French and a certain amount of classical Chinese, with the Confucian saws and maxims expressed in it; but he does not seem to have shown any interest in—and may not in fact have been able to read—contemporary Chinese political writers. This limitation (without which he might have begun where some of them left off) combined with his introvert temperament and his Catholicism to keep him out of the political groupings focused on Cuong De. Diem was appointed in the normal course to be a mandarin himself, and at the age of 30 became Province Chief at Phan Thiet, with charge incidentally of the remnant of the Chams, in whose ancient civilization he showed a certain pride. When Bao Dai returned from school in France to mount the throne in 1932, he made Diem Minister of the Interior, in the aftermath of the Communist disturbances at Vinh; but, though linked factionally with the young Emperor, whose Empress was a Catholic, Diem resigned, never to work again so long as the French Protectorate endured.[e] The bone of contention, he subsequently let it be known, was the Emperor's acquiescence in the assumption of the chairmanship of the state councils of Annam by the *Résident-Supérieur*,[f] in which Dien, despite the security considerations that undoubtedly prompted it, saw an

[a] He was born at Hué on 3 Jan. 1901. (This was not necessarily the actual day but may have been the nearest auspicious date.) The basic facts in this paragraph were obtained from his public-relations staff.

[b] Chesneaux (p. 275) has listed a score of revolts that arose in this area from the thirteenth to the twentieth century.

[c] The given name of the Chinese philosopher Mencius.   [d] *Contribution*, i. 7.

[e] Nevertheless, in 1962 the Communists of South Vietnam put out an historical text (in the author's possession) accusing him of having warmly abbetted, as minister, the French repression.

[f] p. 89 above.

affront to the national dignity and sovereignty—and perhaps a hint of no confidence in himself.[a]

Diem in retirement

Diem's long retirement and meditation yielded no enrichment either of himself (he scorned trade and money as sincerely as any Confucian of the old school) or of literature (there was only a very small intellectual market to cater for, had he had the talent), and he was still living in the isolation of Hué in March 1945, on good terms with the Japanese.[b] He might have been the first Prime Minister instead of Tran Trong Kim, but the 1945 regime could not last, and in Vietnamese politics there are no second opportunities. At the Japanese surrender, on his way south, he was captured at Tuy Hoa by the Vietminh, at the same time as they seized three of his brothers at Hué; Nhu and Can escaped again, but Khoi, the head of the family, who was Province Chief of Quang Nam, was battered to death. Diem was taken to Tonkin in captivity and there met (but not in Hanoi) Ho Chi Minh, whose true identity he knew and who sought his collaboration. In declining, although in Ho Chi Ming's absolute power, he had the unrebuttable argument that filial piety (owed to an elder brother when the father was dead) now forbade reconciliation after what had been done to Khoi. His release by the Communists was timed as an overture to the Tonkinese Catholics in the spring of 1946.[c] He went to live in Saigon and took part in the negotiations for Bao Dai's return in 1949, but again declined the premiership. He next set out on a somewhat mysterious world tour, which took him to pay court for the first time to the aged Cuong De in Japan, to the Philippines, to America, Belgium, and back to America again, where he remained as the guest of the Maryknoll Fathers, waiting. Like Ho Chi Minh and others before and after him, Diem in this way acquired émigré status, for some reason a qualification for power in Vietnam. Towards the end of 1953, as the war at home was moving towards a denouement, he removed to Paris, on what must have been his first visit to France. It was there that he finally agreed to serve under Bao Dai once more.[85]

[a] As against this explanation, Nguyen Qui Hung (1964, p. 20) maintains that Diem's quarrel was a strictly personal one with the *Chef de Cabinet* of that time, who was Pham Quynh, and that his hatred for Bao Dai and the French was thought up afterwards.

[b] Scigliano (1963), p. 16.

[c] Some parts of this episode smack of myth, yet it all originates with Diem himself and is borne out by Communist accounts.

Diem's mandate

The Head of State's appointment of Ngo Dinh Diem to be Prime Minister in June 1954 can hardly have been in accordance with his personal inclination; it was viewed with dismay by French officials, because, like other Vietnamese Catholics, Diem expressed his resentment of the appropriation of Catholicism by the French state through insistent, often publicized, anti-colonialism.[a] This characteristic won him the admiration on the other hand of some Americans, who saw in it a reinforcement of his anti-Communism that made him a kindred spirit. But in making this deduction they were deceived. Some have been inclined since his fall to explain their initial misjudgement by supposing it was Ngo Dinh Diem who changed; this view would divide his stewardship of his country's destiny into two periods at a mid-point in 1959—the first half being a time of democracy, economic advance, and peace, while the second was a time of tyranny, stagnation, and *consequent* Communist resurgence. The truth is that Ngo Dinh Diem underwent no change of character, nor his regime any change of policy; and if certain features of his government did favour the renewal of Communist aggression, they were features America generally applauded rather than the ones it was scandalized by. His own view of his coming to power was undoubtedly conceived in supernatural terms, but whether he believed his intuition to flow from divine guidance, as some foreigners suggested, is hard to tell; he always tried to base his arguments on rational, if sometimes debatable, explanations. His policies are sufficiently accounted for by the Confucian view that faults in a ruler disturb the harmony of nature and forfeit the Mandate of Heaven, whereas piety and purity preserve them. So too, therefore, with the question whether he aspired to the throne for himself: probably he did not, although he envisaged a tenure of office stretching into a conveniently distant future, until his work should be done. In this respect, as in his Christianity, Diem made a worthy third to Chiang and Rhee.

Catholicism and Confucianism

The addition of Catholicism to Confucianism in his upbringing is the key to Diem's political ideas. Like the Jesuits, he was conscious of the similarities between the two ethical systems; but whereas for

[a] Mr Bator is of the opinion (1967, p. 161) that Diem would have gone under without the collaboration he received, his churlishness about it notwithstanding, from French officials.

the Jesuits Catholicism and European social values were central, and Confucianism conformed to them more or less, with Diem the standpoint was the reverse one, and Catholicism brought a trans-cendental sanction to the ethics of a Confucian society which con-stituted his point of reference. At times his view of that society, as revealed in the manipulation of his subordinates, went so far in making use of its defects as to border on the cynical; at others he ex-posed himself to political setbacks through insistence on a falsely idealized image of Vietnamese society. The logic of this distinction was that one standard of political action was appropriate to the life of the village—stronghold of tradition and all that was essentially Vietnamese and the proper care of the mandarinate—while the other developed as an accommodation to modernity and the cor-rupting intrusion of politics and economics which (thanks to the in-sidious legacy of French colonialism)[a] threatened to turn more and more Vietnamese villages into towns. Latent in this contrast was the old Chinese dichotomy between the official and the unofficial, be-tween the orthodox and the heterodox, as well as the Confucian scorn for the political side of government as an obstacle to the work of the mandarinate, which stood for the administrative side and alone had the capacity to preserve stability and so to promote well-being. Diem was in fact grappling here with the same problem of adjustment between Confucian society and the social influences of Western technology that had expressed itself in China in the debate between reformists and revolutionists.

Diem's family

The most important point at which Catholicism touched Con-fucianism was in the pre-eminence both of them assigned to the family as a social unit. Of all the directions from which modernity—synonymous here with mundanity—threatened national stability, the most insidious was the undermining of family life. Ngo Dinh Diem's ambition was both to strengthen and to purify the Vietna-mese family at all levels of society, by restoring it to its Confucian status as the legal personality and responsible entity within the vil-lage community, and at the same time by stamping out polygamy and concubinage in accordance with Christian doctrine. For in-stance, he certainly encouraged, if he did not inaugurate, the cus-tom whereby the armed forces were accompanied by wives and

[a] Devillers points out (1960, p. 307) that this was Diem's principal grievance against France.

children wherever they were billeted and at whatever tactical cost. But the most conspicuous expression of Diem's beliefs in this regard was his attitude to the persons of his own family: in his mind, the teachings of Confucianism and of Catholicism were at one in guiding him to found his state upon them and on the bonds that held them together.[86] His family meant, in the first place, four surviving brothers: Mgr Pierre Martin Thuc, older than Diem, was the third Vietnamese priest to be consecrated in the national hierarchy in 1938 and, through the deaths of the other two, was now the senior among nine native bishops;[a] Luyen, the youngest brother, was an uxorious but otherwise undistinguished person whom Diem employed as an ambassador, latterly in London; Can, unmarried and uncouth, occupied a key security position and was custodian of the family hearth but contributed nothing to the ideology of the regime; most important was Nhu, who never occupied any office of state yet contributed indispensably to both the theory and the practice of the government; and finally, there was Nhu's wife, Tran Le Xuan, her mother (a cousin of Bao Dai) and her father and three of her numerous uncles—a non-Catholic family originally from Tonkin—who all were named in due course to offices of state. Nhu and Xuan shared Diem's official residence, and it was chiefly to Nhu (but also in part to Mgr Thuc) that the task fell of elaborating the ideology believed to be essential to the establishment of Diem as a national leader. In later years Nhu and Xuan also shared with Can the unofficial management of the political services, but Diem generally followed the principle that his 'inner' brothers should support him behind the scenes, while his 'outer' brothers were appointed to positions of public responsibility. Both Nhu and Xuan took seats in the National Assembly.

Ideology of Nhu

Ngo Dinh Nhu was educated in France and graduated at the École des Chartes; like his brother he appeared to be almost totally ignorant of science—what was worse, of scientific method—and had picked up, as part of the legacy of French scholasticism, an exaggerated esteem for his own intuition and eloquence. Unlike his brother, he seemed to have absorbed little of the Chinese heritage. He was in France in the 1930s when the Church, with the encyclicals on Labour, *Rerum Novarum* and *Quadragesimo Anno*, still in the forefront of its debates, was searching for a political philosophy to set

[a] Nguyen-huu-Trong, p. 269.

against Marxism—the age of Catholic trade unions, of *Action Française*, of the many strands of Existentialism, of the 'Corporate States' of Bottai and of Salazar. Traces of all these influences appeared later on in Ngo Dinh Nhu's pronouncements, as did his awareness that in their origins and, where there had been any, in their practical applications to statecraft, all of them took Marxism itself (or Leninism) as their starting point; some did not get far beyond it and appeared to owe their success, not to the conservatism that was their real object, but to promises of social revolution (without benefit of socialism). Nhu was influenced especially by the new review *Esprit*, in which Emmanuel Mounier was expounding with others month by month another un-Communism called Personalism. This doctrine, while admitting its Christian inspiration, claimed independence from Christianity[a] and purported to point a way—'the way of duty which is also the way of true liberty'[b]—whereby the *person* (which was not the same as, but transcended, the *individual*)[c] could liberate himself from the determination alike of capitalism and of Marxism[d] through his participation in the life of social groups—family, Church, trade union, and so on.[e] Personalism, it was claimed, did not set out to be a hard and fast system of ideas, but 'a succession of intuitions marking a road each must follow on his own and as far as he can'.[f] In a 'communal Personalist State', the person would enjoy 'the human dignity and liberty' of living under regulations and controls 'reminiscent of totalitarian regimes', but differing from them because in the latter 'unity and enthusiasm are brought about artificially and by lies', whereas under a Personalist regime they would be evoked as a spontaneous response to the leadership of 'persons of superior moral fibre'.[g] The moral qualities to be specially fostered in a 'Personalist community' were loyalty, courage, humility, renunciation, sacrifice, contentment with their lot.[h] The Personalists took a view of the family and relations between the sexes entirely in accordance with the conventions of French Catholic society.[i]

Personalism and Nhan Vi

The convenience of this doctrine, and its suitability to fit the specification for an ideology surrounding Ngo Dinh Diem as supreme leader, were clear: it sanctioned social discipline and politi-

---

[a] Grevillot (1947), p. 169.   [b] Ibid. p. 230.   [c] Mounier (1950), p. 19.
[d] Ibid. pp. 103–5.   [e] Lacroix (1949), p. 185.   [f] Grevillot, p. 193.
[g] Ibid. pp. 260–1.   [h] Ibid. pp. 242–6.
[i] Ibid. pp. 254–8; Mounier, pp. 106–9.

cal constraint in the name of a nobler liberty; it enjoyed the *nihil obstat* while entailing no offence to Vietnamese tradition; the 'human person' had been honoured in the preamble to the Charter of the United Nations. Personalism was an ideal for which Catholic and non-Catholic could work together. Ngo Dinh Nhu, who had had no occasion to study economics, was convinced that the political structure of the Corporate State was the right remedy for the three national ills of disunity, underdevelopment, and Communist subversion. Personalism would provide an ideological reference for the guidance of the institutions of the state more manageable than practical experience (which he did not yet have), and nobody else in Vietnam could contradict him as the fountainhead of doctrine and therefore of intuitions as to which course was the right one in any situation. He translated the name into Vietnamese as *Nhan Vi*[a]—a neologism of Chinese roots (*jên wei*) suggesting rank and thereby hinting that contentment with one's station might be the quality from the Personalist catalogue the new regime would prize most highly. Diem accepted his brother's ideas as an aid to the exercise of power, but did not expound them himself. Even Nhu failed to commit himself to paper, although a score or so of sycophants endeavoured to make good the deficiency during a brief vogue in 1955 and 1956.[b] In 1957 Mgr Thuc opened a school at Vinh Long for the chastening of ambitious (or possibly conscientiously fractious) civil servants by means of the anti-bureaucratic content of Personalism,[c] but the courses were not published and were hardly recollected a few years later. It was in political action that Ngo Dinh Nhu really elaborated his ideology and combined it with protestations of nationalism in order to justify his brother's dictatorship, in imitation of Ho Chi Minh's orchestration of nationalism with Marxism to justify the Communist regime.

3. THE CONSOLIDATION OF POWER

Ngo Dinh Nhu had already been active politically during Diem's absence abroad: abandoning his civil service post of Assistant Keeper in the Central Library at Hanoi, he had tried to build up a Catholic trade union movement and took a leading part in press

[a] According to Nguyen Thai (1962, p. 129), this phrase was not coined by Nhu himself but by a Dominican professor at Hanoi University who was a devotee of French Personalism on his own account.
[b] Bibliography listed by Donnell, in Fishel (1961, p. 65).
[c] Grevillot, p. 262.

agitation to hasten the end of French tutelage with the intention of 'evoking enthusiasm' for Diem to be appointed Prime Minister.[a] But in spite of the energy he and his wife both put into these efforts, there was neither widespread acclaim nor any party organization behind Diem when he took office in June 1954. The new Prime Minister was most anxious to extricate the *chrétientés* from Tonkin and made a public appearance at Hanoi to appeal to people to opt for the South; he undoubtedly hoped in so doing to gain a ready-made following, for in Vietnamese politics it was still vital to command support through pre-existing social bonds. The brothers therefore set about constructing a network of refugee and other organized interests tied to themselves and dedicated to the maintenance of Diem in office; on the negative side they eliminated, neutralized, or at least kept under discreet surveillance individuals who were not so tied. The network was given a corporate existence in the *Can Lao Nhan Vi Cach Mang Dang*, whose existence was public but its members and activities secret in accordance with tradition, and which operated on principles akin to those of the ICP behind its fronts and 'transitory organizations'; like the cadres of the ICP in the DRV, the *Can Lao* was *de facto* the state.[b87] Certainly, in the absence of a constitution, there was little else in the confusion of Vietnam on the morrow of the Geneva Conference that could have been dignified with that name.

Power and policy

In constructing his first Cabinet as Prime Minister, Diem named three 'outer' brothers to be Foreign Minister (with the immediate, and thankless, task of holding the line at Geneva), Minister of National Economy (and concurrently Ambassador to the US—a significant combination of duties), and Minister of Education. More worthy, conscientious, or talented ministers than these were certainly not to be found at the time, but that was an adventitious circumstance, not the decisive reason for their appointment to a Cabinet comprising at the outset, besides Diem and themselves, only three other members.[c] Outside the capital, Diem turned as far

---

[a] Lancaster, pp. 282 & 309.
[b] *Can Lao* was another phrase like *nhan vi*, hardly less obscure and just as pedantic, suggesting hard work, conscientiousness, and perseverance. The full title of the organization was commonly rendered into English, a little freely, as 'Revolutionary Personalist Labour Party'.
[c] Dr Tran Van Do parted from Diem quite soon (and went to prison briefly on his orders in 1960) but became Foreign Minister a second time in 1965; Mr Tran Van Chuong (Xuan's father) also left the Cabinet but retained his ambassadorship until 1963.

as possible to the Catholic community for reliable individuals to take possession of the townships on his behalf; his solicitude for the *chrétientés* was matched by his giving Catholics their head in the central provinces of Annam—which the Communists had now to evacuate—to work off old scores without questions being asked. Not a few civil servants were received into the Church, or received back, during the next few years.[a] A more sinister method of recruitment to this factional network was through toleration, if not actual encouragement, of the national failing, improbity over custody of cash. It was quickly put about, and repeatedly demonstrated to be the case, that misappropriations unaccompanied by scandal could expect full indulgence so long as the culprits did as they were told in other respects. What was required by the regime was loyalty to the 'leader of superior moral fibre' rather than allegiance to the absent Head of State. If Diem or Nhu had, during their years in the wilderness, reflected on their nation's problems and then pulled out of their pockets at this moment of accession to power a comprehensive outline plan for its exercise in the name of national reconstruction and advancement, it might have fallen on incredulous ears and failed to rally any popular support; but they did not put the possibility to the test, preferring in their turn, on the excuse of pressing problems that called for improvised solutions, the time-honoured ways of their predecessors.

Power and opposition

The negative facets of this consolidation of power similarly focused on the liquidation of rivals: there was no prior appeal for national unity and the pursuit of the common interest. But then it must be added that the previous conduct and present jockeying for advantage which absorbed the energies of most of those rivals did not betoken any useful, or even willing, response had the gesture been made. Ngo Dinh Diem's final object was to be the abolition of the monarchy; this intention was known to Bao Dai,[b] who was under American pressure not to return to Saigon to assert his authority as Head of State.[c] To get rid of Bao Dai altogether Diem had to eliminate French influence on politics, for that had become the source of the monarch's authority, and so long as any part of it remained it would (and indeed was) used to undermine the new

---

[a] However, the extent of this movement quoted by Nguyen-qui-Hung (1964, p. 173) is certainly exaggerated and inaccurate as to names.
[b] Fishel, p. 16.   [c] Lancaster, p. 382.

Government by intrigue.[a] The surviving instruments of French political influence were the Army Command and the Cochin-chinese Sects, both attached by oaths of loyalty to the monarch but by no chain of command to the Prime Minister and his Cabinet. Having no constitution to rely on, and no legislature, the new Prime Minister's control of the army depended on the Head of State's verbal promise[b] which, on the other side of the world, was meaningless; the Commander-in-Chief, over the heads of the Viet-namese service commanders, was in any case still the French High Commissioner, General Ély. General Nguyen Van Hinh had as-pired to the premiership himself, in the footsteps of his father, Nguyen Van Tam; Diem now procured a summons for him to the side of the Head of State in Paris, and, although he returned to Viet-nam once more to intrigue briefly with the Sects, in the end he re-joined the French army. The 'network' penetrated the army thanks, it has been said, to Colonel Tran Van Don[c] with the help of Annamite elements in the officer corps and the inducement of generous promotion for waverers.

Taming the Sects

Whereas the army depended on the Government completely for its pay, the Sects had depended only partly on French subsidies for theirs and proved harder nuts to crack. Deaf to the Prime Minister's appeals, in the national interest, to let themselves be incorporated in the army,[d] they hastily concluded a fresh non-aggression pact of 'spiritual union' among themselves,[e] and several months of intrigue were necessary before they were picked off one at a time. The first to be split up was the Cao Dai; dissident General Trinh Minh The had been running a private 'nationalist' insurrection of his own, independently of both Vietminh and Government, and he now 'rallied' to the Prime Minister.[88] Although more than a year was to pass before the 'Vatican' at Tay Ninh surrendered the autonomous lands of the Cao Dai in mid-1956, the illegal power of the Sect was already broken by then. Its remaining armed forces were either dis-armed or incorporated in the paramilitary forces of the state, and their leader, General Van Thanh Cao,[f] was given a sinecure from

[a] Confirmation that this was the French attitude is contained in Devillers & Lacouture (p. 311) and even Ély (pp. 260, 290, & 295).

[b] Fishel, p. 16.

[c] Devillers & Lacouture, p. 300. Don was an 'outer' cousin destined one day to play the part of Cassius.

[d] Broadcast on 24 Mar. 1955 (Cole, pp. 216–18).   [e] Lancaster, p. 383.

[f] Alias Tran Nhut Thanh.

which he could supervise Government activities in the former Cao Dai domains. The 'Pope' fled to Cambodia, and the Sect's religious work caused no further political disturbance, although sub-sects both in Tay Ninh and in Kien Hoa seem to have provided cover a few years later for resumed activities by the Communists.[a] The Binh Xuyen were shamed into accepting the closure of their gaming houses, known to be a particular object of scandal to American opinion, and were deprived of most of their clientele by the departure of the foreign troops and the end of the war-contract boom; but they rejected repeated summonses from the Prime Minister to surrender the command of the police and of the buildings which had come into their possession with it. Diem called on Ély to order the Vietnamese army, under the command of the Cochinchinese Colonel Duong Van Minh,[b] to evict them[c]—or even the *Corps Expéditionnaire* —but Ély declined to be answerable for battles in the streets, resigned, and conveniently left the country,[d] thereby terminating French tutelage of the Vietnamese armed forces. Le Van Vien's men were brought to battle nevertheless on the outskirts of Cholon, with extensive damage to houses and some loss of life, as Ély had foreseen. The battle itself was inconclusive, but it showed that the Cochinchinese elements in the army had thrown in their lot with the Annamite officers in accepting the command of the Government.[e] What had settled the issue was US insistence on channelling aid through the Exchequer in the proper way; refusal to underwrite the army's pay directly, in the manner of the French until then, still less to pay subsidies and gratifications, had sounded the knell of warlordism. Le Van Vien got away to France, and most of his followers became involved in the Communist underground, on the excuse that they had been persecuted by Ngo Dinh Diem's tyranny. The Hoa Hao, already much divided, declined a handsome quittance,[f] no doubt suspecting that a sprat was being set to catch the mackerel of their previous gains; they made a shortlived stand in the country they had just regained from the Communists under the cease-fire— the original domain of the Dao Lanh. But in the end their unpaid soldiers were persuaded to surrender to Colonel (now General) Minh without much fighting, and the leaders either took refuge in Cambodia or made their peace also on worth-while surrender

[a] The case particularly in the Binh Dai district of Kien Hoa, one-time centre of Col. Leroy's 'pacification'.
[b] In 1963 Minh was to play Brutus to Don's Cassius.   [c] Ély, pp. 305–10.
[d] Ibid. p. 319.   [e] Ibid. p. 314; Lancaster, pp. 393–5.
[f] Lancaster, pp. 393–5.

terms. The last to hold out, Le Van Ngo, alias 'Ba Cut', who had changed sides so many times during the struggle with the Vietminh, was seized at a parley, given a summary trial by court martial on a criminal charge, and guillotined. The Sect gave no more trouble in that guise, but many of its followers remained in touch with the Communists, citing the trial and execution of Ba Cut as persecution and therefore an excuse in later years for not co-operating in the Government's measures against the Vietcong.

Abolition of the Monarchy

The final withdrawal of the *Corps Expéditionnaire*, at Ngo Dinh Diem's request, took place in April 1956. French financial control had been liquidated by the winding up of the Associated States' Currency Board at the end of 1954 and the transfer of state banking functions to the National Bank, which started operations on 1 January 1955.[a] Henceforward the *présence française* was reduced to commercial activities, management of the rubber estates, and the cultural mission, all of which, however, continued to employ numerous French personnel and to make invaluable contributions to South Vietnam economically and educationally. A long campaign of official propaganda had been conducted by the Prime Minister and his brothers against Bao Dai as Head of State, and at Hué Ngo Dinh Can staged a 'spontaneous' public demonstration to break open symbolically the gates of the Great Within[b] and assemble the imperial family in a conclave to dethrone the monarch. In October 1955 a referendum was held to decide the issue: monarchy or republic. The success of intrigues in the army and of manœuvres amongst the Sects, as well as relief in Annam at seeing the back of the DRV and the advent of a Prime Minister from their own region, all seemed to the people to show that Ngo Dinh Diem's horoscope was a lucky one; the conviction was clinched by the unreserved support, moral and financial, of the US, from which so many urban Vietnamese hoped to benefit. Even so, the referendum was so contrived as to give nearly 6 million votes to Diem and a mere 60,000 to Bao Dai. The ballot papers had been printed to portray Diem in lucky red, Bao Dai in unlucky green, while in Saigon the returning officer was the new Commissioner of Police, General Mai Huu Xuan (back from the army), who, according to French

[a] Franco-Vietnamese financial agreement of 29 Dec. 1954. The new Bank's working capital was furnished by French Treasury loans (Cole 1956, p. 199), but the main function of the Bank was to handle American aid (Lancaster, p. 353).
[b] Ibid. pp. 397–8.

reports, returned 605,000 votes by 450,000 voters.[a] The Republic of Vietnam was proclaimed on 20 October 1955, and six days later Diem proclaimed himself President;[b] he waited another year before having this proclamation confirmed by election under a new constitution.

Sovereignty of the RVN

In addition to confirming Ngo Dinh Diem in the supreme executive power, the referendum, by cutting the South adrift from Bao Dai, freed it from any residual links of sovereignty between the monarchy and the North and so went some way towards establishing, by the popular will, the separate sovereignty of the Republic of Vietnam. The Geneva Agreement and its Final Declaration envisaged the holding of elections in both halves of Vietnam the following July (1956) as a preliminary, not very clearly thought out, to unification. But Diem set his face against even the preparatory discussions about elections which the Final Declaration had enjoined (its force, if any, was uncertain);[c] his behaviour was put down in the West most commonly to obstinacy and avidity for despotic power, yet the truth was more complicated than either these critics, or the drafters of the agreement, may have realized. Obstinate and avid for power Diem may also have been, but the decisive factor for him was the balance of population between North and South: before the cease-fire the Communists had had under their control barely a quarter of the total population of the country, and perhaps not that; the cease-fire had awarded them, with their slightly smaller half of the national territory, a clear majority (even taking account of the transfer of population) of close on 2 millions. In the circumstances prevailing in 1955 and 1956—anarchy of the Sects and of the retiring Vietminh in the South, terror campaign of the land reform and resultant peasant uprising round Vinh in the North—it was only to be expected that voters would vote, out of fear of reprisals, in favour of the authorities under whom they found themselves; that the ICC had no hope of ensuring a truly free election at that time has been admitted since by the chief sponsor of the Final Declaration, Lord Avon.[d] Unification after elections would therefore have delivered 14 million Vietnamese in the South

[a] Ibid. p. 399. The accusation is perfectly credible, but the present author has not actually been able to verify it.

[b] He was recognized by the US Government the same day (US, *American Foreign Policy 1950–5*, p. 2404).

[c] The issues are argued in Partan (1966), pp. 289–92.   [d] Eden (1966), p. 24.

to the rule of the DRV irrespectively of whether they had voted for it or not.[a] In point of fact, the pressure to hold elections all came from outside Vietnam and was concentrated against Ngo Dinh Diem, not against Ho Chi Minh. The latter, though glad to blame non-compliance with the Final Declaration on his rival (as well as on the US), can have had no wish to expose his internal problems to the gaze of the ICC and so contented himself with an anodyne protest, in the form of a joint communiqué with Premier Chou En-lai after a meeting at Peking in July 1955, merely reserving his position.[b] Diem, for his part, with the intention of further disarming criticism, followed up the referendum with elections in March 1956 for a Constituent Assembly, at which candidates were also elected for twelve constituencies composed exclusively of Tonkinese refugees,[c] thereby emphasizing the unthinkability of elections of any sort in the North at the time, with or without international supervision.

With these constitutional measures to establish a separate sovereignty in the South went practical measures for its isolation from the North. The DRV, suffering the economic effects of the loss of Cochinchinese rice shipments, sought a resumption of communications and of trade on several occasions, but, for fear of DRV abuse of reopened communications for propaganda, intimidation, and subversion, Ngo Dinh Diem vetoed even postal exchange services, except for Red Cross postcards.[d] Given the number of divided families, the resulting necessity for communications to pass through a third country or by other roundabout means appeared to many Westerners to be carrying caution to the point of cruelty. Diem remained adamant in disregard of protestations which even the US Ambassador felt moved to make.[e] His attitude implied the reversal of his original opposition to partition before and during the Geneva Conference; but he did not expect the Communist Government in China, in the light of her historical vulnerability through Tonkin, substantiated by recent memories of French and Japanese abuse of Tonkinese territory, ever to accept an unfriendly or even neutral regime on her southern frontier.[f] Once partition had come about, here was another reason why it could only be undone on terms acceptable to the Communists. Partition had therefore to be put

[a] The inconsistencies written into the agreement and the equivocations they led to are discussed in Bator, pp. 129–39.

[b] RIIA, *Documents 1955*, pp. 475–9.   [c] Vu-quoc-Thong, pp. 36–40.

[d] Haiphong Protocol of 12 Apr. 1955.   [e] Or so Diem told the author.

[f] Also from Diem himself.

up with for the time being and international recognition to be secured for the sovereignty of the RVN; that in turn seemed to Diem to demand the erection of a frontier between North and South impenetrable by any means, including armed force, and at the same time to exclude any thought on his own part of ultimate intervention in the North by force of arms—a possibility mooted in Saigon military circles from time to time—lest China should step in.[a]

Power and government

In the space of two years Ngo Dinh Diem transformed himself from the powerless and expendable local chancellor of a discredited absentee monarch into the executive Head of State of a sovereign republic. The new state, although he had contrived for it the passive endorsement of a plebiscite, was his personal creation and in no sense reflected public debate. Each step in his transformation had on the contrary entailed a minor coup d'état (within the army, within the Sects, against the French High Commissioner, the former Head of State, the Geneva Agreements), and the whole made up a revolution—little more than a palace revolution, it is true, without active popular participation, but essentially a Personalist revolution, in which the leader of superior moral fibre had 'evoked the enthusiasm' of the people at the confirmatory referendum and elections for a legislature. Coming within weeks of the general stirrings in eastern Europe to loosen the shackles of the Soviet Union, and on the very day of the uprising in Budapest (26 October 1956), Diem's formal assumption of supreme office could be represented to world opinion as the vindication of democratic nationalism, triumphant over the legacies of colonialism and unbowed by the threats of a Communist regime itself menaced by the peasant disturbances of Nghe An and 'many lesser Poznans'.[b] He and his brothers had every cause to congratulate themselves on their recipe for power and on their judicious mixing of its ingredients— intrigue, nepotism, simony, public humbug, and private intimidation. But henceforward it was a question of exercising the power they had won. Unhappily, they determined to carry on as they had begun, governing in their turn by the methods of revolution; they appeared to neglect, if they knew, the Confucian warning given to

---

[a] Still the same source. DRV complaints later on of the activities of sabotage teams from the RVN were probably well founded, but these amounted to no more than nuisance reprisals for acts of terrorism inspired by the North in the South.

[b] The phrase of a Hanoi official talking to Chaffard (1956) at the time of the disturbances in Poland.

the first Han Emperor by his principal counsellor: 'Your Majesty won the realm on horseback, but it can only be governed from the Throne.' But then they were able to foresee that their rule would never encounter opposition over particular measures: any who opposed them would be outright rivals for power, not critics of policy, with no more right to rule arbitrarily, and probably less capacity, than themselves.[a] The popular Vietnamese idea of democracy had proved itself to be identical with the anarchy of factionalism, ceaselessly bargaining with the Government for partisan advantage, unwilling to submit to regulation by law in the national interest, and dangerously expanded into warlordism in the last years of French colonial rule. Unlike, as it seemed to them, their Western collaborators, the Ngo brothers did not overestimate the moral qualities of their fellow countrymen, but counted on superstition, greed, and spite as the mainsprings of action in public affairs. Their policy was to harness these faults to their power structure, for the good of the state they were trying to create. In the event it could be said they merely put a premium on the national faults without assuring the state.

4. THE INSTITUTIONS OF THE STATE

Some American officials congratulated themselves on the advent to power of Ngo Dinh Diem that, in addition to his major qualifications of integrity in regard to money and an unshakeable anti-Communism, his career as a young man had brought him valuable experience of how governments work. In this also they were deceived: Diem's early career in the mandarinate had been short, and he had isolated himself from the main stream of administrative action by his disdainful refusal to co-operate. As President, he used to impute to his subordinates a general scepticism about the principles of democracy and justice supposed to reign in Western counties; most of them believed it was all a sham—that elections and trials, even by jury, were rigged in advance.[b] But he behaved as if he secretly shared that opinion, and the 1956 constitution, although the Faculty of Law also had a hand in its drafting, reflected both Diem's ignorance of the practice of government and a certain am-

---

a Another *obiter dictum* of President Diem to the author.
b The same source. The gerrymandering by which officials could conspire to rig a Vietnamese election, apparently to oblige Mme Nhu and please the President, is related by a candidate at the 1959 election for the National Assembly (Nguyen-tuyet-Mai, 1962). See however note 108.

biguity over principles—not to put a harsher name to it—for which Personalism provided a moral sanction.

Republican Constitution

The constitution proclaimed all the basic Rights of Man and freedoms of belief, association, and property, but with a proviso to each to enable suspension at the discretion of the Executive in individual cases; the concluding article empowered the President to suspend the whole chapter by decree during the initial legislative term. Separation of powers was made much of; however, the legislative power was delegated to the executive when the National Assembly was not sitting (that is, most of the year); the Judiciary was to be independent, but only while on the bench, and there was no word as to appointments or removability.[a] The President enjoyed full executive powers, ostensibly as in the US, but without most of the checks and balances—particularly, of course, without those owed in America to original regional sovereignty. It is in fact hard to think of any power his constitution did not confer on President Diem. He could legislate without the Assembly,[b] but not the Assembly without him; supply required the Assembly's endorsement (chapter by chapter, without specification of items and without knowledge of the extent of foreign aid available, so that the debates meant very little), but the executive's proposals could only be negatived by a minimum of 91 votes out of the total of 123.[c] The members of the Assembly were then required, by their Standing Orders, to sit and vote as two Majority and Minority Blocs of 107 and 16 Deputies[d]—after a second election in 1959, into a Personalist Bloc (80) on the left and a Socialist Bloc (35) on the right (*sic*), with two 'independents' like a cushion in the middle. How the President organized the Government was evidently no concern of the constitution, and his Secretaries of State were answerable only to him.[e] A National Economic Council was created under the constitution, but not actually appointed until 1961; even then it had no powers and played no part in policy-making but, with its membership made up of representatives from professional, industrial, and commercial associations, had probably been intended originally as an

[a] RVN, *Constitution, passim.*
[b] By 'Order in Council' (art. 41); but there was no council.
[c] Arts. 58–61.   [d] Vu-quoc-Thong, p. 29.
[e] Only once, in November 1962, during the National Assembly session to approve the following year's estimates (and make provision for the 'strategic hamlets'), were Secretaries of State required by the President to submit to *interpellation* by the Deputies. The experiment proved the system could have worked.

embodiment of the Corporate State. No laws were ever enacted to prescribe penalties against public officers or others who violated the rights of citizens laid down in the constitution, and although provision was made for impeachment of the President, this could only be for 'treason or high crimes' and, again, no procedure was framed. The constitution established a dictatorship in law; its exercise in fact depended on the organization and direction of the departments of the executive.

Structure of the government

Under Bao Dai's State of Viet-Nam, the ministers had appeared to share responsibility for policy with the Prime Minister, who was *Président du Conseil*.[a] Under the Republic they were all civil servants with the title Secretary of State and much reduced status, ostensibly in imitation of American practice. On the rare, and irregular, occasions when all fourteen met together in the presence of the President they were said to constitute the Cabinet;[b] but the function of such gatherings was limited expressly to tendering advice.[c] French neglect in regard to the legal powers of the executive had continued under the postwar Cochinchinese Governments, and the Republic's ministries were direct descendants of those bodies, usually with the same staff housed in the same offices in Saigon; in fact, the taking over by Ngo Dinh Diem of the Vietminh provinces of Annam was again interpreted by some of the people as the extension to that region of the authority of Cochinchina. Under the Republic, therefore, old procedures were perpetuated by administrative inertia, and where laws dating from the colonial period had vested powers in a *Résident*, a Governor, or the Governor-General, they tended henceforward to be exercised arbitrarily by any official able to impose his will; nobody took the trouble to go through the laws and reallocate such powers by act of the National Assembly. With their uncertain powers and imprecise portfolios, the Secretaries of State found themselves without the protection of collective responsibility and collective policy-making; each had to take decisions on his own, without formal consultation with his colleagues,[d]

[a] Transition from one system of government to the other was made easier by the verbal coincidence *Président du Conseil/Président de la République*.

[b] The ambiguity of French usage, where *cabinet* means private secretariat at the same time as Cabinet, has been carried over in Vietnam.

[c] Vu-quoc-Thong, p. 47.

[d] Many committees were set up, whose proceedings some deemed binding, others merely deliberative; minutes were rarely kept, and both genuine misunderstandings and unconscionable changes of mind abounded, today's victims becoming tomorrow's culprits (Nghiem Dang, p. 298).

and quickly the sole criterion came to be whatever would gratify the President, to whom they were all answerable constitutionally and, in the absence of any popular following of their own, as his creatures, to make or break. Whenever a new policy was adopted, it was not the duty of the department already entrusted with the subject to carry it out; instead a new department would be set up in competition. This was the case first with land reform and later with successive measures for pacification, each of which gave rise to a new department. On few topics was a single policy pursued consistently, and Ngo Dinh Nhu, now invested with the title (but no office) of Political Counsellor, was enabled to establish himself astride all the passages into the palace. The intuition and the commands of the President and his brother took the place of consultation, planned co-operation, and collective responsibility; by keeping the ministers in water-tight compartments they ruled them more effectively, but they took upon themselves a task of co-ordination that lay beyond their capacity; they upheld the patriarchy, but at cost to the nation.

Arbitrary administration

Uncoordinated and changeable policy, accompanied by disregard for the rule of law, made itself felt all through the government machine. Planning was impossible without integration of financial and technical measures and consistency in their pursuit, and if any advance was registered in any matter, it was usually in isolation in some very narrow field. When a technical service could not count on the continuing collaboration of other departments, there was no alternative but to seek or accept special assistance from American helpers and thereby perpetuate or increase dependence on foreign support; so much so that the Political Counsellor is alleged to have been in the habit of proposing that very step, in so many words if perhaps sarcastically, to any who complained. Virements of credits in the budgets of some departments were turned into a habit in order to conceal diversion of funds under other heads to political ends, on instructions from the Palace; they had the additional consequence of making embezzlement easier, and that also the President and his brother looked upon as a potential pledge of loyalty.[a]
The relating of educational policy to the needs of economic develop-

[a] Scigliano, p. 60. Embezzlement was made a capital crime by *Luat* No. 6 of 18 Apr. 1959; on the face of it, this was a gesture of determination to stamp out an abuse that upset foreign advisers; but its practical effect was to render more magnanimous (at no actual cost) the Palace's acts of *noli procedere* in exchange for the pledge of loyalty.

ment was impossible so long as policies for the latter were blocked by indecision and those for the former might be arrived at emotionally, on an inspection away from the capital, for the sake of some local publicity advantage. Gravest of all, in the precarious state of public security outside the townships, was the effect on control of the security forces, from the police up to the army. The President was Commander-in-Chief and his own Defence Minister and gave orders to the General Staff, but was liable at the same time to issue them to lower echelons direct, to the embarrassment of the Staff. Some time after the Communist insurrection had been resumed—and, more significantly perhaps, after the unsuccessful mutiny at the end of 1960—a National Security Council was set up which did bring together the General Staff, the Defence Staff, the Minister of the Interior, and one or two others. However, this body still did not work like a Cabinet, on the principle of collective responsibility; it turned out to be less a device for co-ordinating strategy over the whole field of government and defence than one for enabling the Political Counsellor to take charge as chairman and to exercise the dictatorship on his own account.

Style of administration

Ngo Dinh Diem, in his handling of the civil service, liked to hear talk of high-sounding Confucian principles, and it is to his credit that the treatises on the national history and government from the Hong Duc and later periods were printed with the blessing of his Government, if not his personal patronage, for the first time. But he showed no concern for the consolidation of the civil service as a modern institution that could be turned to practical use. Confucianism had from the earliest times prized the ability to write well as the highest of all qualities sought in members of the bureaucracy, and although we noted before the pedantry that often crept in in China, the ideal of official style was none the less clarity of thought and brevity and directness of expression. The orderly functioning of a modern government depends very much on working methods and standards generally and on the customs in drafting its internal communications and decisions in particular. Many individual Vietnamese civil servants fulfilled this requirement, but in spite, not because, of any lead from the Palace. Formlessness, prevarication, and wordiness became the currency of reporting, and the President derived satisfaction from rambling 'studies' by his Palace aides and favourites on subjects they were rarely acquainted with at first hand. The muddled thinking which flourished in his entourage underlay his habit, deplored outside the Palace, of trying to settle individual cases himself— often after unbearable delays for the persons interested—while neglecting to make up his mind on the general policy in the matter and not allowing any lesser official so to do. There was a corresponding failure of leadership in the control and discipline of departments: no clear principle held superiors responsible for keeping their subordinates on the rails of legality, of policy, of efficiency, and of honesty. Chinese precedent—and to some extent French—justified the creation of inspectorates external to the chain of command, upon whose distant shoulders the distasteful duty of detecting abuses could be shrugged off but who rarely had any idea themselves what ought to be done in departments unfamiliar to them, and so were not answerable for any suggestions they did make. The result was that even corruption, which perhaps was the kind of abuse most susceptible of treatment by an external inspectorate, went almost unchecked.[a] Lack of control made it all the easier for the Communists to persuade government employees to oblige the revolution by simply neglecting their duties.

The Fonction Publique

The constitution of the *Fonction Publique* (*Giam Doc Cong Vu*) in succession to the colonial cadres had been attended to on French initiative early in the life of the State of Viet-Nam and enshrined in a statute[b] that laid down principles for recruitment, promotion, discipline, and the calculation of emoluments. Many of its provisions were modified by administrative circular after 1955, but invariably with the effect of multiplying the opportunities for arbitrary interference from the Palace;[89] the right of civil servants to the safeguard of a fair inquiry before any penalty was invoked against them had been suspended by Ngo Dinh Diem as soon as he took office as Prime Minister.[c] A National Institute of Administration had been opened at Dalat in 1952; transferred to Saigon and enlarged in 1955, it operated as a high school somewhat in the tradition of the *Quoc Hoc* at Hué, but with a staff of Vietnamese university professors, giving three-year courses in a curriculum of economics and social subjects that was an extension of the French Faculty of Law. The civil service had neither a hand nor a say in the

---

[a] The DRV was no less prone to the national failing, and President Ho is the authority for saying so (Ginsburgs, p. 187, quoting him from a Russian publication).
[b] *Du* No. 9 of 1950.   [c] *Arrêté* No. 20 of 1 Aug. 1954.

running of the Institute, whose staff were not themselves practition-
ers of the duties they were preparing pupils to take on; moreover, it
was normal practice for the students to study concurrently for law
degrees, whilst also working several hours a day in odd jobs to sup-
plement their bursaries.[a] However, there was a good deal of direct
recruitment to even the higher ranks of the civil service; the practice of making appointments as a reward for military service
opened the door to patronage of other sorts, and from patronage to
venality. Promotion was rarely by seniority but almost entirely on
the same basis as recruitment: at best promotion on merit meant
service rendered to the Palace, and not necessarily to the President.
The upheavals of the years 1945–54 necessitated new departments
and recruitment of temporary staffs; these were never sorted out
under Ngo Dinh Diem, and by 1963 more than half the public servants were unestablished permanent staff, the majority actually on
daily rates, with no security, meagre pay, and commensurate
conscientiousness. Salary scales throughout remained at a pre-1954
level in spite of the reduced purchasing power of the piastre; senior
ranks were mostly filled by men of independent means, but among
the juniors 'moonlighting' became prevalent, either by obtaining
twin appointments in government service or by working for a
private employer as well. It was observed in the Palace that devotion to duty was growing rarer for all these reasons; remedies were
not sought through reform, however, but through redoubled infiltration of Can Lao agents and more intensive indoctrination in
Personalism—by making it obligatory for civil servants to belong
to the National Revolutionary Movement (*Phong-trao Cach Mang
Quoc Gia*), while their wives joined the Women's Solidarity Movement (*Phong-trao Lien Doi Phu Nu*), and their daughters, from 1961
onwards, the Women's Organization for Military Training (*To-
chuc Ban Quan-su Phu Nu*).[b]

Law Reform

The need for law reform bequeathed by the French administration had become acute since 1946. The financial separateness of
truncated Annam from Cochinchina was terminated in 1955,[c] and

[a] Dr Guy E. Fox, in Lindholm, p. 169.
[b] These movements, whose members owed allegiance to Nhu and Xuan rather than to
the President (still less to the Government or the Nation) were extended from the
beginning of 1962 to take in all the urban middle class and no longer just Government
employees. Mme Nhu never patronized nursing—only the young amazons of the
Womens' Organization.
[c] *Du* No. 17 of 24 Oct. 1955.

a committee of jurists was appointed at the same time to rewrite the fundamental codes on a unitary basis—a task last attempted by Admiral Decoux; but the Committee never presented its work to the President.[a] Other tidying up was put off until that task should be completed and while efforts were made to interest the legislature and public opinion in, first, the Marriage Laws (1959) and, second, the Morality Law (1962), to which the Palace was alone in ascribing either urgency or desirability as embodiments of Personalist ideology. As the Government produced a ceaseless flow of decisions, decrees, and administrative instructions with little apparent regard for suitability of legislative form, for their effects upon existing legislation, for arrangements for execution or for precision in drafting (to some extent a problem of language), the confusion actually increased. It was in any case not always a straightforward matter for officials far from Saigon to be sure what the laws were, even without these complications; printed texts had never been numerous and had been further dissipated by looting and arson in government offices. In 1962, therefore, the Ministry of Justice had the principal enactments concerning law and order reprinted more or less as they stood,[b] although, even so, distribution to those who had a duty to carry them out generally stopped short at the province level, and junior magistrates (usually army subalterns) were dependent on the advice of their clerks who might, or might not, have borrowed a text or made notes from one.

The Judiciary

Aggravations of a legal system already noted for its cumbersome procedures added to the burdens of the Judiciary, where the biggest gaps in personnel had been left by the exodus of French (and naturalized Vietnamese) officers of the court. All the same, the number of indictable offences tried by the criminal courts quintupled between 1954 and 1963[c]—not, it would seem, because of a corresponding increase in the incidence of crime, but because the judicial process was being restored. It was never restored fully, however. In the parts of the country that had suffered most in the turmoil of the previous decade—the Mien Tay and the greater part of Annam—there were not enough judicial staff to go round[90] and

---

[a] The drafts of five codes were not completed until May–July 1966 and were not published even then (*VNP*, No. 5575, 2 June 1966).

[b] Nguyen-van-Hao (1962); repeal or amendment by decree was taken account of but not the effect of other types of regulation.

[c] From 533 charges in 1954 (*Ann. stat. 1962*, p. 376) to 4,148 in 1963 (ibid. *1963*, p. 130).

an insufficient, if any, police force to support them; in these places members of the territorial administration doubled as JPs, while the paramilitary forces, or the local militia, performed the more rough-and-ready police tasks, for whose execution they were answerable to their own commandants, not to the Minister of Justice.[a] In the absence of legal texts, procedures, jurisdictions, verdicts, and sentences all partook of the same quality of rough and—so far as both accused and public could see—arbitrary justice; the best that could be said for these procedures was that they were a degree less rough and ready than the 'justice' meted out in these areas by the Sects and the Vietminh. There were no gazetted prisons—a formality the French administration had not been squeamish about—, and, with only two or three buildings in the country that had been built for the purpose, persons awaiting trial and even convicted persons were housed in improvised camps called Re-education Centres or in any sort of lock-up (sometimes without furniture, sanitation, or feeding), or put to work on parole for want of proper arrangements —or even, if they were lucky, quietly set free, there being no judicial or other inspection to bring the fact to light. As the Communists gradually renewed the unrest in the countryside, the regime succumbed more and more to the temptation to govern as far as possible without recourse to either the ordinary laws or the courts, or else through special tribunals. Apparently with the mistaken idea of overawing and deterring would-be Communist offenders, the State of Viet-Nam had some years before transferred jurisdiction in offences involving the security of the state to military tribunals, presided over by a civilian judge with army assessors and following a simplified procedure.[b] These courts continued under the Republic to relieve the normal Judiciary of its proper duties in the maintenance of law and order, but over them there was set up, within weeks of Ngo Dinh Diem's appointment as Prime Minister, a Special Military Tribunal presided over by a field or general officer of the army (as in the DRV, one with legal training but never a judge) with jurisdiction over charges of sabotage, kidnapping, or assassination (all covered by the Penal Code but punishable more severely under a new law often cited as an example of the regime's 'tyranny')[c] and power to pass the death sentence, whose pronouncement was not subject to appeal, although it must be con-

[a] The Minister of Justice, in answer to an *interpellation* in the National Assembly in Nov. 1962 (quoted by Fall, 1963, p. 369).
[b] Art. 2(3) of *Du* No. 8 of 14 May 1951 (*Bo Quan Luat*).
[c] *Du* No. 10 of 6 May 1959.

firmed by the Head of State.[a] The bringing of cases in any of these courts was a purely political decision, and trials before the Special Military Court—which came under the supervision of the Ministry of Defence, not of Justice—were staged for their publicity effect, as we shall see in the next chapter, sometimes after delays of a year or two or longer.

Territorial administration

In a country at Vietnam's stage of development the key institution of the state was the territorial administration. By 1954 there were 32 provinces south of the 17th parallel, varying in area from under 200 square miles to over 8,000 and in population from under 30,000 to over a million; each province was subdivided into between two and eight or ten districts whose populations ranged from 1,300 to 200,000.[b] It was upon efficiency at this level that the nation-wide application of policy depended, and with it the standing of the Government in the people's eyes as one they could have confidence in. Moreover, the maintenance of province and district government in a robust condition corresponded to traditional ideas. This was appreciated by President Diem. Unfortunately, not content with making certain that no previously existing offices went unmanned, he increased the number of provinces by about a third during the course of his tenure and the number of districts by a fifth. This was done in the interests of closer administration; but by creating more boundaries and limiting administrative jurisdictions, it actually had the opposite effect and exposed a bigger number of villages to Communist infiltration or hit-and-run attacks along the borders of districts and provinces. The measure served to provide a bigger range of offices of reward for loyal followers and, in some sensitive areas, to prevent any one of them from becoming too powerful. Available personnel were put to the least economical use, and insuperable problems of reorganization arose for the land registry and similar departments, leading, for at least a year or two after each change, to near-chaos in the collection of revenue and reallocation of expenditure. Neither the powers nor the responsibilities of Province Chiefs, who in Annam were a combination of the sometime mandarin with the French *Résident*, were worked out; the Ministry of the Interior exercised supervision over questions of finance and supply, but the nature and degree of control technical

[a] *Du* No. 47 of 21 July 1954, amended in 1955 (twice), 1956 and 1959.
[b] Woodruff (1961), p. 13.

departments could exercise over their staffs in the field varied arbitrarily according to the character of particular Province Chiefs. Doubts over ministerial portfolios combined with some resentment of ministerial authority, viewed in Annam as an encroachment from Cochinchina, and with the general inexperience of most of the officials, to give rise to much confusion in the territorial administration. The termination of regional separation between Annam and Cochinchina was beneficial, but difficulties of communication led soon afterwards to its restoration in the modified form of four super-Province Chiefs called incongruously *Délégués du Gouvernement*, appointed one each for the west and the east of Cochinchina and for the highlands and lowlands of Annam. Here again were officials without powers derived from law, whose position was justified on the face of it by vague notions of co-ordination between provinces, but whose real function was to provide the Palace with another set of eyes in the general setting of mutual spying. The *Délégué* for the lowlands of Annam resided at Hué and acted as the front man for Ngo Dinh Can, who was neither informed of nor cared about policies emanating from Saigon and originating with his brother and rival Nhu.

Army Province Chiefs

General shortage of manpower, the conscription of potential administrators of military age, the unpopularity of provincial appointments in the years before province aid-budgets (to be discussed in the next chapter) began, the desire to reward loyalty in the army as well as in civil office, and threats to law and order from well-armed guerrilla bands, Communist and other, all resulted in the secondment of army officers to vacancies in the territorial administration. The Camau province of Cochinchina and the Plain of Reeds were placed temporarily under official Vietminh control in 1954 as a regrouping area under the Geneva Agreement, and these and a few other particularly unsettled provinces never had civilians in charge even in 1954 and 1955. From 1958 onwards, soldiers gradually took over more and more provinces, until by 1963 only five were administered by the civil service; the militarization of the districts was completed more rapidly. In the main, the effect of this policy was to weaken the administration, not to strengthen it as it was obviously expected to do. It emphasized the military aspect of the officer's duties to the neglect of the administrative aspect, and this was the prime cause of the disturbances that made the military aspect important; the new Province Chiefs were tempted to delegate the thornier administrative problems to subordinates instead of the day-to-day military ones and to try to earn a reputation for gallantry in the Colonel Leroy tradition instead of one for efficiency. As army postings were usually for limited periods, few officers gained sufficient experience of public administration before they moved on, and there was a tendency to make the most of a limited tenure by pocketing the cash or furthering family and factional interests, without the restraint of having to live with the consequences of wrong action that tends to deter the professional civil servant from abuse. In the last years of the dictatorship it was widely alleged that interference by Area Commanders of divisions and corps, who considered that all officers of lesser rank must fall under their direct command, could only be resisted by generous gratifications levied on certain items in the provincial budget that were difficult to audit—subheads for intelligence, maintenance of militia, and so on. Civilian Province Chiefs were less liable to these pressures, but their appeals to Area Commanders for defence support against Communist attacks might go unheeded if previous hints that a subvention would be welcome had also gone unheeded.

Local government

Strictly local government was left until 1961 at the discretion of the territorial administration. Province Councils, suspended by Admiral Decoux in 1943, remained in abeyance; this on balance was probably a good thing, for they could have contributed little to village well-being but would have been very exposed to intimidation. The policy followed in regard to village administration was not to interfere with the traditional autonomy of the *xa* but to encourage the villagers—or to leave them—to manage their own affairs and settle their disputes by themselves. On the other hand, the village officials who were to perform these duties were no longer elected, the old procedures having fallen victim to the general confusion of the times. After the anarchy of 1945 and the flight of village notables to the towns, the Cochinchinese Government had in 1947 offered a small expense allowance as an incentive to accept an unpopular job. In the end whether the notables did stay and whether they formed themselves into a village council (*hoi dong xa*) depended on the fate of the village at the hands of the Communists or the Sects. A decree of 1956[a] defined the constitution of village councils more closely; they were to have from four to six paid mem-

---

[a] No. 57A of 24 Oct. 1956.

bers, each of whom would have a specific duty (keeping the peace, collecting the taxes, registering births and deaths, and so on) and would be appointed to it by the Province Chief. Like many Vietnamese constitutional documents, this one did not define what powers it was intended to confer either, so that its execution continued to be as arbitrary as ever. In fact, what heed was paid to it varied from place to place: some councillors actually underwent training[a] and carried out their duties in a fairly regular manner, but in other parts of the country the law was, as so often, not known about. The decree itself—or else an administrative instruction from the Minister of the Interior in the same sense which preceded it— has often been cited by Western writers, as well as in Communist propaganda, as an example of Ngo Dinh Diem's despotic urge to do away with democracy and, more than that, as the main reason why the Communists were able to recruit supporters for their second uprising. The truth, however, is that village administration on the old basis had already broken down in the prevailing confusion and fear, but where elected councils were functioning they carried on. A measure enabling the territorial administrators to reimpose law and order was opposed by all who had profited by the confusion and fear, and Ngo Dinh Diem is to be criticized not for the attempt but for his lack of perseverance. During these years tax collection was resumed over a wide area and many of the tax rolls were brought up to date for the first time for fifteen years. On the other hand, the observance of the traditional ceremonies, agricultural and other, by which village solidarity was annually consecrated, tended to fall further into disuse; only in villages with a strong sense of community were the rites kept up by the traditional celebrants, independently of the council charged with the village administration. Generally speaking, although the Government continued to delegate to the village the collection (though not the assessment) of direct taxes and entrusted the councils with new duties on its behalf, such as administration of the agricultural-credit scheme, it showed little interest down to about 1961 in the actual conduct of village affairs, in the belief that native democratic traditions would keep the councils reasonably honest and immune to subversion. When the change in attitude did come, it was due to the sharp deterioration in law and order and to realization that the Government had hitherto failed to establish its writ over much, if not most, of the territory of South Vietnam.

[a] Hickey (1964), p. 183.

5. ECONOMIC AND SOCIAL DEVELOPMENTS

The material achievements of the Ngo Dinh Diem dictatorship were far from negligible; but they were circumscribed by the administrative limitations of the regime itself, as well as by insecurity fomented by the Communists outside the towns. The failure to get the better of the troublemakers in the early stages was attributable to the regime's reliance on the mystical force of ideology and its belief that righteousness must necessarily be rewarded with providential success, instead of counting on sound policy to win public confidence. But if Diem and Nhu failed to keep their powder dry, it was primarily because they did not know how; ignorant of economics, they depended for their social ideas on religious writers. Substitution of the Personalist philosophy for pragmatic policies led Nhu into the same inconsistency as his spiritual mentors in France of proclaiming himself to be a left-wing socialist politically (in the seating of the Personalist Bloc in the National Assembly, for example), and therefore as much a champion of the underprivileged as any Communist, whilst upholding private ownership of resources, notably in the context of land development, even where private enterprise was less suitable and public control would have been reconcilable with Vietnamese custom. In avoiding economic measures that might be thought to savour of socialism, he and his brother were also avoiding offence to American public opinion.

Economic planning

The main ingredients of economic planning in the early years had necessarily to come from outside the country because of the dearth —though by no means total lack—of experienced Vietnamese economists, bankers, and business or industrial managers, and, more seriously, the limited native capital available in realizable assets: private savings and family fortunes, although built up more rapidly than they would have been if the country had not been so undertaxed, still tended to be locked up in the traditional investment, agricultural or plantation land, while new capital had been absorbed by quick-return war contracts or else was flowing, and would continue to flow, into overseas holdings, through the black market in foreign exchange resulting from the French or American presence and French or American aid. It followed that, whatever economic policy might be pursued, the Government was going to have to provide not merely the planning and the basic services such as transport and public utilities, but also land for new enterprise, whether industrial or agricultural, and both management and a major share of the capital. A twenty-man UN Technical Assistance Board team spent three months at the end of 1955 surveying almost every aspect of the South Vietnamese economy; it catalogued the problems and deficiencies attributable either to the war or to more permanent factors and pointed out that the country was under-taxed, but beyond urging, in a general way, concentration in future on improvements to agriculture as the road towards financial independence, with industry developing primarily in support of that central purpose, it produced no development plan.[a]

Land reform and industry

Both the Vietnamese officials put in charge of economic affairs and their French and American advisers were taken up with pressing separate problems, for which they sought uncoordinated and often short-term solutions. The resettlement of refugees dominated the scene for a long time, and the approach to the agrarian question and to the possibilities of industrial development were alike dominated by the urgency of finding a livelihood for these immigrants. Settlement on the land raised questions of land tenure and land reform; land reform meant compulsory transfer of private rights, but the Government disposed of no reserves from which to indemnify present owners and could secure, for reasons to be explained below, no American aid for this purpose. No objections of principle stood in the way of American finance for industrial purposes, and consequently the ingenious device was hit on of paying expropriated landowners only 10 per cent in cash and the balance in bonds redeemable in cash after twelve years (by which time the Government hoped to be more solvent, if only because it would have recovered the amounts from the new owners) or exchangeable immediately for shares in joint enterprises whose working capital would be derived in part from other private shareholders, but mainly from foreign aid. This arrangement might appear at first sight to constitute an element of economic co-ordination between agrarian and industrial policy; but the links were purely financial, with a political motive uppermost which, whilst perhaps strengthening the regime's support among the refugees, did not of itself foster economic development.

[a] UN & others, pp. 29–30 & 220–4.

New industries

None the less, in the course of a first Five-Year Plan (mid-1957 to mid-1962)—a piece of publicity rather than a detailed programme —the joint-enterprise formula, coupled with tax concessions on private investment in free enterprise, claimed to have attracted more than 1,750 million piastres of local private capital to match an official investment of 2,000 million.[a] The enterprises these investments created included cotton weaving to make good the loss of the product from Nam Dinh in Tonkin and representing private investments in excess of 560 million piastres,[b] paper manufacture, pharmaceuticals, food preserving, and bicycles; the total number of new enterprises set in train down to 1962 was 700,[c] though not all survived the complicated procedure for licensing and the dilatory manner of applying it.[d] A big cement works was erected as a joint enterprise to exploit raw material available near the Gulf of Siam, and exploitation of the coal field at Nong Son, near Danang, replaced imports of 26,000 tons in 1955 by local production of 57,000 tons in 1961.[e] It was hoped to concentrate industrial enterprises at Nong Son and on the outskirts of Saigon; electrical power for the latter was to be supplied from a hydro-electric scheme at Da Nhim in the mountains of southern Annam, which was built and equipped as war reparations by the Japanese Government.[f] The cement works was finished just before, the hydro-electric installation just after, the overthrow of President Diem; both were at once rendered unusable by Communist sabotage.

Public works

Public works undertaken by the Government without private contribution but in effect at foreign expense, and largely under foreign technical direction, included the restoration of the railway from Saigon up to the seventeenth parallel, a great deal of road construction (though with military use predominating over economic) and resumption of improvements to drainage and irrigation for agriculture. In this last sphere also, once the extensive damage

---

[a] RVN, *Bilan* (1962), p. 302. This source also mentions unspecified French investments in the same period totalling 1,300 m. piastres; but that probably covered overdue replanting of rubber estates.
[b] The total for years 1958–61 only (*Ann. Statist. B.*, No. 5, p. 96).
[c] RVN, *Bilan*, p. 47.   [d] Child (1961), p. 136.
[e] *Ann. Statist. B.* No. 5, p. 107.
[f] Reparations Agreement of 10 Mar. 1959.

caused by the Indochina War had been repaired,[a] political considerations, and especially the interests of Tonkinese refugees, dictated their location rather than pursuit of the plans left unrealized
by the French engineers. A number of small schemes were initiated
in parts of Annam that had been under Vietminh domination, but
the major effort, with the aid of earth-moving machinery, was put
forth in the Plain of Reeds. The United Nations team had recom-
mended a low priority for tackling the physical difficulties of this
area,[b] but President Diem was more concerned by its history as the
sanctuary of bandits and revolutionaries threatening Saigon; the
settlement of Tonkinese refugees in the northwestern sector of it
would help put some spunk into the native Cochinchinese peasants
settled on the fertile fringes of the Plain of Reeds, upon whose spine-
lessness he considered the Communists had been preying.[c] In the
event, about forty miles of canal were dug and several thousand
refugees settled. The President's political expectations from these
developments certainly appeared to be fulfilled as long as he lived,
but after his overthrow it became clear that the Tonkinese settlers
had been incorporated by terrorization into the Communist system
as completely as their Cochinchinese neighbours; the mechanical
excavators were wrecked.

Land policy

Three factors conditioned the Republic's land policy: the problem of resettlement of peasant refugees, including Cochinchinese
who had abandoned their cultivations in the fighting,[d] the problem of making new settlements secure against Communist attack,
and the reform of land tenure, exposed as a pressing necessity since
the crisis of 1930 but still not tackled, the formal enactment of a
land-reform law in 1953 notwithstanding.[e] Over land reform no
less than over other questions both Diem and Nhu evinced little
interest at first, and the initiative for changes in what, perhaps more
than any other subject, touched intimately the national life, came
from joint representations by the French High Commissioner and
the American Ambassador early in 1955.[f] Their motives were, in
the case of France, the desire to extricate French interests once and
for all from agriculture now that the big concessions in the Mekong

---

[a] UN & others, p. 209.   [b] Ibid. p. 88.   [c] President Diem to the author.
[d] The UN team believed this to amount to a substantial fraction of the arable acreage
(UN & others, p. 9); it was of the order of a fifth to a quarter of all Cochinchina.
[e] *Du* No. 21 of 4 June 1953.   [f] Ély, p. 279.

Delta and Transbassac had been depopulated by Communist and Sect upheavals and that a return to cultivation by Vietnamese labour on behalf of French landlords was unthinkable. In the case of America, the belief was that Mao Tsê-tung had, as it were, swept to power in China on a land-reform ticket and that the Vietnamese peasants, like their counterparts in other countries of Asia disaffected by unfair land tenure (including the Philippines), would support whichever side in the Cold War gave them land titles first. As we have seen,[a] in reality land reform had been avoided as a Communist talking-point in Vietnam; but, in the New England tradition of family farming, Americans had great faith in any case in 'individualized agriculture as a bulwark of political democracy'.[b] The French Government offered to buy back all concessions from its nationals and to turn the land over to the Vietnamese state domain without further consideration or servitude, while the American Government underwrote the administrative expenses of land reform; the US was not willing to pay for the compulsory expropriations it was urging on President Diem[c]—evidently because of its own public's adherence to the sanctity of private property. An American expert, fresh from organizing land reform under Chiang Kai-shek in Taiwan, was appointed to draw up a scheme for Vietnam.

Problems of tenure

Circumstances in Vietnam presented some intractable problems. Firstly, land registration had made no headway since 1940, and the cadastral survey was still confined practically to towns and domain lands and concessions; the *dia bo* had been further interfered with or destroyed; the staff of the Land Registry was too small in most provinces to carry out any kind of investigation. Secondly, virtually all big landowners had had to abandon their estates and dwellings in the villages for the safety of the towns and in very few cases were sufficiently reassured by the nominal regrouping of the Vietminh north of the 17th parallel to return. On the other side, much of the labour, whether tenant-farmer or hired, had disappeared as well, so that the fields were either fallow or had been squatted on by new peasants, with or without the authority of some Vietminh cadre or one of the Sects. Thirdly, the 1953 reform existed on paper, and although it might not even be known about in some parts of the countryside (extraordinarily, it contained no provisions for its own execution), its failure was sufficient precedent for middle-class

[a] p. 163 above.   [b] Gittinger (1961), p. 195.   [c] Ibid. p. 197.

vested interests at the capital to ignore any new measure in the hope of its remaining a dead letter likewise. Fourthly, in Annam such big landholdings as there were constituted the communal property either of whole villages or of the *chrétientés*. In the former, periodical reallocation was by auction, for rents bid up often to half the crop, the proceeds being credited to the village budget and consequently applied to the reduction of local taxes; in the *chrétientés* property was recognized by custom to be vested in the Church, whose priests had in some notable cases (for instance the Tuy Phuoc district of Binh Dinh) themselves organized the reclamation and drainage of the land from what previously was tidal swamp, with not much more encouragement from the French or Vietnamese territorial authorities than recognition of their property in what they had in fact created.

Measures of reform

The reforms that were now enacted[a]—somewhat hesitantly, for the President took a full year to make up his mind to sign the third decree[b]—had three effects. The first was that abandoned land could be rented on Government order in a landlord's absence without his consent, the money being held on his behalf by the provincial administration until he reappeared to claim it. The second effect was that, in future, all agricultural rents must be based on a model lease, registered with the nearest provincial authority, to run for three or five-year periods, the rent not to exceed 25 per cent of the yield. The third effect was that holdings in excess of 100 hectares were compulsorily bought back into the domain by the Government at 7,000 piastres a hectare (only 1,000 piastres if untilled) and then sold to the tenants in occupation (or to veterans or refugees if they did not want it, but on no account to squatters) for a capital sum fixed by regional arbitration committees and payable in six annual instalments.[c] Interpretation of the intention of this transfer was made more difficult by its exceptions and its imprecise definitions. Thus, each landowner might retain an additional 30 hectares for cultivation himself (that is, by paid labour, not by sharecropping or tenant-farming) and up to 15 more if it formed the object of a trust to maintain the Confucian family altar; rice land turned over to livestock or plantation use was exempted, although it was not certain whether

---

[a] *Sac-lenh* No. 2 of 8 Jan. 1955, No. 7 of 5 Feb. 1955, and No. 57 of 22 Oct. 1956.
[b] Gittinger (1961), p. 204.
[c] Extended to twelve in 1964 (*Sac-luat* No. 008 of 20 Oct. 1964).

this included coconut groves; and expropriation was to apply to 'legal entities' (thought to include both village communes and *chrétientés* but not actually defined in the law), even though the President told some of his advisers that he wished to preserve, and if possible encourage in Cochinchina, the communal tenure practised in Annam which he regarded as characteristic of the nation.[a] A special agency was set up to administer the reform, outside the Land Registry—an administrative error made worse by the fact that hasty creation of new provinces, coupled with poor facilities in some of the older ones, meant that there might be a land registry but no land reform office in some provinces, or a land reform office but no land registry, or neither. To have proceeded with the reform gradually, area by area, would not have been in the character of Ngo Dinh Diem, and it might have disappointed the hopes for quick, spectacular results of his American helpers.

Rent reduction

In the short run, the results of work done on rent reduction did come quickly and were very rewarding: by mid-1959 four-fifths of all tenanted land had been brought under the new controls and 800,000 contracts registered.[b] Unfortunately, many of the beneficiaries owed their landlords big arrears for the war years and in fact went on paying the old rent in consideration of the extinction of this debt, whatever might be written on the contract; and when it came to renewal at the end of the first five-year period few contracts were deposited for re-registration—although this could not be blamed on Ngo Dinh Diem, for by then he was dead. Exorbitant bidding for communal lands ceased for a year or two but was resumed once the dust had settled.[c] The rent on abandoned land was not collected by the Land Offices but by the security forces in exchange for a percentage of the sums recovered—a deplorable source of misunderstanding, abuse, and hostile propaganda by the Communists. The French rice estates were all liquidated by the end of 1960 at a purely nominal figure in francs paid to the title-holders by the French Government direct;[d] the land had not been farmed in the past by long-lease tenants, and the annual sharecroppers and casual labour had mostly disappeared, so that there were no urgent claims to be satisfied in Vietnam. In any case it had been planned to hold this land in reserve for experiments in the future in 'com-

[a] Gittinger, p. 17.   [b] Dr Wolf Ladejinsky, in Fishel, p. 162.
[c] Hickey (1964), p. 192.   [d] Ladejinsky, p. 170.

munity development', about which neither Diem nor Nhu had clarified their ideas by the time deteriorating security overtook them. The former French estates then became *agrovilles*, and as such pivotal points for the first of several pacification plans which will be dealt with later.

Transfers of ownership

Redistribution of Vietnamese-owned lands eventually took in 425,000 hectares—a figure certainly on the low side but obtained from declarations by landlords which there was often no check on in the *dia bo* or the cadastral registers. Only temporary titles were issued to the beneficiaries, the full title being retained until they had paid off what amounted to a hire-purchase debt to the Government, itself reckoned to be the landlord temporarily until the payments were completed. But many ex-tenants had been living in fact rent-free, their landlords far away, and now, as new-fledged landowners in their own right, fell into arrears despite the agricultural credit supposed to be available through village councils from Government funds to tide them over bad years; others sold their land back to the owner in order to realize the cash value and either went on paying rent or disappeared; and even issue of temporary titles fell behind because the Ministry had to depend on the Land Registry which, having had its staff seconded to other duties and not being answerable itself for the land reform, did not always give this survey work priority. By and large, it could be claimed at the end of 1961 that the Government had reallocated all the expropriated land—about 30 per cent of the arable area—but the administrative task of taking in the purchase money and issuing full titles would have taken many years even without Communist meddling and, later, the second armed uprising. As it was, the 'strategic hamlet' climax to the regime similarly overtook the land reform at this point.

Land settlement

At the same time as the land reform was going on, schemes were started in 1957 to settle about 50,000 otherwise landless peasants from the coastal estuaries of central Annam in the highlands to the west of their homes. These *dinh dien* ('Centres d'Implantation'), in which each adult male received an equal divisible but inalienable share,[a] were a scheme personally dear to President Diem's heart

---

[a] Both the name and the practice go back to the vast land resettlement in China in the eighth century.

(less so to his brother's), for he believed that pioneering, as a traditional Vietnamese way of life, would of itself give rise to nationalis-
tically-minded communities impervious to Communist influence.
But the land was often unsuitable for wet paddy, so that the settlers
had usually to fall back on the bread-and-water diet of the ubiqui-
tous but savourless tapioca. Nobody had the capital or technical
skill essential for exportable plantation crops, and there were no
public resources available for clearance and preparation of the land
before planting, but a suitable undemanding industrial crop was
found in *kenaf*, a substitute for imported jute. This form of land development was not viable economically,[a] and few if any of the resettled families ever emancipated themselves from cash subsidies
paid indirectly out of foreign aid. The real considerations here were
political—the desire to establish a Vietnamese racial presence in
the aborigine country and at the same time rid the coastal provinces,
formerly under complete Vietminh control, of families the new
authorities considered unreliable—a question with which the land
interests of the *chrétientés* sometimes became confused. As a result, the
settlements, though reinforced by a sprinkling of demobilized
soldiers, took on the wretched aspect of banishment camps, and
many families slipped away again, even though subject to an unexpressed restricted residence. Paradoxically, the settlements in the
highlands which did survive were the ones whose presence served
the ends of the Communists, and it was their commands rather than
the Government's which kept the families there, continuing to draw
subsidies and supplies in kind and passing on a share to any guerrillas in the neighbourhood. On the other hand, development
schemes farther south, on irrigable land in the plains formerly
covered by jungle, tended to get on better because the settlers were
volunteers, largely refugees from the North, and were able to grow
wet paddy. But here too the President's faith was unfulfilled, and
these communities were destined to keep going only at the cost of
complaisance towards the Communists.

Social legislation

Social policies during these years bore the same ideological stamp
as economic policies. There can be no doubt that the measures most
dear of all to the hearts of the President and his family were the
Marriage Law, which 'abolished' polygamy, concubinage, and

[a] The opinion of the chief American adviser responsible, W. Henderson (in Fishel,
p. 124).

divorce in 1959,[a] and the Morality Law, which, in 1962, took in a wide range of 'abuses' from fortune-telling and gaming[b] to dancing in private houses and to the use of contraceptives.[c] Forthright attacks were made in other enactments on the practice of Chinese medicine[d] and the consumption of opium[e] (though not its far more dangerous derivatives, morphine and heroin). These laws were steam-rollered through the National Assembly, but most of them were loosely drafted and none was endowed with adequate means of enforcement, so that they ended by irritating important sections of the public and making the dictatorship look silly; their intended use was shown, by the prosecutions subsequently made under them, to be a means of penalizing individuals who had fallen foul of the regime for acts or expressions of opinion that were not in themselves unlawful. Affiliation to the International Labour Office dated from 1949, in the twilight of the transfer of power, and the 1936 labour legislation had been replaced by a comprehensive Labour Code enacted soon after;[f] excluding domestic and agricultural workers, it dealt with workmen's compensation, accidents, health, night work, trucking, conciliation, arbitration, and the practice of industry-wide bargaining. Unfortunately, amendments introduced by Ngo Dinh Nhu[g] were not designed for such practical ends, but for the promotion of the mystique of Personalism.[h] The 300 new unions that were registered between 1954 and 1962[i] were founded from above, as branches of one or other of three federations controlled ultimately by the Can Lao, as in a Communist country. Arbitration was compulsory, and the one trade in which the unions attained a modicum of freedom of action was the rubber industry; they almost certainly owed this exceptional latitude to their potential as an embarrassment to the French managements.

Public health

Medical education and the medical and health services developed as far as deepening insecurity allowed, but rather on their

[a] *Luat* No. 1 of 2 Jan. 1959. The DRV was enacting a similar law at the same time.
[b] Gambling is a national vice, as in China; the purpose of this measure was not to stop it altogether but to concentrate it on the National Lottery, whose profits financed certain intelligence operations (see note 99).
[c] *Luat* No. 12 of 22 May 1962.   [d] *Nghi-dinh* 1795 of 4 June 1962.
[e] *Du* No. 60 of 27 Sept. 1955.   [f] *Du* No. 15 of 8 July 1952.
[g] *Du* No. 37 of 8 Nov. 1954 and Nos. 9 & 10 of 8 Feb. 1955.
[h] Admitted to be the case in RVN, *Bilan*, p. 535. Hendry points out (in Fishel, p. 197) that French unions, with which alone Nhu was familiar, also are more concerned with general social conditions than with actual contracts of work.
[i] RVN, *Bilan*, p. 541.

own initiative than as part of any general plan directed from the Palace. Universities with medical faculties were started at Saigon in 1954 and at Hué in 1956, sharing between them much of the former staff of the University of Hanoi but with improvised facilities; Saigon had produced over 750 graduates by 1963 (half of them dentists or pharmacists),[a] but the first graduates issued from Hué only in 1966. Provincial health services were also helped by an American-sponsored project—disapproved of by the majority of Vietnamese doctors—for medical assistants who underwent a course of three years' training only. New hospitals and re-equipment of some of the old ones were achieved with foreign, including UN, assistance, but as a rule without provision for maintenance, renewal, or even staffing;[91] the training of nurses lagged behind. There was a big demand in the rural areas for dispensaries and lying-in wards; villages usually provided buildings from their own budgets, as well as part-time local orderlies who drew supplies, somewhat erratically, from the province stores on their private visits to town, without much prospect of professional inspection or encouragement; the initiative for inspection was lacking even where the opportunity was not. Health campaigns, generally undertaken at foreign prompting, met with a high level of public co-operation— as had been the experience in the colonial period—and the country-wide anti-malarial campaign might have been completely successful, so highly was it prized by the peasantry, if its command had not been placed in the hands of a General of the Military Intelligence, innocent of the least scrap of medical or entomological science, thus lending support to the Communists' contention that it was all a spy network and providing them with the justification for assassinating a number of the field workers and frightening off most of the rest.

Education

The demand for general education was immense, even if it was the ultimate diploma that counted most in the seeker's mind. Considerable progress was made by the Government in catering for it, but here too results were circumscribed by the President's own lack of experience and of vision on one hand and by the wrecking activities of the *dich van* on the other. Diem appreciated the publicity to be gained from ceremonial inaugurations of smart new colleges, and in addition to Saigon and Hué a third university was founded with his

[a] *Ann. stat. 1963*, p. 375.

approval by Catholic educationists at Dalat; specialized technical schools were opened in Saigon, and the French trade schools in provincial centres were reopened and enlarged. The war had damaged rural schools even more seriously than dispensaries, and when it ended the school population was thought to have fallen to fewer than 550,000[a] (out of a population of school age of about 3 million);[b] by 1963 the figure had almost touched 2 million.[c] The share of the national budget allocated to education rose from well under 1 per cent in 1954 to over 10 per cent in 1962;[d] on the other hand the elementary schoolteachers this larger sum was paying for were, almost to a man, untrained.[e] The aloof scholasticism of the Vietnamese professional classes remarked on earlier, whether its origin was French or Chinese or indigenous, continued to stamp educational developments at all levels under Ngo Dinh Diem's leadership; civil servants were trained in academic disciplines without regard to the duties they were to perform, doctors to an international standard fitting them to practise in France, schoolteachers to teach only in the secondary schools. The Government never worked out or even contemplated an integrated education policy geared to national needs and applied on a nation-wide front, whose first steps would be taken in the village classroom, and as a result its achievements (such as they were claimed) added up to a disjointed catalogue of separate initiatives. In secondary education the changeover from a curriculum taught in French to one taught in Vietnamese—a challenging but feasible operation—made little headway against the problems of an incompletely modernized language and poorly developed literature, and although the Government conducted literary competitions on such themes as sentimental verse, its imagination did not rise to offering a prize for science or other technical textbooks. In 1958 a Textbook Bureau was set up under American auspices; it quickly produced one or two provisional texts in relatively limited editions, but its first set of integrated books for elementary schools, designed and printed abroad but with some Vietnamese collaboration over the contents (composed more or less to a planned vocabulary), was not ready for distribution until the end of 1965.

---

[a] *Ann. stat. 1962*, p. 367.
[b] Reckoned as a quarter of the whole population, as in neighbouring countries, the whole population being estimated (ibid. p. 353) at over 12 m.
[c] Ibid. *1963*, p. 71.   [d] RVN, *Bilan*, p. 406.
[e] Some primary schoolteachers were trained, but this grade in Vietnamese usage falls between the elementary and the secondary.

6. COMMUNIST REVENDICATIONS AND THE SECURITY SYSTEM

Communist action to obstruct, and ultimately destroy, the Diem regime was initiated within ten days of the signing of the Geneva Agreements: a 'Committee for the Defence of Peace' was set up in Saigon on 1 August 1954.[a] General Vo Nguyen Giap has explained to readers in the Communist world quite recently that Ngo Dinh Diem was to be regarded as a puppet set up deliberately by the US 'to oust the French and suppress our compatriots' patriotic struggle', which there had never been any intention of relinquishing in the South even after victory in the North.[b] 'Defence of Peace' was evidently another of the Party's changeable 'watchwords' and the 'Committee' (whose members were not revealed then or later) one of those 'transitory organizations' through which Truong Chinh applied the Leninist line to Vietnam.[c] The 'particular immediate problem whose solution would ensure the solution of other problems confronting the Party'[d] was reunification and extension of the DRV regime to Vietnam below the 17th parallel. The Vietminh's underground structure of cells was never dismantled; it was no part of the Agreement that it should be, for the negotiators had been concerned only with the regrouping of formally embodied fighting forces.[e] It is unlikely that the eventual armed uprising was planned at this early stage, but a Marxist-Leninist party holds itself in readiness for such a possibility, which in this case is said to have been foreshadowed in 1954 by Le Duan, successor to Truong Chinh as First Secretary of the Workers' Party.[f] The Party organization was kept in being, and in trim, against whatever might befall: a Resistance Fighters Veterans' Association helped to keep in touch with former guerrillas, and not later than 1958—by which time a fresh uprising definitely was projected—the People's Revolutionary Youth of thirty years before[g] was active again; a Liberation Front publication tells us that, in April 1960, this organ 'was said to be an arm of the Party'.[h] Thus, as in Tonkin between 1945 and 1951, so in Cochinchina between 1955 and 1961, the Party was, like the metaphorical pregnant woman, to be seen if not heard.[i]

[a] Nguyen Huu Tho (nominal leader of the insurrection in the South) to Communist reporter Wilfred Burchett (*VNA*, 9 June 1964).
[b] Vo-nguyen-Giap (1965), p. 13.
[c] The policy is attributed to Lenin through Stalin, in Truong Chinh (1962), p. 27.
[d] Lenin/Stalin again, ibid. p. 29.   [e] Burchett (1965), pp. 146–8.
[f] Honey (1967), p. 5.   [g] p. 142 above.   [h] Phan-nhu-Bang (1966), p. 11.
[i] See note 55.

Many villages previously under complete Vietminh control when the Communist soldiers were regrouped to Tonkin were given up; but in others families remained behind (including young brides wedded in haste on the promise 'We'll be back!'), waiting and watching like the families of any traditional Sect, secret society or *chrétienté*; no village was allowed to forget that it was observed and would be wise not to compromise itself with a Communist regime that would inevitably come to power one day soon. There was no period when selective assassination of village authorities, incautious about concealing their antipathy to the DRV, ceased to occur frequently; but after Ngo Dinh Diem repudiated demands for all-Vietnam elections, the rate at which murders were committed (hardly ever humanely) seems to have increased faster; although the Government's limited administrative control obscured much of what was going on, it is now generally thought that during the nine years that Diem was in power close on 20,000 people lost their lives in this way—the equivalent of an annual murder in every administrative village. The steady psychological impact of this terror on the countryside as a whole was, as those responsible have callously boasted,[a] immense. Murders were always accompanied by denunciation of the victim as an 'enemy of the people'—one, that is, who did not agitate for reunification but respected the authority of the Government, central or local, which in turn was the tool of the few hundred Americans working to help the country recover from the Vietminh war. The message such 'armed propaganda' was intended to convey was that it was not safe for anybody to rely on protection by the authorities and disregard the cadres' behests; the object was to 'resist' the restoration of law and order and to make the detection of the culprits as difficult as it had been in the days before independence.

External defence

After a lifetime spent dreaming of himself as the chivalrous champion of nationalism, it would have called for great flexibility on the President's part, when faced with this situation, to act on the principle that the essence of his problem was law and order and the most effective means of safeguarding it anything so unglamorous as an efficiently-run administration with down-to-earth economic and social policies, to which the issue of colonialism and anti-colonialism, and arguments about political ideology, were in reality irrele-

[a] Burchett, pp. 146–8.

vant. It was not surprising if he thought of Ho Chi Minh and himself as rival patriots, struggling for dominion over their people (North and South) on an equal footing primarily with ideological weapons, secondarily with their armies, supposedly dedicated to the rival doctrines. Once he had put the election issue behind him, Ngo Dinh Diem's immediate anxiety was that Ho Chi Minh might try to wrest his country from him piecemeal, by direct onslaught across the demilitarized zone against the provinces of central Annam, including Hué. Terrorization and subversion of the countryside were deplorable, but in the President's mind the priority for the security system was an army strong enough to hold off invasion by the renowned victors of Dien Bien Phu while the force of argument of his ideology, promoted at the same time by official propaganda and by community development (along lines whose practical forms he never clarified properly) so conditioned the people's minds as to make them impervious to Communist blandishments and to give them the will to resist with their lives attacks on their homes from the hills and jungles and swamps. He missed the point that the security of his threatened provinces, like the security of his army and of the regime itself, rested basically on the personal security of the individual citizen—of that 'human person' his propaganda paid so much lip-service to. If the army of the DRV had attacked the South directly at this time, it would have done so only in the certainty that the areas to be invaded were already sufficiently under the control of the masses-activation cadres to guarantee supplies and intelligence for the invading force.[92]

Political security

The Communist menace was viewed as one, if certainly the sharpest, of half a dozen assassins' knives the patriarch felt were pointed at his throat; political security was not, therefore, a matter for the whole administration, working as an integrated machine to prevent or detect crime harnessed to a single political purpose, but the concern of separate agencies entrusted with this task in isolation, in the same way as military security in Annam was a task that fell to the army in isolation. More than that, the departments of the administration presented opportunities to organize cliques and must therefore be kept divided among themselves lest they grow too powerful and turn against him, whether under the banners of the Sects and parties it had been his first task to tame, or under new banners. Even the agencies that were charged with security duties could not be trusted implicitly but—both intelligence services and armed forces—were played off against one another; they then devoted to mutual spying much of the energy that might have been concentrated against the Vietnamese Communists—the Vietcong as they now came to be called for short. All this orchestra of suspicions could admittedly be justified as Vietnamese custom; but Ngo Dinh Diem was not the leader to break with it—he preferred to turn it to account.

The armed forces

Traditional attitudes also influenced Diem's reliance primarily on the army for security; it was a question of prestige, for Vietnamese monarchs had always disposed of big armies, and the reluctance of France to give back that symbol of authority had been one of the most resented assertions of colonial rule. Besides, there was a frightening problem of underemployment, more particularly in central Annam; not all the idle hands could be drawn off by the land-development schemes, and it seemed wiser to take them into the government forces than to leave them open to Communist subversion.[a] On the other hand, the army must not grow too strong; fear that it might try again to dictate to him as General Hinh tried in 1954, regarding itself as the ally of the state rather than its servant, was a compelling reason for Diem to channel some of this manpower to paramilitary forces under a separate command. The colonial *Garde Indochinoise* had been reformed under Tran Trong Kim in 1945 as the *Bao An* or Civil Guard, and the same title had been used by the Hoa Hao militia. The remnants of these forces formed the nucleus of a new Civil Guard in May 1955; it differed from the army in being composed entirely of volunteers. A third group of armed forces, bearing different names at different places and times but known collectively as the village militia or Local Defence Corps (at first *Tu Ve*, later *Dan Ve*) was made up of poorly-trained hamlet guards with a maximum operating strength of a platoon, supervised by the nearest contingent of the Civil Guard but nominally 'commanded' by the village administrative committee. In fact this concept of a three-tiered security force, whose fighting merits will be considered in the next chapter, was a long-established system common to all regimes, and above all to the Communists:

a The President told the author in 1961 that he considered rural underemployment (a largely seasonal phenomenon) to be the major social factor in traditional disorder in Annam.

the Defence Corps kept watch within the village; the Civil Guard provided garrisons under the provincial authority and went to the help of Defence Corps platoons under attack; and the army, in theory, sought out big formations of the enemy, of which there were none in South Vietnam between the regrouping and the outbreak of the second uprising in 1960. The separation of command between Civil Guard and army ran from top to bottom, the former being responsible through the Province Chief to the Minister of the Interior, the latter through conventional command echelons of battalion, brigade, division, and corps to the Minister of Defence, who was now the President himself; lateral lines ran from each echelon direct to the Palace, but rarely from one area command to the next. The appointment of military officers as Province Chiefs gave area commanders a lever by which the military was able to influence the civil administration, but not a converse one by which the civil administration could even know what the military was up to, let alone influence it. At village level as many as nine different defence forces might be stationed next door to each other but under independent commands[a]—or none at all—and each pursuing its own operational objectives. The President purposely preserved political disunity, for which co-ordination of operations was reckoned at the time a low price to pay; indeed, he fancied there was an advantage in this policy if it resulted in emulation between the armed forces to catch and eliminate the revolutionaries.

Intelligence services

The same principle of mutual emulation was applied to organization of the intelligence services, and these in turn were isolated from the ordinary machinery of government, except that some of them were in contact with agents of their own in the various departments, supposedly on the look-out for Communist agents. In theory all the services—of which by 1962 there were at least ten whose existence was not publicly avowed—came under the general direction of the *Service des Études Politiques, Économiques et Sociales* (SEPES), which pulled the strings of the Can Lao network; but in practice each communicated direct with the President or his brother, in whose hands SEPES became the tool of the Can Lao rather than the other way round, much as the organs of the state were and are subordinate to the Party in the DRV. All these services competed to show off their 'kills' to the Palace, avoiding communication with their rivals

[a] Donoghue (1959), p. 17.

even if they knew about them and deliberately neutralizing the latters' efforts, and even liquidating their agents, while Diem and Nhu posed as eight-eyed spiders at the centre of a skilfully-spun web of intelligence; and yet many of the vital pieces in the jigsaw were deliberately withheld from the Palace if they reflected to any degree on the lack of success of the reporting officer. Meanwhile, the territorial administration and the various security forces, who had to cope with the practical problems of disorder and might have taken some action on the information if it had come into their hands, had to find funds, by misrepresentation of the nature of their expenses, to run their own networks, which operated even less professionally than those of the Palace and were, if possible, more exposed to penetration by the Vietcong. In central Annam the scene was further confused by the activities of Ngo Dinh Can who, never seen in public and having no official position, dominated every department from the Great Within.[a] Though presumably he was loyal to the President, it was whispered that Can excluded Nhu's agents from his territory and even turned the tables by infiltrating his own spies into high places in Saigon. For all the intelligence services it is a valid criticism that the Vietcong were generally a secondary target, priority being given to surveillance of other enemies of the regime or of one another, partly because the Palace wanted things that way, partly because such targets were easier to deal with and less able to take reprisals when an operation miscarried. While the market places were glutted with spies, the security forces were starved of substantial intelligence.

Detention without trial

Most of the intelligence services were active clandestine agents as much as they were collectors of intelligence; several of them included strong-arm gangs modelled on the Communist *cong tac dac biet*, and one or two possessed lock-ups, although rumours about torture-chambers, widely credited during Diem's lifetime, were not substantiated after his death. No legal authority was responsible for camps, and although allegations of arrests without trial were frequent and borne out to some extent by persons released later, the

---

[a] He used to be referred to by the rather puzzling title 'Adviser and Tutor to Organizations in Annam' (*Co-van Chi-dao cac Doan-the Mien Trung*). He made use of the *chrétientés*, whom he helped with economic advantages of various kinds, to keep in check the Dai Viet and VNQDD as well as the Vietcong; he was accused after his death of a virement of 65 m. piastres for these political 'expenses' mulcted from the head of Refugee Resettlement (*Dan Chu*, 7 May 1966).

fact that they were carried out arbitrarily by anybody in authority and that no department was responsible for administering places of detention makes it impossible to find out how many there were.[93] The significant aspect of the affair was the arbitrariness of the procedure rather than the total number of detainees. In the circumstances of Vietnamese village life, no government would have been able to bring to book members of a criminal organization of the proportions of the Vietcong, based as it was on intimidation of all in its path, if it bound itself not to act beyond the rules of evidence deposed in open court—even the French rules of evidence; it is basic to the Leninist technique of revolution for the Party to provoke the authorities into a quandary where security can only be safeguarded by disregard of habeas corpus and then to charge them with repression. On the other hand, there can be, and in many countries are, fair and duly-enacted temporary rules for detention without trial but with other safeguards consistent with the rule of law; no obstacle prevented Diem from copying them. His real difficulties lay in his character: he wanted to preserve his own discretion unfettered and, with that, the possibility of locking up other rivals for power besides those who were implicated in criminal acts; keeping the door open for his own discretion, he left it open for his subordinates as well, especially in the provinces, and then had to take the blame as self-appointed patriarch and dictator. Another difficulty seems to have been his doubt whether, if detention camps had been gazetted and subjected to regulation in their management—a condition that we have seen did not even apply to the jails (which often served for detention as well, as they had under the French)—, they would have been run well enough by Vietnamese administrators to escape condemnation abroad as 'undemocratic' concentration camps. On the other hand, not infrequently, murderers and saboteurs against whom witnesses were not willing to give evidence did benefit from judicial procedure: they were charged before military courts, not for the actual felonies, but for mere membership of the illegal Vietcong underground, to which they would then plead guilty, be convicted, and serve a sentence of a year or two's imprisonment, after which they returned to their old haunts. Thus Diem weakly let things drift, and, in the result, though some tens of Saigonese conspirators from the VNQDD, Dai Viet, and Sects were confined wrongfully for long periods, many hundreds of Vietcong in the countryside who ought to have been put away for the duration of hostilities were left at large. In December 1958, at Phu Loi

Re-education Centre, Communist detainees staged a riot; the Civil Guard in charge, not trained for their duties, panicked and machine-gunned a score of inmates, not necessarily Vietcong; the 'massacre' received such publicity in the West as well as in Communist propaganda that the whole armed Communist intervention has been explained on occasion by it. But Diem, when faced with this materialization of the danger he had feared, ordered no impartial inquiry and learnt no lesson for when his unsympathetic Providence dealt him the same card a second time, at Hué in May 1963.

Police

Languishing in the confused shadows cast by the various armed forces and intelligence services was the one body all ought to have been subordinated to, which alone had any standing in law and which alone might have provided the personal safety and local confidence it was the principal aim of Vietcong anarchy to undermine —the police. The defects of the pre-war French police organization had become accentuated, and in 1954 the total strength was well under 10,000, of whom few had been trained and the majority were on daily pay; they were split up between three separate commands and without proper accommodation for police stations or housing, with the shoddiest equipment and with the slenderest of administrative frameworks. For practical purposes, the jurisdiction of any of the three forces had been confined to the towns, even the Judicial Police entrusting their hazardous duties in the rural areas to one or other of the armed forces. The *Sûreté* had discredited itself in the eyes of the President by continuing to work, even after its transfer to Vietnamese control in 1953, for interests he identified with France and with the Sects.[a] The urgency of equipping village life with the protection of a professional police force was impressed on Diem personally by foreign consultants at an early stage,[b] and he was urged to have the Civil Guard retrained and deployed for this role; but the proposal cut across the premise on which the security system was being developed and so was turned down. After that, the different police forces struggled on with shrinking authority for another six years, until Diem belatedly decided (in 1962) to combine the remnants of the *Sûreté* with the other forces into a National Police (*Canh Sat Quoc Gia*) under a single Commandant; but although the circumstances surrounding this decision were the outbreak of renewed

[a] The President to the author.   [b] See p. 281 below.

fighting with the Vietcong, the Civil Guard were still not brought into the new force, and police protection continued to be denied the villager. When the National Police did come into existence, it, like every other Vietnamese armed body, was accused of 'liquidating' captives in its secret cells in Saigon, and the Director-General, Colonel Nguyen Van Y, and three of his subordinates at their subsequent trial confessed to the charge; the number of victims was thirteen.[a] These and the twenty mown down at Phu Loi a few years before make the sum total of verified unjudicial executions attributable to the regime.

Community Development

The regime's main weapon of defence against the Vietcong became the combination of ideological propaganda with community development; it evolved by stages, the failure of each of which diminished peasant confidence in the experiment but spurred the Government's determination to carry it to greater lengths. Several influences were at work in conjunction. First came faith that Vietnamese village traditions, if once reinstated, would of themselves expel the Vietcong and their alien doctrine like natural antibiotics; there appeared to be fewer Vietcong in Annam, where tradition was strong, and a way must be found to make it take hold again in Cochinchina, corrupted by colonialism and its product, the Sects. Diem was, of course, misled about the state of affairs in Annam, mistaking rarity of incidents for absence of cadres. Another influence on his mind was his knowledge of the *pao chia* system of village co-operation which the KMT had introduced into parts of China; under this, neighbouring families were supposed to be grouped in tens (one *chia*) for mutual aid and joint defence against brigands, and ten *chia* into a *pao*, with a leader recognized by the Government as the head of each. The real intention was that the families so brought together should keep watch on each other politically; this was distasteful to the Chinese, and the arrangements were disregarded in practice.[b] Thirdly, there was the consideration of finding some institutional embodiment for Personalism. Finally, community development was a fashionable slogan during the 1950s as a context for generous aid from advanced countries to the under-

[a] See p. 359 below.
[b] Yang (1945), p. 150. The *pao chia* was also employed by the Japanese in occupied China (Ch'ên, p. 247), and it has been suggested to the author in Vietnam that their interest in the Dai Viet was as a means of introducing it into Tonkin and Annam in 1945.

developed; with the fruits of foreign aid as reward, peasants might be persuaded more easily to enrol in the local militia, thereby committing themselves to the Government cause and in its ranks become accessible to official indoctrination, indoctrination-through-discipline being among the successful methods of the Vietcong. Out of these strands were woven a series of plans, all rather scanty as to detail, for organizing the land-development centres and, at the same time, for organizing *lien gia* (linked households) among established communities. The difficulty was to breathe life into these arrangements for co-operation so as to make them work after the ceremonies for their inauguration had died away; in practice, the *lien gia* repeated the experience of the *pao chia* in China, and even where villagers obediently erected inconvenient fences between one group of houses and the next and a more than usually energetic Can Lao organizer was able to gather intelligence through the heads of the wards, difficulties of liaison in any other direction than upwards to Hué or Saigon usually rendered the results sterile.

Propaganda services

Part of the trouble was the ineptitude of the propaganda services. If a new ideology was going to play so big a part in holding the country together, effective means of projecting it were essential; they never emerged. The French administration in Indochina had a record for incompetence in the field of public information[a] and bequeathed to the State of Viet-Nam a broadcasting station and some other equipment, but no reservoir of professional skill and experience in its handling. In the absence of other guidance as to method, and cut off by the departmental isolation that affected the whole administration from knowledge of the non-political work of the government, the propaganda services took the Communists as their model and the content of Communist propaganda, which they merely negatived, for their content. Apart from broadcasting, whose technique was never mastered because of frequent changes of staff to ensure political reliability, the chief medium of communication was the small team touring villages and addressing the inhabitants by loud hailer, usually in direct response to a known visit shortly before from the Vietcong. Personalism was little understood by these operatives, and in the event the regime made no progress in projecting either it or the policies of the Government, even though in the course of a single year an average of twenty sessions

[a] Pinto, p. 68.

might be held in every hamlet in the country.[a] Invitations to denounce Vietcong cadres by name and in public, but without specifying their misdeeds—in imitation of the Communists' carefully prepared 'armed propaganda', perhaps the previous night—went unheeded. What should have been a police investigation was being turned into an ideological argument, with the lives of the listeners as a stake; propaganda obviously could not prevail against terror in the absence of personal safety.

Agrovilles

By late 1958 there had been no invasion of Annam, but the heightened frequency of sabotage in Cochinchina began to alarm the President where terrorism and subversion had not. He therefore decided to isolate families suspected of close intercourse with the Vietcong, whether as a result of these denunciation sessions or on reports of agents. But this time he had been to Kuala Lumpur and heard about the part 'closer settlement' into 'new villages' of squatters previously spread out along the jungle fringes had been playing in the isolation of the Malayan Communists from their willing or unwilling suppliers. Out of this example were born, in the middle of 1959, the 'Closer Settlement Areas' (*Khu Tru Mat*) or, for foreign ears and tongues, the *agrovilles*—a term borrowed from French pacification in Tonkin. Province Chiefs were instructed to cause heads of *lien gia* to 'demand' the rounding up of unreliable families, until within a few months 43,000 had been made to leave their scattered homes in the more newly settled areas of Cochinchina and build new houses on twenty-three resettlement estates marked out on the former French concessions, still uncultivated; digging wells and drains and making access and internal roads was done by *corvée*, henceforward called 'community development'. These removals did at least have the effect of transferring to the Government some of the taxes that in the immediately preceding years had been exacted by the Vietcong.[b] Yet the scheme had several flaws in its logic and inevitably petered out: isolated security measures had as little prospect of lasting results as government departments working in isolation, and Government propaganda, intelligence, and defence detachments did their jobs no more efficiently on the *agrovilles* than anywhere else. Moreover, the resettled families con-

[a] Between 1 July 1957 and 30 June 1958 well over 300,000 such sessions were conducted (RVN, *Bilan*, p. 494).
[b] Based principally on Zasloff (1962).

tinued to work on the land and so were exposed again every day next cultivation season to the old pressures. After the first pilot schemes had been tried for a few months, plans drawn up to re-settle 150,000 more people were allowed to die. The significance of the experiment was that it showed Ngo Dinh Nhu—who later de-clared that he had not approved of it[a]—that as great a physical effort of *corvée* could still be imposed on Cochinchinese peasants by the Government as by the revolutionaries, and so paved the way in his mind for the idea of the 'strategic hamlets' which, in the next period of this story, marked the climax of the patriarchy's struggle against the Communists.

7. STATE AND NATION UNDER THE NGO DICTATORSHIP

As 1939 was the year in which to strike the balance of France's record in Vietnam, so the eve of the mutiny against Ngo Dinh Diem in November 1960 is perhaps the fairest moment for drawing up the account of his stewardship—before, that is, the Vietcong uprising had assumed warlike proportions. Even earlier than 1960 it is likely that Ngo Dinh Nhu already appreciated the limited authority the Government actually exercised in the villages: the state was under control but not the nation.

Factionalism

The control he and the President exercised over the state was in any case negative: the concentration of power in the Palace failed to identify the government services in any active sense with what was going on, and even Secretaries of State were reduced to report-ing some administrative requirement, shrugging their shoulders, and sitting back to wait for instructions that might never come. They were disillusioned with an independence that represented for them no advance on colonialism, and with them were disillusioned the politicians—both in and out of the National Assembly—and the whole middle class, save any the system happened to privilege. The ramshackle edifice of factional allegiance, vested interest, and pat-ronage, resting on the shifting sands of foreign aid, opposed to the ever-present Communist threat, not a shield of national unity, but a host of additional 'internal contradictions' waiting to be exploited by the revolutionaries in accordance with Leninist doctrine. An in-

---

[a] In an address to civil servants at Phan Thiet on 10 Feb. 1962, in the presence of mem-bers of the Diplomatic Corps and of aid missions.

stitutionalized state, seen to rely robustly on its own revenues in the first place for the realization of social and economic plans of practical scope and unswerving priority might have provided the common ground on which hitherto divergent interests could have been brought together to co-operate in a common purpose; Personalism, had its content been defined, would still have been too abstract to fill this need, while the personality of the President—patriarch and father figure though he tried to be—lacked the sanction of tradition and was no substitute for the abolished monarchy, even if the latter also had meant relatively less to the people of Cochinchina than to those of Annam.

Regionalism

Of the general 'contradictions' standing in the way of national unity, regionalism, though always felt to some extent, did not prove to be so serious as it became immediately the dictatorship was brought to an end; Diem somehow got the mixture approximately right. The same cannot be said of sectarian dissensions. His reliance on Catholic allegiance in preference to appointments and promotions on merit, and the sycophantic genuflexions that that led to, did not exactly outrage any rival Buddhist hierarchy—none existed to be outraged—but it did disgust idealists in the public service and the armed forces not committed to a faction, and it set a low standard of public morality; it was a pity the President never esteemed public morality so highly as private. The breaking of the military power of the Cochinchinese Sects can only be applauded; yet it ended there, with no further provision for their absorption into activities with a national focus than enlistment in the Civil Guard, or more commonly just the local militia, subject to a minimum of discipline and supervision and manning in underpaid (often unpaid) idleness little defence posts situated in their old retreats.

Chinese and Khmers

The biggest threat of disunity came from the ethnic minorities. Here too the criterion of policy was usually not what it would be wise to ask of them but what the regime had the right to demand— an attitude often put down by foreigners to mandarin tradition, of which it was not actually characteristic, whereas it had been very noticeable in French official conduct. The Chinese, partly because they had been encouraged by the French, were now treated in summary manner; the President took his cue from the policies being followed at the time by his neighbours in Indonesia, the Philippines, and Thailand, abolished the extraterritorial administrative arrangements of the *bangs* and brought the schools, hospitals, and welfare bodies they managed under Government control; individuals were offered the choice between returning to China or taking on Vietnamese citizenship, including the attendant duty of military service, the latter becoming a condition for the continued practice of their trades. Except that many Chinese families succeeded in buying themselves reprieves from some of these implications, especially from military service, the measures went through and had no untoward consequences for the Government.[a] Another group who proved on the whole docile were the Khmers. The influx of Vietnamese settlers during the colonial period had not been allowed by the French authorities to disturb the Khmer communities, who generally retained their traditional land rights and village life, under the secular as well as spiritual influence of the Theravadin clergy. They had become involved in Cambodian politics after 1945, certain of the groups from across the frontier being subject, in the background, to Issarak, ICP, and Lien Viet manipulation; but the villages situated along the lower reaches of the Bassac, far from the frontier, succeeded in staying out of the Vietminh conflict. The Diem Government's policy was also to leave them alone in most respects, taxing them lightly, offering them few amenities, paying for education only in Vietnamese, but not interfering with the schools run by their bonzes.

The hill tribes

A bigger racial problem was presented by the aboriginal tribes of the highlands of Annam. Never administered by the Vietnamese monarchs and only superficially under the French (largely through Catholic missions), the hill tribes had been wooed by the Vietminh immediately after the Japanese *coup de force*,[b] and during the Indochina War, through cadres from the hill tribes of Tonkin, villages of the Jarai and Radé especially had harboured Communist forces on the move from time to time. Nor had the French Generals been idle on their side: irregular companies of tribesmen, under a French command which sometimes included officers of Vietnamese race, had fought alongside the *Corps Expéditionnaire*. In 1954 large numbers of young men from these two tribes (between 5,000 and 6,000

[a] Only about 1,600 retained Chinese nationality—that is, Nationalist Chinese.
[b] Bourotte, p. 87.

Radé alone),[a] as well as smaller numbers from other tribes, were taken to Tonkin as part of the regrouping of Vietminh forces. There they were trained as cadres themselves, side by side with tribesmen of similar race and language from parts of Cambodia and Laos adjacent to their own homes.[94] The return of these cadres to their villages in about 1957 marked the genesis of the line of way stations, to be known subsequently as the 'Ho Chi Minh Trail', whose maintenance has provided the Pathet Lao with one of its major purposes and thus stood in the way of implementation of the various international arrangements for peace in Laos.[b] Ngo Dinh Diem was aware, from 1954 onwards, that it was imperative for him politically to gain and keep control of the PMS: Bao Dai's hastily enacted special statute for the highlands[c] had been a reminder of the state's tenuous hold over an area where many historical grievances rankled, with many reasons to regret the withdrawal of French protection, and lying astride any invasion route from Tonkin. He decided on a policy of cultural assimilation of the area, but one lacking details except the settlement in it of as many ethnic Vietnamese as it could absorb (the traditional process of expansion into the lands of the Chams and Khmers) and the substitution of Vietnamese for native languages in the few schools that had survived the end of colonial rule. Some administrators filled in the details with sensible forbearance, others tried to jolt their charges abruptly out of their un-Vietnamese ways and persuade them, for instance, to wear trousers over their loincloths[d] or to stop living in long houses.[e] Under these conditions the agents of the DRV were able to enlist voluntary support, without recourse to much intimidation. In 1957 the People's Government in China went through a phase of declaring the supposed autonomy of Thai minorities within their borders, and the DRV followed suit in Tonkin: cadres thereupon promised similar independence from encroachment and cultural extinction to the tribes of the PMS.[f] During 1958 demands for autonomy were widely canvassed among the Radé, as a revival of Champa and in recognition of the enactments in that sense of d'Argenlieu and of Bao Dai. President Diem, who probably was sincere in his paternal

[a] Hickey (1957), p. 16.
[b] Report of the Sub-committee of the UN Security Council (dated 4 Nov. 1959), compiled after a fact-finding visit to Laos.
[c] See note 79.   [d] Hickey (1957), p. 32.
[e] A senior army officer appointed 'technical adviser' to the territorial administration in 1961 made this his contribution to a national policy for the hill peoples.
[f] Article in *Hoc Tap* (organ of the Workers' Party), 8 July 1956.

attitude to the Chams he had administered on the coast and to certain of the Khmer-speaking tribes of the PMS (for example, the Sedang, though he despised the Bahnar for some reason), paid frequent visits to the highlands to mollify the leaders;[a] he turned aside discussion of the difficult constitutional position but promised closer association of tribesmen with their own administration, and this appeared to lower the pressure. The promises were not fulfilled afterwards, more because of the inherent difficulties (language, inexperience, mutual suspicion) than from prevarication; even if they had been, the Vietcong could have found other 'contradictions' to justify continued subversion of the highlands; as it was, they carried on unhindered into 1960.

Outbreak of hostilities

By 1959–60 the Vietcong, who down to that time had comprised, according to General Giap, only 'self-defence units' and 'armed propaganda units',[b] were ready to 'escalate' their violence into a guerrilla campaign—from single criminal acts of sabotage or terror into the maintenance and steady expansion of a force permanently under arms and no longer disavowed by the DRV. They were henceforward assured of the unsuitability and ineffectiveness of the Government's security system, which they had put to the test from all angles, and of the 'contradictions' and other weaknesses, unlikely now ever to be eradicated, that were at work within the machinery of command; with their own underground complete and at work in every locality of the country, including the Ho Chi Minh Trail, they lacked only arms. On 27 January 1960, which was New Year's Eve that year and the season of relaxed and sentimental goodwill for Vietnamese people, a sudden attack on an unprecedented scale was made against a battalion headquarters of the army near Tay Ninh in Cochinchina; taken unawares, the camp and garrison were overrun and looted of over 500 weapons and an unknown quantity of ammunition.[95] This attack was meant to stir memories of the attack of Emperor Quang Trung, with whom the Vietcong claim affinity, on the invader Sun Shih-i; it was evidently a signal, and on the following nights scattered posts all over the Mekong Delta were similarly overrun for the same purpose. Sabot-

---

[a] In 1957 an attempt was made at Banmethuot on the President's life, but by a plainsman; he was never put on trial but kept in close confinement in expectation of execution. After Diem's own death, he was taken to a camp for political detainees and finally set free in January 1965 (*SDN*, 8 Jan. 1965).

[b] Vo-nguyen-Giap (1965), p. 56.

age of roads and bridges was stepped up, and villagers were rounded up at night to do the demolition work with spade or hatchet; recalcitrant communities were attacked and had their houses set on fire, isolated garrisons guarding installations were overpowered and disarmed. Even more village councillors went to live in the towns (or bought off the revolutionaries with their complaisance), ambushes and hold-ups on roads became daily occurrences, and the landowners of Saigon—many of whom the land reform had spared—again stopped receiving their rents.

The Caravellistes

It was obvious that the Vietcong uprising was gathering a planned momentum, and the articulate classes in the capital recognized the signs of the Vietminh turmoil all over again. The Palace began to be bombarded with pacification schemes from members of the civil service and the army, and on 29 April a group of eighteen former politicians, now out of office and including Dr Tran Van Do, published to the foreign press gathered at the new Hotel Caravelle (whence their collective designation *Groupe Caravelliste*) a set of petitions remonstrating with the President over the resurgence of Communist violence, which they maintained had been helped by incompetent government, and demanding, among other measures to combat it, an end to press censorship, to detention without trial, and (by allusion) to Can Lao undermining of the discipline of the army, to which the recent Vietcong successes were largely attributable; one member of the group put them down in part to peasant resentment of *agrovilles*, but no practical alternative measures were suggested for dealing with the disorders, although there was a general inference to be drawn that things would go better if the signatories were taken into the Government.[a] Diem and Nhu took note of this opposition—which was entirely negative—and intensified all the measures complained of. During the next six months Vietcong incidents in Cochinchina multiplied and took in the whole region, interfering for the first time with the rice harvest;[b] it became plain that in certain areas adherents of the Cao Dai and Hoa Hao must be collaborating with them. There were also a few incidents in the coastal provinces of Annam, but the highlands remained quiet until the end of October. Then suddenly a group of Civil Guard

---

[a] List of signatories and main text are given in Fall (1962), pp. 432–8; additional details in Nguyen-qui-Hung (1964), p. 164.
[b] *NYHT*, 12 Nov. 1960.

garrison posts along the southern end of the Lao frontier was attacked and overrun by tribal guerrillas, supposedly led by North Vietnamese officers. This event was the signal for a general outbreak of hostilities in Annam.

The 1960 mutiny

In the eyes of the President, the attack in the highlands was more serious than the one at Tay Ninh: it was a near threat to Hué and seemed to him to presage the long-awaited invasion of the northern provinces. Army reinforcements were ordered from Saigon to Kontum, including parachutists. The Area Commander in the highlands in fact recovered the posts without reinforcements—the Vietcong only wanted the weapons and withdrew of their own accord—and seems to have connived in the decision of the parachutist commander, Colonel Nguyen Chanh Thi, to stay in Saigon and, in the early hours of 11 November, overpower the barracks of the Presidential Guard and lay siege to the palace itself. The Colonel was commonly believed to have been influenced by the ease with which Captain Kong Lae had carried out his coup d'état in Laos two months before; unlike the Captain, however, he did not declare for neutralism, but, in a broadcast manifesto claiming that the whole army was behind his seizure of power, he declared that he was acting in the interests of the anti-Communist struggle hitherto misdirected; he did not announce any programme for further action. Diem parleyed, called up other troops from the South, and promised unspecified reforms. The mutiny collapsed through indecision and internal dissensions, and a number of politicians were arrested, including all the *Caravellistes*. Although some of these apparently were not connected with the incident, it came out later that the VNQDD had been ready with an inner plot to set up their own Government with Brigadier General Le Van Kim as Prime Minister—a plot which had been betrayed to the Palace through the network of the Can Lao. Diem and Nhu saw in these events reasons, not for reforming their administration as their foreign advisers kept urging them, but for intensifying the dictatorship. Within the next few weeks certain changes in the Government were indeed put into effect, but all amounted to substitution, for the scapegoats now sacrificed, of officials more devoted to the person of the President; some were more competent men, others less. Finally, in February 1961, it was given out that the President would submit himself on the due date in April for election for a second term in office.

The NFLSV and the PRP

But the Communists' extension of the fighting to Annam and the unsuccessful mutiny it set off were harbingers of more significant decisions than these, both on the side of the revolution and on that of the Government. In the middle of the mutiny Hanoi had declared its interest by stating, quite gratuitously, that its 'regular forces would not move south'.[a] Clearly the DRV was staking a claim. During September the Lao Dong had held its Third Party Congress in Hanoi; in his concluding address President Ho Chi Minh had spoken of the connexion between the Second Party Congress and the final victory against the French, and said the Third would be the 'source of a new dawn in the struggle to achieve reunification';[b] his welcoming address to delegates had already declared that 'so long as we have not driven the American imperialists out of the South and liberated it from the barbarous My-Diem clique,[c] our people can know no peace of mind'.[d] Ho Chi Minh issued this obvious war cry only when the Cochinchinese insurrection was firmly established; in response to it, on 12 December, a clandestine broadcasting station announced that the Vietcong had 'formed a Races' Front for the Liberation of South Vietnam'[e] (for which the Communists' own English translation has since become 'National Liberation Front'). The NFLSV was the tenth front behind which the ICP had operated in Vietnam[f]—the seventeenth if all the 'Liberation' and 'National Salvation Committees' are included—and like many of its predecessors consisted entirely of faceless men, not one of the thirty-one names broadcast being an eminent Vietnamese and barely a handful identifiable by the Government at all.[g] It was not long before the Party revealed its presence in Cochinchina in a manner similar to its reappearance in Tonkin in 1951, to reassure Communists at home and abroad that its hand was

[a] *Le Monde*, 12 Nov. 1960. [b] NCNA, 10 Sept. 1960. [c] See note 85.
[d] NCNA, 5 Sept. 1960.
[e] *Mat Tran Dan-toc Giai-phong Mien Nam.* 'Races' included Khmers, Chams, and hill tribes, on the analogy of the 'Malayan Races' Liberation Army' and of the five races making up the Chinese nation, which were a theme of Peking propaganda at this time. Subsequently, the NFLSV and the DRV have always named 20 Dec. as the founding day.
[f] The list is given in Pike (1966), p. 11.
[g] The Central Committee was to have 52 seats, but only 31 could be filled (DRV, *Declaration*, 1962, p. 32).

still at the controls on this eve of momentous events: in July 1962 the same 'Liberation Radio' announced the formation on the previous 1 January of a 'People's Revolutionary Party of Marxist-Leninists to lead the work of the Front'.[a]

'General uprising'

These announcements were heard by very few people in Vietnam and had no practical significance for the authorities or the population, for bloody clashes had long been a daily occurrence. It may seem, therefore, that the move was one of public relations only; it was no less important for that, marking an important stage in the Marxist-Leninist revolution. DRV forces infiltrated through Laos were already engaged in open fighting south of the demarcation line, and it was imperative to establish for the high command a distinct identity that did not admit that the DRV was behind it, although the latter had, as it were, still reserved the right to keep order in the South. The titular chief of the Front, Nguyen Huu Tho, explained to Wilfred Burchett four years later that the Front had existed previously, but that after the successful 'generalization of the uprising' it was necessary to have a body which could look forward to setting up its own Government and having its own representatives abroad.[b] This was in fact the fifteenth anniversary of the *khoi nghia* in Haiphong and an auspicious moment, when the probabilities of victory in the South so outweighed the risks of defeat, to make the irrevocable commitment to guerrilla war, without which the Party could not make further progress. Sympathy and aid could be sought abroad, while at home any supporters of the Government inclined to throw in their lot with a cause beginning to look like the winning side again could be offered a 'united front struggling against tyranny' as an excuse. Between them, the *Caravellistes* (of whom at least three had once been in the Vietminh and four in other revolutionary groups, including the VNQDD, in 1945) and the mutinous 'paras' had unintentionally demonstrated, as impartial witnesses, the Vietcong's main charge against the patriarchy to be no mere Communist propaganda line but an accepted fact; all who rallied to the Front could plausibly claim from now on to be motivated by freedom-loving patriotism. As it turned out, of course, nobody of any standing in the community did so rally, but

[a] Mr Kuno Knoebl (1967, pp. 101–3), inquiring in a VC-held village near Saigon in March 1966, was unable to elicit any real distinction between Front and Party.
[b] VNA, 9 June 1964.

that disappointment was not foreseeable. The manifesto included in the Front's original broadcasts—drafted in a tone of reasonableness totally different from the strident tones of following years—repeated the points of the *Caravellistes*, except that it added an appeal for 'peaceful reunification'.[a] Any measures the Government might take in the future to deal with the insurrection or to protect the lives and property of the Vietcong's victims would, without any gloss from Communist propaganda, look like repression for repression's sake; if the US continued to pay for them it would, in the eyes of the world, be subsidizing tyranny. The timing of the announcement of the Front had boomeranged on to a target of opportunity offered by the army, itself intent on exploiting the opportunity created by the Vietcong attacks in the highlands. From the opposite point of view of Diem and Nhu, their various opponents had proved what the two leaders had always claimed, namely that anybody who withheld co-operation from their plans was *ipso facto* striking a blow for Communism.

Diem and Nhu betrayed by no outward sign at the time any new anxiety over these developments, but certainly Nhu soon came to the conclusion that the regime would have to forge itself a new weapon if it was to survive. It took him a whole year to work out what the weapon would be—it was in fact the 'strategic hamlet'—, and in the meantime the Vietcong advanced a long way in strength. But the next phase in the political tragedy is only comprehensible in the light of the mounting quantity and the effects of American aid, American advice and American initiative, lavished on Diem's Government from now on in the hope of stemming the Vietcong advance.

[a] Text in Fall (1962), pp. 439–43.

6

THE BOUNTY OF AMERICA

I. AID AND ADVICE WITHOUT COLONIALISM

THE defeat of Japan brought to an end the wartime interest of the US in Indochina. President Roosevelt's ill-defined vision of the emancipation of the Indochinese peoples from the colonial yoke of France—based, as it was, largely on misinformation[a]—seemed to have died with him,[b] and the rekindling of American interest several years later was due to considerations arising outside Indochina. These considerations were, firstly, the urgency of 'containing' Chinese aggression which had chosen to assert itself in Indochina, as it was urgent to contain it in Korea, after the disastrous defeat of Chiang Kai-shek; and, secondly, of supporting France financially in the discharge of this particular burden lest she should falter in her contribution to the holding of the Western line against the Soviet Union in Europe. If America refused French requests for aid, the inclination to withdraw troops from Europe to reinforce Tonkin might extend to withdrawals of equipment also. The first year of American aid to France under the Mutual Defense Assistance Act of 1949 on account of the Indochina War was 1950[c] and amounted to only just over $20 million.[d] The money was quickly followed by token supplies of military equipment, and the channelling of these was the occasion for setting up, late in 1951, the first military mission, the Military Assistance Advisory Group (MAAG), and an Economic Co-operation Administration.

Franco-American relations

There was all along a good deal of impatience with France in American circles. The Communist enemy was a ragged one whom a modern army ought to be able to crush, given a little determination On the other hand, he was sustained, notoriously, by contributions from the mass of the Vietnamese people; it was assumed that these contributions were given voluntarily and that the reason for giving them was patriotic solidarity with an anti-colonial rebellion, of

---

[a] p. 131 above.   [b] Schlesinger, p. 11.   [c] US fiscal year 1951.
[d] Lancaster (1961), p. 207.

whose Communist direction, and its perils for them, the majority of the contributors must be ignorant. The French Government was therefore under constant pressure from the US to speed up the devolution of power to the Associated States and take the wind out of the Communists' sails—a process already under way but which the French Government thought, on the contrary, must be slowed down, for otherwise Vietnamese (or Lao or Cambodian) inexperience might give victory to the Vietminh by default. These opposed modes of thought persisted long after Vietnamese independence and the Geneva Conference to exacerbate Franco-American relations—already difficult because so few could talk the other's language—during periods when the interests of Vietnam called for the closest collaboration between her helpers: the French were suspicious of predatory designs on their former empire on the part of America, while Americans blamed French rule, more than Japanese intervention, for letting the Communists get their foothold in the first place and for the intrigues and general state of corruption in Cochinchina, during the years 1950–4, which had contributed so significantly to the supplies of the Vietminh. A still more serious consequence for Vietnam was that this mutual irritation misled American advisers into disregarding French experience, either political or military: if things had gone badly for the French it was because of their false position as selfishly-motivated colonial oppressors (French valour could never be questioned, any more than could American valour when the time came), and even military lessons learnt by the *Corps Expéditionnaire* were not applicable to American or American-taught operations. This injudicious attitude was passed on from generation to generation of American advisers over the years, with considerable cost in dollars and in lives. In 1960 the Vietcong were confident that if they led with the same card again, the American aces would fall to their trumps as had the French ones.

Objects of aid

After 1954 all American aid went straight to the State of Vietnam —the Republic as it soon became. The objects to which it was directed, summarized in the phrase 'defence of freedom'—a sort of antonym to 'defence of peace'—were primarily military and economic, since it was on these two fronts that the new state seemed vulnerable as a victim of the Cold War. The opinion of Ngo Dinh Diem that what he had to fear most was direct invasion from the North was shared in Washington. It was also appreciated there that a subsidiary threat existed in the possibility of subversion, at least in the years before Diem had consolidated his position. However, with the colonial yoke removed, the principal appeal of the would-be subverters must be to the legacy of poverty and economic underdevelopment—as Americans viewed the situation—bequeathed by France; consequently, the second priority, after help with the equipping and training of the army, was for technical and financial assistance so to raise living standards that Communist propaganda would fall on deaf ears. For the same reason, technical assistance would be given with projects to improve the social services, especially education and public health. On matters touching the government of Vietnam more intimately, Americans were cautious: it would be right to offer advice on aspects of public administration where technical skills could be said to be involved—such as the presentation of public accounts—and also financial help with specific problems like settlement of refugees and land reform; but that was all. Three considerations came into play here: first, nothing more than that was seen at the time to be necessary—all peoples are able to govern themselves if only they are left alone; second, it would be both morally wrong to take any step in derogation of the absolute independence and self-determination of the South Vietnamese and imprudent to invite, from Communists or critics at home, the stigma of colonialist intentions; and third, trust was and had to be placed in the capacity of Ngo Dinh Diem personally to govern as he thought fit, for in the somewhat emotional state of the 'public philosophy' of America in 1954, more than in any other year (the McCarthy 'hearings' were going on at the same time as the Geneva Conference), the capacity to withstand Communism was connected with loyalty above all other qualities, and loyalty was guaranteed by ideological reliability—which in Diem's case was unimpeachable.

Military aid

The forms which American assistance took were also determined by what she had to offer. Financial credits were limited as to quantity or purpose only by the will of the American legislature; in fact the Congress and Senate interfered much less with the manner of the executive's spending in Vietnam than later controversy over the US commitment might have led the public to expect. But the Administration safeguarded itself against the susceptibilities of public

opinion by such rules as that aid must not be spent by the Vietnamese Government on compulsory acquisitions of private land[a] or on
improved production of rice or other food exports which might
compete with American commercial interests.[b] Moreover, in spite
of its objections to the Geneva Agreement, the US Government
honoured the limitations on the scope of military aid permitted
under it. The agreement had laid down that no fresh military forces
must be introduced into either South or North save by way of
rotation of units and groups of personnel, and no new equipment
save in replacement of what was worn out.[c] After the withdrawal of
the *Corps Expéditionnaire*, the only foreign forces remaining in the
South were the French military training mission; this included
MAAG, and the combined personnel totalled 888.[d] The US
Government appears not to have made public the details of its
military assistance to South Vietnam, but the numbers of its military staff did not exceed that maximum until 1961, a full year after
the Vietcong had taken up arms openly against the Republic.[e96]
Similarly, in regard to military equipment, the most heinous alle-
gation that the DRV was able to register with the ICC against the
US was that five or six airfields had been built for the RVN in the
provinces and that a Temporary Equipment Recovery Team had
stayed on suspiciously long after the cease-fire.[f] Again, it was only
in 1961 that the US began seriously to rearm the RVN, when the
scale of Vietcong operations in the South gave rise to fears that the
uprising might prove to be a preparation for the long-awaited onslaught directly across the demarcation line—an eventuality that
would have called for sophisticated weapons of defence, including
substantial air and naval forces.

Technical assistance

There were no formal limitations to be reckoned with on the
type or quantity of non-military technical assistance America
could give, but what the US had to offer here was limited by the
more subtle internal factor of the personnel she had available for
secondment. The national feeling against colonialism was so strong
that even American colonies had always been denied specialized
administrative services and—perhaps to their detriment—were run
instead through departments of the home Government. In its deal-

[a] p. 243 above.   [b] Scigliano, p. 200.   [c] Arts. 16–18.
[d] ICC, *11th Interim Report* (1961), para. 50.   [e] ICC, *Special Report* (1962), *passim*.
[f] ICC, *6th Interim Report* (1957), p. 25.

ings with underdeveloped countries since the Second World War, a professional body of overseas officers had been built up inside the Agency for International Development (AID);[a] but they were professional aidsmen, expert in the channelling of American resources to the recipient governments but hardly experts in (though they might be shrewd observers of) the problems of those Governments. Technical assistance had mostly come from consultants hired job by job, the majority of whom had practised their vocations only in the US and even the minority of whom were unaccustomed to taking account of factors outside their specialized field. Consequently, there were to hand to furnish the manpower for the American partnership in Vietnam only the US army—whose unavoidable employment overseas for want of any other disciplined body of men may contribute to the false impression of 'militancy' America creates in the Soviet Union and elsewhere[b]—, the staffs of home departments, professional aidsmen, *ad hoc* consultants, and university teachers. The agencies put to work, besides MAAG, were a United States Operations Mission (USOM—a branch of AID), a Michigan State University Group (MSUG) engaged to give Prime Minister/President Ngo Dinh Diem advice on problems of public administration under a contract to which he was the other party (although the US paid), and two departments of the Federal Administration, namely the Central Intelligence Agency and the United States Information Agency; officers from other Federal departments, and more rarely from state or local administrations, were seconded from time to time to work in USOM. The staffs of these bodies, though perhaps lavish by non-American standards, were before 1961 minute—possibly 300 all told—by comparison with their successors in the years after the Communists took up arms again. A substantial segment of the aid programme in all fields was reserved for study courses for Vietnamese personnel in the US.

The aid record

The nine-year association with Ngo Dinh Diem's Government can be divided into phases. The first two years of it constituted an operation almost of emergency relief. The next five years, from 1957 to 1961, witnessed the consolidation of the dictatorship, the revelation of its political vices, the disappointments over its economic

a Called earlier by other titles of no consequence in this context.
b Shulman (1966).

development, and a general decline in the sympathy felt for it by the American public as well as by many individual officers serving in Vietnam; several MSUG consultants published unfavourable accounts at home of what was going on and so angered President Diem that he refused in 1961 to renew the contract.[a] But the rising anxiety roused by the obvious successes of the Vietcong reversed this trend, and the last two years of the dictatorship, 1962 and 1963, brought a renewal of American generosity and resolve to assist a sorely-pressed ally in the Cold War, even if it was then used to overturn President Diem personally. The total sum of what was given during the eight years probably cannot be worked out, but the trend of costs is indicated by the budget for economic aid—until 1962 the bulk of the cost; from $325 million in 1954–5 the figure fell below $200 million for 1957–8, below $150 million in 1960–1, and was still only $210 million in 1962–3—a total over the whole period of about $1,700 million.[b] This detail is worth noting because it brings out the fact that the 'escalation' of aid into full financial support, of advice into combat—and of uncolonialism into kingmaking—were far from American intentions at the beginning, and their occurrence at all was a consequence, not a cause, of Communist aggression. The variations in the amounts of aid were due to assessments of what the Vietnamese economy could absorb.

Failure of aid

Yet, taken all in all, the aid programme must regrettably be reckoned to have failed; the subsequent 'escalation' is, in a sense, a measure of the failure. It may be argued that some features of the programme were successful, for a time, and that others failed through sabotage by the Vietcong; but it was precisely to obviate the latter danger, and to make South Vietnam viable to the point of resisting aggression, that the programme had been embarked on. At this point (the end of 1961), American inability to achieve a self-appointed aim bears some resemblance to the French failure to 'modernize' Vietnam. It may be pleaded that the extenuating factor is the wrongheadedness of Diem and Nhu. But this too was no bolt from the blue: President Eisenhower had warned Diem from the beginning that American aid must be matched by Vietnamese performance.[c] Unfortunately, the diplomacy of that particular

[a] It expired nominally in May 1962, but work had ceased several months before.
[b] Figures taken from an internal working paper of USOM. Published versions of some of the figures vary from source to source, but not substantially.
[c] US, *American Foreign Policy 1956*, pp. 2401–2.

communication stopped short of indicating what would be done in the event of non-performance; the omission contains a clue to the causes of the failure.

Lack of a treaty

At the head of the list of these causes comes the lack of a definition of the principles that were to regulate relations between American advisers and Vietnamese officials; no 'capitulations' were spelt out —all was left to mutual goodwill and to the reasonableness expected to flow from the loyalty, ideological convictions, and consciousness of a common interest with the US which, in the atmosphere of 1954, were believed to move Ngo Dinh Diem and his collaborators as they moved Chiang Kai-shek, Syngman Rhee, and all 'freedom fighters' by definition. The Geneva Agreement might have been said to stand in the way of drawing up a treaty in so far as it prohibited South Vietnam from engaging in any military alliance;[a] but the prohibition did not apply to non-military aid. The truth is that the US Administration deliberately backed a personal leader in preference to impersonal programmes in the belief that to do so would be more conducive to stable government. In the event, however, having no specific reserve sanction to invoke, the US Administration had to watch the appropriation of its aid to purposes that rendered it 'counterproductive'; individual advisers faced with obstructionism found they had no treaty article they could quote and were reduced to buying collaboration of Vietnamese officials in programmes for the furtherance of Vietnamese national interests, either by the procurement of supplements to the programme or by the offer of tours abroad or similar private advantages. At the time, this situation was treated as a disappointing weakness of character in the recipient but one that American generosity could take in its stride; how in fact it contributed to the symbiosis of the revolutionary war might have been realized in time if French experience had not been scorned.

Politics and administration

The US Administration was also misled by a faulty analysis of the constituents of government in Vietnam and of Communist methods of subversion; too much weight was given to the political side of government and what American officials liked to call 'the realities of power', by extension from the US constitution, regarded

[a] Art. 19.

as a norm of the human political condition which only the aberration of colonialism had temporarily obscured in Vietnam. Any abatement of the principles underlying American democracy—of the pyramid of balanced vested interests at various political levels— would be wrong, would provide material for Communist propaganda, and therefore would make the Communist hold over the people stronger. With concentration of American support on the leader as the rallying point for vested interests harnessed to a national endeavour went disregard for the impersonal institutions of the state and underestimation of the value of the civil service; the majority of American advisers were at one with the Vietnamese politicians in looking upon the civil service and the kind of regulation that, ideally, it stood for (resistant to manipulation) as a bureaucratic straitjacket inherited from colonialism. This further deepened the gap between colonial rule and independence—the transition to democratic institutions over which, Professor Lucian Pye has pointed out, America has so often been unable to guide her protégés by practical steps—an inability all the more calamitous when the Communists are waiting on the sidelines with just such a formula.[a]

Lack of self-confidence

This proved to be the case in Vietnam. Few American advisers had experience of actual answerability for public acts or of the exercise of powers conferred by law; even the MSUG professors, who as a body came the closest of any of the agencies to a professional insight into problems of public administration, had not actually done the work themselves. There was no common *esprit de corps* binding staff culled from dissimilar backgrounds, and short tours of duty prevented the growth of either practical procedures for working together or of an institutional memory; there was no methodical storing of advice, much of which was tendered *viva voce* at conferences, and no sense of having to live with the consequences of what one said. Realization of their own inexperience undermined some advisers' self-confidence, so that they not only forbore to press the soundness of the advice they had come to give but they began to accept as their own doctrine the proposals of their Vietnamese pupils, which they lacked the knowledge to examine critically, and to content themselves with holding open the taps of financial support. The roles were then completely reversed, for, if relations had

[a] Pye (1962), p. 71.

been on a healthy basis, the Vietnamese Government would have been paying for both implementation of the proposals and any foreign advice they called for. Insidiously, quantity was creeping in to make up for quality, public generosity was paying for private shortcomings, and the might of the Vietnamese army was counted on unconsciously to retrieve mistakes in the running of the country. The idea that the major threat to South Vietnamese independence came from outside made it possible psychologically to condone the mistaken policies of the Diem Government outlined in the last chapter, upon which few foreign advisers felt qualified to pass judgement anyway.

American domestic politics

American aid and advice were hampered to an increasing extent by domestic politics and press comment. However clear the insight of the US Administration into the real nature of the problems of Vietnam might have been, the preconceptions and prejudgements of public, press, and politicians at home would still have made the running. Here too anti-colonialism made matters worse: unwillingness to accept that foreign countries could be dependent territories with a need for special kinds of administration at variance with the US constitution logically excluded any sense of special responsibility towards them. If domestic politics had plagued the last years of French tutelage in Indochina, this became true of the American partnership no less.[a] The agencies in Saigon were at all times answerable by direct speech telephone to their headquarters conscience in Washington, rather than for a clearly-defined policy in the Vietnamese interest—to a degree probably never reached in any colonial territory. MAAG was a limb of the US army, and the CIA—which it has been revealed controlled the MSUG[b]—as guardian of American security, acted with single-minded attention to what it deemed were American interests; the interests of independent Vietnam were not identical in every respect. The probings and criticisms of Senate and Congress—or, what was more stultifying than the reality, the apprehension of them—continually conditioned US policies in Saigon in a manner calculated to neutralize any deeper understanding of the needs of Vietnamese nationhood that might have evolved within the American agencies. The ability of the Communists to play on American vulnerability in this respect was possibly less than they themselves have always imagined; yet

[a] Schlesinger, p. 65.   [b] *Daily Telegraph*, 15 Apr. 1966.

we have a convincing inside testimony how, at a moment of great decision, when the lack of a treaty to invoke forced a choice between saving and jettisoning President Diem in 1963—a situation it is possible was engineered by the Communists with an eye to the US press—, heavy pressures were exerted on the Kennedy Administration by both press and party interests at home; these pressures, in the light of memories of Senator McCarthy's inquisition into the past attitude of American officials in China to Chiang Kai-shek at the time of the Geneva Conference, bore heavily on the minds of officials in Vietnam.[a]

Want of a policy

If we can isolate the crux of the failure resulting from these cumulative difficulties facing the American effort in Vietnam, it was want of co-ordination and want of direction in the application of aid and advice. 'Defence of freedom' was a slogan but hardly a policy, still less a programme of action; it had no positive goals to work towards—only the negative one of deterring the Communists from renewed aggression from outside. What the Vietnamese Government was most in need of after independence was minds able to grasp its structure and machinery as a working whole and to see the separate functions of its parts in relation to each other, not in laboratory isolation. Diem and Nhu were not of that calibre; the US felt no duty to seek a way of making good the deficiency—felt rather a duty not to interfere, but to treat 'defence of freedom' as a problem separate from the governing of Vietnam. A very early example of the harm done by this lack of perception escaped attention at the time but was a serious matter because it concerned the police. In April 1956 two professors in the MSUG submitted to Diem (at that time still Prime Minister) a memorandum pointing out the connexion between Communist subversion and the lack of a nationally-organized rural police force; they urged forcefully the retraining of the Civil Guard as rural police. For all its wisdom and cogency, Diem rejected this advice—for two reasons: the first was that he had the other uses for the Civil Guard in mind that we have seen,[b] and the second that the advice came to him in isolation, on the sole authority of the two consultants, as a private opinion carrying no more weight than the advice of a carpenter on how to hold a

[a] Mecklin (1965), pp. 230–2. The pernicious converse influence of Vietnam on America has been explored by Schlesinger (pp. 119–27).
[b] p. 254 above.

screwdriver—not as the advice of the US Government in accordance with a general policy drawn up under a formal agreement. The
air of benign detachment of one American agency from the concerns of another, manifested very often by the US Embassy itself
(since an agency of the State Department could not be answerable
to the White House for the agencies of other departments, least of
all the Department of Defense), degenerated later on into a sometimes malign detachment when agencies found their spheres of concern overlapping and did not shrink from tendering advice in conflict with one another.[a] Vietnamese antipathy to teamwork was
nourished by the mutual detachment of their counterpart tutors,
and the shortcomings of one partner amplified those of the other.
Security intelligence has suffered consistently from this rivalry, but
the most glaring example of it was the encouragement—and the
wherewithal in equipment—given to the Vietnamese army to engage in what was euphemistically called 'civic action' but evolved
in course of time into full-scale usurpation of the functions of government and, later still, into a tendency to avoid encounters with the
enemy on the pretext of more pressing duty.

American criticism of Diem

In the end, therefore, aid and advice without any formal agreement to ensure consistent policy, co-ordination, and guidance,
which ill-wishers might have condemned as 'colonialism', tended to
harden the defects of the Diem regime rather than to correct them,
and to reinforce its defeats. But American expressions of dissatisfaction with the Government dwelt almost exclusively on its unwillingness to share power with other politicians or to establish representative institutions or to allow freedom of non-Communist political
expression. Certainly, the complaints of the *Caravellistes* appeared
to confirm that the Vietnamese people were resentful of this
restriction when they put the resurgence of the Communists down
to it; but the *Caravellistes* were a small minority of city dwellers
addressing the American press and hardly concealed the fact that
their diagnosis of their country's political sickness contained a big
element of special pleading for a personal share in the spoils of office.
But these were questions of political philosophy rather than of
practical administration, and Ngo Dinh Diem resented American
strictures over his handling of them as the very interference the US
Administration sought to avoid. It is necessary to consider the im-

[a] A serious conflict of policy was reported within USOM itself in *NYHT*, 6 Dec. 1964.

pact of American support on Vietnamese finance, economic development, and the armed forces before narrating the opportunities that administrative neglect, and the deliberate avoidance of coordination among the security forces, opened up for the perfection of 'symbiotic insurgency'.

2. FINANCE, ECONOMY, AND THE ARMED FORCES

American prognostications in 1954 for the finances of the State of Viet-Nam had been discouraging. The conditions of anarchy prevailing in the countryside made it improbable that adequate revenue could be collected from direct taxation for the next two or three years, while sources of foreign exchange would be confined, until rice production recovered and substitutes were found for Tonkinese exports, to whatever share of the yield on rubber could be negotiated back from the French banks who had controlled the exchange up to then.[97] It was questionable whether even ordinary expenses of public administration could be met; there was no possibility of covering the cost of defence—with a standing army then numbering 200,000 besides other forces—, still less of providing investments for development. Consequently, a device was required that would permit the subsidizing of all extraordinary expenditure, including maintenance of the armed forces, and at the same time facilitate the purchase abroad of essential commodities, including raw materials for new manufactures (such as cotton yarn) and of industrial equipment by entrepreneurs whose capital was held in piastres; it must be a device, in other words, to make the private Vietnamese investor's piastres available to the US Government for payment of the piastre cost of the armed forces, while making the US Government's dollars available to the investor. The whole operation must be under the control of the Vietnamese Government without its incurring any drain on its meagre piastre revenue from taxation.

The CIP

The device that was applied to these problems was the Commercial Import Program (CIP)—a variation of the Marshall Aid formula and of arrangements in effect in certain other Asian countries. It was both ingenious and comprehensive because it resolved all the difficulties in what was essentially one simple transaction; it was a device to tide Vietnam over her temporary embarrassment but is still in operation today, on a vaster scale than ever. The two Governments agreed first on the size of the allocation of dollars. Vietnamese importers—preferably industrial investors—applied for licences to import from the US, or, in a variety of circumstances arising out of Washington's own balance-of-payments position, from a list of third countries that might change from year to year, the commodities they required, depositing at the National Bank in Saigon thirty-five piastres for every dollar on the pro-forma invoice. The US Treasury reimbursed the supplier in dollars, while the RVN Government encashed the deposited piastres, crediting them to what was known as the Counterpart Fund, and incurred on the other side of the account such expenditure as had been agreed with the US—in the main, the pay and the food of the armed forces. It was expected that the restoration and expansion of Vietnamese production would, by raising the standard of living, simultaneously increase revenue from taxation while reducing the security threat and, with that, the liability to maintain so many men under arms; the rise in exports would gradually improve the Government's own holdings of foreign exchange, and US subsidies under this head could be phased out.[98]

The CIP and financial dependence

There was one assumption behind this argument that proved unjustified: that the RVN Government wished to become independent financially of the US. We saw at the beginning of Chapter 5 that it did not. Without coincidence of viewpoint between the two parties there could not exist the mutual goodwill on which alone the informal partnership was based. First of all, the exchange rate was too favourable to the piastre: the latter stayed at 35 to the dollar throughout Ngo Dinh Diem's rule, even though for most of that time there was also an official 'free' rate of 67 in effect and an unofficial rate of 100. Management of the Program on this basis, it is true, prevented inflation and kept the piastre on a more even keel than might have been expected during the early period of the Vietcong insurrection and the coup d'état of 1960, which both tended to undermine internal confidence;[a] but this advantage was bought at the expense of the American taxpayer and by compromising the aim gradually to phase out the scheme. The importer could afford

[a] When a galloping inflation did set in (1965), it resulted from the spending of US combat troops and logistical support services for them, not from the CIP. See however p. 372 below the paradox that, in the end, the CIP destroyed much of the industrialization it had at first helped to build.

to, and actually did, pay much more than 35 piastres for his goods; but he paid the extra money under the heading of customs duties and other special levies, and Diem did not have to assign those to upkeep of the armed forces if he had other uses for the money—political uses, for instance.[99]

The CIP and taxation

At the same time as the CIP perpetuated Ngo Dinh Diem's financial dependence on the US, it helped him towards independence of the people he was governing by making it less necessary to tax them. The French system of crediting indirect taxes to the all-Indochina budget and direct taxes to regional budgets—the circumstance we saw had provided the trigger for the outbreak of the Indochina War—ceased automatically when the regions were abolished; but no corresponding change was effected in procedures for assessment and collection, and these continued to lie within the competence of the hierarchy of the territorial administration. The Indochina War had resulted in widespread neglect to assess or collect direct taxes.[a] Ngo Dinh Diem had in the increased yield from customs duties produced by the CIP a strong disincentive to reform the system of tax collection, for if the state revenues had gone up to the proper level he would not have needed so much foreign aid; it was less trouble, did not incur unpopularity in the countryside, and afforded another instrument for binding wealthy citizens to himself if he left things as they were. In 1955 wages-and-salaries tax should have brought in 16 million piastres, but only 500,000 was collected; 19 million was collected out of 108 million due on land tax.[b] Public finance was the field in which American advice was at its most confident, and between 1958 and 1961 a procession of experts tore their hair out to persuade President Diem to adopt reforms to make the country stand on its own feet,[c] but to no avail. By 1963 land tax was being assessed at an average of 1 per cent of the agricultural yield, and of the amounts assessed only a third was being collected;[d] periodical reassessment even of urban property tax had fallen into disuse, and well under half the amount due on assessments for Saigon was actually taken in.[e] Insecurity was a contributory factor, but obviously a minor one compared with administrative incom-

---

[a] p. 205 above.   [b] Murphy & others (1956), p. 6.
[c] Including, through the Brookings Institution, British experts, one of whom had had experience of the collection of taxes during the Communist insurrection in Malaya.
[d] Davis (1965), i. p. vi.   [e] Ibid. iii. 11–18.

petence, dishonesty, and lack of vigilance; far from wishing to correct these faults, Diem and Nhu had reasons for perpetuating them, and the CIP provided them with the means. It is hardly an exaggeration to say the two brothers paid for this policy with their lives.

The dollar hoard

Out of dependence on American aid there grew, ironically, independence from American advice. Vietnamese exports did expand as had been hoped and earned dollars of their own; some of these also were credited to the financing of imports—as much as $102 million in 1961[a]—but sizeable sums were at the same time laid aside out of CIP funds; in the single year 1959, for example, $40 million were left unspent, or close on a quarter of the grant for that year,[b] and by 1963 the regime was reputed to have built up dollar reserves of about 300 million,[100] besides reserves in francs, sterling, and other currencies. Ignorance of public finance was certainly at work on the minds of Diem and Nhu—unfortunately, they mistrusted both their American and their small circle of highly-trained, but American-orientated, Vietnamese advisers—to persuade them that a dollar holding in a bank abroad was a more valuable asset than equivalent investment in the productive capacity of the country they ruled. But they were also amassing these reserves against the possibility that US dissatisfaction with their style of government might, in the absence of treaty stipulations, vent itself some day in a definitive suspension of aid; when that actually happened in September 1963, Counsellor Nhu was able to plan continuation of the war effort by spending these savings.[c]

Capital and consumer goods

A third snag in the system concerned the nature of the imports that were licensed. American planners had anticipated that 40 per cent of the CIP money would be devoted to capital equipment, while 60 per cent bought raw materials and consumer goods to generate piastres for the armed forces.[d] In the event, aid administrators had to be content when even 16 per cent was reserved for capital equipment;[e] local investors lacked capital and enterprise, foreign entrepreneurs lacked confidence in the face of the continued

[a] *Ann. Statist. B. 1961*, p. 64.
[b] Jordan (1962), p. 110; according to an oral communication to the author in 1963, that same year witnessed the addition of $75 m. from Vietnamese exports.
[c] Mecklin (1965), p. 238.   [d] Rosebery, in Lindholm, p. 194.
[e] Taylor (1961), p. 247.

Communist menace. Thus finished textiles persistently exceeded in value raw materials for the local mills as the major import of the country; vehicles and petroleum and building materials stood high; but year after year industrial machinery was far outstripped by such single items as pharmaceuticals (which did not include industrial chemicals or agricultural fertilizers) and even dairy produce. The needs of defence, on whose dimensions Americans and Vietnamese entertained similar if not quite identical views, ruled out any measure that imperilled the Counterpart Fund of piastres, there was joint determination to manage the finances by free-enterprise economics, and President Diem set himself against deficit financing. Consequently, American economic aid found its own channels to flow down, to the exclusion of financial planning, and had soon become a regular institution on which South Vietnam counted to prop herself up indefinitely.

The beneficiaries of aid

By 1961—the year in which, it will be recalled, Ngo Dinh Nhu also was searching for a new policy—it was apparent to American advisers that the CIP had achieved only one of its three objectives, namely the financing of the armed forces; industrialization was reckoned to be unnaturally slow,[a] and the consumer goods that were being imported stayed in the towns, whose middle-class tastes alone were being catered for, so that no benefit was accruing to the peasants, improvements to whose well-being, it was hoped, side by side with the land reform, were going to stop the gradual enlargement of Vietcong strength. American advisers observed that even direct aid handed over to the ministries in Saigon rarely seeped through the tight controlling fists to those it was intended should use it: either it would be stored away for some unexplained contingency, or it would be metamorphosed into private property by an alchemy familiar to older USOM hands once privileged to advise the retainers of General Chiang Kai-shek.[101] The aid programme was due for revision, if not because it was seen to be undermining the advice it had been intended to support and the very purpose for which the combined operation had been started, then at least because supplies were going astray and because the security situation was rapidly getting worse, not better.

[a] In 1962, leaving out of account handicraft production, domestic manufactures were valued at US $94·7 m. against imports of manufactured items valued at US $198·2 m. (USOM/Rozental, 1964, pp. 68–74 & 83–85).

The armed forces

The armed forces whose upkeep was the principal focus of the aid programme gave less cause for disappointment, but this was in reality because the development of the security threat had not put them to the test yet. There had been general agreement between Ngo Dinh Diem and American military experts that the major threat to security would be attack from the DRV and that consequently a strong conventional army, backed by small conventional naval and air arms, should make up the chief line of defence. Such differences as there were arose over aid to, rather than the duties of, the paramilitary forces. There were in fact three points of view on this latter subject: President Diem, as we saw earlier, looked on the Civil Guard as a political counterweight to the army and would have liked it armed at American expense as a Praetorian Guard; the MSUG continued to view it as a rural police force; and MAAG remained apprehensive of its potential for interfering with the growth of the army and drawing Vietnamese resources away from it. As was to be foreseen, the Civil Guard fell between all the stools; its numbers were reduced from 68,000 in 1955 to 40,000 in 1959, and would have been reduced further to 30,000 in 1960 but for the Vietcong uprising.[a] It was supposed to be responsible for all law enforcement in the countryside, except where the army had charge, and also policed the frontier.[b] Units were armed with weapons surplus to army requirements, given short training in firing (but not in police duties),[c] supplied with a little motor transport out of the MAAG budget,[d] and then left to do the best they could. Since the Civil Guard was not responsible for external defence in the context of the Cold War, the US Government had no more reason to pay for its maintenance than for that of any other government department.

Air and naval forces

The French forces had been training Vietnamese pilots for some years before 1954; this nucleus was added to with American help, until by 1960 the air force had about 10,000 personnel of all ranks and specializations.[e] The force was equipped for reconnaissance and transport duties, the unarmed single and four-seater craft, together with a score of Dakotas, being supplied at American expense. Flying the President and military leaders round the country was the main duty of the transport wing. Fighter aircraft and light fighter-

[a] Hoyt (1957), p. 5.   [b] Ibid. p. 16.   [c] A French mistake too, p. 101 above.
[d] Hoyt, p. 17.   [e] 13,000 in 1967.

bombers were added in response to the Communist aggressions of 1960, jet-propelled craft from 1964. The Vietnamese navy took shape more slowly and along lines owing more to considerations of national prestige than of practical usefulness. Equipped with lightly-armed inshore vessels and landing-craft, it eventually attained a strength of over 15,000 but was never able to take on the burden of coastal patrols—totally neglected through almost the whole length of President Diem's dictatorship—and never penetrated north of the cease-fire demarcation line, possibly out of deference to his policy of not provoking the North. Such service as the Vietnamese navy has been able to give in resistance to the Communists has been in a support role for American naval units or in civic action among coastal villages.

Manning the Army

The ideal which MAAG set itself was the creation of a Vietnamese army that should be a duplicate of the American army; one day it might have to withstand more than the battalions of Vo Nguyen Giap (or so it seemed in 1954)—possibly an invasion directed, supplied, and even manned from China. The army of 200,000 that Ngo Dinh Diem had taken over was judged by the American Department of Defense to be too big to bring up to these standards—85,000 would be enough;[a] reluctantly, the Prime Minister agreed to a compromise of 150,000, at which figure it stayed until 1961. Conscription remained in force from before the Geneva Conference, but it was to be several years before it became necessary to call men up for the ranks; at the beginning the opposite process of demobilization and resettlement was the Government's chief preoccupation, and even after that sufficient recruits were usually available from volunteers to fill the annual intake. Recruitment for commissioned rank presented more problems: the Vietnamese point of view (not only Ngo Dinh Diem's) was that, as in France, only holders of a school-leaving certificate were qualified to be officers, and promotion from the ranks was abhorrent; all certificate-holders automatically became officers. But there were more opportunities for employment for those with qualifications, and consequently, on the whole, conscription had to be invoked in order to get officer material. There resulted a tendency for the ranks to be long-servicemen and the cadre to be less experienced soldiers than the men they led, although prospects of promotion,

[a] *NYT*, 17 Dec. 1954.

visits to the US, or staff appointments (all of which were matters determined by patronage or politics rather than by service merit) attracted some officer cadets to sign on for longer.

Training and equipment

American training and equipment were conditioned less by study of local experience than by the recent war history of the US. Nobody seems to have questioned the appropriateness to the Vietnamese situation of a conventional command structure, this being right by French tradition as well as American. The army was fitted up with a General Staff and a Field Army divided into 3 (from 1962, 4) Corps and 7 (from 1962, 9) Divisions; the Divisions mostly subdivided into 2-battalion regiments instead of brigades. Not only their American advisers, but the senior Generals of Vietnam also looked on their army as the medical profession looked on their student-doctors: the men should be trained to figure as soldiers by world-wide standards, without concessions to conditions prevailing nearer home for the time being. These conditions would get better as a result of political and economic measures in hand and must not stand in the way of the army's preparedness for the more challenging struggle hereafter. With the conventional command structure there went a variety of branches to be found in the US army, particularly an apparatus for supply, military government, and psychological warfare such as an expeditionary force requires when engaging an enemy outside its home country. By contrast, the morale and discipline of the army adhered more closely to national attitudes: there was no lack of courage, and when the challenges did come later on, although capricious behaviour under fire might lose many a skirmish, it was rare in the thousands of small engagements that any cowardice was exhibited, even in ambushes; but discipline was affected by distaste to inflict punishment on the slack or insubordinate and, with that, loss of face, so that such misdemeanours as absence without leave (outright desertion was rare) and neglect to carry out operational orders became very common.

Equipment similarly was on an expeditionary force scale; although every new American weapon was not supplied to the Vietnamese army—limitations on technical skill were a sufficient impediment—, the army was rendered completely mobile by motor transport (without regard to the greater density of waterways in Cochinchina) and fitted with a complex logistical supply line whose purpose was to make sure the regiments and battalions would want for nothing when the days of battle should dawn again. The support of artillery was taken for granted in the army's training, although really big guns were not available to it until after 1961. The Vietnamese soldier learnt to fight always wearing his American boots, his full pack, and his steel helmet, even when wallowing in the flooded clay of paddy nurseries. That there might one day be a greater need for swamp and jungle fighting and the tactics of patrol and ambush was not generally foreseen; the doctrine of the US army relied on armour and transportation as the foundation of tactics, and the experience of the major anti-Communist war dominating everybody's mind, that of Korea, had shown the rightness of that approach. Surprisingly, it was an initiative from the presidential Palace—apparently Ngo Dinh Diem's own, after his visit to Kuala Lumpur—which resulted, in 1960, in the formation of 'ranger' battalions specially trained for limited jungle penetration (for which the professional trainers were obtained from Australia); more than a year passed before this liability was taken over by MAAG and added to the US bill for maintenance. As the war eventually turned out, what was really required was that the whole army should have been trained so to fight; but that would have conflicted with American strategy, which looked upon ranger-type operations as a temporary concession to abnormal conditions imposed by the initiative of the Communists, which these were very soon going to lose again when the American-advised army got into its stride.

Deployment of the Army

During the years of waiting, down to the end of 1959, the army's three Corps and seven Divisions were deployed in Special Military Areas, with single battalions detached for particular garrison duties from time to time. American advisers were stationed in training establishments and at Corps and Divisional headquarters, but not lower down. In addition to the practice of a good deal of ceremonial with which American military tradition associated unit morale, and to listening to long courses of political instruction on the lines followed in indoctrinating the army of Nationalist China with which President Diem and the Vietnamese Generals associated unit morale, army units performed certain duties in connexion with internal security in the Military Areas and in 'civic action', much as the French garrison had before the Second World War. Internal security came to mean garrison duty in districts where there were believed still to be formidable bands of Vietminh to mop up; actually the duty was discharged by the maintenance of static defence posts in positions reckoned sensitive, and very little seems to have been done to identify, locate, and round up the Communists—a type of operation MAAG would have been embarrassed, in the absence of a militarized enemy and of military intelligence about him, to give any advice on. Areas in which the Communists confined themselves to terrorization of the inhabitants and refrained from sabotage of bridges or military installations were deemed to be pacified and were lightly garrisoned only by the Civil Guard. In the Military Areas the army was supported by American equipment and supplies in the supplementing of health services, minor public works, and other government duties where the civilian staff were either too few to get round the villages or too indolent or too frightened. The American idea was that if the Vietnamese army performed services useful to the peasants—as the Philippine army had with American guidance under Mr Magsaysay—these would be dissuaded in future from siding with the Communists. On the whole the effect was the opposite: supplies underwent the same alchemy when passed down through the chain of military command as through the ministries; and while the individual soldiers on the contrary lived off the peasants they ought to have been protecting and wooing, the High Command was encouraged by the military-government and psychological-warfare apparatus with which MAAG had equipped it to regard itself as an army of occupation in its own country, exempt from observance of the rules and usages of war that protect enemy territories,[102] and with the right to give orders to the government officials of the neighbourhood. The army owed little to the local people, since its pay, like everything else it had, came out of American aid, not out of taxation.

Army and politics

Thus American equipment and training added their weight to the setting up of military courts and the appointment of army officers in the territorial administration to turn the army's thoughts towards the running of the country at the administrative level. Some of its officers would have been in the Civil Service in any case if they had not been conscripted automatically into the army; rational direction of manpower was not proposed by American advisers and would have lain beyond the capacity for organization of the RVN Government; all young professional graduates were enlisted into the army, which then controlled most of the manpower to do the jobs and had to be allowed to make good the civilian short-comings engendered by conscription.[103] The army had not been set up on lines that fitted it to protect the peasants from the real dangers menacing them and pushed on to the Civil Guard such unreward-ing tasks as the pursuit of Vietcong murder squads, while waiting for the enemy in the North to offer it and its American advisers a target more worthy of them. At the political level too, the idleness of the General Staff, superfluous to the problems facing the country, bred more vaulting ambitions still. In 1954 General Nguyen Van Hinh, when Bao Dai was Head of State and he himself at the head of the army, had hoped the US would channel its support direct to the Army Command, making of it a power within the state inde-pendent of Ngo Dinh Diem as Prime Minister and of his Govern-ment;[a] President Eisenhower refused to countenance this.[b] But although for the next few years the Generals accepted that Ameri-can aid was conditional on their supporting the Diem regime and bowed to his manipulation of promotions and to infiltration of their ranks by the Can Lao, their ambition for power was unabated and tended to increase all the time because their formation, equipment, and training were for other circumstances than those prevailing.

The fact that the army marched, as it were, on its Counterpart Fund did not secure its exclusion from politics after all, therefore, and in the end the army killed Ngo Dinh Diem when the US sus-pended the CIP in order to bring him to his senses. Already the mutiny of November 1960 had been embarked on by Colonel Nguyen Chanh Thi in the belief that, after the protests and revela-tions of the *Caravellistes*, American resolve to support Ngo Dinh Diem had slumped into a position of neutrality as between all anti-Communist contestants for power.

3. SYMBIOTIC INSURGENCY

The Vietnamese Communist Party had long since penetrated most organized bodies in the country—from the civil service to the trade unions, the Sects, and even the Legion of Mary[c]—and was presumably as well informed about the political ambitions of the Generals, on whose staffs it had some, if relatively few, agents, as it was about the long-standing factional differences perpetually

[a] p. 220 above.   [b] *NYT*, 18 Nov. 1954.
[c] Revelation by Mgr Ngo Dinh Thuc (*NYHT*, 15 Sept. 1963).

gnawing at Vietnamese official minds; taken with the other weaknesses of the security system reviewed in the last chapter, these differences made a fertile field of 'contradictions' to turn to advantage in the type of insurrection for which the Party considered, at the end of 1959, that the time was ripe. Understanding by the Party's cadres how the insurrection was to be conducted was all the more important at this stage because of lack of the speedy communications necessary for a rigid command structure. Messages could only be sent by wireless or by runner, and the development of either was itself dependent on capture (or purchase) of equipment and the organization of reliable stages; neither was available at the beginning. The guerrilla command was the Party hierarchy, and so informal and decentralized did the command appear that many Western observers, persuaded incorrectly that the Party no longer existed, supposed the scattered guerrilla bands to be quite independent of one another. In reality there was a peripatetic headquarters in the Tay Ninh forest, but it 'led' the bands, through province and district committees, by a combination of doctrine, periodical directives as to the Party line, and the characteristic Communist arrangements for discipline—criticism and self-criticism, hero-making or disgrace, rarely execution. After 1962 'battalions' (simply big companies) were kept under arms the whole time, and a military command began to be superimposed, leading eventually (in 1964) to a High Command, at least for Annam where units from the DRV were in action, under a North Vietnamese General; but even then the principle of independent guerrilla action, adapting itself to immediate conditions, was preserved at the village level to cater for the big formations' logistical requirements in labour and food.[a]

Revolutionary Warfare

Many useful studies of Communist revolutionary warfare have been written in Western countries in recent years, and some of the maxims, especially those garnered from the 'thought of Chairman Mao', have become commonplace in and outside military circles. Whilst the study of Mao Tsê-tung's military writings is of some interest in the history of revolutionary warfare, however, it can also be misleading as an explanation of Communist insurrections else-

---

[a] The very efficient security of the VC, combined with the inefficient intelligence services of the Government, make it impossible to write of these matters except in general terms. There is a full discussion of the subject in Pike (pp. 210–52).

where than in China. There are two sides to a war, and if the Communists' adversaries in another country do not make the same countermoves as did Chiang Kai-shek or the Japanese (even though Mao would assert that historical laws determine that they must), then the revolutionaries also may have to change strategy or tactics. But even on the Communist side itself, there is an element of idealization in these analyses, and the derivative treatises of Truong Chinh and Vo Nguyen Giap are not completely reliable either: the fighting since 1960 has developed along its own lines and has differed in a number of important ways from the first Indochina War. Particularly misleading has been the belief on one hand that the Vietcong would be pursuing a phased development of guerrilla warfare into mobile warfare and thence into positional warfare, the interruption of which by the defence would knock them off balance; and on the other hand that attacks on villages or garrisons must necessarily start out from bases hidden in mountain, jungle, or swamp whose discovery and destruction would deprive the fighting man of his essential supplies. In fact, the remarkable characteristic of the second Indochina War has been the absence of any distinction between 'liberated' and 'free' zones—even though a small number of villages have in practice remained under uninterrupted domination by the Party—and the intimacy with which the revolutionary organization has enmeshed itself into the economic and political life of the Government and of the community it proposed progressively to take over. The Tonkinese campaign was already a considerable refinement of the practice of Mao Tsê-tung, and the campaign of the NFLSV has been an equally considerable further refinement of that.

Vietcong objectives

The problem always facing the Vietcong can be split into three parts: how to make recruits and hold partisans so that their co-operation can be counted on all the time; how to neutralize the defence, politically as well as militarily; and by what strategy and tactics to maintain the movement's momentum and steady growth. All three parts of the problem have been tackled on the principle of getting control of part of the Government's own resources: that is to say, getting possession of part of the security forces' weapons and supplies, making part of the Government's manpower—military and civilian—work for the revolution, and so manipulating 'internal contradictions' on the Government side that solidarity and loyalty are compromised and the antagonists spurred into mutual destruction on other issues than that of the revolution. It is this method that is meant by 'symbiosis'; if it is followed with skill, any 'escalation' of the fighting by the Government should, almost automatically, increase the strength of the revolution by a proportionate amount. The pursuit of such a strategy was not so much a matter of choice or of doctrine for the Vietcong as of necessity. Although accusations that the insurrection was inspired, and to some extent manned, from the North do little more than repeat statements by DRV leaders themselves,[a] it would have been impossible to keep it supplied from there because of the enormous distance. Important personnel and selected weapons could make the risky journey by sea or the safer, though more arduous, one by land; but if the uprising could not maintain itself basically from local resources—in manpower, food, and arms—the time was not ripe to embark on it: supplying it from the North was physically impossible and politically inexpedient—even disastrous if the US should make of this dependence an excuse to retaliate against DRV territory.

Recruitment of cadres

What was said earlier about the Party's methods of recruitment[b] remained substantially true of the Vietcong, except that the proportion of the voluntary element has been smaller throughout and tended always to diminish. Since the 1930s no Vietnamese group has shown any interest in, still less contributed to, the study of Marxian political economy—any more, of course, than was formerly the case with Confucianism:[c] the intellectual curiosity of the student element in the Communist movement in China has been absent in Vietnam. The appeals of anti-colonialism—patriotism, ambition, xenophobia—contained no reason for working to overturn the Government of Ngo Dinh Diem; more than that, the Party's true purpose of unification, which was its constant 'watchword' after 1954, far from stirring enthusiasm in young Cochinchinese breasts, has stung regional sentiment into antagonism to such an extent that NFLSV propaganda has had to adopt a more ambiguous attitude over this point in recent years. Although Ngo

[a] The Workers' Party magazine, *Hoc Tap*, wrote in Mar. 1963: 'North Vietnam is the firm base for the revolution in the South and the point on which it leans; our Party is the steady and experienced vanguard unit of the working class and is the brain and factor that decides all victories of the revolution.'
[b] p. 177 above.   [c] p. 69 above.

Dinh Diem's dictatorial ways made him many enemies in the towns, extremely few, if any at all, felt so oppressed as to take to the jungle with the Communists—least of all any of the *Caravellistes*, who were the most vocal on the matter. Consequently, the Vietcong suffered from the beginning from a shortage of the trained technical men and middle-level leaders who had helped the Vietminh in its early days, and it was these who had to be made up for by infiltration from the DRV.

Masses mobilization

The rank and file of the Vietcong have been recruited by further adaptation of Truong Chinh's 'Marxist-Leninist methods of mobilizing the masses'.[a] In central Annam, the endemic unemployment noted earlier as a characteristic of the region was all the easier for the Party to exploit because it had its infrastructure of *chi bo* intact from the days of the DRV administration; some cadres had been detained in 1955—out of revenge rather than thought-out policy on the part of the Government—and others had been removed to the development areas in the highlands, but by the end of 1959, in both Quang Ngai and Binh Dinh, all were home again.[b] In Cochinchina demobilized bands of the Binh Xuyen and Hoa Hao joined the Vietcong rather than settle down with government help on the land. Everywhere peasant grievances against authority, or feuds with other groups often identified with authority in the uniform of the militia or the Civil Guard, as well as credence for Vietcong offers of land, added their quota, if not a large one, of malcontents vulnerable to a sympathetic ear and helping hand. But the essential feature of the Vietcong adaptation of the revolutionary method was that they did not set up a zone apart from government territory this time; as a result, supporting them entailed no definite and irrevocable act like taking to the hills 'to join the resistance'. It was of the very nature of the symbiotic situation that the majority of the rank and file should carry on their everyday lives as little changed as possible, performing only certain services—or desisting from certain duties—as directed by the cadres. This arrangement increased the 'surplus value' flowing to the revolution and made it possible to enlist support from entire hamlets, every individual contributing, to be on the safe side, enough to insure with the revolution but not enough to seem to make any difference to the Government, and

[a] Truong Chinh (1962), p. 8.
[b] Private communication from a district chief in Binh Dinh.

thereby providing the sea of confusion for the cadre fish (in Mao Tsê-tung's now hackneyed metaphor) to swim about in freely. There was a good deal of backsliding in these conditions, but news of a garrotting in an adjacent village would bring the masses into line again over a wide area. Families would offer a son to the regular Vietcong forces—who *were* away in the jungle—whenever pressure of 'armed propaganda' increased, while another might join the security forces. The peasants tended to work to appease both sides, putting off as long as they could their absolute commitment to either, but Vietcong coercion invariably entered into the relationship sooner or later to hold the partisan when life became uncomfortable or dangerous. From 1961 onwards the Vietcong began to extend the areas from which they levied actual conscripts. At first this was done by rounding up the villagers at night and shaming the young men into joining in the adventure with a patriotic sanction; when, in 1964, the supply of volunteers for the Government forces began to dry up and conscription had to be employed more extensively, the Vietcong imitated the authorities by introducing the same system of time-serving, for three years, sometimes offering those who went quietly a promise that they would not have to fight far from their homes, so that, if they had the misfortune to get wounded, their own families (and local faith-healers) could look after them; recovery is more commonly put down to good luck than to medical skill. This effect of conscription was one example of the operation of 'symbiosis'. Finally, since 1965—sporadically in earlier years—the Vietcong have secured recruits regularly by pressganging, those already tied to the guerrilla force having no compunction about visiting the same fate on others in a midnight swoop on an adjacent village.

Intimidation of authority

Neutralization of the defence involved both village authorities and security forces; mostly all that was demanded of either was that they should not interfere with Vietcong comings and goings, although of course neglect of their duty could expose them to blackmail in the future. It is surprising how many village notables stood out against intimidation—a foolhardiness for which they often paid with their lives. Only in close proximity to towns were village notables fairly safe, and the majority, from 1960 onwards, resumed the habit of the Indochina War of living near the Civil Guard garrisons and only visiting their villages in the daytime. The psychological

effect of this terrorization of notables was, of course, to convince all
the villagers that nobody was safe if their leaders were not and that
obedience to the terrorists was the only practicable course of action;
since the village council was in charge of the militia, the same message was borne in upon them too. As soon as open hostilities began,
the Government reacted much as the Vietcong would have hoped
and expected: defence posts were strengthened and multiplied—
outside villages, at road intersections, on bridges, along the frontiers—, and to man them the paramilitary forces were split up into
smaller units and spread more widely and therefore thinly over the
countryside. The new posts in turn were attacked or intimidated
into a *modus vivendi* (so much ammunition to change hands so often
as the price of immunity from further attack) on condition that they
did not intervene to resist Vietcong murders or waylay the couriers
and cadres going about their business.[a] When, in the hope of keeping the static garrisons from annoying the villagers too much,[b] the
Government allowed their families to go to live with them inside the
barbed wire and earthworks, defence of the posts became more
pressing than defence of frontier, bridge, road, or villagers, and
many a man's loyalty was undermined through intimidation of his
less resolute wife. The Government position was further weakened
by dishonesty in the provincial administration over the handling of
funds for the paramilitary forces, which often went without pay or
supplies and demanded that deficiencies be made good by the villagers—and from then on that the villagers should pay them just
the same, which created an ideal situation for rumour-mongering
and 'agitprop'.[c]

Tagorism

Bold attacks to seize weapons were important at the beginning of
the insurrection for several reasons. As long as the Government remained off balance, the advantage of surprise, falling to the Vietcong over and over again, made attacks on outposts the most
abundant source at a cost of only the lightest casualties; later on the
ambushing of rescue columns became more rewarding, and in 1962

[a] Graphically described by Party cadre 'Sam Nao' in Burchett, p. 146.
[b] In both Phan-nhu-Bang and *Heroes and Heroines* (1965), the VC propagandists give
examples of their female cadres' hardbitten astuteness in enticing idle militiamen
away from their posts and then either ambushing them or having them denounced
to their superiors, ignorant of the cadres' two-faced activities.
[c] The first VC poster the author of this book ever saw, in 1961, read simply: 'Militiamen,
demand your pay on payday!'

opportunities for purchase became common. Secondly, boldness stimulated morale by impressing on the movement the David-and-Goliath relationship of Tagorism; the generous equipment enjoyed by the army weighed the soldiers down in their static shelters and made fools of them, showing the truth that austerity, under the leadership of the Front or the Party, would always be more than a match for mechanization in the field and soft living in the billet. Thirdly, boldness established the viability of the insurrection in the eyes of the world at large: the Vietnamese peasants, who had watched the Communists win before, recognized the old tricks again and from then on expected them to win in the end this time as well; the DRV, which would have hesitated to infiltrate even guerrillas from outside until it could rely on the local logistical base, now had an organization to which arms and special equipment could be channelled with much less risk that local villagers would give away the secret of their origin and the routes by which they arrived; this in turn made it safe for the Communist powers to champion the NFLSV when it was proclaimed as an indigenous uprising, its genuineness proved by these very feats of daring.

Security-force morale

Inversely as they built up morale among the guerrillas, the Communist tactics of ambush of moving columns and hit-and-run assault on lonely garrisons, dovetailed to facilitate one another, disheartened the army, ill adapted to deal with them, and from that point led up to neutralization of the defence at the political level also. This strategy was not destined to be crowned with easy victory, but it had nevertheless many incidental successes, thanks in the main to the soundness of the tactical base. Engagements were never begun unless the local Communist Commander was sure of pulling it off without heavy loss. The success of such tactics is not surprising, for every advantage was with the guerrilla: he always knew where the security forces were—in their camps or posts or else in their lorries—, whereas they never knew where he was and only rarely who he was; he could choose his moment, and enforced withdrawal involved him in no loss—it took only a fraction of the organization, work, and courage to blow up a bridge on one moonless night of the year that it took the security forces to keep it from being blown up every night and every day, or to rebuild it if once they had been caught napping. As soon as the local garrison had been made to look foolish or afraid, it was an easy matter to overawe the people close by, however inclined they had been up to then to send the cadres packing. In fact, though this was not generally appreciated by either army command or Palace, the aim of the Vietcong in attacking the security forces was not simply to capture weapons, but even more to win domination over the people the weapons were supposed to protect.

Towards 'neutralism'

It is unnecessary to postulate a deliberate Vietcong plot in order to account for either the remonstrance of the *Caravellistes* or the mutiny of Colonel Thi; on the contrary, both named disquiet over Vietcong successes as their reason for moving against the Palace. But these were also expressions of discouragement at the failure of the security forces to halt the Communist advance; they demanded that the Government should relax its security measures out of hope that magnanimity would prove more effective. The morale of the soldiers was already shaken, and they were beginning to react as Chiang Kai-shek's army had reacted—by hitting out at what *was* within reach from frustration at always missing the proper target. The very occurrence of the remonstrance and of the mutiny proved the tenability of a position lying somewhere between the Government and the revolution and, by that much, weakened the solidarity of the defence. The thought 'neutralism' occurred to many minds, and the word itself began to be whispered; some at least of the whisperers probably were agents of the DRV. The Vietcong certainly did not engineer the political manœuvres in Saigon, but it is equally certain they had worked in such a way that something of the sort would happen and that its very spontaneity would appear to support their cause.

Situation in Cochinchina

And yet, throughout 1960 and much of 1961, for all the boldness of its attacks and its claims to have been created by the will of the whole people, the Communist organization in South Vietnam was still in a precarious position, with the majority of supporters far from committed once and for all. There had been a limit to the preparations for the uprising that could be made before the first blow was struck without revealing to the authorities what was going on. In the districts of Cochinchina where the Vietminh had never been driven underground—in Camau, the Plain of Reeds, the mouths of the Mekong and Bassac, and in the two jungle belts north and north-

east of Saigon known as War Zones C and D—the old organization
was probably intact though unseen. In other districts agents had
been infiltrated into possibly two-thirds of the villages, but there
had been little chance in the majority of them to train guerrillas on
the spot; only after the flag had been raised was it feasible for the
cadres, and the nucleus of men from each district held in the peri-
pheral bases, to infiltrate home to organize their fellow villagers, for
only then was the population generally frightened enough to help
them on their way and not tell the authorities. The number of Communists bearing arms in the spring of 1960 will not have been many
more than 5,000. Relations between the Vietcong and the Sects
were on a basis of mutual non-interference, but it would take little
in any locality to induce the local Sect commander to give the Vietcong away.

Situation in Annam

In Annam plans may have been well advanced before 1960 but
not their implementation. It will be recalled that the coastal provinces from Cape Varella almost to Tourane had been regarded
during the Indochina War, from the viewpoint of the caves of Thai
Nguyen, as territory administered by the DRV. Ngo Dinh Diem's
apprehension that this region might be designated for 'liberation'
again sooner or later was probably well founded, but for the present
the guerrillas were determined to avoid creating the sort of war
front that had marked off the 'liberated zone' during the Indochina
War; moreover, the active hostility of various sections of the population—Catholic, adherents of rival parties (Dai Viet and
VNQDD), supported by all those who had old scores to pay off
against the Vietminh from the years before 1954—had to be neutralized by subtler methods. The maintenance of a Communist
presence in the intervening years by the periodical murder of active
opponents which had been possible in Cochinchina had not worked
so well in Annam, because of these factors and of the transportation
to the highlands of so many Communist families. Reorganization
had to be undertaken by cadres returning secretly from Tonkin,
and although many landed by sea during 1960 and took control of
coastal villages in Quang Ngai and Binh Dinh again, their activities remained subdued, by comparison with incidents in Cochinchina, until 1964. In the highlands the whole operation seems to
have been organized from Tonkin; although the order for the uprising in Cochinchina was given from the same command post, it

would have been impossible to co-ordinate the preliminary work in the two regions more closely than to reach the same stage of preparedness within a year or so of one another.

Preparation for infiltration

The announcement of the founding of the NFLSV in December 1960 will have coincided roughly with the moment when the necessity for co-ordination between these widely-scattered centres began to make itself felt, and with it a reliable system of communication by surface in addition to the permanent wireless links. Before the end of 1961 way-stations able to guide, feed, and pass along groups of perhaps fifty or a hundred men at a time linked all the provinces of Cochinchina, and similar numbers were reported to be moving between the Ho Chi Minh Trail and the coast of Annam.[104] The population along the southernmost stage on the route from Annam to Cochinchina was suitably cowed into compliance when, on the night of 17 September 1961, a raiding party from War Zone D 1,500 strong overran the little township of Phuoc Vinh, burnt down the public buildings, hanged and disembowelled the Province Chief in the main square, shot his wife, and marched off the young men to the jungle.[a] Whether the Vietcong already anticipated at this date the expansion of their communications to handle the rate of infiltrations reached in Annam by 1965 is uncertain; but, in the meantime, the purpose behind their operations would have made a vulnerable target for the Government's intelligence services if the nature of the opportunity had been appreciated by either pupil or tutor in the defence partnership, and the insurrection might at this stage, with luck, have been stopped from getting out of hand.

4. AMERICAN STRATEGY AGAINST THE GUERRILLAS

Whereas the strategic dispositions of the Vietnamese security forces down to the end of 1960 were a Vietnamese responsibility, the year 1961 rapidly brought a greater American influence to bear on them. It is important to note how this came about. It did not result from any deliberate new agreement whereby American advice must be given and must be acted on, or even from any closer informal association of the officers of MAAG with Vietnamese de-

---

[a] *NYT*, 19 Sept. 1961—which, however, does not report the manner of killing the Province Chief.

fence planning. Instead it came as the incidental consequence of the 'escalation' of American aid, conditioned as that was by the characteristics described earlier in this chapter. America was determined to support the RVN with all the means at her generous disposal, and Ngo Dinh Diem and his Generals, in spite of occasional misgivings, accepted everything that was offered; the equipment America had to offer implied a mechanized style of fighting, and the strategy set itself the objective of creating conditions in which to apply the tactics the equipment was designed for. It is doubtful whether any overall appraisal of the situation was made in the American mission during the presidency of Ngo Dinh Diem; nobody, and no office, had the oversight of the whole field the Vietcong were at work in—the American partnership was active only in connexion with fighting, and if questions of government appeared relevant at all it continued to be because of political criticism of the unrepresentative nature of the dictatorship, rather than of administrative weakness. Such studies as were made confined themselves to assessments of the relative strengths of the two forces and to considerations how to increase the Government's numerical advantage.

Strategic objectives

Although so little interest was shown in the lessons of the earlier Indochina War, American strategy did follow French strategy closely. The central idea was to force the guerrillas to fight a positional war so that the superior firepower of the defence could be brought to bear on them; if a front could be established between friendly and enemy territory, Vietcong strength could be eroded by inflicting heavier casualties on it than could be made good locally or by infiltration from the DRV. In this view the growing points of the insurrection were the armed Vietcong units operating from retreats in uninhabited wildernesses, and the networks in the villages subordinate to them; if the armed units could be rendered harmless, the subversive political wing would collapse and peace return. Government measures to make the villages secure, either by posting garrisons to them or by carrying out civic action or other welfare campaigns to win popularity, were subsidiary to the principal task, which was the military one of searching out and destroying the command posts and of inflicting casualties to wear down the rank and file. The civilian duties of government came gradually to be thought of as incidental to the fighting and the civil departments of the administration ancillary to the army; comfort was taken in battle statistics without regard for the imponderable psychological elements in popular morale. In any case, popular morale continued to be understood in terms of ideological persuasion rather than of confidence in the Government as the guardian of personal safety. If the Vietcong were exploiting administrative weaknesses in the Government in the country and political grievances in the towns, rebuffs from the Palace over administration of the aid programmes made it wise to tackle the Vietcong directly first and to rectify the weaknesses at leisure afterwards; dishonesty in high places was notoriously intractable even in advanced countries, and the 'war' (as it was beginning to be thought of) obviously could not wait that long. No general strategic plan to bring all the resources of the Vietnamese nation to bear on eradicating the Vietcong appeared to be called for at that stage.

Tactical deployment

So, from 1960 on, the deployment and tactics of the security forces were governed by the concept of a war front enabling use of the superior weaponry and technology of the West against a guerrilla force that was potentially the spearhead of a more massive thrust out of North Vietnam. The militia were given rudimentary training by the Civil Guard for close defence of hamlets, which they carried out from the supposed safety of reinforced guard posts, occasionally housed in the village *dinh*, more commonly in the microscopic strongpoints just outside the hamlets left behind by General Latour; although there was dissatisfaction in American circles over this static deployment, its exposure to exploitation by Vietcong symbiosis was not so immediately apparent. The Civil Guard itself was based on district or province towns, except that guard duties at important bridges or, in the Mekong Delta, at intersections of important canals, were also entrusted to them; the companies at base were, in theory, a strike force to rush to the defence of beleaguered platoons of militia. The army was redeployed on a grid that converted the whole country into one big Military Area, divided into tactical zones each under one of the Corps.[a] It also had companies on detachment for protective purposes, but mostly it operated as a strike force in support of the Civil Guard and to conduct sweeps through open country in search of Vietcong units and bases. The chief endeavour of American training and equipment was to render the army as swift and effective as possible in reaction to the

[a] *Sac-lenh* No. 98 of 13 Apr. 1961.

reported appearance of Vietcong forces, and for this Civil Guard posts were linked to divisional headquarters by wireless; the wretched militia, however, did not even have Verey lights with which to summon help. The initial Communist assault in January 1960 had counted on army slackness; for the next two years every piece of equipment was furnished to the army that could have compensated for its heavy-footedness; but attachment to creature comfort, inability to move except by lorry, and the demoralizing lack of a strategic plan continued to inhibit local initiative and to bring the soldiers to the scene of Vietcong attacks always long after the culprits had made off again with whatever was their prize; 'sweeps'—usually undertaken in hot pursuit—were notable for their brevity in both space and time. Since the army moved only by road—considerations of speed were sufficient justification for that—and kept getting mined and ambushed, it began to be necessary to convoy a rescue column of company strength with half the rest of the battalion. Although the intention of MAAG had been to fit the army eventually to bear the brunt of attacks by the DRV's regular battalions (the *chu luc*), while the Civil Guard engaged regional guerrillas and the militia were called on to cope only with untrained local bravoes, the Vietcong inconsiderately played the game the other way round, invariably attacking with locally overwhelming strength the softest targets they could isolate; by the end of two years of fighting nearly all the casualties had been sustained by the paramilitary forces—who, incidentally, were denied military surgical facilities.[a]

Intelligence

The conventional-war starting point of this strategy was an additional impediment to evolving a useful intelligence system, already severely hampered, as we have seen, by the machinations of the Palace. The information required by a conventional army concerns the strength, armament, location, and impending plans of the enemy's battle formations. Military intelligence seeking this kind of information was able to tell the security forces relatively little about an enemy who spent most of his time working in the fields and possessed none of the attributes of strength, armament, location or plans. By its own criterion, therefore, the military intelligence

---

[a] See note 103. No doubt one of the nails in Diem's coffin was a circular telegram he told the author in March 1962 he had addressed to Corps and Divisional Commanders of the army asking them to explain their comparatively low casualties.

operation in Vietnam failed, and the Communists slipped through its net just as they eluded conventional shot and shell. The real core of the Vietcong movement was its organization, its growing points the village cells, and its strength the individuals whose labour it commanded, now for fighting, now for other tasks. The identification of the network through interception of its communications, leading to its eradication from the villages, called for procedures owing more to criminal investigation of the sort it takes a police force to collect and collate over a number of years than to ephemeral tactical intelligence; that point of view would have relegated the army to a subordinate role unacceptable to either Vietnamese or American thinking. A certain amount of political intelligence was gathered at this time, but it was concerned mostly with generalizations and 'studies' of typical Communist methods, or with the organization of the DRV, rather than with the down-to-earth comings and goings—the food supplies, the communications, the hospital arrangements—of the enemy on the doorstep; the product of these researches was not generally communicated to the security forces, but it would have been of little use to them if it had been.

Thus with intelligence, as with operations, responsible Vietnamese were doing their best to keep away from the sharp end of the conflict and its perplexities; regrettably, many of them also looked on American equipment as a substitute for grit and toil. By the spring of 1961 there was disquiet on all hands at the continued intensification of Vietcong activity, its momentum evidently little slowed down by the existing defence mechanism and strategy. There was particular anxiety over the deterioration of security in the PMS, for this was linked with Communist activity in Laos and constituted an unpredictable international threat, its direction possibly traceable to China.

Increased military aid

This disquiet expressed itself in American circles in characteristic fashion when, as the first step towards a reappraisal of the situation, the Secretary of State announced in May 1961 that the aid programme would be stepped up.[a] A few days later, Mr Lyndon B. Johnson, at that time Vice-President, paid a visit to Saigon to show solidarity; he announced that the US would from now on support the Civil Guard financially and that MAAG would retrain both it and the militia; that the army itself would be underwritten for an-

[a] *TVN*, 9 May 1961.

other 20,000 men, to whom guerrilla training would be given; and that, in addition to more money and supplies for social services, American engineers would relieve the strain on the Vietnamese army by helping with the repair of sabotaged bridges and installations.[a] The number of MAAG advisers was doubled at this time, Communist aggression being deemed to have proceeded far enough to nullify the previous limitation. During the summer a thorough survey of the economy was carried out by American experts,[b] and in the autumn the American Chief of Staff, General Maxwell D. Taylor, made a parallel estimate of the military forces. Again, increases in aid were the result—a dozen aircraft, for instance, and the first helicopters (to reduce exposure of army rescue columns to mining on the roads)—but this time the more intangible among Vietnamese needs were looked at as well: doubt was cast on the country's ability to absorb increases in aid indefinitely,[c] and President Diem was supposed to have been urged at last to reform not the political but the administrative side of his Government, especially where it was corrupt. Offended at fresh hints that reform should include dismissal of Nhu, he had replied 'Let us defeat the Vietcong first.' Much as the plight of the Tonkinese refugees in 1954 had helped obscure the real issues of independence, so in 1961 Diem was enabled by an almost unprecedented flood of the Mekong to invoke sympathy for the victims at the crucial moment of negotiation and get let off, once again, what President Eisenhower had referred to as 'performance'. The US, it was rumoured in Saigon, had even discussed introducing her own combat troops,[d] but now stopped short at 'putting Ngo Dinh Diem in a position to win his own war'. However, early in 1962 the most important result of this American reappraisal turned out to be the introduction of a second military mission (Military Assistance Command Vietnam—MACV) to provide the Vietnamese forces with operational advice—MAAG had been concerned only with training—and the support of American transport and logistical services.

MACV and escalation

The setting up of MACV, commanded by four-star General Paul D. Harkins, was the step that transformed aid into support of the

[a] *Time*, 19 May 1961.

[b] The Staley Report was not made public, though often referred to in Communist propaganda.

[c] *Time*, 27 Oct. 1961.   [d] Confirmed later by Schlesinger (p. 29).

RVN and committed US military forces—even if not yet infantry—to participation in the hostilities. The Rubicon had been crossed, and from now on it might be said that American aid contained the seeds of its own escalation. At the time the extent of the NFLSV's dependence on North Vietnam was thought to be greater than it really was, extending, some believed, to food supplies, and there was a sense of alarm that the security forces were too few to out-number their assailants by a viable ratio; as many as possible of them must therefore be released from non-combatant duties. What seemed important about the new commitment was that it was so much less in the short run than a complete take-over would have been, and liability for yet further support did not really matter, so boundless was the generosity of American feeling. But this reasoning left out of account the principle of symbiosis, and unless the Viet-cong's taproots into the storehouses of the recipients of the aid, civilian and military, could be severed, the ferocity of the fighting might be intensified but the balance of forces would remain the same.

Vietnamese irregulars

Better adaptation of tactics to the Vietnamese terrain was talked of, but this on its own, or even accompanied by other tricks of the 'counter-insurgency' trade, imported from Greece or the Philip-pines or Malaya, would be wasted unless there was a new strategic integration of the whole defence effort. Unhappily, General Har-kins, far from becoming the director of all operations his rank might have betokened, did not even command MAAG, still less agencies responsible to other departments in Washington. In an effort to improve tactics, the CIA had begun to sponsor irregular forces of its own among the hill tribes of the PMS,[a] and although the finan-cial support of these was eventually debited to MACV, the com-mand was not, and large numbers of weapons had meanwhile gone astray through them.[105] These irregulars became part of a wider project of the CIA[b] to bring to bear the guerrilla tactics of the US Special Forces against infiltrators making use of the Laotian and Cambodian frontiers for sanctuary;[c] trainers were sent to Vietnam to form élite local units to fight under their own commanders, but

---

[a] Civilian Independent Defense Groups (CIDG); in Vietnamese, *Luc Luong Biet Kich* (Commando Forces).
[b] *The Times*, 10 Sept. 1963.
[c] Operations are described, somewhat colourfully, with changes of place and personal names, in Moore (1965).

with a strong American advisory cadre and paid from American-owned piastres outside the CIP framework. The experiment achieved some notable successes in hampering Vietcong traffic, thanks in part to manipulation of the bands of brigands, heirs to Pu Kombo, who still frequented the frontier zones; but a political price had to be paid: the RVN's already bad relations with Cambodia were aggravated through this entanglement, and the operation was placed, because of its clandestine aspects, under the control of Counsellor Nhu instead of the army, cutting it off from co-ordination with operations round the infiltrators' destinations and enabling Nhu to transfer it for strong-arm retaliation against the Buddhists in Saigon the following year, leaving the frontier exposed. In fact, the previous lack of a treaty became an even more serious matter after the setting-up of MACV than before: there was no joint American-Vietnamese command—to this extent the Geneva Agreement still carried weight—, and consequently no sanction for the advice which the 5,000–8,000 new military advisers were supposed to impart to Vietnamese commanders, down to battalion level, and to Province Chiefs. The temptation to make advice acceptable by securing extra equipment to go with it was carried so far that some advisers became mere channels for aid, and each new item brought into the country, though intended to strengthen the professional bonds between operational and advisory counterparts, tended in compensation to deepen the rifts between rival Vietnamese interests by making them independent of one another; it was as if each member of a football team had been allowed to have his own ball to kick. This was not unwelcome to President Diem in the pursuit of his divisive policy in regard to the security forces and intelligence services.

Uncoordinated operations

Uncertainty about the command structure of all these different forces, the continuing omission to elaborate a definite strategic plan or even a general tactical doctrine, and the American majors' and captains' inexperience of the problems which they found to their surprise faced the Province and District Chiefs they were told off to advise, all combined to give operations a discontinuous, experimental character. There being no general policies, each Vietnamese commander was encouraged to conduct one operation after another, in pursuit of the spoor left by worthwhile Vietcong game on the move; his own operations did not have to be co-ordinated with those of neighbouring commanders, of other forces (for instance, the army, the Special Forces, or the Civil Guard), or of other departments of the Government, and he could report his bag to the Palace as evidence of personal prowess or acumen, without regard to whether the operations carried the Government's cause any nearer to victory. On the other hand, where no prospect of this kind of reward was discernible, the slow entrenchment of the new Vietcong full-time units in hill or swamp redoubts was left unmolested. If a strategic plan had existed, it would have served as a criterion for measuring the effectiveness of experiments, it would have shown up negligence, and it would have afforded means of ensuring that further operations were planned in advance and not haphazard.

Strategic plan

At the beginning of 1962 a strategic plan was discussed in Vietnamese circles—and promptly rejected—, but it did not come from the American advisory machine. This plan was the work of a very small British Advisory Mission, headed by Mr (now Sir) Robert Thompson, invited by President Diem in September 1961 to contribute its opinion to the Vietnamese 'studies' and American surveys. The essence of the plan was that the whole security system should be pulled together under the discipline of a planning and operational mechanism with clear-cut objectives, so that it would be plain to themselves and others when the weaker brethren strayed. The Government was to regain its lost initiative by employing the armed forces in support of the civil power, and this would have reversed the drift towards military government. The plan would have ended the preoccupation with static defence of military installations and strongpoints, while proposing priorities and phases for its own implementation whose economy and concentration on progressive targets was too radical for the prevailing mood of broad sweeps, mechanization, and prodigal logistics.[106] The importance of the British Advisory Mission was, however, that it became associated with Ngo Dinh Nhu's campaign for strategic hamlets, as President Diem's outside referee and reporter on progress.[a]

5. STRATEGIC HAMLET CLIMAX

It was between the visit of General Taylor and the assumption of command by General Harkins that Ngo Dinh Nhu, to use his own

[a] R. Thompson (1966), pp. 130–9.

phrase, stepped out of the shadows. We referred at the end of the last chapter to the regime's need after 1960 for a new weapon; several other considerations combined to induce Nhu to take on a more overt direction of the defence against Vietcong advances. There were many signs at this time that even the Palace was becoming aware of the desirability of strategic direction, especially as the American contribution promised to increase so greatly the resources to be deployed: common prudence—not to speak of national pride—required that an eye be kept on what all the new foreigners would be up to in the country, and perhaps a counterweight found to their influence. Moreover, Nhu was aware that, although the CIA might be his friend and approve his aims, the State Department and the Department of Defense distrusted him profoundly. It would, at the same time, be tactful to give the American Generals an earnest of goodwill and unflagging determination—the more so because determination was flagging in fact. The whole apparatus of government could do with the impetus of a programme with easily verifiable objects which the simplest minds could comprehend and whose attainment could be ticked off day by day. Army morale itself would benefit from a new fillip, but, yet more impelling, the Civil Guard was no longer a sufficient insurance against fresh coups d'état by the army, especially as the latter was about to increase its manpower and, through American training arrangements, get a stronger say in the Civil Guard's deployment;[107] Vietnamese Generals might start intriguing again with their newly-arrived American advisers in the tradition, and with the same purpose, as General Hinh in 1955. The Government had never really established its writ in the countryside, and Nhu wanted to expand the network of the Can Lao so as to create a vehicle to carry the message of Personalism there; these steps could be looked at either as security measures or as measures to put down new roots for the regime. If the Government could in some way extend its administration to the lowest echelons, it stood a better chance of committing sections of the people not yet disaffected to working actively for its cause before the Vietcong reached them.

Nhu's ambition

Furthermore, though this is less certain ground, it seems likely that Nhu had already taken thought by 1961 for his own public image against the day when he would be a candidate for the presidency himself. Although Diem was in the habit of telling selected foreigners that he would not relinquish the presidency, whatever else might happen, until the Communist peril was averted for good, the constitution of which he was the author set a limit for re-election at three terms,[a] and he had entered the second of these in April 1961; if the regime was to be preserved, it was desirable for Nhu to prepare himself for the succession. But, in the meantime, the President might be assassinated: another attempt was made when two disgruntled airmen bombed the palace on 27 February 1962, wounding Mme Nhu and making the President's official residence, to which he was deeply attached, uninhabitable.[b] And if neither of these possibilities terminated the presidency, the day might still come when Nhu wanted to usurp it in his own coup d'état. What was wanted, therefore, was some new measure that, in addition to its other aims, could be managed by the Counsellor himself and would bring him opportunities to tour the country to inspect progress and accustom the people to the sight of him as an alternate for the President.

Origins of strategic hamlets

The concept of isolating the peasants from the guerrilla bands who preyed on them was an old one in Vietnam—and not only in Vietnam, of course. In Annam the people had lived in stockaded villages ever since their conquest of the land from the Chams, and compactness of settlement had been imposed additionally by pressure of population along the narrow coastal plain and the bringing under the plough of the greatest possible area of land. As we have seen, Ngo Dinh Diem—himself an Annamite—believed the intensity of communal relationships to which these physical conditions gave rise to be the foundation of the Vietnamese way of life; Cochinchina had been exposed to subversion by banditry, he thought, through the topography of the settlement pattern—the different wards of a village (called *ap* or hamlets) were often scattered in Cochinchina across the arable or stretched out along a canal and in only occasional contact with the centre and with one another. The *agrovilles* (closer settlement areas) were looked to, over a very limited acreage, to pull the villages back to national tradition. Nhu believed the idea could be improved on and universalized: it underlay the policy of Lyautey (oil-spot pacification), and Nhu thought

[a] Art. 32.
[b] There was a constitutional Vice-President, but nobody at this time would have expected him to succeed on Ngo Dinh Diem's demise.

it could be argued for by reference to the *kibbutzim* of Israel[a] and the 'new villages' of Malaya. The Malayan reference was useful because Malayan success in defeating a Communist insurrection, though the ingredients of that success were generally misread, was a fashionable object of study among both Vietnamese and American officials at the time, and the presence in Saigon of the British Advisory Mission would be opportune if its moral support could be enlisted on the assumption that its practical advice was going to be followed.[b]

Village government

Perhaps even more weight in the framing of the strategic-hamlet 'programme' in Ngo Dinh Nhu's mind came from the conviction that the age-old problem of village administration was insoluble: if the village commune (the *xa*) could be bypassed and left to wither, the much smaller hamlet, especially in Cochinchina, stood a better chance of self-defence on a *lien-gia* or neighbourhood basis—less open to treachery—and also of political domination from the capital, for entire hamlets could be set to watch one another and the village neutralized. Nhu did not conceal his disagreement with the President over this—and incidentally, by his tactlessness, forwent the wholehearted co-operation of some officials who were loyal personally to Diem and resented Nhu's unconstitutional intrusion. It soon became clear that Nhu's efforts to bring the countryside under a close administration were not going to extend the writ of the ministries of the central Government but to cut them out at the same time as the village committees, and to substitute a special hierarchy culminating in himself. But the most cogent factor of all in Nhu's mind was the success of Vietminh methods in dominating village life and cowing village leaders into collaboration; the Vietcong had developed a stage further the organization of the menfolk for harassment of patrolling Government forces and the organization of women, children, and elderly people for dispersal in near-by hills or woods or for concealment in underground tunnels—the routine of what they were beginning to call 'defensive villages' (*xa chien dau*). Nhu was not one to appreciate the contrast of intention that divided the art of government from the tricks of revolution, and in any case he gave himself out to be a revolutionary and derived his whole political philosophy from the desire common to European

[a] He was a little confused over this; what he had been told about was really the *Nahal* movement.
[b] Explanation given the author at the time by a Palace spokesman; this was a typical attitude to foreign advice, by no means confined to the Palace.

Personalists of harnessing Communist method to defence against the political objects of Communist movements.

Ap chien luoc

The name 'strategic hamlet' (*ap chien luoc*) seems to have been used first in the late summer of 1961 in Vinh Long province—a Cochinchinese province which, since Mgr Thuc's days as bishop there, had been a kind of nursery province for pilot schemes. In February of that year Nhu had taken the first step by founding the *Thanh Nien Cong Hoa* (Republican Youth)—a uniformed organ for enrolling young men, that could serve for any purpose for which organization and discipline were required; owing something perhaps to the Boy Scouts, something to the Black Shirts, and even more to Admiral Decoux's youth movement, the Republican Youth was thought to have stood in the way of Vietcong recruitment to the Revolutionary Youth in the few districts where it was organized. In Vinh Long, in the chosen villages, its functions were expanded to include organization of an alarm and evacuation system, and also the *lien-gia* reporting machinery; registers of all the population were drawn up ward by ward, and in them was set down the sectarian adherence of each family and which ones had members away with the Vietcong. While this experiment was proceeding in Vinh Long, two Catholic priests were launching experiments of their own in widely separated parts of the country—both of them called, confusingly, 'Operation Sea Swallow'. The first was a Chinese, Father Hoa; his little refugee *chrétienté* was composed of ex-soldiers of Chiang Kai-shek's army who had fled to Tonkin in 1950, together with their Tonkinese wives and families. In 1959 he led his flock, strongly motivated by anti-Communist sentiment, on to uncleared land on the west coast of Camau, in the very jaws of the Vietcong, and by dint of courage and determination made a self-supporting and self-defending fortress out of it. In the Song Cau district of Phu Yen province another Father Hoa[a] had similarly stockaded his *chrétienté* and, with the help of the Province Chief, increased their share of communal land so as to be able to welcome refugees from the surrounding hills under pressure from the Vietcong trying to link up their inland and coastal communications.[b]

[a] The two names were in reality quite different and distinguished in Vietnamese by their tone marks.

[b] Official support for these Catholic communities came under attack during the Buddhist crisis in 1963 as a form of privilege based on religious allegiance. The symbolism of the name Sea Swallow was that the nesting of swallows in a Chinese house is a harbinger of impending success.

The bringing together of the Republican Youth and of these experiences in 'highly-motivated' stockaded defence, produced the idea for the definitive strategic hamlet.

Scope of the hamlets

On 3 January 1962, the President's 61st birthday and the eve of the agreement with the US Ambassador over MACV, Ngo Dinh Nhu began a publicity campaign to announce, popularize, and elaborate the extension of the strategic-hamlet regime to every inhabited place in the country, not excluding either the long houses of the PMS or the boroughs and wards of Saigon. There were estimated to be 16,000 hamlets in South Vietnam, and, allowing for an element of rationalization here and there, 14,000 stockaded strategic hamlets were to be made of them; all was to be completed in fourteen months. That this radical proposal was viewed in the Palace as a gamble was given away in a speech by the Minister of the Interior when he spoke of it ominously as South Vietnam's last chance to preserve its independence;[a] there can be little doubt that, in the mood of the Palace at the time, he meant independence from direct action by the US as well as from the Vietcong and the DRV.

Strategic-hamlet theory

Nhu and the members of a special secretariat he set up to cut across the ordinary machinery of government, so as to get his wishes through to the territorial administration more directly, now began to tour the country and address meetings of government staff—a surprising method of communicating policy to subordinates, but a reflection no doubt of difficulty in committing abstract ideas to paper. Nhu unfolded his ideas—it is no exaggeration to say he preached them—under three heads: the strategic hamlet was to provide defence against outside attack by organizing its own militia in the ranks of the Republican Youth; it was to be a vehicle for the betterment of village life, both through expansion of government-aided public services and through the inculcation of clean living (every family had to start boiling its drinking water and exhibit a bottle of it where the neighbours could see it); and it was to be the vehicle of political and social change, displacing the old village hierarchy (Nhu was, unlike Diem, opposed to the Confucian rites) and bestowing honour and office only on merit in the furtherance of hamlet interests, especially hamlet defence. All this

a *TVN*, 4 Feb. 1962.

was expressed in slogans made up of three catchwords each—a Communist mode of expression in dealings with the masses, but also of course a classical Confucian one. The three basic purposes just described comprised the Three Sufficiencies (*Tam Tuc*)—self-sufficiency in organization, self-sufficiency in equipment, and self-sufficiency in ideology (that is, traditionalism); the appeal to autarky took note of the moral force of Tagorism in the Communists' ideological armoury. The Three Sufficiencies were to be instructed by the Three Enlightenments (*Tam Giac*)[a]—Morality, Knowledge, and Mettle—which constituted the Three Motivations (*Tam Nhan*)[b] of what Nhu always referred to henceforward as 'the Personalist Revolution' and a kind of anti-Communist 'masses mobilization'.

Practical aspects

The new hamlets were at the same time to keep their powder dry. Each one was to be stockaded with ditch and fence, whose alignment would follow the established administrative boundary, avoiding risk of offence to any local animistic prejudice and taking in rice fields as well as dwellings in such a way as to cut it off psychologically from neighbouring hamlets of the same administrative village, even when contiguous; the fence might be made of barbed wire if the hamlet could afford to pay for it, but otherwise sharpened stakes must do. Approaches must be safeguarded with hidden nail-boards and simple booby traps in the manner practised by the Vietcong—and by generations of revolutionaries before them. Labour was to be by *corvée*, but the employees of Government offices in the administrative townships were ordered out on Sundays to help near-by villages dig their ditches through the clay.[c] The Republican Youth was to extend its recruiting from towns into each hamlet and set up women's and old people's and farmers' associations, as in Communist practice. The Republican Youth would organize alarm, evacuation, and defence and would be armed in the first place with staves until it could capture its own rifles from the Vietcong, as the Vietcong had captured its from the army. In a few cases the squads might be lent weapons by the Civil Guard (who would also give drill and training in their use), but only until they had won their

[a] The phrase was borrowed from Buddhism, but not the concept.
[b] Another Buddhist phrase emptied of its original meaning, which is sinful not virtuous; the *nhan* of this expression is not connected with *Nhan Vi*.
[c] Previously Nhu had tried to 'motivate' slack public servants—and, indeed, the diligent ones without distinction—by making them sweep the slum streets and noisome market-places of Saigon at weekends when the Municipality was short of scavengers.

own.[a] At province headquarters, the Republican Youth was from the beginning organized round the nucleus of the Can Lao. It also included the staff of the Information Department and of a new department called Civic Action; the two were now expanded by the introduction of teams of 'cadres', as they were called deliberately to sound like the Communists, and it was these who took charge of the administrative and training duties in the hamlets, the rate of 'establishment' of hamlets depending on how fast the cadres could get round.

American attitude

Nhu undoubtedly inspired a wide segment of the government machine with his own enthusiasm, and the new spirit might have changed the situation radically if that machine had not already been demoralized. The Counsellor began to include in his homilies expressions of his confidence that the strategic hamlet, armed with the Three Three's of Personalism, would make of Vietnam the exemplar of the underdeveloped world at large and provide the deterrent to aggression by revolutionary war that American arms had not yet discovered, just as the leaders in the DRV viewed the Liberation Front as a model for 'weak and small nations'.[b] After some slight hesitation, the US agencies accepted the strategic hamlets as the token of intentions to do better in future that was asked as the price of increased aid. By May 1962 extra piastres were available through the January increase in economic aid, and these were allocated to the administrative expenses of the strategic hamlets, especially for training cadres. However, instead of crediting them to the accounts of ministries in Saigon or even of the special secretariat, the US Government showed its dissatisfaction at Diem's rejection of its requests for reform to eliminate corruption, as well as its distrust of Nhu, by entering into direct agreements, through USOM, with each Province Chief separately.[c] Help with the fencing of hamlets also became available during the rest of the year from the Military Assistance Program of MAAG: as the Civil Guard was re-equipped for mobile fighting and the militia moved up into its place in the security system, older firearms slipped back

[a] Explanation given the author by Nhu personally. Needless to say, no contingent armed with staves ever did capture VC weapons, although they may have picked up some abandoned ones.

[b] A theme repeated many times; one occasion is Vo-nguyen-Giap (1966) (but writing in mid-1964), p. 70.

[c] Not agreed to formally by President Diem until the following year (*TVN*, 18 May 1963), the policy was in force informally by May 1962.

down the line to the Republican Youth, and later, when some of the new hamlets had given a good account of themselves that surprised many foreign observers, it was agreed to supply barbed wire wherever the villagers asked for it.[a]

Strategic aspects

As originally conceived, the strategic-hamlet programme was anything but a strategic plan: it was to apply to the whole country as fast as the work could be carried out, without consideration of manpower resources or of the military situation. One effect of the addition of American aid was to make some planning essential, not for strategic reasons but for logistic ones. Every Province Chief had to indent for aid, and the bigger his bid the bigger the proportion that would be delivered; that meant inflated targets and an atmosphere of feverish competition between provinces. Hamlets which felt themselves exposed to danger begged to be first, and such requests were always acceded to; the two Fathers Hoa were helped out of strategic turn, and there was grafted on to the Phu Yen project an extensive scheme for resettlement in an isolated valley, the lines of communication with which were then tapped by the Vietcong. 'General' Cao of the Cao Dai early espoused the strategic-hamlet programme as a means of enforcing the writ of his sub-sect and was given a free hand in scattered villages of Bien Hoa province. In other places ease of access by road was the criterion; in others again Province Chiefs—almost every one of whom by now was an army officer of field rank—would set up an isolated strategic hamlet to establish a presence, like planting a flag, in the middle of 'enemy' country. In yet other districts villages under sporadic Vietcong domination were ordered to move their houses to land closer to roads or garrison posts—a fatigue that the majority seemed to undertake with gratifying cheerfulness. Everywhere haste was the main driving force—to be first with a full house to show the Palace —, so that both organization and labour were skimped. Nevertheless, by the spring of 1963, over 8,000 hamlets—nearly two-thirds of the total—had been stockaded and had some degree of organization for self-defence and means of warning a garrison in the vicinity if they came under attack. The hill tribes of Annam proved very receptive to the idea of the strategic hamlet, and, without help from anybody else, erected fences of astonishing thickness. In the western

[a] A good deal of barbed wire was left to rust in depots in the towns because there was no means of transporting it to the hamlets.

provinces of Cochinchina even the Khmers dug ditches and submitted to simple drill with carbines under Vietnamese sergeants.
At no previous time since 1954 had the domain controlled by the
Government reached so far, for even the most persistently dissident
lands of the Hoa Hao, in the great plain west of the Bassac, were
reoccupied and the national flag planted for the first time ever on
top of the isolated *phnoms* overlooking the ruins of Funan.

Usefulness of the hamlets

The strategic hamlet was like a tool: its success in defeating the
Communist insurgency—in so far as that was truly what it was being
fashioned for—depended on the use the Government, and American advisers, made of it. As a gesture to show the Government's resolve, a state of national emergency had been declared in October
1961 on the eve of the visit of General Taylor; but it turned out to
be no more than a gesture, and no emergency legislation followed
to facilitate summary justice or, conversely, to reduce to the rule of
law action by the security forces in the rural areas; on the contrary,
Special Forces and Republican Youth alike were encouraged to get
on with their respective tasks in the villages in the knowledge that
no questions would be asked. Control measures had been in operation since 1959 to blockade Vietcong jungle camps, but without success; Nhu and Diem expected the strategic hamlet to provide a
fresh chance to cut the guerrillas off from their supplies at the
source, in the village. To some extent the rambling, unguarded
fences did hamper infiltration among the houses and coconut
patches; but still the Palace neglected to give either powers or instructions to the Republican Youth on guard at the gates—a poor
substitute for trained police—on how to deal with suspicious goings
and comings, so that little use was actually made of the new tool in
practice. A means had been mistaken for the end—and so the
situation was represented, to good effect, in Vietcong propaganda,
which pointed out the ultimate defencelessness of those within the
hamlets for all their putting up with the 'tyranny' of restrictions on
their movements. The establishment of the central Government's
authority at last in the hamlets opened many routes through which
surrenders might have been stimulated, both to reduce the guerrillas' strength and to gain information; but Diem long resisted proposals that an offer of surrender terms should be made, partly because he mistrusted the administrative capacity of the 'cadres' at
the lower echelons, partly because he could not reconcile the idea

with his image of the conflict in terms of absolute loyalty against absolute rebellion, or with what he expected would be the objections of the army. Finally, an offer of surrender terms was published in February 1963; both of the President's apprehensions proved well founded, and although surrenders took place after the offer, the scheme was neglected and real numbers (after deduction was made for refugees from bombing, sometimes hard to distinguish) were scarcely greater than they had always been, and no better use was made of their knowledge.

Strategic hamlets as a war front

Once the stockades were up round the hamlets, they were treated psychologically as the war front so long desired by both the army and MAAG. There were inevitably areas into which the province authorities would not be able to penetrate until the Vietcong had been decisively weakened; such areas were declared to be 'open zones', and the villages in them were subjected to random bombardment by the newly-arrived artillery and aircraft so as to drive the inhabitants into the safety of the strategic-hamlet belt.[a] This policy had some effect in Annam (in connexion with Sea Swallow II, for example) and was the principal cause of a huge migration of tribesmen in the summer of 1962, which gave the President the personal satisfaction of being voted for by about a quarter of a million feet.[b] On the other hand, it added refugee problems nobody was prepared for to the burdens of an administrative machine already strained to fulfil its 'hamlet' targets and, at the same time, made the Government appear cruelly vindictive towards peasants who found themselves under Vietcong domination without any choice in the matter, while it was casual over the peasants in the hamlets who could no longer plead any excuse for the help some went on giving the guerrillas in secret. Projection in a favourable light of this particular manifestation of Diem's wrongheadedness—'white terror', as the Liberation Front called it—would have taxed the most skilful of public-relations machines; unfortunately, the one that was available was not of the most skilful.

Propaganda

Largely on American initiative, renewed zest was injected into

---

[a] President Diem took great comfort in the use of these two weapons in this manner as the bringing to bear on the enemy of 'engins de la guerre totale'.
[b] According to Ngo-dinh-Nhu (1963, p. 19), 148,927 hill people joined in the 'Exodus from bondage'; Pike (p. 251) believes the reality may have been twice that number.

the Government's information and propaganda services. But domination of operations by equipment resulted in the regime merely continuing to make a fool of itself more loudly.[a] A network of half a dozen wireless stations was installed by USOM, a film unit was set up, and fleets of loudspeaker vans and equipment for producing posters and even local newspapers was given to Province Chiefs to 'help' them publicize the strategic-hamlet programme—as if they were not overworked already. Like the main programme itself, this activity was haphazard and unintegrated, planned only from the viewpoint of quick procurement of the equipment, not from that of its sustained utilization. The American expectation was that, by fostering local self-expression, all this equipment would immediately stimulate local democracy, as in the US, and strengthen the anti-Communist resolve of its audiences. The trouble was, as we have seen, that independent Vietnam had inherited no nucleus of professional talent, none had been developed before 1961, and the equivocal broadcasts of Radio Saigon during Colonel Thi's mutiny had been followed by a complete purge of the information services in favour of persons of guaranteed loyalty, but possessing no other qualification. The bustle of American support during 1962, despite the willingness of USIS itself to do so much of the work on behalf of the Vietnamese Government, made demands on Vietnamese manpower for the provision of 'counterparts' for American experts and for tactical operation of the new equipment which could only be met by drafting to the job individuals who were, professionally, mere hewers of wood and drawers of water. From the Palace, meanwhile, came appeals to the population to co-operate in building strategic hamlets, not as a way back to the law and order they all yearned for, but as an act of faith and solidarity with the 'cause of righteousness' (*chinh nghia*)—antonym for *khoi nghia*, the 'general uprising' of the Communists—and the Personalist revolution, championed by 'Ngo the Patriot'. In every context, Diem projected the conflict in ideological terms, as an extension of the Cold War or a personal quarrel between himself and Ho Chi Minh, over the heads of the people and of the rest of the Government.[b]

Intelligence

No progress was made with the rationalization of intelligence;

---

[a] p. 260 above.
[b] It will be remembered that Ho Chi Minh for a long time called himself 'Nguyen the Patriot'; Diem used different words to convey the same idea.

the prejudices of the regime in this respect tended to deepen all the time, whilst the big increase in MAAG advisers on one-year tours in the provinces underlined still further the conventional, transient, military objectives, particularly now that American personnel were beginning to come under fire, both on the ground and in MACV's helicopters and spotter planes. On its own account, the Government developed at this time an unascertainable number of *dich van* killer squads which claimed to have 'liquidated' Vietcong cells in uncommitted villages and to have penetrated some 'enemy' ones. Such activities yielded quicker and more spectacular results ('carrying the war to the heart of the enemy' etc.) to show off to a President and his Counsellor in a hurry than the toil of collection and brain-racking collation of information that might have contributed more to the erosion of Communist strength in the long run. The choice in Cochinchina of the areas for these activities suggests that they may have owed something to secret-society vendettas. In the vicinity of Hué, Ngo Dinh Can, from his own secret finances, expanded and armed his clandestine spy organization, its guerrillas, and its *dich van*; although their activities had been directed at first against the VNQDD and the Dai Viet, they were said in 1962 to be blocking Vietcong efforts to infiltrate and subvert districts not previously under the DRV. On the other hand, long-range penetration by army patrols was not attempted on a scale to constitute any substantial threat to Vietcong rest and training bases in the War Zones; the longest absence from their own base that Vietnamese units could put up with, whether to gather intelligence or to harry camps and installations, was seven days at a time, and little jungle lore was ever mastered.

Mobile tactics

While the strategic hamlets were being built, the hunt for Vietcong bases and units by conventional forces was stepped up, however. The improved transport and logistics services manned by MACV aimed at making the Vietnamese defence less static by ferrying army units into battle rather faster than before. Experiments with amphibious vehicles for negotiating the flood plains of Cochinchina were, on the whole, a failure. Helicopters were swifter but more vulnerable to ambush, until the most suitable model was lighted on. Many contacts were made with larger formations of Vietcong, especially in Cochinchina, and their appearance in more than battalion strength was wishfully interpreted by President

Diem as a sign that strategic hamlets had made things difficult for smaller Vietcong formations. Province Chiefs began to neglect their perplexing administrative tasks in order to go out after these formations at the head of their Civil Guard companies (all now being retrained by MAAG as infantry), in competition with battalion commanders of the army who, for their part, were often jealous of their fellow officers enjoying the supposedly softer, and definitely more lucrative, jobs in the territorial administration and did little to help them. Divisional commanders began to establish strategic hamlets on their own account, by way of civic action, in competition with the Province Chiefs; the sites chosen tended to be in remoter and conspicuously unstrategic localities, with which the officers responsible considered communications had been adequately restored if they could go there now by helicopter—a repetition of the old mistake that the matter turned on their own safety rather than on that of the peasants on the ground.[a]

Battle of Ap Bac

The whole apparatus of strategic hamlets and MAAG-advised and MACV-supported army was put to the test after a year, probably by accident, on President Diem's 62nd birthday, 3 January 1963. On the 2nd the Vietcong were spotted passing a column about 200 strong through the village of Ap Bac, between the Plain of Reeds and the Mekong. Every weapon of the security forces was trained on the village, where the Communists dug themselves in; but American support proved fruitless, advice went unheeded, bombs and shells fell infallibly off target, and the infantry (army and Civil Guard) refused to attack on foot. The outnumbered Vietcong suffered some casualties, and may well have had a fright, but they continued their march otherwise little the worse for the affray, while the foreign press corps, recording in the very cannon's mouth the imprecations of infuriated advisers, gave the battle and all about it the biggest coverage of the war up to that time, sparing the Vietnamese army little of its ignominy as it trailed back to its billets.[b] In itself, the battle was of no strategic importance—in a revolutionary war battles hardly ever are—, but the psychological repercussions rippled far afield. The army had shown itself to be still timorous and incompetent, as well as ill commanded and undisciplined; the adviser-counterpart relationship had been shown up as a false one; and the superior firepower and tactical mobility

[a] p. 187 above.   [b] For instance *Newsweek*, 14 Jan. 1963.

in the air available to the defence had laid bare its own inherent superfluity. Some civilians had been killed. Vietcong propaganda was jubilant. The army's confidence in itself sank again, and American official confidence received a shock at the same time. Both were tempted to look for a scapegoat. President Diem reacted with meanness, spreading spiteful gossip about the senior American adviser. To add to his chagrin, Senator Mansfield visited Saigon shortly after the battle and, on his return to the US, told Congress that American efforts to set independent Vietnam on its own feet were, after eight years elapsed and $2,000 million spent, 'not even at the beginning of a beginning'.[a] Diem was stung to the quick;[b] it was not in the character of Nhu ever to pardon such a home truth, and soon he was arranging the transfer back to fighting units of Province Chiefs reported to him as getting on too well with their American advisers.[c] On all sides the 'internal contradictions' were gaping open.

Weaknesses of the hamlets

Much had gone wrong in the implementation of the strategic-hamlet idea. Ngo Dinh Nhu expected the fences to bring victory over the Vietcong without supporting measures, by moral force alone, provided the whole people underwent the same regime. As soon as the Province Chief of Binh Thuan reported that there was a stockade round every hamlet in his province and that 98 per cent of the people dwelt inside, Nhu declared the province pacified, in disregard of two sizeable guerrilla formations in the surrounding wilderness still living off the villagers. The stockades winding among the fields followed administrative boundaries and the accidents of field ownership, not tactical considerations. The digging of ditches became an expression of Personalist 'enlightenment' and 'community development' in itself, and Province Chiefs sometimes made villagers carry them on for five, six, or more miles; the colonel in charge of Vinh Long, author of the pilot scheme, began a fence and ditch right across his province which he intended should ultimately reach for fifty miles, in the canal-digging tradition. There was nothing strategic about the siting of the hamlets, and the security forces were encouraged to pursue the Vietcong kinetically, without bothering to consolidate the defence of the belt of hamlets; big unguarded gaps were left in between, and in the

[a] USIS communiqué, 26 Feb. 1963.   [b] Based on an interview with him in March.
[c] R. Thompson, p. 137.

gaps even more of the isolated watchtowers and outposts were overrun—and weapons lost—than in the previous period. The new security forces that were embodied after the setting up of MACV gave rise by 1963 to eight or ten separate commands, each fighting its own war; for every one of them also defence meant defence of their camps, families, and selves, not of the surrounding peasantry. In the administrative confusion of substituting the hamlet for the village[a] and the rush to pay militia and cadres in training, auditing was out of the question and defalcations became common—though probably not this time to the gain of the Vietcong. In trying to cover the whole country in just over a year, the programme exhausted everybody and left no work over to do the following year.

Merits of the hamlets

Yet if these faults could have been put right, the attitude of the peasants was evidence enough that they appreciated the intention to free them from the exactions of the Vietcong and the crossfire of battle. Confidence in the scheme was manifested in the cheerful labour put into it—'the Vietnamese are inveterate diggers', a French Governor-General once wrote[b]—and in the money collected to finance its 'self-sufficiency' aspects; in hamlets where families had been moved some distance it was visible in the investment in permanent structures for their new homes.[c] Both in Cochinchina and in Annam, villages under the domination of Sects or parties that had previously been keeping out of trouble in the face of the Vietcong now committed themselves to the Government by asking to be included quickly in the defence arrangements. The yield from land tax doubled from 1961 to 1962[d] and contributed its quota towards the Government's financial independence as relations with the US began to deteriorate. Vietcong recruitment fell off for perhaps the only time after 1959, the collection of subscriptions and blackmail 'squeeze' became difficult for them in all but the most slackly managed hamlets, and in fact contact with the masses had to be planned anew before it could be resumed.[e] Nguyen Huu Tho subsequently admitted that the strategic hamlets had reduced the effectiveness of Communist domination in some districts to such an extent that the NFLSV had had to reappraise entirely the possi-

---

[a] Not formalized until 3 May 1963 (*Sac-lenh*, No. 45NV).   [b] Pasquier, p. 289.
[c] This was commonly done by building one wall in brick and three in *nipah* palm, with a view to substituting more brick walls later.
[d] *Ann. stat. 1962*, p. 434.
[e] Article in clandestine NFLSV magazine *Chien Dau*, No. 4, Baria, July 1962.

bilities of the armed uprising; only after the windfall of Ap Bac did the Party conclude that it ought to carry on after all.[a] Certainly there had been no change in army tactics that could be credited with this improvement in village security.

Army morale

One implication of the strategic hamlet programme was that, in the teamwork it undoubtedly imposed on much of the Government machine in the provinces, the military tacitly became subordinate to the civil side of the territorial administration, notwithstanding the Corps and Divisional Commanders' efforts to maintain their command over the army officers seconded to it. The army was, moreover, getting knocked about more and more in ambushes by a despised enemy whom, to quote an American General's words later on, it 'would blast if only he would stand up and fight'.[b] The Vietnamese Generals had many grievances against the Palace and could see clearly Ngo Dinh Nhu's hope, if not to squeeze them out of the national picture altogether, at least to set up a balancing power in the rural areas, hitherto their preserve. Thus, by the spring of 1963, the situation was that the strategic hamlets had succeeded, in spite of maladroit propaganda but because of the prospect of personal safety for the average villager at last, in facing the Vietcong with an obstacle they urgently wanted out of the way, and at the same time in bringing the authority of the regime into many South Vietnamese villages for the first time. But within the security system, over the heads of the hamlets, there were growing dissensions which, apart from the Can Lao and the loyalty to Diem of the majority of the Catholic officers, only the American presence was keeping in check. Nobody foresaw from which direction the dénouement would come; the Vietcong could not have supplied it by themselves. When it came it brought into play in turn every flaw in the patriarchy's system of administration and in its relationship with the US.

6. THE BUDDHA IN THE FIRE

The Buddhist crisis that led to the overthrow of Ngo Dinh Diem, punctuated at each stage by the gruesome self-immolation in the streets of half a dozen monks one after another, began with the jubilee of Mgr Ngo Dinh Thuc, which he celebrated at Hué on

[a] Burchett, p. 194.   [b] Gen. W. C. Westmoreland, quoted by Schlesinger (p. 49).

23 April 1963. For about a week churches and public places were hung with bunting, as if that far-off event at Vinh Long in Cochin-china in 1938 had had some national significance. Schools were given holidays, and so were units of the security forces; in accordance with custom,[108] military transport was used to carry the faithful from the *chrétientés* into Hué, and photographs and reports of all this rejoicing were pushed by the press officers in Saigon to show the popularity of the President's family and to offset the mounting criticism of the past three years. Prominent in the bunting were the yellow and white of the Vatican, which a few years before had formed the standard of the militant *chrétientés* in Tonkin. Even some Catholics put this show of personal adulation down more to the Primate's connexion with the President than to reverence for his spirituality, and found it sickening.

The flag dispute

The Buddhists of Hué also found it sickening—at least the monks of the Tu Dam Pagoda did. Wesak, or the Birthday of the Buddha, an annual public holiday in recent years, fell that year on 8 May, and the monks urged their followers to put out Buddhist bunting as profusely as they could, such bunting consisting of the multi-coloured Wesak flag flown by members of the World Fellowship of Buddhists.[109] This flag had been flown in all the towns of Vietnam for more than a decade at Buddhist celebrations and was becoming an even commoner sight than the Vatican flag, usually flown at Christmas. There existed a regulation dating back to the formal adoption of the national flag in 1950 which prohibited the flying of any other flag in public unless with the national flag beside it; that had been the period of the private armies allied with the Government against the Vietminh, each of which flew its own standard.[110] Although, strictly speaking, the archdiocese had just been at fault on this account, the President chose 1963 to circularize the provinces telegraphically on 6 May, through the Ministry of the Interior, instructing that the regulation must be observed this Wesak. The Province Chief at Hué sent the municipal police round the several pagodas and to private houses pointing out the infraction. The Tu Dam group at once formed a committee, in which the leader was one Thich Tri Quang,[111] to protest to the Province Chief, who was a Catholic. The Minister of the Interior (also a Catholic) happened to be in Hué and was consulted about this innovation, following as it did particularly colourful Buddhist celebrations in 1962. The Minister interviewed the monks and told them that, not having powers to decide himself,[a] he could not vouch for future years, but for this year, so late in the day, the bunting could stay up.[b] Thich Tri Quang undertook to refrain from his threat of making a public issue of the matter in his sermon scheduled for broadcasting on Wesak Day.[c]

The riot at Hué

But the Tu Dam group was not going to let a good pretext be quashed so artlessly; if it was so late in the day, the arrangements already made for mischief could also be allowed to stand. On the morning of the 8th, several columns of the faithful were marched round the town, marshalled by the Buddhist Youth Movement and carrying banners demanding religious equality with the Catholics. Thich Tri Quang delivered a sermon in which he avoided spiritual subjects and spoke only of the Government's discrimination against Buddhists. The crowds were kept on the streets till evening, when Tri Quang was to broadcast another sermon over Radio Hué; knowing all broadcasts were precensored by Ngo Dinh Can,[d] the monk withheld his script until he was to go on the air, so that the terrified director of the station had to cancel the programme. The crowd assembled outside were informed and began to storm the building. The Province Chief summoned the Civil Guard, with instructions to disperse the crowd by force.[e] Their commandant—like, in fact, all the authorities at Hué, a Catholic—hesitated over this order given by a civilian Province Chief and telephoned the Corps Commander (the intervening Divisional Commander being absent), who replied something like 'You are a soldier—do as you are told'.[f] At that moment, of course, Major Dang Sy was, by function, not a soldier, but a policeman; however, he interpreted the Delphic pronouncement to mean he should give the order, and his men, not trained for riot control, pushed the crowd away from the building with the aid of tear gas. In the stampede there was an

---

[a] p. 228 above.

[b] This all-important detail is attested by the Buddhists themselves in their official account of the troubles (*Lua Thieng*, 1963, p. 4).

[c] UN, *Violation of Human Rights* (1963), p. 61.

[d] The precensorship was a fact, and so was its notoriety; it is not credible that the monk, who had been through the procedure before, did not also know it.

[e] Years later it was alleged that Thich Tri Quang, the Province Chief and Ngo Dinh Can's principal assistant had all been comrades together in the Vietminh before 1950 (*NYHT*, 12 Apr. 1966).

[f] Evidence at the Major's subsequent trial (*SP*, 3 June 1964).

explosion, leaving eight corpses, including some children; the causes of death were, in the absence of any formal inquest procedure, not established. This episode need not have brought down the regime and removed the strategic hamlets from the path of the Vietcong but for two factors: the skill as revolutionaries shown by Thich Tri Quang and his accomplices[a] and the incapacity of Diem and Nhu to govern administratively and impartially by process of law, relying instead on political manipulation and repression.

Modern Buddhism

It is necessary to understand the background to this episode. Organized Mahayana Buddhism in modern Vietnam has relatively little strength in the countryside. Although Gia Long had encouraged the building of pagodas by the more respectable sects,[b] especially at Hué, Buddhism, as in many other Asian countries at the time, was at a very low ebb in Vietnam when the French occupied it, and the disciplining *Sangha* defunct. It was a faith for the well-to-do, served by monks who were mostly recluses and had no contact with the laity; until after 1940 the teachings of the Mahayana could be read only by the minority literate in Chinese—those of the Theravada by the two or three monks who knew Pali.[c] There appear to have been few pagodas in villages and none in towns to the south of Nha Trang—perhaps none farther south than Qui Nhon. Cochinchina was, apart from the Theravada villages of the Khmer minority for whom religion was a matter of race, given over to the bonzes and Sects described in Chapter 3, who incorporated bits of Buddhism in their practices but were disowned by the Mahayanists of Hué and of Tonkin. But after the First World War the Buddhists of the Far East generally set about building their Church, as one aspect of the political renaissance of the time, and this movement affected Vietnam also; in 1931 an Association for the Study of Buddhism brought together Mahayanists and Theravadins of all three regions for a while in an effort to find for Buddhism a secular role in conformity with the socializing tendencies of the age.[d] The Vietnamese of Saigon founded a Theravada group of their own. Competition with Catholicism cannot have been far

[a] Mr Burchett has been reported as confirming that the accomplices included the VC (*Chicago Daily News*, quoted Higgins, 1965, p. 281).
[b] Mai-tho-Truyen (1962), p. 9.
[c] See the bibliographies of Vietnamese translations of Buddhist texts prepared by the Buddhist authorities for Berval 1959, pp. 1010–13.
[d] Mai-tho-Truyen, p. 12.

from the thoughts of the promoters of these associations, especially in their cult of the infant Buddha connected with the Christmas-like celebrations of Wesak, to which new emphasis was being given in Ceylon and other Buddhist countries. But the capacity for what was essentially political organization was deficient among the Vietnamese monks, and a new initiative was necessary after the Second World War, during which even the communities of monks had become dispersed again.

The Vietnamese Buddhist church

The *Sangha* was revived first at Hanoi in 1948, and the Buddhists there joined in the founding of the World Federation of Buddhists at Colombo in 1950. The following year the *Sangha* visited Hué and at a congress held during Wesak in the Tu Dam Pagoda, attended by monks from Saigon, founded the General Buddhist Association,[a] with a pan-Vietnamese *Sangha*, which took over the Tonkinese membership of the World Fellowship. Wesak became a public holiday in the State of Viet-Nam. Attendance at the World Fellowship's congresses in different countries, and the passage through the port of Saigon in 1952 of the ship bearing the Buddha's Tooth as a gift from Theravadin Ceylon to Mahayanist Japan, put the Vietnamese monks in touch with world-famous personalities of the faith and gave their domestic celebrations that foreign cachet Vietnamese movements seem to require in order to qualify for popular adherence; for, as in those other countries, success in establishing the *Sangha* on a firm basis resulted from drawing the urban laity into active participation. With lay collaboration, the Youth Movement,[b] started in 1940 with the blessing of Admiral Decoux, flourished again; schools and other works of charity were opened. Most important lay work, the Xa Loi Pagoda was rebuilt in Saigon during 1961 as a reformed secular centre of Buddhist fellowship, providing a *pied-à-terre* in the capital for the Hué bonzes as it did for all other Buddhists. A key role in what amounted to setting up the Chinese Mahayana in Saigon was played by refugee monks from Hanoi who came south in 1954, notably Thich Tam Chau. However, these secular works, including the building of Xa Loi, ran into a legal difficulty: neither the pagodas nor the charitable organizations were incorporated for the purposes of French civil law; this meant

[a] *Ton Hoi Phat Giao Viet Nam*—literally 'Vietnamese Association of Worshippers of Buddha'.
[b] *Gia-dinh Phat Tu* (Family of the Disciples of Buddha).

that property could not be held in the institution's name, nor could legacies be bequeathed, for only legal persons could hold title. Catholic churches and associations had been incorporated by extension of the laws of France, but the only form of incorporation open to Buddhists was through registration as a society under a Societies Ordinance of 1950.[a] It appears from its provisions that this enactment was basically a security measure, possibly to provide the authorities with a weapon against extortion and misappropriation of funds by the Cochinchinese Sects and the Vietminh for the purposes explained in Chapter 4. Annual steps were required to re-register office-bearers and to lodge accounts for scrutiny by the territorial authorities. The Ordinance had for long—perhaps since enactment—been a dead letter, and the General Buddhist Association, though registered originally, had let its certificate lapse.[b] Unfortunately, the concluding article of the Ordinance exempted Chinese Catholic and Protestant associations from registration pending enactment of a special law to govern them.[c] Although no demands for amendment had ever been made in the name of the Buddhists before 1963, this detail enabled malevolent persons to argue that it was the Government's policy to persecute 'native' Buddhism in order to promote the social work, the proselytism, and the political solidarity of the 'alien' Church and its *chrétientés*.

The Sangha's demands

When he heard of the riot and bloodshed at Hué, Diem did not know what to do; he had no Cabinet to share the burden of decision —only his brothers—, and the American partnership did not provide anybody whose duty it was to tell him. Instead of ordering an immediate judicial inquiry—such procedures were unknown—he left the running to the Tu Dam Pagoda and the local authorities to the mercy of its demands for compensation, public funerals, and other foreseeable pretexts for mob-manipulation. In communiqués to the press, the monks demanded that the Government admit out of hand official responsibility for the loss of life, that the flag regulation be rescinded, and that Buddhists be given equality with Catholics over endowments;[d] in conjunction with the Saigon *Sangha*, led by Thich Tam Chau, an appeal for 'human rights' was telegraphed to the Secretary-General of the UN.[e] At Xa Loi a press-relations

[a] *Sac-lenh*, No. 10 of 6 Aug. 1950.
[b] Bui Van Luong (Minister of the Interior) to the UN Mission (UN, *Violation of Human Rights*, p. 64).
[c] Art. 44.   [d] *AFP*, Saigon, 15 May 1963.   [e] *NYT*, 19 May 1963.

office was set up and contact made with the hundred or so resident Western journalists, avid for a new angle to the Vietnam story. 'Nation-wide masses' for the eight dead were made the occasion for processions in Saigon, Hué, and several other towns in Annam. Confronted with mounting agitation, the President received a delegation of monks and dismissed the Province Chief from Hué without a hearing; but he offered no redress for the more fundamental grievances,[a] and, hoping the fuss in the towns would subside—in Cochinchina not even the towns were affected, outside the capital—took no step to try to align the majority of the public with the Government against the troublesome minority; the vulnerability of his patriarchal organization of the Government stood revealed, for with none to share the responsibility he became the sole butt of animosity. Understanding this, the monks determined to strike on a wider front while the iron was hot. Tri Quang told an American official he would not rest until Ngo Dinh Diem was overthrown.[b] Tam Chau gained allies by forming an Inter-Sect Committee with the Theravadins of Saigon and with some of the Hoa Hao and Cao Dai, whom the *Sangha* had not previously recognized as Buddhist sects but who had their own vendettas to work off against the regime.

The auto-da-fé

It was now early June. On the morning of the 11th there occurred the first of the immolations; in the presence of the foreign press, alerted to stand by, and helped by other monks, while hundreds more diverted the attention of the police, the elderly Thich Quang Duc set fire to himself with petrol and burnt to death. The marvel made a journalist's photograph that was reproduced in newspapers all round the world and later won a prize as the press picture of the year. The impact was immediate: abroad it was plain that persecution of Buddhism in Vietnam must be a serious matter if a monk would martyr himself in such grisly protest—and Communist claims to be resisting tyranny gained credence. At home, a signal had been given: Quang Duc had made the highest bid for Buddhist merit as laid down in the *Lotus Sutra*, most popular of Mahayana canons, when, addressing itself to 'young men and women of good family', it enjoined self-anointment and immolation by fire as 'the most sublime worship of the Buddha'; Vietnamese lay demonstrators, content with lesser merit, took their cue 'to worship with

[a] Ibid. 2 June 1963.   [b] Higgins, p. 101.

flags' as befitted their lesser spirit.[a][112] Under pressure from the US Government,[b] Diem agreed to meet the monks again; but he chose to bargain with them, appointing a committee of Vice-President Nguyen Ngoc Tho (a Buddhist) and two ministers (one Catholic, one neither) to negotiate with three monks headed by Thich Tinh Khiet of the Co Son sect at Hué, the senior monk and most respected sect in the country. By this step the Palace appeared to admit its partisanship and to be abandoning its proper position of authority, for what it was now seeking was terms on which to buy an unstatesmanlike peace.

Steps towards anarchy

After two days of argument, an agreed joint statement was issued: an inquiry would at last be held by the Vice-President into responsibility for the Wesak episode; the flag would in future only be flown with the national flag; and the question of incorporating the Buddhist Church would be referred to the National Assembly.[c] The third point conformed with constitutional procedure but lacked conviction because there was no precedent and the Assembly was reputed to act solely on instructions from the Palace. Extremists did not want peace, and while the agreement was being signed there was fresh provocation in the streets outside by supposedly Buddhist crowds, followed by several score arrests, though no charges or prosecutions: the magistrates were not organized to deal summarily with disorderly behaviour, and every stone hurled through a plate-glass window was elevated into a political issue by the Government's own handling of the situation. Events at Hué, allegations of persecution of organized Buddhism, and each endeavour of the police to keep order became an excuse for the venting of spite, after so many years of enforced calm in the towns, by anybody at all over any grievance at all or none; the cover of street marches blessed by the *Sangha*, and the anonymity of the mobs, were an opportunity for mischievous persons to join in any riot that was afoot, for few were arrested unless they courted it. Two plastic charges were planted by Vietcong, profiting from diversion of police attention elsewhere.[d] The monks' friends in Ceylon organized an eleven-nation meeting at Calcutta to appeal to the UN General Assembly, which eventually resulted in the dispatching of a Fact-Finding Mission to Saigon in October. Arrested persons were

---

[a] *Saddharma Pundarika* (1894), pp. 378–80.   [b] *NYT*, 14 June 1963.
[c] Ibid. 16 June 1963.   [d] *NYHT*, 30 June 1963.

not held long, but every calming concession by the Government was hailed with further trouble at Hué or Saigon. At a loss, Diem ordered the dismissal of the Rector of the University at Hué, a Catholic cleric, for siding with the Buddhists, and then the arrest of Buddhist dons for siding with the Catholic Rector. To divert attention, he staged one of his show trials, this time of persons implicated in Colonel Thi's mutiny, and one of them (not in custody) hanged himself.[a] Into the general hysteria that took possession of the capital was injected periodically the unconsidered and ill-mannered vitriol of Mme Ngo Dinh Nhu, in the name of her Women's Solidarity Movement, through the columns of the *Times of Vietnam*— the regime's organ for projecting itself to the foreign community. The President had lost the Mandate of Heaven; he could not long keep that of the US.

American antagonism

For American opinion no less than for Vietnamese, the quarrel of the Buddhists became, unconsciously, a peg on which to hang a long-standing exasperation with Diem and Nhu. But, like these two, American officials as well tended to view the situation in political terms rather than as one of how to restore order. The troubles were interpreted as another sign that Diem was at loggerheads with his own people; it was argued that, since everybody must have a religion and less than a fifth of the population was Catholic, four-fifths must be Buddhist. It followed that army morale might become affected, and in support of that apprehension the foreign press began to report scraps between Buddhists and Catholics in the army in the field, although their source was not authenticated.[b] There was disagreement within the US Mission in Saigon: MACV and the CIA pointed out that the *Sangha's* following, which in reality counted barely a million souls, or half the number of Catholics,[c] was confined to the towns, at a distance from the war against the Vietcong; the Embassy, perhaps realizing that town members of long-repressed factions (VNQDD, Dai Viet, Hoa Hao, and Cao Dai) might muster rural mobs to agitate under the banner of the monks, believed the whole country was disaffected.[d] In the US, public and politicians, not familiar with Asian rioting, assumed that

[a] *Le Monde*, 2 July 1963. [b] For instance, the *Observer*, 25 Aug. 1963.
[c] Mai-tho-Truyen, p. 53; even non-registered Buddhists brought the total, according to this lay chairman of Xa Loi, only to 3 m.
[d] Based on Mecklin, pp. 213–14.

depth of feeling could be measured by the courage of the suicides,[a] the impressive silence of the monks, or the rowdiness of the mobs, and believed that disaffection from the patriarchy America had sponsored in South Vietnam was the source of Vietcong strength, as disaffection from French colonialism had been that of the Vietminh. Opinion in America held the casting vote; it gave the thumbs-down. The wholehearted support extended to Diem in 1955 had become little better than neutrality in 1960; now it became antagonism. The slogan 'Put Diem in a position to win his own war' changed into 'Put the Vietnamese people in a position to carry out their own revolution', and the US Government moved towards financial sanctions. Ambassador Nolting, consistent admirer of Diem, was reassigned and Mr Henry Cabot Lodge, leader of the party that had presided over Ngo Dinh Diem's advent to power—Mr Lodge had, of course, other qualifications as well—was appointed to lead the US Mission during the forthcoming crisis. Ngo Dinh Nhu was fully alive to the implications of the change of Ambassadors and, no doubt taking stock of the dollar hoard, decided to clear the decks before Mr Lodge could arrive. He planned as always to act politically, not by invoking the process of the law on the several charges that could by now have been preferred against the monks in the courts.

The pagoda raids

Obviously, the *Sangha*, though it might have the capacity to create confusion, could not seize power by itself—not even its militant members like Thich Tri Quang—and the danger for the Palace came as always from the army, its morale shaken by the discomfitures the Vietcong continued to visit upon it throughout the summer. Nhu invited the senior Generals to sign a remonstrance calling on the Government to seize and silence the Buddhist ringleaders.[b] The signatories included, besides some others, the Staff Generals Duong Van Minh, Tran Van Don, Le Van Kim, Tran Tu Oai, and also the Commander of III Corps at Bien Hoa, Brigadier General Ton That Dinh. Nhu published this prior endorsement and then, as if in response to it, declared a state of siege in the capital—a gesture, it may be said, of uncertain legal effect since the Government had already taken arbitrary powers in 1961.

[a] Nobody thought to look into the physiological aspects of death by burning; suggestions from the Palace that it could be rendered almost painless were dismissed without examination.
[b] *NYT*, 20 Aug. 1963.

General Don was made responsible for administration of what amounted to martial law,[a] while General Dinh was appointed Military Governor, with the Commandant of the Special Forces, Colonel Le Van Tung, and his men (paid directly by the CIA[b]— that was why Nhu so employed them) as a strike force. On the night of 22 August the Xa Loi and three other pagodas were broken into, papers were sequestrated, and the monks were detained—all except Thich Tri Quang and three companions, two of whom escaped over the Xa Loi wall into adjacent USOM. The outcry against persecution redoubled, and not-quite-eyewitness accounts of outrage done to sanctuary and cloth made headlines again round the world. But Nhu had not misjudged: the raid broke up the centre of the agitation for the moment, calm returned to Saigon under curfew and General Dinh and a Government-sponsored Buddhist group quietly took charge of the pagodas, with elder monk Thich Tinh Khiet, now ranged on the side of authority, presiding. The whereabouts of Thich Tri Quang remained a mystery until he pushed in at the door of the US Embassy in mid-September and asked for asylum, instantly accorded. The curfew was lifted after three weeks, and the situation might still have been saved but for pressure coming from overseas, which further fed the flames in Saigon and Hué. As the UN assembled its Fact-Finding Mission, there were demonstrations in Saigon University, and agitators stirred up a number of school children ('of good family', in the phrase of the *Lotus*), many of whom, below the age of criminal responsibility, the Government also detained briefly, and stupidly, to the consternation of their parents, largely civil servants. National Assembly elections due at the end of August were actually held at the end of September and gave the usual spectacular mandate for the Government's action.[c]

American sanctions

But the raid on the pagodas was the last straw for Washington. The fact that General Dinh had withdrawn to take part in it a unit in garrison at a strategic village set up eighteen months earlier in an isolated position thirty miles north of Saigon (under pressure from MAAG for quick results to show in Washington when the setting up of MACV was under consideration),[d] and that the Vietcong had

[a] *The Times*, 22 Aug. 1963.   [b] Ibid. 10 Sept. 1963.   [c] Ibid. 28 Sept. 1963.
[d] Ben Tuong, part of the controversial Operation Sunrise, intended to regain control of the district known as the 'Iron Triangle'.

promptly sacked the place,[a] was a piece of evidence, however solitary and ambiguous, that repression of the Buddhists was damaging the war effort. Recognizing the trend of American opinion, the Vietnamese Ambassador in Washington (still the Palace's 'outer cousin', Mme Nhu's father) resigned, followed by all his staff; so did the Foreign Minister in Saigon, after shaving his head. Earnest debates took place in the US Government's inner councils,[b] and General Taylor paid another visit with Secretary of Defense McNamara; early in September a resolution to take sanctions against Ngo Dinh Diem by cutting aid was introduced into the Senate.[c] Various official American statements were made to exonerate the Vietnamese Generals for responsibility over the pagoda raid Nhu had procured their signatures to (as they themselves promptly confirmed in their own statement to the foreign press),[d] and a Voice of America broadcast went on from that to a warning (immediately retracted, but in vain) that aid would be cut off if 'those really responsible for the pagoda raid' (that is, Nhu and Xuan) were not dismissed.[e] Nhu retorted with a strident attack on American in the *Times of Vietnam*,[f] predicting an army coup and alleging it had been paid for in advance by the CIA—his firmest America friend for the past nine years—whose responsibility for the Special Forces now stood revealed as a spearhead, so the article complained, through the CIDGs, of autonomy for the PMS—an eventuality that did materialize the following summer. It was widely canvassed that the US Government was indeed signalling to the army to carry out a coup d'état,[g] and at the beginning of October somebody disclosed to the press that President Kennedy had put a stop not only on the pay of the Special Forces (because they were no longer defending the country against Vietcong aggression from outside),[h] but also on the CIP upon which the rest of the army's pay depended.[i] The US had put a tourniquet on the army's main artery, not to bind it closer to the President as in former days, but to incite it to mutiny.

Coup and counter-coup

The next six weeks saw the passage of the eye of the typhoon,

[a] *NYT*, 21 Aug. 1963.   [b] Mecklin, pp. 200 ff.   [c] *NYHT*, 13 Sept. 1963.
[d] *NYT*, 28 Aug. 1963.   [e] *The Times*, 27 Aug. 1963; Mecklin, p. 194.
[f] *TVN*, 2 Sept. 1963.   [g] *Le Monde*, 2 Sept. 1963.
[h] Not passed on to the press for another fortnight (*NYT*, 22 Oct. 1963). The sum of money was, however, only US $250,000 a month.
[i] *TVN*, 7 Oct. 1963, and *NYHT*, 8 Oct. 1963.

before the fury of the wind turned to blow the other way. As is customary in moments of instability in Vietnam, feverish consultations were had with fortune-tellers (especially by wives on behalf of civil servants and soldier politicians desperate to know which way the wind was going to blow next), and rumours were credited of ominous natural prodigies;[a] two more 'bonze-fires' occurred, bringing the total to five or six—the hand had been overplayed, and, caring less now, people had lost count. Both Mme Nhu and Mgr Thuc had business that took them abroad, she eventually to America, he to the Oecumenical Council at Rome, where, having accused the US Government of laying out $20 million inside Vietnam to promote a coup d'état,[b] he was instructed by the Curia to hold his peace.[c113] In Saigon, rumours of conspiracies to unseat the regime were whispered loudly on all hands; at least some of them originated in the Palace, where Nhu, in conversations with delegates to a meeting of the Pacific Anti-Communist League opportunely held in Saigon during October, threatened portentously that if the US brought him low he and his Republican Youth would drag all South Vietnam into the cataclysm with them. Once the *Sangha* had tempered the axe for other hands to wield, Thich Tri Quang sat things out in the unascetic safety of the US Embassy. The only plot with guns to back it as well as American sympathy was that of the Generals; they took their time, for the prestige of Ngo Dinh Diem still stood high among their men and in the country, where hundreds of thousands of peasants, their hearts unwrung by denial of their human right to wave the flag of the World Fellowship of Buddhists on Wesak Days without the national flag, slept every night with new-found peace of mind behind their hamlet fences and dutifully gave thanks to the patriarchy of Ngo Dinh Diem for it, as the Republican Youth told them to. While the Generals were still polarizing other plotters to the leadership of Duong Van Minh, Tran Van Don, and Le Van Kim—moves the Can Lao must have kept the Palace informed about—, they themselves found out that Nhu was making diplomatic inquiries through third parties on what terms the DRV might agree to a cease-fire.[d114] This news (certainly known to the US through other channels as well) knocked away America's basic reason for supporting Ngo Dinh Diem in the first place.

[a] Mecklin, p. 239.
[b] *Giornale d'Italia* quoted by AP, 7 Sept. 1963.
[c] *The Times*, 12 Sept. 1963. [d] Halberstam (1965), p. 251.

Calends of November

Adhesion to the army plot by the Corps Commander and Military Governor of Saigon came late, and the National Day Parade on 26 October (anniversary of the end of the monarchy) was allowed to pass before the blow was struck; Ngo Dinh Diem made his last public appearance, realization that his doom must soon befall written on his lonely face. The next weekend was chosen, the Friday siesta, on All Soul's Day, at the full moon. Few troops were needed since General Dinh had now come in as a principal conspirator, and General Oai, Director-General of Psychological Warfare, another; the latter was answerable for the loyalty of the troops to the President and controlled the army's propaganda equipment. He took possession of Radio Saigon, to which his men had access in the course of their duties, and broadcast that President Diem had abdicated to a military Junta of sixty-odd names and would speak to the nation that evening before flying off to exile the next day; military and civil authorities should telephone in their allegiance to the Junta. The capital breathed a sigh of relief that all was over swiftly, bloodlessly, and reasonably; many, including inner confidants of the regime, believed what they heard and did telephone in—even the Commander of IV Corps, Ngo Dinh Diem's own godson, whose troops had tipped the balance against Colonel Thi in 1960—, and the provinces remained quiet. But it was not quite all over. Tanks and infantry cordoned off the Palace, whence the guard kept the cordon at bay all night while Diem and Nhu escaped to a house in Cholon. The Presidential barracks having surrendered in the early hours of the morning, the infantry made a bayonet charge against the Palace itself soon after dawn—with the foreign press corps suitably in the van—to find halls and corridors deserted.

Death of the President

If things had not turned out quite as General Oai's tape-recording had been repeating over the air the previous afternoon, Ngo Dinh Diem did nevertheless surrender by telephone to Joint General Staff Headquarters during the morning of 2 November. He and his brother were collected by the Commandant of the Civil Guard—oaths of personal loyalty, even Can Lao ones, were forgotten in this moment—, and he consigned them to a Captain Nguyen Van Nhung with an armoured car.[a] Later in the morning

[a] Higgins, pp. 217–19.

the Captain delivered their corpses to the Generals, battered and shot. General Oai announced that they had committed suicide inside the church;[a] the Captain was arrested shortly afterwards on a charge of corruption, and soon General Oai's staff were putting it about that he too had committed suicide, after confessing to the regicide.[b] Mgr Thuc stayed on at Rome; Xuan went there too, and the Generals, who were compassionate men, allowed her children to leave Vietnam to live with their mother. Ngo Dinh Can appealed to the American Consul at Hué for asylum; but different rules applied to him from those applicable to Thich Tri Quang, and he was handed over to the Junta, eventually tried and shot (in public)[115] for responsibility for the death of a man who had committed suicide while in police custody at Hué; a local editor commented that a Western court would have found him not guilty on the evidence, but that in Vietnamese eyes he was guilty because his wickedness was common knowledge.[c] The frail widow of Ngo Dinh Kha did not long survive the battering to death of her second and third sons and was already dead herself, from old age, by the time they shot her fourth.

[a] *JEO*, 4 Nov. 1963.   [b] Higgins, p. 220.   [c] *SDN*, 27 Apr. 1964.

7

FAILURE OF NATIONHOOD

THERE is an old Chinese aphorism, known to Vietnamese classical scholars, which runs: 'Dominion of infamous men over the state is like a goitre on the neck of some unlettered rustic; he cannot stand it, stabs at it rashly with a knife, and then dies from the wound he has given himself.'[a] Many former mandarins must have reflected on this truth as they watched the nation's cohesion crumble after the regicide; that fateful deed—fraught with Buddhist *karma*, one might have supposed—had lifted the lid from the cauldron of cliques and factions again and, in the name of Democracy, put the country back where Ngo Dinh Diem had found it. Within two years, many were prepared to admit that, if he had not been killed, he would by then have been President a second time. Far from removing the major obstacle to united resistance against Communist aggression, his death had removed the only source of collaboration and dynamism, as the opponents of his overthrow in the US Mission had feared it would. Vietnamese people saw in the issues that had so worried Westerners only arguments to take up or cast aside again as might suit the course of what to them was a factional vendetta; most of the Generals who had just liberated the land from its tyrant had been mixed up in his campaigns of so-called repression at one time or another, and half a dozen of them in episodes in this very Buddhist crisis; their guilt, if it can be called that, was carried into limbo with the sacrificed President. Diem had been deposed to gratify American opinion, and from now on, whether the US Government wished it that way or not, the question was not going to be how to encourage a regime in South Vietnam that America could support, but of finding one that would support her in keeping up the struggle against the jubilant Communists. This shift of balance manifested itself in subtle ways not only in the ministries and Joint General Staff at Saigon, but also in provinces and districts, where only the framework of MACV and USOM stood fast to provide a skeleton for government; the eventual commitment of the US armed forces to battle became the foregone conclusion

[a] Su Tung-p'o, writing about 1080.

Vietcong propaganda had all along proclaimed: 'contradictions' among the Generals, they confidently predicted, would be the prelude to a US take-over.[a]

If the story of South Vietnamese independence down to 1963 was a sad chronicle of villainies and follies, the stages by which national cohesion has been eroded since then makes no more cheerful reading. No fault of Diem's patriarchy was reformed: instead whatever was already bad became worse—patronage, corruption, detention without trial or review. The Buddhists did not become more law-abiding as concession after concession was made to them, but less so, and more immolations and demonstrations took place after 1 November than before. Where administrative, agrarian or other reform was called for, the task was shelved in the name—but hardly the substance—of more radical social revolution. Nor did aid or advice take any new direction: whatever had gone wrong up to now was blamed on Ngo Dinh Diem in American circles as loudly as in Vietnamese, and old efforts were simply redoubled. Vietcong strength also doubled—and so, tragically, did the bloodshed. The power blocs following each other during those years in undignified procession through the patched-up halls of the Gia Long Palace—the second palace bequeathed by the French that the armed forces had wrecked—each obliterated their predecessors' traces, so that few of their acts had any lasting effect, unless to spread chaos a little farther afield and deepen the general foreboding. The well-to-do who could go abroad got out; those who could not got by. The Ministries and constitutional 'Charters', the riots, the pacification schemes, the 'operations' and the battles could fill many pages of concentrated history; yet they merit only summary consideration, for they have all been overtaken. What is of significance, however, is the condition in which their chief actors have left the Republic of Vietnam and its machinery of government, since it is on that mined and blasted foundation that a permanent political settlement has to rest.

I. JUNTA AND JUGGERNAUT

After commending the troops employed in the coup d'état for their heroism and distributing promotions and decorations to those of their own members whose scruples would, in default of this reward, have deterred them from joining in, the Junta produced

[a] USIS, *Communist Reaction* (1963), pp. 3–6.

two resolutions and a proclamation over the signature of General Duong Van Minh; the resolutions, somewhat superfluously, destituted Ngo Dinh Diem of his offices, substituted for the Presidency a *Conseil Militaire de la Révolution*, and abolished the 1956 constitution and the recently-elected National Assembly. The proclamation promised respect for treaty obligations and an anti-Communist foreign policy, while, internally, the army would 'uphold national unity' until an elected government became practicable, as well as equality of religious faiths, freedom of political association (except for Communists), and freedom of the press.[a] A military order at the same time announced strict censorship of all printed matter.[b]

The Tho Government

This was apparently as far as pre-coup constitutional planning had been thought through, and how actually to carry on the Government had not been worked out. It had not been worked out by the Generals' American sympathizers and advisers either: the desire of American opinion had been to see the termination of the unrighteous patriarchy of Ngo Dinh Diem; once that was accomplished, normal, democratic conditions would re-establish themselves among the freedom-loving Vietnamese. The Ambassador, Mr Lodge, is reliably reported to have secured from Washington a moratorium on pressure of any kind for two to three months while the Generals 'did things their own way'.[c] In fact the initiative in keeping the government machine at work seems to have been taken by the former Vice-President of the Republic under Diem (and constitutional successor to him), Nguyen Ngoc Tho, who on 4 November 1963 decreed himself Prime Minister and Minister of Finance, with a list of fourteen colleagues, of whom three (Generals Don, Dinh, and Oai) took charge of the political Ministries of Defence, Interior, and Information, while the technical ministries were placed under the charge of civil servants. Mr Tho's intention was plainly to reduce as much as possible the disruptive effects of the coup d'état; unfortunately other steps taken by the Generals set this intention at naught.

Party politics

What preoccupied the Generals was the question of popular representation; more than on their conduct of the fighting, they

[a] *JEO*, 4 Nov. 1963.   [b] Ibid.   [c] Mecklin, p. 283.

guessed—not entirely without reason—that they would be judged in America principally on the concessions they were able to make to the forms of representative government. Furthermore, the *Caravellistes* and other non-Communists under detention had to be set free, while *émigrés* quickly began to flock back from Paris and Washington; these all joined the home teams of VNQDD, Cao Dai, Dai Viet, Hoa Hao, and the new contestants—Mahayanists and students—in the clamour for a sounding-board from which to make their long-silent voices heard. As in 1954, none had any plan or programme to urge, and, once the garlands hung by schoolgirls on the tanks patrolling the streets had wilted, it was obvious that no spirit of national renewal was going to sweep the country this time either. The best known among the politicians were invited by the Junta to belong to a Council of Notabilities, with the somewhat forlorn hope that, forgetting their rivalries, they would eventually sit down together in two or three coalitions capable of playing the part of the Democrats and Republicans in the US.[a] The Junta, like all their successors, promised future elections once the country was more settled.

De facto constitution

In this way a new constitutional pattern took shape—not explicitly, since, apart from a shortlived 'Charter' that saw the light of day in August 1964, no new draft replaced the suspended constitution, but by inference. National sovereignty was arrogated by a Council of the Army, which began as the twenty-two man Junta but later expanded into an Armed Forces Council with representatives from all the regiments and field formations; a select committee of the Council actually made all the decisions—in the early days Generals Minh, Don, Kim, and Dinh—, and the senior of them (General Minh) exercised the titular functions of Head of State. The Council of Notabilities—later the High National Council— was appointed by the Junta merely as a forum for the expression of opinions and played no part in the governing of the country. The ministries functioned at the pleasure of the Junta in any technical spheres the Generals saw no reason to impinge on. There was no apportionment of powers, and relations between these different bodies were at all times arbitrary.

[a] The manœuvres to this end were conducted on behalf of the Junta—somewhat incongruously by Western standards but not so by Vietnamese—by the Military Security Service. The principal executive in these manœuvres, Communist-turned-Catholic Lt. Col. Pham Ngoc Thao, later tried his own coup, was outlawed, then perished in a vendetta.

Military government

The pre-eminence of the Junta rested on its control of force, and this in turn depended on the army chain of command running through the Tactical Zones and Areas introduced by the old regime. This hierarchy of Corps and Divisional command, whose overweight had been made to feel its own unsuitability through the daily pricks and prods of the Vietcong, acquired a meaning for the first time when it became the political framework for outright military government; the elimination of the Palace from political decision and control, and the usurpation of its role by the Joint General Staff, transferred to the Army Command control of communications on political and administrative as well as military subjects. Prime Minister Tho tried to salvage administrative jurisdiction over the running of the provinces for his own office, while conceding that, where internal security or politics came in, the Divisional Commander was the appropriate authority;[a] but the attempt was not a success because the Commanders now asserted to the full their command over the territorial administration (was it not right that everything else should be subordinated to the interests of the war?), appointing and removing officers to and from it as suited them, for there was involved not only the stake of regional influence and power but also, as American aid began to rise in quantity again, control of big sums of money. Whereas Ngo Dinh Diem's original error of judgement in agreeing to a conventional command structure had provided the army with a path to power, the seizure of power created a new vested interest in resisting any radical reform of the command structure to suit the fighting.

Attitude to the war

The political supremacy of the army did not bring forth any revolutionary change in its attitude to the war and pacification in other directions either; the way had, on the contrary, been opened for the building of still bigger, more heavily equipped forces, stalwartly vowed to maintenance of uncompromising resistance to the DRV at the side of the US. The strategic hamlets were regarded by the Junta as an embarrassment that they could not wish away with the old regime but that still did not fit into their image of the war. While the Joint General Staff hesitated what their policy should be, the Vietcong, who *had* thought things out, began within a few days of the coup d'état an intensified campaign of propaganda support-

[a] Circular No. 9-TTP of 29 Nov. 1963.

ing the overthrow of Diem and Nhu and arguing from it the abandonment of local defences.[a] The Republican Youth had melted away in Saigon, and with it went the organization and close defence of almost all the hamlets; they fell apart at a pace determined only by the capacity of the Vietcong to take advantage of the confusion. In the past, the army had blamed its own ineptitudes on the interference of the Palace, and so rather had the US; but when freedom of action came, it did not adapt itself in any way to the realities of the peril, but blundered on as before, a Juggernaut with no steering wheels.

The Khanh coup d'état

For all their concentration on political affairs, the senior officers of the army were unable to keep up, for construction of a new regime, the collaboration among themselves that had led to destruction of the old; if a leader of Ngo Dinh Diem's prestige had been so easy to topple, lesser men would be easier. So thought General Nguyen Khanh, now commanding 1st Corps. He had commanded the defence of the Palace in 1960 against Colonel Thi, had played no part in the recent 'Revolution', and was rumoured to have urgent reasons for getting possession of Can Lao records and destroying them. In close alliance with General Tran Thien Khiem of the Junta—a Catholic who had recently taken command of IIIrd Corps while General Dinh allowed himself to be appointed Minister of the Interior and thereby unguardedly renounced his command of troops—with the sympathy of various others and with help from Colonel Thi himself, newly returned from exile in Cambodia, Khanh swooped down from Tourane on 29 January 1964 and seized the persons of Generals Minh, Don, Kim, Dinh, and Xuan (now Director-General of National Police for the third time); he accused them also of plotting to negotiate with Hanoi for a peace settlement. All but Minh were bundled off to confinement at Dalat, Mr Tho and his Ministers (except three) were dismissed, and the Council of Notabilities was dissolved. General Khanh set up General Minh again as his Head of State, while he declared himself Prime Minister and General Khiem Defence Minister; other

[a] As late as 25 Jan. 1964 the Junta's principal planner, Gen. Le Van Kim (who had associated himself with the *Caravellistes'* remonstrance against the *agrovilles*), told the author priority for the military Government's attention had had to be given to securing foreign diplomatic recognition, and after that to setting up the Council of Notabilities; with those more urgent tasks accomplished, the Junta was now on the point of giving its attention in earnest to pacification.

ministers were appointed from the Junta, from leaders of the
VNQDD, Cao Dai, and both local and émigré wings of the Dai Viet
(the dominant group),[116] and from among professional men whom
the US Government persuaded to return from abroad to take office.

The Khanh administration

This coalition survived as the titular Government until the end of
August 1964, but reluctance on the part of the majority of factions
to acquiesce in Khanh's right to rule found expression in constant
intrigues within the armed forces and in civil disturbances at
Saigon and at Hué; these developments justified him in ruling as a
dictator, which in turn discredited him further. For six months after
the overthrow of Diem, the General Association of Buddhists
busied itself with the consolidation of a Unified Buddhist Church
while circumstances were propitious;[a] the half-hearted Theravadins were included, and the Hoa Hao and Cao Dai proved capricious allies. The Junta was persuaded to allocate gratis valuable
land for an Institute of Propaganda (*Vien Hoa Dao*) and some new
pagodas; it gave way at the same time over the appointment of
Buddhist chaplains to double the Catholic ones in the armed
forces,[b] and the faithful were organized on Communist Party lines,
into a self-conscious force available for demonstrations; but the
Mahayana's strength in Saigon was still practically confined to
Tonkinese and Annamese residents, and no headway was made in
converting (if that is the right word) the Cochinchinese, who still
regarded the Hué movement as regionally alien. The Catholics too
strengthened their militant wing, and marches and counter-
marches became usual on feast days, political anniversaries, and
most Sundays. The demise of the Can Lao removed restraints from
trade unions and student associations—for the authorities to have
let the law take the place of the Can Lao would have been greeted
in the prevailing atmosphere as tyrannical. All these groups provided manpower in traditional Vietnamese style for vested interests desiring to put pressure on the Government, all were exposed to incitement by Vietcong agitators,[c] and some were re-

---

[a] *Giao Hoi Phat Giao Thong Nhat Viet Nam*; the term *giao-hoi* for 'church' is a Catholic
one, Buddhism not previously having had any use for such an expression.

[b] Foreseeably, the chaplains became another pressure group within the Army and by
1966 were going on hunger strike against the military government (VNP No. 5561,
19 May 1966).

[c] For example, in the notorious riot in Saigon when youths in a jeep rushed from
Catholic to Buddhist headquarters 'warning' each that the other was about to attack
it (*Tu Do*, 28 Aug. 1964).

putedly hired by the Prime Minister himself. In August, interpreting the co-operativeness of the American Generals towards
him as of the same quality as the Eisenhower commitment to Ngo
Dinh Diem, and having quarrelled with his Dai Viet ministers, the
Prime Minister met the agitators' demands for more representative
government by producing a 'Charter' that would have made him
President of the Republic with what amounted to absolute powers.[a]
A furious wave of rioting was set in train in Saigon; Khanh
abolished the Military Revolutionary Council and, behind the
screen of a supreme triumvirate of himself flanked by Generals
Minh and Khiem, gave out that his ministers would carry on by
themselves under the sovereign authority of the Triumvirate.

Khanh steps down

With Buddhists and Catholics locked in conflict throughout
Annam and demonstrations or riots every week in Saigon, Khanh
promised to hand over power to a civilian Ministry by the end of
October and meanwhile replaced the Generals in the Cabinet with
self-styled elder statesmen acceptable to the Cao Dai and VNQDD.
In mid-September another coup d'état was attempted under the
leadership of one of the émigré Generals, but failed; ten days later
there was a general strike in Saigon; the CIDG wing of the Special
Forces rebelled in the PMS under the leadership of a Radé official,
seized Banmethuot broadcasting station, massacred thirty-five of
their Vietnamese officers, and demanded federal status for a 'Republic of Champa';[b] Buddhist mobs attacked government offices
all over Annam, and, in their wake, the Vietcong seized and held
for several hours the port of Qui Nhon. If MACV had been per-
turbed by the withdrawal of one battalion of troops from the Iron
Triangle for police work in 1963, they had now to watch whole
divisions so diverted in 1964. At the end of October Khanh retired
from the premiership 'to concentrate on being Commander-in-
Chief'—a position of political eminence but no military significance. He turned the Government over to an all-civilian *Convention*
under a new Head of State (Mr Phan Khac Suu, *Caravelliste*) and a
new Prime Minister (Mr Tran Van Huong, likewise a *Caravelliste*)—
both of them connected with the Cao Dai and so champions of the

[a] Text in *SDN*, 17 Aug. 1964.
[b] *SP*, 25 Sept. 1964; Y B'ham, the leader, called his organization *Front Unifié pour la
Lutte de la Race Opprimée* (FULRO), spurning the Vietnamese language for French.
The casualty figure, denied at the time, was confirmed the following year by the
regional commander, Gen. Co (VNP No. 5296, 26 Aug. 1965).

Cochinchinese against the Tonkinese and Annamese—under a new 'Provisional Charter' destined never to go into effect.[a] On 1 November 1964 General Minh, as outgoing Head of State, addressed the nation on the anniversary of the glorious Revolution against Ngo Dinh Diem; attainment of civilian government, he said, marked the fulfilment of the army's promise a year before to hand the state back to the people.[b] Alas, all there was to hand back by that time was the broken pieces of the state.

The Huong administration

Mr Huong held office for three months as Prime Minister and Minister of Armed Forces (which, incidentally, the new Charter laid down should be held by different persons), but the agitators were not to be appeased. To add to his misfortunes, unprecedented rainfall in Annam in November 1964 caused disastrous floods, carrying away fields, livestock, hamlets, and whatever bridges, roads, and stretches of railway had not already been blown up by the Vietcong. MACV and USOM made superhuman efforts to repair the damage and rescue and house the victims—with other refugees, soon to number three quarters of a million; but normal land communications between Saigon and Hué were never restored. Neither the Annamese of the towns nor the permanent demonstrators of various self-styled persuasions on the streets of Saigon ever accepted the authority of the Huong Government, and on 20 December General Khanh carried out another coup d'état by arresting the members of the High National Council (which had the effect of invalidating the October Charter) and setting up in its place an Armed Forces Council, while leaving the hapless Mr Suu and Mr Huong to hold the administration together as best they could.[c] This they contrived to do, despite the mounting ferocity of Vietcong attacks and the breakdown of several army regiments under the strain, until the end of January 1965. Then the Prime Minister secretly took refuge in the residence of the British Ambassador and only emerged again when the Commander-in-Chief personally guaranteed his safety. His place as Prime Minister was taken—after yet another abortive army coup[d]—by Tonkinese Dai Viet and *Caravelliste* Dr Phan Huy Quat, who formed a Cabinet in which every major faction was intended to be represented. Though

[a] *JEO*, 22 Oct. 1964.   [b] *SDN*, 2 Nov. 1964.
[c] Joint protest by them issued through VNP (No. 3275, 28 Dec. 1964).
[d] By Pham Ngoc Thao.

General Khanh eased the situation by going abroad at this stage and the US relieved the pressure on the army's fighting forces by introducing the first American troops, Dr Quat found himself deprived of the authority to conduct public affairs in the face of the continuous turmoil, still headed by Thich Tri Quang and the Buddhists of Hué (although these were represented in his Cabinet),[117] and on 8 June 1965 he dumped the mandate back in the lap of the Armed Forces Council.

The Ky administration

Air-Force Brigadier Nguyen Cao Ky had taken a lead at every coup d'état or riot since 1964 on the side of whoever represented authority for the moment, and more than once his control of aircraft had proved decisive. Having established his name, especially with foreign observers, as a factor for stability, he now undertook to form a *Directoire*, under the authority of the Armed Forces Council and a military Committee of National Leadership, and, being himself Tonkinese, appointed Annamese General Nguyen Van Thieu as titular Head of State and Cochinchinese General Nguyen Huu Co as Minister of Defence. This Junta, freed by the mounting strength of American combat forces from the immediate peril of being overwhelmed by the People's Army of the DRV, was destined to become the most lasting Government since Ngo Dinh Diem's, although twice within the next year professional or civil-servant members of it had to be sacrificed to rivals for power from Sect or party.[a] The Saigon public seemed by mid-1965 to have had enough of civil disturbances for the moment, but more serious threats than ever lay ahead in Annam. During the spring the Cambodian Government had held a Conference of Indochinese Peoples at Phnom Penh, inviting representation of Vietnam only from the DRV, the Vietcong, and FULRO. In August FULRO agitators reappeared among the CIDG and repeated the demand for an autonomous Champa; but this time they were swiftly isolated from the CIDG, no longer able to play off their generously-disposed American officers against the Vietnamese authorities as they had the previous year, and they withdrew as American combat forces began to take up positions in the PMS. Meanwhile a secessionist movement was taking shape at Hué and, more menacingly, at Tourane (Danang) beside the base under construction for US

[a] Reallocations of office had to be made in Feb. and July 1966 and in Jan. 1967, and on the last date Gen. Co was dismissed and exiled (*The Times*, 28 Jan. 1967).

troops. Ostensibly the dissatisfaction of the troublemakers was over the slowness of progress in moving from military control to representative government—a complaint to which the new Prime Minister lent substance by promising elections to a legislature and then insisting it was only to be a Constituent Assembly.[a] The Mahayanists of Tu Dam Pagoda were prominent again, and a disquieting feature of their pronouncements was the anti-American neutralism with which they appealed to a war-weary public in the villages round Tourane.[b] But much of the impetus undoubtedly came from local struggles between factional interests—within the Buddhist movement, within the VNQDD and Dai Viet, within the University of Hué, and within the army[c] (inside which all of the others had subversive cells). The Commander of 1st Corps, now General Nguyen Chanh Thi, at once member of the *Directoire* and rival of General Ky, adopted an equivocal attitude at Hué while a 'Civilian and Military Revolutionary Force' intimidated government departments, the police, and the armed forces, ravaged Danang, and for weeks on end denounced the Government from Radio Hué (in whose administration an embarrassed USIS had a share). The VNQDD suffered casualties in gang fights at Hué—allegedly over the sharing-out of American handsels[d]—and its leader was murdered at Danang.[e] Dai Viet elements organized upwards of 20,000 people to march round the outskirts of the town defended by their own 'Revolutionary Armed Forces' sporting machine guns[f] borrowed from the army. Independence for Annam was demanded by the Vien Hoa Dao from Saigon[g] as Buddhists and Catholics resumed their marches and counter-marches in the capital, both blaming their grievances on the US. The Vietcong made a determined effort to subvert the troops siding with the Hué dissidents[h]— without success. The American Consulate at Hué was attacked.

Reoccupation of Hué

Early in May, General Ky directed troops to 'recapture' Hué and Danang (after depriving General Thi of his command) and raided student and union offices in Saigon.[i] This resolute action, though

[a] He admitted this prevarication explicitly in VNP, No. 5516, 4 Apr. 1966.
[b] Thich Nhat Hanh (1967), p. 74.
[c] With frankness unusual in these matters, a Saigon newspaper put the trouble down to 'war weariness and economic deterioration combined with selfish contention for power' (*Quyet Tien*, 7 Apr. 1966).
[d] VNP, Hué bulletin, 20 Apr. 1966.   [e] *SDN*, 29 Apr. 1966.
[f] *Tu Do*, 26 Apr. 1966.   [g] *Dat To*, 7 Apr. 1966.
[h] Liberation Radio bulletin, 9 Apr. 1966.   [i] *SDN*, 3 May 1966.

conducted in the same extra-legal manner as Ngo Dinh Nhu's raid on the pagodas, was generally applauded by the Saigon public and the foreign press; the current phase of disorder subsided, allowing preparation for the Constituent Assembly elections to take place on 11 September 1966 as planned, although quiet was bought in Hué at the price of ceding both civil and military command to nominees of the Dai Viet.[a] There can be little doubt that a factor in the disturbances had been the desire of the Vien Hoa Dao and some other groups to prevent any election from taking place because of their unpreparedness to face an electoral campaign. In the absence of regular party memberships to support Western representative politics, an election in Vietnam is a gamble liable to result in sudden eclipse for even the most vocal politicians.[118] The members of parties and sects invited to sit in the various councils during these years never proclaimed the affiliations they stood for, as if wanting still to preserve the secret-society character of their organizations. The clamour for democracy in which the Mahayana Buddhists had made the running, and for which they had held successive Juntas guarantor, had not been accompanied by any effort to found a political party with a programme such as Western observers might have supposed was their intention; it had served more immediate purposes of nullifying the initiatives of the authority of the moment.

Weakness of military government

Several causes contributed to the failure of the army to keep order, or to stem the advance of Vietcong domination of the countryside, which continued disastrously throughout the period. The more obvious ones were the administrative inexperience, and possibly political immaturity, of individual officers who held the reins; less obvious was the military inexperience of men who did not owe their rank to promotion on account of service and who were treated with indifferent respect by the men under them. Widening scope for corruption as foreign aid increased, without the controlling hand of a 'tyrant' in Saigon, was another cause, for it offered a spur to ambition for power and a seduction from duty. The endemic factionalism of an army that could not but be a cross-section of traditional society added its hazards. But the decisive causes arose from the army's position as government and combatant at the same time; both functions were jeopardized by their combination. Mili-

[a] *The Times*, 14 Apr. 1967.

tary governments are not necessarily made stronger by reliance on *Lex Wellington* (that the only source of law is the will of the Commander-in-Chief); in Vietnam this reliance has greatly weakened the army as a peacekeeper. Many countries in recent years have resorted to military government at home, and there are Western political writers who would go so far as to prescribe it for backward countries as a prophylactic against disorder. But even an army invading somebody else's country will be faced by enormous difficulties if it has to administer territory in which it is fighting battles at the same time; an army undertaking both tasks at home in circumstances of civil war cannot escape from the daily quandary, over hundreds of matters, that forbearance lets the enemy in, whereas firmness identifies the people with the enemy—an acceptable state of affairs in hostile territory, but a calamity in one's own. The arbitrary rule of the gun creates an atmosphere in which no official has any guide as to the proper course to follow. Nor has it been any help in Vietnam to set up civilian Councils of Ministers with neither political authority nor executive machinery at their command, as was the situation of Nguyen Ngoc Tho, Tran Van Huong, and Phan Huy Quat: their repudiation as scapegoats was bound to occur soon rather than late.

2. GOVERNMENT AND SOCIAL REVOLUTION

The arbitrary character of military rule in South Vietnam came about through the suspension of the constitution and the proclamation on 1 November 1963, in effect, of a revolution instead of a Government; the casting away of legitimacy that these steps entailed might have been of purely academic consequence but for the fact that it spun the wheel for anybody to try his luck. Existing laws remained in force, but the legislation of new ones became more, not less, uncertain than under the old regime; fortunately, few serious problems seem to have been posed, however, and the great majority of enactments required were dealt with adequately by temporary regulation or administrative instruction. The extent of ministerial responsibility was always in doubt. There had been no Council of Ministers under Diem; Mr Nguyen Ngoc Tho tried to start one but was unable to bring within its purview the portfolios of three ministers who were Generals and members of the Junta. The failure of this experiment was covered up by the overthrow of the Junta upon which its limited authority depended. It was complained against General Khanh that he consulted his colleagues less and less as time went on, and certainly there was no regular Cabinet procedure. Mr Huong revived the Council of Ministers, and it has remained a formal institution ever after; however, its jurisdiction did not include defence, pacification, law and order, or any other political question reserved by the Junta of the day, and consequently the overall planning of Government action remained as imperfectly co-ordinated as under the old regime, and in this rendered the Government weaker, not stronger, by reason of its military character.

The Civil Service

The civil service fared rather worse after 1963 than before. The first Junta arrested several score senior officers believed to have enjoyed too much of the confidence of Diem or Nhu and confined them at first in disused offices, later in prisons. Others were compulsorily retired or given gipsies' warnings to resign, forgoing their pension rights. The witch-hunt to find evidence that would justify revenge against them through process of law went on all through 1964, and in one or two departments was the sole activity for months on end. Libellous campaigns in the press were tolerated, if not encouraged, by the first Junta.[119] However, no criminal charges appear to have been brought against established members of the *Cong Vu*—although there were several against army officers occupying administrative positions—, and by the end of 1964 the majority of the victims had been set free again, a few even rehabilitated; the last residue were released for Tet 1967. The loss of experienced personnel by that time had been serious, however, and the annual intake of sixty administrators through the NIA could not make it good for several years, especially as liability for military service took everybody for a few months after graduation and some for longer. A second, more frightening, witch-hunt was that of the People's Salvation Committee, set up in the coastal towns of Annam late in August 1964; this movement was part of the Buddhist turmoil but, ominously adopting the same title as the Vietminh riot committees of 1945,[a] started a clamour against 'Can Lao remnants' in the territorial administration and the police; certain among the leaders were themselves professional men in government employment who did not conceal their personal ambition to gain political office for themselves. The designated victims, un-

[a] Coincidence of name pointed out by *Chinh Luan*, 12 Oct. 1964.

protected by their army superiors,[a] mostly fled from their posts, and a shortlived seizure of Qui Nhon in September by the Vietcong (resulting in destruction of the houses of the Public Prosecutor and other officers concerned with law enforcement) was due to the paralysis of the police and to the army's inability to protect anything but public buildings. None of the Generals or Prime Ministers of these disastrous years ever made any declaration of appreciation of conscientious work in the civil service, but several did issue gratuitous threats as to what they would do about bribery if it came to light; the intention appeared to be to give the public and the foreign advisers an impression of energetic rule. In practice, each change of Government led to fresh dispensations of patronage, on a scale much in excess of that reached under Ngo Dinh Diem; the protests of the Civil Service Directorate that the beneficiaries could not all be fitted into the establishment or the budget provoked Dr Phan Huy Quat into suppressing that Directorate altogether in May 1965 and transferring all public offices to the gift of ministers.[b] Meanwhile, requests from civil servants for restoration of their Disciplinary Code, suspended by Ngo Dinh Diem,[c] met only prevarication, until in March 1966 General Ky silenced them by handing over the discipline of public officers to the military courts.[d]

Territorial administration

The Province and District Chiefs who had served under the old regime were all turned out, and in some provinces there were three or four changes in the space of a year. Confusion and uncertainty went all the deeper because, as in the ministries in the capital, there was extensive destruction of files at the same time. Whereas under Diem a high proportion of the army officers in civil posts were actually well qualified to fill them on educational grounds, regard could no longer be had to that criterion because the supply had run out; instead, two other considerations governed staffing under the army: patronage to facilitate corruption within the chain of command, and the desire to grant self-determination to factional interests predominant in each region. Corruption was based partly

[a] The commander of II Corps was accused at the same time of Can Lao affiliations (*SDN*, 26 Sept. 1964), was dismissed, and then tried to commit suicide. His detractors also accused him of 'inordinate dishonesty'—a mode of expression which reflected the traditional Vietnamese, and Chinese, point of view that corruption is not wrong in principle, but only when its degree exceeds what is customary.
[b] The change itself was made public, but not of course the motive.
[c] p. 231 above.   [d] VNP No. 5112, 31 Mar. 1966.

on the distribution of American aid—although the officers of USOM took strenuous steps to prevent it—but more substantially on faked payrolls for paramilitary forces or training programmes in connexion with pacification; these spoils of office were alleged to be divided between all echelons of command up to Corps Commander, either on a regular-income basis or on an outright-fee basis.[a] The political element in territorial appointments arose from the deliberate reversion to the conditions of 1955; the Generals preferred to give the sects and parties their head in what the latter regarded still as their domains instead of challenging them to show their boasted patriotism shoulder to shoulder with other citizens—this in spite of evidence that the various groups' claims to unanimity of local support were based on exactly the same traditional formulae of intimidation as were those of the Communists. Military Province Chiefs were appointed in Cochinchina from the ranks of the Cao Dai and Hoa Hao or from lists of officers acceptable to them, and this became the practice in regard to Dai Viet, VNQDD, and certain family cliques in coastal Annam; only the hill tribes did not profit from this form of what foreigners were invited to understand as local self-determination. The ranks of the Civil Guard and Militia were similarly manned and officered, with a view to restoring the warlord policy pursued by the French, even if it was not thought of in those terms; the turbulence that took possession of Annam in 1964–6 can hardly be reckoned a recommendation for the policy. In Cochinchina there occurred as a result of it some surrenders of Hoa Hao groups previously allied to the Vietcong,[b] and the Long Xuyen and Chau Doc provinces entered a long period free of 'incidents'; however, evasion from the official granaries of the 1965 rice crop, taken with other signs, left few in doubt that the policy amounted to a *modus vivendi* at one remove between authorities and Communists. These arrangements were made by the army command alone; the Ministry of the Interior lost its authority over the territorial administration, except in matters of routine dealt with by civilian deputy Province Chiefs, and from early in 1964 onwards the Corps Commanders became *de facto* regional governors, though without legal sanction.[c]

[a] Scandals in Saigon over embezzlement have been ceaseless, and an American source was reported as recently as *The Times* of 17 Mar. 1967 as complaining that the alchemists of the black market, following in the footsteps of Gen. Lu Han (pp. 60–61 above), were reselling at 16 piastres a kilo imported rice supplied to the army at only 7 piastres thanks to subsidies by the US.

[b] *SDN*, 20 Feb., 1 Apr., & 23 June 1964.

[c] Minutes of a Ministry of Interior conference, 11–12 Oct. 1965.

Government by appeasement

This partial reversion to the French policy of feudalization was accompanied by a host of inactivities believed to be pleasing to various partisan interests in the country. Although direct taxation already ran at such ridiculously low rates,[a] the Tho Government instructed certain provinces to waive rural taxes altogether, and by mid-1965 it was complained that Province Chiefs preferred to suspend all collection and to demand subventions from Saigon.[b] The administration of justice also felt the gentle touch of this policy of appeasement, accused persons tending to be judged according to their political standing rather than the criminality of their deeds. Thus Major Dang Sy was convicted of the Wesak homicides at Hué in spite of conflicting evidence[c] and of the exoneration available to him in law that death had been caused (if it had been caused at all) in the course of duty.[d] To appease with a spectacular and vigorous gesture popular outcry against the profiteering and corruption consequent on the entry of American combat troops into Vietnam, General Ky had a Chinese merchant, Chia Eng (Ta Vinh in Vietnamese), arrested and then set up a Special Court to try him under a draconian and inappellable war-crimes law;[e] the accused's specific 'war crimes' were, in substance, an unspectacular foreign-exchange offence and the offering of a bribe at the moment of his arrest for it; half the Cabinet sat in the front of the court for its opening, the accused was quickly convicted, and the execution was carried out a few days later in the street.[f] On the other hand, the first Junta passed a law condoning retrospectively all offences of whatever nature committed with the purpose of opposing the Diem regime,[g] and under this law the Saigon Court of Appeal saw fit, at the instance of one of the civilian Prime Ministers, to rehabilitate posthumously Le Quang Vinh ('Ba-Cut')[h] of the conviction for murder and arson for which he had been guillotined in 1956.[i]

The police

The police enjoyed no higher regard after the revolution than before it. The force continued to be deployed only in the towns,

[a] p. 285 above.

[b] Minutes of a Ministry of Interior conference, 14–17 July 1965.

[c] *JEO*, 8 June 1964.

[d] Penal Code art. 327; actually he was tried in Saigon but by the Code of Annam, which contains no such safeguard—although a humaner justice might have arranged matters otherwise.

[e] *Sac-luat*, No. 4 of 1965.   [f] *SP*, 8 Mar. 1966.   [g] *Sac-luat*, No. 3 of 1963.

[h] *JEO*, 8 June 1964.   [i] *SDN*, 19 Mar. 1965.

where, in accordance with the pattern running through the whole administration, it often found itself playing the part of an ancillary to units of the infantry drafted to do its work for it. Fear of witch-hunting was prompted not only by the arrest and trial of the former Director-General, Colonel Y (not a member of the regular force), but also by the arrest of Mr Tran Van Tu (who was), commandant of the Saigon police, without any charge being preferred against him. The result of this vindictiveness was the total paralysis of the Criminal Investigation Department, and for more than a year burglars and other thieves—their numbers swollen by refugees from the surrounding villages under artillery or Vietcong attack and by young men in hiding from military service—were assured that little effort would be made to detect, still less to punish, them. Members of all the Juntas were inclined to condone police in-activity in the pursuit of common criminals, lest the antagonizing of street gangs should add to their political problems. During 1965 the police on beat or guard in all the big towns became a special target for Vietcong terror attacks; but by this time their nadir was passed, and USOM was trying to rehabilitate and expand the force as an indispensable buttress for stable government, in rural as well as urban areas. At the end of 1964 the force numbered 34,000; the American plan was to double this by the end of 1966.[a] How-ever, enough recruits could not be found, as the army (American as much as Vietnamese) demanded the pick of the manpower;[120] the period of training never extended beyond three months and for many of the men was limited to three weeks' weapon drill; the force was built up as a number of separate wings so independent of one another that they did not even wear the same uniform; and the chain of command on the Vietnamese side was subordinated to the army in such a way as to make the force available as a counter-weight to other military factions with a mind to carry out coups d'état, on the same principle that had shaped Ngo Dinh Diem's security system. All senior positions in the force were political appointments, no regard whatever being had to the need for con-tinuity in the conduct of police operations against the Communists.

Social revolution

It should be clear from this survey that the proclamation that the coup d'état of 1 November 1963 was to be a revolution (the

---

[a] A small mission of British officers formerly in colonial police forces was employed to help—note 103.

'November Revolution') amounted to a boast of little substance. The word provided a temporary psychological bond between the Generals and their American partners, but it was soon apparent that, whereas the latter understood from the word the political and social emancipation of their own history in 1776, the former were thinking of the freedom to fight for power that was inaugurated by the French Revolution in 1789: the alternate manipulation of the mob and surrender to them, the machinations of émigrés, much of the nomenclature (*Assemblée Nationale, Assemblée Constituante, Convention, Directoire*), and the faith of French-educated soldier after soldier that he had it in him to be his country's Bonaparte. The revolution had in fact less substance, if that was possible, than the Personalist revolution had had; the impetus to give it substance came entirely from American advisers, still sharing the conviction— from which the Generals did not dissent anyway—that the halting of the advance of the Communists required betterment of the life of the common people on a scale exceeding anything the Communists could offer through the promise of their revolution. American ideas were tied mostly to schemes for pacification, and there was no question of urging the various Vietnamese Governments to inaugurate measures based on native resources: the object was still that the Government should appear to its people as the dispenser of benefactions that did not have to be paid for in the harsh kind extorted by the Vietcong; this was the message of many joint American-Vietnamese communiqués culminating in the 'Honolulu Declaration' of President Johnson and Generals Ky and Thieu at the beginning of 1966.[a] The ideal was to be a 'social revolution'; the most practical measure for giving it an objective reality seemed to be a resumption of land reform.

Land reform

Not a great deal could be done to take up again the problem of rent control: the eighteen months' concentration of administrative effort on building strategic hamlets, and the confusion resulting from occupation of other tenants' land by Government order in many villages (oral, not recorded anywhere), had been followed during the course of 1964 by loss of access to their land by owners now resident in the towns and able to lobby behind the scenes against officious reformers. In Annam, however, the overwhelming waves of refugees entering the towns from the autumn of 1964 on-

[a] VNP No. 5462, 8 Feb. 1966.

wards demanded land to till in the vicinity; in many places this could only be found by allotting them a share of the communal lands (the *cong dien*), hitherto put up to auction and frequently sublet to the wealthy bidders at rack rents. Auctioning of communal land was therefore prohibited in the summer of 1965, and village authorities were ordered to charge rents only on the basis of the crop, within the limits of the existing law (that is, on five-year tenancies at no more than 25 per cent).[a] Extensive observance of this reform was claimed, although its conflict with the ancient tenures of common land held by the *chrétientés* provided the occasion at Qui Nhon—and possibly elsewhere—for renewed tension between Catholics and Buddhists, the latter not being above denouncing officials who upheld the claims of the former as 'Can Lao remnants'.

Land transfer

The main concentration of effort in pursuit of land reform was in Cochinchina on the land-transfer aspect. Loss by the Government of proper control of practically the whole countryside in the course of 1964 brought collection of the quotas due on redistributed land almost to a standstill, because the debtors were physically unable, or forbidden by the Vietcong, to visit Government offices and could only resume contact during the relatively brief duration of various pacification schemes or military operations to show the flag; the extension of the period of repayment from six to twelve years[b] merely covered up the authorities' inability to collect the money—it did not bring any nearer the day when the land would become the peasant's own. The Vietcong, for their part, proclaimed the rule of 'land to the tiller' for the period of the armed struggle and pocketed the sums due to the Government as an item of taxation due to themselves. Their propaganda on the subject was by now no longer directed against the remaining landlords because, as in Tonkin in 1945, the support of landowners as part of the 'whole people' was needed and demanded; instead the Government was their butt for having appropriated the big estates to the state domain under Ngo Dinh Diem and for having withheld titles to redistributed lots until the purchase money was fully paid up; the aim of the agitation was not to hasten reform, of course, but to justify collecting the money

[a] VNP No. 5284, 14 Aug. 1965. Pressure was also put on villages to give preference to war victims.
[b] p. 244 above.

themselves. This was understood by the Ky Government, and during the summer of 1965, therefore, under American pressure, the Minister of Agriculture announced what amounted to bowing to force of circumstances: temporary titles would be converted to permanent ones wherever survey was in order without waiting for completion of payment, but on the understanding that the land was mortgaged back to the Government; there would be a moratorium on repayment (extendable indefinitely), but peasants could meanwhile pay off their putative mortgage—there was no time to draw up land certificates—by selling the crop to the Government direct to help it out of what by this time was a serious difficulty over rice supplies.[a] Simultaneously with this easement, the Government began to issue titles for the old *agrovilles* and land settlements deliberately held back by President Diem.[b] Unfortunately, by no means all the land concerned fell within the areas included in the French cadastral survey, and new survey work could not be carried out because of insecurity and the dispersal of the technical staff of the Land Office to 'war work'. Publicity was given to the handing over by Prime Minister Ky of several hundred[c] permanent titles over former domain land on the outskirts of the towns (Tay Ninh, Phan Rang); but it remained an open question whether American faith was justified that absolute proprietorship (still encumbered and therefore not alienable) would triumph in the beneficiaries' unsophisticated minds over the pressure of their other unsolved problems, including personal safety, and whether the Vietcong would as a result have less of their own way in future.

3. PACIFICATION AND ESCALATION

The unexpressed justification for General Khanh's seizure of power in January 1964 was his willingness to allow MACV and USOM to try belatedly to salvage what was left of the strategic hamlets. It was very difficult to assess what really was left. Generally speaking, the dissolution of the Republican Youth had been ignored in hamlets wholly or largely Catholic; in quite a number of other places, where there were no Catholics, the same courageous vitality continued, surprisingly, to be shown by the villagers and deterred the Vietcong from pressing their dominion for the time

[a] VNP No. 5245, 6 July 1965; *Sac-luat* 020 of 8 Oct. 1965.
[b] *Sac-luat* 021 of 8 Oct. 1965; see pp. 245–6 above.
[c] Many thousands by mid-1967.

being: but such localities were disconnected islands in a sea of uncertainty. By Christmas 1963 the Vietcong had convinced, directly
or by example, the bulk of the residents of the hamlets that in case
of attack they could no longer expect support from the Civil
Guard, caught up in its own command purge[a] and further para-
lysed by the confusion prevailing in the territorial administration
that gave it its orders. It is reasonable to assume that in many
localities where no incidents occurred a *modus vivendi* had been
arrived at. A prodigious national effort had been put forth on the
stockading of the strategic hamlets, and in some cases on moving
houses and building new schools, dispensaries, and fortified accommodation for the garrison as a *corvée*, besides the contributions in
money (some of which had been embezzled); even if the Government pulled itself together again under the leadership of General
Khanh—which in the event it did not—it was not to be expected
that the villagers would repeat the effort with any confidence.
Emphasis in the new doctrine (the work mainly of American
advisers) was therefore on what the Government—in practice
USOM and MACV—could do for the peasants rather than on
what they should do for themselves, as in the days of the Three
Sufficiencies. The *ap chien luoc* was changed to *ap tan sinh* (already
invented before General Khanh seized power)—'new life hamlet'
in place of 'strategic hamlet'.[121]

Hamlets and aid

The change of phrase foreshadowed a new attitude to close
defence. Many stockades were destroyed by, or by order of, the
Vietcong at the end of 1963, and the Joint General Staff had at one
stage forbidden their restoration, as smacking of a concentration
camp;[b] the new-life hamlets had no stockades, unless the old ones
happened to be intact—a detail which ruled out the operation of
controls on the movement of agents or the diversion of supplies.
The somewhat sketchy records of the inhabitants also were dropped.
Much uncertainty seemed to prevail over the hamlet militia;
wherever possible, it was turned over to Sect or other partisan control—otherwise its continuation depended on the villagers' own
resolve. But the main use of the hamlets during 1964 was to provide a channel for distributing aid and making sure it reached the

---

[a] The Commandant himself was a member of the Junta, but not a few company commanders were changed.
[b] According to members of the territorial administration in Cochinchina.

hands of those the US Government intended it to benefit. Even military advisers were to be seen touring hamlets with their Province Chief counterpart, notebook in hand, listening to 'the people's aspirations', which meant taking orders for hogs, fertilizer, or cement. The civic-action teams of the Vietnamese armed forces were reinforced, and some units seemed to spend more time in offering medical assistance or distributing aid than in chasing the enemy: the Junk Force, whose duty was to help intercept arms shipments from the DRV, did sterling civic action among the fishing villages of Camau, but somehow the Vietcong weapons shipments still slipped through. In the spring of 1964 bombing of hamlets lost to the Vietcong in Cochinchina and in the PMS was intensified, and civic-action teams were sent in with the mopping-up patrols to tend the wounds of the civilians and compensate for damage their own comrades had just inflicted.

Symbiosis of aid

There was, of course, no means of knowing how much of the stepped-up aid was being diverted to the Vietcong. Most of the stores could hardly be reckoned munitions, and there was therefore little disquiet in American circles over this risk: the pressure of generous impulses from Washington was overwhelming ('the money has been voted—it must be spent'), and Saigon planners consoled themselves that every item of what by now was being called euphemistically 'rural reconstruction' carried the US clasped-hands label and the Vietnamese torch emblem to identify the benefactors. But the villagers, whose all-absorbing preoccupation was with their personal safety, knew that American generosity was no measure of their own army's strength, while the share each received only enhanced the exactions of the Communists whom they could see applying the money to the steady expansion of their own army.[122] There can scarcely have been any other source for the cement used to line the scores of miles of tunnels in the Vietcong Iron Triangle stronghold north of Saigon than the uncontrolled distributions of 'self-help' cement in 1964 and 1965.[a]

Symbiosis of conscription

The year 1964 also brought a manpower crisis, felt equally by Government and Vietcong. For both sides it was a question not

---

[a] *The Times*, 18 Jan. 1967. Every hamlet was allocated 20,000 piastres to spend on projects of its choice, but cement came as a supplementary gift *ad lib*.

only of expanding their own ranks but of denying combatants to their adversaries. The strength of the Vietnamese army rose from about 300,000 at the end of 1963 to 565,000 at the end of 1965,[a] that of the Regional Forces (a Communist term borrowed for the Civil Guard since the revolution) from 75,000 to 140,000.[b] At the same time Government estimates attributed an increase in strength to the Vietcong from 30,000[c] to 240,000 over the same period.[d] Although the rival forces were absorbing men faster than youngsters were growing up, even this rate could not have been maintained if the gathering ferocity of the fighting had not interfered with agriculture, making mobilizable refugees out of two more men for every one man killed in battle. The administrative shortcomings of the Vietnamese Government and army were mitigated by closer association between MACV and the Joint General Staff.[e] But the tightening of call-up regulations that resulted (men were drafted to army, regional forces, or local militia according to the number of dependants they had to support), and the participation of American advisers sometimes in the round-ups through the villages, were exploited by the Vietcong, who promised shorter 'engagements' nearer home. When these Communist undertakings were broken by drafting Cochinchinese units to Annam in 1965 to oppose newly-landed US troops, it was reported (by captured or surrendered Vietcong) that it had become the practice to desert back to the village guerrilla bands, whose local commandants welcomed them because otherwise they had to content themselves with low-grade recruits. The necessity of conscripting village manpower was given in Communist propaganda as the excuse for collectivizing land previously made over to tenant cultivators in their own 'land reform'[f]—the Party's new policy at this moment in the DRV;[g] both these Communist measures reflected the fading of Government authority from the hamlets.

Pacification setbacks

This last process gathered momentum all through 1964; Ameri-

[a] MACV communiqué, 1 Jan. 1966.   [b] Private communication.

[c] Gen. Minh to *Newsweek*, 9 Dec. 1963.

[d] Joint General Staff assessment, 1 Jan. 1966. Three months later, the VC Commander, Gen. Thanh, reported his strength as 330,000 (speech quoted on p. 2 above).

[e] Sharing of offices for military planning became embarrassing for MACV advisers during Gen. Khanh's bid for supreme power in August 1964, with pressmen clamouring inside and demonstrators clamouring outside.

[f] *Nhan Dan*, 20 Dec. 1964 (quoted in Pike, p. 293); see also p. 16 above.

[g] Le Duan (1965), pp. 56–66.

can field officers—now constituting a double network of military and civilian advisers rarely under thirty strong in any populous province and generally outnumbering their responsible Vietnamese counterparts—reported over and over again the reluctance of army commanders to persevere in the identification and ambushing of their locally-based adversaries, wasting their time instead on 'operations' known in advance to lead away from the enemy.[a] The certainty that, in the absence of any strategic plan, no effort could be rewarded with lasting success—though any might be with personal disaster—induced in the Vietnamese community an *ohne mich* frame of mind ('la démobilisation des esprits', as some French observers dubbed it) and diversion of attention, especially in Annam, to politics. American effort was therefore directed to putting new heart into the territorial administration by revival, and improvement, of Ngo Dinh Nhu's schemes for buttressing rural administration through the training of 'rural-development' cadres to live temporarily in the new-life hamlets, organize a local militia again, and reopen schools, dispensaries, and other channels for American bounty. But the problem became then how to protect the cadres and control the enlarged scope for corruption (inflated payrolls and unauthorized disposal of stocks were the commonest misdemeanours), and scheme after scheme was frustrated—even one in the provinces surrounding the capital; its name, *Hop Tac*, was meant to signify co-operation between Government and people, but it hardly got beyond co-operation between Government and foreign advisers in the handing out of benefits, and the domination of the people by the Vietcong was little affected.

American intervention

During the first few months of 1965 it appeared to many foreigners that independent South Vietnam was on the verge of collapse. The north–south railway could only operate over three short lengths; roads all over the country were being blown up faster than they could be repaired; refugees crowding into provincial towns, not counting the ones in Saigon, exceeded three-quarters of a million; wholesalers were no longer delivering rice from the Mekong Delta, so that, from being an exporter, South Vietnam now became an importer of rice, with the Vietcong operating 'control measures' against the Government instead of the

---

[a] During 1964 contacts with the VC, even of the most fleeting kind, averaged only one per hundred and fifty 'operations' (R. Thompson, p. 88).

other way round; and the rank and file of the army, though able to inflict quite heavy casualties from time to time on the now much bigger Vietcong formations,[a] felt it was dividing its time between riot control in the towns and being flown by US helicopter from ambush to ambush in the country. The interception at Cape Varella of a sea barge loaded with 100 tons of munitions from the DRV revealed the scale on which the DRV was now able to supply war material to the NFLSV;[b] interrogations of captured prisoners showed that reinforcements in manpower were arriving through Laos on a comparable scale—2,000 a month late in 1964, destined to rise to 7,000 in 1966.[c] Whilst for purposes of public relations it might be asserted by the US Government that this massive intervention by the DRV was responsible for the Vietcong's domination of the countryside, the truth was that cause and effect were the other way round: it was the collapse of Ngo Dinh Nhu's security system, with all its weaknesses, that had put the Vietcong organization into a position to receive, conceal, feed, and deploy professional reinforcements from General Vo Nguyen Giap's army; the task of these reinforcements would be to hasten victory in the field, at some fresh Dien Bien Phu, against an army demoralized in the rear by its commitment to politics in the face of never-ending civil disorders and the economic problems created by its bombing, under provocation, of its own villages.[d] Whether the DRV was justified in believing the failure of South Vietnamese nationhood had advanced so far that the NFLSV could shortly have rolled its log over the brow of the hill will never now be known;[e] the US took no risks, and President Johnson gave the orders for punitive bombing of the DRV (the operation planned early in 1954 to relieve Dien Bien Phu, but never carried out) and for American combat forces to be committed to battle in the South in February 1965.

American aims

The immediate purpose of the combat forces whose introduction gave the world the new word 'escalation' was to hold the line against the recent intensification of the permanent fear of direct, Korea-

[a] Over 5,000 killed in November (MACV communiqué, 1 Jan. 1966)—subject to the general caveat over battle 'statistics'.
[b] *SP*, 21 Feb. 1965.
[c] Figures often named in military briefings but not based on very specific intelligence.
[d] On 14 Feb. 1965, Liberation Radio broadcast a rousing 'Order of the Day' from Nguyen Huu Tho calling for the *coup de grace*.
[e] Doubt whether this was quite so is expressed, for what his opinion may be worth, by Schlesinger (p. 37).

type invasion of central Annam; a foreign expeditionary force should not be liable, to the same extent as the Vietnamese forces, to 'symbiotic' exploitation by the Vietcong. American troops were quickly engaged in head-on assault of brigade-sized formations that included DRV reinforcements and began to inflict on them a rate of casualties even higher than before. The parallel of Korea was further brought out by internationalization of the American force: South Korea itself contributed a tenth of the eventual American strength, Australia a tenth of that, and New Zealand not quite a tenth again of that.[123] The long-range purpose of the intervention of these forces, once they should have blunted the external aggression of the DRV on the chosen battlefields in the sparsely-inhabited PMS and the forests north of Saigon, was 'attrition' of the Communist forces to the point where they would 'fall silent' and melt away, leaving the South Vietnamese people to shape their own destiny free from outside menaces.[a] In support of this, the principal purpose, the Vietnamese army would have a second chance to recover and pacify ground lost to Communist subversion in the estuaries of Annam and the plains of Cochinchina, rather in the manner of the 'Plan Navarre' a dozen years earlier. Viewed in this light, the role of the Junta headed by General Ky[b] amounted to providing the political stability behind which American advisers could reorganize the territorial administration and the various paramilitary forces in a reinvigorated programme of pacification.

Revolutionary development

Inspiration for the new policy came from experience in the Philippines, and the agency chiefly responsible there for planning, the CIA, took the lead in Saigon as well.[c] Pacification donned a new publicity garb, 'revolutionary development'; 'new-life hamlets' kept their name in English but changed it again in Vietnamese, for they were to be called henceforward *ap doi moi*, which meant literally the same thing but enjoyed the patriotic overtone of an all-Vietnamese locution, unlike its sinicizing forerunner.[d] The ingredients of the new policy were not original in themselves, but the emphasis was different, and the whole made up one of those periodi-

[a] Speeches and interviews of Ambassador Cabot Lodge 1965–7.
[b] The nominal head of the Junta was Gen. Nguyen Van Thieu, but Gen. Ky was its dominant personality.
[c] Earlier reticences over this identity appear to have been discarded later on—see, for example, *Newsweek*, 21 Feb. 1966 and *Sunday Times*, 15 Jan. 1967.
[d] Actually, *ap* is a word of Chinese derivation, but it is felt by Vietnamese people to be completely assimilated to their tongue.

cal revitalizations the American machine had always appeared to stand in need of, perhaps because its fuel mixture contained more spontaneous enthusiasm than calculating perseverance. The priority allotted to aid in previous schemes was now taken by representative government, the direct distributions of commodities being concentrated mainly on the colonies of refugees under closer supervision and more accessible than outlying villages. The resumed land reform came next. Third was the programme for the special motivation of the agents who were to carry out revolutionary development. Last, there was the expansion and partial retraining of the National Police mentioned in the previous section.

Local democracy

Representative government was envisaged at three levels: the national (as soon as the constitution drawn up by the Constituent Assembly should go into effect), the provincial, and the village. The village was restored during 1964 to its status as the basic administrative and fiscal unit and was supposed to be managed by a committee made up, as previously, of local notables each with a designated function (spokesman, keeper of records, treasurer, constable) and each in receipt of a nominal indemnification. Where resident villagers could no longer be found to fill these positions because of Vietcong intimidation, rural-reconstruction cadres had been doing the work. Village councils were intended to be a check on the committees, whichever way they were constituted, to forestall both dishonesty at the other villagers' expense and underhand relations with the Vietcong. Similarly at province level, councils elected by electoral colleges composed of the village councillors were intended to keep an eye on corruption within the territorial administration and to 'guide' Province Chiefs in the exercise of such discretions as disposal of captured Vietcong and the allocation of project aid to this or that community.[a] It is to be feared, however, that the powers of these councils were not drawn precisely enough, and consequently councillors were inclined to take opportunities for obstruction more often than opportunities for co-operation.[b] The American faith, which these arrangements honoured, in the power of local self-determination to lead back to the paths of righteousness communities subverted by the Vietcong during the

[a] *Sac-lenh* No. 203 of 31 May 1965 and a communiqué by the Minister of the Interior on 7 June 1966.
[b] Reproach addressed to them by the Minister of the Interior at conference 11–12 Oct. 1965.

tyranny of Ngo Dinh Diem thus received little confirmation in practice.[a]

Masses activation

Teams of 'revolutionary-development' cadres each comprised fifty-nine individuals in two groups: the technical cadres, who were the majority, and the political cadres, who were designated by the Communist term 'masses-activation cadres'.[b] The principal duty of the second category was to gather intelligence and identify Vietcong agents.[c] Nevertheless, the men were not trained as interrogators and were personally controlled by the overloaded Province Chief, whose facilities for collation with intelligence from other sources were usually meagre and his means for taking action, just as in the days of Nho Dinh Diem, almost nil.[124] The cadres underwent three months' training intended to instil in them deep emotional dedication to the anti-Communist struggle and to personal integrity in the handling of public money, so that, in the field, they should become 'the impenetrable shield that protects the people from the terror of the Vietcong and the exploitation of the corrupt'.[d] This monumental task, which had baffled generations of advisers up to now and might be said to beg the whole question of pacification, was to be accomplished by teaching villagers a new, specially made-up national mythology and by interrogating every inhabitant of a hamlet in a private booth every ten days, inviting him to denounce corrupt officials and Vietcong agents.[e] The hope was that action taken on denunciations of the former would so win 'hearts and minds' that denunciations of the latter would flow more readily. Villagers refusing to co-operate might themselves 'be denounced to the Vietcong as government agents or otherwise liquidated'.[f] In the event, the rumour ran that the scheme was penetrated by the Vietcong, and a later report says that it was the cadres who, once adrift in the countryside, were being liquidated at the rate of fifty a month.[g]

Cadres versus government

Both these measures—revival of local councils and introduction

---

[a] This faith of the US Government was reiterated by President Johnson on his way to the Guam Conference (BBC News Bulletin, 10 Mar. 1967).

[b] The *dan van* mentioned on p. 143 above. US publicity on the subject calls them 'People's Action cadres'.

[c] Laid down in *Sac-lenh* No. 2164 of 10 Dec. 1965.

[d] USIS communiqué issued at Saigon (in press kits), May 1966.

[e] As told to *Newsweek*, 21 Feb. 1966.   [f] Ibid. Cf. p. 187 above.

[g] *Sunday Times*, 15 Jan. 1967.

of politicking cadres—partook of the same underlying defect: negatively, they poured more scorn on government in the country-side, where feebleness of administration was already at the bottom of the trouble, and they further fragmented authority in the face of an enemy noted for his ruthless discipline and monolithic policy-making. Yet again, 'contradictions' were being handed to the Com-munists by this fostering of 'the spirit of Tammany', as some of its advocates called it; what was being done was rather like leeching a patient ill with anaemia. The shaky foundations of an international expeditionary force operating against guerrillas, with no better intelligence than could be furnished by a Government network improvised since 1963 on lines such as these, were revealed in the inconclusiveness of one bloody encounter after another on the same battlegrounds, many of them well fought over years before by the *Corps Expéditionnaire*; the world at large learnt something was wrong through repeated 'erroneous' bombings of 'friendly' villages.

Economic crisis

Meanwhile, the mechanism of the CIP was being put to its severest strain so far: the piastres that the Government ought to have been collecting in direct taxes were being converted in the towns into black-market dollars and were being demanded in the country by the Vietcong; more and more piastres were required to pay not only the security forces (700,000 of them) and other public employees (200,000) but, now, contractors to the American forces, besides (if a relatively small item) providing spending money in exchange for the dollars of the half-million foreign troops. These piastres could only be drawn from the public by increased importa-tion of commodities, but, even when licensing delays were over-come, congestion in the ports held up delivery for weeks and months and exposed the cargoes to large-scale pilfering—which meant that the imports were sold below market price, and the Government lost the piastres.[a] Spiralling expenditure on the war made it necessary to license any import that would attract piastres to the Treasury, so that, by early 1967, the situation had been reached where concentration on consumer commodities—the quickest source of piastres under conditions of inflation and lack of confidence about the future—was killing the very industries the CIP, under Ngo Dinh Diem, had been designed to create as a pillar

[a] The *NYT* alleged (13 Nov. 1966) that the proportion going astray might be as much as 40 per cent.

for South Vietnam's economic independence: 6 of the 10 new mills had to close because they already held enough stocks to last 3–5 years and could not sell them in competition with the flood of imports.[a] Rice production fell by a fifth between 1963 and 1966–7, whilst Vietcong control of what was produced—control aimed both at feeding their own huge army, including the troops from the North, and at providing them with revenue—swung South Vietnam's balance from exports of 322,570 tons in Diem's last year to imports of 800,000 ordered for 1967. There was in this a paradoxical advantage for the Government, however, in that imported rice could now be sold for scarce piastres in competition with the Vietcong's local supplies and paid for in dollars, of which American aid (under Public Law 480) furnished a readier source. Rubber exports fell from 78,000 tons in 1960 to 46,440 in 1966.[b] The piastre had to be devalued under the multiple strains upon it, by two stages, to 118 to the dollar, although it did remain stable thereafter. Warlike stores found their way direct to the Vietcong at certain provincial ports. Theft, black marketing, and the traffic in foreign exchange reminded many urban Vietnamese of conditions a dozen years before, and they wondered whether the affair might end the same way.

Vietcong reaction

The Communist reaction to American participation in the fighting was the opposite of what had been hoped for: far from melting away, the Liberation Front transferred battalions from Cochinchina to Annam, and the drafting of units of the People's Army from the North gathered momentum; a former DRV organizer of rural co-operatives on the staff of the First Secretary of the Workers' Party, General Nguyen Chi Thanh,[c] made his appearance as Commander-in-Chief of the combined Communist forces.[125] The main, if temporary, strategic success of this reinforcement was that it preserved the symbiotic balance and neutralized, yet again, the American design to secure an advantage. Not only the drain to Vietcong units of warlike stores, which it had been hoped foreign forces could stop, but the capacity of the Communist organization to supply this army with its basic wants, however simple by comparison with the logistics of its adversaries, was a measure of the Party's control over an alarmingly wide area of the country. The explanation was that the Party, amid all the signs (exultantly high-

[a] Ton-That-Thien (1967).   [b] Ibid.   [c] Le Duan, p. 126.

lighted by Western commentators) of progress from guerrilla to mobile warfare—even from mobile to positional warfare—had never lost sight of its real target (domination of 'the broad mass of the people', 'annihilation of the puppet army', 'disintegration of the puppet administration')[a] and, unlike the foreigners, considered the big battles a diversion from the main struggle, not its centre-piece.[b] It followed that whatever ratio of casualties might be in-flicted by the Government and its allies on either 'main' or guer-rilla forces under General Thanh, there would still be no 'attrition': 'South Vietnam's resources in manpower and *matériel* lie in the North', wrote Party Secretary Le Duan to General Thanh from Hanoi, 'and can never be exhausted because we have on our side the Socialist Bloc and the full potential of the Chinese people.'[c] Local defeats registered against these forces—defeats because the Communists always ran away in the end, if only to reappear some-where else—were, again in Le Duan's words, 'like stabbing at water because, when the sword has been withdrawn, the water re-mains unchanged';[d] they could not affect the issue of ultimate vic-tory or defeat unless they contributed, by isolating the Vietcong from 'the broad masses', to restoration of government, elimination of revolutionary cells, and curbing of factionalism. Unhappily this was not the case, and, whereas the Communists regarded the war as incidental to the revolution, the Government and the Americans continued, as they had done since 1960, to conceive their arrange-ments for pacification and preparations for a 'return to democracy' as ancillary to the needs of their war machine: in June 1967 General W. C. Westmoreland took command of all American operations in Vietnam, including all aid programmes, the better to integrate them with the fighting. There was virtual deadlock while each side waited for the other's civilian morale at home to crack.

4. PROBLEMS AND DILEMMAS OF FUTURE PEACEMAKING

Even Germany's Thirty Years' War, to which the war in Viet-nam bears notable resemblances, came to an end at last; presum-ably the Vietnamese conflict will also. But as these pages are writ-

---

[a] Top-secret letter dated Mar. 1966 on proceedings at the 12th Congress of the VWP Central Committee at Hanoi; it was captured by US forces in the Tay Ninh GHQ on 21 Jan. 1967, released by USIS, Saigon, 14 Mar. 1967, pp. 12–13.
[b] In the speech quoted on p. 2 above, Gen. Thanh rejected the doctrine of 'phases' in revolutionary warfare (pp. 4 & 6).
[c] Le Duan, p. 18.   [d] Ibid. p. 16.

ten, it is impossible to predict by what road peace will arrive; the US Government is continually under pressure from many quarters to negotiate and commit South Vietnam to some, or indeed any, settlement, much as France committed the State of Viet-Nam in 1954; however, North Vietnam refuses to negotiate on her side, and her Generals tell their own forces that even when at last the time is judged to be ripe, she will still continue to fight while negotiating, as happened in Korea:

Fighting while negotiating is aimed at opening another front, at making the puppet army more disintegrated, at stimulating and developing the enemy's contradictions and thereby depriving him of propaganda weapons [that is to say, so that he can no longer point to Communist intransigence as the obstacle to peace], isolating him further, and making those who misunderstood the Americans see clearly their nature.[a]

As if this cynical approach to the process of negotiating a peace were not disheartening enough, the guerrillas are told that the agreement, once negotiated, might not be allowed to last any longer than that of 1954 if under it the Communist demands were not satisfied in full: 'Whether or not war will resume after the conclusion of agreements depends on the balance of forces; if we are capable of dominating the adversary, war will not break out again, and the converse also holds true.'[b] With one side unwilling to honour a settlement it has agreed to if, by it, it gains less than total cession of the South to the North, immediately or by stages, peace will not necessarily follow even if agreement is reached, and true reconciliation seems far off indeed.

It is not proposed here to speculate on the military and diplomatic possibilities that could, in present or changed circumstances, lead to a settlement in Vietnam, still less to suggest how the parties to the conflict might be constrained to honour it. The purpose of this book has been to trace the factors that have brought the country to its unhappy condition. Although Professor Schlesinger has warned us recently, in the context of Vietnam, how inscrutable is history and how elusive its lessons,[c] it may still be useful to end by pointing out some of the characteristics of the national life of Vietnam in the past that can, with reasonable certainty, be expected to continue into the future and influence the working of any fresh

[a] Address by Gen. Nguyen Van Vinh of the People's Army at the PRP Congress in Mar. 1966 'somewhere in South Vietnam' at which Gen. Thanh spoke; notes captured by US forces at the same time in Feb. 1967 (USIS communiqué, Saigon, 30 Mar. 1967), p. 13.
[b] Gen. Nguyen Van Vinh (ibid.).   [c] Schlesinger, pp. 84–101.

peace settlement—more especially the characteristics about which there has been, outside Vietnam, general misapprehension or misrepresentation. Obviously it is at the very least debatable whether domestic harmony can be brought to any country by foreign powers, and its preservation must, short of some form of colonialism, depend in the last resort on the willingness of private and sectional interests inside the country to sink their differences and collaborate in a common interest.

One might expect a common interest to be found in nationalism; scores of political writers in recent decades have discovered in nationalism the dominating factor shaping the history of all Asia in the twentieth century, and there has been no lack of talk about nationalism in Vietnam. Nationalism has been the battle-cry of Sect and party, of the monarchy and the army, of Ngo Dinh Diem and of Ho Chi Minh (though the latter at one time was a class-struggle internationalist), of Buddhists and of Catholics. Unhappily, it has not provided a common focus for national endeavour: the conclusion to be drawn from this study of Vietnamese history is that nationalism has been entirely negative and an excuse for sectarian bids for power. Vietnamese leaders of all persuasions invite foreigners to sympathize with their country as the victim all through its history of one predatory invasion after another, fought off sooner or later by the valiant nationalism of the Vietnamese people. The historical facts hardly bear out this interpretation, valid at best for the Mongol invasion; Chinese interventions all occurred at the request of Vietnamese monarchs against rebellious factions and were undertaken in the hope of bringing about what the Chinese Emperors sincerely believed was a righteous settlement. The intentions of Pigneau de Behaine and of Napoleon III were of the same kind, and, although predatory private interests quickly asserted themselves under the protection of the tricolor, France never quite lost sight of her mission to modernize and to maintain law and order. America has not introduced a dollar or a man to Vietnam unless invited to, and the same is true of the foreign backers of the DRV.[a] It is no stain on the motives of any of these powers to say that they would not have intervened in what they regarded as a good cause if to do so had gone against their own interests: all have been prodigal of both men and treasure on their

[a] Premier Chou Ên-lai of China was reported as telling Mr Simon Malley in Mar. 1967 that if the DRV looked like concluding a 'sell-out' peace with the US, China might intervene (*NYHT*, 16 May 1967); but if that did happen, it would be a completely new departure in Chinese national policy.

protégés' behalf, and their gains have not been tangible ones. If predatory invasions feature in Vietnam's history, she has been more sinning than sinned against, and it is her very nationalists who have been the ones to seek moral support abroad, as well as material, to commend them in the eyes of their own people.

As with nationalism, so with political and religious ideologies: Marxism-Leninism, Personalism, Catholicism, Buddhism, Cao Dai—these have all served as justificatory systems for groups of leaders seeking power, and their adepts have either sought their protection in a clique-ridden society or have bowed to it when it was thrust upon them, with or without pretension to supernatural advantage as well. Dialectical materialism and the Labour theory of value are unheard of in Vietnam, while the philosophical and economic canvas of homegrown Personalism remained almost blank; Cao Dai is made up by its leaders as they go along, and the numerous temple cults that have emerged in certain towns of Annam and in Saigon since the overthrow of Ngo Dinh Diem have little to do with religious faith; they are a product of the free-for-all atmosphere of politics, offering their members organization and solidarity in response to the freemasonry of longer-established groups and, in the important case of the Tran Hung Dao Sect for example, a nucleus to uphold Tonkinese interests in the midst of the Cochinchinese. Some of these groups may have gained adherents from the dissolution of the organizations centred on Personalism; all have been characterized by hostility to Buddhist, Catholic, Dai Viet, and VNQDD power groups; and, it is specially significant to notice, none have turned to the Vietcong for satisfaction of their needs.

Factionalism, as it has been called all through this book, is the most constant characteristic of Vietnamese society; on one hand it is the source of revolutionary movements to upset stable government—not excluding, in the circumstances we have described, the originally Russian-inspired Communist movement—and on the other hand is a reaction to the inadequacies of government. Vietnamese anarchy has preserved, through all the vicissitudes of colonial rule, wartime occupation, independence and civil war, a kind of steady state. This anarchy may be no worse in reality than is to be found in certain other, more truly, underdeveloped countries; the difference is, of course, that their anarchy has not been exploited by a Marxist-Leninist rebellion. The dangers of anarchy in this situation, and its effect on national development and social progress, is generally appreciated by foreigners; the mistake has been made of seeking a cure primarily in political instead of administrative terms. The solution to the problems of ordinary people in Vietnam, which they seek through factionalism, does not lie in self-determination at the level of local government, for that on the contrary has been the initial cause of their trouble. The first duty of government is the protection of the citizen's life and property, and it is at that point that the Government has failed under each successive regime; the real fault of Ngo Dinh Diem was not that he was tyrannical but that he did not know how to administer. The misjudgement of the US was to decide that Diem's greatest needs were money and a big army, when what he really required was an efficient civil service; the failure of the *agroville* experiment was due in the main to administrative incompetence, only rectified to a very limited extent in the strategic hamlets; the colossal dishonesty rampant since Diem's death and the success of Vietcong symbiotic insurgency are a product of administrative inefficiency. Diem believed the problem could not be solved—he understood it imperfectly himself—and so, like the metaphorical grass of China, he bent before the east wind and tried to govern by manipulating factionalism and imitating the Communists, which compounded the disaster.

New national leaders in South Vietnam find their problems more difficult today than in 1954, as they were then than in 1945, but hardly changed in kind. They are, first, to elaborate a constitution that concedes lawmaking to representative government but entrusts its execution to a strong Judiciary and administration not swayed by fear or favour; it remains to be seen whether the decentralized 1967 constitution will work in this manner in practice.[126] How to police the country honestly and effectively, after all it has gone through in the last few years, is an enigma to tax nerves of iron. Closely entangled with these problems is that of village government—the permanent challenge to Vietnamese nationhood; this is linked in turn with the abiding problems of human geography—both the wide separation of Annamites from Cochinchinese in space and custom and the many practical obstacles to assimilation of the racial minorities, so long shrugged off in Saigon by blaming the country's ethnology on to French colonialism. Propaganda about land reform still holds the stage where radical rationalization of tenure and a scientifically-based agricultural policy have been required for forty years. All these problems have a fundamental bearing on the great issues of national solidarity and internal peace. But all of them also are practical problems calling for administrative and technical solutions applied over a long period of time: their intractability has been persistently underestimated by American helpers, analysing Vietnamese problems in ideological terms. The true lesson of the Diem–Nhu regime must surely be less the personal wickedness of the two brothers as politicians than the general futility of stabbing at major problems one by one from a viewpoint bounded by the horizon of some immediate crisis.

Few foreign observers believe the South Vietnamese can put their house in order by their own unaided efforts; the devastation of the war is reason enough for the continuation of foreign aid, and the cost sooner or later of demobilization is another. But the physical devastation in the country is much less than the moral, and the danger of foreign aid given for physical reparation has been in the past—at least since the days of Emperor Minh Mang—that it adds to the moral damage. The positive element in the unpopularity of Ngo Dinh Diem as Prime Minister in 1955 in Cochinchina was certainly his having stifled the private profits made down to that time from foreign aid; the joy in the same quarters at his overthrow proceeded, if we may judge by subsequent developments in Saigon, from the prospect that more hay could be made now that the sun was shining again. There have, unfortunately, been a large number of individuals in Vietnam with a vested interest in the continuation of the conflict that earned the foreign aid—many of them in humble walks of life; that a quota of the aid should be diverted to the hands of their antagonists was not without its advantages from their point of view. None the less, if this attitude began to be penalized on all sides—but it would have to be genuinely on all sides—, these same citizens would at once become conscientious collaborators with the authorities again. There is no place in Vietnamese society for the lone idealist: being no more honest than the next man and allying oneself from moment to moment to the party in any conflict that looks like winning is not only a human code of behaviour, it is the only practical one in Vietnam today; for a foreigner to ignore these factors and insist on analysing Vietnamese problems in idealistic or ideological terms is paradoxically to exhibit lack of true sympathy.

The great dilemma facing peacekeepers in Vietnam in the future, therefore, will be how to make the country economically viable without priming the spiral of disorder once again. Vietnam counts among her own intellectuals an abundance of technical talents, thanks to her Chinese and her French traditions; but so far she has produced relatively few political leaders and no ideas on government and still depends for ideas even more than for money—as was shown in the DRV's doctrinaire land reform—on foreign countries, Communist or Western. The profits of foreign aid have somehow to be made to accrue on a national, not a private, plane—and in the future, when the work has been done, peace restored and the aid tapered off, not here and now, as virtually a bribe for collaboration, while the conflict is still going on. But if foreign aid and protection are to end in a measurable space of time, what confidence can the common people repose in them as a protection against trouble-makers on their doorstep who for sure will never go away?

To break out from this vicious spiral, prophesied so long ago in the verse with which this book began, foreign helpers may have paradoxically to jettison some of the political principles which are the very reason why they want to help. This is no greater paradox, however, than that of the recipient Vietnamese themselves who revere their sovereign nationhood in the symbol of a white elephant supporting an alms bowl and a magic jewel to grant their private wishes.

SUPPLEMENTARY NOTES

[1] p. 26. *Chinese settlement.* It is in Cochinchina that the bulk of the Chinese community has settled; during the last days of French rule, there were fewer than 20,000 Chinese in Tonkin and a negligible number in Annam. Similarly, in the rest of Indochina, there are far more Chinese in more southerly Cambodia than in Laos, which has a common frontier with China. Chinese migration, even to Tonkin, has rarely been overland, for that path was until the development of railways interrupted by brigands and unfriendly aborigines. Instead movement has been by sea, from Canton or the ports of Fukien, as part of the general drift of the coastal Chinese of humble class to the *Nanyang* or 'South Seas'—whence the contemporary Vietnamese reference to China and the Chinese people disparagingly as *Nuoc Tau* and *nguoi Tau* or plain *Tau* ('Boatland' and 'Boatfolk'), as for instance throughout Dr Tran Trong Kim's history (1964).

[2] p. 29. *Aboriginal ethnography.* The linguistic division between Malay-speaking peoples of Indochina and the Mon–Khmer does not extend to other cultural elements: the essentials of the social organization in autonomous villages, like their agricultural practices, tools, and long houses, cannot easily be differentiated, and even then not on linguistic lines. It is tempting to look on the Malay-speakers (Radé, Jarai, Koho) as island folk pressing northwards from the Eastern Archipelago, and the Khmer-speakers (Mnong, Sedang, Halang, Bahnar) as a continental people pressing southwards from the mainland of Asia. But they are so similar in appearance and way of life that it must be concluded they are essentially of a single race, although the language of the different groups has been affected by domination of the great states of the plains in the days before the coming of the Vietnamese.

[3] p. 31. *Names of medieval states.* No native name has come down to us for any of the medieval states of Indochina; Vietnam is hardly an exception, and the hesitation over its Chinese names (note 15 below) supports the view that these states did not have indigenous names. *Angkor* is a corruption of Sanskrit *nagara* (government); *Chanla*, known only from Chinese, is explained as Khmer *Cham rap* or 'Chams defeated', as modern *Siem Reap* near Angkor means 'Siamese defeated' (Pelliot, 1951, p. 81). *Funan* is guessed to be a Chinese rendering of the Khmer word *phnom* ('hill'); around 500 AD, both the Khmer and the Chinese words will have been pronounced something like *bhunam*. *Funan* is thus not a name either but a reference to the Indian idea of the realm radiating from a royal hill, token of Kailasa or the Himalaya, and pretending to universality without boundaries and therefore

without a name. Vietnamese statehood was influenced by these Indian ideas as well as by Chinese.

⁴ p. 32. *Chinese residing at Angkor.* One French scholar has pointed out that the final stages of the vast bas-relief frieze inside Angkor Wat bear signs of having been executed by Chinese craftsmen (Goloubew, 1925, p. 519). Chou Ta-kuan, a visitor who spent a year at Angkor in 1296, describes the homely practice of the Chinese male community making the Siem Reap river the object of their evening's walk in order to watch the Khmer girls unashamedly bathing in the nude; he mentions incidentally one Chinese resident having lived there for thirty-five years (Pelliot, 1951, p. 33).

⁵ p. 35. *Cham place-names in Annam.* The principal coast towns of Annam all had euphonious Indian names in Cham epigraphy: Tour Cham was Panduranga, Nha Trang was Kauthara, Tuy Hoa was Vira-pura, Qui Nhon was Srivinaya. There must also have existed versions of the Indian names in the mainly monosyllabic Cham language, but only *Pan Rang* (Phan Rang of the Vietnamese) has survived in modern Cham usage.

⁶ p. 36. *Cham war fleets.* Both Chams and Khmers possessed equally fleets and armies, the latter running to brigades of elephants as well as of horse-drawn chariots (Coedes, 1948, *passim*). Bas-reliefs at Angkor commemorate both the land battles and the 'sea' battles on the Great Lake, whither the Chams must have sailed down their own coastline and up the Mekong. Cham art was less developed than Khmer art and its representations less elaborate.

⁷ p. 40. *Status of the Dinh.* Some writers question whether the Dinh represent more than the assumption, by themselves, of the function of Vietnamese Governors in place of Chinese Governors, still considering themselves to be administrators of Tonkin in the name of the Son of Heaven (e.g. Buttinger, 1958, p. 140, and Le-thanh-Khoi, 1955, p. 145).

⁸ p. 41. *Tran Hung Dao as a national hero.* The final victory of Tran Hung Dao was in the David–Goliath tactical tradition of Vietnamese resistance to superior foreign forces; but the modern interpretation of it as a national uprising against the Chinese has to be set against the stronger likelihood that the Vietnamese at this time thought of themselves as making common cause with the Chinese against the same barbarian invader. The Tran family was a strongly sinicizing influence in Vietnam and would have considered itself more Chinese than the Mongols usurping the Government in China. The cult of Tran Hung Dao has become a shamanistic one and a powerful focus for Tonkinese regionalism.

⁹ p. 42. *Le Loi's triumph.* Although luck played some part in the victory of Le Loi, in the main it was the reward for perseverance and skilled deployment of his guerrilla force; the Chinese commander, Ch'ên

Hsia (the same surname as Tran), commanded throughout the Ming occupation and in defeat committed suicide from shame. When the war was over, possessing no royal temple to decorate with a victory frieze like his contemporaries at Angkor, Le Loi had a triumphant proclamation penned by his Confucian Chief Minister, Nguyen Trai; he gave it the title 'The Daunting of the Men of Wu' (a disparaging reference to the site of the Ming capital at Nanking, as if they were not authentic Chinese). After reproaching the invaders for their gratuitous design to tame Tonkin—gratuitous because, 'although our realm has had its strong times and its weak', it had never strayed from the paths of Confucian orthodoxy—the proclamation summarizes the people's griefs at the hands of the Ming; chief among these griefs was exploitation of the country's mineral resources—a surprising modern touch. Evidently the Ming nevertheless had numerous supporters among the Vietnamese 'whom they had bought', and it was on these 'bandit cliques' that Le Loi and his guerrillas first turned their wrath, in order to isolate the occupying forces. Once the Chinese had been cut off from their supplies, the proclamation goes on, their main forces were tackled, and such fights were fought that 'the corpses tumbling down the slopes of Lang Son choked all the torrent and the gorge below, while the blood from battles in the plains so ruddied the waters of the Xuong that wind and cloud took on its hue, and the sun and moon in sorrow ceased to shine'. Now that the Men of Wu are dead or fled, honour is due to 'the whole army' and rest to the people mobilized to support them. 'When incense burns anew for spirits of hearth and field, when all traces of the occupation have been wiped from the landscape, then Heaven and Earth will be at one again and sun and moon break through the clouds.' (Taken from the Chinese text as given by Tran-trong-Kim, 1964, pp. 224–8.) In the event, the peace lasted just under two years before the next rebellion gave substance to a laconic comment on these events by the official historians of China: 'The Tonkinese are an incurably turbulent lot' ('*Chiao-jênku hao luan*'— *Ming Shih*, quoted by Li Chêng-fu, 1945, p. 148).

[10] p. 42. *Early Nguyen designs on the monarchy*. This was not because the ambition had not been entertained. According to Gaspardone (1950, p. 21), *chua* Hien-Ton sent a tribute mission of his own to Canton in 1702, entrusted to two Chinese retainers, one of whom was a Buddhist bonze. These envoys sought investiture of the *chua* as sovereign over Annam, and presumably over the newly-annexed portions of Cochinchina in process of settlement with Overseas Chinese help. The request must have been turned down or ignored—it may never have reached Peking.

[11] p. 46. *Intellectual Buddhism*. This is not to depreciate the speculative achievements of Buddhism in China. During the Sung dynasty especially, but also at most other periods, Buddhism has attracted some

of the finest intellects, including many officials and princes who reckoned themselves good Confucians at the same time. Buddhist thought has influenced the conduct of government in China at many periods, and its observances have crept into court life during certain reigns at the expense of the Confucian 'rites'. Yet Chinese Buddhism has never quite emancipated itself from what might be called barbarian status. In Vietnam poverty of intellectual tradition has prevented in equal measure any contribution to Buddhist or Confucian philosophy; on the whole, the periods when the Vietnamese court was trying to observe a Confucian rule have been shorter than when Buddhism was in the ascendant, as it was during most of the two centuries, after 1550, when the Le 'Emperors' reigned but did not rule.

[12] p. 50. *Triad Society*. So called by Europeans because it revered the triad of Heaven, Earth, and Man; in Chinese and Vietnamese it is usually just 'Heaven and Earth Society', *T'ien-ti Hui/Dien-dia Hoi*; these words contain a pun, for with other characters substituted the name becomes 'Add-Comrades Society', suggesting recruitment by 'bead-stringing' (see p. 143). Many other names have been current in China at various times, mainly to facilitate concealment. Secret societies were a feature of Chinese life at least 1,500 years ago, and many of them are known to have taken a decisive hand in the rise and fall of dynasties; but none probably has been so persistent at the Triad, still an active force among the Overseas Chinese and until recent years among the Vietnamese of Saigon as well.

[13] p. 54. *Quang Trung as a national hero*. It is less for his intentions of reform that Quang Trung is admired by his fellow countrymen today than for having outwitted the Chinese, first by his tactics in dealing with Sun Shih-i, and immediately afterwards in his relations with Ch'ien Lung himself. Following his investiture at Hanoi, he asked for and obtained an invitation to the latter's 80th birthday celebrations at Jehol in 1790; in reality, however, he sent an understudy called Pham Cong Tri, whom, on the latter's return from carrying off the part successfully, he put to death, along with all the retinue, lest they be tempted to boast and the truth reach Ch'ien Lung's ears and call down another punitive expedition (John Barrow, in Devéria, 1880, p. 40 n. 1, and Tran-trong-Kim, p. 376).

[14] p. 54. *Confucianism and the national history*. A sidelight on the Confucian attitude of the Nguyen is cast by the commissioning of a national history by the fourth Emperor, Tu Duc. The great mandarin Phan Thanh Gian (of Minh Huong extraction) was in charge, and his terms of reference were based on the principles of historiography enunciated in China by Ssu-ma Kuang in the eleventh century; these included a perfect Chinese style and the portrayal of all unsuccessful rebels as scoundrels, all successful ones as being virtuous and in the line of true legitimacy leading to the reigning dynasty. Even the

Trung Sisters, so long legendary heroines of the Vietnamese, are put in a poor light in this work because they were rebels against the constituted authority of China (Durand, 1950, p. 33; *Kham-dinh Viet-su* 1859/1960, pp. 32–40 & 51).

[15] p. 55. *Names for Vietnam.* The Vietnamese monarchs never stuck to one name for their realm for very long at a time. *An-nam/An-nan* was used first by the Chinese of the T'ang dynasty for Tonkin, in place of earlier *Chiao Chih/Giao Chi.* The Dinh rulers used *Ta Ch'ü Yüeh/Dai Co Viet.* The shorter *Ta Yüeh/Dai Viet* began with the Ly, was replaced under the Ho by *Ta Wu/Dai Ngu,* under the Chinese interregnum by *Annam* again, but was restored by the Le; under the overlords it fell practically into disuse, for in their relations with the monarchs the Chinese continued to refer to *Annam.* Gia Long, according to Vietnamese authorities, would have liked to revive the very ancient *Nan Yüeh/Nam Viet,* but the Chinese objected to its irredentist overtones, and *Yüeh Nan/Viet Nam* was a compromise. Minh Mang substituted *Ta Nan/Dai Nam* on his succession, and that lasted until the French occupation, when once again the unitary name fell into disuse as it had under the *chuas.*

[16] p. 62. *Succession to Gia Long.* Lemonnier de la Bissachère reported (1812, ii. 198) that the succession to Gia Long was already a delicate issue in 1807. The choice lay between his fourth son, by a concubine (the future Minh Mang), and the eldest bastard of his only son by the Empress, Pigneau de Behaine's protégé Prince Canh (see p. 79). The Empress favoured the latter, and it was from him that Prince Cuong De was descended who became the nominee for the throne of the Vietnamese émigrés in Japan after 1900 (p. 124).

[17] p. 65. *Sino-Vietnamese vocabulary.* There are some 50,000 character-words in Chinese, comprising the 44,000 in the K'ang Hsi Dictionary of 1716, less about 4,000 totally obsolete but plus close on 10,000 made up in the modern period. The standard Vietnamese dictionary of Father Gouin (1959) gives, besides a selection of 8,775 Chinese characters in frequent use in Vietnamese, some 14,364 words not of Chinese derivation.

[18] p. 67. *Quoc Ngu as official language.* In the colonial period the official language was French, but the vernacular language could not be ignored in official business, especially as the native administrations of Annam and Tonkin, nominally undisturbed by the French presence, used Chinese for their internal correspondence in the early days. The vernacular was the only practical medium for popular education, once that came into fashion. The romanized script was made obligatory first in correspondence with the colonial authorities of Cochinchina in 1882; although literacy in it was made a necessary qualification for appointment under French auspices to positions of village notable in Cochinchina, *quoc ngu* made its way much more

slowly in the two Protectorates (Le-ngoc-Tru, 1961, p. 132). It was the practical requirements of printing (notably of newspapers), of the telegraph and of the typewriter more than French encouragement to sever the links with China that secured its adoption all over the country by the time of the First World War. Knowledge of Chinese continued to be insisted on by the French, however, as one of the qualifications for appointment in the mandarinate until 1940.

[19] p. 67. *Transliteration of Buddhist terms.* When Buddhism first came to the Far East 1,500 years ago, the Khmer, Cham, and other Indo-chinese languages tried to adjust their monosyllabic grammar to the polysyllabic vocabulary of Sanskrit–Pali, just as their rulers had adopted the polysyllabic names of Hindu kings; it is significant that there resulted no native development of the intellectual heritage of Buddhism. China, and later Japan, made the opposite choice and were enabled to make their own outstanding contributions to Budd-hist thought. As an example of the ingenuity employed by the Chinese literati of those days, we may take a word known to the West in its Japanese form, *Zen.* The original Sanskrit word that had to be con-veyed was *dhyana*, and it meant sitting with one's legs crossed and meditating according to special rules. The Chinese already possessed a word *dhan*, one of whose meanings was suggestive of something vaguely similar, namely the abdication of a prince from public affairs. This character (pronounced *zen* in modern Japanese, *ch'an* in modern Chinese, *thien* in modern Vietnamese) was borrowed by the Chinese lexicographers of the sixth century for the Buddhist idea and so absorbed into the semantics and phonology of the language that devotees do not feel it to be foreign.

[20] p. 68. *Vietnamese dialects.* Vietnamese also shows differences of dialect between Tonkin, Annam, and Cochinchina; considering the dis-tances involved, these are minor, but they have been developing only for 500 years. Whereas Tonkinese leans more towards Chinese in its vocabulary, it is Cochinchinese which preserves the most characteris-tics of archaic Chinese pronunciation.

[21] p. 68. *Frequency of surnames.* An inquiry was made in 1931 (Gourou, 1932) into the frequency of family names in Bac Ninh province, thought to be the homeland of the Vietnamese in Tonkin. Among a total population of 450,000 living in 76,300 households, it was found that 93 names were in use; 12 of them accounted for 85 per cent of the families and the single name *Nguyen* for no fewer than 54 per cent, leaving 31 per cent for the other 11 and 15 per cent for all other sur-names. The incidence of *Nguyen* in Tonkin as a whole, however, was thought on other evidence to be only 37 per cent.

[22] p. 73. *Early Japanese in Indochina.* Japanese settlers, if only in small numbers, were already to be found at this period to the west of Viet-nam, in Cambodia and Siam. In those countries also they seem to

have acted as intermediaries between Portuguese and Spanish missionaries and the native inhabitants (Groslier, 1958, pp. 27–62). Some of the Japanese émigrés were already Christians (Marucci, 1651, p. 95) and no doubt spoke Portuguese themselves.

[23] p. 77. *Rites Controversy*. This was the main issue in the so-called Rites Controversy (the other being the Chinese, and therefore Vietnamese, translation for *God*); it became the bone of contention which the other Orders picked on as the vehicle for their long and rancorous struggle against the Jesuits. Matteo Ricci and his followers in China feared they had little prospect of ultimate success in that country if they clashed with Chinese susceptibilities over ancestor worship and its attendant ceremonies. They therefore made up their minds to tolerate continued practice of the rites by converts after baptism, arguing that they were secular observances, not in conflict with any sacrament. The rest of the Church, including the Société des Missions Étrangères, took the opposite view, that the Confucian rites were a pagan idolatry and must be banned to those who had received baptism. As if in substantiation of Ricci's fears, it was the Pope's ultimate ruling against tolerance of the Rites, and the dispatch of a French bishop, Mgr de Tournon, to China to make it known, which was construed by the Emperor K'ang Hsi as interference in the spiritual affairs of China and led him in 1717 to declare the practice of Christianity unlawful— which it remained until the peace treaties following the second China War of 1858. In Vietnam the Jesuits tolerated the Rites, while the French Fathers forbade them, and the issue, though less deeply felt, especially among peasant communities where Confucian practices were somewhat attenuated, was an irritant and a ready excuse to be rid of foreigners unwanted for other reasons.

[24] p. 77. *Supplies of artillery through Missions*. A fifteenth-century Papal prohibition on the sale of arms to non-believers had become a dead letter in Asia (Boxer, 1966, p. 161), and the head of the mission in China, Belgian Fr Verbiest, himself added the founding of guns to his many other talents and wrote a treatise on the subject in Chinese (Bosmans, *Ferdinand Verbiest*, quoted in Couling, 1917, p. 588).

[25] p. 78. *Native clergy*. Hereby hangs another controversy within the Church. The religious Orders in the missionary field in Asia, including the Jesuits, reserved ordination for native seminarists who were ready also to take the vows of the Orders and accept the same discipline as themselves in all its particulars. The French Fathers, on the other hand, trained secular native priests, although their efforts to found an independent Vietnamese hierarchy were thwarted at Rome; the first native bishop was not consecrated until 1933.

[26] p. 79. *Warren Hastings and Vietnam*. It was not entirely original, however, but something that was in the air at the time. Late in 1777 two Vietnamese mandarins took passage at Tourane in an East Indiaman

bound for Saigon. But the ship could not sail into the Donnai against the wind and carried the two passengers to Calcutta. There they were kindly cared for by Warren Hastings and sent back to Vietnam under Chapman (p. 52 above), who was to assess prospects of securing commercial advantages for the Company in exchange for a helping hand to Nguyen Anh. The French at Chandernagore got wind of this, and Pigneau de Behaine's idea occurred to them already at that time, although they did not act on it (Lamb, 1961, pp. 13–24).

[27] p. 79. *Pigneau and Conway*. The French Commander-in-Chief who finally stifled the Bishop's scheme for official French aid to the Prince of Vietnam was the same Comte de Conway, an Irishman, who had served in America beside Lafayette as a private volunteer officer on George Washington's staff. Perhaps knowledge of his personal enemy's background gave Pigneau the idea for his alternative plan.

[28] p. 83. *The Canton trade*. The Manchu system of licensing trade through monopolies granted at Canton began in 1702 and was felt with full effect after 1757, when Ch'ien Lung banned all foreign intercourse at other Chinese ports absolutely (Morse, 1913–19, i. 63–67). Tourane had a long history as entrepot for trade between Japan and South China, direct intercourse having been stopped by the Ming.

[29] p. 86. *Lao-Siamese frontier*. Franco-Siamese treaty of 3 Oct. 1893. Lao territory to the west of the Mekong, however, passed under Siamese protection for the first time by virtue of this treaty, so that, from the point of view of Laos, French protection lost her as much as it gained.

[30] p. 88. *Cambodian frontier*. The frontier between Cochinchina and Cambodia defies delineation on an ethnic basis; laid down first in 1873 for the mainland and in 1874 for the islands in the Gulf of Siam, it had to be reaffirmed repeatedly until actually demarcated in 1936. Even this demarcation proved impermanent, and there have been many mutual accusations of frontier violations in the fighting since 1960. The frontier between Cambodia and Annam was not fixed until 1911, when Stung Treng and Ratanakiri provinces were recognized by France as under Cambodian sovereignty (Le-thanh-Khoi, 1955, p. 405); the line passes through the tribal lands of the Jarai, favouring irredentist claims as well as the infiltration of subversive elements on terms with the tribesmen.

[31] p. 89. *France and the Cambodian succession*. For example, Admiral Decoux's nomination to the throne in 1941 of Prince Norodom Sihanouk, the present Head of State in Cambodia, in preference to Prince Monireth chosen by the national leaders themselves, and the Admiral's insensitively presumptuous account of how he crowned him (Decoux, 1945, p. 287).

[32] p. 89. *The Emperor's Sovereignty*. Franco-Annamite Conventions of 6 Nov. 1925, 10 Sept. 1932, and 11 Oct. 1932. These conventions, imposed unilaterally when French colonial power was at its height,

appear to conflict with art. 16 of the original treaty of 6 June 1884: 'Sa Majesté le Roi d'Annam continuera comme par le passé à diriger l'Administration intérieure de ses États'.

[33] p. 91. *Corvée*. An important French reform was the abolition of the *grande corvée* (unregulated pressganging for major public works) in Cochinchina in 1881 and the commuting of the *petite corvée* (five days' labour a year on village maintenance) for a small tax payment to the budget of the *xa*, which then hired labour instead—the system known as *prestation* and in operation in France. The reform was delayed in Tonkin and Annam, however: reduction to 48 days a year (Tonkin 1886, Annam 1889) and, after intermediate reductions, total absorption as a tax in Annam in 1918 and in Tonkin not until 1920 (ILO *Problèmes du Travail*, 1937, pp. 29–30).

[34] p. 91. *Chinese extraterritoriality in southeast Asia*. Arrangements for the administration of the Overseas Chinese in different European dependencies in southeast Asia were the result at the same time of their traditional community organization and of whatever treaty arrangements as to their nationality were in force between China and the respective European powers (including, in regard to the Philippines, the US). A treatise on the legal position in Indochina (Levasseur, 1937) emphasized the anomalies that could arise. The government of the *bangs* was regulated by an *arrêté* issued in Cochinchina in 1906; it was extended to Tonkin in 1913 and Annam in 1928.

[35] p. 95. *Labour Code*. The Labour Code was called *Décret Organique sur le Travail Indigène*. Enacted by President Lebrun on 30 Dec. 1936, its applicability to Tonkin and Annam was confirmed by two *du* of Emperor Bao Dai dated 6 Sept. 1937 and 22 Dec. 1937, at the same time as regulations made under it on the authority of the Governor-General (a series of *arrêtés* all dated 31 May 1937) were extended, also by *arrêté* of the Governor-General, to European workers as well as native (Indo-China, *Réglementation du travail*, 1937, pp. 12–36 & 338). Although there were not many laws like this one, inspired by the aims of social reform of the *Front Populaire*, the Labour Code nevertheless exemplifies the complexities of the legislative process in French dependencies.

[36] p. 96. *Social legislation*. France never ratified the international Opium Convention of 1912—possibly because the Opium Monopoly contributed a quarter of the all-Indochina revenue (Roubaud, 1931, p. 205) and consequently cut down the incidence of taxation under other heads. The regulation of conditions of labour in the 1930s—the Labour Inspectorate was set up in 1927—took on the aspect of a response to the conventions of the ILO rather than to spontaneous social conscience.

[37] p. 97. *Special courts*. The empowering decree was dated 11 Oct. 1904 (quoted by Jean, 1944, p. 119). The power to set up special courts

appears, however, to have been confined to the Protectorates, or at least only to have been made use of there; in the Colony of Cochin-china, where the Judiciary was fully under the control of the French executive, jurisdiction was never taken away from the criminal courts even temporarily.

[38] p. 103. *Term of office of Governor-Generals.* French colonial practice was open to criticism in another, closely related, particular. During most of its history, the *Union Indochinoise* was administered by Governor-Generals whose average term of office was less than two years; indeed, Admiral Decoux claimed (1949, p. 353) that Governor-General Doumer and himself were the only two heads of *any* French administration in any part of the world since 1789 to have stayed in office for five years at a stretch. Moreover, the men appointed to this paramount position were nearly all proconsuls whose previous careers had brought them little experience relevant to the problems of colonial administration. The desire to crown a career of public service given by a capable leader of the Establishment is understandable but would not suffice to explain the appointment of miscellaneous admirals, generals, and plain party leaders whose names came to figure on the list of Indochina's Governor-Generals beside the much rarer men of established professional standing.

[39] p. 103. *Privilege of expatriates.* The most famous was Laotian Prince Souvannavong, destined later to become leader of the Communist Neo Lao Hak Sat and Pathet Lao. The controversial Admiral Decoux (p. 399) was a bitter critic of this discrimination against Indochinese in their own country; he found that an unlettered and uncouth French sergeant received more pay than a first-class mandarin, but his efforts to introduce more equitable salary scales during the war bore no fruit.

[40] p. 103. *The number of Catholics in Vietnam.* Devillers considers (1952, p. 185) that by 1945 20 per cent of the population of Tonkin and of Annam north of the Col des Nuages was Catholic. A Catholic public-relations communiqué dated 31 Mar. 1966 gave the proportion of the population of South Vietnam believed to be members of the Church as 10·5 per cent.

[41] p. 104. *Reliability of French colonial statistics.* Some authors refer to an Indochina census taken in 1936; although more care than usual may have attended the count in that year, it still did not amount to a house-by-house enumeration but rested on the traditional method of counting (and taxing) families through the commune. The gap between theory and practice in regard to the reliability of demographic information—and sometimes economic statistics—upon which colonial governments based their policies appears to have been a widespread feature of the French empire (e.g. Hailey, 1945, pp. 122–3, and Brunschwig, 1960, p. 87). Inconsistency and doubt under-

lie a great deal of the statistical data of all kinds published on Vietnam at any period, despite a superficial appearance of meticulous precision. It is not only the unsettled state of the country that is to blame, but also vested interest, slackness, and contrariness which the authorities, French or Vietnamese, have not checked.

[42] p. 106. *Modern education systems.* In fairness to the French educationists, it must be pointed out that the difficulties of evolving a valid, modernized education system—for which no local demand existed at the time—would have been immense. The problem of creating a national, yet modern, system, complete with curricula, books, properly-trained teachers and a basis for research and spontaneous further development, out of translated materials, has, save for Japan, still been solved nowhere in eastern Asia. The failure of France to do better in this respect than governments in neighbouring countries, from Burma to the Philippines, Indonesia to Korea (or, for that matter, China), is due far more certainly to the intractability of the problem than to her desire to assimilate the Vietnamese, wholly or in part, to her own cultural pattern.

[43] p. 107. *Exposure of unwanted babies.* Exposure of unwanted babies was for long a custom of the urban poor in China that disturbed foreign residents during the nineteenth century. Urbanization in Vietnam during the twentieth century has reproduced the same evil in, if anything, aggravated degree. In both countries French Catholic missions have always made special efforts to rescue these foundlings, at times with painful consequence for themselves in China but with financial support from the authorities in Vietnam. References to *orphelinats* in literature on Vietnam are as a rule to religious homes for foundlings.

[44] p. 108. *The Hongkong Bank.* The Hongkong Bank already had an agency at Saigon in 1866, and it is an historical curiosity that when the Catholic Basilica was to be erected there in the 1870s, the Bank was alone in being able to find the money in advance—in those days necessarily in the form of silver specie (Collis, 1965, p. 87.)

[45] p. 108. *History of the piastre.* The piastre remained on the same silver standard as the majority of Far Eastern currencies from its introduction until the collapse of silver in the world depression of 1930, when the piastre was given a gold standard like the franc. Both currencies left the gold standard again in 1936, and henceforward the piastre was quoted only in terms of the franc—at ten francs to the piastre. This period saw the closest bonds of any between the Indochinese economy and that of France in all respects. The piastre was revalued to 17 francs on 26 Dec. 1945, but then underwent the same devaluations as the franc it was still tied to, in 1948 (twice) and 1949. The unilateral devaluation of the piastre yet again to 10 francs on 11 May 1953 was regarded by the Vietnamese as the ultimate gesture of highhandedness by the colonial power (Vu-do-Thin, 1954, pp. 44–46).

[46] p. 110. *Canal-digging.* As in so many matters, the French were in this perpetuating a Vietnamese tradition. Robequain (1944, p. 110) quotes the report of John White, an American living in Cochinchina in 1819–20, that he witnessed the digging of the first Cho Gao canal; 26,000 coolies laboured in shifts night and day to complete the eleven miles in six weeks, and 7,000 of them perished. Re-excavation and re-alignment of the ancient Khmer canal from Chau Doc to Ha Tien, the Vinh Te (about 40 miles), under Gia Long's famous mandarin, Nguyen Ngoc Thoai, on the other hand, took 22,000 labourers more than a year (1819–21), and half of them died of enteric (Malleret, 1959, pp. 27–28). It took 40,000 coolies two months to dig the Cua Tien Canal in 1875 under French supervision (*Cochinchine française*, 1878, pp. 56–60). A not dissimilar spectacle was still to be observed periodically under President Ngo Dinh Diem, despite possession of mechanical excavators as well; it differed only in the freedom from epidemics and resultant high mortality—not in any other particular.

[47] p. 111. *Paddy yields.* Henry (1932, ii. 390) compares the average Vietnamese yield (two-crop paddy taken with one-crop) of 12 quintals a hectare (just under half a ton an acre) with 15 for Java, 17 in Burma, 18 in Siam—and, not surprisingly 33 in Japan. By 1938, however, the Agricultural Services claimed to have caught up Burma and overtaken Siam (France, *Premier rapport* (1948), p. 41). Since independence it has been asserted that the yield for South Vietnam on its own (actually less productive than Tonkin) reached 0·84 tons an acre in 1962 (*Ann. stat. 1962*, p. 121); this is still low by comparison with Chinese cultivation in Hong Kong, which obtained between 1·2 and 1·8 tons an acre in the same year (*Hong Kong Ann. Report 1962*, p. 103).

[48] p. 112. *The fortunes of chettyars.* Governor-General Lanessan remarked (1889, pp. 502–3) that, in his time, Indian immigrant coolies turned chetty had been able, in the space of twenty years, to rise from the position of cabman to a controlling interest in land and buildings in the township of Saigon, and that, more than Vietnamese, their victims had been Europeans and even Chinese businessmen.

[49] p. 115. *French and Vietnamese land grants.* The proportions held by metropolitan French interests and by Vietnamese with French nationality are worth noting: in 1938 they came to 334,000 ha. and 2,262,000 respectively (Devillers, 1952, p. 32 n. 2). As the French interests were mostly in the hands of finance companies by that time, while the total number of naturalized Cochinchinese was only about 1,600, it is plain that the big private landowners were primarily native rather than European.

[50] p. 116. *Interest on agricultural loans.* Gourou (1940, p. 279) gives examples of loans in cash, as distinct from loans in grain. An annual loan of 100 piastres would be repayable as 130 piastres, even when paid back long before the stipulated term—a fact which confirms the

lender's prior concern with a steady income. Commoner, however, were monthly loans repayable at 40 cents a day from the second day—which work out at 240 per cent per annum. Day loans also were known: a piastre advanced early in the morning would be repaid with ten cents interest in the evening—and that of course makes 3,650 per cent per annum.

[51] p. 122. *Hoa Hao observances*. In its religious aspects, Hoa Hao is of an extreme simplicity and fundamentalism. Its full title is *Phat Giao Hoa Hao*, in which the place name can be understood in its literal meaning, to give 'The Buddhism of Reconciliation'. It stands for reaction against all ideas of progress or acquisition of wealth. There are few temples—only shrines at holy places having some animistic significance—and all pomp or display is shunned. Life may not be taken. Observances consist of daily reverences before the family altar, as in all Vietnamese homes but with the embellishment of a red banner with the inscription *Buu son ky huong* (Magic fragrance from the Jewelled Mountain) which also appears on the Sect's *bua gong*. Participation in the Confucian celebrations in the village *dinh*, whether of the tutelary spirit or the harvest, is, like the taking of alcohol or opium, abhorred (Savani, 1953, p. 100). While at work in the fields, the faithful chant or hum catchy tunes to which moral or political slogans are set in rhyme. Expectation of the messianic reincarnation of Minh Vuong seems to have faded, but reverence for Huynh Phu So himself is a cardinal dogma, and the stages of his exaltation in the Seven Mountains and final transfiguration as the 'Buddha in the flames' (see note 112) can be studied, in brightly-coloured plaster, in the little 'mother' pagoda at Long Xuyen. Male followers in the villages often identify themselves by wearing long hair gathered in the old-fashioned chignon, but followers outside their home territory are usually reticent about their membership.

[52] p. 125. *Emperor Duy Tan*. Duy Tan was deposed for his involvement, in favour of Khai Dinh, father of Bao Dai; but he lived on to become a gallant, loyal, and much respected officer of the French air force.

[53] p. 127. *Political consequences of language reform*. The fact is, of course, that the development of popular education in Vietnam at this time spread knowledge of progressive Chinese ideas as much as of French because of the *pai-hua* (clear language) reform in China and the teaching of *quoc-ngu* in Vietnam. Chinese became easier to read and more accessible through newspapers and popular magazines; rendering into Vietnamese and circulation through similar media in Tonkin was a natural development, infecting the student class with some of the Brave-New-World excitement of the 1919 May 4th Movement in Shanghai.

[54] p. 137. *Public opinion and the Throne in Tonkin*. A proposal in 1930 to restore the royal authority to administration of the Protectorate in Tonkin, suspended with the office of *kinh luoc* in 1897 (p. 90 above),

was opposed by Tonkinese public opinion (Pinto, 1946, p. 131).

55 p. 141. *Names of Ho Chi Minh.* Although almost any auspicious combination of Chinese words is valid to make a personal name from in Vietnamese, *ai-quoc* as a given name would sound as forced as Puritan names in England and America used to; it is instead to be understood as a revolutionary's alias, and McLane states (1966, p. 109) that articles so signed in *L'Humanité* were in reality by several hands. Ho Chi Minh is said to have adopted this name out of deference to French Communists upset by his first choice, *O-Phep* or 'Francophobe' (Fischer, 1956, p. 178). When Ho Chi Minh was first heard of in the West by his new name, in 1945, his identity was not spotted at once and for a time was not avowed in Communist circles; a Party directive of 1951 (see p. 170) quaintly explained that 'President Ho is like a pregnant woman—he does not boast about the fact, but everybody knows it.' Since 1954 the identity of Nguyen Ai Quoc and Ho Chi Minh, long attested by photographs (e.g. in *Contribution*, v), *has* been 'boasted about' officially. Mohan Das (1950, p. 3) quotes the Indian Communist M. N. Roy as mentioning the use of 'Ho Chi Minh' at Canton in 1925, in Borodin's time, also as a collective imprint for political articles.

56 p. 144. *Trotskyism and Stalinism in Vietnam.* Although, in their original struggle for power inside Russia, Trotsky had stood for world revolution and Stalin for 'socialism in one country', their roles became reversed in the Sino-Vietnamese context: Trotsky became the symbol of Marxism (of Communism as a system of economics and social organization) while Stalin, perhaps because of difficulty in controlling the Ho Chi Minhs of the Comintern, became the symbol of Leninism (of Communism as a method for revolutionary seizure of power).

57 p. 149. *Britain and Japan in 1940.* It will be recalled that Britain also gave way to Japan momentarily at this time by closing the Burma Road for a few weeks, and even the US was loath to antagonize her.

58 p. 150. *Indochina and German-occupied France.* After the Germans occupied Vichy in November 1942, Admiral Decoux found himself in a difficult constitutional position and obliged to exercise some of the attributes of sovereignty. The reforms he considered politically desirable ran into obstruction from those of his advisers who were sticklers for form, and there was no metropolitan authority to settle the issue and enact legislation that French colonial practice reserved to Paris.

59 p. 152. *Fascist proclivities of Admiral Decoux.* Decoux belongs more to the history of France than to that of Vietnam, but it is clear from his memoirs that his sympathies were with the Fascists and that he copied Pétain's compulsory organization of the *Volontaires de la Révolution Nationale* because he was persuaded personally that that was right. He enacted legislation against Jews and Freemasons and conducted witch-hunts against persons sympathetic to the 'Anglo-Saxons' (Legrand, 1963, pp. 166 & 175).

[60] p. 153. *French and British wartime intelligence compared.* These French intelligence operations fitted at the time into the same framework as those undertaken by Britain in Malaya; but there was, from the point of view of the future government of Indochina, a crucial difference. The European community in Malaya was interned, and the intelligence officers who landed secretly were gazetted officers of the Government, with extensive local knowledge, legal executive powers, and a future answerability beyond the mere interests of military intelligence; they made contact with the Asian population. Their French counterparts, though not strangers to the terrain, were military officers keeping in touch with the European population still at large, without contacts among an Asian population they did not trust, and concerned much more with the internal divisions between Frenchmen than with the destinies of the Indochinese peoples (Mordant, 1950, p. 117).

[61] p. 153. *Movements of Ho Chi Minh before the war.* There is some mystery about Ho Chi Minh's movements between 1931 and 1941 and, hardly less, his early relations with the American Office of Strategic Services. An account of the conflicting stories is given by Fall (1962, pp. 97–103); the points selected in these pages are not generally in dispute and are perhaps all that is necessary to account for the development of the Vietminh.

[62] p. 155. *Japanese behaviour after March 1945.* The Japanese army was in no mood at this stage of the war to scruple over the obligation of care and maintenance in the occupied territory according to the usages of war. They permitted looting of French property, private and public, and their own soldiers took part, turning even the government archives to account by selling them as wastepaper by weight.

[63] p. 157. *Allies' support for the Vietminh.* What this support amounted to in fact has been much argued since, but as all the agencies concerned were as secretive as the Vietminh itself, the full facts are not likely to be made known. That arms, money, and training were all given in some measure is, however, certain; Britain too may have contributed.

[64] p. 158. *Changes of Communist façade.* Every few months since 1942 the Vietminh had gone through some reshuffle of its name or implied support; there had been a succession of 'brotherhoods' (*dong minh* or *dong-chi hoi*). All were façades, without any formal membership: there would scarcely have been time to enlist individual adherents, and, in any case, the Comintern years before, in the resolution quoted on p. 178 below, had instructed that in dependent territories the Party should 'attempt to co-ordinate and to unite the activities of national revolutionary organizations with the help of common action committees'. Moreover, the words *hoi/hui* (association) and *dang/*

tang (party) both have a long and dishonourable history in China, and in only lesser degree Vietnam, in the senses of what in the West are called cliques or secret societies. Even today, a Vietnamese political party has little formal organization but is a *tendance* that one supports or breaks with from moment to moment out of personal considerations rather than conviction or principle; the Vietnamese Communist Party would have been no exception had it not always had the character of a disciplined fighting force. (See also note 108.)

65 p. 164. *Admiral Thierry d'Argenlieu*. Gen. de Gaulle's choice of yet another proconsul with no relevant experience—he had divided his career between the navy and the Carmelite Order (Sabattier, 1952, p. 328)—was apparently based on d'Argenlieu's loyalty as a *résistant* due for reward and on his animosity towards Decoux. The choice was regarded as rather a slight by educated opinion in Vietnam.

66 p. 166. *French Communists and the Vietminh*. The Vietminh uprising put the French Communists in a dilemma on their side too, for they could not both support Ho Chi Minh and remain members of a coalition administration in Paris organizing the defence against him. The Communists chose to stay in the Government, and, on balance, the Soviet leaders seem to have approved a decision which kept their foot in the constitutional doorway to power for the time being (Rieber, 1962, pp. 322–30). But even if the French Communists had won the election outright, it is open to doubt whether they could have conceded the independence the Vietminh wanted, on account of the jingoist aftermath of the World War and the spreading suspicion of Communist intentions, fast deepening as Stalin intensified the Cold War. Thus *L'Humanité* was prepared to advocate a policy of 'fraternal and democratic collaboration' with the Vietminh, as it had fifteen years before, but explicitly not full independence (Hammer, 1954, p. 190).

67 p. 167. *French military objectives*. In 1950 it was revealed in the French parliament that the *Corps Expéditionnaire* had been under instructions not to try to extend the areas under French control (Chesneaux, 1956, p. 267). This seems tantamount to an admission that the French intervention was temporary and that the DRV was a legitimate Government.

68 p. 168. *Constitution of the DRV*. The present constitution of the DRV went into effect on 1 Jan. 1960; it claims jurisdiction over all Vietnam. Except for its long historical preamble, this second constitution owes a great deal to the 1954 constitution of Communist China, which in turn was inspired largely by Stalin's 1936 constitution for the USSR.

69 p. 169. *Terms for Communist cadres*. Various terms have been in use for Party activists in Vietnam, all owed to Communist usage in China; the three commonest are *can bo*, *dan van*, and *dich van* (p. 143 above). They can be distinguished by nuances of meaning: *can bo* is unspecific; *dan van* suggests a local leader organizing voluntary support among his

fellow 'masses'; and *dich van* implies an emissary from the centre mobilizing support among a more distant population; although *dich van* was usually applied to Communist agents penetrating French territory or French organizations, distinctions have never been precise.

[70] p. 169. *Records of decisions in the DRV.* Communications and instructions were rarely written, however. The complete administrative break with the past deprived the regime of a tradition of documentary forms, even if the run of the cadres had been educated enough to express themselves on paper. Instead, administrative decisions were reached by consensus at interminable meetings between cadres, in a manner not unlike that of Communist Parties in other countries. Since no records of decisions were kept, no precedents existed, and government remained to that extent arbitrary (Tongas, 1961, pp. 97–101).

[71] p. 170. *The ICP's subsidiaries.* The truth about these two organs was that their cadres, never numerous, were ex-students won over by Vietnamese comrades while attending the University at Hanoi or colleges in France; up to this time, they had still failed to gain a hold over any mobilizable 'masses' in Cambodia or Laos and lay down bases of their own. Being still in a position analogous to that of the ICP before it transferred its weight from its foot in China to its foot in Vietnam, they were evidently content to accept the discipline of membership of the Lien Viet along with its financial support.

[72] p. 174. *Manipulation of terror in the DRV.* Relief is usually so great when terror is suddenly turned off that there is an upsurge of popular enthusiasm for the hand responsible. Ho Chi Minh and Vo Nguyen Giap appeared to derive personal kudos from the gesture, partly at the expense of Truong Chinh who, as Secretary-General of the Party, could not escape blame. Truong Chinh stood down from his position for a while, and Ho Chi Minh took his place (Honey, 1963, pp. 44–45).

[73] p. 177. *Quality of Chinese advisers.* The quality of Mao Tsê-tung's experts is sometimes questioned by former Vietminh officers who have since broken with the DRV. It is suggested that political soundness played a large part in their selection: one former divisional medical officer in the People's Army, a Vietnamese fully trained to Western standards, found himself being advised by a tactless Chinese orderly trained only to perform a few simple emergency procedures. Whilst the purpose of the Chinese Communists was to pass on their own hard-won experience of improvisation, they were exultant over their recent victories against Chiang Kai-shek, and their dogmatic insistence on the virtues of austerity scared many sensitive, and not all that backward, Vietnamese.

[74] p. 181. *Binh Xuyen and the Communists.* The appearance on the Saigon scene of the Binh Xuyen was so sudden as to suggest that some pre-existing clandestine body was mixed up in their beginnings. They

collaborated closely with the Communists during the Japanese interregnum and, according to Bodard (1963, p. 122), placed their underground network at the disposal of Nguyen Binh as a nucleus for his own. Following several years of inactivity after 1955, they became part of the VC in the 1960s.

75 p. 184. *Vietminh revenue in Cochinchina*. Bodard estimated (p. 184) that total Vietminh income in Cochinchina amounted by 1950 to 'several million piastres a month'. Despuech (1953, p. 132) put it even higher, at 500 m. for the year 1948. Leroy (1955, p. 155) believed the Vietminh collected 40 m. piastres in Kien Hoa province alone during 1950 but, thanks to himself (p. 144), only 151,000 by 1951. Whatever the exact figures, the Vietminh paid the non-local costs of their war in Tonkin by taxing Cochinchina and remitting the proceeds abroad at the cost of the French exchequer. Allegations of fraudulent complicity on the part of French bankers resulted in scandals, judicial inquiries, and suits for criminal libel in Paris, but in no clear disclosure of the facts (Laurent, 1954, *passim*).

76 p. 187. *Gen. de Latour's defence system*. Again according to Bodard (p. 121), the General had, like most of his colleagues, spent a lot of his service in the Sahara (whence no doubt the propensity of all the Generals to rely on 'Beau Geste' forts in the Vauban tradition). He thought mistakenly he discerned in the Vietnamese warlords a counterpart to the Berber *qaids* and took it for granted that their rules of loyalty and chivalry applied in Vietnam.

77 p. 189. *Career of Col. Leroy*. The Colonel's organization was called *Unités Mobiles pour le Défense des Chrétientés* but did not confine itself to protection of Catholics and was not approved of by the Catholic hierarchy (Savani, 1953, p. 113). Three causes led to the discomfiture of Leroy: internal rivalries as his domain expanded, impingement on Cao Dai and Hoa Hao territory, and bankruptcy of the public services whose finances he tampered with.

78 p. 189. *Opium*. M. Bodard also reported on this skeleton in the French cupboard. The power of the Tonkin warlords rested at this time—and probably for a century before that—largely on the control of the opium traffic. The French Government had had two unadmitted reasons for not ratifying the Opium Convention (note 36 above). In the first place, the growing of the opium poppy provided the livelihood of whole tribes in Laos and Tonkin (as well as northern Siam and Burma—Hong Kong, *Problem of Narcotic Drugs*, 1959, p. 7). The traffic in the smuggled export of the surplus not consumed within Indochina—the greater part (Sabattier, p. 163)—was a highly-lucrative business for the underworld of Haiphong before the war. One consequence of the fighting in Tonkin was to divert this traffic through Bangkok, where it has remained; but not without a long struggle between the Vietminh and the *Corps Expéditionnaire* to get their

hands on it, both for the sake of its cash value to their unit 'goat-bags' and for the control of the hill peoples who grew it, which would result from denying it to the other side.

[79] p. 192. *Administration of the PMS.* Presumably with the consent of the French High Commissioner, Bao Dai safeguarded these special areas against victimization by Vietnamese politicians of the future (who might force him otherwise, as a constitutional monarch, to sanction measures detrimental to the defenceless inhabitants) by declaring the highlands (in *Du* No. 6 of 1950) to be 'domains of the Crown of An-nam' and expressly not of the State of Viet-Nam. (Blanchet, 1954, pp. 117–18.)

[80] p. 194. *Prime Minister Nguyen Van Tam.* How broad or narrow would be the horizons of the individuals who by themselves made up these Governments may be judged from the career of the second Prime Minister. A poor but brilliant product of the French education system, he joined the Cochinchinese Administrative Service and in 1939–40 was *doc phu* in charge of a densely populated district astride the water-way linking the Mekong with Saigon. He watched with disgust the methods by which the Cao Dai spread its network in his home town of Tay Ninh, in the civil service, and finally in his district. When the Communists also shattered the peace with their uprising at My Tho (p. 150 above), Tam took part in repressive measures in which regard for the forms of justice were not conspicuous (Lancaster, 1961, p. 431). In 1945 the Vietminh took their revenge and murdered two of his sons. In 1948 he became the first Vietnamese Province Chief, in the same province, and in 1949 Minister of Internal Security, in 1952 Prime Minister; in both the first two capacities he again got a reputa-tion for extra-legal action in the name of law and order. As Prime Minister, he engineered the appointment of his eldest son, Hinh, who had had a distinguished career in the French air force and on whom he could count not to betray him but to get on with the job ener-getically, as first Commander-in-Chief of the new Vietnamese army. Nguyen Van Tam typified—in the conflict between his French-orientated idealism as public administrator and his tragic personal feud, against the background of the realities of Vietnamese rural society—the dilemmas with which his junior colleagues in their turn are still grappling in South Vietnam, while he himself and his equally talented but unsuccessful son have found a permanent haven in the citizenship of France.

[81] p. 198. *The French High Command.* During the seven years of the war there was no change in the Vietminh Commander-in-Chief, but there were seven on the French side, with six changes in the top civil office (Navarre, 1956, p. 32); the two positions of command were closely connected and bound up in turn with the nineteen changes of govern-ment which took place in Paris during this time. Leclerc and de Lattre

both combined civil with military command; at other times the commands were separate. While Salan was Commander-in-Chief, the Commissioner-General had been Letourneau, and he, doubling as Minister of Overseas Territories in the Mayer Cabinet, was thus the General's superior as well as his colleague. Letourneau 'fell' with René Mayer, and Navarre, partnered with a diplomat Commissioner-General, Maurice Dejean, again had greater freedom of decision. In the final phase, after Navarre's disgrace, Gen. Ély became High Commissioner with supreme powers in both fields; Gen. Salan returned with him as explicitly his subordinate. These vacillations over the high command rendered all the harder the proper direction of the total war effort, the more so since they were backed by incoherent policies and objectives at home.

[82] p. 204. *Conditions for French withdrawal from the South.* At the final session, France undertook 'to withdraw its troops from the territory of Cambodia, Laos, and Viet-Nam at the request of the Governments concerned'. This could be said to take care of the issue of command of the army in the South, but not of political, administrative, or financial questions. A second undertaking given by France at the same time, to 'proceed with the principle of respect for the independence and sovereignty, the unity and territorial integrity etc.', added nothing to previous declarations to the same effect going back to December 1947 (Bollaert–Bao Dai Convention, Bay of Along), and on the contrary appeared to be at variance with a cease-fire whose very foundation was partition.

[83] p. 206. *Exports of Rubber.* The value of the export quadrupled from 1949 to 1951 (*Ann. stat. 1949–50*, p. 257, and *1952*, p. 232). By 1956 quantity and value were higher still (ibid. *1956*, p. 238) and continued to rise until 1963. The present estates, whose area has remained constant for twenty-five years but which have been extensively replanted, are capable of producing 75,000 tons a year and in 1961 reached 85,000 (*Ann. Stat. B. 1961*, p. 79).

[84] p. 207. *The flight from Tonkin.* Made up predominantly of the inhabitants of the autonomous Catholic dioceses, this massive migration seemed to parallel in political significance the exodus from south China into Hong Kong going on at the same time in reaction to the establishment of Communist rule there too. The exodus of the Tonkinese is justifiably portrayed as a similar 'vote with their feet' against the Communist regime; yet it was necessarily more sudden (the Geneva Agreement allowed only 100 days) and more organized (the distance to be travelled could not be negotiated on foot), and these factors made it less spontaneous. The Government in Saigon used its last weeks of control over Hanoi to encourage people in all walks of life to leave (Lancaster, p. 344), while the Vietnamese hierarchy, rejecting the decision of the foreign bishops to stay behind (Fall, 1966,

p. 59), gathered up the faithful in their dioceses by whole *chrétientés* in lorries provided by the *Corps Expéditionnaire* (Tongas, p. 161) for transport to the South in ships provided by the French Government in accordance with the agreement. The DRV on its side retained improperly about 15,000 Vietnamese prisoners (Ély, p. 214) and put many obstacles in the way of anybody under its control wanting to leave (Lancaster, p. 359); the ICC reported that most of these obstacles were removed in the end, but sometimes too late (*4th Interim Report*, 1955, p. 16). In other words, the situation in the two zones of Tonkin illustrated the riddle that hangs over all adhesions to sect, party, faction, or cause (as also over voting at elections) at any period of Vietnamese history: are the circumstances of Vietnamese society ever of a kind to permit a free choice? For many of the intellectuals in Tonkin the decision was taken as much out of conviction as of ambition and perfectly reasonable self-interest, since both alternatives were consistent with patriotic duty; for the peasants in the *chrétientés* it was taken no doubt out of dread of what might befall them if they were separated from their spiritual leaders. Yet for many who decided to stay behind, it was taken out of misgivings over reprisals (perhaps not threatened explicitly) against their families in North or South, or out of duty to relatives who could not travel. It is hard to judge how far the arguments used at the time by the advocates of the conflicting courses was legitimate persuasion, how far intimidation.

[85] p. 212. *The Communist gibe 'My-Diem'.* The identity of Ngo Dinh Diem's benefactor during these years has not been acknowledged, but the surmise of the curious that it was one of the discreet hands of the US Government (for an explanation more positive than surmise, see Robert Scheer in Gettleman, 1965, pp. 246–52) seems to have been at the source of the Communist propaganda trick whereby they always referred to Diem while he was in power as '*My-Diem*'—a pun meaning on the face of it 'American Diem' (or 'America and Diem'), but containing as well the innuendo 'strumpet'. Diem's return to Saigon from Paris rather than from Washington delicately avoided drawing attention to the similarity between this operation and the one which had seated Syngman Rhee at the helm of the South Korean ship of state after an exile in the US of forty years.

[86] p. 215. *The President and his family.* One day, when the dictatorship was already in obvious decline, a foreign diplomatic representative (neither British nor American) hinted to Ngo Dinh Diem that the state might be saved if he would sacrifice, not the persons or the private interests, but the power of his family. His retort was that to sacrifice his family in any manner would be turpitude, and Heaven would not long preserve the state to which he had sacrificed it.

[87] p. 218. *The Can Lao.* As far as can be ascertained in the face of its members' secretiveness (and of the destruction of its records early in

1964), the organization owed more to the French *Sûreté* than to the Communist Party. It was divided into four *bureaux*: the *Premier Bureau* was the administration, the *Deuxième Bureau* collected and collated information, the *Troisième Bureau* carried out 'operations', and the *Quatrième Bureau* handled revenue and paid out rewards. The members had to swear the same kind of oath of 'loyalty unto death' as did members of the ICP, the VNQDD, and the Dai Viet; some who refused to join held out on the ground that their conscience demurred at the superstitious sanction for the oath—a sort of 'Rites Controversy'.

88 p. 220. *Trinh Minh The.* This picturesque ruffian endeared himself to some Westerners and distinguished himself as the inventor of plastic charges stuffed into bicycle frames and motor cars with a time fuse to blow up in crowded streets. He operated in this way in Saigon two or three times—in the French view in support of the Vietminh, in the American view out of patriotic fervour against colonialism. It is possible that his submission to Ngo Dinh Diem was prompted by patriotism, but it is hard to find any Vietnamese who believes that his motive was other than venal, even if the funds were not a charge on the national exchequer. He was killed before he could tell any tales himself.

89 p. 231. *Recruitment to the civil service.* The 1950 rules, based on French models, prescribed competitive examination as the normal entry. However, a *nghi-dinh (arrêté)* of 10 June 1953 admitted army veterans on the strength of meritorious service or wounds. They were given priority for places under further regulations of 12 Apr. 1955 and 29 May 1956 made by President Diem to facilitate the entry of certain veterans as a reward for personal loyalty to himself. Nevertheless, of 2,835 permanent civil servants recruited to the most senior class, 481 entered by graduation from government training schools, 1,430 by competitive examination or on the basis of university diplomas, and only 924 by the back door; moreover, even the back-door entry included many good men. (Based on RVN, *Ann. Report 1958*, pp. 40–52.)

90 p. 233. *Provincial courts.* On paper, the number of courts set up in the provinces actually exceeded that of any previous regime; but of ten courts supposedly set up in Cochinchina by three decrees between 1955 and 1958, not one was functioning by the end of the dictatorship in 1963. Reluctance to serve as a magistrate in distant, and possibly uncomfortable or unsafe, places played a large part in this failure. Needless to say, it was rare for a defence lawyer to put in an appearance in an out-of-the-way province for any altruistic motive.

91 p. 249. *Block votes and maintenance.* All department budgeting was by block vote—not only as far as the voting of supply and the publishing of accounts went, but even for the keeping of accounts within the departments themselves. Consequently, it could never be said with confidence in any year or for any item whether provision had or had not been made for maintenance: spending was fluid within the total amounts—and also quite impossible to audit.

[92] p. 253 *Village and state in Confucianism*. Confucianism in Vietnam, as in China, is fully aware of this order of priorities. Village *dinhs* are decorated, like other temples, with painted 'flowery' boards on which are carved, in gilt calligraphy, saws and maxims from the Chinese classics. So common as to be found in nearly every *dinh* in Vietnam is one which reads as a palindrome: from left to right it says 'Defend the realm and protect the citizen' (*Hu kuo, pi min*), but from right to left: 'The citizen protected, then the realm defended' (*Min pi, kuo hu*).

[93] p. 257. *Numbers of prisoners and detainees*. Both Vietminh and VC have held detainees for several years at a stretch in distressingly squalid camps far from villages in all parts of the country on the excuse of 'indoctrination'; from time to time security-force patrols have stumbled on them, sometimes in time to release the captives, more often to discover them dead or dying at the hands of their fleeing guards. But Communist propaganda has made great play over detention without trial by the Government, and its intemperate generalizations have often been accepted as true in the West though unsupported by details. The truth is hard to get at. Statistics of the prison population in Vietnam ceased to be published after independence. Figures that seem to throw light on the matter are those for 'cours de rééducation des détenus' included by the Ministry of Civil Action in RVN, *Bilan* (1962, p. 437). These report a rise from 12 individuals in 1955 to over 3,000 in 1959; then a jump to 40,000 in 1960 and 276,000 in 1962. The entry was meant to do the regime credit and should probably be interpreted (at least for the later years) as numbers of people released after listening to one or more 'lectures'. How these people came into captivity would vary from properly-sentenced criminals to women and children rounded up by military patrols through villages empty of men (away with the Vietcong) and held overnight for simple questioning and hectoring. After the overthrow of Ngo Dinh Diem, the Government of Mr Tran Van Huong claimed (in a statement broadcast on 16 Jan. 1965) that 46,240 political detainees, against whom no charges had been preferred, had been released since the coup d'état of 1 Nov. 1963; the statement did not clarify whether all the detainees had been in confinement before the coup d'état or whether the figure included some of the many persons detained without trial by more recent Governments, including Mr Huong's own. On 1 May 1965, after Mr Huong's fall, there were 212,000 persons in places of detention, besides 1794 convicted of political offences (private communication).

[94] p. 265. *Ethnic divisions of hill tribes*. The hill tribes of the PMS are not only different racially from the Vietnamese, but also from the hill tribes of Tonkin, who are mostly Thai; on the other hand, they are

closely akin to the people of Stung Treng and Ratanakiri (Cambodia) —who, though Khmer by race, have not been incorporated culturally in the indianized kingdom—and to the hill peoples of Champassak (Laos). The Lao themselves are Thai but differ from the hill tribes of Tonkin by their indianized civilization, which they share with their Siamese cousins. The potential for mischief-making in the ethnic composition of Laos can be judged from the fact that only one person out of four in the country is Lao, while three out of four of all Lao are subjects, not of the King of Laos, but of the King of Thailand.

[95] p. 266. *VC headquarters.* Tay Ninh is for the VC what Thai Nguyen was at one time for the Vietminh—a jungle region, with villages and sources of supply on one side and an unguarded frontier on the other, in which the command post could wander ceaselessly—easy to find for its friends, impossible for its enemies.

[96] p. 275. *American military strength in Vietnam.* The US Government treated information about the actual strength of its military staff in Vietnam as confidential. However, when the French Mission withdrew in 1956, the combined Franco-American strength had evidently fallen to 685—half French, half American—, and it was only to that lower figure that the American contingent was made up. It stayed at the same level until towards the end of 1960, when another 100 advisers and trainers were added. After President Kennedy took office —that is, a few weeks after Col. Nguyen Chanh Thi's mutiny—the figure was quietly tripled (*Washington Post*, 7 Feb. 1965). That this had been done was only admitted at the end of 1961, in connexion with the decision to add a second mission, MACV. Thereafter year-end strengths have been:

1961	1,364	1964	23,000
1962	9,865	1965	184,000
1963	15,500*	1966	389,000†

* According to Schlesinger, 1967, p. 29.
† According to Washington correspondent of *The Times*, 26 May 1967.

[97] p. 283. *The Vietnamese rubber market.* Rubber is, of course, a world raw material like non-ferrous metals or wool, with a world-wide market and a world-wide price. However, concentration of production in Indochina in the hands of French financial groups meant that almost the entire yield was exported on forward contracts negotiated in Paris, where any non-franc exchange earned by the companies remained at the disposal of the Government of France, not of Vietnam. Latex and sheet rubber produced in Cambodia were exported in the same consignments. The financial emancipation of Vietnam had now made all the foreign exchange earned by Vietnamese rubber (two-

thirds of the value of all exports in 1962) available to the Republic. However, the pattern of the trade has been little affected by the change and there is still no local market in rubber, as there is in other producer countries. As a result, the VC have had no outlet for stolen rubber (a source of income for the Communists during the early stages of the Malayan insurrection), and their efforts late in 1965 to take control of the Michelin crop appear to have broken down because of their inability to find their own buyer.

[98] p. 284. *Titles of American aid.* Dollar expenditure on direct military assistance to Vietnam (additional to expenditure on American forces posted or, later, operating there) is controlled by the Department of Defense, and details are not available.[a] Economic aid, which has contributed to the piastre costs of Vietnamese defence in the manner described, is given under different heads, all controlled by AID. The biggest item is the CIP, which generates piastres owned by the Vietnamese Government. Next come US surplus agricultural products, sold in Vietnam for piastres owned by the US Government and used to meet the in-country expenses of USOM technical-assistance projects (e.g. payment of rents in Saigon); the so-called 'project aid' from which the dollar expenses under this head are paid is not included in the economic-aid grants. Another title has been Food for Peace (Public Law 480), under which not only food but tobacco for manufacturing have been channelled to Vietnam. Totals for monies administered by AID during the years covered by this chapter (1954–62) are given below (as they appear in *Ann. Statist. B.*, No. 5, p. 120); but they still only represent about nine-tenths of the economic assistance of the US. A very small proportion of the allocations was technically a loan, but 99 per cent was outright grant.

(million dollars)

CIP	1,589·3
Food for Peace	111·7
Project aid	139·8
Total	1,840·8

It is believed that in roughly the same period (1955–64) Soviet economic aid to the DRV amounted to $350 m. and Chinese to $450 m. (Parry, 1967, p. 81), making with aid from Eastern Europe close on half the American contribution to the RVN; according to a Communist source (quoted in Prybyla, 1966, p. 91), this foreign aid represented 20 per cent of the DRV budget, and that in turn was half

[a] Not, that is, until Fiscal Years 1967 and 1968, when expenditure was published as being $19,500 m. and $21,800 m. respectively (*NYHT*, 5 May 1967).

the proportion of foreign aid in the budget of the RVN (see note 99).

99 p. 285. *Aid in the Vietnamese budget.* The importance of US financial aid to the Vietnamese budget year by year was as follows (in m. of piastres):

Year	National revenue	CIP piastres	Customs duties
1956	13,625	6,303	2,115
1957	14,160	5,699	1,801
1958	14,133	5,103	2,223
1959	15,276	5,051	2,405
1960	15,214	4,515	2,181
1961	16,600	4,163	2,915
1962	20,883	7,275	4,287
Total	109,891	38,109	17,937

Source: Ann. stat. 1962, pp. 432–3.

Although not all the products of Customs duties can be put down to the CIP—other countries were giving aid, the Government was financing some of its own imports, etc., etc.—the discrepancy is more than offset by American contributions that did not pass through the public accounts. Thus American aid provided something like half as much again to the state revenue of the Ngo Dinh Diem regime, in addition to equipping its armed forces and making gifts to many other departments; some authorities rate the proportion rather higher (e.g. USOM/Taylor, 1961, p. 245).

100 p. 286. *The dollar hoard.* Neither the actual amount nor the nominee are easy to ascertain. In 1960 the National Bank had admitted to Mr Child of MSUG (1961, pp. 16–18) to a total of $222 m., of which $125 m. had been in their accounts already on 31 Dec. 1955 (a share of the Currency Board's reserves, presumably) and only $97 m. had been added as a result of CIP operations, including $40 m. in 1959. But these figures do not correspond with the published accounts. The *Ann. stat. 1956* shows (p. 210) a foreign-exchange holding at the close of 1956 valued at 4,598 m. piastres—the equivalent of $131 m. at 35:1; in corresponding tables over the following years the entry moves between piastre equivalents of $150 m. and $175 m. at which it still was at the overthrow of Ngo Dinh Diem (*Ann. stat. 1963*, p. 278). These low figures, which do not even cover known sterling balances, may be due to undervaluation in terms of piastres (at 35:1); but they may also confirm rumours that dollars were somehow being converted to other currencies deposited abroad otherwise than in the name of the National Bank. Even in regard to its piastre transactions, the Bank held more than thirty Government accounts, running to 1,000 m. piastres at a time, which did not appear in the budget (USOM/Rozental, 1964, p. 5). About the biggest was the account of the National Lottery, whose enormous profits were credited to SEPES, especially for operations abroad whose allocations of foreign exchange had been diverted to other uses; probably the hoard played some part in these arrangements analogous to the old piastre-franc transfers. There was a public scandal over the Lottery in 1962 and again in 1964, but few facts came to light.

[101] p. 287. *Political funds.* Many rumours were current about defalcations of cash from special funds like the one for refugees from the North and were confirmed privately by foreign helpers with a close insight into their management. It is uncertain whether these monies were being used for political purposes or were being pocketed (e.g. the case of Ngo Dinh Can quoted on p. 256 above).

[102] p. 292. *Army behaviour.* The North Vietnamese forces had treated their French prisoners with studied brutality, and the forces of the South, especially the army, have earned a similar reputation abroad as bullies. Without going into such difficult questions as the applicability of the Geneva Conventions on Prisoners of War to interrogation of a member of an ambush party seized by the force caught in the ambush, it must be admitted that the South Vietnamese have been guided in their treatment of their own civilian population by native traditions which American influence would have liked to curb but has not been able to; this was due to omission to foresee the problem and tackle it, not by moral exhortation, but by the practical means of getting written into the security laws the right of the aggrieved to sue for compensation.

[103] p. 293. *Army monopoly of doctors.* For example, the establishment for medical officers in the army of Vietnam was, like everything else, based on requirements for an expeditionary force. Virtually every graduate from the Faculty of Medicine was taken into the army every year; this deprived the hospitals of house staff, broke the continuity of training of potential specialists, and, since there were hardly any army casualties at this period, let the young graduates drift into professional idleness. Meanwhile the government hospitals were acutely understaffed following the withdrawal of French Government doctors (except from the Grall Hospital in Saigon) and unable to provide surgical facilities for normal cases; when victims of VC terror became more numerous, and a little later casualties among the Civil Guard and the militia, they were added to the overcrowded wards, for the army excluded even the paramilitary forces (who were taking all the losses) from its facilities. Only after 1964 did the army begin to treat paramilitary casualties, and in 1966 to relax imper-

ceptibly its throttlehold on professional personnel. (On 31 Dec. 1965 there were 533 Vietnamese doctors in the army, 233 in Ministry of Health hospitals, 78 in teaching hospitals, and 180 in wholly private practice, according to a private communication from the Ministry.) At the same time, doctors in private practice in the towns were, many of them, adding to the fortunes of the Indochina War in the growing boom conditions, without doing a hand's turn in the hospitals for the war wounded. It was mismanagement of local resources that led, from 1962 onwards, to American requests for foreign medical teams.

[104] p. 303. *Feeding the VC.* Western military planners usually reckon that Asian fighting men consume rice at the rate of 5 tons a month for every 200 men. VC rations necessarily varied at times according to local conditions, but the ration for main-force units of 18 kg. a month mentioned in a captured document dated 18 Aug. 1965 (15 kg. for non-combatants) is probably a rough average. Thus, even when total VC armed strength had reached 300,000 men, their consumption of paddy would still only be 30 per cent of the annual surplus of Cochinchina normally exported overseas.

[105] p. 309. *Unrecorded distributions of arms.* Slackness and venality more than disloyalty and cowardice were the Vietnamese sins Vietcong symbiosis relied on for weapons. But both sins were fostered by American generosity, which laid down no rules for the custody of armouries and made good the losses without murmur. By mid-1962 some 10,000 weapons had been given out in the PMS; it was estimated that perhaps 3,000 were in authorized hands, and various schemes to buy back the remainder for cash or in exchange for agricultural tools netted another 2,000; the balance of 5,000 were presumed to be in VC hands—a neat symbiotic equilibrium.

[106] p. 311. *The British Advisory Mission.* Beginning with three retired civilian officials from the Malayan Civil Service who had served through the Communist insurrection in that country (and of whom the author of this book was one), the group expanded at one time to six members and ended with four. Its life span was from 16 Sept. 1961 to 31 Mar. 1965. The British Government placed the Mission at the disposal of the Vietnamese Government to advise it how to adapt its organization and methods so as to re-establish the rule of law in circumstances that had cost so many peasants and village authorities their lives (*The Times*, 18 Sept. 1961). A large part of the Mission's contribution dealt with the remoulding of the police and its progressive extension into rural areas accustomed to the presence only of garrisons. When the Mission was wound up its name was transferred to a small British police mission, still at work today in Vietnam but devoted to this one aspect of the problem and closely identified with American efforts in the same field.

[107] p. 312. *Control of the Civil Guard.* The Civil Guard began under the

control of the Minister of the Interior, as did the territorial administration that gave it its operational orders; now the Minister of Defence was given control of training and equipment, in order to make the channelling of American aid easier. In 1964 the Civil Guard was transferred completely to the Army Command.

[108] p. 328. *Vietnamese implications of 'popular support'*. One of the peculiarities of political life in modern Vietnam, as in that of China before the Communists, is the dependence of parties and religious institutions on the transport, equipment, and other facilities of the Government for organization of their supporters. At an election, it is the Government that organizes the meetings and publicity for the candidates' 'campaigns' (see note 118). There was nothing objectionable in Vietnamese eyes in the use of public resources for a Catholic celebration; what was objectionable was the withholding of facilities from other groups. This peculiarity is connected with the implications in Vietnam of what in other countries would be called 'popular support'; the Western concept of subscription to party or church to meet the organization's expenses is not shared by the Vietnamese, who expect rather to be paid, in money or other perquisites, for their adherence (*'panem et circenses'*)—by extortion from those who are well off, from the Government or some foreign agency, or by general levy on everybody in hamlet, village, or district. This attitude to political organization is universal and not reckoned to be venal; the Communists have played on it, and so did President Diem. It must not be lost sight of when the numbers of supporters of any political or religious body are under consideration, for formal memberships are almost unknown outside the modern Catholic and Buddhist Churches. When, under the provisional administration of Gen. Nguyen Khanh, the organization of political parties was made legal again, it was suggested by some politicians that the Government should help them consolidate their position by withholding recognition in kind from splinter groups (*Dan Chu*, 8 May 1964).

[109] p. 328. *The Buddhist flag*. The flag has two similar sets of stripes (dark blue, yellow, red, white, and orange) set at right angles to each other. The design was the joint work of the American founding president of the Theosophical Society, Col. H. S. Olcott, and Mr De Silva of Colombo eighty years ago. The intention was to provide bunting for the celebration of Wesak, which Col. Olcott had been instrumental in having declared a public holiday in Ceylon from 1888 onwards as part of the secular revival of the faith in that country. When the World Fellowship of Buddhists was founded on Ceylonese initiative in 1950, the flag of Col. Olcott and Mr De Silva was adopted for Wesak decorations. (Information kindly supplied by The Buddhist Society of London.) That the example of Christmas underlay the modern revival of Wesak (see p. 331) is borne out by the

fact that, traditionally, the Enlightenment and the Extinction of Buddha, as well as the Birth, had been celebrated on the same day of the year, that is to say the full moon falling in the Hindu month of Vaisakha; for the Vietnamese laity today it is only the Birth that is associated with Wesak.

110 p. 328. *The regulation about flags.* Presumably this regulation, in whatever form it was made, had been published in the *Gazette*; but it was not reproduced in the *Bo Hinh Luat* 1962, and the present author has been unable to trace it. Typical of the doubt about legislation in Vietnam and the cavalier manner of its application is the declaration of the Minister of the Interior to the UN Fact-Finding Mission (*Violation of Human Rights*, 1963, p. 63) that the regulation was contained in *Du* No. 10 of 1950; it is not.

111 p. 328. *The meaning of Thich.* The monk's whole name is a name-in-religion meaning 'very clever'. *Thich* (Chinese *Shih*) is the surname taken by all Mahayana monks: it is the *Shakya* of *Shakyamuni*, family name of the Buddha; it is usually translated into Western languages as 'Venerable'. This particular monk had had a number of aliases; his worldly name is believed to be Pham Van Bong.

112 p. 334. *Buddhist traditions of immolation.* Foreigners in Saigon mostly shared the idea that immolation was an aberration for Buddhists, and even contrary to Buddhist teaching altogether. This was mistaken; in addition to its exaltation in the *Lotus Sutra*, the unlettered knew the sacred fable of the little hare (Buddha in a former existence) which offered its flesh for cooking to a hungry beggar (a god in disguise)—*Jataka* No. 361 (1895–1913, iv. 34–36); 1963 was the Chinese Year of the Hare, although in the Vietnamese calendar the animal is called a cat. Tonkinese Mahayanists in bygone centuries had burnt themselves to death for merit, and the 'Mad Bonze' of the Hoa Hao portrayed himself figuratively in this guise (note 51 above). For ancient and modern Chinese precedents, see Welch, 1967, pp. 327–9.

113 p. 339. *The Vatican and the crisis.* The Vatican had obvious cause to be apprehensive over the repercussions on the Church of the conflict between the Buddhists and the Government; President Diem's patriarchy was looked upon in Vietnam as a family administration, and the head of the family was not Diem but Thuc, who was also head of the Vietnamese hierarchy. Immediately after the raid on the pagodas, two or three veiled warnings about 'rights and liberties of all' were issued, and then, after the rebuke to Mgr. Thuc by the Curia, the Pope himself issued an appeal for tolerance in the form of a letter to the Vietnamese bishops (*The Times*, 14 Sept. 1963). Their graces replied that what was going on was not a religious dispute but a political one—that Catholics and Buddhists were not in conflict as such (*Le Monde*, 26 Sept. 1963). Whilst literally true, this affirmation begged the question, for, in Vietnam, adherence to church or

pagoda was primarily a political, or factional, gesture, not a religious one. This reality became much clearer in the course of 1964, when, Diem out of the way, the faithful of the two groups broke one another's heads in the streets and set fire to one another's newspaper offices at the same time as their spiritual leaders were appearing in public arm in arm.

[114] p. 339. *Ngo Dinh Nhu's contacts with the DRV*. The diplomatic gossip of the moment reported that Nhu's feelers had been listened to in Hanoi. If this was so, the DRV's subsequent public disowning of any control over the fighting in the South and its insistence—strenuously backed up for some reason by French Government representatives, businessmen, and press—that the NFLSV was an independent body, shows either a change of policy or—more plausibly—a hardening attitude once America had become chief protagonist in place of the RVN.

[115] p. 340. *Public executions*. Westerners have been shocked from time to time by public executions that have appeared to be staged in Vietnam for political reasons; but in part the law, which dates back to French times, provides the explanation. In the Penal Code of Cochinchina (art. 12) the guillotine is the only lawful mode of execution—so that, strictly speaking, the shooting of Can in Saigon was perhaps irregular —, but there is no stipulation that it should be in public, although it seems usually to have been so. In the Penal Code of Annam (art. 6), execution can be by guillotine or by shooting but *must* be in public in either case.

[116] p. 348. *The Dai Viet Party*. The Dai Viet at this time was even more split than the VNQDD, the Sects, the Catholics and Buddhists, or even the army. Having still no mass membership, it found itself without a territorial base of family and secret-society ties in the provinces such as the VNQDD commanded in central Annam; it consisted in fact only of its half-dozen leaders and their personal clients, and these divided broadly in two ways: firstly into Tonkinese, Annamite, and Cochinchinese, and secondly into émigrés and those who had stayed at home. Dr Nguyen Ton Hoan was the leading Cochinchinese; he was also the leading émigré. He returned from Paris in February 1964—with an official French send-off, since he expected to become Prime Minister under the patronage of Gen. Khanh. But nobody else was willing to work under him, and so Khanh took the premiership and made Hoan Deputy Premier in charge of pacification. His ignorance of the state of the country (and perhaps of contemporary intrigues) made his position untenable, and after a few months he was forced to resign. He went to the Dai Viet base at Tokyo and thence back to Paris. Dr Phan Huy Quat (Tonkinese) and Mr Ha Thuc Ky (Annamite) fared better as non-émigrés, but each in turn was squeezed out again by regional rivalries.

[117] p. 350. *Thich Tri Quang and the VC.* It had been the contention of Ngo
Dinh Nhu that Tri Quang had engineered the Buddhist crisis
deliberately to help the VC; Western observers had generally preferred—in the hardly surprising absence of direct evidence of col-
lusion (Mecklin, 1965, p. 160)—to see in his actions only religious
fervour. His prominent position during the much more severe agita-
tions of 1964, after the Buddhists' demands on the religious issue had
been met, brought many foreigners round to agree with Nhu after all.
In Oct. 1964, therefore, Tri Quang published a statement in his
newly-founded periodical, *Lap Truong* (Foundation), that Communism in South Vietnam would be the end of Buddhism, as it had
been in the North, but without mentioning his own reaction to such
an eventuality (quoted in *Dan Ta*, 21 Oct. 1964). During 1965 and
1966 he became outspokenly anti-American and was detained while
on hunger strike to force the Prime Minister to resign (*NYT*, 23
June 1966). In Sept. 1967 he again led demonstrations aimed at dis-
crediting newly-elected Pres. Nguyen Van Thieu in the US.

[118] p. 353. *Vietnamese electioneering.* Against the background described in
notes 84 and 108, it is hard to see how a free election as understood in
the West could be held in Vietnam. In the disturbed state of the
country, campaigning by private candidates, even if they could
afford the expense, would be impossible without recourse to use of
official transport, including helicopters and other facilities such as
armed escorts. The current electoral law (*Sac-luat* No. 022 of 19 June
1966 for most of the country, *Sac-luat* No. 028 of 22 July 1966 for the
districts of Annam inhabited by ethnic minorities) therefore provide
for the payment of all costs of electioneering by the Treasury. The
security situation also necessitates vetting of candidates—a further
derogation from freedom, however unavoidable.

[119] p. 355. *Press policy.* Press policy was an example of the harmful consequences of the army's inexperience at governing. There was, of
course, no strong press tradition, for which the national failing of
quarrelsomeness was chiefly to blame. By the end of December 1963
the Minister of Information (a rather inappropriate authority to
make Registrar of the Press if he was to be the press's friend) had received over 100 applications to start newspapers; most of these were
granted without financial guarantees of good behaviour, in order not
to displease the applicants, who might have made trouble on grounds
of discrimination. Registration was thus meaningless, and was justified in fact only by the shortage of newsprint, which the Junta controlled and rationed in order to keep the price down and give everybody a 'fair' share—instead of decontrolling it and letting the fly-
by-nights go to the wall. (Admittedly, decontrol was made more difficult by the urgency of finding more imports to license on account of
the CIP and the army's pay.) Libel and blackmail became the prin-

cipal source of income of some of these exercises of 'democratic rights'—a situation all the more disreputable because the official pre-censorship of news and comment was kept up, and whatever was printed consequently carried an *imprimatur*. Libel expanded from time to time into sedition and defeatism, which the Junta was averse to controlling by judicial process; instead it closed the offending journals down, in spite of the censorship—a sanction applied in the single year 1964 to about ten times the number of papers suppressed in all the years of the Ngo Dinh Diem 'tyranny'.

[120] p. 359. *Effect of conscription*. During 1964 the army's requirements for manpower to meet its programme of expansion led to curtailment of the grounds on which exemption from military service might be granted. There were no reserved occupations, and the only grounds that remained arose from the personal situation of the conscript: he might be let off because of family commitments or have his service deferred if he was a student. Students secured further protraction for their period of exemption, whether deliberately or not, whenever their courses were suspended on account of their political agitation against the Junta of the moment. Student status was reckoned to extend to apprentices and other classes of trainee in skilled trades, so that managers soon found their factories and workshops had to be kept going with relatively abundant trainee labour while all their skilled and experienced workers were called up. This in turn meant that demands for artisans for military construction work had to be met in part by recruiting American workmen. There is some evidence that a similar process has been at work in the DRV since 1965, as more men were called up for combat service in the South and their place was taken in part by Chinese workmen.

[121] p. 363. *'New Life' and China*. Vietnamese titles and slogans usually have overtones inaudible to the foreign ear; *tan sinh hoat* was the slogan of the 'social revolution' of Chiang Kai-shek in China, and the in-fluence of Formosa was strong in Vietnam at this time, both directly and through USOM.

[122] p. 364. *VC taxes and administration*. The year 1964 appears from inter-rogations and captured documents to have been the easiest for the VC, for aid was at its peak, the rural population had not taken refuge in the towns yet, and Government vigilance was at its lowest ebb. Tax was derived from levies on all goods moved by road or waterway, and it is said to have covered even the oil companies' aviation spirit on its way to helicopter bases; USOM aid that had not paid such duties was liable to confiscation as 'booty' (*cua cuop*). In 1965 the NFLSV seems to have been less satisfied with its finances: a general survey for Cochinchina, captured in Mar. 1966, gives the overall 'norm fulfilment' as only 75 per cent; however, the 'norm' had been set at 150 per cent of 1964, so there was certainly no drop in the

absolute figure. This document does not give the actual sums involved, but the evidence of other documents that do would indicate total collections running into several hundred m. piastres per annum —£1,000 m. in the opinion of Pike (1966, p. 304). Do these operations justify occasional VC claims to be 'administering liberated areas' in their propaganda to the West? Not really: tax rolls existed only with reference to concessions and plantations, for which they were abstracted from government revenue offices surreptitiously (or else from the management) and copied, the managers being required to pay to the VC the figure named in them. Elsewhere, the cadres tried to fulfil their norm as best they could, hoping those from whom big sums were exacted would not complain to VC headquarters. But the lack of facilities for keeping records of public business—something the DRV suffered from itself before 1954—makes it doubtful whether the activities of the NFLSV merit the description 'administration'.

[123] p. 368. '*More flags*'. The 'more flags' policy had previously brought aid to South Vietnam of one kind or another from some 40 countries, largely in response to an appeal circulated to nearly 100 countries by President Diem in 1962. But whereas in his days the emphasis had been on helping Vietnam independently of the US, the emphasis since 1964 has been on helping the US with its Vietnam commitment.

[124] p. 370. *Resources control*. An intensive programme of Resources Control was manned at the same time by the National Police and was intercepting large quantities of supposedly VC supplies. Like all pacification and security measures, Resources Control was put into effect at random all over the country at once; it was confined to roads and waterways, was not co-ordinated with other security measures, and was judged successful or otherwise according to the quantity of supplies confiscated from passers-by—which did, however, include arms and ammunition now and again. No attempt was made to intercept movement of supplies by coolie columns through the hills.

[125] p. 372. *DRV command over the NFLSV and PRP*. It was inevitable that a DRV General would have to take overall command when regular formations were drafted to the South, armed with weapons 'from the Socialist bloc', and when the North began to contribute half the NFLSV's expenses (People's Army Gen. Nguyen Van Vinh, p. 374 n. (a) above); all this could hardly have been put under the guerrilla commanders of the South. Gen. Thanh's identity was given away by a number of prisoners of war and surrendered personnel, and in Feb. 1967 a photograph of him in camp was captured, together with portraits of three other People's Army Generals, by American forces at what appeared to be GHQ near Tay Ninh (USIS communiqué, Saigon, 18 Mar. 1967). Gen. Thanh received his directions as to policy from the Politburo of the Party in Hanoi through Gen. Vinh;

the letter from First Secretary Le Duan in Mar. 1966 contained the political background, as laid down at the Party Congress, to the campaigns that were to be planned for 1966 to lead to a position of strength from which the next stage, of 'fighting while negotiating', could be embarked on. This stage had not been reached, however, when the General died in Hanoi on 6 July 1967 (VNA, 8 July 1967)—
—or, according to the suggestion of the authorities in Saigon, in an air raid on his GHQ in the South (*SP*, 9 July 1967)—mourned by the PRP as 'a loss for the Southern Armed Forces and people' (Liberation Radio, 8 July 1967). The funeral oration pronounced in Hanoi admitted he had been 'leading the army against the aggression of US imperialism' (NCNA, 9 July 1967), and the Chinese Government leaders' appreciation of the gravity of the loss 'to our common revolutionary cause' (Chairman Mao, ibid. 8 July 1967) of this 'outstanding Marxist-Leninist' (Chinese Party Central Committee, ibid.) and 'fighter for mankind's cause of Communism' (Prime Minister Chou Ên-lai, ibid.) is shown by the long list of senior Peking officials who called at the DRV Embassy to express their condolences. At the time of writing, his successor has not been identified.

[126] p. 377. *RVN Const. 1967*. The Constituent Assembly elected in Sept. 1966 drafted a new constitution to replace the 1956 one suspended on 1 Nov. 1963; it was promulgated on 1 Apr 1967, amid no public enthusiasm, but in fulfilment of promises to the US Administration, desirous of justifying its support for the RVN against charges at home that the Saigon Junta was a military dictatorship. The new constitution follows the old in proclaiming the national sovereignty and territorial integrity of all Vietnam, the fundamental rights of its citizens, and the separation of powers. The American model is followed more closely, with an executive President and almost sinecure Vice-President, a bicameral National Assembly (Senate and House of Representatives), and hopes for a two-party balance of power. The most radical change from 1956, however, is the extension of the elective principle to the office of province chief, besides mayor and village chief (all answerable to elective councils), but not district chief. A prime minister and other ministers are appointed by the President, answerable to him, not to the Assembly. Either left over for further legislation or ignored are (*a*) procedures for ensuring independence of the Judiciary, (*b*) responsibilities of ministers—especially in regard to the henceforward decentralized territorial administration—and (*c*) the powers of the Armed Forces, National Security, and Cultural Councils. The President is C-in-C, but relations between army and Government are not spelt out. He may take emergency powers as before but, this time, subject to ratification by the National Assembly. The first President to be elected is Lt. Gen. Nguyen Van Thieu; his election (on 3 Sept. 1967) was attended by the same

charges of gerrymandering from unsuccessful rivals as the elections of Ngo Dinh Diem, and, it is to be feared, with similar effect on public opinion abroad.

GLOSSARY

(An asterisk in the Chinese column indicates that, as far as the author is aware, the expression is not used in Chinese in quite the same way.)

Vietnamese	Chinese	English
ap	*yi	hamlet
ban dac-cong	*t'ê-kung pan	special work team
bang	pang	Chinese *congrégation*
Bao An	pao an	Civil Guard
Binh Dinh Vuong	p'ing-ting wang	Prince of Pacification
bua gong	—	talisman of invulnerability
Buu Son Ky Huong	pao shan ch'i hsiang	magic fragrance from the precious hill
cach menh (or mang)	kê-ming	revolutionary
can bo	kan pu	Communist cadre
Can Lao	*ch'in lao	hardworking
Cao Dai	*kao t'ai	high altar
chi bo	chih-pu	cell
chien dau	chan tou	defensive
chien luoc	chan lüeh	strategic
chinh nghia	chêng yi	correct line (Com.); righteousness (non-Com.); originally, the orthodox interpretation of the classics
chu luc	chu li	main force
chu nho	*ju tzu	Chinese characters
chu nom	*nan tzu	non-Chinese ('southern') characters
chua	*chu	Vietnamese *shogun*
Cong An	kung an	Communist security police
cong dich	kung yi	*corvée*
cong san	kung ch'an	Communist
cong tac dac biet	t'ê pieh kung tso	special tasks
cua cuop	—	booty
Dai Co Viet	*ta ch'ü yüeh	medieval name for Vietnam
Dai Noi	ta nei	the imperial palace
dan bo	*pu min (=tsi min)	owners of village land
dan lau	liu min	landless peasants
dan trung van dong (dan van)	min-tsung yün-tung (min-yün)	masses mobilization or activation
dan ve	*min-wei (=min ping)	local militia
dang	tang	party
dao noi	*nei tao	secret sect
den thanh	— shêng	sacred fane

Vietnamese	*Chinese*	*English*
Di	yi	eastern barbarians
dia bo	ti pu	land register
dich van	yi yün	Party activist
dinh	t'ing	village hall
dinh dien	*ting t'ien	pioneer settlement
doc lap	tu li	independence
doc phu	tu fu	district officers
don dien	t'un t'ien	demobilization settlement
dong chi	t'ung chih	comrade
Dong Duong	*tung yang	Indochina
dong minh	t'ung mêng	brotherhood
Dong Son	tung shan	eastern hills
du	yü	imperial decree
duc	tê	mode of address (=virtue)
duy tan	wei hsin	reform
Giac Van Than	— wên ch'ên	War of the Civil Mandarins
Giam doc Cong Vu	kung wu chien tu	Directorate-General of the Public Services
Giao Chi	Chiao Chih	ancient Tonkin
giao hoi	ch'iao-hui	religious society
Gia Tong	chiao-tsung	Pope
ho duong	—	Catholic parish commune (*chrétienté*)
Ho Phap	hu fa	Defender of the Faith; medium
hoc tap	hsüeh hsi	indoctrination
hoi dong xa	*shê hui t'ung	village council
hop tac	hê tso	co-operation
Hué	hoa	place name (=transformed)
Hung Vuong	hsiung wang	legendary dynasty
huong dich	*hsiang yi	village elders
khoi nghia	ch'i yi	revolt
khu tru mat	*ch'ou-mi ch'ü	close settlement (*agroville*)
kiem thao	chien t'ao	criticism and self-criticism
kinh luoc	ching-lüeh	area commander
lap truong	li ch'ang	laying foundations
lien gia	*lien chia[a]	linked households
linh	ling	infantryman
luat	lü	permanent law
luc luong biet kich	pieh-chi li-liang	commandoes
mon	mên	sect (=door)
Nam Giao	*nan chiao (=chiao t'an)	Altar of Heaven
nam tien	*nan chien	expansion southwards
nghi-dinh	yi-ting	regulation
ngoai nhiem	wai jên	provincial appointment
nhan dan	jên-min	the people

[a] A Chinese phrase *lien chia* does exist, as an alternative to *pao chia* (q.v.), but the *chia* is a different word, corresponding to Vietnamese *giap*.

Vietnamese	Chinese		English
Nhan Vi	*jên wei		station in life
nuoc phep	—		holy water (early Cath.)
nuoc thai	—	t'ai	holy water (Buddh.)
nuoc thanh	—	shêng	holy water (later Cath.)
o-Phep	wu fa		Francophobe
—	pao chia		policing by wards
phan canh	fên kêng		sharecropping
phong thuy	fêng-shui		geomancy
Que That	kuei t'a		gynecaeum
Quoc Hoc	kuo hsüeh		college for sons of mandarins
quoc ngu	kuo yü		romanization[a]
Quoc Truong	*kuo chang		Head of State
sac-lenh	ch'ih-ling		decree
sac-luat	*ch'ih-lü		decree-law
ta dien	tso t'ien		tenant farmer
Tam Giac	san chüeh		the Three Enlightenments
Tam Nhan	san yin		the Three Promptings
Tam Phu	san fu		the Three Realms
Tam Tuc	*san tsu		the Three Sufficiencies
tan sinh (hoat)	hsin shêng (huo)		new life
Tay Son	hsi shan		western hills
Tet	*tsieh		New Year's Day
thai hon	t'ai hun		great spirit
thich	shih		Hindu *shakya*
Thien Dia Hoi	t'ien-ti hui		Heaven and Earth Society
thu hien	shou hsien		territorial prefect
—	t'ung chih		adviser, coadministrator
tong tran	tsung chên		provincial governor
Tra Son	*cha shan		a hillside suddenly alight
trinh sat	chên ch'a		security police
tu ve	*tzu wei		self-defence
uy ban hanh chanh	hsing-chêng wei pan		administrative committee
uy ban khang chien	*k'ang chan (=k'ang chêng) wei pan		resistance committee
Vien Hoa Dao	hua tao yüan		Buddhist *propaganda fide*
Viet gian	yüeh chien		Vietnamese traitors
xa quan	*shê kuan		village mandarin
xa truong	*shê chang		village chief

[a] The Chinese equivalent does not refer to the system of writing but means standard speech.

BIBLIOGRAPHY

1. *Vietnamese Periodicals and Newspapers*

Bulletin des Amis du Vieux Hué (Hué).
Bulletin de l'École Française d'Extrême Orient (Hanoi and Paris).
Bulletin de l'Institut de Recherches Historiques (Saigon).
Bulletin de la Société des Études Indochinoises (Saigon).
Chinh Luan (Saigon).
Dan Chu (Saigon).
Dan Ta (Saigon).
Dat To (Saigon).
Hoc Tap (Hanoi).
Journal d'Extrême Orient (Saigon).
Nhan Dan (Hanoi).
Revue Indochinoise Juridique et Économique (Hanoi).
Saigon Daily News.
Saigon Post.
Times of Vietnam (Saigon).
Tu Do (Saigon).
Xay Dung (Saigon).

2. *Official Publications*

DEMOCRATIC REPUBLIC OF VIETNAM

South Viet-Nam National Front for Liberation. *Declaration of the First Congress*. Hanoi, 1962.
Thirty Years of Struggle of the Party. Hanoi, 1960.

FOREIGN MINISTERS' CONFERENCE, GENEVA 1954

Further Documents relating to the Discussion of Indo-China at the Geneva Conference, June 16–July 21, 1954. Cmd 9239, 1954.

FRANCE

Les Accords franco-vietnamiens du 8 mars 1949 [Élysée Agreements]. *Notes et études documentaires*, no. 1147, 1949. (RIIA, *Documents, 1949–50*, pp. 596–608.)
Conventions inter-États conclues en application de l'accord franco-vietnamien du 8 mars 1949. *Notes et études documentaires*, no. 1425, 24 Jan. 1950.
Présidence du Conseil. *Premier rapport de la Sous-commission de modernisation de l'Indochine*. Paris, 1948.

HONG KONG

Problem of Narcotic Drugs in Hong Kong. Hong Kong, 1959.

INDOCHINA

Comité Agricole et Industriel de Cochinchine. *La Cochinchine française en 1878*. Paris, 1878.

Direction Générale de l'Instruction Publique. *L'Annam scolaire.* Hanoi, 1931.
—— *La Cochinchine scolaire.* Hanoi, 1931.
Gouvernement-Général. *Contribution à l'histoire des mouvements politiques de l'Indochine française.* Hanoi, 1933–4. 5 vols.
—— *L'Indochine scolaire.* Hanoi, 1931.
—— *Réglementation du travail en Indochine.* Hanoi, 1937.
—— *Organisation judiciaire de l'Indochine.* Hanoi, 1938–9.
Service de Statistique Générale. *Annuaire statistique de l'Indo-Chine 1936–7.* Hanoi, 1938.

INTERNATIONAL CONTROL COMMISSION

4th Interim Report, Apr. 11, 1955 to Aug. 10, 1955. Cmd 9654, 1955.
6th Interim Report, Dec. 11, 1955 to July 31, 1956. Cmnd 31, 1957.
9th Interim Report, May 1, 1958 to Jan. 31, 1959. Cmnd 726, 1959.
10th Interim Report, Feb. 1, 1959 to Jan. 31, 1960. Cmnd 1040, 1960.
11th Interim Report, Feb. 1, 1960 to Feb. 28, 1961. Cmnd 1551, 1961.
Special Report to the Co-Chairmen of the Geneva Conference on Indo-China, June 2, 1962. Cmnd 1755, 1962.
Special Report to the Co-Chairmen of the Geneva Conference on Indo-China, Feb. 13, 1965. Cmnd 2609, 1965.

REPUBLIC OF VIETNAM

Violations of the Geneva Agreements by the Viet-Minh Communists. Saigon, 1959.
Directorate-General of the Civil Service. *Annual Report 1958.* Saigon, 1959.
Information Services Press. *Bilan des réalisations gouvernementales 1954–62.* Saigon, 1962.
Institut de la Statistique et des Études Économiques. *Annuaire statistique du Viêtnam, 1952–3; —1956; —1958–9 —1962; —1963.* Saigon, 1955–65.
Institut National de la Statistique. *Annuaire statistique du Viêtnam, cinquième volume 1954–5.* Saigon, USOM, 1961.
Ministry of Labour. *Bo Luat Lao-Dong.* Saigon, 1958.
Secretariat of State for Information. *The Constitution* [of 1956]. Saigon, 1958.
Société de Recherches Historiques, ed. *Hong-Duc Thien Chinh Thu.* Saigon, 1959.

STATE OF VIET-NAM

Inst. de la Statistique et des Études Économiques. *Annuaire statistique du Viêt-Nam, 1949–50; —1950–1; —1951–2.* Saigon, 1951–3.
—— *Budget de l'année 1953.* Saigon, 1953.

UNITED NATIONS

Fact-Finding Mission to S. Viet-Nam. *Report on the Violation of Human Rights in South Vietnam.* A/5630. New York, 1963.
UN and others. *Towards the Economic Development of the Republic of Viet-Nam; Report of the Economic Survey Mission . . . organized by the United Nations, the International Labour Office, and the Food and Agriculture Organization.* (Chief of Mission: Carter Goodrich.) New York, 1959.

UNITED STATES

Dept of State. *Aggression from the North; the Record of North Vietnam's Campaign to Conquer South Vietnam.* 1965.

—— *American Foreign Policy, 1950–5: Basic Documents.* 1957. 2 vols.

—— *American Foreign Policy: Current Documents, 1956; —1961; —1962.* 1959–62.

USIS. *Communist Reaction to the End of the Diem Government.* Saigon, 1963.

USOM. *Studies on Land Tenure in Viet Nam; terminal report by J. P. Gittinger, Agricultural Economist.* Saigon, 1959.

—— *Taxation in South Vietnam,* by Milton C. Taylor. Saigon, 1959.

—— *Studies in Vietnamese Economy,* ed. by Alek A. Rozental. Saigon, 1964.

—— *Analysis of Property Tax in Vietnam,* by Ray E. Davis. Saigon, 1959.

—— *The United States Assistance Program for Vietnam,* 1965.

3. Books and Articles

AUBARET, G. *Histoire et description de la Basse Cochinchine* (the *Gia Dinh Dong Chi*). Paris, 1863.

—— *Le code annamite (Hoang-Viet Luat-Le).* Paris, 1865. 2 vols.

AUROUSSEAU, Léonard. La première conquête chinoise des pays annamites. *BEFEO* (Hanoi), xxiii (1924), pp. 137–264.

—— Sur le nom de *Cochinchine. BEFEO* (Hanoi), xxiv (1925).

AUVADE, Robert. *Bibliographie critique des oeuvres parues sur l'Indochine française.* Paris, 1963.

BATOR, Victor. *Vietnam: a diplomatic tragedy, origins of US involvement.* London, 1967.

BERNARD, Paul. *Le problème économique indochinois.* Paris, 1934.

—— *Nouveaux aspects du problème économique indochinois.* Paris, 1937.

BERVAL, René de. *Présence du Bouddhisme.* Saigon, 1959.

BETTS, Raymond F. *Assimilation and Association in French Colonial Theory.* New York & London, 1961. (Columbia Studies in the Social Sciences No. 604.)

BLANCHET, M.-Th. *La naissance de l'État Associé du Viet-Nam.* Paris, 1954.

BLET, Henri. *France d'Outre-Mer.* Grenoble & Paris, 1950. (Vol. iii of *Histoire de la colonisation française.*)

BODARD, Lucien. *La guerre d'Indochine—l'Enlisement.* Paris, 1963.

—— *L'Humiliation.* Paris, 1965.

BORRI, Fr. Cristoforo. *Relation de la nouvelle mission des Pères de la Compagnie de Jésus au Royaume de la Cochinchine.* Rennes, 1631.

BOUDET, Paul. La conquête de la Cochinchine par les Nguyen et le rôle des émigrés chinois. *BEFEO* (Hanoi), xlii (1942).

BOUDILLON, A. *Le régime de la propriété foncière en Indochine.* Paris, Ministère des Colonies, 1915.

BOUROTTE, Bernard. Essai d'histoire des populations Montagnardes du Sud-Indochinois jusqu'à 1945. *BSEI*, xxx (1935).

BOXER, Charles R. Asian Potentates and European Artillery in the 16th–18th Centuries. *JMBRAS*, xxxviii/208 (1966).

BRIMMELL, J. H. *Communism in South East Asia.* London, OUP/RIIA, 1959.

BRUNSCHWIG, Henri. *Mythes et réalités de l'Impérialisme colonial français 1871–1914,* Paris, 1960.

BURCHETT, Wilfred. *Vietnam: Inside Story of the Guerrilla War.* New York, 1965.

BUTTINGER, Joseph. *The Smaller Dragon: a political history of Vietnam.* New York, 1958.

CADIÈRE, Abbé Léopold. *Croyances et pratiques religieuses des Vietnamiens.* Saigon, 1955–8.

CAMERLYNCK, C.-H. L'Option en faveur de la loi française par des contractants annamites. *RIJE,* 1937.

CATROUX [Gov.-Gen. (Army General)], Georges. *Deux actes du drame indochinois.* Paris, 1959.

CÉLERIER, Pierre. *Menaces sur le Viet-Nam.* Saigon, 1950.

CHAFFARD, Georges. Le gouvernement nord-vietnamien doit à son tour affronter le mécontentement populaire. *Le Monde,* 30 Nov. 1956.

CH'ÊN, Jerome. *Mao and the Chinese Revolution.* London, 1965.

CHESNEAUX, Jean. *Contribution à l'histoire de la nation vietnamienne.* Paris, 1956.

CHILD, Frank C. *Economic Growth, Capital Formation and Public Policy in Vietnam.* Saigon, MSU, 1961.

CH'Ü T'UNG-TSU. *Law and Society in Traditional China.* Paris, 1961.

—— *Local Government in China under the Ch'ing.* Cambridge, Mass., 1962.

COEDÈS, G. *Les États hindouisés d'Indochine et d'Indonésie.* Paris, 1948.

COLE, Allan B. *Conflict in Indo-china and International Repercussions 1945–1955.* Ithaca, 1956 (mimeo.).

COLLIS, Maurice. *Siamese White.* 2nd ed. London, 1951.

—— *'Wayfoong', the Hongkong and Shanghai Banking Corporation.* London, 1965.

COULET, Georges. *Les sociétés secrètes en terre d'Annam.* Saigon, 1926.

—— *Bonzes, pagodes et sociétés secrètes en Cochinchine. Extrême Asie,* 1928.

—— *Cultes et religions de l'Indochine annamite.* Saigon, 1930.

COULING, Samuel. *The Encyclopaedia Sinica.* Shanghai, 1917.

CROWDER, Michael. Indirect Rule: French and British Style. *Africa* (London), xxiv/3 (1964).

CULTRU, P. *Histoire de la Cochinchine française des origines à 1883.* Paris, 1910.

DANG-CHAN-LIEU. Annamese Nationalism. *Pacific Affairs,* xx/1 (1947).

DAS, S. R. Mohan. *Ho Chi Minh: Nationalist or Soviet agent?* Bombay, 1950.

DAUDIN, Pierre. Un Japonais à la cour des T'ang. BSEI, xl (1965).

DAUFÈS, E. *La garde indigène de l'Indochine.* Avignon, 1933–4. 2 vols.

DECOUX [Gov.-Gen. (Admiral)], J. *A la barre de l'Indochine.* Paris, 1949.

DE GROOT, J. J. M. *Sectarianism and Religious Persecution in China.* Amsterdam, 1903–4.

DELOUSTAL, Raymond. La justice dans l'ancien Annam. *BEFEO,* viii–xiii, xix & xxii (1908–23).

DES MICHELS, Abel. *Annales impériales de l'Annam.* Paris, 1880.

DESPUECH, Jacques. *Le trafic de piastres.* Paris, 1953.

DEVÉRIA, G. *Histoire des relations de la Chine avec l'Annam-Vietnam du XVIe au XIXe siècle.* Paris, 1880.

DEVILLERS, Philippe. *Histoire du Viet-Nam de 1940 à 1952.* Paris, 1952.

—— Vietnamese Nationalism and French Policies, *in* W. J. Holland, ed., *Asian Nationalism and the West.* New York, 1953.

—— The Struggle for Unification. *China Quarterly,* No. 9, London (1962).

BIBLIOGRAPHY 425

—— & LACOUTURE, Jean. *La fin d'une guerre*. Paris, 1960.

DONNISON, F. S. V. *British Military Administration in the Far East 1943–6*. London, 1956.

DONOGHUE, John D. *My Thuan, a Mekong Delta Village*. Saigon, MSU, 1959.

DORSENNE, Jean. *Faudra-t-il évacuer l'Indochine?* Paris, 1932.

—— *Le péril rouge en Indochine*. *Revue des Deux Mondes*, 1932.

DOUMER [Gov.-Gen.], Paul. *Situation de l'Indo-Chine (1897–1901)*. Hanoi, 1902.

DUMOUTIER, G. *Les symboles, les emblèmes et les accessoires du culte chez les Annamites*. Paris, 1891.

DURAND, Maurice. *Miroir complet de l'histoire du Viet*. Hanoi, 1950.

—— *La Dynastie des Ly antérieurs*. *BEFEO*, xliv (1954).

—— *Technique et panthéon des médiums vietnamiens*. Paris, 1959.

—— *Imagerie populaire vietnamienne*. Paris, 1960.

DUTREB, M. *L'Amiral Dupré*. Paris, 1924.

EDEN, Sir Anthony (Earl of Avon). *Memoirs*, iii: *Full Circle*. London, 1960.

—— Letter to *Sunday Times*, 14 Apr. 1964.

—— *Towards Peace in Indo-China*. London, 1966. (Chatham House Essay No. 14.)

ÉLY [High Commissioner (Gen.)], Paul. *Mémoires: l'Indochine dans la tourmente*. Paris, 1964.

ENNIS, Thomas E. *French Policy and Developments in Indochina*. Chicago, 1936.

ESCARRA, Jean (*see also* Maspéro, H.). *Le droit chinois*. Peking, 1936.

FAIRBANK, J. K. & TÊNG SZE-YÜ. *Ch'ing Administration: Three Studies*. Cambridge, Mass., 1960. (Harvard-Yenching Inst. Ser. No. xix.)

FALL, Bernard. *The Viet-Minh Regime*. New York, 1956 (mimeo.).

—— *Le Viet Minh*. Paris, 1960.

—— *Street without Joy: Insurgency in Indochina, 1946–63*. 3rd ed. London, 1963.

—— *The Two Viet-Nams*. London, 1963.

—— *Viet-Nam Witness, 1953–1966*. London, 1966.

FAVRE, B. *Les sociétés secrètes en Chine*. Paris, 1933.

FERRY [Prime Minister], Jules. *Le Tonkin et la mère-patrie*. Paris, 1890.

FIELDHOUSE, D. K. *The Colonial Empires*. London, 1966.

FISCHER, Ruth. *Von Lenin zu Mao: Kommunismus in der Bandung-Ära*. Cologne, 1956.

FISHEL, Wesley R., ed. *Problems of Freedom: South Vietnam since Independence*. East Lansing, MSU, 1961.

GALEMBERT, J. de. *Les administrations et les services publics indochinois*. Hanoi, 1931.

GASPARDONE, Émile. Bonzes des Ming réfugiés en Annam. *Sinologica* (Basle), ii (1950).

GAULTIER, Marcel. *Gia Long*. Saigon, 1933.

—— *Minh-Mang*. Paris, 1935.

GERNET, Jacques. *Les aspects économiques du Bouddhisme dans la société chinoise du Ve au Xe siècle*. Saigon, 1956.

GETTLEMAN, Marvin E., ed. *Vietnam*. London, 1965.

GINSBURGS, George. Local Government and Administration in North Vietnam, 1945–1954. *China Quarterly*, No. 10 (1962).

GIRAN, Paul. *Magie et religion annamites*. Paris, 1912.

GITTINGER, J. P. United States Policy toward Agrarian Reform in Under-developed Nations. *Land Economics* (Madison, Wis.), xxxvii (1961).

GOBRON, Gabriel. *Histoire du Caodaisme*. Paris, 1948.

GOLOUBEW, V. *Mélanges sur le Cambodge ancien. BEFEO*, xxiv (1925).

—— Le peuple de Dong-son et les Muong. *Cahiers de l'École Française d'Extrême Orient* (Hanoi), No. 10 (1937).

GOSSELIN [Capt.] Charles. *L'Empire d'Annam*. Paris, 1904.

GOUIN, Abbé Eugène. *Dictionnaire vietnamien-chinois-français*. Saigon, 1957.

GOUROU, Pierre. Les noms de famille ou 'ho' chez les Annamites du delta tonkinois. *BEFEO*, xxxii (1932).

—— *L'utilisation du sol en Indochine française*. Paris, 1940.

—— For a French Indo-China Federation. *Pacific Affairs*, xx/1 (1947).

GREVILLOT, Jean-Marie. *Les grands courants de la pensée contemporaine: Éxistentialisme, Marxisme, Personnalisme chrétien*. Paris, 1947.

GROSLIER, Bernard Philippe. *Angkor et le Cambodge au XVIe siècle*. Paris, 1958.

HAILEY, Lord. *An African Survey*. London, OUP/RIIA, 1945.

HALBERSTAM, David. *The Making of a Quagmire*. London, 1965.

HALL, D. G. E. *A History of South-East Asia*. London, 1964.

HAMMER, Ellen J. *The Struggle for Indochina*. Stanford, Calif., 1954.

HARMAND [Gov.-Gen.], Jules. *Domination et colonisation*. Paris, 1910.

HARRISON, James P. Communist Interpretations of the Chinese Peasant Wars. *China Quarterly*, No. 24 (1965).

HAUDRICOURT, André-G. De l'origine des tons en Vietnamien. *Journal Asiatique*, ccxlii (1954).

HENDRY, James B. *The Small World of Khanh Hau*. Chicago, 1964.

HENRY, Yves. *Économie agricole de l'Indochine*. Hanoi, 1932.

Heroes and Heroines of the Liberation Armed Forces of South Vietnam. Hanoi [?], 1965.

HICKEY, Gerald Cannon. *Les pays montagnards du sud*. Saigon, MSU, 1957.

—— *Village in Vietnam*. New Haven, Conn., 1964.

HIGGINS, Marguerite. *Our Vietnam Nightmare*. New York, 1965.

Histoire sommaire du Caodaisme, publ. by Trung Hung Giao Ly Vien, Danang (Tourane).

HO-CHI-MINH [alias NGUYEN-AI-QUOC]. *Le procès de la colonisation française*. Paris, 1926. (Reissued Hanoi, 1962.)

—— Le chemin qui m'a conduit au Léninisme. *Écho du Vietnam* (Paris), July 1960.

—— *Prison Diary*. 3rd ed. Hanoi, 1966.

HOANG-VAN-CHI. *From Colonialism to Communism; a case history of North Vietnam*. London, 1964.

HOGARD, J. Guerre révolutionnaire et pacification. *Revue Militaire d'Information* (Paris), No. 280 (1957).

HONEY, P. J. Progress in the Republic of Vietnam. *World Today*, Feb. 1959.

—— *North Vietnam Today*. New York, 1962.

—— North Vietnam's Workers' Party and South Vietnam's People's Revolutionary Party. *Pacific Affairs*, xxv/4 (1962–3).

—— *Communism in North Vietnam*. Cambridge, Mass., 1963.

—— Hanoi and the Vietnam War. *Mizan* (London), Jan.–Feb. 1967.

HOYT, Howard W. *Civil Police Administrative Program*. Saigon, MSU, 1957.
HUANG HAI-AN. *Liu Yung-fu li-shih ts'ao*. 1936. Reprinted in *Chung-kuo chin-tai shih tzu-liao ts'ung-k'an*, vi. Shanghai, 1955.
HUGHES, E. R. *The Invasion of China by the Western World*. London, 1937.
HUMMEL, Arthur W. *Eminent Chinese of the Ch'ing Period*. Washington, 1943.
HU SHIH. *Wên Ts'un*. Shanghai, 1934.
HUYNH-VAN-CAO. *People's Strategy*. Saigon, 1960.

INTERNATIONAL LABOUR OFFICE. Problèmes du travail en Indochine. Geneva, 1937.
ISOART, Paul. *Le phénomène national vietnamien*. Paris, 1961.

JANSEN, Marius B. *The Japanese and Sun Yat-sen*. Cambridge, Mass., 1954.
The Jataka, or stories of the Buddha's former births, ed. E. B. Cowell. Cambridge, 1895–1913.
JEAN, M.-L. *Le régime législatif, administratif et judiciaire de l'Indochine*. Hanoi, 1944.
JOINER, Charles A. *Human Resources Needs in Vietnam*. Saigon (MSU), 1962.
JORDAN, Amos A. *Foreign Aid and the Defense of Southeast Asia*. New York, 1962.
JUMPER, Roy. Mandarin Bureaucracy and Politics in South Viet Nam. *Pacific Affairs*, xxx/i (1957).

KITAGAWA, Joseph M. Buddhism and Asiatic Politics. *Asia Survey* (Berkeley), ii/5 (1962).
KNOEBL, Kuno. *Victor Charlie: the Face of War in Vietnam*. London, 1967.
LACHEROY, Col. La guerre révolutionnaire. *Revue Militaire d'Information* (Paris), No. 281 (1957).
LACOUTURE, Jean (*see also* Devillers, P.). *Vietnam between Two Truces*. London, 1966.
LACROIX, Jean. *Marxisme, Existentialisme, Personnalisme*. Paris, 1949.
LAFONT, P.-B. Contribution à l'Etude des structures sociales des Chams du Viet-Nam. *BEFEO* (Paris), lii (1964).
LAMB, Alastair. *British Missions to Cochin China, 1778–1822*. Singapore, *JMBRAS*, 1961.
LANCASTER, Donald. *The Emancipation of French Indo-China*. London, OUP/RIIA, 1961.
LANESSAN [Gov.-Gen.], Jean Louis de. *L'Indo-Chine française*. Paris, 1889.
—— *La colonisation française en Indo-Chine*. Paris, 1895.
LANIEL [Prime Minister], Joseph. *Le drame indochinois*. Paris, 1957.
LAURENT, Arthur. *La Banque de l'Indochine*. Paris, 1954.
LE CHAU. *Le Viet Nam socialiste: une économie de transition*. Paris, 1966.
LE DUAN. *On the Socialist Revolution in Vietnam*. Hanoi, 1965.
LEGRAND, Julien-Joseph. *L'Indochine à l'heure japonaise*. Cannes, 1963.
LEMONNIER DE LA BISSACHÈRE, Abbé P. *État actuel du Tunkin, de la Cochinchine &c.* Paris, 1812.
LE MYRE DE VILERS [Gov.]. *Institutions civiles de la Cochinchine*. Paris, 1908.
LE-NGOC-TRU. Chu Quoc-ngu tu The-ky XVII den XIX. *BIRH*, No. 2 (1961).
LEROY [Col.], Jean. *Un homme dans la rizière*. Paris, 1955.
LE-THANH-KHOI. *Le Viet-Nam, histoire et civilisation*. Paris, 1955.

428 BIBLIOGRAPHY

LE-THANH-TUONG. *Un patriote annamite, admirateur de la France*. Hanoi, 1938.

LEVASSEUR, G. Les répercussions des accords de Nankin sur les problèmes de droit international privé en Indochine. *RIJE*, i (1937).

LEVY, Howard S. *Biography of Huang Ch'ao*. Berkeley/Los Angeles, 1955.

LI CHÊNG-FU. *Chün hsien shih-tai chih An-nan*. Shanghai, 1945.

LINDHOLM, Richard W. ed. *Viet-Nam; the first five years*. East Lansing, MSU, 1959.

LOUVET, Abbé Louis-E. *La Cochinchine religieuse*. Paris, 1885.

Lua Thieng. Saigon, Buddhist Publishing House, 1963.

LURO, Eliacin. *Le pays d'Annam*. Paris, 1876.

LYAUTEY [Maréchal], Hubert. *Lettres du Tonkin et de Madagascar*. Paris, 1921.

MADROLLE, Claude. Le Tonkin ancien. *BEFEO*, xxvii (1937).

MAI-THO-TRUYEN. Le Bouddhisme au Viet-Nam, *in* Berval, *Présence du Bouddhisme*. (Reissued separately 1962.)

MALLERET, Louis. Les fouilles d'Oc-Eo (1944). *BEFEO*, xlv (1951).

—— *L'archéologie du Delta du Mékong*. Paris, 1959.

MAO TSÈ-TUNG. *Selected Military Writings*. Peking, 1963.

—— *Selected Writings*. Peking, 1965.

MARINI, Fr. Giovanni Filippo de'. *Historia et relatione del Tunchino e del Giappone*. Rome, 1663.

MARITAIN, Jacques. *Humanisme intégral*. Paris, 1936.

MARUCCI, Fr. Giovanni. *Relation de ce qui s'est passé dans les Indes orientales*. Paris, 1651.

MASPÉRO, Georges. *Le royaume du Champa*. Paris/Brussels, 1928.

—— *Un empire colonial français: l'Indochine*. Paris/Brussels, 1929-30.

MASPÉRO, Henri. Phonétique historique de la langue annamite. *BEFEO*, xii (1930).

—— Études d'histoire d'Annam. *BEFEO*, xviii (1918).

—— Les régimes fonciers en Chine. *Études Historiques* (Paris), 1950.

—— & ESCARRA, Jean. *Les institutions de la Chine*. Paris, 1952.

MASSON, André. *Histoire de l'Indochine*. Paris, 1950.

MAYBON, Albert. *L'Indochine*. Paris, 1931.

MAYBON, Charles-B. *Les marchands européens en Cochinchine et au Tonkin (1660-1775)*. Paris, 1910.

—— *Histoire moderne du pays d'Annam*. Paris, 1919.

McLANE, Charles B. *Soviet Strategies in Southeast Asia*. Princeton, 1966.

McVEY, Ruth T. *The Calcutta Conference and the Southeast Asian Uprisings*. Ithaca, N.Y., 1958.

MECKLIN, John. *Mission in Torment*. New York, 1965.

MOORE, Robin. *The Green Berets*. New York, 1965.

MORDANT [Gen.] G. F. *Au service de la France en Indochine*. Saigon, 1950.

MORGAN, W. P. *Triad Societies in Hong Kong*. Hong Kong, 1960.

MORSE, Hosea B. *The International Relations of the Chinese Empire*. London, 1913-19. 3 vols.

—— *The Trade and Administration of China*. 3rd ed. London, 1921.

MOUNIER, Emmanuel. *Personalism*, tr. by P. Mairet. London, 1952.

MURPHY, Marvin & others. *Administration budgétaire au Viet-Nam*. Saigon, MSU, 1956.

Mus, Paul. The Role of the Village in Vietnamese Politics. *Pacific Affairs*, xxii/3 (1949).
—— *Viet-Nam; sociologie d'une guerre.* Paris, 1952.

Navarre [Gen.], Henri. *Agonie de l'Indochine.* Paris, 1956.
Navarrete, Fr. Domingos. *Travels and Controversies*, ed. J. S. Cummins. Cambridge, 1962. (Hakluyt Society.)
Nghiem Dang. *Viet-Nam; Politics and Public Administration.* Honolulu, 1966.
Nghiem Tham. Rapport sur les trésors Cham. *BIRH*, No. 1 (1960).
Ngo-Dinh-Diem. *Message to the National Assembly, 1 October 1962.* Saigon, 1962.
Ngo-Dinh-Khoi. L'Ambassade chinoise qui conféra l'investiture à Tu-Duc. *BAVH* (1916).
Ngo-Dinh-Nhu. *The Highland Refugees.* Saigon, 1963.
Ngo-Van-Chieu. *Journal d'un combattant viet-minh*, tr. Jacques Despuech. Paris, 1955.
Nguyen-Huu-Khang. *La commune annamite.* Paris, 1946.
Nguyen-Huu-Trong. *Les origines du clergé vietnamien.* Saigon, 1959.
Nguyen-Phut-Tan. *A Modern History of Vietnam.* Saigon, 1964.
Nguyen-Qui-Hung. *Neuf ans de dictature au Sud-Vietnam.* Saigon, 1964.
Nguyen Thai. *Is South Vietnam viable?* Manila, 1962.
Nguyen-Trung-Truong. *Handbook for the Village Council.* Saigon, 1963.
Nguyen-Tuyet-Mai. Electioneering Vietnamese style. *Asian Survey*, ii/9 (1962).
Nguyen-Van-Hao. *Bo Hinh Luat Viet Nam.* Saigon, 1962.
Nguyen-Van-Tam [Prime Minister]. Caodaisme et Hoa Hao. *Éducation* (Saigon), iii/14 (1949).

O'Ballance, Edgar. *The Indo-China War, 1945–1954.* London, 1964.

Park, George K. Divination and its Social Contexts. *JRAI*, xciii.
Parmentier, Henri. La religion ancienne de l'Annam. *Conférences du Musée Guimet.* Paris, 1906.
Parry, Albert. Soviet Aid to Vietnam. *The Reporter*, 12 Jan. 1967 (reprinted in *Survival* (London), Mar. 1967).
Partan, Daniel G. Legal Aspects of the Vietnam Conflict. *Boston University Law Review*, xlvi (1966).
Pasquier [Gov.-Gen.], Pierre. *L'Annam d'autrefois.* Paris, 1929.
Peautonnier, M. Contribution à l'Étude des conditions d'Exploitation de la Rizière en Indochine, in *L'Information d'Indochine Économique et Financière* (Saigon), 1946.
Pelliot, Paul. *Mémoires sur les coutumes du Cambodge de Tcheou Kouan.* Paris, 1951.
Petit, Robert. *La monarchie annamite.* Paris, 1931.
Pham Van Dong. *The Banner of Independence and Peace.* Hanoi, 1965.
Phan-Huy-Chu. *Lich-Trieu Hien-chuong Loai-Chi*, ed. Vu Van Mau & others. Saigon, 1957.
Phan-Nhu-Bang. *Ta-thi-Kieu, an heroic Girl of Bentre.* Hanoi [?], 1966.
Pike, Douglas. *Viet Cong: the Organization and Techniques of the National Liberation Front of South Vietnam.* Cambridge, Mass., 1966.
Pinto, Roger. *Aspects de l'évolution gouvernementale de l'Indochine française.* Saigon & Paris, 1946.

430   BIBLIOGRAPHY

Pouvourville, Albert de. *Les défenses de l'Indo-Chine at la politique d'association.* Paris, 1905.

Prybyla, Jan S. Soviet and Chinese Aid to North Vietnam. *China Quarterly,* No. 27 (1966).

Purcell, Victor. *The Chinese in Southeast Asia.* London, OUP/RIIA, 1965.

Pye, Lucian W. *Guerrilla Communism in Malaya.* New Jersey, 1956.

——— Armies in the Process of Political Modernization, *in* J. J. Johnson, ed. *Role of the Military in Underdeveloped Countries.* New Jersey, 1962.

Rhodes, Fr. Alexandre de. *Histoire du royaume de Tunquin.* Lyons, 1651.

Rieber, Alfred J. *Stalin and the French Communist Party, 1941-7.* New York, 1962.

Royal Institute of International Affairs. *Documents on International Affairs, 1955.* London, OUP/RIIA, 1956.

Robequain, Charles. *The Economic Development of French Indo-China.* Oxford, 1944.

Roberts, Stephen H. *History of French Colonial Policy, 1870-1925.* London, 1929.

Roubaud, Louis. *Viet Nam.* Paris, 1931.

Roussel, Anh-Van & Jacqueline. *Mouvements nationaux et lutte de classes au Viet-Nam.* Paris, 1947.

Sabattier [Gen.], Gabriel. *Le destin de l'Indochine.* Paris, 1952.

Saddharma-Pundarika or the Lotus of the True Law, trans. J. H. C. Kern. Oxford, 1884.

Sainteny, Jean [alias Jean Roger]. *Histoire d'une paix manquée; Indochine 1945-1947.* Paris, 1954.

Saletore, B. A. *India's Diplomatic Relations with the East.* Bombay, 1960.

Sarraut [Gov.-Gen. (& Min. of Colonies)], Albert. *La mise en valeur des colonies françaises.* Paris, 1923.

——— *Grandeur et servitude coloniales.* Paris, 1931.

Savani, A. M. *Visage et Images du Sud Viet-Nam.* Saigon, 1953.

Schlesinger, Arthur M., Jr. *The Bitter Heritage; Vietnam and American Democracy.* London, 1967.

Schram, Stuart. Mao Tsê-tung and Secret Societies. *China Quarterly,* No. 27 (1966).

Schreiner, Alfred. *Les institutions annamites en Basse-Cochinchine avant la conquête française.* Saigon, 1901.

Scigliano, Robert. *South Vietnam; nation under stress.* Boston, Mass., 1963.

Shulman, Marshall D. American Militancy—the Soviet View. *Washington Post,* 27 Nov. 1966 (reprinted in *Survival* (London), Feb. 1967).

Southworth, Constant. *The French Colonial Venture.* London, 1931.

Taboulet, Georges. *La geste française en Indochine.* Paris, 1955-6.

Tanham, George K. *Communist Revolutionary Warfare; the Vietminh in Indochina.* London, 1962.

——— *War without Guns.* London, 1966.

T'ao Wei-ying. *Yüeh-nan ku-tai shih.* Shanghai, 1959.

Tarling, Nicholas. British Relations with Vietnam 1822-1858. *JMBRAS,* xxxix/1 (1966).

Taylor, Milton C. South Viet-Nam: lavish aid, limited progress. *Pacific Affairs,* xxxiv/3 (1961).

TEXIER, Muriel. Le mandarinat au Viet-Nam au XIXe siècle. *BSEI*, xxxvii (1962).

THICH NHAT-HANH. *Vietnam; the Lotus in the Sea of Fire*. London, 1967.

THOMAZI, A. *La Conquête de l'Indochine*. Paris, 1934.

THOMPSON, Sir Robert. *Defeating Communist Insurgency*. London, 1966.

THOMPSON, Virginia. *French Indo-China*. London, 1937.

TONGAS, Gérard. *L'enfer communiste au Nord Viet-Nam*. Paris, 1961.

TON-THAT-THIEN. South Vietnam's Economy. *Far Eastern Economic Review*, 25 May 1967.

TRAGER, Frank N. & others. *Marxism in Southeast Asia*. Stanford, Calif., 1960.

TRAN-CHANH-THANH. Organisation et compétence des jurisdictions mandarinales de l'Annam. *RIJE*, iii (1943).

TRAN-QUANG-VINH. *Le Caodaisme, troisième amnistie de Dieu en Orient; la constitution religieuse du Caodaisme*. Paris, 1953.

TRAN-TRONG-KIM [Prime Minister]. *Viet-Nam Su-Luoc*. 7th ed. Saigon, 1964.

TRAN-VAN-GIAP. Le Bouddhisme en Annam des origines au XIIIe siècle. *BEFEO*, xxxii (1932).

—— Les chapitres bibliographiques de Le-qui-Don et de Phan-huy-Chu. *BSEI*, 1937.

TRINQUIER, Roger. *Modern Warfare; a French View of Counterinsurgency*, trans. by Daniel Lee. New York, 1964.

TRUONG-BUU-LAM & others, eds. *Kham-Dinh Viet-su Thong-Giam Cuong-muc*. Saigon, 1960. (*See also* Durand, 1950.)

TRUONG CHINH [personal name DANG XUAN KHU]. *The August Revolution*. 2nd ed. Hanoi, 1962. (1st ed. 1946.)

—— *March Ahead under the Party's Banner*. Hanoi, 1963.

—— *The Resistance Will Win*. 2nd ed. Hanoi 1966. (1st ed. 1948.)

VAN DER SPRENKEL, Sybille. *Legal Institutions in Manchu China*. London, 1962.

VANLANDE, René. *L'Indochine sous la menace communiste*. Paris, 1930.

VIAL, Paulin. *Les premières années de la Cochinchine*. Paris, 1874.

VIOLLIS, Andrée. *Indochine S.O.S.* Paris, 1949. (1st ed. 1935.)

VO-NGUYEN-GIAP [Gen.]. *People's War—People's Army*. Hanoi, 1961.

—— *The South Vietnam People Will Win*. Hanoi, 1965.

—— Le Mouvement s'arme. *Récits de la Résistance Vietnamienne*. Paris, 1966.

VO-NHAN-TRI. La politique agraire du Nord-Vietnam. *Tiers Monde*, i/3 (1960).

VU-DO-THIN. *Évolution économique du Viet-Nam*. Paris, 1954.

VU-QUOC-THONG. *La Décentralisation administrative au Viet-Nam*. Hanoi, 1952 (mimeo.)

—— *Viet Nam Government Organization Manual 1957–58*. Saigon, 1958.

VU-VAN-MAU & others. *Quoc Trieu Hinh Luat*. Saigon, 1956.

WALTER, Gérard. *Histoire du Parti communiste français*. Paris, 1948.

WELCH, Holmes H. The Reinterpretation of Chinese Buddhism. *China Quarterly*, No. 22 (1965).

—— Foreign Relations of Buddhism. *Journal of the Hong Kong Branch of the Royal Asiatic Society*, vi (1966).

—— *The Practice of Chinese Buddhism, 1900–50*. Harvard, 1967.

432   BIBLIOGRAPHY

WOODRUFF, Lloyd W. *Local Administration in Vietnam the number of local units,* East Lansing (MSU).

WRIGHT, Arthur F. *Buddhism in Chinese History.* London, 1959.

YANG, Martin C. *A Chinese Village.* New York, 1945.

ZASLOFF, Joseph J. *Rural Resettlement in Vietnam—an agroville in development.* East Lansing (MSU).

—— Rural Resettlement in South Viet Nam; the Agroville Program. *Pacific Affairs,* xxxv/4 (1962).

INDEX

agriculture: methods, 111, 114; yields, 111, 392; development, 115; government credit schemes, 116; private indebtedness, 116, 392. *See also* money-lending.

agrovilles, 186, 246, 261–2, 267, 313, 362.

AID (ECA, USOM), 276, 322, 357, 359, 405.

Air force, 288–9.

Angkor, 31, 34–35, 37, 56, 381 f.

Ap Bac (battle of), 324–5.

army:
conscription, 13, 59, 101, 289, 407–8, 413; desertion, 60, 209; form of employment, 254;
under the Nguyen, 59–60;
Vietminh and DRV, 153–4, 166, 175; State of Viet-Nam, 196;
RVN: chain of command, 219–20, 254–5, 290, 346; army and Can Lao, 220; in internal security, 254; efficiency, 266; finance, 283–4; US policy towards, 288; manpower, 289; training and equipment, 290–1; indoctrination, 291; deployment, 291–2; behaviour, 292, 407; in politics, 292–3, 337, 343 ff; bid for independence under Diem, 293; morale, 300, 327.

assimilation and *association*, 86–87, 94, 97–98, 109, 127, 132.

Associated States of Indochina, 192, 198, 202, 222, 273.

Ba Cut, *see* Le Van Ngo.

Bahnar, 31, 266, 381.

bang, 91, 264, 389.

banking, 108, 222.

Banque de l'Indochine, 108, 161, 199.

Bao An, *see* Civil Guard.

Bao Dai: abdication, 54, 158; escape to Hong Kong, 166; Head of State, 192, 195; and French aid, 204; and Ngo Dinh Diem, 211; dethroned, 222.

Behaine, Mgr Pigneau de, 78–80, 83, 375, 385, 388.

Bidault, Georges, 165.

Binh Xuyen, 157, 159, 179, 187, 221, 297, 397–8.

Black Flags, 61, 85, 118–20, 160.

bonzes, 48–49; in the Catholic Church, 75–77.

Britain: co-chairmanship of Geneva Conf. 8, 202; occupation of Cochinchina, 159–60; advice on taxation, 285;

British Advisory Mission, 311, 408.

Brotherhood for an Independent Vietnam, *see* Vietminh.

Brotherhood of Revolutionary Youth, 142–3, 251, 315.

bua, 76, 121; *bua gong*, 121, 180, 393.

Buddhism, 33, 47–48.
Theravada, 37, 47, 264, 331.
Mahayana, 47, 331, 348, 353; *Sangha*, 48, 330 ff; Japanese subversion, 151; hierarchy, 263; against arming *chrétientés*, 315; World Fellowship of Buddhists, 328, 331, 339; the flag, 328–9, 409; Youth Movement, 329, 331; availability of texts, 330; extent of, 330, 335–6; Vietnamese Church, 331, 334, 348; General Buddhist Association (*Ton-hoi*), 331; *Giao-hoi*, 348; *Lotus Sutra*, 333, 410; political organization, 345, 352; Vien Hoa Dao, 348, 352 f; intellectual Buddhism, 383–4; translation of terms, 386; traditions of immolation, 410.

Bui Quang Chieu, 123.

Bui Van Luong (Minister of the Interior), 207, 328–9, 410.

Buu Loc, Prince, 195, 210.

cabinets and ministerial procedure: DRV, 168; RVN, 228–9, 354–5. *See also* ministerial responsibility.

cadres:
Communist, 143, 168–70, 249, 253, 296–7, 298, 302; terms for, 396–7.
RVN: under Diem, 318, 323; after Diem, 366, 370; versus government, 370–1.

cadres, French, *see* Civil Service.

Cambodia: religion, 48; French protectorate, 84; succession to throne, 89, 388; irredentism, 117, 264; Associated State, 192; VC subversion of tribesmen, 264; Indochina Conference, 351; first Christians, 386–7; frontier with Vietnam, 388. *See also* Angkor.

canal-digging, 110, 242.

Can Lao: compared to ICP, 218; infiltration of army, 220, 267–8, 293, 327, 339; and trade unions, 248, 348; controls SEPES, 255; extension to countryside, 312; and Republican Youth, 318; destruction of records, 347; vacuum left by, 348; persecu-

433

community development, 245–6, 259–60.
Confucianism: the sovereign, 24; social philosophy, 33, 44; literature, 69, 296; rites, 77, 244, 383, 387, 393; and Catholicism, 213–14; administrative principle, 230; individual and State, 253; slogans, 316.
cong dien, 114, 245, 361.
conscription: by the VC, 13, 296–7, 365; under the Nguyen, 59–60; under French rule, 91, 100; in State of Viet-Nam, 196; competition for manpower, 288; under Diem, 289–90; after Diem, 364; American role in, 365; manpower resources (RVN and DRV), 413.
Conseil Militaire de la Révolution, *see* Councils.
Constituent Assembly:(1956),225;(1966), 353, 415.
Constitution: Union Indochinoise, 88; DRV, 168, 174, 386; Repub. of Cochinchina, 190–1; State of Viet-Nam, 191–2, 210, 228; US model, 227, 278; RVN: (1956), 227–8, 344; after Diem, 346; (1964 Charters), 344,350;(1967),377,415;*Convention*, 349; *Directoire*, 351.
Corps Expéditionnaire: tasks of, 175, 193; fighting strength, 185; high command, 185, 198, 399–400; deadlock with Vietminh, 198; after Dien Bien Phu, 210; under Diem, 221; withdrawal, 222, 275, 400; tribesmen enlisted in, 264; experience disregarded in US, 273; old battlegrounds, 371; limitation on operations, 396; battles for opium, 398.
corruption: under the Nguyen, 63; under French rule, 135, 273; as an instrument of policy, 219, 229; in the DRV, 231; under Diem, 231, 287; military exactions, 237; American attitude to, 287, 305; forms of embezzlement, 298, 357; flourishing after Diem, 356.
corvée (cong dich): under the Nguyen, 58, 61–62; under French rule, 91, 98, 389; in the DRV, 172, 175; under Diem, 261,317; after Diem, 363.
councils: of the Nguyen, 89; under French rule, 92–94, 211; *Grand Conseil des Intérêts Économiques et Financiers*, 93, 116; provincial, 135, 237, 369, 415; *Conseil de Cochinchine*, 191; National Economic, 227, 415; National Security, 230, 415; village, 237–8,369,415; *Conseil Militaire de la Révolution*, 344; of Notabilities, 345; High National, 345, 350; Armed Forces, 350, 415; Committee of National Leadership, 351.

Cuong De, Prince, 124, 149, 150 f., 211 f., 385.
customs duties, 101, 132, 165, 284.

Da Nhim hydro-electric scheme, 241.
Dai Viet (party): origins, 151; break with Vietminh, 165; in power in Tonkin, 189, 195; kept in check, 256, 323; and *pao chia*, 259; in Khanh Government, 348–9; internal dissensions, 352; 'Revolutionary Armed Forces', 352; government of Hué, 353; loyalty oath, 402, divisions, 411.
Dalat Conference, 164.
Dang Lao Dong, *see* VWP.
Dang Sy, Maj., 329, 358.
Dang Xuan Khu, *see* Truong Chinh.
Dao Lanh, 121–2, 206, 221.
D'Argenlieu, Adm. Thierry, 164, 265, 396.
Decoux, Adm. Jean, 149 ff., 155, 331, 388, 390, 394.
De Gaulle, Gen., 162, 165.
De Lattre de Tassigny, Gen., 178, 185.
délégués du gouvernement, 236.
DRV: strategic interests, 4; cost of war to, 4; invasions of Laos, 5, 184, 201, 270; claim to RVN, 8, 251; flag, 150; extent, 167; government of, 167 ff.; 1956 insurrection, 174; effect of Geneva, 204; and VC 266 ff.; infiltration of RVN, 270, 303, 367, 372; complaints of US intervention, 275; and 'neutralism', 301; and Cambodia, 351; arms shipments to VC, 364, 367; aggression, 368; administrative records, 397.
De Rhodes, Alexandre, 67, 74.
detention without trial: under French rule, 130; under Diem, 256–8; after Diem, 403; by Communists, 403.
De Tham, 120, 147, 189.
dia bo, 133, 243.
Dien Bien Phu (battle of), 2, 177, 200–2, 367.
dinh (village hall and temple), 205, 305, 393, 403.
Dinh, 382.
Dinh Bo Lanh, 40.
dinh dien, 246.
doctors, 106, 208, 407–8.
don dien, 60.
Dong Khanh, 88.
drainage and irrigation, 23, 102, 107, 110, 133, 241–2, 244.
Dulles, J. F., 5.
Duong Van Minh, Gen., 221, 336, 339, 344, 347, 350.
Duy Tan (Vietnamese emperor), 124, 132, 393.
Duy Tan Hoi, 124.